P9-DNU-183

DALRYMPLE'S SALES MANAGEMENT

Tenth Edition

DALRYMPLE'S SALES MANAGEMENT

Tenth Edition

William L. Cron
Texas Christian University

Thomas E. DeCarlo
University of Alabama, Birmingham

JOHN WILEY & SONS, Inc.

VICE PRESIDENT & EXECUTIVE PUBLISHER	George Hoffman
EXECUTIVE EDITOR	Lise Johnson
EDITORIAL ASSISTANT	Carissa Marker Doshi
MARKETING MANAGER	Carly DeCandia
DESIGN DIRECTOR	Harry Nolan
SENIOR DESIGNER	Kevin Murphy
SENIOR PRODUCTION EDITOR	Patricia McFadden
SENIOR MEDIA EDITOR	Daniel Haag
PRODUCTION MANAGEMENT SERVICES	Katie Boilard, Pine Tree Composition, Inc.

This book was set in 10 pt. Times Roman by Laserwords Private Limited, Chennai, India and printed and bound by R.R. Donnelley & Sons. The cover was printed by R.R. Donnelley & Sons.

This book is printed on acid-free paper. ♾

Team exercises that appear in each chapter were prepared by William L. Cron of Texas Christian University and Thomas E. DeCarlo of University of Alabama, Birmingham.

To order books or for customer service please, call 1-800-CALL WILEY (225-5945)

ISBN-13: 978-0470-16965-0
ISBN-10: 0-470-16965-6

Printed in the United States of America

10 9 8 7 6 5 4 3 2 1

PREFACE

In this tenth edition, we continue with our tradition of providing readers with a comprehensive, practical approach to sales management. In doing so, we have refined the focus of the book by meticulously editing and rewriting each chapter with the goal of streamlining the presentation of the topics. As always, the goal is to present the material as clearly as possible so that students can effectively learn and apply sales management concepts to solve business problems. While most marketing students will likely start their career as salespeople, we believe it is important to gain an understanding of the sales manager's role in order to function effectively in sales and prepare oneself for promotion. Effective management of salespeople is a key weapon in marketing strategy and critical to business success because many goods and services demand personal contacts to close the sale. However, selling costs are growing rapidly and sales forces must become more efficient and effective. The manager who understands how to effectively plan and direct the actions of salespeople will have an advantage in moving up the executive career ladder.

Approach and Objectives

Sales Management begins with a review of the current business environment in which organizations must operate and the sales force must compete. This sets the stage for discussing the possible roles of the sales force in developing and executing a firm's strategy, as specified in an organization's sales program. This discussion is relevant for either existing firms or new start-up organizations. Execution of the sales program occurs at the point of customer contact whether this involves sales managers, as is often the case with strategic accounts, or salespeople. This is why the next section of the text focuses on the topics of sales opportunity, customer relationship, and customer interaction management. Particular emphasis is given to the impact of alternative sales programs on these topics. The remainder of the text addresses the efforts of sales management to facilitate the execution of the sales program through recruiting, training, leading, motivating, compensating, and evaluating the sales force.

An important objective in writing the tenth edition of *Sales Management* was to continue to provide comprehensive coverage of sales management practices by combining the latest findings in sales force management research with examples of current sales management practices. Our approach is to not only present the theoretical concepts, but show how they are operationalized with real-world examples in an easy-to-read style. One way we do this is to embed in each chapter, as boxed inserts, short team-based exercises that are designed to stimulate class discussion of the topics in the chapter. We also conclude each chapter with competency-based problems and an application exercise designed to build on a featured case study presented in the first chapter. In addition, we have included twenty-six other comprehensive cases that provide students additional opportunities to apply what they have learned in resolving realistic business dilemmas.

Features of the Tenth Edition

Although the basic objectives, approach, and style of earlier editions have been maintained, several noteworthy changes have been made. First, all chapters have been thoroughly scrutinized and rewritten for easier reading and retention. In addition, there has been a major updating of examples that reflect both the emerging trends in sales force management practice as well as the growing body of published research.

Second, the discussion in some chapters has been streamlined while in others it has been expanded to incorporate new developments. For example, in chapter 7 we have incorporated a running example using one company's hiring procedures throughout our discussion of recruiting and hiring. This provides a much tighter discussion of the material. In other chapters we have added or expanded discussion in topics such as:

- Sales networks
- Customer lifetime value
- Solutions selling
- Marketing-sales interaction
- Marketing-sales shared responsibilities
- Leadership

We have also removed redundant or outdated material in an effort to focus more directly on relevant issues. Finally, we have summarized the discussion of certain topics by using tables and have significantly increased our use of figures and graphs, which were designed help the reader more easily understand the relationships between key concepts.

Third, we have added a new, featured case, Shield Financial, at the end of chapter 1. We have also preserved the running case concept from the ninth edition. In doing so, we have added modified the situations at the end of each chapter to fit with the new case. This unique pedagogical feature allows for a more in-depth case analysis and provides students the opportunity to thoroughly develop a case throughout an entire course.

Finally, we have over twenty new Team Exercises that are designed to enhance in-class discussion. In addition, two-thirds of the introductory case vignettes at the beginning of each chapter have been reworked. The end result of these modifications is a text that is comprehensive, but more concise and reader friendly.

Chapter Objectives. Each chapter begins with a set of objectives to show students what they will learn. Instructors can use these to develop expectations in terms of discussion questions and exam items.

Boxed Team Exercises. Each chapter has at least two boxed inserts that highlight real-world issues related to one or more topics discussed in the chapter. These exercises can be used in class as a small group assignment to stimulate discussion and enhance learning of various chapter topics, or as assigned homework exercises.

Shield Case Exercises. As mentioned above, a feature of this edition is a running case question included in at the end of each chapter. The questions were developed to extend the issues in the featured Shield Financial case introduced in chapter 1 and call for students to solve a new issue facing the firm that focuses on topics relevant to the chapter topics discussed. That is, students will be able to apply each chapter's material to a case they have been familiar with all semester.

Developing Your Competencies. Each chapter includes problems related to each of the sales management competencies. These are written to include a wide variety of questions. Some are application questions that provide students the opportunity to solve a sales management problem. Others are thought-provoking questions that require students to reflect on a competency-based issue related to the material they have just read. Still others are experiential exercises that direct students to conduct active learning activities on their own.

Summaries. All chapters end with a summary for each of the chapter objectives listed at the beginning of the chapter. These summaries are useful to ensure students understand the key points made in each chapter.

Case Studies. Over half of the cases are new or have been significantly reworked and, similar to the previous edition, all cases appear at the end of the book in alphabetical order. Immediately preceding the cases is a guide designed to indicate the topics each case covers. These meaty cases cover a number of topics and the guide can be a helpful integrative tool for instructors and students.

Key Terms. Key terms are highlighted in the text and listed at the end of each chapter. These can serve as a quick reference to important terms developed in the chapter.

Indexes. Cases, Author, Company, and Subject indexes help students find information and examples.

Excel Problems. Excel-based numerical problems have been updated and refined to help students develop their technical competency in Excel and to work with numerical data. Edited worksheets are available for student use when working on the problems at the end of selected chapters or when performing data analysis on the cases. The solutions to the problems are available to instructors only. These can be downloaded from the book's website at *www.wiley.com/college/cron*.

Instructor's Resources. The instructor's resources include suggested course syllabi, chapter outlines, lecture notes, lecture enhancement examples, case notes, suggested solutions to the end-of-chapter competency problems and Excel problems, and in-class exercise instructor notes. In this edition, not only have we increased the content, but we have made significant changes to the teacher's manual to make it even more user friendly. For example, we have found that instructors tend to use the lecture note enhancement examples as a stand-alone teaching tool. To this end, we have added more than fifty new lecture enhancement examples to the Instructor's Resource. We have included these in a separate web link for downloading by chapter. We have also significantly revised the test bank to include a wide assortment of new multiple-choice and true/false questions. The test bank, along with all other instructor resources, is available to download from our Web site, *www.wiley.com/college/cron*.

Powerpoint. Presentations for lecture planning and note taking are available to both professors and students and may be downloaded from the book's Website at *www.wiley.com/college/cron*.

Personal Selling Videotapes. A set of 17 short (three- to five-minute) selling tapes prepared by Wilson Learning Corporation. These tapes provide models of good sales skills, mistakes to avoid, and coaching suggestions for sales managers. Ask your Wiley representative for more details.

ACKNOWLEDGMENTS

This book could not have been published without the spirited comments and suggestions of our reviewers. A special note of appreciation is due to Joseph Fola Aiyeku, Salem State University; F. Rick Brous, Fairleigh Dickinson University; Jeffrey Kulick, George Mason University; Lynnea Mallalieu, University of North Carolina, Wilmington; Michael Mallin, University of Toledo; Victor J. Piscitello, University of Arizona; Daniel Ricica, Sinclair Community College; Ian J. Scharf, University of Miami; John Summey, Southern Illinois University, Carbondale; and Douglas W. Vorhies, University of Mississippi.

We would also like to express our appreciation to a host of colleagues as well as numerous reviewers on previous editions, whose comments and suggestions live on:

Avery Abernethy, *Auburn University*

Kenneth A. Anglin, *Minnesota State University, Mankato*

Anne L. Balazs, *Mississippi University for Women*

Tim A. Becker, *Point Loma Nazarene University*

Robert Cook, *West Virginia University*

Ned J. Cooney, *University of Colorado, Boulder*

Kevin Coulson, *Northeastern Illinois University*

Kevin M. Feldt, *The University of Adron*

Eli Jones, *University of Houston*

Maryon King, *Southern Illinois University*

Lewis Neisner, *University of Maryland*

Robert S. Owen, *SUNY Oswego*

Leroy Robinson, Jr., *University of Houston, Clear Lake*

Raymond Rody, *Loyola Marymount University*

Richard Spreng, *Michigan State University*

James A. Stephens, *Emporia State University*

Michael J. Swenson, *Brigham Young University*

Ron Taylor, *Mississippi State University*

Zafar Ahmed
Ramon A. Avila
Robert Collins
Jill W. Croft
Daniel Gardiner
James Gray
Bill Greenwood
Jon Hawes
Karen E. James
Madhav Kacker
Thomas Leigh
Richard Leventhal
Elaine Notorantino
Keith Paulson
Robert Roe
Jose Rosa
Bob Smiley
Fred Smith
Winston Stahlecker

A special acknowledgment is due to the sales and marketing executives and consultants who served as chapter consultants to this book. They both reviewed the chapters and offered important insights into the chapters' subject matter. The result of their efforts is a text that is both practical and cutting-edge with respect to current sales and sales management practices. We are deeply indebted to the contributions of the following people:

Bob Braasch
Manager Sales Planning
SABRE

Carol Caprio
Software Business Unit Executive
IBM

Randy Cimorelli
President/COD
Massey-Fair Industrial, Inc.

Joseph P. Clayton
President & CEO
Sirius Satellite Radio

Robert Conti
Vice President
The Alexander Group, Inc.

Nein Cronin
Director of Training and Specialist Manager
John Wiley & Sons

Liz Crute
Vice President
Pitney Bowes Credit Corporation

Kevin Cummings
National Sales Manager
ABTco, Inc.

Russel Donnelly
Sales Manager, Central Region
Ericsson Inc.

Robert P. Eschino
Executive Vice President
Gold

William I. Evans
Principal
The Evans Group

Elizabeth Forbes
Director, International Results & Analysis
GTE International

Keith Hall
Area Manager
Anderson Chemical Co.

David Henry
General Sales Manager
CBS Radio: KVIL

Don James
Principal
Human Dimensions, Inc.

Christopher Jander
National Account Manager
GTE

Michael Mahan
Account Manager
IBM

George Michaud
Director of Environment/ Health Safety & Ethics
Northern Telecom

Greg Miller
Senior Vice President, Strategic Planning and Human Resources
Sunburst Hospitality Corporation

George Petagrew
Sales Training Manager
Johnson & Johnson Medical

David Pinals
President
TTG, Incorporated

B. J. Polk
Associate Director, Marketing
Proctor & Gamble Distributing Co.

Tim Prevost
Director, Sales & Marketing
Stuart C. Irby Co.

Jonathan Scarborough
District Marketing Manager
Federated Insurance

John Schreutnyekker
Partner
Ray & Berndtson

Scott Smith
Vice President, Sales & Marketing
SABRE Group, Inc.

Howard Stevens
President
Chally Group

Paulette Turner
Sales Operations Business Unit Executive
IBM Corporation

Ken Whelan
Director, Business Development
Qwest Communications

Jerry Willet
National Sales Manager
Software Spectrum

We also want to thank all the people at John Wiley & Sons who helped develop this book. Carissa Doshi, our Assistant Editor, worked tirelessly to upgrade and improve the tenth edition. Our Production Editor, Trish McFadden, has also been a great help in guiding the book through the many steps of the production process.

Finally, we want to thank our wives, Deborah and Tiffany, for their help and encouragement.

ABOUT THE AUTHORS

William L. Cron is Professor of Marketing in the M. J. Neeley School of Business at Texas Christian University. He received his MBA and DBA from Indiana University and his BSBA from Xavier University in Cincinnati, Ohio. Professor Cron has also taught at Southern Methodist University, the University of Wuhan, Universitat Bern Switzerland, and the University of Dijon France. His research on motivation in general and a variety of sales force issues has been published in the *Journal of Marketing Research, Journal of Marketing, Academy of Management Journal, Journal of Applied Psychology, Journal of Psychometric Classifications, Harvard Business Review, Journal of the Academy of Marketing Science, Journal of Personal Selling & Sales Management, Journal of Vocational Behavior, and Journal of Occupational Behavior* among others. Professor Cron has been a member of the Editorial Review Board for the *Journal of Marketing, Journal of the Academy of Marketing Science, Journal of Personal Selling & Sales Management*, and *Journal of Business and Industrial Marketing*. He has also coauthored four sales management books.

Thomas E. DeCarlo is the Ben S. Weil Endowed Chair of Industrial Distribution at the University of Alabama at Birmingham. He received his Ph.D. from the University of Georgia and his BA from North Carolina State University. Professor DeCarlo has also taught at Iowa State University and the University of Wuhan. His research in sales force management and related topics in marketing communications has been published in the *Journal of Marketing, Journal of Consumer Psychology, Journal of International Business Studies, Journal of Personal Selling & Sales Management, Journal of Service Research, Industrial Marketing Management, Marketing Letters*, and others. Professor DeCarlo is currently a member of the Editorial Review Board for the *Journal of Personal Selling & Sales Management*. He has also coauthored a personal selling textbook.

BRIEF CONTENTS

CONTENTS

INTRODUCTION TO SELLING AND SALES MANAGEMENT

> If you sincerely believe that "the customer is king," the second most important person in this kingdom must be the one who has a direct interaction on a daily basis with the king.
>
> Michael Bon
> Chairman & CEO, France Telecom

Chapter Consultant:
Paulette Turner, Sales Operations Business Unit Executive, IBM Corporation

LEARNING OBJECTIVES

After studying this chapter, you should be able to:

- Describe the major changes taking place in selling and the forces causing these changes.
- Define sales management.
- Describe the sales management process.
- Discuss the competencies required to be a successful manager.

CHIEF SALES EXECUTIVE FORUM

At a recent Chief Sales Executive Forum, executives from leading companies responded to some fundamental questions about their sales forces. The executive panel consisted of sales leaders, vice president and higher, from Honeywell, Siemens AG, General Electric, Oracle, and Xerox. Let's listen in on some of their answers.

"As sales leaders, what is the biggest challenge facing you today?"

- (General Electric) Without a doubt, the biggest challenge for GE is making the sales force realize that we're in a global business. Not everything is invented in America. There's a lot of work to be done outside the United States, and we're really focusing a lot of energy on emerging markets.

- (Xerox) At Xerox, we are putting much more experienced sales leaders on our largest global accounts to focus on that globalization. We're also moving resources. I just assigned someone to work in Singapore to coordinate activities in that growing market. I think this whole focus on globalization is huge.
- (Siemens AG) Selling is no longer about the portfolio and quarterly performance; it's about an ongoing relationship with the customer. Our mission is to become a trusted advisor to our top customers, and that becomes more difficult when you're working on a global scale.
- (Oracle) One thing we're struggling with at Oracle right now is finding the right level of specializing to ensure that we're giving customers what they want and need, and we're really exploiting all the products that the sales reps carry in their portfolio, but balancing that with not having too many people calling on the same customer.

"Is this a good time to be in sales?"

- (Honeywell) At Honeywell, sales eats first. We are in charge until someone says we're not. Other divisions in the company will have to take that ring away from sales, and believe me, they won't.
- (General Electric) At GE, it is a wonderful time to be a salesperson. We have no issue with top-level buy-in since our CEO (Jeffrey Immelt) came up through the ranks as a salesperson. As a result, I think we are a lot more customer-driven than we have been in the past. Sales leaders have the ability to say to product design, "That won't fly with our customers." That's a powerful thing to have in your favor. We have to make sure our sales force realizes that we're there to help our customers solve their problems instead of just trying to sell them product.

"Have the responsibilities of the sales position expanded at your company?"

- (Siemens AG) That's absolutely right. Our account executives plan a business strategy for each of their accounts. Then we require them to sit down and do a four-year business plan, and that's been very effective. It puts them in the other seat. What we're really trying to do is avoid the "one-size-fits-nobody" style of selling.
- (Xerox) I'm a believer in allowing the people who are actually managing the customer to make more decisions about how to handle an account. I think we should be empowering our teams more. Xerox customers have many different corporate structures, and I think a lot of times we try to do a cookie-cutter approach. It just doesn't work.
- (Xerox) I see a bigger issue in getting more people into management, accelerating the development of top salespeople, moving them along quicker. I think we tend to keep people in their jobs too long at the first-line level.[1]

These are very exciting times to be in sales and *sales management*. According to a recent survey, the average pay for a salesperson is $94,872, while sales executives earn on average $150,882.[2] Beyond compensation, this is an exciting time of change in the sales profession. Many organizations are finding that sales force changes are needed for more demanding customers in an increasingly competitive world. Giant retailers such as Wal-Mart and Target are leveraging electronic data technology and are requiring manufacturers sales forces to assume responsibility for "just-in-time" inventory control, ordering, billing, sales, and promotion. Like other companies, Hewlett-Packard now rents an office in a key customer's headquarters building and stations an account manager there.

These innovations in the way suppliers and customers interact have necessitated changes in the way sales forces are organized, compensated, developed, and evaluated. Our goal in this textbook is to explain how the sales team operates in this new environment and how they may be supervised for maximum efficiency and effectiveness. We begin by defining personal selling and describing its role within a firm's promotion mix. We then turn to some of the changes taking place that have had an important impact on the sales function. Next, we direct our attention to the sales management function by describing the activities they perform, a process of sales management, and the competencies needed to successfully perform these activities and the sales management process. The final section of the chapter profiles career paths that you may find in your first sales job.

PERSONAL SELLING

According to the U.S. Department of Labor's Bureau of Labor Statistics, people working in sales number close to 12 million, or about 10 percent of the total workforce in the United States. *Personal selling* is critical to the sale of many goods and services, especially major commercial and industrial products and consumer durables, and can be defined as:

> Direct communications between paid representatives and prospects that lead to transactions, customer satisfaction, account development, and profitable relationships.

The relationships between selling and other elements of the marketing mix are highlighted in Figure 1-1.

Marketing programs are designed around four elements of the marketing mix: products to be sold, pricing, promotion, and distribution channels. The promotion component includes advertising, public relations, personal selling, and sales promotion (point-of-purchase displays, coupons, and sweepstakes). Note that advertising and sales promotions are non-personal communications, whereas salespeople talk directly to customers. Thus, where advertising and sales promotion "pull" merchandise through the channel, personal selling provides the "push" needed to get orders signed. With public relations, the message is perceived as coming from the media rather than directly from the organization. Personal selling involves two-way communication with prospects and customers that allows the salesperson to address the special needs of the customer.

It is often the job of a salesperson to uncover the special needs of the customer. When customers have questions or concerns, the salesperson is there to provide appropriate

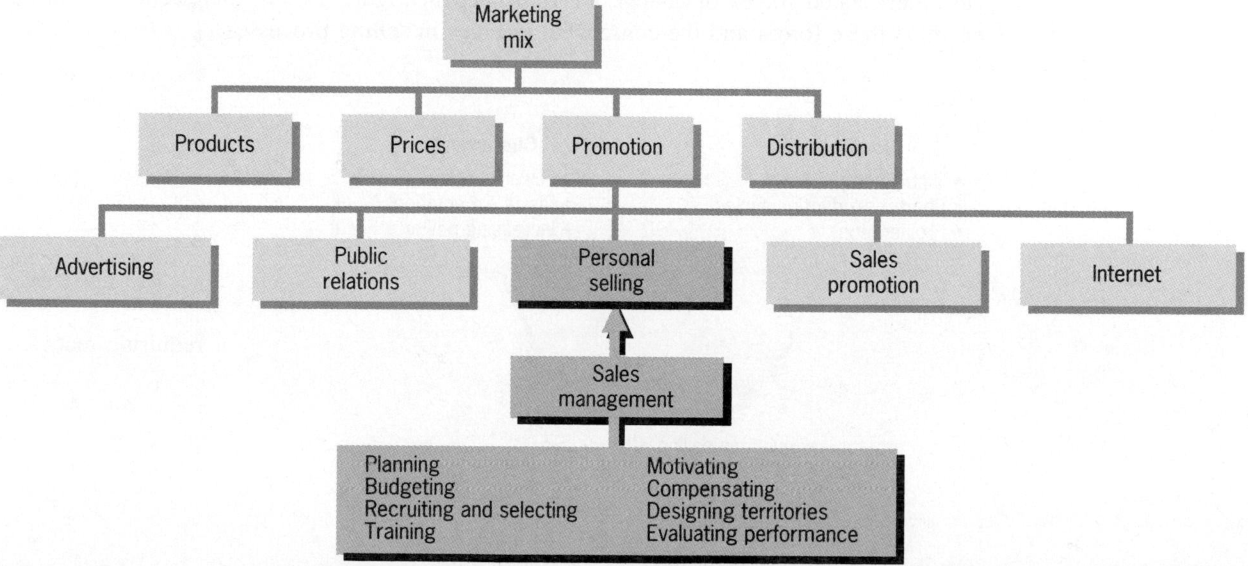

FIGURE 1-1 Positions of Personal Selling and Sales Management in the Marketing Mix

explanations. Furthermore, personal selling can be directed to qualified prospects, whereas a great deal of advertising and sales promotions are wasted because many people in the audience have no use for the product. Perhaps the most important advantage of personal selling is that it is considerably more effective than advertising, public relations, and sales promotion in identifying opportunities to create value for the customer and gaining customer commitment.

The person responsible for management of the field sales operation is the *sales manager*. He or she may be a first-line manager, directly responsible for the day-to-day management of salespeople, or positioned at a higher level in the management hierarchy, responsible for directing the activities of other managers. In either case, sales management focuses on the administration of the personal selling function in the marketing mix. This role includes the planning, management, and control of sales programs. Sales management can thus be defined as:

> The planning, organizing, leading, and controlling of personal contact programs designed to achieve the sales and profit objectives of the firm.

Regardless of whether the sales manager directs salespeople or other sales managers, all managers have two types of responsibilities:

- Achieving or exceeding performance goals for the current period.
- Developing the people reporting to them.

Each of these responsibilities includes a number of more specific activities that will be discussed throughout this book. It is important that you understand the context in which sales managers execute these two responsibilities. In the next section we discuss some of the more consequential changes taking place in the marketplace and in selling operations.

A CHANGING MARKETPLACE

It is certainly a time of change. Powerful forces are at work that are irrevocably changing the way that salespeople and sales managers understand, prepare for, and accomplish their jobs. Few sales forces will be immune. Some of the more important competitive and customer-related forces of change are illustrated in Figure 1-2. In this section we briefly examine these forces and the consequent changes in selling processes.[3]

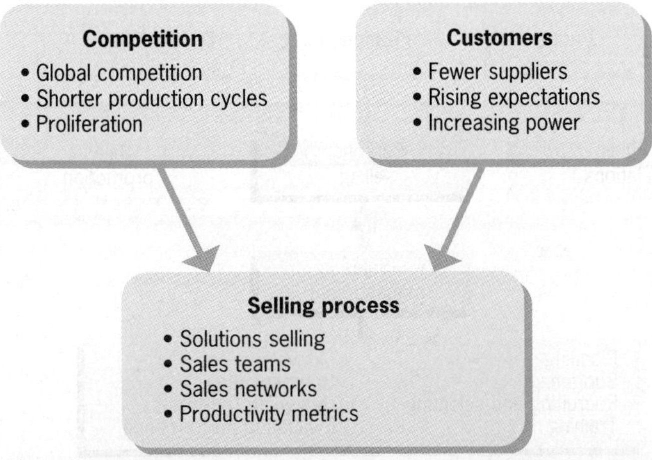

FIGURE 1-2 Marketplace Changes and Selling Consequences

Competition

The 1980s and early 1990s were generally a seller's market. Today, the number of competitors in most markets has literally exploded. In this section, we explore three key reasons for this development—*globalization* of markets, shorter product cycles, and a blurring of market boundaries.

Globalization. Companies that compete only in the United States or even in a region of the United States are feeling the effects of globalized competition. It is not unusual to compete with companies from other countries, to use suppliers located in other parts of the world, or to sell to customers that are selling in other countries. Any of these situations may result in intensified competition and require that the sales force adjust from a local to a global focus.

The most obvious need for a global perspective is for those companies competing in other countries. World trade accounts for more than 20 percent of U.S. gross national product. This is because almost 95 percent of the world's population and 75 percent of its purchasing power are outside of the United States. The majority of sales by such well-known companies as Coca-Cola, Colgate-Palmolive, and Avon Products are made outside the United States. Chief Sales Officers (CSOs) know that their companies' growth is likely to depend on how well they manage customer relationships in global markets. This means more traveling, hiring the right people, defining new roles and duties, and developing a global perspective and world-class skills at addressing an increasingly eclectic sales force.

Shorter Product Cycles. The rate of technology transfer is increasing. Process and products that were once proprietary are quickly becoming available to competitors. As a result of the porousness of technology, product cycles are shorter, imitation is more rapid, and as a consequence, the window of product differentiation has narrowed considerably. This development has important implications for sales management. Sales and customer relationship skills are most important when a product is new and again when it is late in its life cycle. New products need careful presentation because a buyer's risk is highest owing to lack of experience with the product. The sales force's task is to help customers understand that the benefits of the new product outweigh the risks and costs associated with the requisite business changes. In the late stages of the life cycle, the salesperson again becomes very important. With very few important differences in competing products, the personal relationship and intimate customer knowledge of the sales force become the primary point of differentiation and leverage for a supplier. As a consequence, sales forces are constantly balancing competing and changing sales priorities.[4]

The Proliferation Challenge. Recent advances in technology, information, communications, and distribution have created an explosion of new sales and service channels, media, products, and brands. Consider the wireless-telecommunications market. The number of discrete offerings has ballooned into the hundreds: prepaid and postpaid calling plans; family-friendly and nights-and-weekend plans; text-, data-, and message-capable mobile telephones; video and music phones, and so on. The number of distribution touchpoints has increased from three to more than ten, including company-owned stores, shared and exclusive dealers, telemarketing agents, affinity partners, and the Web. As a result, the number of price points exceeds 500,000. The same picture holds for most other businesses as diverse as packaged goods, pharmaceuticals, retail banking, and others. The number of chocolate candy brands in the United States increased from 407 to 537 over a four-year period of time.[5]

The implications for sales and sales management are profound. Product and competitor knowledge demands on salespeople are greater. Developing solutions for customer problems becomes more complex as does the need for better understanding of customer needs. Most fundamentally, the sales force increasingly must understand their company's marketing program in order to successfully execute the firm's marketing plan in the field. The remainder of this book will discuss efforts by companies to successfully meet this challenge.

Customers

The increase in competition clearly calls for new selling and sales management approaches. However, identifying the correct selling and sales management approach is further complicated by customer developments such as purchasing from fewer suppliers, rising expectations, and increasing power.

Fewer Suppliers. The traditional practice of buyers rotating purchases across multiple supplier sources is increasingly being questioned in many industries. Motorola's Personal Communications Sector group, for example, has reduced its supplier base from 300 to 100 suppliers.[6] On September 29, 2005, the *Wall Street Journal* ran a front-page story on Ford Motor Company's decision to reduce its supplier base from 2,500 vendors to 1,000. The lucky survivors will be given long-term contracts and a larger share of the $90 billion Ford spends on global purchases annually. Everyone else will be on the outside. Keep in mind that Ford has been working on this consolidation process since the late 1980s, when it had over 13,000 vendors. Xerox Corporation, GE, General Motors, and most other major corporations have followed suit in reducing their supplier base by one-half or more. These companies are finding that the costs of maintaining relationships with a large number of suppliers far exceed any possible price savings. Consider the results of a Department of Defense study that found that it costs hospitals $1.50 in administrative costs associated with $1.00 worth of medical supplies.

At first glance, customers purchasing from fewer suppliers would appear to benefit suppliers. But what if you are not chosen as one of the "in suppliers"? Among wholesalers of periodicals and magazines, for instance, the shift by large retailers to single-sourcing has resulted in intense consolidation. Contract-winning wholesalers rapidly acquired former competitors in an effort to cover larger territories and service larger accounts. As a result, the number of wholesalers in the United States has dropped to one-third of the number operating in 1990. In other words, the revenue stream from individual customers had become so important that survival had become dependent on maintaining the supplier-customer relationship.

Rising Expectations. Despite a focus on quality and service, customer satisfaction remains low, according, to research by J. D. Power and Associates. Customer satisfaction is difficult to manage because as customers receive good treatment, they become accustomed to it and demand even better treatment. In other words, the bar is being constantly raised. Customer expectations are raised not just by how well a business performs versus competitors, but also by the higher standards set in other industries. People are aware of the standard in the consistency of service at McDonald's, the cleanliness at Disney, and the product quality at Sony. Customers are aware of the product and service quality they receive from these companies and are holding everyone else to a higher standard.

The good news is that these rising expectations are very apparent. Customers expect salespeople to be professionals who are adept at identifying and satisfying their buying needs. The H. R. Chally Group, a sales and sales management consulting firm, conducted extensive research into customer purchasing behavior. Figure 1-3 lists some of the most important expectations of salespeople in the customers' own words.

Increasing Power. Fewer than 10 percent of all retail stores, for instance, account for more than half of U.S. retail sales. Wal-Mart, Target, Sears, Costco, and many other dominant

"Be personally accountable for our desired results"

"Understand our business"

"Be on our side"

"Design the right applications"

"Be easily accessible"

"Solve our problems"

"Be creative in responding to our needs"

FIGURE 1-3 Customer Expectations of Salespeople

retailers have grown bigger and more powerful than the manufacturers that supply them, and they are now dictating the supplier-customer relationship.

This shift to large powerful customers has had dramatic impact on suppliers. Procter & Gamble, for example, has well over 100 people located in Bentonville, Arkansas, to sell and service Wal-Mart. When the accounts are huge, consumer goods companies are finding that marketing and sales must make joint decisions about product, price, brand, and all kinds of support. Pricing, product and service customization, and merchandising programs cannot be entrusted to either marketing or sales alone. The economic impact of these large accounts requires an integrated approach.

Selling Process

The changes discussed so far are rapidly dooming the traditional sales attitude of "I can sell anything to anyone." The financial stakes are too high and the problems too complex for a single salesperson to handle. In this section we briefly discuss several important changes that are taking place in many companies' selling efforts: relationship selling, sales teams, inside selling, and productivity metrics.[7]

Solutions Selling. The traditional selling model emphasizes selling products in the short term. The value added by the sales force was in communicating the benefits of the product or service to the customer, helping customers make a purchase decision, and making the whole process convenient and easy for the buyer. In many situations, especially when the product or service is not of strategic significance to the buyers, this type of relationship is appropriate. However, many buyers and sellers are finding that this selling model does not work for all customers, particularly those that are most important. This has led to the development of an alternative selling model referred to as solutions selling. Solutions selling involves creating customer value by addressing important customer problems and opportunities through a supplier-customer relationship that is much more intimate than that of traditional transactional selling. In a recent survey of sales executives, 64 percent rated implementing a *solutions selling model* as one of the top three challenges facing sales forces today.[8] Figure 1-4 contrasts some of the differences between the traditional *transactional selling model* and the solutions selling model.

Perhaps the best way to understand what is meant by solutions selling is by describing one company's experience in transitioning from a traditional to a solutions selling model. Procter & Gamble's (P&G) sales model with retailers was traditionally transactional. As a result, buyers and P&G salespeople operated at an arm's-length buying-selling environment. The sales force took orders and aggressively pursued shelf space, while buyers negotiated

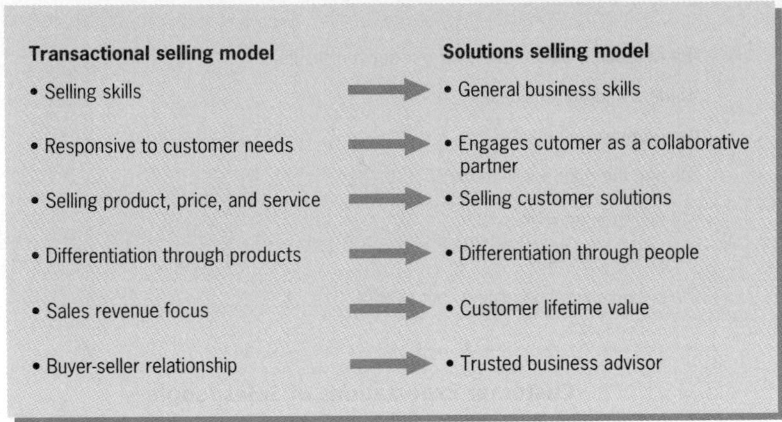

FIGURE 1-4 Contrasting Transactional and Solutions Selling Models

fiercely for lowest prices and sought the highest shelving allowances in the form of fees for premium shelf facings. In contrast, solutions selling involves a collaborative effort to create added value from this synergy. P&G has reorganized into Customer Business Development Teams composed of a variety of functional areas and organizational levels focusing on individual customer needs. This system has increased customer product turnover by 20 to 30 percent, and the retailer often sells the inventory before paying for it.[9] Of course, for this program to be successful, customers must share critical inventory data with P&G and trust that P&G will operate in the customers' best interest.

The factors associated with success in selling are also changing as sales forces change from a transactional to a solutions selling model. In a recent survey of over 200 sales executives in a variety of industries, the top five factors judged to be important to success in sales were the following in order of importance:

Listening skills
Follow-up skills
Ability to adapt sales style to the situation
Seeing a task through to its completion
Well organized[10]

This is a vastly different list from that associated with success in the traditional transactional selling model and is reflective of the greater sophistication and business knowledge that today's salespeople must possess in order to provide their customers with solutions. The qualities of top sales professionals run a close parallel with the qualities of top leaders.

Sales Teams. As the P&G experience suggests, the importance of the "lone-wolf" salesperson winning and losing on the strength of his or her own efforts and skills is likely to diminish in the future. In the case of relationship selling, no one person possesses the necessary knowledge and resources to address the bigger opportunities to create value that go beyond selling the product. Figure 1-5 illustrates the change made by P&G. Under the traditional buyer-seller interface model, all of P&G's capabilities and communications with the retailer were funneled through one salesperson whose customer contact was a purchasing agent. With *sales teams*, the model is reversed, with multiple contacts being established between P&G and retailers. This model allows for a broader transfer of capabilities and communications. Notice also that both the seller and buyer must change, so the degree and extent of interaction expand dramatically. Obviously, not all buyers and sellers are prepared to make these adjustments.

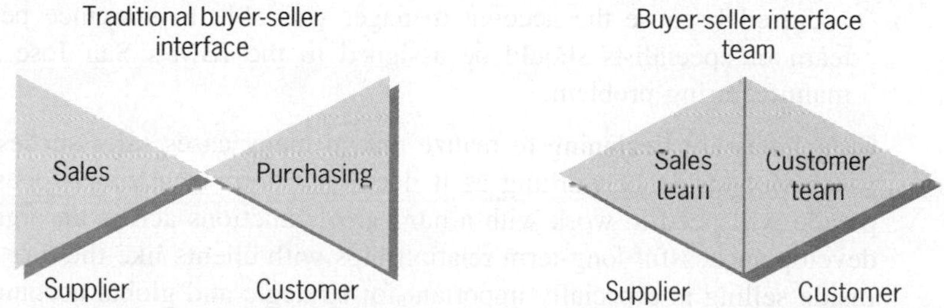

FIGURE 1-5 Traditional Buyer-Seller Interface versus a Team Interface

The switch to sales teams incorporating a relational sales orientation has a number of critical consequences for a firm's sales program and management processes. Sales teams require changes in a firm's organization structure, selection process, training program, compensation plan, and evaluation processes. Even with strong top management commitment and support, it took P&G five years to transition relationship selling and sales teams, and there is still a commitment to constantly revisit progress and make further adoptions. In recognition of its importance, we will discuss team building later in this chapter as an important competency for sales managers.

Sales Networks. Anyone in sales will tell you that networks are critical to his or her success. The more contacts you have, the more leads you generate, and ultimately the more sales you'll make. While this is true, the situation today is more complex because of the changes noted previously with customers and the marketplace. Today, sales networks are needed to not only prospect for new customers, but networks are also often required for closing the complex deal and for providing customer solutions. To complicate matters even more, research is finding that the type of sales network needed to find prospects is different from that needed to close the deal and to provide customer solutions.[11]

Specifically, successful prospecting depends on the salesperson's acquiring precise and timely information about opportunities from contacts outside the seller's organization. We discuss this type of sales networking more in Chapter 5, Customer Interaction Management. The sales network for closing the complex sale, however, is quite different. At this point the salesperson needs to secure meetings with key decision makers so that the proposal gets serious consideration. This involves knowing who in the customer's company makes the decisions, who has influence, and who is involved in implementing and working with the solution. Because answers must come from inside the customer's business, the salesperson must develop a network inside the business to help achieve the sales goal. This type of networking is discussed in greater detail in Chapter 4, Account Relationship Management. Yet a third sales network is needed to provide the customer solution because rarely does the salesperson come up with the complete solution in a complex sales situation. Success depends on the salesperson knowing where within his or her own organization the solution resides.[12] Consider the following example involving 3M and IBM:

- The 3M account manager for the IBM account discovered that one of IBM's major manufacturing problems involved electrostatic discharge. Thinking that proprietary 3M technologies might help address the problem, the account manager brought in a core group of four people from 3M's Technology Group to study and solve the problem. The group spent over two years addressing the problem and was able to significantly reduce IBM's problem, translating into several million dollars of savings for IBM. As a result, IBM asked 3M to supply the manufacturing system components throughout its worldwide operations. As a result, 3M increased sales to IBM by 300 percent over two years, generating more than $10 million in incremental revenue. This increase in revenue occurred because the account manager was able to convince people inside 3M that a team of specialists should be assigned to the IBM's San Jose facility to address the manufacturing problem.

Companies are beginning to realize that in many cases sales success depends as much on successful inside networking as it does on external customer-focused networking. Salespeople will need to work with a number of functions across an organization if they are to develop successful long-term relationships with clients like the one between 3M and IBM. Inside selling is especially important for strategic and global account selling.[13]

Productivity Metrics. Historically, sales performance metrics were simple—increase revenue over the previous year. Sales managers typically rewarded and compensated salespeople by evaluating sales volume over a certain period of time. Although sales volume is still important, companies are discovering that not all sales are equally profitable. Profitability often depends on the following:

- The amount of time necessary to complete the sale
- The gross margins associated with the sale
- The level of price discounting
- The amount of promotional support
- The amount of post-sale support
- The potential for future sales

The sales force has an important influence on all these issues through their account selection, account penetration, account retention, pricing, and servicing decisions. In effect, salespeople are resource allocators. First, they decide on which customers and prospects they will spend time selling and how much time they will allocate to each customer. These decisions and the metrics for making them are discussed in Chapter 4. Second, the sales force also has an important role in the allocation of marketing resources to individual customers.

For example, sales forces for large food manufacturers selling through grocery stores are responsible for trade promotion spending decisions, such as coupon promotions, newspaper advertising, display racks, and price promotions. These trade promotions typically account for close to 50 percent of the marketing budgets for consumer goods companies. Spending this money effectively is critical to these firms' profitability. As a result, salespeople are being evaluated on a wider array of performance metrics, which places greater emphasis on gathering more and better performance data. We discuss these performance metrics further in Chapter 13.

As indicated at the beginning of this chapter, it is an exciting time to be in sales and sales management. The breadth of skills and knowledge required to excel in sales has increased dramatically. As a consequence, sales is becoming an important proving ground for top marketing and operating officers in many companies. In the next section we try to provide a picture of what sales management is all about by first describing the functions they perform, followed by a discussion of the activities in which they are involved, and finally the competencies a successful manager needs to develop.

THE SALES MANAGEMENT PROCESS

As stated earlier, the two primary responsibilities of sales managers are to achieve their firm's goals for the current planning period and to develop the people reporting to them. One field sales manager described the job as follows:

> People development is my main mission in life: 50 percent people development, 30 percent sales and product leadership, 10 percent administration, and 10 percent compliance—you go to jail if you are not the policeman on the block.[14]

To better understand how sales managers execute these responsibilities, in this section we describe a fundamental process for sales management, the activities in which sales managers are engaged, and the competencies needed to be a successful sales manager.

The sequence of activities that guides managers in the creation and administration of sales programs for a firm is known as the sales management process. This text is organized around the steps in this sales management process. Each step is briefly described here.

Focusing on the Big Picture

An effective sales force is a powerful asset for any company. Physicians have consistently ranked Pfizer's sales force as one of the best in the pharmaceutical industry. As a result, when Parke-Davis launched its blockbuster cholesterol-lowering drug, Lipitor, it entered into an alliance in which Pfizer's sales force pitched the drug to physicians throughout the United States.

A company's management process is fundamentally affected by the firm's overall business strategy and its strategy for accessing its target markets. The relationship between business strategy, a firm's marketing strategy, and a firm's strategic sales force program is discussed in Chapter 2. Two management resource presentations follow Chapter 2: sales force investment and sales forecasting. Put together, Chapter 2 and sales forecasting and sales force investment constitute the "big picture" focus of top sales force executives.

Roles of the Sales Force

To be successful and produce profitable results, a firm's business strategy and market access strategy must be implemented by the sales force. In other words, strategic plans are implemented through the activities and behaviors of the sales force. Key sales force behaviors include calling on certain types of customers and prospects, managing customer relationships, and creating value for individual customers. The role of the sales force in implementing a firm's market access strategy is the focus of the second section of this text. This section is organized hierarchically to first look at managing multiple sales opportunities (Chapter 3), account relationships (Chapter 4), and customer interactions (Chapter 5). Together, these chapters examine the activities and behaviors of successful sales forces.

Structuring the Sales Force

To meet customer needs efficiently and effectively and to sell the firm's products and services, a sales force must be well organized. Sales force structure decisions influence how customers see the firm because sales force structure will affect the selling skills and knowledge level required of salespeople. In turn, sales management activities such as compensation, recruitment, training, and evaluation are affected. Alternative sales force structures are presented, and their implications are discussed in Chapter 6. Following this chapter is a management resource describing a process for aligning sales territories, that is, assigning customers to salespeople.

Building Sales Competencies

Sales managers are responsible for hiring salespeople with the appropriate skills and backgrounds to implement the sales strategy. Good sources must be found for new hires, and those who are weak in these areas must be carefully screened out. These and other recruiting issues are covered in Chapter 7.

In addition to hiring qualified people, salespeople's competencies are usually developed through training before they are sent into the field. Sales managers are responsible for making sure that training is completed, and they often conduct some of the classes.

Most initial training programs are designed to familiarize salespeople with the company's products, services, and operating procedures, with some time devoted to development of selling skills. Because sales training is expensive, the sales manager is responsible for selecting the most cost-effective methods, location, and materials. A detailed discussion of training is given in Chapter 8.

Leading the Sales Force

Effective sales managers know how to supervise and lead their salespeople. Sales managers provide leadership by inspiring people to grow and develop professionally, while achieving the revenue goals of the firm (Chapter 9).

In addition to leading the sales force in business results, sales managers are also expected to lead by example in encouraging ethical behavior within the sales force. Salespeople are continually confronted with ethical dilemmas; Chapter 10 provides some background on these problems so that informed decisions can be made.

Sales managers use a variety of tools in their efforts to motivate salespeople to work more efficiently and effectively. Chapter 11 describes a proven process for achieving goal-directed effort. The chapter also discusses other techniques that have proved to be effective motivators, including sales meetings, quotas, sales contests, and recognition awards.

The most powerful motivator for salespeople is often a well-designed compensation package. Money is an important consideration for attracting and motivating people to work hard (Chapter 12). A key task for sales managers is to devise an effective mix of salary, bonuses, commissions, expenses, and benefits without putting the firm's profitability in jeopardy.

The final step in the sales management process is to evaluate the performance of the sales force and develop the skills of their people. This involves analyzing sales data by account, territory, and product line breakdowns (Chapter 13). It also means reviewing selling costs and measuring the impact of sales force activities on profits.

Based on the prior discussion of the sales manager process, which person would you promote in the Team Exercise "Who to Promote?"

THE SALES MANAGEMENT COMPETENCIES

We've talked about the sales management process, but you may be wondering what it takes to be an outstanding sales manager. So, let's look more closely at the competencies that managers need in order to succeed.

Sales management competencies are defined as sets of knowledge, skills, behaviors, and attitudes that a person needs to be effective in a wide range of industries and various types of organizations.[15] People use many types of competencies in their everyday lives. Here we

FIGURE 1-6 A Model of Sales Management Competencies

TEAM EXERCISE
"Who to Promote?"

Your company has experienced fantastic growth during the past year, with sales jumping an average of 60 percent per month because of the added exposure a new product, StarDuster, has given to all of the company's other products. Introducing the new product has also had salespeople working double-time.

Assume you are the vice president of sales. Lately, you have been spending most of your time interviewing and hiring new salespeople. After adding ten new salespeople, you realize that you need to promote one of your senior reps to be an area sales manager. You want to choose the person who will keep sales growth high and the reps motivated, but also someone who can maintain records and budgets as if the area were his or her own business. You have narrowed your choices down to the following two people. Which would you choose to promote to manager and why? Remember to consider the duties of a sales manager and the skills that sales managers need to perform effectively. You also do not want to lose one rep by promoting the other, so how would you handle the discussion with the person you do not promote?

LISA BELL	Lisa is very persistent, won't take "no" for an answer, and is one of your best closers. She has been a President's Club member (top 10 percent in sales each year) every year since she was hired five years ago. Her dynamic personality is an inspiration to other reps, and she has had great success with the two rookie reps she has mentored. Her "take-charge" personality has been of benefit to you and you have often asked her to help you plan sales meetings.
STEVEN BELLACH	Steven is a six-year veteran with the company and a solid producer who is looked up to by many of the younger reps. He is great at building customer relationships and always has supportive words and suggestions for his peers on how to improve their sales techniques. He is surprisingly detail oriented for a salesperson; his sales reports are always filled in perfectly and turned in on time.

focus on six competencies (Figure 1-6) that you will need for today's sales management responsibilities. Exercises are included at the end of each chapter focusing on each of the six competencies. Let's examine the dimensions of each of these competencies more closely.

Strategic Action Competency

Understanding the overall strategy and goals of the company and ensuring that your actions and those of the people you manage are consistent with these goals involves strategic action competency. Strategic action competency includes:

- Understanding the industry
- Understanding the organization
- Taking strategic actions

Today's sales managers are being challenged to think strategically in order to improve their job performance. One dimension of strategic thinking is to anticipate strategic trends in the industry and to make the appropriate adjustments to take advantage of these changes. Failure to do so may be very costly.

The plight of Encyclopedia Britannica Corporation is a good example of the possible penalty for ignoring important industry trends. First published 225 years ago in Edinburgh, Scotland, sales of *Encyclopaedia Britannica* peaked in 1990 at $650 million. As CD-ROM technology gained acceptance, however, Britannica's management failed to respond and continued to market through a direct sales force of 2,300 people. Part of the reason Britannica found it hard to change is that a typical sale pays the salesperson a commission of $300. With CD-ROM encyclopedia packages priced from $99 to $395, commissions would have dropped significantly. It also would have required marketing through competing channels of distribution such as retail outlets, direct mail, and telemarketing, a change the powerful direct sales force would have resisted. As a consequence, however, sales declined dramatically, profitability has been a problem, and the sales force has been reduced to less than half of its former size. Britannica has also reduced its price and production costs, and developed electronic versions on CD-ROM, DVD, and the World Wide Web.[16]

This competency also involves understanding the organization—not just the sales unit in which the manager works. Goals and standards will cascade from above. Unless you are well connected and can influence them, your point of view goes unheard at the top. The first five chapters of this text are organized to reflect the hierarchical nature of goals, strategies, and tactics. After examining the competitive environment (Chapter 1), a strategy or plan for achieving specific goals must be developed (Chapter 2), which will have implications for how resources are allocated across various market opportunities (Chapter 3), what types of customer relationships are developed (Chapter 4), and how the account interaction is executed (Chapter 5).

Coaching Competency

Comparisons are often made between the competitive worlds of sports and business sales. Athletes compete against opposing players to win the game, whereas salespeople compete with other companies' salespeople to win accounts. Like the athletic coach, the sales manager plays an important role in this competition by helping to develop the skills of the sales team.[17] The president of a large distribution company developed the habit of calling a district sales manager into his office and bringing up an account on his computer. He then asked the manager to comment on what he or she had done to support the salesperson's relationship-building efforts in that account. He didn't tell the district managers how to help salespeople build better account relationships. He wanted to reinforce the importance of this management responsibility. At first, managers were unprepared, but as soon as the message was understood, helping salespeople build better customer relationships became a priority among the district managers. Soon other senior officers began copying the president's actions.

Coaching is defined as a sequence of conversations and activities that provide ongoing feedback and encouragement to a salesperson or sales team member with the goal of improving that person's performance. Performance improvement is achieved by

- Providing verbal feedback
- Role modeling
- Building trust

Coaching helps salespeople develop through one-on-one feedback and encouragement. The best coaches don't tell salespeople what to do; rather, they collaborate with them to achieve mutually agreed-upon goals. In this role, a sales manager works with each person to create and implement a developmental plan to improve performance. This process often includes providing ongoing training and coaching in selling skills, sales strategy, and product and market knowledge.

Sales coaching, however, involves more than just providing verbal feedback on what a salesperson has done. Successful sales coaches also provide a role model of positive example through their own behavior or that of others. According to one successful sales manager:

> I believe in the power of personal example. You can rant and rave and threaten, but the most effective way to get results is to show someone what you want done.[18]

Many sales managers believe that being a good role model is the most effective way to gain the respect of their salespeople.

Still, a salesperson must be open to coaching, taking feedback constructively, and following the sales manager's example. This requires a level of trust between a salesperson and a sales manager.[19] A climate of trust is created when a manager is honest and reliable, and shows a genuine concern about the needs of the salespeople. This is achieved by listening and maintaining an open, two-way channel of communications. As the saying goes: "They won't care what you know, until they know you care."

Team-Building Competency

Accomplishing tasks through small groups of people who are collectively responsible and whose work is interdependent requires a team-building competency. Sales managers in companies that utilize sales teams can become more effective by

- Designing teams properly
- Creating a supportive environment
- Managing team dynamics appropriately

Over the past decade, companies have increased their use of teams. In sales the primary reason for the use of teams is to improve customer service and sales force productivity. To help its customers focus on patient care, Allegiance Healthcare includes a wide range of functional experts on its customer teams. Financial experts monitor regional economics, for instance, while information service specialists help customers with their information systems needs. Marketing liaisons analyze product-specific data such as usage trends and pricing options, and the logistics experts help customers streamline their logistical processes.

A well-designed team is capable of high performance, but it needs a supportive environment to achieve its full potential. In a supportive environment, team members are empowered to take actions based on their best judgment. This means that it is very important to hire people who can get along with others and who work well within a team environment. These salespersons are quite different from the traditional salespersons who survived by relying solely on their own abilities. A recent study concluded that approximately 25 percent of the performance of sales teams was a function of the diversity within the sales team, with more diverse sales teams expressing greater job satisfaction.[20] Successful team development undoubtedly will require team training, which is necessary to allow team members to assume each other's roles and to work interdependently.

Conflicts and disagreements among team members are natural, which means that managing team dynamics is necessary for effective team building. Essentially, this means maintaining cooperative relationships while pursuing a common goal. If managed well, conflict can be productive; if managed poorly, however, it can destroy the team. Demonstrate your team building skills on the Team Exercise: "Prima Donna."

Self-Management Competency

Taking responsibility for your actions at work and elsewhere involves self-management competency. When problems arise, people often blame their difficulties on the situation or on others. Effective managers don't fall into this trap. Self-management competency includes

- Integrity and ethical conduct
- Managing personal drive
- Self-awareness and development

TEAM EXERCISE
"The Prima Donna"

You manage a team of salespeople located throughout a twelve-state area in the Midwest. You stay in touch with your people via regular conference calls and weekly progress reports. Fran Lowe, your star salesperson and a bit of a prima donna, often misses meetings and is late with reports because her territory is particularly difficult. You are starting to sense some resentment from your other salespeople that Lowe gets a free pass on her administrative duties because of her sales success. What should you do?

Sales managers are in a particularly sensitive position with respect to integrity and ethical conduct. To achieve success, the sales force must trust and respect a sales manager. How is it possible to respect people you feel have no integrity and do not conduct themselves ethically? As a person who influences or controls the rewards salespeople receive, a manager's ethics and integrity are constantly under review. As the leader of the sales team, salespeople take their cues from the sales manager with respect to the ethical treatment of customers. If salespeople are aware of instances in which a sales manager has bent the rules to make a sale to one customer, they are more likely to model this behavior. At the same time, there is increasing emphasis on ethical professional behavior, and important penalties are associated with unethical behavior.

Business is responding to the public's increasingly negative view of business ethics due to recent scandals by developing and enforcing codes of ethics, instituting formal ethics training programs, and maintaining standing ethics committees. Evidence of industry's interest in ethics is also seen in the establishment and continued growth of the Ethics Officers Association (EOA), which is dedicated to promoting ethical business practices.[21]

A sales manager's job is more than just balancing the many issues that arise each day. The most important part of his or her job is achieving a balance between personal goals and those of the organization and of the people he or she manages. After being promoted to sales management a year earlier, one manager responded as follows to the question of what satisfied him:

> What satisfies me about the job? Well, you do get feedback. Every month you can see how much your team has generated and you can see which people have developed and maybe even been promoted. You know you are doing something that is important to the company, something that needs to be done—both making money and helping people grow and move—both aspects bring their own satisfactions.

Self-awareness is a critical element of being a good sales manager. This begins with the reason for wanting to be a sales manager in the first place. People are attracted to management for a variety of reasons, including being tired of their present job, the opportunity to assume more authority and make more money, and the opportunity to exercise power and influence. New managers quickly discover that these reasons don't help them much in the day-to-day life of a sales manager, which often leads to self-doubts and a focus on the question, "Will I be good at it?" Following are comments from three new sales managers regarding what they discovered about themselves through their salespeople:

- I saw my style as very aggressive, demanding, interested, and involved. They saw me as a dictator, a tyrant on their backs.
- I was just being myself. But after three weeks on the job, it was coming back to me that people thought I was harsh, harsh. I needed to soften.

- What an eye-opener. People were trying to tell me I was too indecisive. I made them nervous because I seemed timid. No one had ever called me timid before.[22]

To help you in your own self-awareness, a number of self-assessment exercises have been included in the following chapters. The best way to develop self-awareness, however, is to do something: take some action. A number of experiential exercises are suggested at the end of the chapters along with in-class exercises in which the feedback from other students and your instructor will be helpful in developing self-awareness. The Developing Your Competencies section at the end of this chapter poses challenging problems and self-assessment exercises. Real-word, practical challenges are also posed in each chapter's Team Exercises, which are designed for small teams to tackle. How would you handle the issues posed in "How to Handle Rumors?"

TEAM EXERCISE
"How to Handle Rumors"

One of your salespeople tells you about an interesting conversation he had this morning with a long-time customer about a competitor's salesperson who used to work for you, but was discharged for underperforming. The sales rep had criticized your company and you, as a sales manager. He told the customer that the quality of your company's products had diminished significantly in recent years and that consequently your salespeople were having a hard time selling to prospects and are relying on past reputations to sell to current customers. He also added that your make-quota-or-leave mentality is forcing reps to push products that customers don't really need, such as updates of new parts before old parts are worn out. Your salesperson indicated that this particular long-time customer was unmoved by the competitor's accusations and, in fact, thought that his approach was in bad taste. She also was insulted by the suggestion that she's one of the customers being duped by your company, which implies that she isn't doing her job properly.

After thanking your salesperson for telling you about this, you head back to your office to consider what to do with this information. Will other customers react as this one has? What about prospects—how will they react? Have other customers heard this story and not told your salespeople? What, if anything, should you do now? In addition, should you say anything at your next Monday morning sales meeting with your sales team? If so, what will you say?

Global Perspective Competency

Drawing on human, financial, information, and material resources from multiple countries and serving customers who span multiple cultures requires a global perspective competency. Not all companies compete in global markets or service customers who sell throughout the world, but during the course of your career, it's likely that you will work for an organization that has a global sales component. To be prepared for such an opportunity, you should begin to develop your global perspective competency, which in sales is reflected in

- Cultural knowledge and sensitivity
- Global selling program

By the time you become a sales manager in your home country, your own culture has become second nature to you. However, unless you have traveled extensively, or studied other cultures as part of your education, you probably have much less general knowledge and understanding of other countries, even those that share a border with your own country. Yet because business is becoming global, many managers are now expected to develop a knowledge and understanding of at least a few other cultures, such as where the company is marketing its products or where customers are selling their products. For example, Wyeth-Ayerst International sells pharmaceuticals in 100 countries and employs 50 international sales trainers. The skills component of their training programs emphasizes that listening, asking the right questions, and probing for needs are the same throughout the world. Nevertheless, the company adapts training to local conditions in response to cultural differences. Salespeople are taught when to drink tea, when to schedule appointments, and when to close.[23]

Selling globally or to global accounts affects almost everything a sales manager does. Selection, for instance, becomes more difficult. One study reported that sales executives rated only half of expatriates as effective.[24] Coordination also becomes problematic as issues arising between sales efforts at global headquarters and in individual regions and locations are exacerbated. In recognition of this complication, global issues are discussed in each of the following chapters.

Technology Competency

Understanding the potential for technology to improve sales force efficiency and effectiveness and knowing how to implement the integration of technology into the sales force is referred to as possessing technology competency. Consider the following examples in which technology has significantly increased sales force productivity:

- The TaylorMade Company, a marketer of golf equipment, increased sales force productivity by 25 percent through the use of a handheld wireless activity inventory system to take the inventory of retail stores automatically, allowing salespeople more time to focus on helping retailers increase sales.
- The Vanguard Group offers a Web interface that is accessible to both customers and the sales force. Customers use it to open new accounts, purchase and redeem fund shares, and gain access to account performance. The sales force is freed up to devote time to higher value interactions. Vanguard's Web customers invest 150 percent more than non-Web customers, and the cost to serve them is just 5 percent of what is spent with a human interface.

Technology competency includes:

- Understanding the productivity potential of new technology
- Implementing sales force automation (SFA)
- Implementing customer relationship management (CRM)

Many experts consider the integration of communications technology, more commonly known as *sales force automation (SFA)*, as not only a source of competitive advantage but increasingly as a necessity to stay competitive. According to a recent survey of top sales executives, 83 percent of respondents' companies plan to upgrade existing sales and marketing servicc and customer relationship management systems. The average budget companies have slated for these initiatives is $1.5 million.[25]

Sales and marketing adoption of technology tends to evolve over the years. In the first stage, sales force automation systems often focus on efficiency and consist of call reporting systems focused on tracking activities that are designed to automate repetitive and error-prone sales tasks such as order processing. In the next stage, a company may adopt an electronic territory management system to increase sales force effectiveness by assisting with targeting and customer profiling. In the third stage, a company may adopt a customer relationship management perspective to technology in recognition that a firm's relationship with a customer is a many-to-many relationship. Sales, service, marketing, finance, product development, as well as a company's partners, all need to collaborate and share information in order to meet customer needs. A major focus of CRM systems is to ensure a consistent experience for a customer across multiple sales channels. If a customer gets product information over the Internet, makes an inquiry over the phone, sees a technical specialist for product design assistance, and sees a salesperson for pricing information, CRM systems seek to ensure that all the parties have the same information for seamless collaboration. This helps companies be more effective in communicating with a customer and more efficient in transacting business.

When implemented correctly, SFA and CRM can streamline a company's entire selling process. Although most companies can't afford not to automate, an estimated 61 percent of automation projects fail to deliver the expected benefits.[26] According to experts, company efforts to automate are jeopardized by one of three reasons, each of which causes sales force resistance. One reason for resistance is that the sales force does not understand how SFA and CRM will help them in their efforts to sell. Research indicates that appropriate technology training and improved salesperson effectiveness will cause resistance to technology and job insecurity to abate.[27] In other words, management has not clearly identified and communicated what they want to accomplish. Second, sales management may expect SFA and CRM to allow better control of remote and mobile salespeople. Experience shows that when the balance shifts to management control and data collection from increasing sales-rep productivity, the sales force will resist. Third, resistance is likely when top management is not committed to automation by adapting technology themselves. Unfortunately, it is still almost a badge of honor among top corporate officers to not know how to use their own personal computer.

Proficiency in working with and presenting numerical information is increasingly demanded of new sales hires in many companies. To help you in developing this proficiency, problems have been included in the appropriate chapters accompanied by Excel spreadsheets. The companies we have talked with and the sales managers who have been chapter consultants for this text have indicated that they expect their new hires to have a basic proficiency in the use of spreadsheets, which is why we have included the problems along with Excel files for your analysis.

CAREER PATHS

Sales is a great way to start a career. We believe it is important for students to understand how someone moves into the position of sales manager and what the opportunities are for further advancement. Sales managers almost always begin their *career paths* as salespeople. The median age of newly appointed first-line field sales managers is about 30 with about three to five years of prior sales experience with the company. Many selling and sales management experts will testify that there is a significant positive correlation between salespeople's success and the quality of their sales manager.[28] Because of their enthusiasm and fresh ideas, new sales managers are often able to boost the sales of the salespeople they supervise. The bottom line is that you can make a difference with a career in sales management. That the average total compensation for sales managers is over $150,000 also testifies to the importance of this position.[29] Following is one person's story.

The Path to CEO

Lisa Cash started in sales with Club Corporation of America in the early 1980s. She worked her way up to regional sales and marketing manager by 1991. In 1992, she joined Bell Atlantic, now Verizon, where she managed two separate $100 million divisions. Intrigued by the fast-growing high-tech sector, Cash took a position with a software company. She was hired as East Coast sales manager of Princeton Softech in 1997. After a short time, she started taking on additional projects that utilized her experience. One of these projects was implementing a telemarketing channel (outbound sales calls) for the company, which eventually led to an appointment as vice president of sales in 1999. When the company's CEO decided to leave, it was Cash he recommended to replace him. According to Cash, "I think we are seeing more CEOs from sales and marketing because they have highly developed communication and persuasion skills. And they have a high level of awareness about the importance of the customer."[30]

Procter & Gamble

Sales careers with consumer product firms begin in the field. At P&G, the role of sales is to deliver brand volume and market share at a competitive cost. The sales force is a part of the Market Development Organization, which is organized as shown in Figure 1-7. As you can see in the figure, there are only four levels of management below the executive management level. An account manager, either as a part of an account team or a geographic unit, is responsible for influencing decisions affecting P&G brands at individual retail outlets. An account manager is expected to develop and execute merchandising and promotional programs that grow the profits and sales for the customer and the brand.

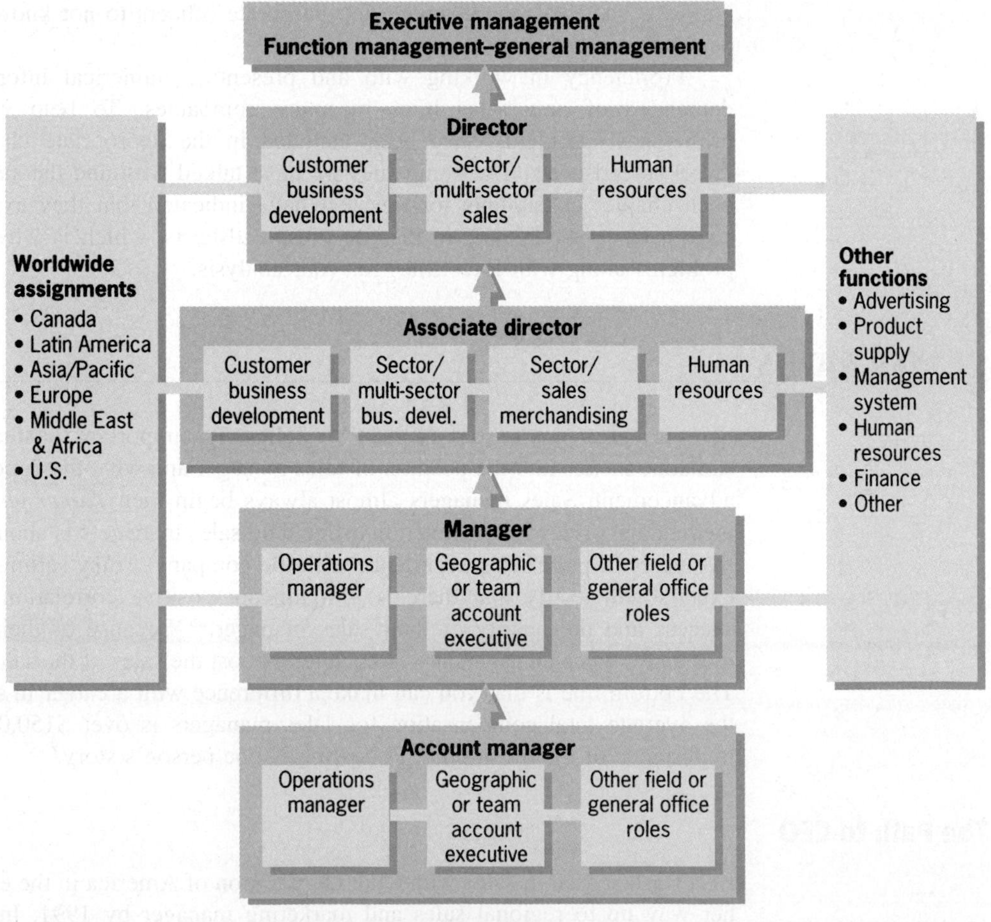

FIGURE 1-7 Career Paths at Procter & Gamble

The account executive level influences P&G brand decisions at the customer headquarter level, while also coordinating local store activities of the account managers. An associate director is responsible for all the brand, customer, and functional strategies in a particular business sector, such as major food distributors, national chains, wholesale clubs, and discounters in a particular region of the country. A director leads the sales organization of multiple sectors and influences brand merchandising strategy and customer strategy. A director would be involved in decisions such as the overall structure of the sales force, the development of sales force competencies, and performance emphasis.

Opportunities for personal growth and development may be found within each of the four organizational levels at P&G. So, a new recruit might start as an account manager in the Midwestern Kroger customer team. After several years, he might be promoted to head up the Southeastern Safeway customer team as an account executive. This promotion might be followed by an assignment in Europe or in human resources as a trainer. A key advantage of a career at P&G is the wide variety of positions available that provide experience needed to climb the ladder of success.

PREPARING FOR SALES MANAGEMENT SUCCESS

Sales Management was written to prepare you for a successful sales management career. To accomplish this objective, its chapters provide comprehensive coverage in a manner that is both interesting and engaging. In addition, each chapter has been reviewed and enhanced by the experiences and suggestions of highly successful people in sales and marketing, including, among others, Paulette Turner, Sales Operations Business Unit Executive, IBM Corporation; B. J. Polk, Director-Sales-Marketing, Procter & Gamble Distributing Company; and Joseph Clayton, Chairman of the Board, Sirius Satellite. They have passed along the lessons they have learned to help you be a success.

Success in business is directly related to the competencies that you develop. The remaining chapters build on the competencies introduced in this chapter. These six competencies have been identified as important for success in management. At the conclusion of each chapter, exercises for developing each of the six key competencies are presented. Each exercise relates to the chapter's topic and is designed to help you build your competencies so that you are prepared to assume sales management responsibilities when the opportunity is presented.

To further help in your development, each chapter includes several Team Exercises describing typical situations in the day-to-day life of a sales manager. Each situation calls for you to decide the most appropriate action to be taken and often includes the opportunity to think about the words and phrases you would use when talking with the other people in the exercise. Because more than one person is usually involved, this exercise lends itself well to a team or group discussion and role playing of conversations between individuals.

Each chapter begins with a company or individual vignette introducing many of the concepts and issues discussed in the chapter in a live situation. On the first page of each chapter is a list of Learning Objectives for that chapter. A Summary at the end of each chapter revisits each learning objective, along with a brief description of the topic. Key terms are presented in italics and are listed at the end of each chapter. Comprehensive cases are presented at the end of the book.

Following this chapter is the Shield Financial case describing Doug Bloom's first days after being promoted to sales manager in a financial services company. This first case describes the company, its products, and organization, as well as the "growing pains" Doug goes through in those first months as a sales manager. You are given the opportunity to grow with Doug as he faces challenges described at the end of each chapter. Again, you are asked to make decisions based on the background information presented in the chapter. By the end of the book, you will have matured along with Doug and will have gone through the full cycle of issues common to the sales manager position. In short, by reviewing the material in the chapters and addressing the challenges presented within and at the end of each chapter, you will be much further along the path to success in sales management.

SUMMARY

This chapter has introduced the topics of personal selling and sales management. Where personal selling focuses on direct contacts with prospects, sales management is concerned with the planning, organizing, leading, and controlling of personal contact programs to satisfy customers and achieve the objectives of the firm. You should now be able to do the following:

1. **Describe the major changes taking place in selling and the forces causing these changes.** The competitive marketplace is becoming more globalized, product life cycles are getting shorter, and competitive boundaries are blurring. At the same time, customers are buying from fewer suppliers, their service and performance expectations are increasing, and their power is increasing so that they can not only demand but also obtain higher service and offerings from suppliers. As a result of these forces, the selling process is becoming more focused on relationship selling, selling teams are often necessary to fully address customer needs, people are spending more of their time on internal selling and marshaling resources to develop customer solutions, and sales force success is increasingly measured in terms of productivity and profits as opposed to top-line revenues.
2. **Define sales management.** Sales management is defined as the planning, organizing, leading, and controlling of personal contact programs designed to achieve the sales and profit objectives of the firm.
3. **Describe the sales management process.** For pedagogical purposes and by way of organizing the variety of activities involved in sales management, the sales management process is grouped as follows: seeing the big picture and developing strategic sales plans, defining the role of the sales force in executing a firm's business plan, structuring the sales force for efficiency and effectiveness, building the sales competencies necessary to implement the firm's business strategy, and leading the sales force to achieve success. Although these steps are not usually performed in sequence, this organization of sales management activities provides a good overview of the decisions in which sales managers at all levels in the organization are involved.
4. **Discuss the competencies required to be a successful sales manager.** To be an effective sales manager in a dynamic environment requires six competencies: strategic action, coaching, team building, self-management, a global perspective, and a technology competency. You can develop these competencies through study, training, and experience. By doing so, you can prepare yourself for a variety of sales and sales management positions in various industries and countries. You can continue practicing your managerial competencies by completing the exercises at the end of this and subsequent chapters.

KEY TERMS

Career paths
Globalization
Personal selling
Sales force automation (SFA)
Sales management
Sales management competencies
Sales manager
Sales teams
Solutions selling model
Transactional selling model

DEVELOPING YOUR COMPETENCIES

1. **Technology Competency.** When JVC Company of America, an audio and visual equipment manufacturer, decided to explore sales force automation (SFA) with its 200-plus reps, mostly working from their homes, it asked them two questions: "What would you like to have on your desk at home?" and "What questions do you get asked?" JVC reps wanted to be able to provide answers to their customers' queries about purchase orders and inventory. JVC implemented a software program that lets reps download that information from a mainframe every day, providing them with instant information and saving them considerable time in having to call headquarters and customers the next day. What did JVC do right in this SFA effort, and what other things could they have done to ensure a successful SFA implementation? For more on JVC Company, visit the company's home page at www.JVC.com.

2. **Team-Building Competency.** GoldMine Software Corporation is a leading developer of software solutions for sales and marketing teams. Firms like GoldMine that sell complex analytical software are relying more on sales teams to work with customers, partly because a single salesperson can never know everything about the product. Nonetheless, companies have found it difficult to transition to a sales team-selling effort from a more traditional model. What are some of the problems that GoldMine is likely to encounter with a team sales operation? For more information on GoldMine Software Corporation, visit the company's home page at www.goldminesw.com.

3. **Coaching Competency.** Which sales force situation do sales executives prefer?

   - Average salespeople and an excellent manager

     or

   - Excellent salespeople and an average manager

   Consultants have asked hundreds of sales vice presidents, national sales managers, and regional sales managers this question. Which one would you prefer if you were the top sales executive of your company?

4. **Strategic Action Competency.** Carter Diamond Tool has been a leader in manufacturing and has been designing high-quality synthetic and natural diamond cutting tools and dressers since 1920. Until recently, it employed ten salespeople to call on accounts. Dissatisfied with the results, Carter Diamond discharged all ten in favor of eight independent manufacturer's representatives. (Manufacturer's reps are not employed by the company; they sell for a number of companies.) The reps in this case sold other industrial products along with the Precision line to the same customers. Immediately, sales began to increase, old business was retrieved, and new accounts were acquired. What possible reasons might explain this? What are the advantages and disadvantages of manufacturer's reps compared to an in-house sales force? For more on Carter Diamond Tool, visit its home page at www.carterdiamond.com.

5. **Self-management.** A good way to learn about sales management is to spend a day with an actual sales manager. Contact a sales manager and arrange to observe his or her activities during a typical day. Ask him or her what it was like becoming a sales manager. Why did this person want to be a manager? What did he or she think it would be like? What was it like during the first six months? How did he or she come to his or her present perspective? If possible, keep a log of how the sales manager's time is spent. If you have difficulty finding a cooperative sales manager, contact the local chapter of the Sales and Marketing Executives Club or the American Marketing Association, or ask your instructor for help. A good way to get started is to visit the American Marketing Association home page at www.marketingpower.com.

6. **Global Awareness.** All multinational companies face pressures from customers for globalization and global integration, but the amount of pressure varies by industry. For example, many computer suppliers, such as Hewlett-Packard and IBM, have created some of the most extensive and successful global account management programs. At Hewlett-Packard and IBM, the global account managers have significant line authority relative to national accounts managers. That is, they get involved in the evaluation, compensation, and management of local sales efforts. In contrast, Citibank's long-running "parent account" global management program gives only coordinating responsibility to the parent account managers. That is, they provide information to the local country Citibank employees and gather information from these same people. They are not responsible for hiring, managing, or evaluating local Citibank employees. Why is there this difference between Hewlett-Packard, IBM, and Citibank? The three companies have mostly the same global customers, but the global account managers are given very different responsibilities.

FEATURED CASE SHIELD FINANCIAL

I was having another good year in sales. I've been one of the top four reps at Shield Financial, averaging $150,000 per year for the past four years, and it looked like I would do it again this year. I've always taken pride in getting great results while doing things my way and not necessarily by the book. I really liked the competition and the excitement of sales, but lately I'd been thinking about moving to the next level. After all, many of my college buddies were making it in management. If they could do it, why couldn't I? Plus, I liked the thought of Doug Bloom—Manager emblazoned on my door. As far I as I could tell, a good sales manager would only work a little harder at the same things I'm doing now, but with more power, control, and autonomy. Just work with the worst reps a while, show them how it should be done and bring them up to speed, and everyone would be happy. The more I thought about it, the more I wanted it.

OPPORTUNITY KNOCKS

I was prepared to leave Shield within six months if I received a management offer from another insurance brokerage firm. I didn't want to leave; Shield had been very good to me. As luck would have it, the very next week a branch sales manager opening was posted in the company newsletter for the Midwest region. I wasn't excited about leaving Atlanta to go to Des Moines, Iowa, but the timing was perfect. Lady luck was shining on me again. I was finally going to get in the management game, and I was ready for the move.

I had a good shot at landing the job, since Shield had an unwritten policy to try and hire from within, and I was probably the top producer applying for the job. I did some checking into the position and according to the company statement, the previous manager left because "a change was needed to take the branch office into a new direction." But I heard through the grapevine that the manager was fired because sales were off the previous years. That might have explained the minimal competition from other eager sales reps who were ready to spread their management wings. Maybe they knew something I didn't. It was too late though; mentally, I already had my bags packed.

HISTORY OF SHIELD FINANCIAL COMPANY

In 1919, entrepreneur Howard Driver Sr., of Brooklyn, who just returned from World War I, joined with Tom Mader to found Shield Financial. Howard's vision of an insurance company was closely tied to the emerging popularity of the automobile industry and auto dealerships.

In subsequent years, the company grew into an insurance group, adding subsidiaries through strategic acquisitions that enhanced its geographic reach,

This case was prepared by Thomas E. DeCarlo of the University of Alabama at Birmingham and William L. Cron of Texas Christian University.

EXHIBIT 1 Sampling of Business Products

Accounts Receivable Protects against inability to collect outstanding balances as a result of lost or damaged account records.	**Brands and Labels** Pays the cost of removing the brands and labels from damaged stock so that it can be salvaged.	**Business Property** Pays for property (e.g., inventory, office furniture, etc.) if damaged by fire or other covered loss.
Business Income Reimburses earnings when a shutdown is caused by a covered cause.	**Sales Rep Protection** Protects business items, samples, and laptop computers when traveling.	**Computer Fraud** Protects against "electronic" theft of property through a computer.
Contract Penalties Pays penalties when contract promises are not met due to covered cause.	**Denial of Service Attack** Protects against computer attacks that prevent normal business operation.	**Dependent Properties** Insures against loss of income when a major supplier suffers a covered loss.
Electronic Vandalism Protects against hackers sabotaging the company's computer system.	**Employee Dishonesty** Covers loss of money or property due to employee dishonesty or fraud.	**Equipment Breakdown** Repairs or replaces damaged equipment (e.g., computer, phones, etc.)
Forgery Protects against forged or altered checks, credit card receipts, or bank drafts.	**Good Faith Advertising** Covers advertising needed to restore reputation after a covered attack.	**Money and Securities** Covers lost, stolen, or destroyed money and securities.
Newly Acquired Property Covers newly acquired buildings, even when under construction.	**Replacement Cost** Covers property without deduction for depreciation.	**Web Site Income** Protects against loss of income due to web provider disruption.

strengthened its selling and marketing capabilities, and broadened its product offerings. The most recent acquisition was the 1998 purchase of substantially all of the Commercial Lines Division of Great American Insurance Company.

Shield specialized in servicing the insurance needs of all sizes of commercial enterprises by offering customized insurance and risk management programs. Shield has products in a variety of areas, including property, auto, general liability, and workman's compensation. Exhibit 1 describes a sample of the programs Shield offers to businesses.

Headquartered in New York City, the company was organized into four regional areas with a regional vice president heading each region. Spread throughout the regions are 84 sales offices headed by a branch sales manager responsible for supervising office operations and from 8 to 12 salespeople. The company also sold through independent brokers in the less populated states of Montana, Idaho, Wyoming, Utah, and Colorado. Two broker sales managers were responsible for supervising and managing these independent brokers.

SALES MANAGER TRAINING

After signing my new contract on February 1, the company flew me and six other manager wannabes to Shield's headquarters in New York City for five days of management orientation. The training schedule was chaotic, to say the least. I think they relished the idea that more information was better. The manuals alone reached close to 3 feet high when I stacked them up in my hotel room. I could have read the materials nonstop all week and still only be half finished. They gave us manuals on strategic analysis, competitor analysis, external environment analysis, product positioning, pricing, promotion, personnel problems, coaching, feedback, performance evaluation techniques, and hiring and firing tips. Other than the consultants who wrote these books, I doubt anyone in the company has read them cover to cover. It didn't matter, they would look impressive on my office shelf.

The majority of the new manager training amounted to Shield's rollout and promotion of the new First-Plus account program. Basically, it was a renewed effort by Shield to increase revenues by encouraging sales reps to focus on larger accounts. All-Safe, our major competitor in the full service market, had already implemented its version of First-Plus and now Shield was repositioning itself as well. The VP of Marketing expected us to redirect our staff's selling efforts on this new product line as soon as we started our jobs. I thought to myself, how in the world am I going to get all 25 salespeople interested in selling this new program? I remember that I felt intimidated by the larger, more sophisticated accounts back when I first started.

In those days the smaller accounts were my bread and butter. I knew this was going to be a big change for some people.

On the last day, George Treadgold, Shield's CEO, showed up to make a few remarks and shake our hands to wish us luck. As he was shaking my hand he smiled and offered his life-in-the-trenches line, "bring in the numbers every month and everything else takes care of itself." He also mentioned using the company policy manual to avoid any personnel problems. I thought to myself what an odd combination of send-off messages. The VP of Human Resources, Ray Cody, gave me his card, slapped me on the back, and told me to call anytime if I had any problems. I had met him during my interview process five years ago; he said the same thing then. He didn't remember me.

MOVING TO DES MOINES

When I returned to Atlanta, I spent the next few days finalizing the details of my move to Des Moines. It was a hectic time. I had to bring the Atlanta office up to speed with my accounts, break my lease on my apartment, notify everyone of my new address, close bank accounts, shut off utilities, and find a new apartment in Des Moines. At first, moving sounded like a good idea, but after all the small hassles, you understand why people stay where they are. Plus, I was really going to miss Atlanta, I had some good friends there.

When I arrived in Des Moines near the end of February, I felt like I had moved to the North Pole. It was 10 degrees below zero. My first stop was to the nearest mall to buy the warmest coat I could find, then to the office to scope it out. Shield's branch office was on the 27th floor of a new high-rise office tower that overlooked the Des Moines River. I had a corner office with a huge picture window overlooking the city. I thought, this is it. The big time. My hoop dream was becoming reality and I couldn't wait to get started. As I was unpacking and organizing my office, Liz Shute, my district director, walked in. We exchanged chitchat for a few minutes, then she invited me to lunch to get acquainted.

During lunch I tried to impress her with my understanding of sales management. I made sure that she understood that I was going to be an action-oriented manager and that the majority of my job is sales and sales leadership. The next biggest part of the job is fire fighting and solving salespeople's problems. Maybe 5 percent is human relations and counseling and another 5 percent is other administration duties such as recruiting. She smiled and nodded. I didn't understand why she wasn't getting as excited as I was. I got the sense she had heard this all before from previous managers. As I was finishing the last bite of my chocolate torte, she summed everything up by stating, "Doug, I like everything that I'm hearing; just remember, though, you are accountable for the production of this office. I'll give you whatever support you need. You just get the reps to come up with the numbers and everything else should take care itself." I thought, first the CEO, now the district manager; is that the company slogan, or what?

MY FIRST SALES MEETING

After lunch, I spent the rest of the afternoon organizing a presentation to the sales staff about the new First-Plus account program. I built in some humor, stories from my background, and a model on how to operationalize the new strategy. I was thinking, what's not to like? This was going to be the perfect introduction—a new manager and a new direction. Liz was planning to introduce me, then I would take over and not look back. I was starting to get the feeling that management just might be my calling.

Liz gave me a great introduction. As I walked up to the podium, I could feel that all eyes in the room were sizing me up. I wondered if everyone could see how nervous I felt. I launched into the new strategy and provided color graphs, charts, and percentages on how the new program works and how sales reps, if they followed just the minimum of my performance model, would be compensated. Some people were actually taking notes, some were staring blankly. I thought, good time to get them involved. "Any questions?" I asked. Big mistake. Tiffany Williams, the top performer for the past eight years, raised her hand and said, "Doug, I make more than ten times the income level you just described, and I have a lot of smaller to medium-sized accounts that have taken me years to cultivate. They throw off a ton more commissions to me than my larger accounts. Why would I want to follow that model?" The room was silent. I cleared my throat. "This isn't my idea, the directive came from corporate." Tiffany responded, "I can't see why corporate would want us to completely abandon the smaller accounts." I pointed out that Shield doesn't want us to neglect the smaller accounts, but the company was moving in a new direction. Someone in the back snickered. More questions followed, some of which only Liz could answer. Overall, not what I had planned. I knew I had to do something to stop the flood of questions. I recommended that people hold their remaining questions for the individual meetings planned for Thursday and Friday so we could finish on time. One by one the hands went down.

MEETING THE REPS

The rest of the week I spent preparing for the meetings. I pored over each rep's account history and revenue numbers for the past year to find ways to sell each one on the new program. I knew that if I could find ways to get most to buy into the plan, then everyone else would eventually get on board. I scheduled the lower performers for my first meetings on Thursday morning. I figured they would help me warm up and gain confidence for the bigger hitters to follow. I was pretty sure I could get the lower performers to refocus their efforts on my model, but the higher performers might take more persuasion. Based on what I've seen, however, everyone would benefit by implementing aspects of the First-Plus program into their sales strategy. I just had to show them how.

Around 8:00 A.M. Thursday morning I was thinking how excited and nervous I was to be having my first official one-on-one meeting as a sales manager. Bill Johnson, my lowest performer, was first. I had plans for this guy and I couldn't wait to see him begin implementing this new strategy. But before I could talk about my ideas, Bill starts telling me how the First-Plus program won't work. He said he was on the verge of a breakthrough and that changing course now would destroy all of his hard work. I couldn't believe what I was hearing. If the worst performer was telling me this, I could be in for a long two days. After he finished, I gave him my pitch for the future and how he could become a player by changing strategy with his larger accounts. He said he would give it a shot and left. As he was walking out, I thought, he wasn't going to change a thing. I made a note to myself that I was going to have to spend more time with him to show him how the program would work.

Much to my surprise, most of the remaining meetings went smoother. A few were excited about the change, some just wanted to know how I pulled off the promotion, others wanted specifics about my expectations. One thing struck me though: I was not at all prepared for the individuality of my reps. No two were alike. Each one had different motivations and talents, and I spent most of each meeting figuring out each rep's hot buttons. I felt like I was dealing with 25 customers. When the final sales rep left on Friday afternoon, I was worn out. Some meetings went better than others, but all in all, not too bad.

TRYING TO KEEP UP

The first few weeks flew by, and I was putting in a lot of overtime. I routinely stayed after 5:00 P.M. Monday through Friday and worked most of the day on Saturday. I always felt it was the manager's duty to set the example and, as a sales rep, I lost respect for managers who would leave at 5:00 P.M. while others were still working. Plus, the workload was much more than I expected, so it wasn't merely an act. In between the 25 reps constantly vying for my time, I had to deal with system crashes, approve salesperson expense reports, review budgets, and prepare a three-year strategic plan due to the home office at the end of the next month. I could have worked 24 hours a day and still not be caught up. I felt like I was speeding along a curvy highway at the top of a mountain at night with no signs such as slow, curve, narrow bridge, and stop. If I drove off a cliff, the entire branch office would follow me right over too.

The results for my first month were not good—revenues slipped 15 percent. I felt like my wheels were slipping off the road. Based on the numbers, though, the sales force was not implementing the new program. I knew the reps would not like the First-Plus program to be forced down their throats, but I didn't want a repeat performance next month, so I had to take action. It was time I showed them who was running the office. I fired off a memo to all sales personnel requiring them to complete a weekly sales planning report, including their First-Plus activities for the week. Although I didn't need additional work, I was sure they would read between the lines and start focusing on the First-Plus program. The next morning Tiffany Williams called me from her car phone. "Doug," she said, "I got your memo yesterday." "Good, looking forward to seeing your plan," I said. She said, "Look, Doug, I can't control when my clients want to meet with me and I'm just a little bit too busy to be filling out reports about how I'm going to spend my time." Based on the sarcasm in her tone, I could tell she wasn't happy about the memo. I explained that some reps (including Tiffany) reached their overall quota, but everyone was behind on their First-Plus targets last month and that people need to take some steps to work toward those goals. She responded by informing me that she single-handedly produced 20 percent of the office's revenue last year, so she was exempting herself. I said, "I don't think so, Tiffany, have it on my desk first thing in the morning." As I hung up, I stared at the phone thinking, why did I say that? I shouldn't have demanded she fill it out, but too late.

HELPING REPS RESCHEDULE THEIR TIME

The following Monday everyone, except Tiffany, turned in their weekly reports. I worked through lunch making comments and reprioritizing the reps' week. I couldn't believe the inefficiencies in their schedules. Some were spending too much time with smaller accounts. Others had large chunks of time devoted to "administrative." No wonder we didn't make quota last month. It felt like this was my first real management breakthrough. Later that afternoon Bill Johnson appeared in my office, obviously upset. I had completely reorganized his schedule. He said, "Doug, what are you trying to do?" I told him I was just trying to help. His voice rose. "Maybe I'm not the best rep in the office, but I'm not incompetent. I'm close to getting things turned around." I told him I wasn't suggesting that, I was just showing him how to implement the First-Plus account management principles. He clenched his jaw and said, "Let me know when you want to take over my accounts too." He threw the reorganized schedule on my desk and stormed out of the room. I sat in my chair in disbelief for a few seconds; I could feel myself tightening up. I dashed after him and motioned him back into my office. I lost it. I started hollering, "You're lucky I'm even helping at all." He looked completely surprised. I continued: "Corporate wants you fired. But I've been covering your ass." The rest was a blur. It felt like I was on the outside looking in while this lunatic occupied my body. It wasn't me.

I figured a salesperson has to always be as cool as a cucumber while dealing with problem clients, but it's nothing compared to management. One of the fundamental lessons in management training was that the manager, more than anybody else in the branch, stands for professionalism. Finding and maintaining composure under every situation are all you've got. But, it was too late and I couldn't have a "do over." I wished the entire Human Resources Department was working down the hall.

BILL JOHNSON RESIGNS

The next Monday I got a call from Liz to let me know that she'd had complaints from corporate. I wasn't getting my expense forms in on time. I told her I've been swamped. Not only was I busy working with the reps so we could make our quarterly quota, but that I was also trying to be meticulous before I sent them over to corporate. She shot back, "You're job is to make quota and have the reports in on time." As soon as I hung up the receiver, my secretary brought in Johnson's letter of resignation. What a relief. It was just a matter of time before I had to let him go. I immediately called the top rep at AllSafe, our biggest competitor, and tried to lure him away with the promise of his own corner office and an excellent compensation package. I had met him at a conference a few years ago, and I knew I could work with him. He accepted immediately. I think he liked the idea that if he continued to perform as he did at AllSafe, he would be the highest paid rep in our office. The very next day, Tuesday, rumors were flying around the office that I hired my buddy and threw lots of guaranteed cash at him. Needless to say, most of the reps were not happy about it—Williams in particular, though she didn't say anything.

The rest of the quarter was a constant struggle to get something completed. Someone always needed a "minute" to resolve a crisis—which usually meant sorting out head-on collisions reps had with clients. But there were malfunctioning computers, squabbles over accounts and commissions, and basic jealousies I had to constantly deal with. I thought that a sales manager had the primary responsibility for taking care of the customer, but I wasn't prepared for the sheer volume of fires to be put out every day. I could count on about fifteen totally different conversations within any 2-hour time span. The only place where I could get some peace was the men's room. Not only was I falling even farther behind on paperwork, but I needed to update the reps on some new policies and come up with a new sales idea for our Friday afternoon sales meeting. At times I felt like a babysitter who was also running his own $30 million business.

The day after my first quarterly numbers came in, Liz called me. "Bloom," she said, "you're under quota. What are your plans for turning it around next quarter?" A fair question, I thought, but I didn't like the tone of her voice. I told her I'd looked over the numbers and a few of the reps are close to landing some big accounts. If I have to, I'll close those accounts myself. I also said that my reps don't like having the First-Plus program pushed on them. She said, "Look, Bloom, this is our new direction. It's your job to sell it to the reps and get the branch back on track with First-Plus account volume. If you need anything from my end, just call." "Will do," I said.

CLOSING THE TOP 10 FIRST-PLUS ACCOUNTS

My first plan of action was to identify the top 10 unclosed First-Plus accounts with the most revenue potential. I couldn't afford to lose those accounts. As a sales rep, I was the big account guru, so why not handle those accounts personally? Plus, the customer would love it if the sales manager was their primary contact person. If I was going to get fired, it wasn't because my office couldn't sell the large accounts. I knew some reps weren't going to be happy, but at this point I didn't care whose toes I stepped on. They would just have to understand. The following Monday morning I circulated a memo explaining the new policy for the ten accounts. Later that same morning, just as I have started working on some salesperson expense reports that were already a month overdue, Williams and another rep named Bill Barone walked into my office. They had the memo in their hands and were obviously upset about it since two of the biggest accounts came from them. Williams started out, "Doug, what's going on here?" I said, "For two months now I have been trying to get people to close more First-Plus accounts, but it's not happening. Corporate wants me to take responsibility, so I am." Bill responded, "Everybody in the office is pissed about the lost commissions on the account." I said, "As of right now, nobody is getting any commissions on those accounts because no one seems able to close them. Once they're on board, everyone will get them back." I thought, didn't they even bother to read the memo? Williams said as she was walking out the door, "Doug, this isn't a threat, but I can guarantee you that if you keep pulling this stuff, you'll find yourself taking over more accounts than you can handle." This is getting ridiculous; as a rep I would have accepted it and moved on. These ungrateful reps were resenting the fact that they were going to get a big account handed to them on a silver platter after someone else closed it.

DOUG BLOOM PLANS FOR THE FUTURE

I was glad when the month ended. Not because I made quota for the first time, but because I had a chance to rethink this whole management thing. I didn't want to quit, but I'd rather quit than get fired and I saw nothing but a downward trend. I was working 80-hour weeks, but I constantly felt like I was treading water. Plus, Williams was probably going to leave soon, and it would take time to replace her volume. I also got word that some of my other reps had been looking around. If I stay, I've got to do something about Williams and the other reps who might leave. I had to get a handle on my time and most of all, put the fun back into my job. Was it possible?

STRATEGY AND SALES PROGRAM PLANNING

"Sharing a Vision"
Two men were struggling to get a large crate through the door. They struggled and struggled, but the crate would not budge. Finally, one man said to the other, "We'll never get this crate in." Replied his partner, "I thought we were trying to get it out."

Chapter Consultants:
Scott Smith, Vice President–Sales & Marketing, SABRE Group, Inc.
Joseph P. Clayton President and Chief Executive Officer, Sirius Satellite Radio

LEARNING OBJECTIVES

After studying this chapter, you should be able to:

- Describe the major elements of business strategy.
- State the basic elements of strategic marketing planning.
- Explain what is meant by strategic implementation process decisions.
- Describe the purpose of a sales force program and list its major elements.
- Tell what an account relationship strategy is and explain its purpose.

AN AWARD-WINNING ACCOUNT

Reynolds and Reynolds is a $1 billion company headquartered in Dayton, Ohio, providing integrated information management solutions. The Enterprise Solutions Group at Reynolds is responsible for sales to Reynolds' customer accounts generating more than $90 million in annual revenue. The Group has 15 Partnership Executives who work with the 20 largest automotive retail and distributor groups in North America, helping them achieve outstanding business results.

The Strategic Account Management Association recently presented the Account Performance Award to the Reynolds-Southeast Toyota Distributors (SET) account, located in Deerfield Beach, Florida.[1] SET has 163 dealer locations in the southeastern United States with an annual sales volume of $7 billion. Reynolds put together a dedicated account team from nine functional areas, including sales and marketing, Web services, financial services, CRM solutions, and software solutions. Together with this account team, Reynolds' Partnership Executive developed an account playbook for SET that laid out how Reynolds needed to sell, deliver, and support its business solutions. SET bought the Reynolds dealer management system because it was a critical step in a long-range strategy that would lead to a solid partnership and greater business results for many years. The basis for the partnership was the account team selling SET corporate on developing the next generation of the dealer management system.

Over the next two years Reynolds installed its dealer management systems in 80 percent of the SET dealerships. While these installations were going on, Reynolds people were interviewing more than 200 SET associates to capture their requirements and to develop the next generation of solutions and services. After the systems had been in place for a period of time, SET and Reynolds sat down together to quantify the value that Reynolds had delivered to SET. Some of the performance metrics utilized in this review were annual net profits and new business from the Internet lead generation system. It was discovered that dealers using the Reynolds system were, on average, realizing $200,000 more in annual net profits than dealers not using the system.

The benefits of the relationship to Reynolds are equally impressive. After the partnership began, Reynolds' sales to SET jumped from $1.8 million to more than $16 million in five years, resulting in a compounded annual growth rate on sales of 53 percent per year.

The Reynolds account team is currently implementing a plan to provide financing and support services to all SET dealers for Toyota's Technical Information System. This is the first time Reynolds has ever financed and supported a third-party system. Reynolds' goal continues to be that of helping SET meet its business objectives. SET is also a solid reference for new Reynolds prospects.

The Reynolds-SET account case exemplifies many of the changes in the sales force role that will be discussed in this chapter: sales teams, selling to top management, partnering for mutual benefit, and extraordinary supplier-customer intimacy. It is also important to note how the role of the salesperson, the account executive in the Reynolds case, has changed. Salespeople still communicate and close the sale with the customer, but notice that salespeople must also spend much more time getting to know the account and working with many different areas of the account. The other side of the coin is that the account executive is also spending more time gathering and coordinating the resources and expertise inside Reynolds that can be brought to bear on a customer opportunity. The financial commitments being made to the account and the revenue opportunities are very significant and important to Reynolds' overall performance. The actions of the account executive and account team therefore must be consistent with Reynolds' overall business and marketing strategy. Achieving this consistency and its impact on the sales force is one of the primary focuses of this chapter.

There is a recommended sequence when making sales force and sales program decisions as depicted in Figure 2-1. The level 1 decisions, business and marketing strategies, are made by the firm's top management along with the participation of the top sales executive, sometimes referred to as the chief sales officer (CSO). Level 2 decisions are concerned with implementing a firm's business and marketing strategy. Because strategy implementation is likely to be cross-functional, top sales executives participate along with managers from other functional areas in the firm in making these decisions. Level 3 decisions are largely under the control of the sales management team and are the focus of the remaining sections of this text. This hierarchical sequencing of decisions also guides the organization of the book.

This chapter shows that a firm's business and marketing strategy and implementation decisions impact sales force program decisions. In other words, a firm's strategy and implementation decisions provide the context within which sales program decisions are made and implemented. We do not attempt to fully explain business or marketing strategy; this is better accomplished elsewhere. Instead, we offer an overview of marketing strategy, while focusing mostly on the four-strategy implementation decisions because they more directly influence a firm's sales force program.

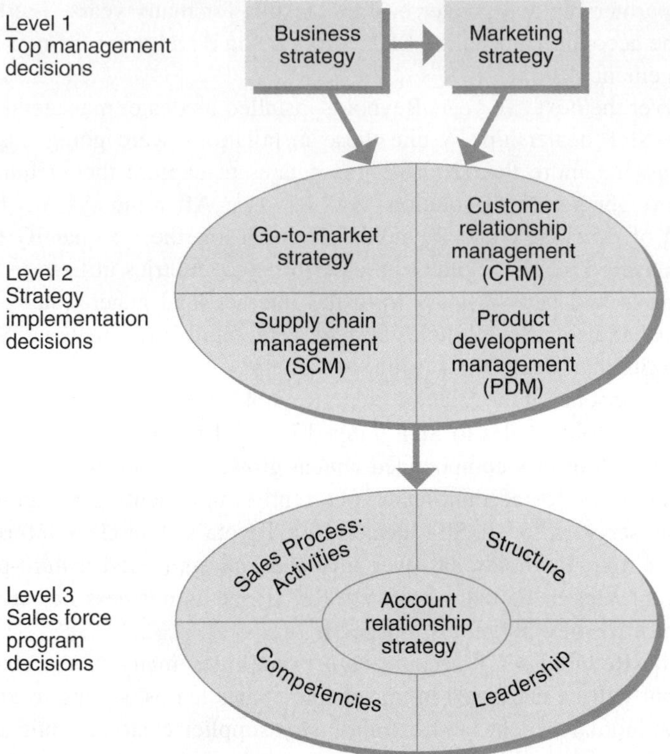

FIGURE 2-1 The Sales Force Decision Sequence

Following this chapter, two Management Resources are presented: "Estimating Potential and Forecasting Sales" and "Sales Force Investment and Budgeting." These are considered important resource topics because sales executives need to know how to perform these activities when either starting up a new sales force or completing their annual planning exercises.

BUSINESS STRATEGY

Strategic planning is employed to make better use of company resources and to create and sustain an advantage over the competition. Business strategy involves defining and articulating an overall business mission, developing specific business goals, and designing a strategy for achieving these goals. The factors influencing the strategic management planning process are depicted in Figure 2-2. Both marketing and sales personnel should be intimately involved in an organization's strategic planning process because they understand the customers' requirements and the sales force is often responsible for implementing key aspects of a firm's strategic plan. This is especially the case when the product is expensive, complex, and of high risk to the customer.[2]

Business Mission

A well-defined business mission provides a sense of direction to employees and helps guide them toward fulfillment of the firm's potential. The basic character of an organization's business is defined by the three Cs—customers, competitors, and the company itself. Top

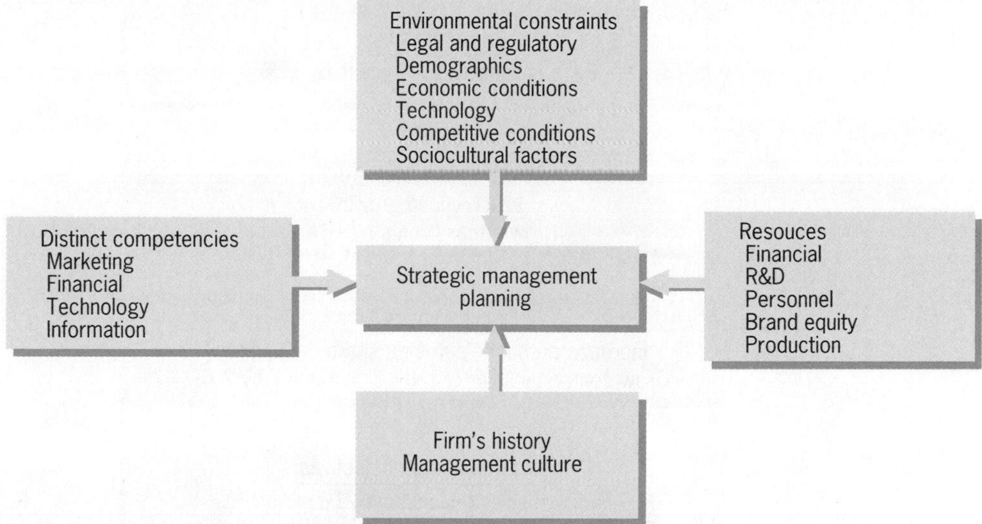

FIGURE 2-2 Factors Influencing Strategic Management

managers should ask, "What is our business?" and "What should it be?" A *business mission statement* should include information regarding (1) the types of customers it wishes to serve, (2) the specific needs to be fulfilled, and (3) the activities and technologies by which it will fulfill these needs. Thus, organizations will not only know the focus of their business, but they will also be able to identify strategic opportunities.

Establishing Goals

Once the mission for an organization has been decided, the next step is to translate the mission into the *organization's goals*—specific objectives by which performance can be measured. These objectives are usually stated in terms of profits, sales revenue, unit sales, market share, survival, and social responsibility. Firms will typically pursue multiple objectives. Procter & Gamble, for example, has historically sought a 10 percent after-tax profit and a 6 percent increase in revenues each year. In a recent survey, 200 B2B senior executives indicated that their most important goal for the current year was increasing sales and revenues.[3]

When priorities change, the sales force is often affected. Faced with major competitors such as Procter & Gamble, demanding retailers, and mature markets, Scott Paper Company switched its mission from gaining volume at any cost to profitability. This called for massive changes in how Scott's 500 salespeople related to the retail trade. "It's no longer a volume or promotional approach to customers," states one Scott marketer, "it's a lot more than that. It's understanding brands and how the consumer's response to various actions on our part is timed so we can eliminate waste and improve profit."

The Scott Paper example illustrates another important characteristic of organizational goals: the hierarchical nature of the goals. Measurable organizational goals must be communicated down the organizational structure. Figure 2-3 illustrates this point by showing how an organizational sales goal is translated into a major account goal.

Strategies

Once business objectives have been identified, the next step is to translate them into strategies. A *strategy* is the means an organization uses to achieve its objectives. Several strategy

FIGURE 2-3 Hierarchy of Sales Objectives

typologies have been developed to describe the overall thrust of a firm's strategy. One of the most popular is Porter's *generic business strategies*.[4] According to Porter, all successful businesses focus on creating superior customer value by achieving one of the following market positions: *low cost, differentiation*, or a *niche*. Each of these positions is described in Figure 2-4.

To successfully execute a firm's strategy in the marketplace requires that the sales force program be properly aligned with the strategy. This assertion was recently tested with a sample of business-to-business organizations. The results supported the idea that different sales programs are associated with high-profit execution of each of these strategies.[5] The high-profit sales program characteristics associated with each strategy are summarized in Figure 2-4.

MARKETING STRATEGY

Marketing strategy is the set of integrated decisions and actions a business undertakes to achieve its marketing objectives by addressing the value requirements of its customers.

Low-Cost Strategy:	High-Profit Sales Programs:
Vigorous pursuit of cost reductions from experience and tight cost control.	• Extensive use of independent sales agents • Focused on transactional customer relationships • Structured so that managers supervised a large number of salespeople • Compensation was largely incentive based • Salespeople were evaluated primarily on their sales outcome performance
Differentiation Strategy: Creating an offering perceived as being unique, leading to high brand loyalty and low price sensitivity.	**High-Profit Sales Programs:** • Selective use of independent sales agents • Focused on long-term customer relationships • Structured so that managers intensely supervised a limited number of salespeople • Compensation was largely salary based • Salespeople were evaluated on their behaviors as well as their outcomes.
Niche Strategy: Servicing a target market very well, focusing all decisions with the target market needs in mind, dominating sales with the segment.	**High-Profit Sales Programs:** Experts in the operations and opportunities associated with a target market. Otherwise the firm adopted the program characteristics associated with the appropriate value creation strategy above.

FIGURE 2-4 Business Strategies and High-Profit Sales Force Programs

As such, marketing strategy is concerned with decisions related to market segmentation and target marketing, as well as development and communication of a positioning strategy.[6] Each of these decisions has important selling and sales management implications, as discussed in this section.

Segmentation and Target Marketing

Because marketing programs require a customer focus to be effective, companies segment the market and select target markets on which they will concentrate their marketing efforts. *Market segmentation* involves aggregating customers into groups that (1) have one or more common characteristics, (2) have similar needs, and (3) will respond similarly to a marketing program. *Target marketing* refers to the selection and prioritizing of segments to which the company will market.

The Graham Company, a Philadelphia-based commercial insurance broker, provides a good example of how important target marketing is to the company and the job of the sales force. Graham, an insurance broker in the United States, has an annual premium volume of more than $200 million. Remarkably, Graham generates these premiums from only 200 clients. It typically contacts only 350 prospective clients a year, seeks relationships with only 35 of those prospects, and earns the business of 28. In pursuing clients, Graham invests substantial resources diagnosing the customer's situation. The broker sends a sales team that may include, in addition to an account manager, attorneys, risk managers, engineers, CPAs, and experts in the customer's business to evaluate the prospect's insurance issues and exposures. How well does such a selling strategy work? Graham enjoys a 75-percent conversion rate in an industry with a 15-percent average and maintains a 98 percent customer retention rate.[7]

Positioning Strategy

Having settled on specific marketing goals and identified target markets, the third step in the planning process is to develop and implement a positioning strategy based on product, price, distribution, and promotion decisions. *Positioning* occurs in the mind of the consumer and refers to how the consumer perceives the product, brand, and company vis-à-vis competitors. Some of the fundamental questions that customers ask about brands are: (1) Who are you? *(brand identity);* (2) What are you? *(brand meaning);* (3) What do I think or feel about you? *(brand responses);* and (4) What kind of association and how much of a connection would I like to have with you? *(brand relationships).*[8]

A clear and strong position in the customer's mind is achieved by designing the proper *marketing mix*—price, product, promotion, and channels. A significant change in any of these elements will usually have ramifications for the sales force program. When a new product is introduced, for instance, it is often necessary to establish new sales quotas, adjust the sales force compensation plan, and create new sales support material.

In some cases, repositioning involves helping your channel partners to reposition themselves as well. Due to commoditization of its network products, Cisco found it necessary to reposition itself to providing network-related solutions for leveraging voice-, video-, and data-based applications. To accomplish this repositioning, Cisco needed to help its more than 36,000 resellers redefine their business as providers of value-added network-based solutions. Cisco now helps each reseller partner select appropriate target markets, and then it provides the reseller with the appropriate training, tools, and support to succeed.[9]

Up to this point we have talked about Level 1 decisions, business and marketing strategy, and how these decisions will impact the sales force. Although sales executives have a voice in Level 1 decisions, they have a much greater voice in Level 2 decisions, which focus on the implementation of an organization's strategy. The Strategic Implementation or Level 2 decisions require cross-functional cooperation and coordination. Sales executives will likely work with top executives from marketing, finance, operations, logistics, engineering, customer service, and other areas of the organization in making these decisions. We now turn our attention to these critical Level 2 decisions.

STRATEGIC IMPLEMENTATION DECISIONS

Strategic implementation decisions refer to a set of processes that organizations will develop to create customer value and achieve a competitive advantage. The fundamental decisions that most companies will have to make with respect to these level 2 processes include: (1) How will customers be accessed? (go-to-market strategy); (2) How will new offerings be developed and existing products be improved? *(product development management [PDM]);* (3) How will physical products be created and delivered to the customer? *(supply chain management [SCM]);* and (4) How will customer relationships be enhanced and leveraged? *(customer relationship management [CRM]).*[10] We address these interrelated strategic process decisions in this section. Although we will discuss each of these decisions in sequence, it is important to realize that decisions in one area will likely have an impact on the other areas.

How a company chooses to develop and execute each of these processes will have an important influence on the activities required of the sales force and around which the sales program is built. In this section the implications of these Level 2 decisions for the sales force are discussed. In addition to the sales force's traditional role of articulating the value proposition to customers, the sales force is being asked to provide customer and market information to their companies to facilitate development of key processes and to orchestrate and coordinate the company's efforts to create customer value.

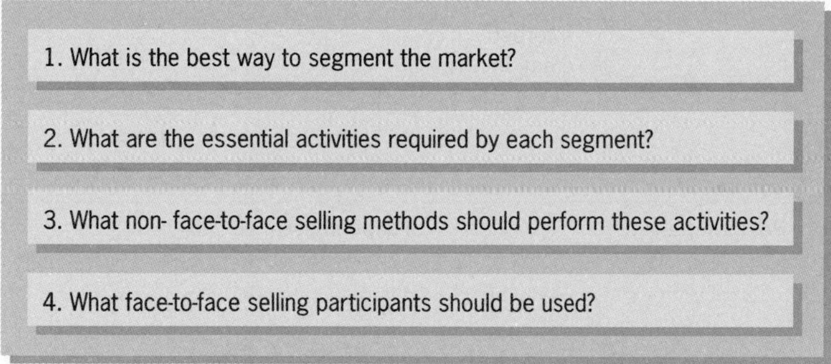

1. What is the best way to segment the market?
2. What are the essential activities required by each segment?
3. What non- face-to-face selling methods should perform these activities?
4. What face-to-face selling participants should be used?

FIGURE 2-5 Steps in Developing a Go-to-Market Strategy

Go-to-Market Strategy

A world-class sales force is a powerful resource for any company, but the sales force is only one of the options companies have for going to market. In addition to direct sales force, advertising and promotions, value-added resellers, the Internet, and telemarketing can all play roles in connecting a supplier with its customer base. An essential set of activities must be performed in order to attract and retain customers. A *go-to-market* strategy defines who will perform these activities and for which customers. The process for determining a go-to-market strategy consists of answering the four major questions shown in Figure 2-5.[11]

Segmenting the Market. The first step is to identify market segments. As described earlier in this chapter when discussing marketing strategy, market segmentation involves identifying different groups of customers with similar characters, product needs, and responsiveness to marketing efforts. Since segments are identified in developing an overall marketing strategy, we can also see here the fundamental relationship between a firm's overall marketing strategy and its go-to-market strategy.

Customer segments and go-to-market strategies will vary depending on the product sold. Adult diapers and baby diapers are very similar in how they are manufactured, but they have very different go-to-market strategies. Most adult diapers are sold in bulk to nursing homes via distributors, and with very little advertising. Most baby diapers are sold at retail with massive advertising support.

Customer characteristics commonly used to segment a market for purposes of developing a go-to-market strategy include, but are not limited to, the following:

- *Industry* What business is the customer in?
- *Size* What is the revenue size of the customer? How many employees? What is the sales potential?
- *Geography* Where is the customer located? Does the customer have global operations?
- *Behavior* Who are the key decision makers? What are their adoption tendencies? Does the customer currently use our product? A competitor's product? Does the customer buy centrally for all its plant locations?[12]

For purposes of developing a go-to-market strategy, the best approach to segmenting a market is one that generates groups of customers whose members require similar customer attraction and retention activities. For example, some segments may require significant prospecting and attraction activities because the customer is still learning about the offering, while other segments may require significant servicing activities because they are already current customers.

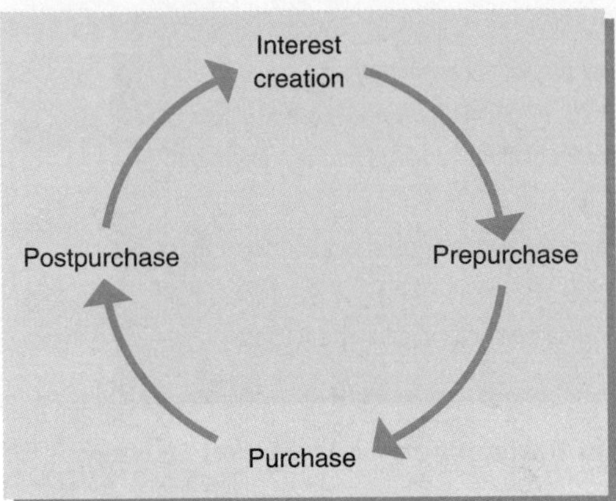

FIGURE 2-6 Essential Activities

Sales Process Activities. From the first time a prospect is identified to the first time a customer hears about a product, to the first sale, to the last service and system upgrade call, many activities must successfully take place. The *sales process activities* consist of all the activities needed to serve a customer properly.

Essential activities can be divided into four groups: interest creation, prepurchase, purchase, and postpurchase. These activities roughly mirror the selling cycle and are shown in Figure 2-6. Notice that the activities recycle, because good postpurchase activities and support can lead to interest creation, building a continuing relationship with the customer.

Interest creation activities include all the ways that customers can learn about the benefits of the product and the company. After all, only customers who want to buy will buy. Specific activities involved in interest creation include prospecting, generating leads, creating awareness and interest, and providing information about the company's products and services. The prepurchase phase is different from interest creation in that customers are actively considering and evaluating competitive product offerings. Essential activities in the prepurchase phase include explaining features and benefits, qualifying prospects, assessing customer needs, cooperating in problem solving, and demonstrating company and product capabilities. The purchasing phase includes the set of activities culminating in a purchase. As such, it is the set of activities most likely to involve direct salespeople. Activities in this phase include negotiating, bidding, finalizing terms and conditions, and writing proposals. The essential work does not conclude with the purchase. The postpurchase activities may include delivery, installation, and servicing of products; addressing customer questions that need answering; providing information about new features; and collecting payment. These and other essential activities are discussed further in Chapters 3 through 5.

Go-to-Market Participants. Once the set of essential activities has been identified, the next question is, who will participate in performing these activities? Figure 2-7 provides several go-to-market participants, including the Internet, telemarketing, advertising, promotion, direct mail, and face-to-face selling (including a direct sales force, independent agents, distributors, integrators, and alliances). Most large companies today access their markets in more than one way. To defend their customer base, expand market coverage, and control costs, companies today are adopting multiple methods for reaching different target markets. IBM, for example, once sold all its computers through the company's 5,000-person sales force. When low-cost computers hit the market, IBM reacted by expanding into new channels. Now they sell through dealers, value-added resellers (VARS), catalog operations, direct mail, telemarketing, and the Internet. In total, IBM added over eighteen new channels in addition to its own sales force to communicate with customers.

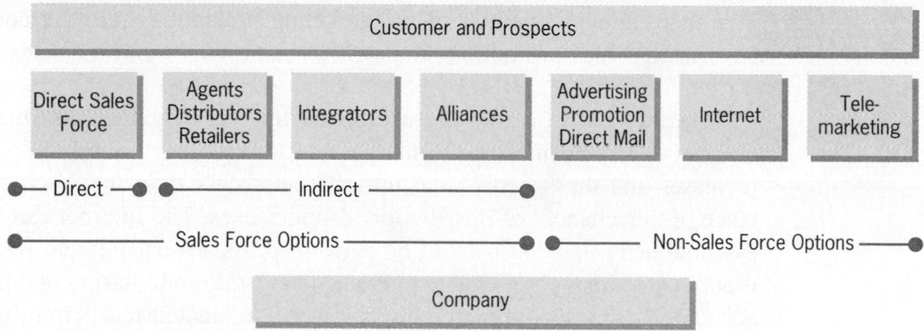

FIGURE 2-7 Potential Go-to-Market Participants

The combination of go-to-market participants that is most appropriate for each customer segment and type of essential activity will depend on a number of factors, including cost, efficiency, and effectiveness. The efficiency of a participant refers to its ability to generate customer contacts for the money spent. On the other hand, the more results created from the number of customers contacted, the more effective the participant is. Figure 2-8 illustrates the relative efficiency and effectiveness tradeoff for the major go-to-market participants. Following is a brief discussion of the major non-sales force go-to-market options: advertising and promotions, telemarketing, and the Internet.

Advertising and Direct Mail. Advertising and direct mail consists of instruments such as broadcast media, magazines, trade publications, newspapers, and direct mail. As shown in Figure 2-8, advertising and direct mail is very efficient in that it is inexpensive per customer contact. It is estimated to cost around 32 cents per contact to reach business markets through specialized business publications.[13] Direct mail is estimated to cost only $1.68 per business contact. Although advertising and direct mail are efficient, they are not always very effective. This is why companies ask these marketing instruments to raise awareness and interest, and then utilize other means to drive the purchase behavior. Consider Hewlett-Packard's go-to-market efforts in a recent introduction of a new printer. First, Hewlett-Packard sent sales kits to customers and dealers, followed by a mailing program and telemarketing. Next, it sent sales reps to the dealerships to make follow-up calls and

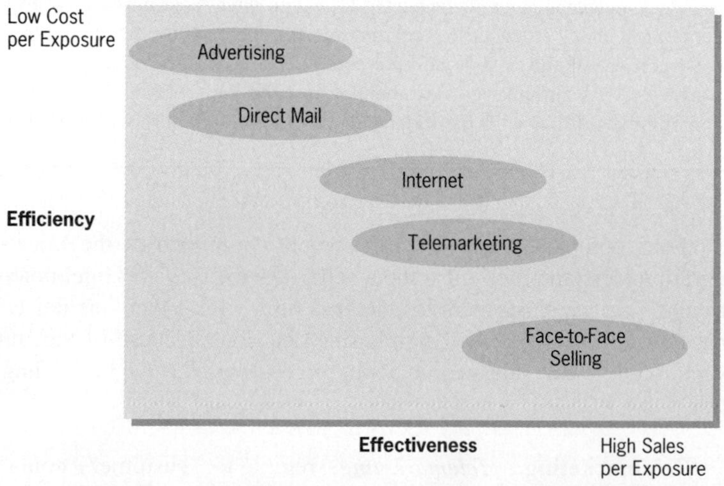

FIGURE 2-8 Comparing Various Go-to-Market Alternatives

give management briefings. This marketing program required a coordinated effort among advertising, sales promotion, channels of distribution, and the sales force.

Internet. The extensive use of the Internet to gather information and to make purchases is a key business go-to-market development. As household penetration of computers increases and the speed of the information access over the Internet increases, the importance of this channel of distribution also increases. The Internet can be used in all phases of essential activities that need to be performed. Its advertising and streaming qualities can be used on a company's Web site to create interest. Prepurchasing and purchasing activities are accomplished on e-commerce buying sites. Automated reordering, tracking of transactions, billing information, and other post-transaction activities are also efficiently and effectively executed on the Internet. Although the Internet costs a little more per contact than direct mail, overall it is more effective at generating desired customer behaviors.

TEAM EXERCISE
"Web Sales"

Creative Communications Inc. (CCI) is an Atlanta-based manufacturer of consumer electronic devices, most notably digital audio players. In recent years, these devices have exploded in popularity with their increase in memory capacity and as prices declined to affordable levels. A key element in the CCI success story is the growth of major retailers such as Wal-Mart, Target, and Best Buy. CCI uses major account teams to serve these and other major retailers, which account for 60 percent of CCI's sales. The remaining sales come from smaller retailer accounts who have traditionally purchased from independent reps with whom CCI has a contract for a commission of 4 percent of sales.

In an effort to reduce costs, last year CCI established a Web site as an alternative channel for small retailers. Cost of sales on the Web site was a modest 2 percent of sales. Sales volume on the Web site amounted to 3 percent of CCI's sales last year, but it is forecasted to increase to 7 percent this year, and perhaps as much as 15 percent the following year.

Many of the salespeople selling to smaller accounts are upset by the move to Web sales since they receive no commission on these sales. Although not all of CCI's product line is offered over the Web, this did not appease the salespeople. Some of the stronger salespeople are threatening to go to a competitor who is offering compensation on Web sales.

As national sales manager for CCI, you have been asked to keep sales costs at 5 percent of sales. Sales force costs are running at 7 percent for the major account sales teams, and 90 percent of the cost is compensation related—salary plus incentive pay. How would you assess CCI's alternative sales channel over the Web? What changes would you recommend to minimize conflict with the independent reps and still stay within your budget?

Even companies that are 100 percent committed to the Internet are finding that they need to understand their customers better. An executive at Intel noted, "Today we notice that trying to get our customers to purchase through the Web has not worked. But we do know that buyers will make their purchasing decisions because of the Internet. They continue to want to talk to our salespeople about price—maybe if we had a 'haggle' button on the Web, they'd use it."[14]

Telemarketing. *Telemarketing* refers to customer contacts utilizing telecommunications technology for personal selling without direct, face-to-face contact. Business-to-business telemarketing is estimated to cost \$31.16 per contact. It is growing at a rate of 30 to 40 percent a year and generates sales in excess of $100 billion yearly.[15] The greater effectiveness of telemarketing is indicated by the over $1,000 value of the average business-to-business telemarketing sale. Corporations such as IBM, Procter & Gamble, Chase Manhattan Bank, and Union Pacific Railroad have all developed extensive telemarketing systems.

Face-to-Face Selling Alternatives. Upon deciding that a face-to-face sales force should perform some of the essential activities, a company must still address another question. Should the selling be performed by a direct company sales force, a selling partner, or some combination? The main outsourcing options available to most companies are agents, resellers, integrators, and alliances. A brief discussion of these indirect sales options follows.

Independent Sales Agents. An important alternative to the direct sales force is to hire *independent sales agents* (sometimes referred to as manufacturer's reps, reps, or brokers) to perform the selling function. Independent sales agents are not employees, but rather independent businesses given exclusive contracts to perform the selling function within specified geographic areas.

Resellers. *Resellers* are channel members, retailers, and distributors, who take title to the offerings they sell to end-users. They perform many functions within the channel, including warehousing, breaking bulk, extending credit, and providing information, but one of their primary functions is to market their suppliers' offerings to their own customers.

Integrators. In a number of industries new channel members have arisen called integrators. An *integrator* is a service supplier unaffiliated with specific products, whose advice end customers has sought to help them with a complex choice. Earlier in this section we have already introduced one of these integrators, value-added resellers (VARS) in the computer industry. They may advise a client to buy an IBM computer one day and advise another client to purchase a Dell computer the next day. Other examples of integrators are Personal Financial Advisers, Building Contractors, and Systems Integrators.

Alliances. An increasingly popular alternative for accessing markets is to establish an *alliance* with another organization in a joint venture to sell products to specific markets. This strategy has often been used to expand globally. AT&T, for example, negotiated a variety of sales partnerships with companies in France, Germany, Italy, Belgium, and the Netherlands. General Mills and Nestlé SA have set up a joint venture to form a separate company for marketing breakfast cereal throughout Europe. Alliances have also been formed to sell new products. This has become a fairly common practice in the ethical drug market.

When Parke-Davis launched its blockbuster cholesterol-lowering drug, Lipitor, it entered into an alliance for Pfizer's sales force to perform many of the essential sales activities.

The number of different go-to-market arrangements continues to mushroom. The net effect has been extremely important to the sales force and sales management. First, many large firms have reduced the size of their field sales forces by focusing them on only certain essential activities and on medium- and large-size accounts. Second, efforts to coordinate the various participants have affected the sales force. IBM, for example, attempts to limit the direct competition between its value-added resellers and its direct sales force by crediting 85 percent of the volume generated by resellers in the salesperson's territory against the salesperson's annual sales quota.[16] Third, valuable company resources must be allocated to the various channel partners. In the commercial airline industry, for example, one of the biggest challenges is allocation of passenger seat inventory to Internet sellers, travel agencies, and bulk buyers, such as corporate customers. Airlines are finding that their "distressed" inventory is a valuable commodity to resellers because of the market draw potential. Depending on one's view, this may be a marketing decision, but this sort of channel allocation has huge ramifications to the sales organization as well.[17]

When designing a sales force program, management also needs to consider the interactions and relationships that the sales force should have with other functional areas within the organization. The next sections describe three core processes that firms must develop to create customer value—product development management, supply chain management, and customer relationship management—and the role of the sales force in these processes.

Product Development Management (PDM)

The success of a company often depends on how it develops, produces, and markets new product offerings. This is why 3M, for instance, encourages its researchers to spend up to 15 percent of their time on projects of their own choosing. They call it "bootlegging time."[18] At the same time, studies indicate that new product failure rates are around 50 percent of all launched products and that on average it takes 3,000 new product ideas to produce one successful new product launch.[19]

Figure 2-9 lists some of the subprocesses involved in PDM. The arrows in the figure indicate that the sales force is most likely to be directly involved in the initial and final steps of the process. Although the sales force has traditionally played a large role in the introduction of new products, especially business-to-business products, its role in identifying new and modified product opportunities is growing with the emphasis on customizing products to address individual customer needs. In fact, executives in business-to-business firms rate the sales force as the most important source of information for new product development, more important even than primary research.[20]

One notable example of sales involvement in new product development is the case of an alert U.S. Surgical Corporation (USS) salesperson. The salesperson saw an opportunity to satisfy a surgical need that was not being met with existing products as a result of working closely with surgeons in operating rooms. The salesperson observed surgeons inserting a tiny television camera into a body with very small laparoscopic instruments. USS responded quickly to the need by designing and introducing a laparoscopic stapler for skin closure. The product is now used regularly for internal surgical applications.[21]

The other phase of the PDM process in which the sales force is most likely to be directly involved is the launching of a new product into the marketplace. The sales force will almost always play a major role in the launching of new products. Some of the changes

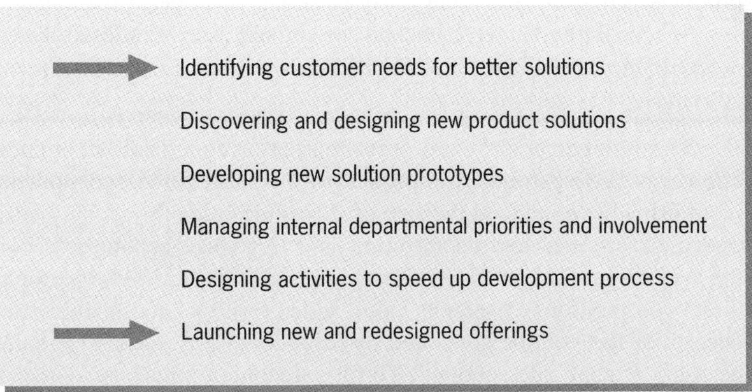

Identifying customer needs for better solutions
Discovering and designing new product solutions
Developing new solution prototypes
Managing internal departmental priorities and involvement
Designing activities to speed up development process
Launching new and redesigned offerings

FIGURE 2-9 Product Development Management Subprocesses

companies are likely to make in their sales force programs when introducing important new products include the following:

- Sales quota systems, most likely adjusted upward to include new product sales.
- Training program adjusted to develop new sales competencies.
- Supervision program is altered to allow management to spend more time accompanying salespeople on sales calls for purposes of training and coaching.
- Compensation plan changes including commission rates, sales incentive programs, and guarantee draws.
- Sales force organization structure is changed, often to organize around different types of customers.

The next section addresses another key management process, supply chain management (SCM), that is becoming increasingly important in today's competitive environment.

Supply Chain Management (SCM)

In recent times, many companies have experienced the whiplash of too much or too little inventory to satisfy demand, missed production schedules, and ineffectual transportation and delivery schedules. To get a handle on the problem, companies are turning to supply chain management. Supply chain management is the integration and organization of information and logistics activities across firms in a supply chain for the purpose of creating and delivering goods and services that provide value to customers.[22] In short, supply chain management is about producing world-class products that are available at the right time, at the right place, and in the right form and condition.

How is the sales force involved in supply chain management? Figure 2-10 lists some of the subprocesses involved in SCM and the arrows suggest that the sales force's involvement is largely at the tail end of the process when interfacing with the customer and channel members. This generalization, however, is changing somewhat as companies adopt more of a market-driven focus to SCM. This entails a shift from sourcing inputs at the cheapest possible prices to designing, managing, and integrating the firm's supply chain with that of both suppliers and customers. The benefits experienced by the end customer is becoming the

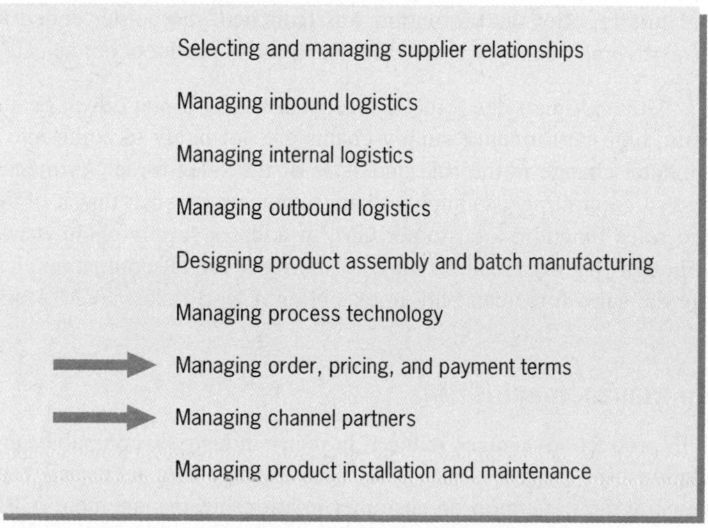

Selecting and managing supplier relationships
Managing inbound logistics
Managing internal logistics
Managing outbound logistics
Designing product assembly and batch manufacturing
Managing process technology
Managing order, pricing, and payment terms
Managing channel partners
Managing product installation and maintenance

FIGURE 2-10 Supply Chain Management Subprocesses

driving objective, as opposed to internal goals such as delivery cycles, production schedules, and operating costs.

Lucent Technologies, for instance, has developed one of the most advanced supply chain capabilities. Lucent has created a position called a customer general manager (GM) whose job is to identify ways in which the supply chain can help customers address their issues. The GM is an advocate of the customer inside Lucent[23] and is getting involved in bids and demand planning and developing the implications for the back end of the supply chain. The customer now has one point of contact for all its supply chain issues.

As the Lucent case suggests, a shift to an SCM perspective raises the level of complexity that salespeople must face. Following are some of the important implications of SCM for the evolution of the sales force.

- **Knowledge of the entire upstream and downstream supply chain.** The experience of a leading consumer foods processor is a good example of the opportunity that is available to firms. This company makes a perishable product with no more than a twelve-month safe shelf life. As a consequence, it shipped the product two to four days after its manufacturing. What it didn't know was that the distribution chain was exceptionally sluggish. It took anywhere from two to twelve months for the item to reach grocery shelves.
- **Thinking strategically about partnering.** Consider again the case of the food processor. The most important "success item" for this company's sales force should not have been generating more orders, but working with distributors and retailers to decrease the time it took for the product to get to the grocery shelf. This necessitates talking to people other than the purchasing agents and merchandisers for their product, the traditional customer targets for this sales force.
- **Establishing good lines of communications and influence with senior corporate management.** In a benchmark study by consultants Meritus-IBM, suppliers and customers all recognized and emphasized the importance of openness, honesty, good communications, and mutual strategy creation. But the study found that in reality, suppliers and customers were rarely entirely open and honest with each other and often didn't even try. To understand why this is the case, consider the example of the retailer who planned a special promotion but refused to tell the beverage bottler which of its products was involved. Why would the retailer not share this information? Because he was afraid that details would leak out to other retail competitors. So the bottler had to build up inventory levels of several possible products and be prepared to incur extra costs of fulfilling late-breaking orders. Naturally, after the promotion was launched, the bottler ended up with excess inventory for several weeks, or even months, in those products not selected for the promotion.

Although the sales force is mostly involved in the downstream processes of the supply chain, high-performance supply chains are not likely to come into existence without a fundamental change in the role and style of the sales force. As mentioned earlier, Lucent has made a commitment to supply chain management such that it organized a separate specialized sales function, a customer GM, to address supply chain issues for specific customers. Although this organization may not be right for all companies, it does suggest the critical role the sales force can play in executing a world-class SCM program.

Customer Relationship Management (CRM)

With product advantages reduced in many industries, companies are realizing that customer relationships are assets that have to be managed for increased value. Many companies are focusing their attention on customer relationship management (CRM) as a strategic competency. This is a major shift in thinking for most companies, and one that is being fostered by the investment community and enabled by technology.[24] Figure 2-11 lists the major

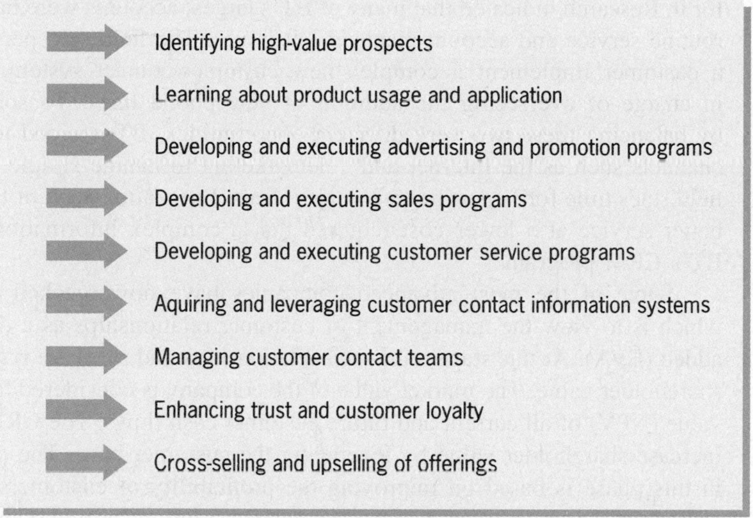

Identifying high-value prospects
Learning about product usage and application
Developing and executing advertising and promotion programs
Developing and executing sales programs
Developing and executing customer service programs
Aquiring and leveraging customer contact information systems
Managing customer contact teams
Enhancing trust and customer loyalty
Cross-selling and upselling of offerings

FIGURE 2-11 Customer Relationship Management Subprocesses

subprocesses involved in CRM. The sales force is involved in many of these subprocesses as indicated by the arrows.

What is CRM? Although its implementation may differ among companies, it is essentially a comprehensive set of processes and technologies for managing relationships with potential and current customers and business partners across marketing, sales, and service regardless of the communications channel. Successful CRM efforts depend on a combination of people, processes, technology, and knowledge. At the heart of the CRM process is information. As one executive has put it, "Information is the currency of the relationship." Information must be readily benchmarked, analyzed, critiqued, and shared among all the constituencies in the buying process. The processes involved in customer relationship affected by CRM technology include:

Marketing Targeting and acquiring prospects through data mining, campaign management, and distributing leads to sales and service.

Sales Developing effective selling processes using proposal generators, knowledge management tools, contact managers, and forecasting aids.

Service Addressing service and support issues with sophisticated call center applications and Internet-based customer service products.

As the functional unit often held responsible for all customer relationships, the sales force is intimately involved in a company's CRM efforts, and CRM has likewise had an important impact on the sales force. The nature of this impact, however, is likely to differ between companies according to how far the company has progressed in the CRM process.

According to CRM Group Ltd., CRM efforts tend to evolve through three phases. First, companies look to manage customer relationships as a driver of revenue. The focus is on utilizing cross-selling and up-selling opportunities and on finding new solutions to customer situations that could be packaged as new offerings.

In the second phase, companies look for possibilities to manage customer relationships as drivers of profits. Successful CRM initiatives have focused on using customer knowledge and emerging new channels to decrease cost to serve and frequently on using advanced price mechanisms. A good example of a second-phase CRM program is the Major Business Division of BT plc (formerly known as British Telecom). It concluded that it was relying too heavily on a long-standing face-to-face selling model and was also paying too much for it. Research indicated that many of BT's largest accounts were having difficulty resolving routine service and account management issues. The field salesperson in charge of helping a customer implement a complex new customer-contact system, for example, was also in charge of overseeing the addition of new phone lines. To solve the dilemma caused by balancing these two very different opportunities, BT decided to add low-cost, efficient channels such as the Internet and Telemarketing to handle simple transactions and free up field sales time for larger, more complex deals. Integrating each of these channels to provide better service at a lower cost required that a complex information backbone be added to BT's CRM program.[25]

Some of the most advanced companies have now reached a third phase of CRM, which is to view the management of customer relationships as a driver of economic value added (EVA). At this stage, customer relationships and sales are regarded as a true driver of shareholder value. The market value of the company is considered the sum of the net present value (NPV) of all current and future customer cash flows. The CRM task in this phase is to increase shareholder value by leveraging the customer base. The driver of business profits in this phase is based on improving the profitability of customers. A phase 3 CRM sales professional adds value by being a customized solutions provider and a business relationship manager who oversees and nurtures all the players and processes in the sales, marketing, and customer service continuum.

The GartnerGroup recently studied the skills that distinguished top salespeople in a phase 3 CRM environment. Some of the traditional skills are still on the list, but they are enhanced by new, critical management skills. The four skills most important to top sales professionals in a phase 3 CRM environment are the following:

- **Collaboration** Truly having each stakeholder's interest in mind—customers, the selling team, the enterprise—is needed for true collaboration. Management must make sure that compensation and motivation strategies reinforce good collaboration fundamentals. At the same time, IT systems for sharing customer information such as Opportunity Management Systems, Web Chat, and collaboration platforms must be in place to provide the necessary infrastructure for broad collaboration.
- **Relationship Management** One of the most critical skills needed in selling today is management of business relationships. The skills needed are effective listening, diagnostic analysis, and interpersonal communications. Sales executives are emphasizing good listening skills in their interviews. As one said, "I look for salespeople that rarely make statements, but orient client communication in the form of a question."
- **Finance and Business Skills** The effective salesperson must speak the vocabulary of business and analyze customer needs in the context of financially viable solutions. Pricing, logistics, inventory management, and customer service must fit into the context of the selling proposition and the related financial proposition to position the offerings well with senior business executives.
- **Consultative Skills** In many industries, the salesperson must apply consultative skills in analyzing customer needs, processes, and operational requirements. A Xerox executive put it this way, "Our business is no longer about selling boxes. It's about selling digital, network-based information management solutions, and this requires a highly customized and consultative selling process."[26]

In short, companies will need to develop a CRM strategy and define the sales force's role within the organization's strategy. The sales force's role will dictate the skills the sales force needs.[27]

Summary. Much of today's business literature focuses on Level 2 strategic implementation decisions that companies make to fully implement their overall strategies. It is not an exaggeration to suggest that these are the most important decisions a firm makes and are instrumental in determining the financial and competitive success of most organizations. As the previous discussion suggests, the sales force is most intimately involved in go-to-market and customer relationship management decisions. As an important source of customer information and contact, the sales force is also involved in a firm's supply chain management and product development processes. Although top sales executives are likely to have an important voice in these decisions, these processes are cross functional in nature and are likely to involve executives from across the organization. In other words, they are not likely to be solely or even largely under the control of a firm's sales management team.

We turn our attention to the sales force program or Level 3 decisions. There are two distinctions between Level 3 decisions and Level 2 decisions. First, the Level 3 Sales Force Program is developed within the context of previous strategic decisions. That is, the various elements of the sales program are based on an understanding of the sales force's role in the Level 2 decisions and the firm's overall objectives and strategies. For instance, a decision to emphasize supply chain management will usually necessitate a certain type of customer relationship. An emphasis on CRM will also affect most every element of the sales force program. Second, unlike Level 2 decisions, the sales management team is largely responsible for developing and executing the sales program, though the sales force must still coordinate its decisions and actions with the other functional areas of the firm.

SALES FORCE PROGRAM DECISIONS

A *sales force program* is a tool for planning how the sales force will perform its role in achieving the firm's objectives. This book is organized around the sales force program. The major elements of the sales force program and how they are related are illustrated in Figure 2-12. The process begins with a careful consideration of the objectives and target markets specified in the marketing plan and estimates of the sales potential and forecast for various market segments. The tools and techniques for estimating sales potential and forecasting sales are discussed in Management Resource: Forecasting Sales and Potential following this chapter. Resulting from the sales forecast, but also influencing the final forecast, are sales force sizing and budgeting decisions. These decisions and techniques for making these decisions are discussed in Management Resource: Sales Force Investment and Budgeting following this chapter. To better appreciate the significance of budgeting decisions see the Team Exercise "Looking Forward to Next Year" on page 50 and the budgeting issues related to selling in new geographies.

The next step of the process is deciding on an account relationship strategy, which involves determining the kinds of relationships the organization wants to build with its target markets. This decision is critical in that it influences and frames decisions with respect to the remaining four elements of the sales program.[28] This is why the account relationship strategies are discussed next in this chapter.

The other elements of the sales force program—selling actions and behaviors, organizational structure, competency development and leadership system—are developed in the remaining chapters of this textbook.

Account Relationship Strategy

A firm's *account relationship strategy* refers to the type of relationship it intends to develop with its customers.[29] This decision encompasses plans for acquiring, maintaining, and developing customers. Most important, this decision determines which customers can be profitably served because it calls for very different levels of investment into customer relationships. Some firms, for instance, take a transactional approach to customers because customers

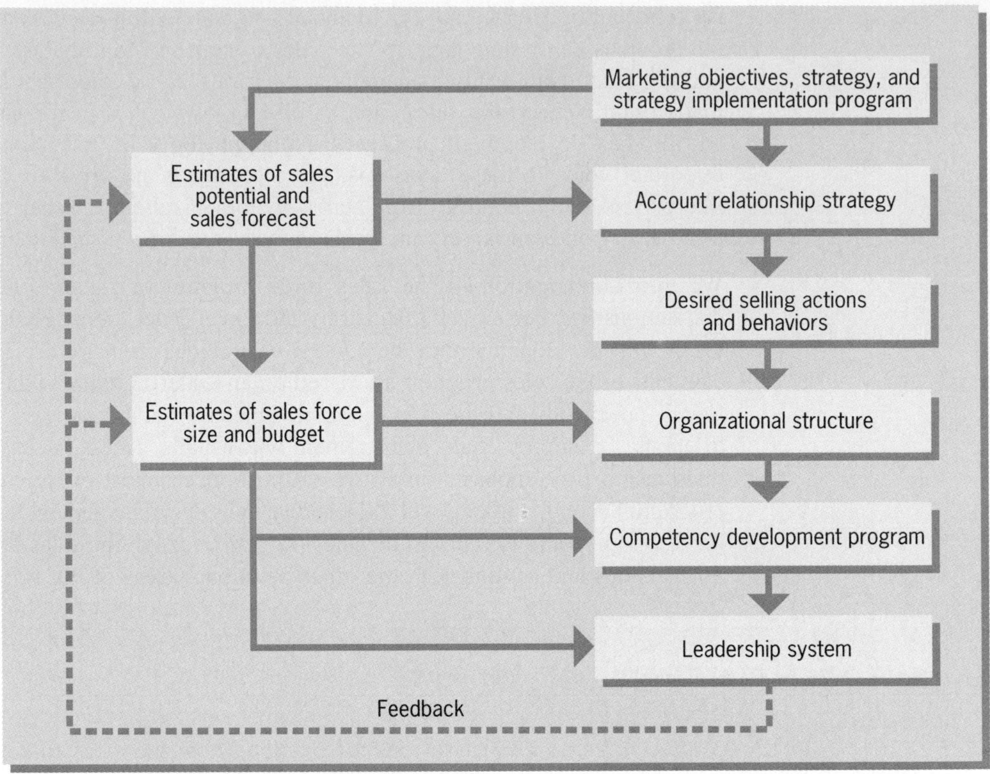

FIGURE 2-12 Sales Force Program

can quite easily switch their business from one supplier to another, depending on which supplier offers the lowest price. Other firms may establish relationships with their key customers involving a close integration of their operating processes. To further complicate the situation, many firms have decided to establish one type of relationship with certain customers and a different type of relationship with other customer groups. Selection of the right customers for the right type of relationship is strategic for both the customer and the supplier.

Account relationships may take a variety of forms, each having major implications for the sales force with respect to recruiting and selection, compensation, necessary competencies, and behaviors. Although many types of relationships are feasible and successful, for illustrative purposes we confine our discussion to three general types of account relationships, as shown in Figure 2-13. Notice that both the supplier and the customer must choose the type of relationship in which they will engage for the relationship to be successful, it is not just a seller's decision.[30] Notice also that the three relationships in Figure 2-13 are depicted on the diagonal. This suggests that an appropriate convergence of selling and purchasing approaches is needed for a particular relationship to be successful. It might surprise some to see that the customer must also invest in the relationship more for consultative or enterprise-type relationships, which are higher on the diagonal. You might get a better idea of the nature of this customer investment by considering the words of a chief information officer when talking about what the customer must do for the supplier in a successful consultative relationship:

> Give the supplier unfettered access to your operations. Let them see what's going on inside your processes. Tell them what you want, how you will measure their performance. In short, train them in your business, so that they know what the solution is supposed to do.[31]

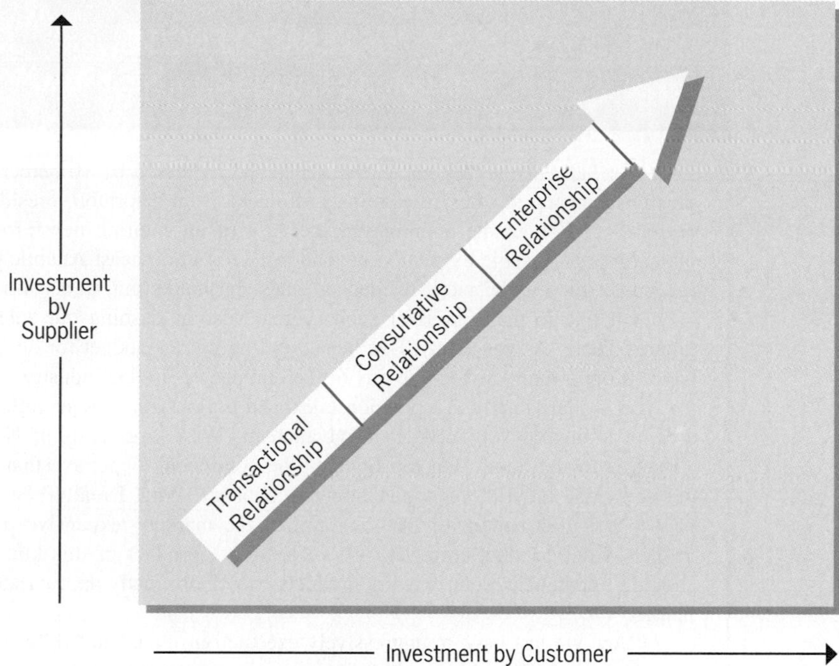

FIGURE 2-13 Alternative Type of Account Relationships

So the investment is not just money, but also time and information. You would be correct in concluding that few firms have the time or inclination to make this level of investment in all their supplier relationships. This is why there must be a coming together or congruency between the investments of the supplier and the customer for each type of relationship to be successful.

To get a better idea of the investments involved, the nature of the relationships, and the role of the sales force, we will discuss each of the three types of relationships described in Figure 2-13.[32]

Transactional Relationship. Most business-to-business transactions take place as part of an ongoing relationship between supplier and customer. A *transactional relationship* is one in which the relationship is based on the need for a product of acceptable quality, competitively priced, and a process and relationship convenient for the buyer. Often a good transactional relationship involves a personal relationship between the buyer and the seller. This type of relationship, like all relationships, is based on the nurturing elements we will describe in Chapter 4, including a history of building trust, creating value, and meeting or exceeding customers' expectations. What distinguishes the transactional relationship from the others is that it is usually based on a personal relationship between individual buyers and sellers. As a Scandinavian executive remarked, "You know, I personally have never bought anything from someone I didn't like." This is at the heart of a transactional relationship—personal relationship.

The advantages and limitations of a transactional-type account relationship are illustrated by the efforts of a salesperson with Holston Building Supply, Jim Roberts, to sell oak balusters and other staircase parts to a chain of lumberyards in eastern Tennessee. Although having long purchased other Holston products, the customer informed Jim that it was quite satisfied with its present supplier of staircase parts and had excellent profit margins on these items. Jim persisted, saying, "Just give me a chance to prove that you could sell even more

TEAM EXERCISE
"Looking Forward to Next Year"

Last year had been a very good year. Sales had increased by 10 percent to $134 million, due mostly to increased sales to existing customers. Tom Thornton, president and CEO, is even more excited about the coming year because of an exciting new product development and plans for a geographic expansion beyond last year's Southeast Atlantic Coast sales area. He is meeting with you, the vice president of sales and marketing, to discuss next year's budget.

"I'd like to thank you for such a great year in pushing our sales over $130 million," greeted Tom. "As you know, I've been working on our budget for next year and feel that we have an opportunity to become one of the real players in this industry. With our earnings from last year, we are finally in a position to expand beyond our present eight-state geographic sales area by adding on New York, Pennsylvania, and West Virginia in the North and Louisiana and Arkansas in the South. On top of that," he continued, "I believe that at least 10 percent of our sales will be in the new packaging technology. What I really like about the new product is that it is best suited for the high end of the market—expensive products that are easily broken if not handled correctly. We've needed a product of this kind for some time and it shouldn't cannibalize our existing products, which are really appropriate for the middle of the market."

"Now we just have to aggressively execute our plan," added Tom. "I've forecasted sales next year for $174 million, which is right at a 30-percent increase over this year's projected sales. We've got to maintain our bottom line to help finance our growth plans, so I'm setting a sales and marketing budget of $19 million, which is the same as this year's projected 10.9 percent of revenue. This is nearly a $5 million increase in your budget, which should be enough to reach our target of $174 million."

As vice president of sales and marketing, what would be your reaction to Tom's budget? How would you begin to analyze this budget? What are the possible budget implications of the expanded geographic selling area? What about the new product introduction?

and make better margins with our products." When the buyer did give them a trial run, they sold so well that he soon switched completely to Holston's stair parts. "I would not have had the slightest chance of getting him to try our line," says Roberts, "no matter how good my arguments might have been, if I had not already established a solid, trusting relationship with him."

Notice that the personal relationship between Jim and the account was critical to obtaining the sale and that trust was a key element in the relationship. On the other hand, another supplier of staircases offering a higher profit margin and able to generate equal demand is likely to take business from Jim in the future. Also notice that the customer's investment in the relationship is mostly at a personal level—that is, between Jim and the customer's purchasing manager, not with Jim's company. Jim's relationship with the lumberyard may become quite tenuous, for instance, if the purchasing agent is no longer there.

Although repeat transactional relationships may appear to be restricted to traditional buyer-seller relationships, this is not necessarily always the case. Michael Dell was one of the first to recognize the enormous opportunity to provide sophisticated buyers with the kind of relationship they were seeking. By offering a direct sales channel for computer equipment, Dell was providing buyers who knew what they wanted with a low-cost and very convenient way to purchase a personal computer. The Dell selling approach through telemarketing and self-customization of the equipment was roughly 15 percent less expensive for Dell than selling through computer retailers.

What types of firms are likely to emphasize a transactional-type customer relationship? A recent study sheds some light on this question. Based on a sample of companies from four countries, the study concluded that 68 percent of all firms focus on a transactional relationship with at least some of their customers. Consumer goods firms and large organizations are most likely to emphasize transactional-type relationships with their customers.[33] The overarching reason for emphasizing transactional relationships in these situations is because the buyers are already quite knowledgeable about the product and the role of the product in meeting their objectives. Consider again the Holston Building Supply example discussed above. The lumberyard's buyer is probably quite familiar with most staircase parts, how they differ, and how to merchandise them in his stores.

Business-to-business firms, especially those selling capital equipment and hightech products are likely to employ a different type of customer relationship strategy. These alternative type of relationships are discussed next.

Consultative Relationship. A *consultative relationship*, a quite common relationship in industrial markets, is based on the customer's demand and willingness to pay for a sales effort that creates new value and provides additional benefits outside of the product itself. Consultative relationships employ the solutions selling approach described in the previous chapter, as do the enterprise-type relationships to be discussed next. The success of consultative relationships rests on the ability of the salesperson or sales team to get very close to the customer and to intimately grasp the customer's business issues. In these relationships, the sales force attempts to create value for the customer in three ways:

- Helping customers understand their problems and opportunities in a new or different way.
- Helping customers develop better solutions to their problems than they would have discovered on their own.
- Acting as the customer's advocate inside the supplier's organization, ensuring the timely allocation of resources to deliver customized or unique solutions to meet the customer's special needs.

The role of the salesperson in a consultative relationship is quite different from his or her role in a transactional relationship. Much more time is spent learning the special needs of the individual customer and marshaling resources inside the supplier's company to meet those needs. A good example of a company implementing a successful consultative relationship program with its key customers is the Boise Cascade Office Products Corporation (BCOP), a business-to-business distributor of office products. BCOP has repositioned its salespeople as business consultants, through the application of value-added techniques. Using database marketing software, the salesperson examines a customer's buying pattern, seeking areas in the customer's organizations where process improvements are possible. Sales usage reports enable the sales representative to advise customers on buying trends in the categories of paper, furniture, computers, and office supplies. Sales representatives also use a software program called Activity-Based Cost Management (ABCM) to measure costs by activity, customer, and product. ABCM enables Boise to directly assign more than 90 percent of actual costs to specific customer-related activities. As a consequence, opportunities for cost savings can be explored and presented to customers, hopefully resulting in improved financial results for both the buyer and Boise.

Boise Cascade's efforts at establishing consultative relationships with its customers illustrate several important characteristics of this type of customer relationship and how it differs from purely transactional relationships. Notice that the additional customer value resides in the nonproduct resources that the salesperson brings to the relationship. This type of relationship also puts a premium on gathering and analyzing information about customers and their business issues. As a result, the selling process is usually longer, so the value of the customer to the supplier must be great enough to cover the higher selling costs. The relationship must usually be long term in nature for the customer equity to justify Boise's investment in the customer. Notice also that the salesperson must have a great deal of skill in gathering customer information, business acumen, and technical competency.

Figure 2-13 indicates that the seller and the buyer's investments in the relationships are greater in consultative relationships than in transactional ones. The Boise Cascade example clearly shows that the seller's investment increases, but what about the buyer's investment? Information sharing to understand the customer's problems and opportunities requires, by its very nature, an investment of time and a sharing of information by the customer. A vice president with a large utility firm put it this way: "It's a big investment of time bringing a new vendor aboard. You need to know that the time you spend with them is worth it. You can't just give a free education to everyone who comes knocking at your door."[34]

It is critical to choose the right situations in which to invest in consultative relationships. Experience indicates that a consultative relationship is most appropriate when one or more of the following conditions are present:

- The product or service can be differentiated from competitive alternatives.
- The product or service can be adapted or customized to the needs of the customer.
- The customer is not completely clear about how the product or service provides solutions or adds value.
- The delivery, installation, or use of the product or service requires coordinated support from the selling organization.
- The benefits of the product or service justify the relatively high cost of consultative relationships.

When these conditions are present, the sales force may have an opportunity to create customer value through consultative selling.

Enterprise Relationship. In recent years, customers have been downsizing their supplier base and replacing their myriad vendors with a very small number of possibly long-term relationships offered only to a select few suppliers. The trend toward purchasing from fewer suppliers has resulted in customers leveraging the volume of their purchases for enhanced services and cost-cutting opportunities. The response of many sellers to the emergence of very large and powerful customers has been to develop a system of enterprise relationships to better meet the needs of their major customers.

An *enterprise relationship* is one in which the primary function is to leverage any and all corporate assets of the supplier in order to contribute to the customer's strategic success. In such a situation, both the product and the sales force are secondary, and the customer must be of strategic importance to the selling organization. Adjectives to describe this category of relationships abound and include Major, Strategic, National, Global, Corporate, and Key Account Programs. To achieve successful enterprise relationships, the supplier must deliver exceptional customer value while also extracting sufficient value from the relationship. This is always challenging, especially when the customer has worldwide needs.

Many of the United States' premier industrial firms such as GE, IBM, Du Pont, Monsanto, and Honeywell have established enterprise relationships with customers such as American Airlines, Ford, Milliken, Procter & Gamble, and the federal government. The customer generally initiates this radically different type of relationship.[35] When Chrysler was on the ropes in the early 1990s, one of its responses was to change the way it did business with its key suppliers. Instead of forcing suppliers to win business anew every two years and focusing on lowest list price, it decided to give suppliers business for the life of a model and beyond. Instead of relying solely on its own engineers to create the concept for a new car and to design all the car's components, Chrysler now involves suppliers. Instead of Chrysler dictating price, the two sides now work together to lower the costs of making cars and to share the savings.

The Chrysler example illustrates some ways in which enterprise relationships differ from traditional supplier relationships. Following are some of the ways in which other companies have made strategic partner relationships work.

- Suppliers are involved in the early stages of need identification, specification, and new-product development.
- In conventional relationships, the primary players were the salesperson, the customer service representative, and perhaps a design engineer. With enterprise relationships, the supplier usually fields a team that interfaces with the customer on a regular basis, and includes a variety of functional areas and management levels.
- In enterprise relationships, there is an unusually high degree of intimacy resulting in immediate responsiveness from suppliers, sharing of information, radical empowerment of suppliers, and termination of the relationship as a remote and difficult option. For instance, a small group of nine suppliers, called "in-plants," work on-site, full-time at Boise. This insider status gives them unparalleled opportunities to grow with the customer and to influence requirements for their products.[36]

The activities of the sales force, the structure of the sales force, compensation, and even the sales philosophy differ for each type of relationship.[37] For instance, as the buyer-seller relationship becomes more sophisticated and complex, the sales force's role as the primary point of contact between customer and supplier often diminishes. The focus also shifts to some degree from sales volume generation to management and maintenance of the relationship and the conflicts that are likely to arise over time.[38] Studies have shown that enterprise-type business-to-business relationships tend to focus on lowering the customer's overall operating costs. Industrial salespeople are typically trained in selling behavior and in how to present technical product features, not in process and cost analysis. Salespeople are needed who can develop a thorough understanding of the customer's operations and the way costs are influenced by the supplier's products and customer interactions. A supplier may also have to analyze whether their sales compensation system rewards salespeople for lowering customer costs, which usually requires a long-term perspective, or short-term volume gains. These and other issues are addressed in the remainder of this book.[39]

Cautionary Notes. In today's business world strategic decisions can be quite complex. At IBM, for example, American Airlines is viewed as both a customer and a supplier; that is, American sells airline seats to IBM, but IBM is also a primary supplier of computer equipment and software to American. This type of relationship requires that the supplier's account manager navigate within his or her own procurement area as well as that of the customer.

A critical mistake is to assume that more investment in the customer relationship will automatically create a better relationship with improved results. The experience of a packaged materials manufacturer provides a typical example of this mistake. Because the manufacturer's costs were slightly higher than competitors' costs, they were losing business. This manufacturer decided that the best way to halt this decline was to upgrade its sales force. Their "packaging consultants" were charged with adding value to their products through providing customers with help and advice. The investment in upgrading the sales force, including retraining and recruiting, together with the development of a new marketing strategy, was in excess of $10 million. The average cost of each sales call increased to $890, and the average sales cost to acquire a new account was $112,000. It turned out, however, that most customers simply didn't want advice or help. They needed packaging material, pure and simple, and that's all they were prepared to pay for. The company was soon taken over at a fire-sale price. Studies suggest that this case is not unusual. As indicated

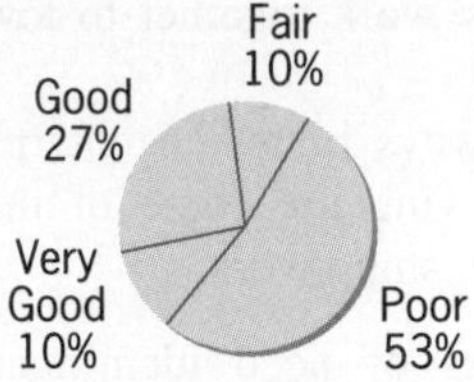

FIGURE 2-14 Partnering Effectiveness Index

in Figure 2-14, more than half of the companies offering enterprise-level relationships to their strategic customers rated the performance of these programs "Poor." The challenges of these programs are significant, and the risks of revenue and profit loss associated with losing these accounts to competitors are often of even greater significance.

SUMMARY

The sales force strategy and management structure should be planned and designed within the context of an organization's overall business strategy and marketing strategy. Competitive advantage resides in the firm's ability to develop and perform a set of basic business processes for implementing a firm's business strategy. As the primary customer contact, the sales force and sales management are likely to play an important role in these processes. This chapter has given numerous examples of how sales force decisions are subject to and contribute to the overall strategy of the company and its marketing strategy. You should be able to do the following:

1. **Describe the major elements of business strategy**. The strategic management process includes defining a business mission, setting specific measurable goals for the organization, and deciding on a strategy for meeting these objectives. A well-defined business mission should provide a sense of direction for the organization. The mission should be defined in terms of customers to be served, competitors with whom an advantage must be achieved, and the processes by which the company will achieve these advantages. Goals should be measurable and should guide goal setting throughout the organization. Strategies should be based on developing a sustainable competitive advantage through creation of customer value.
2. **State the basic elements of strategic marketing planning**. Strategic marketing planning is a process whereby an organization attempts to meet the value requirements of its target markets. This process starts with a situation analysis that consists of taking stock of where you have been, where you are now, and where you are likely to go in the future. The next step is to define market segments from which to target. Once you have made these decisions, an appropriate marketing mix program should be designed, including integration of the various promotion tools.
3. **Explain what is meant by strategic implementation process decisions**. Strategic implementation decisions refer to a set of processes that organizations will need to develop to create customer value and achieve a competitive advantage. The fundamental decisions that most companies will have to make with respect to these Level 2 processes include: (1) How will customers be accessed? (go-to-market strategy), (2) How will new offerings be developed? (product development management), (3) How will physical products be created and delivered to the customer? (supply chain management), and (4) How will customer relationships be enhanced and leveraged? (customer relationship management).

The sales executive team will likely have an important voice in making these decisions, but they essentially involve cross-functional teams. The decisions a company makes with respect to these four processes will have an important impact on the sales job and on the skills the sales force will need to perform their job.

4. **Describe the purpose of a sales force program and list its major elements**. A sales force program is a tool for planning how the sales force will perform its role in achieving the firm's objectives. The sales program planning process begins by reviewing the firm's business and marketing strategies. The major elements in a sales force program include an estimate of sales potential and forecast, an account relationship strategy, specification of the desired selling actions and behaviors, an estimate of the sales force budget and size, the sales force organizational structure, a competency development program, and a leadership program.
5. **Tell what an account relationship strategy is and its purpose**. A firm's account relationship strategy refers to the type or types of relationships a firm intends to develop with its customers. Relationship types differ in terms of how much of an investment a supplier and customer are willing to put into a relationship. The more both are willing to invest in the relationship, the more intimate, difficult to terminate, strategic, and broad based the relationship is likely to be. The economic value of the relationship must usually be very important for both parties to be willing to make these investments. Three types of relationships are transactional, consultative, and enterprise.

KEY TERMS

Account relationship strategy
Alliances
Brand identity
Brand meaning
Brand relationships
Brand responses
Business mission statement
Consultative relationship
Customer relationship management (CRM)
Deseasonalized data
Differentiation
Enterprise relationships
Generic business strategies
Go-to-market strategy
Independent sales agents
Integrators
Jury of executive opinion
Leading indicators
Least squares
Low cost
Market segmentation
Market potential
Marketing strategy
Moving average
Multiple regression
Naive forecast
Niche
Organization's goals
Positioning strategy
Product development management (PDM)
Resellers
Sales budget
Sales carryover
Sales force composite
Sales force program
Sales forecasting
Sales potential
Sales process activities
Smoothing constant
Strategic implementation decisions
Strategy
Supply chain management (SCM)
Target marketing
Telemarketing
Time series regression
Transactional relationships
Trends
Turning point

DEVELOPING YOUR COMPETENCIES

1. **Strategic Action.** Merrill Lynch & Company has finally decided to enter the low-cost business of on-line trading. On-line brokerage firms such as E*Trade Group Inc. have been growing rapidly and taking business from full-service brokerage houses owing primarily to the low price per transaction and the record bull market since 1994. With the Internet now accounting for 30 to 35 percent of all stock trades by individuals, Merrill executives finally decided they could no longer afford not to embrace such trading. Not

only is this a major change in strategy for Merrill, but the move to the Internet could spark rebellion within its army of 14,800 well-paid brokers. An internal Merrill Lynch study, for example, suggests that brokers who are paid chiefly in commissions might see their incomes decline by 18 percent initially. How big a problem does Merrill face? What would you suggest they do about their brokers? For more information on Merrill Lynch, visit its Web site at www.ml.com.

2. **Technology.** The marketing plan for 2004 was recently released to the thirty-person sales force of Access Radiology Corporation. The salespeople were unhappy with what they saw, and Mary Callaghan, vice president of sales at Access, had received more than a dozen angry e-mails, voice mails, and memos from her salespeople. Complaints ranged from not enough money for lead-generation activities and too much image-based advertising to a lack of a comprehensive Web-based marketing initiative. The last issue has salespeople worried about Access's marketing direction. Customers have said that they mainly want to interact and buy products from Access on-line. Callaghan had already relayed this information to Access's senior management in an effort to create new on-line initiatives at Access. It doesn't seem that this is happening, and Callaghan and her sales force are extremely concerned. How should Callaghan address these issues with senior management, and what can she do to ensure that the company's marketing department listens to the needs of the sales force and its customers?
3. **Coaching.** Perhaps one of the best role models for today's sales and marketing managers is Lou Gerstner, the former chairman of IBM. Major problems faced IBM when Gerstner became chairman at IBM, and it was probably tempting for him to turn all his energy inward to resolve these difficulties. Instead, he decided to become actively involved in the company's sales efforts. IBM's relationship with Monsanto, the St. Louis-based agricultural and pharmaceutical giant, is a good case in point. Gerstner hosted a number of one-day strategy seminars for small groups of chief executives from significant companies in a variety of industries. The chairman of Monsanto, Robert Shapiro, who was an attendee at one of these events, asked whether any of IBM's research or cutting-edge technology might have an application for Monsanto, which was involved in genetic research. IBM found some interesting material on gene mapping in both animal and plant cells that IBM thought might be useful to Monsanto. A few weeks later an IBM executive team arrived at Monsanto headquarters, and discussions began. As the discussions progressed, it became apparent that IBM had other more important strategic-level contributions to make. Within a year, Monsanto and IBM signed a contract, reputedly worth several hundred million dollars, that had IBM running the total Monsanto mainframe and PC network of more than 20,000 personal computers. What did Lou Gerstner do right? Which type of customer relationship do IBM and Monsanto have, and what makes it work? IBM: www.ibm.com. Monsanto: www.monsanto.com.
4. **Team Building.** The need for coordination and teamwork has been emphasized throughout the discussion of relationship management in this chapter. WESCO Distribution, Inc., a $3 billion electrical equipment and supplies (EES) distributor, presents an interesting case study on the issues involved in coordinating the implementation of a national account contract with large customers.

   WESCO regularly carries and sells more than 210,000 products from over 6,000 suppliers to satisfy the electrical equipment needs of any customer anywhere in the world. What it is really selling, however, is the capability of a single source of supplies, customized delivery, technical support, application development, and customer product training. In other words, WESCO offers the latest in integrated supply chain systems, including inventory management options, inventory reduction initiatives, and related efficiency improvements to customers such as industrial manufacturers, original equipment manufacturers (OEMs), municipal power authorities, and other utilities.

Recently, WESCO established a national account program for its 300 largest industrial customers, who collectively accounted for almost 70 percent of WESCO's total revenues. The national account contract offered customers a 2 to 3 percent price discount on products purchased from WESCO in exchange for consolidating all their purchases of these product lines with WESCO. WESCO's account penetration with these customers ranged from 60 to 90 percent for the product lines covered by the contract, so the lower prices in the contract could be offset by greater volume through 100 percent penetration. Contracts were signed at the customer's corporate headquarters, but most of the purchasing was left to purchasing agents at the local plants. This is where the coordination problems began. Despite corporate enthusiasm, some plants were reluctant to abandon local distributors with whom they had long-established and close relationships. In addition, the local availability of supplies was often highly valued in case of emergency. Problems in coordinating between corporate and local interests also existed inside WESCO. A customer may purchase a lot of supplies in total, but the volume generated at the local plant level may be fairly small in comparison with larger single-plant customers serviced by the WESCO branch salesperson. The branch salespeople report to the branch manager and are paid a base salary plus commission on sales volume. They are therefore reluctant to call on a relatively low-volume plant, especially one with a long commute, even if they are on a national account contract. What would you recommend the national account manager do to encourage teamwork and local support for a national account in such a situation? What actions would you recommend for the vice president of marketing and sales?

For more on WESCO Distribution, Inc., the products and services it offers, and its customer base, see www.wescodist.com.

5. **Self-Management.** Every baseball player must throw, catch, and hit the ball. Yet what it takes to be a winning pitcher or a great hitter is quite a different matter. The same is true of sales—all salespeople must talk to customers and take orders; however, what it takes to excel at transactional relationships is quite different from that required for enterprise relationships.

   The H. R. Chally Group has built a large database of salespeople information from which they have identified four different sales roles and skills. Each sales job requires a certain amount of each skill to be a top performer. Rate yourself from 1 to 10 in terms of how much each of the following four skills describes yourself.

   - **Closing.** Can aggressively initiate personal contacts. Does not have a high fear of personal rejection. Can quickly establish another person's emotional desire and personal concerns. Has high self-confidence.
   - **Consultative.** Possess a combination of patience, good interpersonal skills, and aggressiveness. Have good persistence. Are very career oriented. Are somewhat academically inclined. Are willing to take risks, but only after careful thought and calculation. Pay a high level of attention to detail. Can handle personal rejection and the fear of failure extremely well. Are team oriented.
   - **Relationship.** Like independence and the freedom of sales (i.e., the feeling that you are your own boss). Exercise discipline and take responsibility for their actions. Once again, have low fear of failure. Have a strong work ethic.
   - **Display.** Are easily bored, need to have something to do. Enjoy people. Possess high physical energy level. Are impulsive. Like work to revolve around home and other goals.

   What is your profile on these four dimensions? Name two types of sales positions (e.g., stockbroker, telephone sales, corporate jet sales, computer software sales) for a person rating high on each of the four dimensions. What would be the composite profile on each of the four skills (rate from 1 to 10) of a person who would be successful at each of the three customer relationships discussed in this chapter: transactional, consultative, and enterprise relationships. For more on H. R. Chally, see www.chally.com.

FEATURED CASE: SHIELD FINANCIAL: "A DIFFERENT KIND OF CUSTOMER"

The First-Plus plan was designed for Shield's larger customers, even though many of the salespeople at Shield were very successful with smaller business owners. Getting salespeople to refocus their efforts on larger customers was a major issue with Doug Bloom when he took over the Des Moines office. Tiffany Williams, the top salesperson for the past eight years, had been particularly upset at the first sales meeting by this change in direction. Doug had a lot of experience with selling business owner, liability, workman's compensation, and other forms of insurance to small businesses when he was a sales rep in Atlanta. Although price was of primary concern for most of these businesses due to their focus on cash flow, smaller accounts were faster to close because one person generally made the decision and the business risks were fairly straightforward and addressable. As a result, the selling cycle—the time it took to close a deal—was fairly short. Even a new account would take only two to three calls to close.

Doug realized that First-Plus was a more complex plan, requiring more time to explain and understand. He also knew from experience that the buying process in large firms could be more complicated. A committee often made the purchase decision and more people could veto the deal or delay the purchase for an extended period. On the other hand, these accounts could potentially be exceptionally large sales opportunities, with high testimonial value. If a large well-known company chose your plan, it was a natural opener for more companies in the same business.

Doug decided to tackle the problem head-on and the next time he was riding with Tiffany to see some of her accounts asked if they could stop to visit a large prospect to which Tiffany had made an initial sales call to determine their interest in purchasing insurance from Shield. He was really pleased when Tiffany agreed and was able to make an appointment with the vice president of Human Resources for that afternoon. After introductions and some initial small talk, they got down to business.

"As I mentioned last time," the vice president said, "we would like to get a better handle on our risks, but we need a lot of help. Every one of our offices is used to doing things its own way, and that includes the liability and workman's compensation plans they've purchased. We don't have a common set of procedures for determining our risks or handling claims. Making matters even more difficult, we haven't got a common information system. We might be willing to write a lot of business with you if your people are prepared to work with each office individually. Study their particular needs and help them get their act together." The discussion proceeded with the vice president explaining the background of how decentralized decision making has traditionally been in his company. This was changing, however, and insurance was one of the issues that he felt should be standardized throughout.

Doug and Tiffany thanked the vice president for his time and the information. Doug promised that he and Tiffany would get back to him with some ideas. In fact, Doug was not sure how to respond to this request. This was an entirely different type of situation than he was used to seeing. On the other hand, he knew that they could not afford to lose this opportunity and that this could really turn things around in the Des Moines office. He also wondered if this situation was typical of other large businesses.

Questions

1. How fundamentally different is the role of the sales force in addressing these new customer needs from that of addressing the needs of more traditional brokers?
2. How will the selling effort change when addressing these new broker needs?
3. How will the changes affect sales management?
4. What are the threats and possible downside of addressing these emerging broker needs?

SALES MANAGEMENT RESOURCE

ESTIMATING POTENTIALS AND FORECASTING SALES

WHY FORECAST?

One of the keys to success in sales is knowing where customers are located and being able to predict how much they will buy. Firms have found that sales potential data are indispensable to developing a sales program, particularly in setting up territories, assigning quotas, developing budgets, and comparing sales performance of individual salespeople. Sales forecasting is so important that most firms include this topic in their sales manager training programs.[1]

Inaccurate demand predictions can have disastrous effects on profitability. For example, Hewlett-Packard was once unable to predict the proper mix of products demanded by its customers for two quarters in a row. Demand for low-end printers and workstations was high, and demand for commercial computers was low. As a result, earnings were 14 percent lower than analysts expected. The stock market was dismayed with Hewlett-Packard's forecasting problems and knocked the company's stock down 5 percent in one day. This case example demonstrates the importance of being able to measure the size of market opportunities. In this Management Resource, we will show you how to measure demand for today and how to forecast sales for tomorrow.

WHAT IS MARKET POTENTIAL?

Market potential is an estimate of maximum demand in a time period based on the number of potential users and their purchase rate. Actual industry sales are usually less than market potential, as shown in Figure SMR2-1. For instance, the U.S. market potential for DVD players could be defined as the total number of households with television sets based on typical purchases of one unit per family. Actual sales are less than potential because it takes time to convince people to buy discretionary items such as DVD players and because some people can't afford them. The industry purchase rate is a function of price levels, overall product quality, promotional expenditures, and the number of stores stocking the machines.

Company *sales potential* is a portion of total industry demand. It is the maximum amount a firm can sell in a time period under optimum conditions. As Figure SMR2-1 suggests, company sales will be lower than industry sales. The ratio of company sales to industry sales is a measure of the market share of the organization.

In your position as sales manager, you will be asked to estimate current values for market and company potential for products assigned to your care. This assignment can be tricky because the number of users and the purchase rate change over time. In addition, price declines, industry promotions, and changing economic conditions can also influence the size of the market. Besides measuring current levels of demand, you will be required to forecast into the future. These predictions are shown as the dashed lines for period 12 in Figure SMR2-1. Our discussion begins with demand measurement and shifts to the issue of forecasting later.

Resource Consultant: Beth Forbes, Director of International Results & Analysis, GTE International

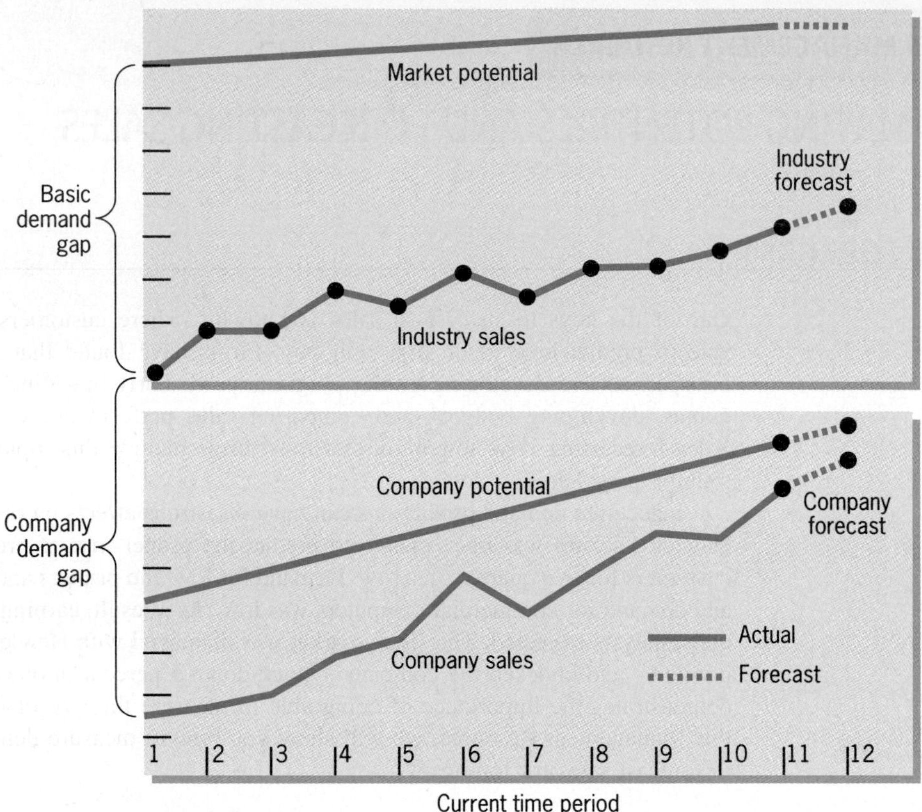

FIGURE SMR2-1 Relations Among Market Potential, Industry Sales, and Company Sales

Estimating Potentials

All estimates of potential are based on two key components—the number of possible users of the product and the maximum expected purchase rate. Sometimes you can get estimates of these numbers from trade associations or commercial research associations, but you have to come up with your own potential figures, broken down by geographical area, industry, and customer type.

The initial approach for estimating the number of buyers is to use secondary sources. A wide variety of commercial data are available that provide the potential number of buyers, size of firms, age of consumers, income levels, and locations. Dun's Marketing Services and *Sales & Marketing Management* magazine sell these data in an Excel format for personal analysis. You can also access potential databases through computer networks on a fee basis. Large firms often have their own databases that can be mined for potential information.

Purchase rates are usually derived from trade organizations or government publications. For existing products, you may wish to use the ratio of current sales to the number of households or sales per person to derive a purchase rate. These data can be obtained from trade publications such as those from the Conference Board, or they can be calculated from published data. For example, average demand per household could be derived by dividing total industry sales for an area by the number of households. In the case of new products, managers may estimate conversion rates from experience with other items. If a similar product was sold to 4 percent of U.S. households during the first year, this rate could be applied to obtain demand estimates for new merchandise.

Duracell, a division of Gillette, is the world's leading alkaline battery manufacturer. Every month, five standard alkaline battery sizes are converted into thousands of stock-keeping units that are shipped to customers. Forecasting's mission at Duracell is to provide management with forecasts to help prepare strategies and set goals. The basic forecasting formula at Duracell is that Shipments = Retail Market × Market Share +/− Changes in Retail Inventories. Thus, forecasts are a function of the size of the market times anticipated market share with an adjustment for retailer inventory changes. The company uses six different statistical models to determine market size. Marketing executives estimate market shares based on plans for advertising, product enhancements, distribution strategies, and pricing. Changes in retail inventories are the most difficult to estimate. Duracell uses five forecasting cycles: competitive view, strategic business plan, tactical plan, latest estimate (monthly), and supply chain management (weekly). To ensure coordination of resources, marketing, finance, and production planning activities all use the same forecasts. Its forecasting toolbox includes judgmental, time series, and causal model approaches. No single procedure meets all forecasting needs, and so Duracell selects methods that best suit the situation. This often means using simple naive methods for tactical forecasts of less than one year. They also use linear regression, exponential smoothing, moving averages, and causal models for long-term situations. Duracell often selects forecasting methods on the basis of those shown through tests to be the most accurate with company data.

Buying Power Index Method

Market potentials for consumer goods are usually estimated by constructing indexes from basic economic data. Perhaps the most popular multifactor index of area demand is the Buying Power Index (BPI), published each year by *Sales & Marketing Management* magazine. This index combines estimates of population, income, and retail sales to give a composite indicator of consumer demand in 922 geographic areas known as Core Based Statistical Areas (CSBSAs). These CBSAs are subdivided into either metropolitan or micropolitan statistical areas.

Data used to calculate the Buying Power Index for the Atlanta, Georgia, area are summarized in Table SMR2-1. The figures show that the Atlanta Metro area has 1.824 percent of U.S. income, 1.768 percent of retail sales, and 1.606 percent of the U.S. population. These three numbers are weighted by 0.5, 0.3, and 0.2 for income, retail sales, and population, respectively, to give a Buying Power Index for Atlanta Metro of 1.7636.[2]

A comparison of the three figures—retail sales, population, and income percentages—provides valuable information about a geographic area. Consider again the Atlanta area percentages that have only 1.509 percent of the U.S. population, 1.784 percent of the national income, and 1.719 percent of retail sales. This suggests that income for the Atlanta Metro area is considerably above average. When retail sales for an area are more than the population for an area, as in this example, there is strong evidence that people are driving in

TABLE SMR2-1 Data Used to Calculate Buying Power Index

	2004 Effective Buying Income		*2004 Total Retail Sales*		*2004 Estimated Total Population*		
	Amount ($000,000)	*Percentage of United States*	*Amount ($000,000)*	*Percentage of United States*	*Amount ($000,000)*	*Percentage of United States*	*Buying Power Index*
Total U.S.	$5,466,880	100.0%	3,906,482	100.0%	292,936	100.0%	100.0
Atlanta Metro	$99,691	1.824%	$69.071	1.768	4.704	1.606	1.7636

from surrounding counties. This suggests that managers should spread their promotional dollars over a wide area to reach most of the customers who shop in the Atlanta Metro area.

Buying Power Index values are used to help managers allocate selling efforts across geographic regions. That is, the Buying Power Index suggests that Atlanta Metro, with 1.7636 percent of the U.S. sales potential, should receive about 1.7636 percent of the personal selling and advertising budgets for products in national distribution.

NAICS Method for Business Markets

Business market potential can be built up from data made available through the U.S. Census of Manufacturers. The Census of Manufacturers, which is available every five years, combines businesses into North American Industry Classification System (NAICS) codes according to products produced or operations performed.

The first step in estimating potentials from census data is to identify all the NAICS codes that make use of the product or service. This is usually accomplished by selecting industries that are likely customers, using judgment to pick codes from the NAICS manual, and running surveys of different types of firms to see where products are employed. Next, the firm must select an appropriate database for estimating the amount of the product that will be used by each NAICS code. A food machinery manufacturer, for example, could review past sales data to determine the relationship between the number of its machines in use and the number of production workers in a particular industry. If the manufacturer found that 24 machines were used for every 1,000 grain milling employees, 15 for every 1,000 bakery workers, and 3 for every 1,000 beverage workers, then the market potential for North Carolina could be determined as shown in Table SMR2-2. The 2002 Census of Manufacturers showed that North Carolina actually had 878 grain milling workers. If 24 machines were used per 1,000 workers, the market potential would be 878 × 24, or 21.1 machines. Similar calculations for other codes yield a total market potential of about 175 machines for the state of North Carolina. The potential built up for North Carolina would then be added to estimates derived for other states to give national figures. These figures can be converted into annual measures of market potential by adjusting for the average life of the machines. If the machines lasted an average of ten years, then approximately 10 percent of the North Carolina potential of 175 units, or 17 machines, would be replaced each year. Multiplying annual demand potential by the firm's current market share would derive estimates of company potential.

TABLE SMR2-2 Estimating the Market Potential for Food Machinery in North Carolina

NAIC Code	*Industry*	*(1) Production Employees*[a]	*(2) Number of Machines Used per 1000 Workers*[b]	*Market Potential (1×2)/1000*
3112	Grain Milling	878	24	21.1
3122	Tobacco Mfg.	9,571	15	143.6
3121	Beverages	3,538	3	10.6
				175.3

[a]The production employee data are from the *2002 Economic Census of Manufacturing, Geographic Area Series, North Carolina*, p. NC1 & 2.

[b]Estimated by manufacturer from past sales data.

QUALITATIVE SALES FORECASTING

Sales forecasting is concerned with predicting future levels of demand. These projections are vital for budgeting and planning purposes. For new products, a few simple routines can be employed. The absence of past sales means that you have to be more creative in coming up with predictions of the future. Sales forecasts for new products are often based on executive judgments, sales force projections, surveys, and market tests. We will begin our discussion of forecasting techniques by focusing on subjective methods that are based on interpretations of business conditions by executives and salespeople.

Sales Force Composite

A favorite forecasting technique for new and existing products is the *sales force composite* method. With this procedure, salespeople project volume for customers in their own territory, and the estimates are aggregated and reviewed at higher management levels. The territory estimate is often derived based on demand estimates for each of the largest customers in the territory, the remainder of the customers as a group, and then for new prospects. Sales force composite forecasting is one of the most popular forecasting methods and is used by 45 percent of the firms in a U.S. survey (Table SMR2-3). This technique is favored by industrial concerns because they have a limited number of customers and salespeople are in a good position to assess customers' needs. This technique was adopted by a medical products subsidiary of American Home Products.[3] Previously, the sales forecast came down from headquarters; now the forecast is built up from estimates prepared by 120 field reps. When salespeople provide input, they buy into the forecast and are more likely to achieve their sales quotas. The net result at the medical products firm has been improved sales forecast accuracy.

Jury of Executive Opinion

This technique involves soliciting the judgment of a group of experienced managers to give sales estimates for proposed and current products. The *jury of executive opinion*

TABLE SMR2-3 Utilization of Sales Forecasting Methods of 134 Firms

Methods	*Percentage of Firms That Use Regularly*	*Percentage of Firms That Use Occasionally*	*Percentage of Firms No Longer Using*
Subjective			
Sales force composite	44.8%	17.2%	13.4%
Jury of executive opinion	37.3	22.4	8.2
Intention to buy survey	16.4	10.4	18.7
Extrapolation			
Naïve	30.6	20.1	9.0
Moving average	20.9	10.4	15.7
Percent rate of change	19.4	13.4	14.2
Leading indicators	18.7	17.2	11.2
Unit rate of change	15.7	9.7	18.7
Exponential smoothing	11.2	11.9	19.4
Line extension	6.0	13.4	20.9
Quantitative			
Multiple regressing	12.7	9.0	20.9
Econometric	11.9	9.0	19.4
Simple regression	6.0	13.4	20.1
Box-Jenkins	3.7	5.2	26.9

was used by 37 percent of the firms described in Table SMR2-3. The main advantages of this method are that it is fast and it allows the inclusion of many subjective factors such as competition, economic climate, weather, and union activity. United Parcel Service forecasts are prepared by a group of senior executives using economic indicators such as the Consumer Price Index, historical sales data, and other trends. These forecasts are then compared with predictions developed by salespeople, and the differences are reconciled.

The continued popularity of the jury of executive opinion shows that most managers prefer their own judgment to other less well-known statistical forecasting procedures. However, available evidence does not suggest that the jury of executive opinion method leads to more accurate forecasting. Perhaps the main problem with the method is that it is based on experience, and it is difficult to teach someone how to forecast using this method.

Leading Indicators

Where sales are influenced by basic changes in the economy, *leading indicators* can be a useful guide in preparing sales forecasts. The idea is to find a factor series that is closely related to company sales, yet for which statistics are available several months in advance. Changes in the factor can then be used to predict sales directly, or the factor can be combined with other variables in a forecasting model. For example, General Electric has found that sales of dishwashers are closely related to the number of housing starts that occur several months earlier. Thus, if GE observed a 4 percent increase in housing starts in California, it could expect demand for dishwashers to increase by about 4 percent two months later. Obviously, the key issue is finding indicators that have forecasting value for particular products. Some of the more useful leading indicators include prices of common stocks, new orders for durable goods, new building permits, contracts and orders for plant and equipment, and changes in consumer installment debt.

Perhaps the greatest contribution of leading indicators is their ability to predict turns in sales trends. If sales have been increasing, for example, a decline in the leading indicators may indicate a leveling-off of sales or a decline. Most of the quantitative forecasting techniques that we will discuss in the next section do a very poor job of telling managers when sales are going to change direction. Leading indicators can be more sensitive to changes in the business environment, and they often signal turns in the economy months before they actually occur.

When Should Qualitative Forecasting Methods Be Used?

Qualitative methods are often used when you have little numerical data to incorporate into your forecasts. New products are a classic example of limited information, and qualitative methods are frequently employed to predict sales revenues for these items. Qualitative methods are also recommended for those situations where managers or the sales force are particularly adept at predicting sales revenues. In addition, qualitative forecasting methods are often utilized when markets have been disrupted by strikes, wars, natural disasters, recessions, or inflation. Under these conditions, historical data are useless, and judgmental procedures that account for the factors causing market shocks are usually more accurate. Managers should calculate and record the forecasting errors produced by the qualitative techniques they employ so that they will know when these methods are best employed.

QUANTITATIVE SALES FORECASTING

We now shift our focus from qualitative-based methods to quantitative techniques. These procedures are based on analysis of historical data to predict future sales.

Seasonal Adjustments

Before we discuss quantitative forecasting techniques, it's important to understand how seasonal factors influence predictions of the future. Sales forecasts are often prepared monthly or quarterly, and seasonal factors are frequently responsible for many of the short-run changes in volume. Thus, what appears to be a good forecast may turn out to be a poor one because of the failure to consider seasonal factors. When historical sales figures are used in forecasting, the accuracy of predictions can often be improved by making adjustments to eliminate seasonal effects.

The first step in seasonally adjusting a time series is to collect sales figures for the past several years. Next, sales for months or quarters are averaged across years to build a seasonal index. In Table SMR2-4 four years of quarterly sales are averaged to give a rough indication of seasonal effects.[4] The quarterly averages are then divided by mean sales for all quarters to give seasonal index numbers. For example, when average sales of 58.0 for quarter 1 are divided by the mean for all quarters of 79.25, a seasonal index of 0.73 is obtained. This number indicates that seasonal factors typically lower first-quarter sales by 27 percent.

Once seasonal index numbers are developed for each time period, it is easy to adjust a set of sales data seasonally. Actual sales, such as those shown in Table SMR2-4, are simply divided by the appropriate index numbers to give a set of *deseasonalized data*. Sales forecast are then prepared using the deseasonalized sales figures. For example the deseasonalized sales data for the four quarters of the first year in Table SMR2-4 would be 67 (49%/.73), 68, 78, and 81 for quarters one, two, three, and four, respectively. The resulting forecasts must be multiplied by the seasonal index for the forecast period to make them comparable with regular sales figures.

Computer programs used in sales forecasting take these indexes and make forecasts for future periods. Nabisco Biscuit Company uses computer programs to forecast sales of new cracker and cookie brands soon after they have been introduced. Because new products have no sales history, Nabisco's program uses an exponential smoothing approach that can start forecasting with only two periods of data. The first six weeks of sales figures are discarded in the Nabisco model because these shipments are used to build store and warehouse inventories. Then the program deseasonalizes the sales figures using weekly

TABLE SMR2-4 Calculating a Seasonal Index from Historical Sales Data

	Year				Four-Year	Seasonal
Quarter	*1*	*2*	*3*	*4*	*Quarterly Average*	*Index*
1	49	57	53	73	58.0	0.73[a]
2	77	98	85	100	90.0	1.13
3	90	89	92	98	92.3	1.16
4	79	62	88	78	76.8	0.97
Four year sales of 1268/16 = 79.25 average quarterly sales						

[a]Seasonal index is 59.0/79.25 = 0.73

seasonal factors from a similar product, brand, or category. Nabisco initially used seasonal indexes based on retail store scanner data supplied by the independent marketing research firm IRI. When these indexes did not significantly reduce forecasting errors, Nabisco decided to calculate the indexes from Nabisco's weekly shipment data. These indexes led to a 14 percent reduction in forecasting errors for four-week projections for cookies and 21 percent reductions in errors for crackers. The Nabisco forecasting program also includes adjustments for trend and sales promotions. Nabisco's new forecasting program led to a 34 percent overall reduction in errors in national weekly projections and a 53 percent reduction in errors in four-week projections compared to their old method. Nabisco's program has been employed successfully for several years and has been adapted for use with existing products that have been hurt by new items or have been affected by mergers or acquisitions.

Some students think that because seasonal adjustments complicate the forecasting process, they may not be worth the time and effort required. However, there are two truths about seasonal adjustments that you should remember:

1. Seasonal adjustments are widely used in business.
2. Seasonal adjustments reduce forecasting errors.

Naive Forecasts

Time series forecasts rely on past data to provide a basis for making projections about the future. The *naive forecast* is the simplest numerical forecasting technique and is often used as a standard for comparison with other procedures. This method assumes that nothing is going to change and that the best estimate for the future is the current level of sales. For example, actual sales of 49 units observed in quarter 1 in Table SMR2-4 can be used to predict sales in quarter 2. Naive forecasts for the last three quarters of year 1 would be

	Quarter			
	1	*2*	*3*	*4*
Actual sales	49	77	90	79
Naive forecast		49	77	90

The error in the forecast for quarter 2 is the difference between 49 and 77. The formula for the *percentage forecasting error* is

$$\text{Percentage of forecasting error} = \frac{\text{forecast} - \text{actual}}{\text{actual}}$$

This means the percentage error for the naive forecast in quarter 2 is

$$\text{Percentage error} = \frac{49 - 77}{77}$$

$$\text{Percentage error} = 36\%$$

The naive approach may also be used with deseasonalized sales figures, such as those calculated in the previous section. Recall that the seasonally adjusted sales figure for the first quarter of year 1 was 67, so the naive forecast sales in the second quarter would also be 67. Seasonally adjusted, the forecast for the second quarter would be 76 ($67 \times 1.13 = 75.7$). The Figure 1.13 is the seasonal index shown in Table SMR2-4. If the data were seasonally adjusted, the forecasting error for quarter 2 would be only 1.3 percent. This example shows that seasonal adjustments can lower forecasting errors for even simple naive forecasts. Because it is simple to calculate, the naive forecast is often used as the "base case" against which other, more sophisticated forecasting techniques are compared.

MAPE

In order to compare forecasting accuracy across several time periods, most forecasting professionals use the *mean absolute percentage error (MAPE)* method. The formula for calculating MAPE is:

$$\text{MAPE} = \frac{\sum_{i=1}^{n} |\text{forecast} - \text{actual}|/\text{actual}}{n} \times 100\%$$

Where n is the number of periods for which forecasts are to be made.

MAPE calculates the percentage forecasting error for each period without regard to whether the errors are positive or negative, adds up the errors, and divides by the number of periods being forecast. The main advantage of MAPE is that it allows easy comparison of forecasting errors across product categories and companies. For practice in calculating MAPE, see the problems at the end of this Resource. Notice also that Excel worksheets are available at www.wiley.com/college/cron. Go to "Student Companion Site."

Trend Projections

The use of *trends* to project sales is a popular technique among business firms. With this method, the analyst estimates trends from past data and adds this figure to current sales to obtain a forecast. For example, in Figure SMR2-2 sales increased from 10 units in period 2 to 20 units in period 3, suggesting a trend of plus-10 units per period. A unit rate of change forecast for period 4 would combine current sales of 20 plus 10 units of trend for a total of 30.

Trends can also be expressed as a percentage rate of change. With this method, the 10 units of trend would be divided by the base of 10 units of sales to give a 100 percent growth rate. A 100 percent growth rate applied to current sales of 20 units would give a forecast of 40 units for period 4. Note that the percentage rate of change method and the unit rate of change procedure give different sales forecasts. When sales are increasing, forecasts prepared with the percentage rate of change approach will normally be higher than those obtained by other projective techniques. Research reported in Table SMR2-3 shows that the percentage rate of change method is the most popular projective forecasting technique,

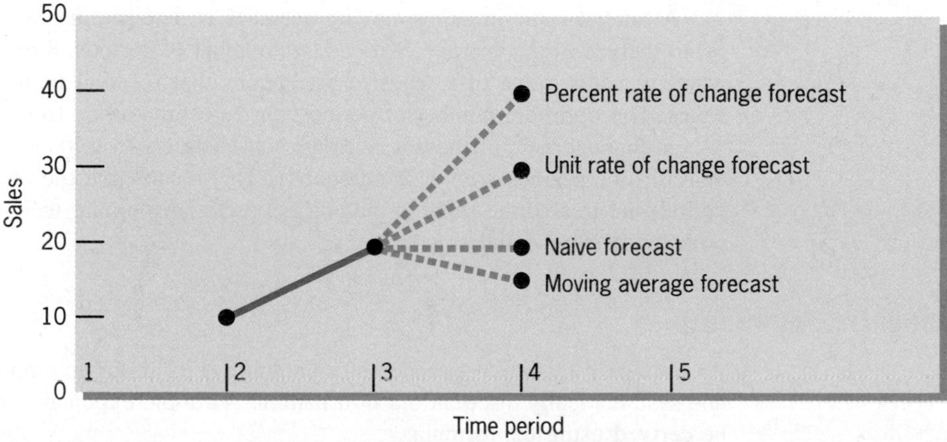

FIGURE SMR2-2 Comparing Trend Forecasting Methods

followed by the unit rate of change. Trend projections are often combined with exponential smoothing and moving average forecasts to help improve forecasting accuracy.

Moving Averages

With the *moving average* method, the average revenue achieved in several recent periods is used as a prediction of sales in the next period. The formula takes the form

$$F_{t+1} = \frac{S_t + S_{t-1} + \cdots + S_{t-n+1}}{n}$$

where
Ft+1 = forecast for the next period
St = sales in the current period
n = number of periods in the moving average

This approach assumes that the future will be an average of past achievements. For example, if sales in the last two periods went from 10 to 20, then a two-period moving average forecast would be 15 (30/2) as shown in Figure SMR2-2. Thus, when there is a strong trend in a time series, a moving average forecast without a trend adjustment lags behind. However, this lag can be an advantage when sales change direction (suddenly increase or decrease).

Students must remember that a moving average really does move. For example, sales data from Table SMR2-4 can be used to make two-period moving average forecasts as follows:

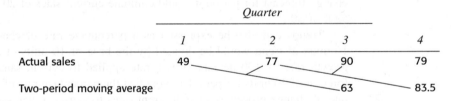

	Quarter			
	1	*2*	*3*	*4*
Actual sales	49	77	90	79
Two-period moving average			63	83.5

Thus, periods 1 and 2 are averaged to give a forecast of 63 for period 3. Then period 1 is dropped, and periods 2 and 3 are averaged to produce a forecast of 83.5 for period 4. This process would be the same when using deseasonalized data, but do recall that the forecast must then be seasonally adjusted. If forecasting for the third quarter, for instance, then the forecast would be multiplied by the seasonal index for that quarter.

A crucial issue in using moving averages is determining the ideal number of periods *(n)* to include in the average. With a large number of periods, forecasts tend to react slowly, whereas a low value of n leads to predictions that respond more quickly to changes in a series. The optimum number of periods can be estimated by trial and error using Excel.

A characteristic of moving averages that distracts from their ability to follow trends is that all time periods are weighted equally. This means that the oldest and and most recent periods are treated the same in making a forecast. A popular technique that overcomes this problem is exponential smoothing.

Exponential Smoothing

An important feature of exponential smoothing is its ability to emphasize recent information and systematically discount old information. A simple exponentially smoothed forecast can be derived using the formula:

$$\overline{S}_t = \alpha S_{t-1} + (1 - \alpha)\overline{S}_{t-1}$$

where

$\overline{S}_t$ = smoothed sales forecast for period t.
α = the smoothing constant, greater than 0 and less than 1
$St - 1$ = actual sales in period $t - 1$
$\overline{S}_{t-1}$ = smoothed forecast for period $t - 1$

The formula combines a portion (α) of current sales with a discounted value of the smoothed average calculated for the previous period to give a forecast for the next period. The following example uses data from Table SMR2-4 with a smoothing constant of 0.4.

	Quarter			
	1	*2*	*3*	*4*
Actual sales	49	77	90	79
Smoothed forecast			60.2	72.1

The forecast for period 3 is obtained by multiplying 0.4 times the current sales in period 2 of 77 plus 0.6 (1 − α) times 49, which is the actual sales for period 1 that can be used as a proxy for the prior period's forecast to get the process started. The resulting forecast for period 3 would be 60.2 units [(0.4 × 77) + (0.6 × 49) = 60.2]. A forecast for period 4 would be obtained by multiplying 0.4 times the period 3 sales of 90 plus 0.6 times the smoothed forecast for period 3. The forecast would be 72.1 units. [(0.4 × 90) + (0.6 × 60.2) = 72.1]. Remember, once again, that if you are using deseasonalized numbers, then you would need to seasonally adjust the smoothed forecast.

The major decision with exponential forecasting is selecting an appropriate value for the *smoothing constant* (α). Smoothing factors can range in value from 0 to 1, with low values providing stability and high values allowing a more rapid response to sales changes. Using a smoothing constant of 1.0 gives the same forecasts that are obtained with the naive method. Forecasts produced with a low smoothing constant, such as 0.2, lag behind, and forecasts generated with high values, such as 0.8, will likely overestimate sales at turning points. When historical data are available, analysts should search for the optimum smoothing constant by trying out different α values to see which one forecasts best.

Regression techniques have advantages in situations in which managers wish to incorporate variables other than just past sales in their forecasting program.

Time Series Regression

In *time series regression*, the relationship between sales *(Y)* and a period of time (e.g., week, month, quarter, or year) *(X)* can be represented by a straight line. The equation for this line is $Y = a + bX$, where a is the intercept and b shows the impact of the independent variable on Y. The key step in deriving linear regression equations is finding values for the coefficients *(a, b)* that give the line that best fits the data. The best fit can be obtained by employing a *least squares* procedure (as illustrated in Figure SMR2-3), where sales *(Y)* have been plotted against time *(X)*. The equation $Y = 63.9 + 3.5X$ indicates that sales are 63.9 plus a trend of 3.5 for every unit of time (e.g., month, quarter, year, etc.). Two variable regression equations can be easily calculated using some pocket calculators, Excel, or other computer programs.

A limitation of simple regression forecasting is the assumption that sales follow a linear pattern. Although this may hold for some series, others have cyclical patterns that are hard to track with linear equations. In this case, the analyst can base the forecasting equation on the logarithms of the time series data to produce improved forecasting equations.

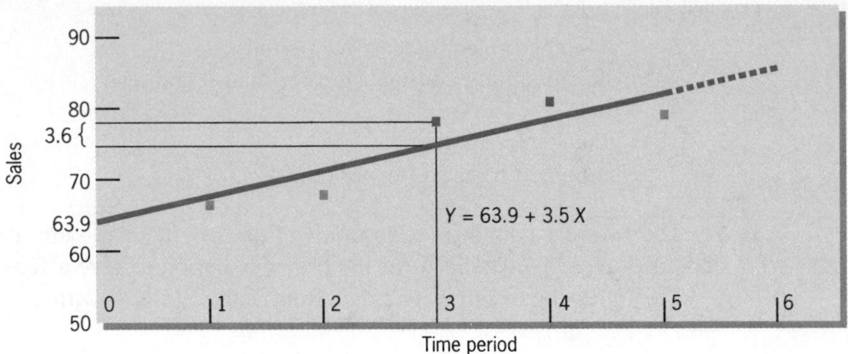

FIGURE SMR2-3 Fitting a Trend Regression to Seasonally Adjusted Sales Data

Another problem is knowing how much past data to include in the calculation of the forecast. Usually, all past data points are used to provide greater stability. Sometimes, however, regressions using data from a shorter period of time will do a better job of tracking changes. For example, Procter & Gamble's Italian division produces powdered and liquid detergents for Europe. It regularly prepares sales forecasts for two powdered detergents and one liquid detergent for use with washing machines. For established products, P&G Italy looks at the history of a product, adjusts for advertising effects, and uses three years of historical data to prepare these forecasts. Forecasts for new products are based on estimates of expected market shares. Sales forecasts at P&G Italy are medium to long term, and its most detailed forecasts are for three years.

The simple regression equations that have been described use time as the independent variable, which is common in sales forecasting. With time as the independent variable, a regression approach becomes a trend forecast. Other variables such as income or the rate of growth in GNP may be used if they are found to closely relate to sales.

When sales seem to be associated with several independent variables, multiple regression procedures should be used to build a forecasting model.

Multiple Regression

With *multiple regression*, a computer model is used to build forecasting models based on historical relationships between sales and several independent variables. Sales managers first have to find an appropriate set of independent factors that are related to the series being predicted. Some of the best variables for multiple regression equations are leading indicators, such as housing starts, new orders for durable goods, and contracts for plant and capital equipment. Leading indicators have the advantage that known values from an earlier time period (e.g., last months, quarter, or year) can be plugged into multiple regression equations to predict the future. However, in some cases, indicator values for the prediction period are needed; then you have to predict these indicator factors for future time periods before loading them into the forecasting equation.

The decision of whether to use a simple or multiple regression forecasting model often depends on the values of three statistics that are calculated by forecasting programs. One of these statistics is R^2. If the R^2 value is .70, your equation explains 70 percent of the variation observed in your data. Forecasting equations with high R^2 are generally preferable to equations that explain only 5 to 10 percent of the variation. Another statistic indicating the quality of your forecasting model is the standard error of the estimate. This statistic tells you the range within which you can expect to find the true value of the variable you are predicting. Yet a third statistic is the error in each of the coefficients. The errors in the coefficients for the variables in your equation should be smaller than the coefficients. If the errors are larger than the coefficients, then there is good reason to drop that variable from your forecasting equation. With regression forecasting, you need five observations for every independent variable in your equation. Thus, an equation with one predictor variable would need five observations, and an equation with three variables would need fifteen observations. If your data set does not meet these requirements, then another forecasting method should be selected.

Despite the complexities of multiple regression forecasting, this technique was the most popular quantitative method reported in Table SMR2-3 and was used regularly by 13 percent of the firms. A real data set that you can use to build a multiple regression forecasting equation is included with Problem 5 (Table SMR2-5) later in this chapter.

Turning Points

At several points in this discussion we have mentioned the idea of turning points. A *turning point* is a sudden change in a trend. For instance, a decline in sales after several years of moderate growth would be considered a turning point, if sales continued to decline in subsequent years. The numerical forecasting methods we have discussed make projections from historical data, and most of them do a poor job of predicting turning points in a time series. Percentage rate of change, unit rate of change, and time series regression are all notoriously poor predictors of a numerical series that changes direction. Naïve, moving average, and exponential smoothing are somewhat better because they tend to lag and then adapt to new information. If the identification of turning points is important to you, then the use of qualitative procedures is often the best approach. These methods can pick up environmental cues that signal turning points frequently missed by numerical methods. Sometimes leading indicators can be included in multiple regression equations to help predict turning points.

For practice in all the quantitative techniques discussed here, see the problems that follow this Management Resource. Excel worksheets are available for working these problems under "Student Companion Site" at www.wiley.com/college/cron.

When Should Quantitative Forecasting Methods Be Used?

Quantitative forecasting techniques are best employed when you have access to historical data. It is also helpful if the time series you are trying to forecast are stable and do not frequently change direction. Quantitative methods have distinct advantages in situations where you must make frequent forecasts for hundreds or thousands of products. Because of the large number of calculations required by quantitative forecasting procedures, analysts need access to computers and appropriate forecasting software. The successful use of quantitative forecasting methods demands that analysts be well versed in the statistical procedures used by these techniques.

SELECTING FORECASTING METHODS

Most initial sales forecasts today are prepared with computer programs. However, most companies allow managers to make adjustments to computer-generated forecasts with judgmental procedures. This same study showed that the average firm uses 1.8 sales forecasting computer systems. Management believes that more than one forecasting program can help reduce forecasting errors. More than half of the companies surveyed use customized forecasting software.

TABLE SMR2-5 Company Sales and Other Variables (Semiannual)

Period	*Company Sales (thousands of dollars*	*Personal Disposable Income (millions of dollars)*	*Dealer's Allowances (thousands of dollars)*	*Price (dollars)*	*Product Development Budget (thousands of dollars)*	*Capital Investments (thousands of dollars)*	*Advertising (thousands of dollars)*	*Sales Expenses (thousands of dollars)*	*Total Industry Advertising Budget (thousands of dollars)*
1	5540.39	398	138	56.2058	12.1124	49.895	76.8621	228.80	98.205
2	5439.04	369	118	59.0443	9.3304	16.595	88.8056	177.45	224.953
3	4290.00	268	129	56.7236	28.7481	89.182	51.2972	166.40	263.032
4	5502.34	484	111	57.8627	12.8916	106.738	39.6473	258.05	320.928
5	4871.77	394	146	59.1178	13.3815	142.552	51.6517	209.30	406.989
6	4708.08	332	140	60.1113	11.0859	61.287	20.5476	180.05	246.996
7	4627.81	336	136	59.8398	24.9579	−30.385	40.1534	213.20	328.436
8	4110.24	383	104	60.0523	20.8096	−44.586	31.6456	200.85	298.456
9	4122.69	285	105	63.1415	8.4853	−28.373	12.4570	176.15	218.110
10	4842.25	277	135	62.3026	10.7301	75.723	68.3076	174.85	410.467
11	5740.65	456	128	64.9220	21.8473	144.030	52.4536	252.85	93.006
12	5094.10	355	131	64.8577	23.5062	112.904	76.6778	208.00	307.226
13	5383.20	364	120	63.5919	13.8940	128.347	96.0677	195.00	106.792
14	4888.17	320	147	65.6145	14.8659	10.097	47.9795	154.05	304.921
15	4033.13	311	143	67.0228	22.4940	−24.760	27.2319	180.70	59.612
16	4941.96	362	145	66.9049	23.3698	116.748	72.6681	219.70	238.986
17	5312.80	408	131	66.1843	13.0354	120.406	62.3129	234.65	141.074
18	5139.87	433	124	67.8651	8.0330	121.823	24.7122	258.05	290.832
19	4397.36	359	106	68.8892	27.0486	71.055	73.9126	196.30	413.636
20	5149.47	476	138	71.4177	18.2208	4.186	63.2737	278.85	206.454
21	5150.83	415	148	69.2775	7.7422	46.935	28.6762	207.35	79.566
22	4989.02	420	136	69.7334	10.1361	7.621	91.3635	213.20	428.982
23	5926.86	536	111	73.1628	27.3709	127.509	74.0169	296.40	273.072
24	4703.88	432	152	73.3650	15.5281	−49.574	16.1628	245.05	309.422
25	5365.59	436	123	73.0500	32.4918	100.098	42.9984	275.60	280.139
26	4630.09	415	119	74.9102	19.7127	−40.185	41.1346	211.25	314.548
27	5711.86	462	112	73.2007	14.8358	68.153	92.5180	282.75	212.058
28	5095.48	429	125	74.1615	11.3694	87.963	83.2870	217.75	118.065
29	6124.37	517	142	74.2838	26.7510	27.088	74.8921	306.80	344.553
30	4787.34	328	123	77.1409	19.6038	59.343	87.5103	210.60	140.872
31	5035.62	418	135	78.5910	34.6881	141.969	74.4712	269.75	82.855
32	5288.01	515	120	77.0938	23.2020	126.420	21.2711	328.25	398.425
33	4647.01	412	149	78.2313	35.7396	29.558	26.4941	258.05	124.027
34	5315.63	455	126	77.9296	21.5891	18.007	94.6311	232.70	117.911
35	6180.06	554	138	81.0394	19.5692	42.352	92.5448	323.70	161.250
36	4800.97	441	120	79.8485	15.5037	−21.558	50.0480	267.15	405.088
37	5512.13	417	120	80.6394	34.9238	148.450	83.1803	257.40	110.740
38	5272.21	461	132	82.2843	26.5496	−17.584	91.2214	266.50	170.392
39	?	485	125	81.6257	20.0000	40.000	85.0000	275.00	180.000

Remember that simple procedures such as naive, moving averages, and exponential smoothing often have lower forecasting errors than other more complex methods. This suggests you should start with the basic procedures and move on to more complex models only when they are needed. It is rare that one technique is best in all situations, so you may want to base your predictions on the average of several methods to help reduce forecasting error.

Finally, you must select techniques that can be sold to management. If managers cannot understand how forecasts are prepared, they are likely to reject the techniques in favor of their own judgmental forecasting methods.

PROBLEMS

Note: Excel spreadsheets for these problems are available at www.wiley.com/college/cron. Go to "Student Companion Site"

1. Using the following sales data, forecast revenue for periods 4 through 7, using naive, trend projections, moving average, and simple exponential smoothing. Compare MAPEs across methods for time periods 4 to 7. What length of moving average and smoothing constant works best? What are your forecasts for periods 8 and 9?

Period	1	2	3	4	5	6	7	8	9
Sales	12	15	17	14	16	19	18	?	?

2. Quarterly sales (thousands of dollars) for the Chester Furniture Company for the past four years have been as follows.

	Year				
Quarter	*1*	*2*	*3*	*4*	*5*
1	230	240	264	328	?
2	245	266	290	344	?
3	193	259	221	275	?
4	174	218	202	281	?

Calculate seasonal indexes and adjust the data. Run seasonally adjusted naive, moving average, exponential smoothing, and linear regression forecasts through the data to see which method has the lowest MAPE. Select the best method and forecast sales for quarters 1 through 4 in year 5.

3. Sales (in thousands of dollars) for the Busy Bee Bakery for the past 15 time periods have been:

Period	*Sales*	*Period*	*Sales*	*Period*	*Sales*
1	2005	6	2360	11	3442
2	2150	7	2354	12	2948
3	1940	8	2682	13	3020
4	1770	9	2504	14	3079
5	2285	10	2329	15	3275

Prepare sales forecasts for periods 6 through 15 using the naive, projection, moving average, exponential smoothing, and regression techniques. What length of moving average and smoothing constant work best? What method does the best job of tracking the data over periods 6 through 15? What is your forecast for periods 16 through 24?

4. The following table shows the first six years of sales of retail optical scanners in the United States. What forecasting method seems to track quarterly sales best over the period from quarter 4 of year 1 through quarter 3 in year 6? What is your forecast for the number of scanners installed in the fourth quarter of year 6?

	Quarter			
Year	*1*	*2*	*3*	*4*
1	0	1	3	1
2	3	4	7	12
3	10	15	17	19
4	27	25	31	23
5	47	67	95	137
6	173	196	235	?

5. You are the sales manager for a manufacturer, and you have been asked to forecast company sales for the next 6 months. You have collected data on company sales and other variables for the last 38 semiannual time periods (Table SMR2-5). In addition, you have estimates for period 39 for most of your variables. Using the Excel spreadsheet file accompanying this text or another multiple regression program, calculate a correlation matrix and explain what it tells you about your variables. Create an equation to predict sales using all or a subset of your variables. Explain why you have included each variable and discuss the power of your equation. Forecast sales for period 39 using your multiple regression model.

SALES MANAGEMENT RESOURCE

SALES FORCE INVESTMENT AND BUDGETING

SALES FORCE INVESTMENT

For almost all firms, the sales force represents a major investment. The largest sales forces spend billions of dollars a year to sustain tens of thousands of salespeople. Sales forces cost companies between 1 and 40 percent of sales and, for many companies, represent the largest part of their marketing budget.

Beyond the financial commitments made to supporting a sales force, the importance of the sales force rests in its role of sales creation, representing the public face of the organization, and being entrusted with the firm's most important asset, the customer. There is not a single company sales force that cannot seriously harm its company's performance. Likewise, there is not a single sales force that cannot significantly improve its company's competitive position.

Deciding how much to invest in a company's sales force is an important decision and one that needs to be made with careful consideration. The purpose of this Management Resource is to provide guidance in making this decision, whether the firm is in a start-up situation or an ongoing concern. This Resource is organized in two related sections: determining the best sales force size and budgeting. There is an obvious connection between the two decisions, as the size of the sales force will greatly affect the budget needed to support the sales force. The sales force size issue is addressed first, though it is important to recognize that a company's budget may not be able to support the optimal sales force size.

Is Your Sales Force the Right Size?

Deciding on the proper size of the sales force is a strategic management issue because it has an important impact on an organization's revenues and its profits. How can you determine if your sales force is correctly sized? For starters, your sales force may be the wrong size if you experience some of the situations listed in Figure SMR2-4.

Top management is concerned with the sales force size issue, and justifiably so since the decision directly affects company profitability. Cost containment and productivity enhancement are common organizational goals, so the sales force size decision is highly salient. At

---

Chapter Consultants: Scott Smith, Vice President—Sales & Marketing, SABRE Group, Inc. and Joseph P. Clayton, Chairman of the Board of Sirius Satellite Radio

You are probably undersized if:

Key customers wonder where your representative is.
Current customers are considering switching suppliers.
New customer development is down.
Your salespeople feel overworked, but costs seem under control.
Your salespeople do not have enough time to determine how customer needs might be changing or providing solutions to those needs.

You are probably too large if:

Your favorite customers are asking, "Didn't I just see you?"
Overall, your customers seem to be getting plenty of attention.
Your salespeople seem to have considerable free time.
Your salespeople don't seem to be sufficiently stimulated.
Finance has noticed that your cost of sales is out of line with industry norms.

FIGURE SMR2-4 Is Your Sales Force Sized Correctly?

the same time, the decision will have an impact on the individual salesperson, for it will affect the salesperson's workload and compensation. Clearly, getting the sales force size decision right is an important issue.

Five Insights for Better Sales Force Investment Decisions

Perhaps no one has more experience with making sales force investment decisions than ZS Associates. With more than 400 employees, ZS Associates have advised hundreds of companies in over sixty countries on issues of sales force size and structure and sales force productivity assessment. Following are five important insights based on these studies.[1]

Sales Carryover. *Sales carryover* refers to the phenomenon in which a portion of current sales is a function of customer relationships established through prior selling efforts. Figure SMR2-5 shows how current sales can be attributable to selling effort in prior years. In some rare instances, ZS Associates reported seeing vacant territories leading their regions in sales.

The amount of sales carryover is likely to vary considerably from one industry to the next and even from company to company within the same industry depending on their customer relationship strategies. To understand why differences exist, consider the case of two pharmaceutical product categories: acute-care and chronic-care products. Acute-care products, such as antibiotics and antihistamines, have low sales carryover. Patients typically

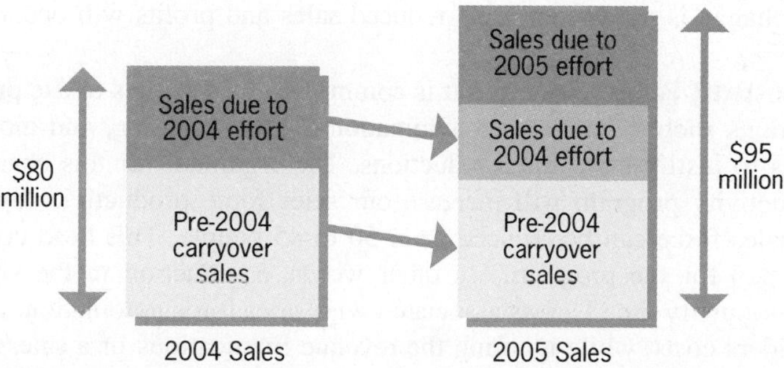

FIGURE SMR2-5 An Illustration of Carryover

Low Carryover	High Carryover
Low switching costs	High switching costs
High levels of new incremental business	Low levels of new incremental business
Many new customers/small purchase volumes/short selling cycles	Few new customers/large purchase volumes/long selling cycles
No maintenance or service activity	High levels of maintenance or service activity
New products	Mature products
High levels of competitive noise	Low levels of competitive noise
Growing market	Flat or declining market
Products similar or nearly identical to competitors' products	Highly differentiated products
Weak brand and/or company loyalty or new brand and/or company	Strong brand and/or company loyalty
Sales force is the only promotion vehicle	Many promotion vehicles in addition to the sales force

FIGURE SMR2-6 Conditions That Affect Carryover

take these medications for a short period of time, so salespeople can often persuade a physician to prescribe a new acute-care medication for their patients, particularly when the medication has very little risk associated with it. On the other hand, chronic-care products, such as diabetes and heart disease, typically have a high sales carryover effect since patients stay on these medications for a long time. The physician is reluctant to switch if the current medication is effective since there is typically some risk involved. Conditions that are likely to influence sales carryover are listed in Figure SMR2-6.

It is important to understand the extent of sales carryover because it will affect the sales consequences of sales force size changes. If sales carryover is high, then there will likely be little short-term sales reaction to a reduction in sales force size. The appropriateness of the decision is therefore difficult to evaluate, and a reduction in the sales force is tempting since short-term profits and productivity are likely to be enhanced. The total impact of the size change is not immediate—reduced sales and profits will occur over time.

Productivity Enhancements. It is common for companies to use productivity enhancement programs such as sales force automation (SFA), targeting, and more effective selling protocols to justify sales force reductions. The argument for this change goes like this: "Our productivity program will increase our sales force productivity by 10 percent. Therefore, our sales force can be reduced from 50 to 45 people. This head count reduction will more than pay for the program." In other words, a reduction in the size of the sales force is used to justify the IT costs associated with sales force automation. However, this logic only considers costs, while ignoring the revenue implications of a sales force IT investments.

It is likely, for instance, that the productivity enhancement of the new sales force IT program actually reduces the firm's selling expenses. Smaller-customers who were previously too expensive to call on are now profitable because of the lower cost per sales call resulting from the productivity program. Therefore, expanding the sales force when implementing a productivity enhancement may actually increase profitability.

The lesson here is that sales force sizing and productivity enhancement are independent decisions and activities. In other words, sales force productivity should be increased regardless of the sales force size. Sales force reduction should not be used as a justification for productivity enhancements.

Gradual Downsizing Is Disruptive. To understand why gradual downsizing is usually disruptive for the sales force, consider the case of six salespeople in a metropolitan sales district. The company chose to downsize gradually by closing one territory immediately and another territory six months later. When the first territory was closed, the accounts were divided among the three bordering territories. These three territories now had more work than the two nonbordering territories, and the company was forced to do another realignment to balance the workload across the five territories. When the second territory was closed, its accounts were divided among the three bordering territories, resulting in these three territories having more work than the fourth nonbordering territory. A fourth realignment was needed to create four balanced territories.

The results of the continuous realignment are potentially devastating for the sales force. Salespeople become frustrated with the constant change, and top performers are tempted to leave the company. There is also a significant threat of alienating customers, since an almost constant shift in territories occurs. In the previous example, some customers saw three different salespeople in just over six months as a result of realignments. The situation only gets worse with each phase of downsizing.

What is the conclusion? If a downsizing is necessary, make all the changes at once. Let your salespeople know the logic for the change and help those who are let go with career placement. Some of them may go to work for a customer.

Launch Hard, But Protect Your Strengths. New product launches almost always require a considerable selling effort. In the short term, the total amount of selling effort is fixed, so that any effort redirected toward new products must be taken from the effort devoted to current products. It is not unusual for a new product launch to take as much as 50 percent of the sales force's time. Sales carryover may sustain the sales of current products for a short period of time, but eventually sales will suffer. Eventually, existing products will fail to make their sales goal.

According to ZS Associates, the best strategy is to "launch hard, but protect your strengths." This means that a company should both support the new product launch with an appropriate sales effort and also continue to put the right amount of support into current products. This necessarily requires an expansion in the total amount of sales effort.

What if the increased effort is only for a short period of time? Often, launching a new product line requires a lot of effort, but then things settle down to a degree and the required effort diminishes. One solution would be to "outsource" selling resources by borrowing salespeople from another division, hiring temporary sales support, or hiring brokers. Outsourcing has several advantages. It turns largely fixed costs into mostly variable costs since temporary salespeople and brokers are paid on commission. Also, some of the temporary salespeople may wish to join the company, thus providing a good pool of potential sales candidates.

In a worst-case scenario, attrition can be used to manage the size of the sales force when the need for increased selling effort is for a restricted period of time. The average turnover rate in sales is about 20 percent. This means that the size of the sales force can be managed by increasing the size of the sales force and then letting attrition systematically bring the sales force size back to a steady-state level. The risk in this approach is the disruption to the sales force and to customer relations that may result from the need to adjust territory balance. Nonetheless, it will produce the temporary support needed for new and existing products.

Watch Out for Company Politics. Consider the following case. The product manager is asked to make a forecast of product sales to help determine the appropriate level of sales support for the coming year. He arrives at a reasonable number but decides to take a little off the number before reporting it to the vice president of sales. "After all," he reasons, "I'll look a lot better if I make my number."

When the vice president of sales sees the number, she decides to reduce the number slightly before making a promise to the company president. "I'll stay out of hot water by making my number," she reasons. Then the president decides to add a little more "cushion" before making a promise to the board of directors. By the time the final number has been agreed on, so much cushion has been added that the sales forecast is drastically lower than the product's real potential. Too little sales effort is allocated to the product, and a significant profit opportunity is lost.

The lesson is to be aware of the individual incentives at different levels in the organization when making a sales forecast. These incentives may undermine efforts to have the right size sales force.

Finding the Right Sales Force Size

At some point, management must settle on a specific dollar amount that will be invested in the sales force. Three methods for arriving at this number are described in this section: the workload approach, the sales response approach, and the percent of sales approach.

Workload Approach. The workload approach to determining a sales force size derives the investment figure from the workload required to meet a revenue target. An example may best illustrate this approach. Loctite North America sells adhesives and sealants to heavy industry. To improve short-term profitability, Loctite allowed its field sales force to decline through attrition. Because of the resulting greater size of the sales territories, however, Loctite's salespeople were unable to provide adequate service to existing customers. Industrial adhesives are a special applications business that requires a lot of technical support. Loctite decided to hire thirty additional salespeople during a one-year period. The added expense depressed profitability for six months, but soon afterward, sales began to grow. Loctite's decision to add salespeople incorporated the idea behind the workload method of calculating sales force size, which is to focus on the work to be done in determining the number of salespeople needed to do the work.

A common method for implementing a workload approach is to determine the size of the sales force based on the amount of activity that a customer segment requires. Customer activities are specified in terms of:

- **Reach:** The number of customers that need to be covered
- **Frequency:** The average number of sales calls per year that should be made on the average customer
- **Duration:** The average number of hours that will be needed for typical sales call

An estimate of the total number of sales people required using the workload approach could be made using the following formula:

$$\text{Number of salespeople} = \frac{\begin{array}{c}\text{Number of}\\ \text{accounts}\end{array} \times \begin{array}{c}\text{Frequency of}\\ \text{sales calls}\end{array} \times \begin{array}{c}\text{Length of a}\\ \text{sales call}\end{array}}{\text{Selling time available for one salesperson}}$$

For example, if a computer software development firm had 5,250 midsized customers to be called on five times per year for 2 hours (including travel time), and if available selling time per salesperson is 1,500 hours per year, the size of the sales force would be:

$$\text{Number of salespeople} = \frac{5{,}250 \times 5 \times 2}{1{,}500} = 35 \text{ people}$$

If the same sales force is also expected to call on electronic distributors and large retail chains, then the workload associated with these additional customer segments will also need to be calculated in arriving at the total number of salespeople the company will need. Remember to consider new customers that you intend to add in the coming year in the above calculation. The sales force investment is then calculated based on the cost of hiring, training, supervising, and supporting the desired number of salespeople.

Some accounts within a segment will require heavier workloads, while others will have lighter workloads. An average workload figure is probably appropriate for sizing the sales force since accounts requiring heavier and lighter workloads tend to cancel each other out. In the end, the salesperson will determine the most appropriate sales coverage for each account. We will pick up this discussion in the next chapter when discussing opportunity management.

Data for developing the workload calculations may be obtained from several sources. Salespeople and sales managers can articulate what has worked in the past and make adjustments for current competitive situations. Channel partners are also a good source of information. Finally, the firm may investigate how competitors treat their customers and how noncompeting sales forces organize their activities.

Sales Response Approach. The sales response approach is based squarely on the concept that the sales force drives sales. If the relationship between sales effort and sales response can be estimated, then different sales force size scenarios can be evaluated in terms of their sales and profit impact.

Figure SMR2-7 shows a simple sales response relationship for two customer segments. To determine the right sales force investment for each segment, the anticipated sales responses to different call frequencies are compared with their associated costs. In Figure SMR2-7 the textile accounts generate incrementally more sales and consequently more profits than a similar investment of selling effort in the carpet segment. The recommended sales force investment depends on the cost of the sales force. For example, assume that all the accounts are now receiving a low call frequency. If the additional sales cost needed to implement a high-frequency call pattern for textile accounts is less than the profit increase, the best sales force investment strategy will be to increase to a high call frequency on textile

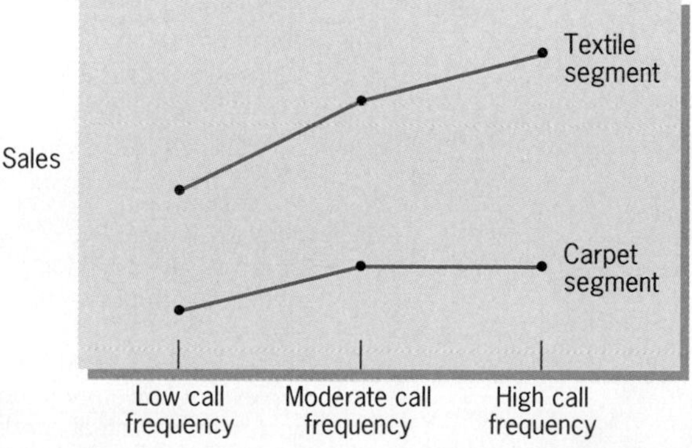

FIGURE SMR2-7 Sales Response Relationship

accounts. On the other hand, the sales response to even a moderate call frequency is modest for carpet accounts, so the best sales force investment will be to keep a low call frequency for carpet accounts, assuming that the additional sales force costs for a higher call frequency are higher than the incremental profit impact.

The data for developing sales response relationships are of two types: historical data and judgmental data. Historical data may be based on variation in call frequency at the territory level or on time-series data showing variation in sales and call frequency over time. Judgment data are derived from interactions asking salespeople and sales managers to judge the response of customer segments to various call effort levels. For instance, salespeople could be asked to estimate the sales expected to arise from zero call effort; 50 percent of the current call effort; 150 percent of the current call effort; or twice the current call effort. From their responses, a sales response curve similar to the curves shown in Figure SMR2-7 can be derived.

Research has demonstrated that historical and judgmental sales response forecasts are almost equally effective. However, historically derived forecasts perform better when markets and products are stable, while judgmental data are most appropriate for dynamic markets and when products are new.

Percentage of Sales Approach. To ensure a certain level of profitability, almost all firms will monitor their sales force costs as a percentage of sales. When used as a tool for determining the sales force size, the sales forecast is multiplied by a predetermined percentage to derive the total amount of money available for the sales force. In other words, this approach bases sales investment on what managers think is a reasonable percentage of planned revenues. The percentage is usually derived from historical spending patterns and industry standards for a particular line of trade Table SMR2-6, for example, provides the average sales force expenses for nineteen major industries. A typical firm selling industrial services spent 6.4 percent of sales on sales force related expenses.

TABLE SMR2-6 Sales Force Selling Expenses as a Percentage of Sales

	Sales Force Total Cost as a Percentage of Sales		*Sales Force Total Cost as a Percentage of Sales*
Company Size		**Industry**	
Under $5 Million (MM)	14.7%	Business services	1.7%
$5–$25 MM	10.5	Chemicals	2.9
$25–$100 MM	7.9	Communications	9.8
$100–$250 MM	3.5	Educational services	47.9
Over $250 MM	6.8	Electronics	4.2
		Fabricated metals	10.8
Product or Service		Health services	19.9
Industrial products	4.1%	Hotels and other lodgings	21.4
Industrial services	6.4	Instruments	2.3
Office products	9.4	Machinery	10.1
Office services	8.1	Manufacturing	13.6
Consumer products	5.4	Office equipment	9.0
Consumer services	7.9	Paper and allied products	6.8
		Printing and publishing	12.0
		Retail	6.1
		Trucking and warehousing	12.2
		Wholesale (consumer goods)	3.7
		Wholesale (industrial goods)	9.5
		Average	**6.9%**

Let's say that the management of a company is trying to determine how much to spend on the sales force next year. They have forecasted sales for $10 million and have noted that manufacturing companies spend 13.6 percent of their revenue on the sales force. Let's also say that traditionally 15 percent of the sales force budget was spent on sales management. In this case, the sales force budget and the number of salespeople the budget supports could be derived as follows:

$10,000,000 Expected sales
$\underline{\times .136}$ Field sales expense ratio(wages, commissions, and travel expenses)
$1,360,000 Sales budget
$\underline{\times .85}$ Percent for sales force(i.e., 15% for supervisor)
$1,156,000 Available for salespeople

$$\frac{\text{Dollars available}}{\text{Wages and expenses per person}} = \frac{\$1,156,000}{\$77,000} = 15(\text{number of salespeople})$$

The preceding example indicates that of the $1,360,000 expected sales budget, $1,156,000 would be available to pay for salespeople after supervisory expenses had been deducted. If salespeople cost an average of $77,000 per year for wages and expenses, then the company could afford a sales force of 15 people.

Despite its widespread use, the sales percentage approach is essentially a backward-looking approach. There are several notable drawbacks to utilizing this approach for setting sales force budgets. First, there is no guarantee that the use of industry percentages in setting sales budgets will lead to optimal results for individual firms. Note in Table SMR2-1 that smaller firms tend to spend a larger percentage of sales on the sales force than do larger firms. Another drawback to this approach is that budget allocation for selling expenses changes in the same direction as sales. This can lead to premature downsizing, resulting in millions of dollars of sales opportunities being left on the table. If a firm is losing market share, for instance, an intensified selling effort may require greater funding than would be appropriated under the percentage of sales method.

Despite its drawbacks, the percentage of sales method is practical and provides useful standards for comparison. A company might adjust the industry average according to its own needs and plans, using sales budgets that are higher or lower than average to see if they lead to greater effectiveness.

Each of the methods for determining sales force size focuses on a particular aspect of the problem—workload, sales and profits, and cost. Since the decision involves consideration of each of these factors, the best approach may be to triangulate the problem by using all three methods to determine the boundaries of the budgeting problem. With the results of this analysis as decision aids, management judgment is needed to determine the final choice of sales force size.

The Profit Impact of Sales Force Size

As was mentioned earlier, the sales force is a sales generator. The sales force is also a cost generator, influencing not only the cost of the sales force but also the variable expenses associated with sales volume. The sales force investment issue therefore affects company profits.

One division president told some consultants that he sized his sales force for profits. When asked how he did this, he responded that he budgeted his sales force cost at 14 percent of sales, so profits were always maximized.[2] You will recognize this as an example of the percentage of sales approach to sales force investment. This is essentially a cost containment approach to sales force investment. Cost containment is not the same as profit maximization.

TABLE SMR2-7 Profit Impact of Adding Ten New Salespeople

Scenario	*80 Current Salespeople*	*Incremental Impact of 10 Additional Salespeople*
Financial Impact:		
Sales per Salesperson	$1.6 million	$500,000
Total Sales	$128 million	$5 million
Contribution Margin	60%	60%
Contribution Dollars	$76.8 million	$3 million
Sales Force Costs	$18 million	$2.25 million
Contribution Dollars after Sales Force Expenses	$58.8 million	$750,000
Total Contributions after Sales Force Expenses with ten additional salespeople: $59.55 million		

To illustrate the difference between cost containment and profit maximization, let's assume that the division has 80 salespeople and has projected sales next year of $128 million. See Table SMR2-7 for the financial figures in this example. This means that the average salesperson will generate $1.6 million per territory. Let's also assume that a fully loaded sales force (including salary, benefits, taxes, bonuses, car, travel, call reporting, administrative support, and field support) costs $225,000 per salesperson. This represents a sales force cost ratio of about 14 percent of revenues.

Suppose another ten salespeople were added to the sales force, increasing its size to ninety people in total. The new people must generate $16 million in sales, or $1.6 million each, to maintain the 14 percent ratio of sales force costs to revenue. It rarely happens that a new person will generate the same revenues as a veteran salesperson, though it may occur in a rapidly growing business or in a company that is woefully understaffed. A more realistic expectation is that the new person will generate perhaps $500,000 in revenue the first year or a total of $5 million in additional revenue from the ten new salespeople. This means that the sales force cost ratio will be higher than the targeted 14 percent of sales. As a result, a company relying on the percent of sales rule for budgeting sales force costs will only reluctantly increase sales force size.

Continuing our example, let's assume that our company has a 60 percent contribution margin (sales minus all variable expenses, i.e., costs that vary with the amount of product sold).[3] Then in our original projection for eighty salespeople, a total of $76.8 million in contribution dollars will be generated, assuming our sales projections are accurate. This means that each salesperson is expected to generate $960,000 in contribution dollars. The breakeven sales volume (i.e., the minimum sales volume at which no contribution dollars are generated in a territory) is $375,000 (calculated by dividing the fully loaded cost of $225,000 by 60 percent). In other words, any sales volume over $375,000 would increase profits.

Revisiting the issue of adding an additional ten salespeople, recall that ten new salespeople are expected to generate $5 million in revenue. This would result in an increase in the sales cost to revenue ratio to about 15 percent ($20.25 million in sales force costs divided by $133 million in revenue). However, contribution dollars after sales force expenses also increase from $58.8 million ($76.8 million in gross margin minus $18 million in sales force costs, i.e., $225,000 times 80 salespeople) to $59.55 million. The $750,000 increase in contribution dollars result from the $3 million in projected gross margin ($5 million in sales times 60 percent) minus sales force costs of $2.25 million ($225,000 times 10 salespeople). So, sales force costs as a percentage of revenue have increased, but so have profits as a result of increasing the sales force.

As you can see, the sales force size issue affects sales, sales force costs, and profits. These measures can be in conflict, as in our preceding example above. Profit increase usually comes at the expense of a total sales costs increase. Management often needs to choose between increasing profits and containing expenses.

DEVELOPING A SALES BUDGET

Budgets are a key element used by sales managers in annual planning programs to reach their objectives. A *sales budget* is essentially a set of planned expenses prepared on an annual basis. The sales budgeting process is described in Figure SMR2-8. Sales budgeting begins when senior management designs a marketing plan and sets spending levels for advertising and sales promotion. Once these demand creation factors are determined, sales forecasts can be made (forecasting is discussed in the Sales Management Resource: Estimating Potentials and Forecasting Sales). The sales forecast, in turn, provides a guide for estimating how many salespeople will be needed. Sales managers must also project travel and other expenses for the sales force. Next, the actual expenditures for a period are compared with the budget. When expenditures exceed planned levels, the sales manager has to revise the categories or ask for more funds. The main concerns in preparing budgets are to decide how much to spend on personal selling and how to allocate the money to various selling activities.

Sales Budget Planning

For budgeting purposes, it is usually necessary to further refine and identify the strategic avenues for achieving an overall sales volume target. For instance, the overall sales target may be broken down by geographic area, region, district, or by product line. For example, if one region represents a greater growth opportunity than others, then management may wish to add more salespeople and spend more on marketing programs in this region. When combined with market share and market growth figures for individual product lines, product-focused avenues for achieving sales targets can be identified, and costs can be budgeted to support product sales targets.

Many companies have found the Customer-Product Matrix shown in Figure SMR2-9 to be very useful for analyzing the basic revenue-generating avenues of the firm. This matrix identifies four strategic sources of sales revenue based on a combination of new and/or current customers and products. Companies have found this to be a useful analysis tool because the sales job and resulting expenses are quite different for each quadrant in the matrix. New business development revenues (new customers and new products)

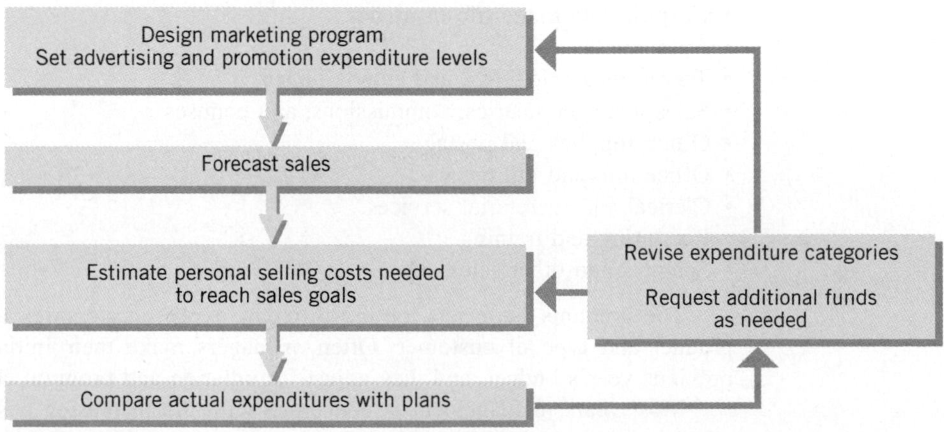

FIGURE SMR2-8 The Sales Budgeting Process

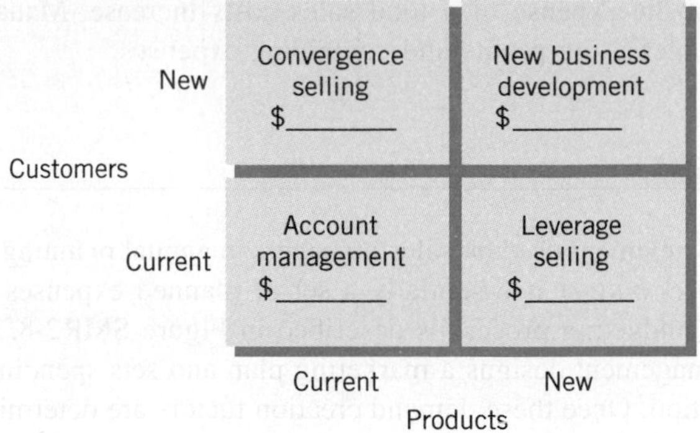

FIGURE SMR2-9 The Customer-Product Matrix

will require much higher training and promotion expenses and may require additional salespeople, for instance, than account management revenues (current customers and products). Conversely, account management revenue development may call for additional sales support such as telemarketers and service people. Even the sales force compensation plan may be quite different depending on the quadrant representing the source of company revenues. When New Business Development is a significant growth opportunity, sales force compensation should include significant incentive opportunities for generating new customers. This and other compensation issues are discussed further in Chapter 12. The point being made here is that a sales figure for each of these four sources of revenue illustrated in the customer-product matrix should be budgeted so that the total of the four quadrants equals the company's total sales volume target. This analysis will help considerably in determining expense budgets and in designing an overall sales program.

Where to Spend It?

Sales managers set target figures for the various selling expense categories for each planning period. The goal is to keep actual expenditures at, or under, the budgeted figures to ensure that overall financial objectives are achieved. Some of the more common expense classifications are the following:

- Sales force salaries, commissions, and bonuses
- Social Security
- Retirement plans
- Hospitalization and life insurance
- Automobile
- Travel, meals, lodging, and entertainment
- Sales manager salaries, commissions, and bonuses
- Office supplies and postage
- Office rent and utilities
- Clerical and secretarial services
- Recruiting and training
- Samples and other sales aids

The amounts budgeted for the different expense categories tend to vary widely by product and type of customer. Often, managers make their initial allocations using the previous year's budget, and they adjust for inflation and program changes.

Most years, management is concerned with the increasing costs of human resources, which put pressure on salary, clerical services, and recruiting. These cost concerns are somewhat abated during a recession, as was experienced in 2000–2003, due to higher jobless rates. During these times, human-resource-related cost concerns are replaced by pressure to reduce travel and entertainment expenses. In the recent recession, many companies—41 percent in a recent survey—have not increased travel expenses, or have even decreased their budgets for travel.[4] Sales managers are adjusting to these budgetary pressures. Videoconferencing, a technology that has been around since the 1960s, is quickly becoming a popular option. AT&T reported a 20 percent spike in videoconferencing services since September 11.[5] As one sales manager noted, "If ten salespeople from around the country traveled to Dallas for a four-hour training session, it would cost us about eight thousand dollars. With videoconferencing, the cost is twenty percent of that."[6]

Budget Administration

One of the prime benefits of sales budgets is that they force managers to think about how marketing funds should be spent. Decisions must be made about whether sales representatives should receive more training, whether more money should be spent to purchase complimentary hockey tickets, whether to provide more sample books, whether to increase bonuses, and so on. Budgets, therefore, aid sales managers in designing the optimal combination of the marketing variables under their control.

A budget also facilitates the control of sales operations. If sales objectives are not being reached, for instance, the manager can see from the budget how much money has been spent in each expense category and where adjustments are needed. In this case the sales manager might be able to use funds from the training budget to buy prizes for a sales contest.

Budget administration has been greatly simplified in the past few years with the development of the electronic spreadsheet. Computer programs, such as Excel and Lotus, have made it easier to keep track of sales force expenditures. Companies have come to rely on these programs for their analyses, and so it is increasingly important for you to be comfortable using these programs, particularly Excel. To help you develop these skills, Excel spreadsheets can be downloaded from the "Student Companion Site" at www.wiley.com/college/cron to work the following problems.

Cost control is so important in today's competitive environment that many companies are rewarding sales managers and salespeople for sticking to their budgets. At one company, for instance, sales managers receive a quarterly bonus that is based on three key elements. One of these elements is ability to control costs. This part of their quarterly bonus starts to pay out if they meet their quarterly travel and entertainment budget, and it increases until they max out at 5 percent below budget. The company feels that this has been very effective in controlling budgets.[7]

PROBLEMS

Note: Excel spreadsheets for working on these problems are available at "Student Companion Site" at www.wiley.com/college/cron.

1. Your company has 2,500 regular customers on which your sales force calls on once every other month. In addition, you would like to obtain 500 new customers to meet your company's growth target. The average number of calls to convert and service a new account for the year is expected to be six calls. Your salespeople are in the field calling on accounts 40 weeks a year. They spend 60 percent of their time calling on customers and prospects, with the average sales call taking 30 minutes. If the average number of hours your salespeople work each week is 50 hours, how many salespeople would you need in your sales force to maintain this level of customer service and also generate 500 new customers?

2. SOMA Inc. has been in business for a little under two years. SOMA is a Web-based information technology training company currently employing one salesperson and a sales manager. It has been successful in two rounds of financing and has a $5 million cash balance. Its target for 2008 is to have revenues of $4 million. Revenues in 2007 are anticipated to be $1.3 million. The issue it is struggling with is to determine a sales force budget for 2008 that will be sufficient to meet its sales projections. Sales force expenses in the training industry average 22 percent of sales, but they can be quite a bit higher. In fact, a recent start-up company in the training field spent more than 50 percent of its revenues on the sales force. An executive recruiting firm supplied SOMA with the following data on typical sales compensation ranges in the computer-based training industry.

	Salesperson	*Sales Manager*
Typical Quota	• $800–$1,200,000	• Sometimes carry personal quota
Cash Compensation		
• Base salary range	• $45,000–$85,000	• $60,000–$110,000
• Commission rate	• Varies by company	• Varies by company
• Total cash compensation	• $65,000–$135,000	• $110,000–$160,000
• Top earnings	• $250,000	• $250,000

SALES OPPORTUNITY MANAGEMENT

> It almost goes against the nature of salespeople to think about time; they just want to hit the road and sell.
>
> Marty Wiley
> Vice President of Marketing and Sales, Loctite Corporation

Chapter Consultants:
Greg Miller, Senior Vice President, Operations Planning and Support, Marriott Senior Living Services
Jerry Willett, National Sales Manager, Software Spectrum

LEARNING OBJECTIVES

After studying this chapter, you should be able to:

- Describe effective steps for generating new accounts.
- Explain how to determine the minimum opportunity a salesperson should pursue.
- Describe four methods for setting opportunity priorities.
- Explain why emphasis is shifting from sales volume to profit flow.
- Tell how salespeople can manage their time more efficiently.

PRIORITIZING OPPORTUNITIES AT HILL-ROM

After seventy years of success, Hill-Rom, headquartered in Batesville, Indiana, found revenue growth slowing and competition increasing and began considering lower priced alternatives. Top management noticed that cost of sales had risen gradually but persistently over the past five years. Hill-Rom decided to take a closer look at its customers and determine if it was allocating its sales resources appropriately and if the sales force was performing the correct set of activities to generate needed revenue and profit growth.

Hill-Rom's product line is patient's beds for hospitals. Sales resources were allocated based on the size of the health care facility because this size influenced the level of spending on Hill-Rom products. This was logical since the more beds a hospital has and the more services it offers, the more likely that capital funding will be set aside on a regular basis to replace or acquire equipment. The sales force was structured into teams calling on all customers in a particular geographic location. Management discovered on closer examination that while size of facility is important, less obvious factors also affected purchasing behavior. These factors included financial metrics such as customer capital spending and profit margins, operating metrics such as occupancy rates, and even a facility's mix of insurance payers.

Based on regression analysis of existing customer data, customers were divided into two groups, key and prime customers, based on overall similarities of needs and priorities. Key customers have far higher capital expenditures for medical equipment, replace equipment sooner, seek out customized consultation, and look for comprehensive solutions to their problems. Prime customers, because of greater cost pressures, are more concerned with paying the best possible price, less able to afford high-end products and services, more likely to buy individual products rather than systems, and often wait to make a purchase until the need is urgent.

A time and cost analysis revealed that the company had been making a significant effort to sell to and serve both segments in the same manner, resulting in a skewed allocation of sales resources and high overall sales costs. Salespeople were expected to cover all facilities in a given geography and felt compelled to make regular calls on each account. As a result, sales teams were often taking a consultative approach when the account's profile and purchase behavior warranted another approach. Not surprising, it was discovered that the cost of sales for prime customers was four to five times higher than for key customers. At the same time, penetration of key customer accounts was less than desired because there was not enough time left to provide the in-depth and customized type of solutions that customers valued. The sales force had basically been treating all customers the same and trying to sell prime customers a level of service and product that they did not value or could not afford, while underselling to key customers.

Armed with a method for prioritizing customers, Hill-Rom decided to restructure its sales force into two separate sales forces dedicated to each type of customer, the team structures, skill sets, compensation plans, the selling process, and the reporting structures of the sales force. All these efforts were designed to ensure that resources were allocated to the size of the opportunity. After two years, the cost of sales is down, short-term revenue growth is up, the outlook for long-term revenue growth appears bright, profit margins are up, and customers are reporting higher satisfaction.[1]

As Hill-Rom learned, it is critical to prioritize sales opportunities in order to effectively and efficiently allocate resources. All sales opportunities are not equally important. Similarly, time available for face-to-face communications with customers is a significant resource that must be managed wisely. Tackling the problem of opportunity prioritization is the focus of this chapter.

We started our discussion of the sales force program at the end of the last chapter by talking about the account relationship strategy element of the sales program. Recall that the relationship strategy decision will influence each of the other four elements of the sales force program. We now turn our attention to the selling process or sales activities element of the sales force program. This chapter focuses on efficiency or "doing the right things." Salespeople have considerable latitude in deciding how they are going to allocate their valuable selling time. Management's job is to get the sales force's priorities in line with those of the company's marketing plan. Nowhere is this more important than with respect to the firm's growth strategy.

There are essentially two paths by which to grow sales: obtain new customers and grow the business with existing customers. This chapter is organized accordingly. The first part of our discussion focuses on strategies for growing a firm's customer base. We begin by discussing the importance of growing by acquiring new customer prospects, and we present various methods for generating qualified prospects. We shift our focus to existing customers by discussing specific tools for allocating effort across a set of sales opportunities. First, we show how to determine the minimum-size opportunity a salesperson should pursue, followed by a discussion of how to allocate time among selling opportunities. We conclude

the chapter with a discussion of the profit impact of these decisions and time management in sales.

One way to increase productivity is to focus sales force time on those prospects that have a high probability of becoming important customers. The next section discusses the importance of building your customer base by acquiring new customers and company efforts to increase sales force efficiency in this area.

A PROCESS FOR GENERATING NEW ACCOUNTS

In the award-winning book *Customer Equity*, the authors point out that the value of a firm is dependent how well a firm manages its customer base. They go on to suggest that there are three ways by which a firm can increase the value of its customer base: acquiring new customers, retaining existing customers, and increasing the profitability of each customer by increasing its purchases.[2] This section focuses on the first of these strategies by suggesting ways that the sales force can efficiently and effectively acquire new customers.

No matter how strong your products, how great your customer service, or how aggressive your sales force, businesses lose customers every year when companies are bought and sold, management changes, industries consolidate, and global economies fluctuate. Few companies can afford to neglect new business development. Indeed, according to recent research findings, firms who have developed effective customer acquisition capabilities are more profitable than those who have the capability of developing close customer relationships, but are not good at acquiring new customers.[3]

The key to building sales through *prospecting* is to spend time with prospects that are likely to become good customers. Therefore, an important first step in acquiring new customers is for salespeople to build a good prospect profile.

Building a Prospect Profile

Not all businesses will want or need your product or services. Some prospects will clearly be a waste of your time, while others will not buy enough to make it worth your time. You must first decide what factors determine who is a good prospect. This means building a *prospect profile*, which is simply a profile of what the best prospect looks like.

A starting place for building this profile is a review of the target markets for your products, as specified in your marketing plan. Allnet Communications Services, a small long-distance phone company in Michigan, defines its target niche as small- to medium-sized businesses that bill between several hundred dollars and several tens of thousands of dollars per month. This target was identified to avoid head-to-head competition with AT&T and Sprint. If a target market has not been clearly identified, a new salesperson may need to rely on the past experience of other salespeople in the company by asking them what types of business became their most valuable customers. Veteran salespeople are probably best advised to examine their own past successes.

If you are selling blood-processing machines, for example, then your best prospects may be hematologists (hospital consultants specializing in analyzing and treating blood disorders). Upon closer examination, the hottest prospects may be young (under 30) and trained at a handful of teaching hospitals.

The blood-processing example points out a few important aspects of building a profile. First, the profile is defined in terms of demographics, the identifiable characteristics that define the individual buying environment. In the blood-processing example, demographics included the customer's business, age, and educational background. This information often can be obtained before meeting with the prospect. Other examples of demographics frequently used to build a prospect profile include the following:

- Size of the business
- Age of the equipment to be replaced
- Geographic distance from shipping points
- Product line specialty

The Internet can also play an integral role in building a prospect profile. Once on-line, you can access databases containing government statistics, journals, books, and up-to-date newswires. There are also about 7,000 newsgroups and any number of bulletin boards, forums, and roundtables that cover almost every subject imaginable. Web sites useful for target marketing and identifying new customers include www.census.gov or www.city.net. A good site for identifying the top business in a geographic market area is www.toplist.com.

Building a Prospect List

With a prospect profile clearly in mind, the next step is to develop a list of prospects matching the profile developed in the first step. The traditional method of generating prospects is through cold canvassing. *Cold canvassing* involves contacting prospective customers without appointments; that is, salespeople call on firms or knock on doors until they find good prospects. Direct sales organizations such as Avon Products have had success with this approach. Salespeople selling office supplies, air conditioning, paper supplies, and insurance also use it with some regularity. Cold canvassing is used in these situations because the target markets for these products are fairly broad. The drawback to this approach is that a salesperson could waste time soliciting low-quality prospects. Canvassing may also be more efficiently accomplished by telephone.

Direct Mail. All companies receive direct inquiries about products or services from potential customers. The fact that the potential customer is giving permission for a sales call allows salespeople to concentrate their efforts on those prospects most likely to purchase. The use of e-mail inquiries has made it possible to dramatically increase the speed with which companies can respond to a *direct mail* inquiry, which helps to increase the rate at which inquiries are converted to sales. At Tribute Inc., a software company in Cleveland, a business development coordinator will analyze the responses from mailings to discern the prospect's critical business issues, including their buying time frame and budget constraints. As a result, Tribute's high-priced salespeople are focusing their efforts only on high-quality prospects.[4]

Trade Shows. *Trade shows* are also an excellent vehicle for generating good prospects. It is estimated that more than 145,000 firms participate in over 8,000 trade shows at a cost of $10 billion annually. The National Restaurant Show held annually in Chicago, for instance, draws more than 100,000 food buyers and business owners. One reason for the growing popularity of trade shows is the relatively low cost per customer contact—approximately $89 per qualified contact. (A qualified contact is a customer contact whose interest in purchasing has been verified.) Although some sales are consummated at trade shows, it is more likely that the lead is passed on to the appropriate salesperson; in fact, some trade shows do not permit the writing of orders.[5]

Directories. Special direct inquiry *directories* and open-to-bid announcements are important sources of leads for many firms. For example, the *Thomas Register of American Manufacturers* provides names, addresses, and other information compiled by types of products and by state. Furthermore, the firms in the *Register* are scored according to their assets, which enables the salesperson to judge the size of each potential customer. Industry trade associations often publish directories of their members by targeted segment or organization function.

Internet. The Internet has revolutionized the process of selling and qualifying prospects. Not only can potential customers make purchases over the Internet, but a wealth of information is available over the Internet at company Web sites. In addition, published information on companies is readily available at Web sites, such as *Business Week* and the *Wall Street Journal*.

One of the hottest lead-generating tools today is Webcasting. Webcasting requires no special equipment on the part of the host company or the audience and can be as simple as sitting at a computer and talking over the phone, which is all that is required at WebEx. Standard features include live streaming video and audio, on-line statistics and reporting, and polling to gather opinions and engage viewers. Inverwoven, a Sunnyvale, California-based content-management company, lured 2,000 information technology pros to sign up and participate in a 60-minute presentation.[6] As broadband connectivity becomes more ubiquitous, this type of lead generation is likely to expand in use.

Referrals. With *referrals*, a satisfied customer is asked to provide the names of others who might be interested in a product. In some cases, the person may also supply an introduction of the salesperson to the prospects. The advantage of referrals is that the person can say things about the salesperson and the product line that might not be as credible coming directly from the salesperson.[7]

Referral programs have gained wide acceptance among companies selling big-ticket goods and services because prospects considering spending six or seven figures on one transaction want all the information they can get. Siebel Systems, Sun Microsystems Inc., and J. D. Edwards & Company are some of the companies with well-developed reference programs. In these programs, reference companies are involved in speaking engagements, videos, white papers, and articles. The benefits to the reference companies include networking with other customers and Siebel executives, the opportunity to expand their brand through speaking engagements and media activities, and previews of new products.[8]

Qualifying Prospects

Regardless of the process used for generating a list of leads, salespeople ultimately must *qualify a prospect*, that is, determine if the prospect is likely to be converted to a buying customer. As described earlier, some companies may initially qualify leads by telephone because of the lower cost of doing so. But ultimately, a salesperson is usually needed to qualify a lead. At Southwest Networks in Austin, Texas, salespeople profile all leads on 12 characteristics, including current vendor, percent savings, equipment specs, and payback period. After the first call on a prospect, the salesperson answers all twelve characteristic questions. The purpose of the profile is to tell salespeople how good a prospect a lead is and when to walk away from the lead. Note from this example that the salesperson needs information about customer needs, buying authority, and ability to pay.

Needs. Qualified leads are those that have a use for the seller's goods or services and are planning to buy in the near future. A prospect that is satisfied with the present supplier and has no desire to change is going to be very difficult to convert into a customer. You will sell such a prospect only if you can discover a desire or need that the present supplier is not fulfilling adequately and you can get the buyer to focus on these needs. This is not an easy task. Even if the prospect has an immediate need that you can meet and a desire to buy, you must still determine whether the size and profitability of potential orders are sufficient to warrant further attention.

Buying Authority. Beyond the question of customer needs is the issue of buying authority. The plant manager may want a milling machine, but if he or she does not have the authority to buy, then a sales call may help create a favorable impression but will not necessarily produce a signed order. Methods for identifying the buying authority are presented in Chapter 4.

Ability to Pay. Finding prospects that want a product and also have the authority to buy will not be productive if they lack the financial resources to buy. Selling products that must be repossessed later for nonpayment of bills is not the way for salespeople to get ahead. Hence, salespeople should make an initial screening of prospects on their ability to buy. The objective is to eliminate prospects who represent too high a credit risk. Credit ratings are readily available from banks and credit services such as Dun and Bradstreet.

Successful salespeople differ from less successful salespeople in the way they think about prospects. Although both groups of salespeople generally use the same cues to qualify a prospect (e.g., income, need), successful salespeople utilize higher qualifying standards and are more likely to cut their losses early. For example, they may require a higher credit rating or a greater need for the product or service to consider a lead to be a hot prospect. This is yet another example of how wasted time can hurt productivity and how time management is critical to sales success.

MANAGING EXISTING ACCOUNTS

Generating new customers is important, but many sales and marketing managers feel that the companies that will prosper will be ones that maintain strong customer loyalty. Loyalty customers are considered to be more profitable because they are less price sensitive and will stick with you in the face of competitive offerings. An additional $100 in revenue to an existing customer is often more profitable than an equivalent increase in revenue from a new customer because some sort of price discount or incentive is often needed to induce new customers to switch suppliers.

As a sales force program moves from a transactional to more of a consultative-type account relationship, the opportunity management task shifts to one of prioritizing opportunities with existing accounts, as opposed to generating new accounts. The need for prioritization and opportunity management of existing accounts is just as important as with prospects. Models for prioritizing account opportunities are presented in this section, but first we address the important issue of determining whether an opportunity justifies an allocation of precious sales resources.

When Is an Account Too Small?

An important starting point in managing existing accounts is determining the minimum opportunity on which you should be spending your time. The individual salesperson is in an excellent position to determine the long-term value of a customer. For example, salespeople should know customers' short-term growth potential, as well as their competitive and demand situations. Salespeople who are supplied with the necessary direct selling expense information are in an excellent position to perform a minimum account size analysis. This analysis involves two steps: calculating a personal cost per sales call and a breakeven sales volume. We turn our attention to these analyses in this section.

Cost per Call. The first step in addressing the minimum customers size issue is to calculate the costs of making a sales call. *Cost per call* is a function of the number of calls you make per day, the number of days available to call on customers, and your direct selling expenses. *Direct selling expenses* include such expenses as compensation, travel, lodging, entertainment, and communications. These expenses are referred to as direct selling expenses because they can be attributed to an individual salesperson. In other words, the company would not have incurred these costs had a salesperson not been present in the territory.

The procedure for computing the average cost per call is illustrated in Table 3-1. In this example, compensation includes salary, commissions, and bonuses, as well as fringe benefits such as insurance and social security. These total $80,020, which is about average for a nonretail salesperson.[9] Other direct selling expenses equal $25,450, for a total direct selling expense of $105,470.

For this salesperson, 205 days a year are available for selling. If the average number of calls per day is 3, then under normal circumstances the total number of calls for the entire year is 615 (3 × 205). Using these estimates, the representative can now compute the cost of an average call as $171.50 ($105,470/615).

TABLE 3-1 Computing the Cost per Call for an Industrial Products Salesperson

Compensation			
Salary, commissions, and bonus		$69,035	
Fringe benefits (hospital, life insurance, social security)	10,985		$80,020
Direct Selling Expenses			
Automobile	8000		
Lodging and meals	6250		
Entertainment	3250		
Communications	4500		
Samples, promotional material	1750		
Miscellaneous	1700		25,450
Total Direct Expenses			$105,470
Calls Per Year			
Total available days			260 days
Less:			
Vacation	10 days		
Holidays	10 days		
Sickness	5 days		
Meetings	18 days		
Training	12 days		55 days
Net Selling Days			205 days
Average calls per day			3 calls
Total Calls per Year (205 × 3)	615 calls		
Average Cost per Call ($105,470/615)			**$171.50**

TABLE 3-2 Sales Force Costs Across Selected Industries

Industry	*Sales Force Costs as a Percent of Sales*	*Industry*	*Sales Force Costs as a Percent of Sales*
Banking	0.9%	Instruments	14.8%
Business services	10.5	Machinery	11.3
Chemicals	3.4	Manufacturing	6.6
Communications	9.9	Office equipment	2.4
Construction	7.1	Paper/allied products	8.2
Electronic components	4.9	Pharmaceuticals	5.6
Electronics	12.6	Printing/publishing	22.2
Fabricated metals	7.2	Rubber/plastics	3.6
Food products	2.7	Wholesale (consumer)	11.2
Overall	**10.0%**		

How does a cost per call of $171.50 compare with that of most salespeople? One survey estimated the average cost for a single sales call to be as much as $242, depending on the industry. This cost is increasing by about 5 percent a year.[10]

Breakeven Sales Volume. *Breakeven sales volume* is the sales volume necessary to cover direct selling expenses. It is necessary to calculate breakeven sales volume in order to determine the minimum size customer that should be pursued. Calculating the breakeven volume requires knowing direct selling expenses as a percentage of total sales.

The basic formula for calculating the breakeven sales volume per sales call is to divide the cost per call by sales costs as a percent of sales. The previous section described how to calculate the cost of a sales call. Selling costs as a percent of sales will vary widely across industries as shown in Table 3-2 where sales costs as a percent of sales are 22.2 percent on average for printing and publishing companies, but only 0.9 percent in banking. Selling costs as a percent of sales will also vary among companies in the same industry. Therefore, it is important to know the target selling cost for a company.

So if the cost of a sales call is $146, and sales costs are 8 percent of sales, then the breakeven sales volume necessary to adequately cover sales costs is $1,825 ($146/.08). In other words, this is the minimum dollar sales figure that a salesperson should expect to generate from a sales call if selling costs per sales call are $1,825 and the target selling costs as a percent of sales is 8 percent. One point of clarification is that sales calls refer to a personal face-to-face contact with a customer. Telephone calls, e-mails, and text messages are not considered sales calls in this case.

How the breakeven sales volume figure is used to determine the minimum size opportunity a salesperson should pursue will depend on the nature of the selling process itself. It is typical in most consumer packaged goods and wholesale businesses for salespeople to be responsible for selling both new products and taking orders to replenish inventory levels of existing products. In this case, the breakeven sales volume can be used to calculate the minimum sales volume needed over a period of time to justify a certain number of sales calls for that period. If a salesperson is making four calls on a particular customer each month and the breakeven sales volume per call is $1,825, then the account should generate an average of $7,300 per month ($1,825 * 4) to meet the minimum sales revenue necessary to justify this amount of salesperson time. A similar calculation can be made for determining the minimum sales volume per quarter or per year depending on the number of sales calls typically made over a period of time.

If the selling process involves selling to new accounts, then the minimum sales volume needed to justify pursuing a prospect can be calculated based on the number of calls typically needed to close the sale. Say the number of calls to convert a prospect is estimated to be

5 calls, then the account must have the potential to generate at least $9,125 ($1,825 * 5) of business to justify being a targeted prospect. Obviously, the more complex the sale, the more time and sales calls it will require to close the sale; therefore, the minimum sales volume will increase accordingly.

I Cannot Afford to Lose This Business. Having performed a breakeven analysis, how can a salesperson use this information? Should a salesperson not call on customers or prospects whose sales volume does not exceed the minimum sales volume?

People, and companies too, are rarely inclined to turn their backs on a sale. Other factors must be considered before dropping a customer or reducing the selling effort. For example, sales to a customer may be growing, which may be due to one of two causes. The customer's business is growing rapidly, so its need for supplies is also increasing. Alternatively, your sales to this account may be growing because you are getting a larger share of the customer's business. If this is the case, then it is important to know how much of your customer's total purchases are with your company and how much more is available. What if a customer is located next door to a major account, so that a call takes little time and no real travel time is involved? Should you walk away from this opportunity, even though it does not take as much time as your average sales call? Another important consideration is that a customer may purchase a mix of high-profit products, so that this customer's gross margins are 25 percent higher than the average for the territory. As you can see, a number of factors must be considered when judging the value of an opportunity.

Top management may choose to address the smaller, less profitable accounts in ways other than reducing the number of sales calls made on these accounts. The Gillette Company's Safety Razor Division decided to hire part-time merchandisers to assist salespeople in calling on individual small retailers. The Commercial Systems Division of Hewlett-Packard hired inside sales and technical reps to work the phones. A plumbing fixtures manufacturer, however, chose to raise prices to discourage the "worthless" small customer orders that were disrupting its production scheduling. These small orders subsequently became the company's most profitable. The new higher prices more than compensated for the costs; customers weren't changing suppliers because of high switching costs; and competitors had shied away from these small accounts because of the conventional wisdom in the industry regarding their profitability.

As you can see from these examples, the minimum-size customer on which a salesperson should call depends on the direct selling costs involved, the number of sales calls made over a period of time, and the cost structure of the company, as well as other considerations. There is rarely a hard-and-fast dollar volume below which a customer's business should not be pursued. However, when supplied with the right information, sales professionals are in a better position to judge whether an account is likely to become a profitable one.

Four Methods for Setting Account Priorities

Breakeven account analysis provides a starting place from which to determine the minimum-size account that should be called on. This analysis does not fully address the issue of how much time should be allocated to prospecting and how much to existing accounts in a territory. Following are four methods for setting account priorities along with the situations in which each is most appropriate.

Single-Factor Model. The easiest and probably the most widely used model for allocating salespeople's time is the *single-factor model*. This model examines a single customer characteristic, often sales volume, to arrive at an initial allocation of sales calls. Thomas Cook Travel, a division of the Thomas Cook Group, an international travel and financial services company based in the United Kingdom, divides its clients into As (those who spend $750

TABLE 3-3 ABC Account Classification

Account Classification	No. of Accts. (1)	Total Accts. (2)	Sales (000) (3)	Total Sales (4)	Total Calls per Classif. (5)	Sales ($) per Call (6)
A	21	15%	$910	65%	105	$8,667
B	28	20	280	20	140	2,000
C	91	65	210	15	455	462
Total	140	100%	$1,400	100%	700	$2,000 (Avg)

or more in annual revenues), Bs (those spending $250 to $749), and Cs (those who spend less than $250). Differentiating its client services according to their classification has freed up travel agents to spend more time with A and B clients.

The basics of a single-factor allocation model based on total sales volume are presented in Table 3-3. This is referred to as an ABC account classification. Customers are arranged according to their total sales volume. In this case, the top 15 percent of all accounts are classified as A accounts, the next 20 percent are classified as Bs, and the remaining accounts as Cs. Column 4 is a calculation of each type of account's sales as a percentage of total territory sales. In this example, As generate 65 percent of total territory sales, Bs account for 20 percent, and Cs represent only 15 percent. Based on surveys of sales executives, these results are fairly typical for a variety of businesses. Notice that if you treat all accounts as equal, say by calling on each account weekly, you will be spending 65 percent of your time on your C accounts. A sales call on an A customer, however, is on average 20 times as productive as a call on a C customer.

The main limitation of using sales volume in setting priorities is that other factors driving your return on invested time are not taken into account, for instance, sales potential. Two accounts may have purchased the same dollar volume last year, but if one is growing at twice the rate of the other, then it probably needs more attention and time. Also not taken into account are differences in account profitability.

Portfolio Model. The *portfolio model* considers multiple factors when determining the attractiveness of individual accounts within a territory. Selling effort is allocated so that the most attractive accounts receive the most effort.[11] For instance, one company classified its portfolio of accounts according to their average gross margin and the cost to service each account. In another company, the Surgical Division of Cardinal Health, Inc., a customer classification system based on the type of hospital (e.g., teaching/research, regional medical center, government/federal, community), location (rural versus urban), and size was instituted. Sales effort and marketing programs were designed for each type of customer within the classification system. The criteria a company uses to classify its customers will depend on its competitive situation, a company's ability to capture and disseminate relevant customer information, and what the sales force is being asked to accomplish.

Figure 3-1 illustrates one well-known portfolio model. This model classifies accounts into one of four categories by determining account attractiveness based on two criteria: account opportunity and competitive position. Account opportunity refers to the magnitude of an account's present and future need for the salesperson's offering. Ratings of account opportunity may be based on the account's present and projected growth rate, its financial health, and its present and future strength in the marketplace. Competitive position, the second dimension on which accounts are classified, refers to the strength of the salesperson's present relationship with an account. Competitive position may be based on outcome measures such as an account's total gross profit dollars, share of the account's total purchases, type of contract, and contract compliance. Additional indicators of competitive position may

Competitive Position

Account Opportunity	Strong	Weak
High	**Core Accounts** Accounts are very attractive. Invest heavily in selling resources.	**Growth Accounts** Accounts are potentially attractive. May want to invest in heavily.
Low	**Drag Accounts** Accounts are moderately attractive. Invest to maintain current competitive position	**Problem Accounts** Accounts are very unattractive. Minimal investment of selling resources.

FIGURE 3-1 Portfolio Model

focus on the account relationship and may include the account's attitude toward the company and familiarity with the decision makers in the account. Once all accounts have been rated on both dimensions, we can proceed to prioritize our accounts by splitting them at the median of both dimensions and forming a four-quadrant grid, as shown in Figure 3-1.

As an extension of single-factor customer classification models, portfolio models offer several benefits:

- Help the sales team to identify the important customer and relationship issues.
- Facilitate communication between salespeople and sales managers.
- Help isolate information gaps and set priorities for customer data collection and analysis.
- Force the sales team to think about the future and consider ways of achieving a more desirable portfolio configuration.

Portfolio models for setting account priorities are most likely to be used in sales force programs with more of a consultative-type account relationship strategy where understanding individual customer needs and the strength of the relationship are critical. As the Cardinal Health case demonstrates, a sales team is likely to be involved, so there is a need for greater depth of analysis than is available in a current sales volume-based model.

To test your understanding of the importance of setting account priorities within a territory, see Team Exercise "Working Hard or Working Smart."

Decision Model. Although portfolio models have the advantage of using multiple characteristics to classify accounts, several shortcomings remain. First, accounts must still be grouped into the four quadrants for the purpose of allocating sales calls. Differences between firms in the same quadrant are therefore not taken into consideration. Second, the process does not arrive at an optimal allocation of sales calls.

The *decision model* for allocating sales calls overcomes these two shortcomings by focusing on the response of each account to the number of sales calls made over a period of time. Although mathematically elegant, these models consist of just two parts. The first part develops the relationship between the number of sales calls over a period of time and sales to a particular account. This is referred to as a *sales response function*. The response function may be derived either through regression analysis on historical data or judgmentally. With judgment-based decision models, salespeople are first given information about how many

TEAM EXERCISE
"Working Hard or Working Smart?"

You have recently been transferred to Chicago as the new district sales manager and have had a chance to spend some time with each of your salespeople. For the most part, the sales team you are managing has done well, but, as usual, there is a big difference in the sales generated by each salesperson. One of your low producers is Tim, whom you are meeting with today. At first, you thought that Tim may just not be right for the position, but after spending some time riding along with him in his territory you believe he has what it takes to be a good salesperson. Observing him during sales calls, you are convinced he has the right presentation skills; he also set a challenging schedule of calls during the two half-days you spent with him.

After some opening chitchat, you ask Tim to explain why he thinks his sales are not as high as they should be. "I really don't know," answers Tim. "My close rate is good. I make as many calls as the next guy. I have a good territory with potential. I work hard. I think I have the right customer service attitude. I try to treat all my customers the same—as if they are the most important customer I have. I work my territory systematically and I call on each customer once a week. I really don't understand how these other agents do it."

How would you respond to Tim? Based on this conversation, describe the steps you would take to guide Tim toward greater productivity.

times they called on a particular account over a period of time and the sales generated. Salespeople are then asked to project sales in the next period of time if the same number of calls are made on the account, if the number of sales calls is decreased by 50 percent, if they make no sales calls, and if they make the maximum number of sales calls possible. These estimates are used to construct a sales response function like the one shown in Figure 3-2.[12]

A close examination of the response function in Figure 3-2 indicates that customers will not respond dramatically when only one or two calls are made per quarter, but sales are expected to increase dramatically when the number of sales calls increases from two to four. The response function flattens out after four calls, suggesting that there is little left for the salesperson to accomplish by calling on the account more than four times in a quarter. Software is available to constructing sales response functions.

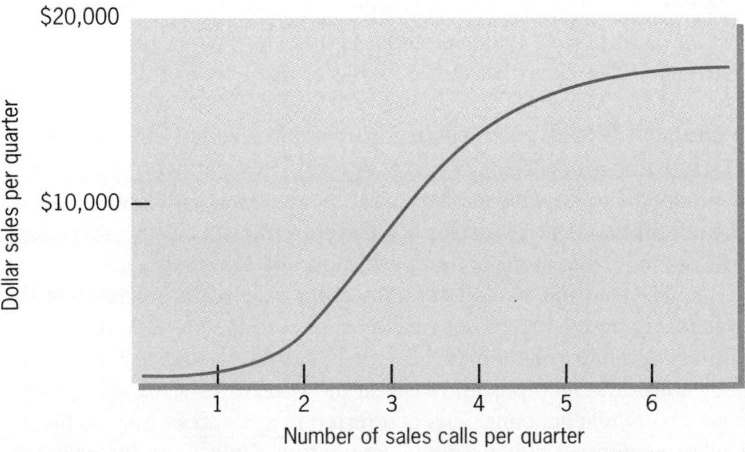

FIGURE 3-2 Number of Sales Calls Response Function

The second part of these models uses the individual response functions to allocate calls so as to maximize sales. Essentially, these models continue to allocate sales calls to an account until more sales can be generated by calling on another account. For example, a third and fourth call may be allocated to the account in Figure 3-2, but greater sales are likely to be generated by calling on another account rather than by allocating a fifth call to this account.

Sales response models are most likely to be helpful in setting priorities when the sales force program is more transactional in nature because the response estimates are most reliable in such selling situations. As the account relationship strategy becomes more complex and involves increased investments from both suppliers and customers, it is not as meaningful to think in terms of the number of sales calls needed to generate a sale. In such situations, a sales process model is more appropriate. We discuss these models next.

Sales Process Model. Despite the advantages of sophisticated call allocation programs, they are not appropriate for all situations. Instead of calling on microprocessor customers, some people in Intel's sales force call on software vendors, information technology buyers, and retail outlets, selling the idea of PCs on every desk and in every household. In the case of these Intel salespeople, immediate and near-term sales volume is not the most relevant measure of the opportunity these sales calls represent.

In other sales situations, the selling cycle can be quite long because of the dollar commitments associated with the sales. This is especially true in industrial goods and high-tech markets, as well as in major account selling where many people may be involved in the purchase decision and where an enterprise-type account strategy exists. In such situations, the focus is on developing opportunities within one or a few accounts, so the focus is not on prioritizing accounts so much as on prioritizing opportunities, all of which may reside in a single account.

Unlike the earlier models, which focus on the relative sales volume or profitability of opportunities, a *sales process model* focuses on where the opportunity is in the selling process. In these models, opportunities are assigned to different stages of the selling process according to the probability that they will ultimately result in a sale. This sort of opportunity categorization is most appropriate when the selling cycle is fairly long and multiple opportunities may exist within the same account.

One example of a selling process model is the sales funnel (see Figure 3-3). Initially developed for training salespeople at Hewlett-Packard, this system categorizes and prioritizes sales opportunities or objectives, not accounts.[13] This is necessary because a salesperson or sales team may have multiple selling objectives at one account at the same time. The account executive may be attempting to get a pilot installation in one of the client's departments, for example, while wanting to upgrade to a more sophisticated piece of equipment in another department.

Each sales opportunity is categorized based on the level of uncertainty in meeting the opportunity:

1. **Unqualified opportunities.** In this case, data suggest that a possible need exists, but this need has not been verified with key people in the account. For example, you have learned that a customer's existing contract with a competitor is about to expire. The selling job needed in this situation is to qualify the account by verifying that a need exists according to the criteria discussed earlier in this chapter.
2. **Qualified opportunities.** A qualified opportunity must meet four criteria:
   - The need has been verified with at least one of the buying influences (e.g., the technical, user, or economic buyers to be discussed in Chapter 4).
   - There is a confirmed intention to buy a new product or service, replace an existing one, or switch suppliers.

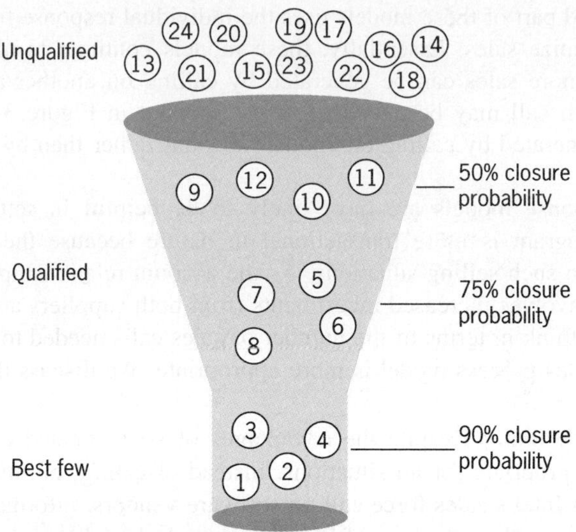

FIGURE 3-3 The Sales Funnel

- Funding for the purchase has been approved or already exists.
- There is an identified time frame within which the purchase will be made.

3. **Best few opportunities.** All the buyers have been contacted and their needs identified, and in your judgment have been sufficiently developed to make the sale. You have all but eliminated luck and uncertainty in the sale and are at least 50 percent along in the selling cycle. That is, it should take you half as long to close these sales as is normal in your territory.

The term *sales funnel* is derived from figuratively placing the sales opportunities in a funnel. Unqualified opportunities appear just outside the top of the funnel, qualified opportunities inside the funnel (depending on the probability of closure and the position in the selling cycle), and the few best opportunities at the bottom of the funnel.

At first glance, it would seem advisable to work on your best few and qualified opportunities, while spending whatever time remains on unqualified opportunities. The problem with this approach is that when given low priority, prospecting rarely occurs. Having closed the best few and exhausted the qualified opportunities, there is nothing left to replace these opportunities. Therefore, experts suggest a prioritization sequence of (1) closing your best few sales opportunities first, (2) prospecting for unqualified opportunities next, and (3) working the qualified opportunities last to ensure a constant and predictable flow of sales over time. It is always important to keep the funnel full by prospecting for new opportunities.

SALES VERSUS PROFITS

There is a tendency in sales to evaluate opportunities in terms of dollar sales. Faced with tough buyers in mature markets, however, some companies are beginning to focus on the bottom line instead of the top line. A recent survey of strategic account sales executives reported that two of the top four customer selection criteria are profit related. Specifically, resources are allocated to strategic accounts as a function of current and potential profits.[14] Profit, of course, is the difference between net price and the actual cost to serve a customer. There can be dramatic differences between the price an account pays and the costs incurred in servicing an account. Why is this true?

Customers may pay very different prices for similar products and services. Although there are some legal constraints, such as the Robinson-Patman Act, some customers are able to negotiate lower prices and higher discounts because of their size. In other words, large customers can demand and get lower prices because a seller cannot afford to lose their business. Other customers are simply able to get lower prices because of their negotiating skills. And still other customers exploit deals and promotions more than others and "forward buy," which means they buy a large amount of their annual needs at one time when the product is on discount.

The cost to serve is also likely to differ between customers. Some accounts are located far from the salesperson's normal route, so more travel time is involved. Some customers place their orders by phone or over the Internet, whereas others require endless face-to-face sales calls to close a deal or to place even a routine order. Some customers demand intensive presale services like applications engineering and custom design support, while others accept standard designs. Costs may also vary according to preferred transportation mode, number of receiving locations for an order, and opportunities to back-haul. (Back-hauling refers to transporting goods back to an origination point after delivering supplies. As a result, a truck does not travel without a load, which wastes time and money.) The list of customer service cost differences sometimes seems endless.

The main point we would like to make here is that companies and salespeople need to be aware of the price, cost, and profit differences between customers and allocate their sales effort accordingly. It is not at all unusual for there to be a 50 to 75 percent difference in the profitability of customers who purchase a similar quantity of product. This is what FedEx found out when it began studying the profitability of its customers. This issue is so important to FedEx that it now searches its database to compare the costs of doing business with particular customers and rates its customers according to profitability. FedEx also now matches transaction information with demographic data to pinpoint the characteristics to seek in prospects or existing customers that might offer more business.

To test your understanding of the profit versus sales issue, try your hand at answering the questions posed in Team Exercise, "Destructive Discounting."

TEAM EXERCISE
"Destructive Discounting"

You have recently been hired as vice president of sales for an Original Equipment Manufacturer (OEM) of small electronic components. After three months on the job, you don't like what you are seeing from the company's nine salespeople. The sales force seems focused on closing as many deals as possible, regardless of whether they provide good solutions for customers. Salespeople are discounting so much that your margins have continued to decline. Clearly, you would be in trouble if this continues since this was precisely what you were hired to change. Further, your bonus is based on achieving profit margin objectives. When you talk with the salespeople, however, they say that they were previously taught to focus on sales volume, not the profitability of the deals. What should you do first? To help communicate the critical financial consequences of price discounting, create a simplified income statement illustrating the effect of a 10 percent discount on profits.

Customer Lifetime Value. You may recall that one of the problems with the single-factor model was that, based on historical sales volume, it was not forward looking enough in considering future sales and profits. Consistent with the shift from a transaction view of revenues and profits to a relationship perspective, marketers are starting to adopt Customer Lifetime Value (CLV) as an appropriate metric for measuring marketing performance.[15] Who cares if profits are good for one period, if the customer is alienated as a result? Taking a long-term view of profitability is the motivation behind using CLV as an appropriate performance and resource allocation metric.

Customer Lifetime Value is based on the notion that the value of a customer is the sum of the customer's discounted flow of profit contributions into the future. Calculating CLV requires knowing or making judgments about the following inputs:

- The company's discount rate (cost of capital)
- The company's planning horizon (3 years, 5 years, 10 years)
- The customer's product category purchases in the future
- The average contribution from purchases
- Each supplier's share of total category purchases[16]

The experience of one pharmaceutical company illustrates the potential significance of switching to CLV as its resource allocation metric from past sales volume. The company had been allocating sales effort according to the number of prescriptions a physician wrote—a surrogate for sales volume—which led to a focus on doctors in midcareer. When they switched to calculating the CLV of a physician, their analysis revealed the importance of young physicians, including residents and new practitioners, who, though not currently big prescribers, were specialists in a given area and could thus be expected to prescribe more drugs over time. This lifetime emphasis brought a whole new set of doctors to the company's attention, displacing a quarter of the physicians it had previously thought were of greatest value.[17]

As mentioned earlier, it is the forward-looking, future orientation of CLV that helps firms develop insights into the optimal allocation of resources across their customer base. After using CLV to analyze its customer base, one U.S. company discovered that it was already the sole or dominant supplier for many of its top customers. The biggest growth opportunities actually rested with companies in the second and third sales tiers where the company had a smaller share of even larger purchases.

Another example of how CLV has helped in allocating marketing resources is Roadway Express Inc., which learned that 30 percent of its "small" customers who were sent only direct mail communications had as much yearly freight volume as its large account segment. Like the previous example, a future focus will often bring to light hidden opportunities for greater return on marketing investment.[18]

TIME MANAGEMENT

In most surveys of business training programs, *time management* is one of the most frequently mentioned training topics. The reason is that significant productivity gains can be made through better time management. Figure 3-4 shows how salespeople spend their time. The time spent selling, either with customers, prospecting, or on service calls, is on average less than 50 percent of a salesperson's time.

Improving the amount of time spent selling is an opportunity for significant productivity gains. A task force for one Fortune 100 company estimated that a 10 percent improvement in the time its sales force spent selling would generate more than a 5 percent increase in overall sales volume. This is one of the main reasons companies are investing heavily in sales force technology.

Consider how things have changed for the salespeople in Quaker Oats' chemical division. In the 1990s, tracing a shipment of solvent for a client meant numerous hours of phone calls and plenty of headaches. Today, Quaker Oats salespeople simply open their laptop, go

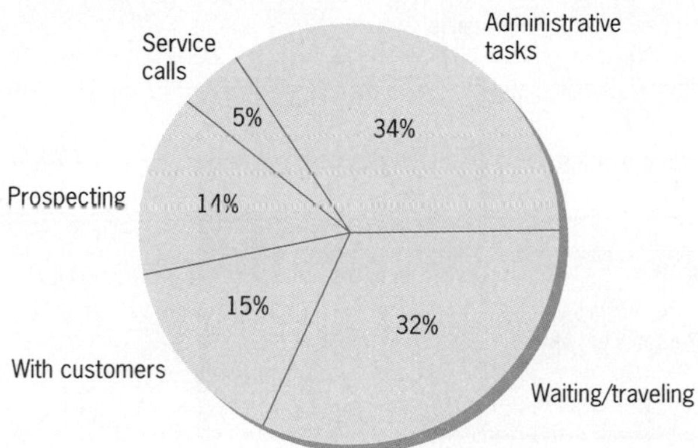

FIGURE 3-4 How Salespeople Spend Their Time

into the company's internal Web site, click on a button that says "shipment information," and in just a few minutes they are able to tell the purchasing agent that the tank car is in Houston, 20 miles away. The importance of this technology is indicated in Figure 3-4, which shows that salespeople spend 15 percent of their time on service calls.

Overall Time Management

Despite all the emphasis companies are putting on increasing selling time, 34 percent of a salesperson's time is spent on administrative tasks. This figure has not changed much during the past two decades. Although it is important for salespeople to provide customer and competitor information to their company, a key aspect of managing time effectively is to recognize and control things that tend to waste time. Following is a list of what many salespeople consider some of the most common time wasters:[19]

1. Telephone interruptions
2. Drop-in visitors
3. Lack of self-discipline
4. Crises
5. Meetings
6. Lack of objectives, priorities, and deadlines
7. Indecision and procrastination
8. Attempting too much at once
9. Leaving tasks unfinished
10. Unclear communication

Note that the top two time wasters are telephone interruptions and drop-in visitors. The rest of the time wasters, such as lack of discipline, lack of objectives, and procrastination, indicate poor self-management by the salesperson. How different is this list from the one you would make for yourself? One aspect of time management that is particularly important in sales is to know when the customer is available. This is the key selling time during the day, and salespeople should strictly adhere to customer contacts during these times. This time must be protected, while other duties and issues are handled at other times of the day.

A key step frequently recommended for improved time management is preparing a list of personal and professional goals and then pursuing them one step at a time. Planning does not have to be elaborate to be useful. Simply writing down a list of things you want to do tomorrow is a good place to start. The next step is to rank the tasks on the basis of their importance. Then when you start the day, begin task 1 and stay with it until it is completed. Recheck your priorities and begin task 2. Continue with tasks as long as they remain most important.

Once people get into the habit of daily planning, the next step is to plan a week or more ahead. Many salespeople, for example, are required to prepare weekly call plans. The idea is to encourage salespeople to plan a series of calls for each day, to call ahead for appointments,

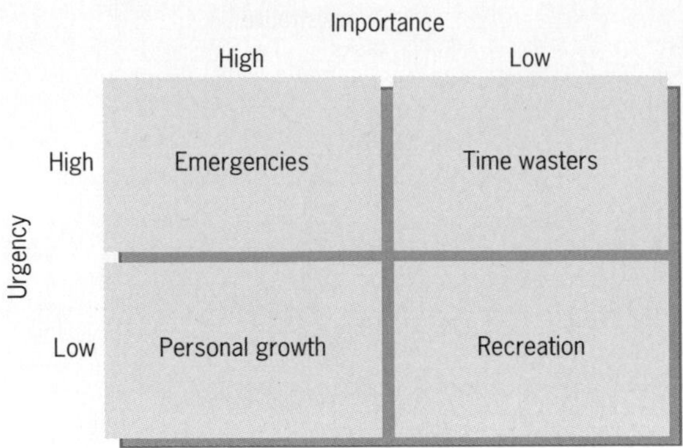

FIGURE 3-5 Time Management

and to make better use of their time. Today technology such as Blackberries and smart phones help time management for busy salespeople because of their size, portability, and ability to sync with multiple personal computers.

Stephen Covey, a well-known consultant in personal and professional development, advises people to analyze their time management using a framework like the one shown in Figure 3-5.[20] "Importance" refers to activities that are of importance to you in meeting your objectives. "Urgency," on the other hand, is the time pressure we feel to perform certain activities. Notice that we may feel this pressure for both important and relatively unimportant activities. According to Covey, activities in the Emergencies and Recreation quadrants will generally take care of themselves. People can gain control over their lives by spending less time on Time Wasters and more on Personal Growth activities. Time Wasters (high urgency but low importance) include phone calls, some meetings, and unnecessary administrative work—in other words, things that demand our immediate attention. Personal Growth activities (low urgency but high importance) are easily put off but are very important to our future growth and development. Activities in this category may include reading professional journals or books, enrolling in professional development or executive courses, learning how other functional areas operate, or prospecting for new customers. Notice that many people can postpone these activities indefinitely. Considering both urgency and importance may provide us with a useful perspective on how we can spend our time more productively.

SUMMARY

Over the past decade, sales force productivity has lagged behind the double-digit increase in selling costs. As a result, top executives are giving added emphasis to improving sales force productivity by increasing the amount of time salespeople spend face-to-face with customers. Salespeople are being armed with laptop computers, cellular phones, and the Internet to fight this battle.

1. **Describe effective steps for generating new accounts.** First, a prospect profile should be constructed that describes the best prospects for your company's offerings. The profile may be based on sophisticated database analysis of the purchasing patterns and profitability of your current customers. With an ideal prospect profile clearly in mind, a list of prospects should be developed using a variety of methods, including direct mail, trade shows, directories, referrals, and cold canvassing. Finally, prospects need to be qualified based on their need for the seller's offerings and intention to buy in the near future, their authority to buy, and their ability to pay for the offering.

2. **Explain how to determine the minimum account opportunity a salesperson should pursue.** Two techniques for making this determination should be used. First, the cost per sales call should be identified. This is calculated by identifying all direct selling costs for the period of time being evaluated and dividing this sum by the number of sales calls that are expected for the time period. The cost per call figure is then included in a breakeven sales volume analysis, which consists of multiplying cost per call times the number of calls necessary to close the sale and dividing this product by the company's sales costs as a percent of sales target. This provides a base figure from which to determine whether a sales opportunity is of sufficient magnitude to warrant a face-to-face selling effort.
3. **Describe four methods for setting opportunity priorities.** The single factor model focuses on sales volume to classify account opportunities and allocate salespeople's time. Portfolio models expand the criteria for classifying account opportunities by considering both competitive position and account opportunity factors. Decision models allocate effort according to a sales response function, which is based on the sales response to different numbers of sales calls during a period of time. The sales process model allocates time to sales opportunities based on their stage in the selling process. The appropriate model will depend on market demand, the competitive, and selling situation of the company.
4. **Explain why emphasis is shifting from sales volume to profit flow.** The main reason for shifting from sales volume to profits as a performance and resource allocation metric is because profits may be quite different for customers purchasing the same total volume of products and services. This is caused by the price concessions some customers obtain, the mix of product they purchase, the services they require, as well as their future profit growth potential. A corresponding shift is taking place from emphasizing past sales and profits to valuing customers based on their future stream of profits. Customer Lifetime Value (CLV) is one method for calculating the discounted flow of future profit contributions.
5. **Tell how salespeople can manage their time more efficiently.** A recent survey indicates that salespeople spend about 54 percent of their time selling either face to face or over the phone. Three avenues for increasing this percentage are incorporating technology into the selling and planning process, more efficient routing of sales calls within a territory, and reducing time wasters through personal time management techniques.

KEY TERMS

Account opportunity
Acquisition costs
Best few opportunities
Breakeven sales volume
Cold canvassing
Competitive position
Cost per call
Decision model
Direct mail
Directories
Direct selling expenses
Minimum account size
Portfolio model
Prospecting
Prospect profile
Qualified opportunities
Qualify a prospect
Referrals
Sales funnel
Sales process model
Sales response function
Single-factor model
Time management
Trade shows
Unqualified opportunities

DEVELOPING YOUR COMPETENCIES

1. **Self-Management.** One of the most important aspects of self-management is to develop a clear understanding of your personal and career goals. One highly successful method of arriving at a better understanding of your goals and of the steps that should be taken to achieve those goals is the time management analysis developed by Stephen Covey.

First, list your personal and professional goals in any order. Next, list the actions that you will need to take to get yourself in position to achieve these goals. Third, draw the Time Management Matrix presented Figure 3-5, labeling the axes as high versus low importance and high versus low urgency. List the activities on which you spent time over the past week or month. Now compare these activities to the list that you developed for achieving your personal and professional goals. In which quadrant would these goal-directed activities fall? How could you adjust your time to put yourself in a good position to achieve your goals?

2. **Coaching.** You are spending the day with a new salesperson in your district who has been with your company, Consumer Research International (CRI), for less than a month. CRI is a marketing research company that competes with the likes of M/A/R/C Group, Market Facts, and Burke Marketing Research. Although CRI has a number of accounts with which it has worked for a number of years, each month between 20 and 30 callers will contact your company to investigate engaging it in a marketing research project; however, only about two or three of the calls warrant further attention. A new salesperson is having a problem determining in a reasonable amount of time, which of these callers is a real prospect and which is a waste of time. Time is precious, however, but you do not want your salespeople walking away from important growth opportunities. Because the salesperson is new on the job, you would like to give him a set of questions that he could ask to determine whether this is a "hot" prospect or one that is "just looking." What would be your advice?
3. **Global Perspective.** Dendrite International is one of the world's leading suppliers of sales force automation software in the pharmaceutical industry. Pharmaceutical firms worldwide are arming their salespeople with laptop computers and looking for software to design call plans and collect call reports to increase sales force efficiency and effectiveness. More than 15,000 salespeople in 40 companies in 11 countries use Dendrite systems. One of the issues Dendrite faces is that software demands differ greatly from country to country. How would software requirements differ in each of the following countries? For more information on Dendrite, see www.drte.com.

   - U.S. pharmaceutical sales forces are among the largest in the world, ranging from 500 to more than 3,000 reps per firm. Sales reps call on medical personnel every 4 to 6 weeks to leave product samples and literature, perform service tasks, and build relationships with prescribing physicians.
   - In Western Europe, sales forces are generally 100 to 200 reps in size. Government funding of health care and large, managed-care organizations are common. In England, a rep sees a doctor once a year, always by appointment, and can only leave one sample.
   - In Japan, sales forces are like those in the United States, and, with fewer doctors, there is one pharmaceutical salesperson for every six physicians. Unlike in the United States, where physicians cannot sell drugs, Japanese physicians combine prescribing and dispensing of drugs. Sales reps negotiate prices with individual physicians, who also derive income from selling free drug samples to their patients. Most Japanese doctors work in clinics or hospitals that require sales reps to wait outside to see the doctor. As a result, "social selling" is very important in Japan. Reps develop face time with doctors by washing their cars, entertaining them, and running all sorts of errands.

4. **Technology.** Wisdom Ware Inc., a small software firm, has developed a slick tool that helps salespeople to be better informed and more efficient. It requires salespeople and their bosses to do things just a little differently. The issue Wisdom Ware attempts

to address is keeping the sales force informed about products, the market, and the competition. Even more important, the software is designed to enable every piece of information to link with any other piece. That way, salespeople can assemble just the right combination of facts necessary for the immediate task without being inundated with information. In short, this software is the interactive equivalent of Cliff Notes. While planning a call, a sales rep makes a few menu choices to identify the customer, the product, and such. One click creates the most up-to-date qualifying questions, another reveals how the competition stacks up, another reports the most common objections, and still another suggests a quick product positioning statement. Though only a few concise sentences pop up on the screen, detailed reports are just a click away. Unfortunately, Wisdom Ware has been less than wildly successful so far. The problem isn't training, which takes less than an hour. Nor is it compatibility; Wisdom Ware works seamlessly with other front-office software. Neither has any customer winced at the price of $500 and up per user. What do you think could be the problem? For more on Wisdom Ware, see www.sellmorenow.com.

5. **Strategic Action.** IBM has proved it can market successfully to fellow corporate giants like General Motors and Citibank. But will the company be successful in selling to the millions of enterprises with 1,000 or fewer employees who make up the world's fastest growing segment? It had better be because for IBM entrepreneurial companies are the future in information technology. In the United States, small businesses are responsible for 50 percent of the gross national product. That segment is growing at 11 percent annually, three percentage points higher than the growth of large companies. What's more, IBM estimates that last year 75 million small and medium-size companies worldwide spent $305 billion in information technology.

   But IBM faces an enormous challenge simply trying to prove to smaller customers that it really cares about them. "My small customers don't feel comfortable with IBM," says Gunther Obhlschlager of TransCat, an IBM reseller in Karlsruhe, Germany. "Unless you spend millions of dollars with the company, you can't get someone on the phone," he says. Richard Laermer, a New York entrepreneur, adds, "I don't believe they're really going after small businesses." He adds, "Their attitude is, 'If you don't have a thousand employees, get out of my face." Should IBM go after the whole market—large, medium, and small firms? Can it? If so, how?

6. **Team Building.** One of the most important jobs of the first-line sales manager is to create an atmosphere in which individual salespeople feel that they are part of a team and are also responsible for carrying their own weight. Perhaps one of the most controversial aspects of this balancing act is the degree to which the sales manager should get involved in territory and account planning.

   The attitudes and advice of sales managers run the gamut from close supervision to a totally hands-off attitude. At Ziegler Tools, an Atlanta industrial distributor, for example, salespeople are required to fill out weekly detailed itineraries and call reports, which are compared with quarterly itineraries. Turner Warmack, vice president of sales and marketing at Ziegler Tools, states, "Generally speaking, salespeople are poor managers and can be thrown off course pretty easily. What we feel our system does is help them focus their efforts." At the other end of the spectrum are sales managers who do not require their salespeople to submit call reports and detailed reviews of customer status. Typical of this approach is Rick Horn, president of Stahl Company, a specialty truck body manufacturer, who states: "I didn't feel I had to tell them what to do. They were big boys and knew their territory. All I wanted to know is where they were in case I had to reach them." Which approach do you feel is best? Does it depend on the circumstances? If so, what circumstances should be considered?

PROBLEMS*

1. You are a rookie salesperson with Associated Medical Supplies, Inc., a wholesaler of disposable medical supplies. As a new salesperson, you are finding it difficult to convince accounts to switch from their current suppliers. The doctors with whom you are having the most success tend to be small, single practices located in rural areas. Competition for these accounts is not as intense, perhaps because their purchases are fairly small. They usually place about $900 worth of business with you every month. Nevertheless, they seem to be most appreciative of your weekly visit to take inventory of their supplies and write an order. Furthermore, it is better than no sales at all. Lately your boss has been hassling you because productivity has not increased as much as he had hoped when he placed you in the territory. In particular, direct selling costs, including compensation, are currently 15 percent of net sales, whereas the total company's target is for direct sales costs to be 10 percent of net sales. In light of this, you are wondering if spending time on small rural physicians is the best way to manage your territory. You have calculated that your cost per call is currently $34.50. Should you be calling on these small physician practices? What is the smallest size customer you should pursue in order to meet your company's selling cost objectives? What actions might you consider in managing your territory better?
2. As a salesperson for Strength Footwear, Inc., you have been very successful. Your commissions are well over $70,000 per year. Demand for your product line is strong, but so is the demand on your time. You work your territory 220 days a year and can make four calls a day. The maximum number of times you need to see any account is every other week, but you need to call on each account at least once a quarter. To help you allocate your time according to sales results, you have gathered the following information on customer sales:

Accounts	*Sales Last Year*
Top 10 accounts	$150,000
Next 10 best accounts	37,500
Next 10 best accounts	37,000
Next 20 best accounts	56,250
Next 20 best accounts	55,500
Next 20 best accounts	18,750
Last 20 accounts	15,000
	$370,000

Develop and justify a call schedule for allocating time across the 110 customers in your territory.

3. You have just finished your annual account review of the telecom purchases of one of your largest customers. It purchased $125,000 worth of telecom equipment from you last year but indicate that it wants a 10 percent discount on next year's purchases or it will switch its business to one of your competitors. Technical, installation, and other account services that were provided to this customer last year totaled $11,000 and are expected to be about the same next year. You earn a commission of 10 percent on sales. Last year this account's gross margin was 40 percent, and they are expected to purchase a similar quantity of equipment next year. Assuming that the list price for the equipment would

*Excel spreadsheets for working these problems are available at www.wiley.com/college/cron. Go to "Student Companion Site."

be the same as last year, but discounted by 10 percent, how would the discount affect the profit contributions this account is estimated to generate next year?

4. Continuing with the account analysis from problem 3, assume that the account purchases some of its telecom equipment from one of your competitors. How much would you need to increase your penetrations of this account through increased sales in order to justify the 10 percent discount the account wants on next year's purchases?

FEATURED CASE SHIELD FINANCIAL: "LEAD GENERATION"

One method by which Shield identified leads on new prospects was through mailing of information to businesses in the area accompanied by a mail-back card and an email address for those interested in learning more about the programs Shield could offer. Since this type of lead generation program had not been used for some time in the Des Moines area, Doug, the sales manager at the Des Moines office, decided to run the program after some disappointing first quarter sales results. To his surprise and thrill, 79 requests for more information were received in the next ten days following the mailing. Doug gave each of the salespeople in the office around ten leads to follow up on.

A month later, at the monthly sales meeting, Doug asked for a progress report on the status of those prospect leads. Only two of the reps had followed up on any of the leads. Of those five leads, three sales were made and two prospects were still being developed. Doug was now concerned. After all the hard work that went into generating these leads, he wasn't about to see them gather dust on his salespeople's desks. Moreover, he didn't want to lose easy sales from prospects that were ready to buy. Doug voiced his concern to the salespeople and said he would be creating a standard plan that the salespeople would have to use when following up on leads.

Questions

1. Should Doug have taken an approach other than saying that he would create a standard plan?
2. If you were the sales manager, what would you do about the reps' obvious lack of motivation to follow up on the leads generated by the mailing?
3. What are the possible reactions from the leads not contacted by Shield?
4. What is an "ideal" course of action given all the issues involved?
5. Write a brief step-by-step plan to handle this situation.

ACCOUNT RELATIONSHIP MANAGEMENT

> The sale, then, merely consummates the courtship, at which point the marriage begins. How good the marriage is depends on how well the seller manages the relationship.
>
> Theodore Levitt

Chapter Consultants:
Ken Whelan, Director, Business Development, Qwest Communications International, Inc.
Chris Jander, National Accounts Manager, Marconi Corporation plc.

LEARNING OBJECTIVES

After studying this chapter, you should be able to:

- Describe the steps in the professional purchasing process.
- Identify the different buying influences in the buying center.
- Explain how relationships are likely to evolve.
- Describe factors critical to gaining commitment to a relationship.

GROWING THE RELATIONSHIP

You're a global IT services company serving a customer many times your size. You need to create an innovative way to manage the customer relationship, and the method must have enough flexibility for the account's unique and constantly changing requirements. You know that, if successful, the relationship will set your company and the customer well ahead of the competition. And while you realize that it might be a difficult business decision to dedicate hundreds of individuals to this account, you also know that the account could use your firm's competencies.

This is not an imaginary situation. The supplier is Satyam Computer Services Ltd., a global IT consulting and services firm. Satyam offers services as diverse as strategy consulting, end-to-end IT solutions implementation, and business process outsourcing.

The account is Caterpillar Inc., the world's largest manufacturer of construction and mining equipment, diesel and natural gas engines, and industrial gas turbines with annual sales of \$20 billion.

The account plan developed by Bipin Thomas, Satyam's Global Account Manager for Caterpillar, was to perform joint IT strategic planning and development with Caterpillar that would yield a competitive advantage for both firms. To this end, Thomas pioneered an innovative partnering model that he named Competency-Driven Strategic Account Management (CDSAM™). Key elements of the process are jointly developing a relationship vision and establishing multilayered relationships between the tops of the two organizations on downwards. The centerpiece of the plan demands that once required competencies (embedded systems, for example) have been identified, Satyam will develop dedicated competency teams designed to link with customer teams to solve customer problems. Over the next five years, the number of Satyam employees focused on Caterpillar jumped to over 200 people.

The financial results for Satyam have been dramatic. Revenues from the Caterpillar relationship increased 8 fold over the next five years to over $15 million annually. Margins also doubled over this time. Caterpillar benefited as well, reducing costs by 409 percent and realizing $37 million in cost savings in developing IT services. For every dollar Caterpillar spent with Satyam, it realized a dollar in savings.

Mr. Thomas, the Caterpillar account manager, started with deep customer knowledge and identified needs that led to an idea. He had the internal marketing skills to sell the idea inside his organization, and the project management skills to bring the idea to fruition in a relatively short time.[1]

This chapter focuses on the sales force activities involved in building lasting and profitable relationships with customers, referred to as *accounts*. The Satyam-Caterpillar relationship illustrates some of the most important developments in business-to-business selling—selling teams, buying centers, identification of opportunities, growing the relationship, creating customer value, meeting expectations, and building trust. This chapter examines each of these issues, identifies related selling activities, and provides practical examples of their significance.

In Chapter 2 we discussed the notion of an account relationship strategy decision as a central element of a sales force program. This chapter focuses on the implementation of the account relationship strategy in discussing the activities involved in managing account relationships. Specifically, we will examine four key aspects of business-to-business relationships shown in Figure 4-1. Although the concepts discussed in this chapter are relevant regardless of a supplier's specific customer relationship strategy, there are differences in the relative importance and execution of these activities. Trust and need recognition, for instance, are relevant regardless of whether there is a transactional, consultative, or enterprise relationship between the customer and supplier, but they fundamentally differ in their processes and activities, depending on the type of relationship sought by a supplier and customer.[2]

One additional point that should not go unnoticed in the Satyam-Caterpillar example is that companies are increasingly looking for significant growth opportunities within current accounts. In a recent survey, over 70 percent of sales executives listed increasing sales to existing customers as one of their top priorities for the next year.[3] Results of a classic study of sales force performance further underscores the importance of existing customers in meeting sales objectives. The study investigated whether the amount of time spent calling

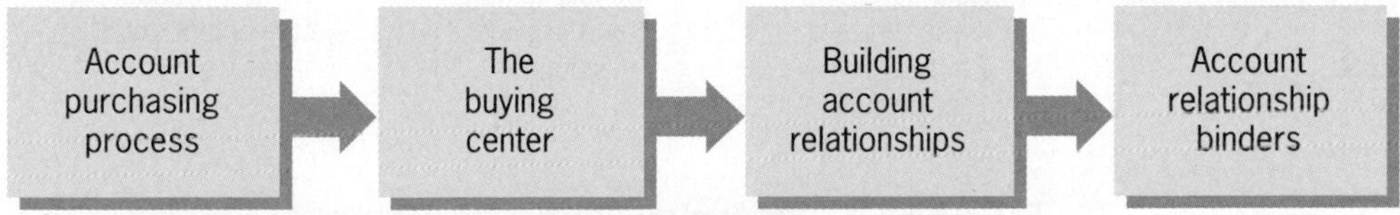

FIGURE 4-1 Account Relationship Management Concepts

on accounts affected sales force performance. The results show that time spent prospecting is not related to performance, but the time spent with established accounts has a positive impact on performance.[4]

Our discussion of relationship management begins by presenting the typical stages in the business-to-business purchasing process. Examples of different types of account relationships will be discussed within the context of each stage. The concept of a buying center is introduced, along with the development of selling teams. Following this discussion, our focus changes to understanding how account relationships typically develop and what steps sellers can take to ensure profitable account relationships.

PURCHASING PROCESS

One of our basic premises is that in order to be successful the sales force must create value for the customer. To better understand how the sales force can create customer value, let's look at the different points in the purchasing process where a sales force can potentially add value. The typical sequence of steps that purchasers go through in business-to-business acquisitions includes the four steps shown in Figure 4-2.[5]

A key determinant of the nature of the purchasing process is the buying situation faced by an account. Three different types of situations are possible, each of which will influence the nature of the four steps in the purchasing process and the opportunity for the seller to provide value to the customer in completing the purchasing process.

In a *straight rebuy* purchasing situation, the product has been previously purchased and there is no change desired in the product or offering; it often involves replenishing inventories of products. In such a situation, the seller can add value for the customer by making the purchase easy, convenient, and as hassle-free as possible. The purchasing department is likely to be responsible for the entire purchasing process in this situation.

A *modified rebuy* purchasing situation occurs when some changes are anticipated in a product that the buyer has previously been purchasing. As a result, the evaluation of options step of the process is much more extensive, and it is here that the seller can add the most value. A group of people from various functional areas of the purchasing organization is usually involved in the purchasing process.

The most complex purchasing situation is the *new buy* purchasing situation. In these purchase situations, the seller has the opportunity to add value for the buyer during three of the four stages of the purchasing process: recognition of the needs, evaluation of options,

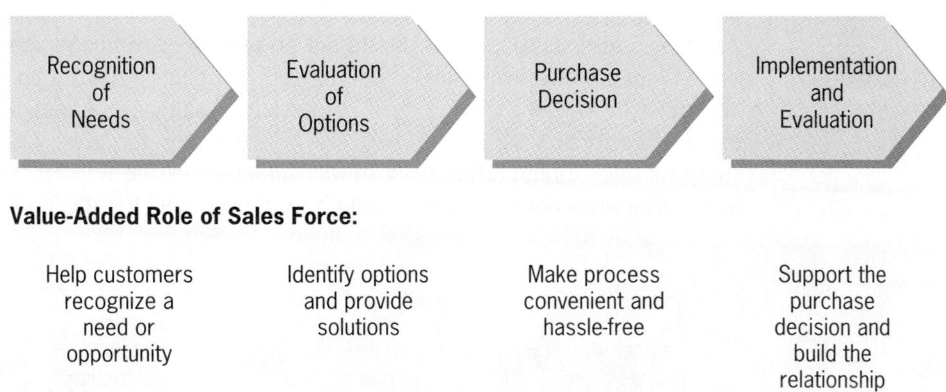

FIGURE 4-2 The Typical Purchasing Process

and implementation and evaluation. The actual purchase decision itself follows naturally from the previous two stages, though the whole purchasing process may take some time to complete.

Recognition of Needs

The first stage in the purchasing process occurs when the account recognizes that a need exists. In some cases, the need is immediate and focuses on resolving a problem, such as when a manager observes a bottleneck in a production process or when existing machinery breaks down. This type of need is more typical of a transactional relationship.

In many consultative-type selling relationships, a customer may not be aware of the extent of the problem or opportunity. It is often up to the sales force to quantify the situation. Transcend Services, Inc., of Atlanta provides hospitals an alternative to in-house medical records. The selling process involves an evaluation of a hospital's operations as to cost effectiveness, quality control, and reliable delivery of a patient's medical records. Cost is not the only issue, however, as the timely availability of patient records are needed for purposes of billing insurance companies, all of which is critical to timely collection for services provided. According to Transcend's President and CEO, Larry Gerdes, an evaluation can be done in a matter of days and includes quantifying not only savings from elimination of in-house staff but also reduction of a hospital's capital investment associated with equipment and software needed for dictation capture and transcription. Transcend is able to provide these savings due to its capabilities in technology, such as speech recognition, as well as managing a global workforce to provide timely and economical medical records. The key for Transcend is getting customers to understand and quantify the magnitude of the problem. This is a good example of a new buy purchasing situation and an enterprise type of selling relationship context in which the issues of cost and efficiency are the main customer problems.

One of the first things a salesperson needs to understand when identifying business-to-business buying needs is the concept of derived demand. Professional buyers do not purchase for themselves but rather help to produce goods and services for resale. *Derived demand* refers to the dynamic in which demand for a product or service is derived from the demand for the customer's products and services. This suggests that suppliers can gain a competitive advantage by knowing and understanding the needs of the customers' customers. Derived demand may influence whom the sales force calls on, what customer benefits are emphasized, and how much of a product or service is ultimately sold. To convince GTE to carry its line of ethernet connections, for example, RELTEC demonstrated to apartment owners the advantages of ethernet connections for the computer needs of their customers. Since this feature could reduce the apartment's client turnover, the apartment owners convinced GTE to include RELTEC's ethernet connection with its product lines. In other words, RELTEC sold GTE by selling to GTE's customers, apartment owners. In this case, the ethernet connections are a new buy purchasing situation for GTE and illustrate a consultative type of selling relationship in which an opportunity was identified by the RELTEC sales team.

Evaluation of Options

Businesses may spend considerable time and money in searching and evaluating alternative suppliers, depending on the strategic significance of the purchase.[6] Purchased materials usually represent from 30 to 80 percent of product costs for an original equipment manufacturer (OEM). The cost of misunderstandings among the parties involved and post-sales problems can be enormous. As a result, it is critical that a supplier understand the buyer's situation. Consider the complaint of one buyer when talking about some suppliers:

> A lot of guys come in and say: "Hey, I am going to solve your problems." But how can you solve my problems, when you don't even know me? A number of times, they don't even understand my business, what I do on a day-to-day basis. It might be a great solution for them, but I know that they are just throwing a cookie cutter at me.[7]

Specifications. One of the key activities taking place during this phase is the development of a precise statement of the requirements and tolerances, referred to as a product's specifications. The exact specifications are usually dictated by the anticipated demand for the organization's products and by the technological requirements of its operations. This stage is often critical for potential suppliers because final specifications will dictate the cost to produce the product and can favor one supplier's product over another. Therefore, getting involved in this phase of the process is often critical.

In most transactional-type relationships, customers have largely developed their own product specifications before a supplier gets involved in the process. In more consultative and enterprise-type relationships, however, customers and suppliers work together to jointly develop product specifications. Take the case of Johnson Controls, Inc., chosen to supply seats for one of Chrysler's models. Johnson was able to meet the customer's cost target but fell far short on safety, weight, and comfort. Ten Chrysler engineers met with ten Johnson counterparts, led by the sales director. After five 11-hour days, they agreed on weight, cost, and performance targets and subsequently helped Johnson meet these targets.[8] This example also illustrates that in more advanced buyer-seller relationships, the supplier is often chosen prior to completion of detailed technical specifications, which may be jointly developed by the supplier and customer.

Proposals. A *sales proposal* is a written offer by a seller to provide a product or service to a purchasing organization. The proposal may represent the culmination of sales activities spanning several months involving extensive client analysis. On the other hand, a proposal may result from receiving a *Request for proposal (RFP)* from a buyer. An RFP is a notice that a customer sends out to qualified suppliers asking them to bid on a project with a certain set of specifications. Regardless of how the process was initiated, it is important that the proposal development process be integrated into the selling process. In purchasing materials and equipment, for example, building contractors may consider service, quality of product, supplier support, low price, and/or reputation for fair dealing among their most important purchasing criteria when choosing suppliers. The proposal is actually the outcome of the first two phases of the purchasing process: identification of needs and evaluation of options.[9]

Purchase Decision

The purchase decision is the final flurry of activity culminating in a sale. Purchasing activities involve writing orders, persuading, negotiating, finalizing terms, and closing the sale. As mentioned earlier, this is where a seller can create value for customers in a straight rebuy situation and in a transactional type of relationship by making the purchasing process easy, convenient, and hassle free.

To facilitate the straight-rebuy-type purchase, many companies are turning to *extranets*. Extranets link trading partners' internal Internet computer networks to provide a secure private electronic environment for real-time communication. By connecting with the customer's computer system and accessing a customer's inventory information, a supplier is able to automatically ship product for purposes of inventory replenishment. More companies are in fact requiring their suppliers to support just-in-time inventory practices, improve supply chain management, and furnish instant order-status information via extranets. Heineken recently initiated a system that allows its 450 distributors to forecast and order over the Web, reducing order cycle time from three months to four weeks.[10] Marshall Industries, a leading distributor of steel products, has gone one step further with its extranet, which allows customers to track order status, expedite shipping by linking to freight forwarders, participate in live engineering seminars with video and audio, and get live on-line support.

Price is usually a crucial factor in business-to-business marketing, especially for commodity-type items, for which one can choose from many comparable alternatives. The role of price in many buyer-seller relationships is changing in today's competitive environment. Instead of looking for the lowest price, some buyers are realizing that, by working together with key suppliers, they can operate more efficiently and effectively in satisfying the needs of the ultimate consumer and may do so at a lower overall cost. Grief Brothers Corporation, which manufactures fiber and plastic drums, routinely conducts what it calls cost-in-use studies to document the incremental cost savings that a customer gains by using Grief's more expensive products and services, rather than a less expensive alternative. One of Grief's technical service managers works with customer managers to estimate the customer's current total costs and to identify system solutions for the customer. Solutions might include just-in-time deliveries, a new delivery system, or drum recycling. In giving the customer a variety of service alternatives together with estimates of cost savings, Grief helps the customer make a more informed purchase decision based on the total worth of the system solution to the customer.[11]

Implementation and Evaluation

The purchasing process does not end with the purchase. During the immediate post-purchase phase the seller's obligation is to ensure that all promises are fulfilled and customer expectations are met or exceeded. This will include making sure that the product has no defects, arrives on time as promised and at the right place, warranties are honored, repairs or exchanges are handled quickly and smoothly, needed information is provided, and adequate training is provided. A senior manager with a health care firm complained, "Support is the Achilles heel for most suppliers. They come, deliver, and go. But what happens when I am in trouble? We need solution providers, not fair weather friends."[12]

After the immediate post-purchase activities are performed, the seller's focus should shift to customer retention and growth. Activities focus on nurturing a continuing business relationship with the customer. This may include performing customer market analysis, developing joint customer marketing programs, monitoring inventory, providing customer service, providing ongoing training, and handling complaints.[13] Listen to what one satisfied senior manager has to say about the company's best suppliers:

> They are there to give us updates on our network status. They are there to give us updates on security issues. They are there to cover up for us in case of disasters. They are there to cover up for us when our servers are down. They are there when we need them. They are our partners.[14]

Value Analysis. Many organizations evaluate their suppliers by a formal value analysis and/or a vendor analysis. *Value analysis*, developed by General Electric as a basis for cost reduction, is a detailed analysis of a product. It focuses on the relative cost of providing a necessary function or service at the desired time and place with the necessary quality. Value analysis focuses on total cost, not just invoice cost. For repetitively purchased items, possession costs (i.e., costs related to holding inventory) and acquisition costs (e.g., costs associated with originating requisitions, interviewing salespeople, expediting deliveries, receiving and editing invoices, following up on inaccurate and late deliveries) usually far exceed the price on the invoice that the customer pays for the product.

Vendor Analysis. *Vendor analysis* is similar to value analysis but focuses on the vendor by looking at such items as delivery reliability, price, service, and technical competence. In addition to reporting a supplier's product quality, delivery, and cost competitiveness, Deere & Company also measures something it calls "wavelength." Wavelength measures such values as attitude, responsiveness, and follow-up on details. Deere feels that such information is usually not communicated, but is important in today's tough markets.[15]

The greater importance of the implementation and evaluation stage of the purchasing process has key implications for the sales process. A broader perspective is needed with multiple goals: short-term goals, such as winning the sale and ensuring that the value the customer is expecting is actually delivered; and long-term goals, such as creating new value delivery opportunities and positioning yourself and your company's capabilities to enlarge the customer relationship. This duality is inherent in most consultative- and enterprise-type customer relationships.

One last thought regarding the purchasing process: Knowing and understanding the purchasing process is necessary, not just a identifying where you are in the process and pushing it along toward the sale. The most important part of understanding the purchasing process is to enhance the quality of this process. In the absence of a quality purchasing process, the purchase decision will degenerate to the lowest common denominator, price.

Supplier Tiers

Increasingly, companies today are borrowing a page from marketing when working with their supplier base. They are segmenting their supplier base according to the importance of the supplier's product and the difficulty of finding alternative sources for the product. Recognizing that groups of suppliers should be treated differently, customers are starting to place their various supplier relationships into separate *supplier tiers*. This practice is illustrated in Figure 4-3. Organizations are explicitly recognizing that some suppliers are much more important than others to their success. This being the case, it is in the organization's best interest to establish special relationships with these suppliers. On the other hand, there are many products and services that make little difference in the quality of the organization's offering and for which there are many qualified suppliers. In this case, controlling procurement costs and maintaining a reliable source of supplies take priority. Depending

Tier	Type of Supplier	Nature of the Relationship
A	In-Supplier	• Traditional arms-length relationship • Individual level relationship dominates • Standardized, nonstrategic products
B	Preferred	• Relationship focus on products • High level of familiarity • High level of trust
C	Extended	• A bundle of products • Several collaborative processes, e.g., product design, inventory management • Supplier is viewed as best in class
D	Partner	• Supplier is viewed as key to customer's competitive position • Business relationship is rarely challenged • Some degree of exclusivity

FIGURE 4-3 Tiers of Suppliers

on which tier the supplier is in, the relationship and the purchasing process will be quite different. Note also that the tiering of suppliers is the mirror image of a supplier's account relationship strategy.

Selling in each type of customer relationship requires a high degree of customer intimacy—knowing the customer's problems and priorities, expectations, needs, and culture.[16] Similarly, it is important that salespeople know who within the customer's organization is involved in the purchasing decision and understand this person's role in the process. This consideration is particularly important in complex sales situations. *Complex sales situations* are those in which several people in the customer's organization must give their approval before the sale can take place. Complex sales situations refer to the structure of the purchase decision, not a particular product or its price. Consider selling basketballs, for example. The salesperson selling a dozen basketballs to Mr. Jones, owner of the local sporting goods store, is making a simple sale. But the salesperson selling a hundred gross of basketballs to Wal-Mart is probably involved in a complex sale because making the sale will require not just one approval, but several, especially if this is a new line of basketballs. The added complexity of selling to more than one person in an organization and a framework for doing so are discussed in the next section.

BUYING CENTER

The term *buying center* refers to all of the people formally or informally involved in the purchasing decision—that is, all the people who must say yes for a sale to occur or influence the people who will ultimately say yes or no to the purchase. The buying center changes over time and is not a formal department in the organization. The number of people included in the buying center may vary, depending on a number of factors, including how many departments use the item, the dollar value of the purchase, and the product's degree of technical sophistication. Furthermore, each of these people is likely to have different concerns depending on his or her level in the organization. For instance, if I'm selling manufacturing equipment, one of the symptoms of a problem associated with overused equipment is leaking oil. The significance of the oil on the floor changes as we move up the command hierarchy. To the machine operator we might be talking about oil on the floor, but to the CEO we would need to translate the impact of overused equipment and leaking oil on Earnings per Share (EPS). See Figure 4-4 for how the performance indicator in this selling situation might change as I move up the customer's hierarchy.

A *purchasing role* refers to the set of issues or concerns that a member of the buying center will consider when deciding whether to approve or recommend either a purchase or a specific supplier. For purposes of clarification and simplification, these concerns may

Level	Need Indicator
CEO	EPS
CFO	ROI, EBITDA
VP Operations	Cost of Goods Sold
Plant Manager	Machine Availability
Maintenance Manager	Maintenance Expense
Machine Operator	Oil on the Floor

FIGURE 4-4 Impact of Oil on the Floor

be grouped into one of three purchasing roles: economic buyers, user buyers, and technical buyers. An individual buying center member may occupy multiple purchasing roles, but each purchasing role is expected to be held by at least one individual in any major purchasing situation.[17] A fourth person must also be present for the sale to be successfully concluded; this person is referred to as an advocate.

Economic Buyer

An *economic buyer* is the person or committee with the power to give final approval to buy your product or service. These people have the money to make a purchase and are able to release the cash to buy should they choose to do so. The focus of the economic buyer is not exclusively on price or technology but is also on performance; that is, what will the organization get in return for spending this money?

The economic buyer's role in the sale is unique, in that this is the person who:

- Establishes the priority of projects
- Is concerned about the economic health of the business
- Focuses on the future
- Asks "Why?"
- Can say "yes" even if everyone else says "no"
- Can also say "no" when everyone else says "yes"[18]

Obviously, this buyer must be identified in each sale. Although these people are rarely very far down the organizational ladder, their exact organizational position will depend on a number of factors. The economic buyer is likely to be farther up the organizational ladder in the following situations:

- The more expensive the product
- The more depressed the organization's business condition
- The less experience the customer has with you, your firm, and the product
- The greater the potential impact a wrong purchase decision will have on the organization

Consider the situation the telecommunications industry faces as a result of movement to distributed data processing and networked computer systems. Many companies now view telecommunications as a strategic asset rather than as just "utilities." This has far-reaching implications for sales and marketing in the industry. "In the last three years," says a vice president of operations at AT&T, "we have changed from selling to purchasing agents and dealing with only the communications managers. We have expanded our horizons to where we must gain acceptance with people in the customer organization who are policy makers." This change in focus has necessitated many changes in AT&T's sales practices. For instance, the RBOCs' sales force training has been beefed up to place more emphasis on strategic business decision making in addition to the usual technical training of salespeople.

User Buyer

The role of *user buyers* is to determine the impact of the purchase on the job that they or their people perform. Their focus is much narrower than that of the economic buyer because they are concerned primarily with their own operating areas or departments. Users typically:

- Are personnel whose daily work will be affected by your product or service
- Are implementation oriented
- Take a tactical view versus a strategic one
- Focus on the past and present rather than the future, except to ask, "How will this affect me?"

In general, users want to know how your solution will affect them, but they likely will not be concerned about how the solution affects their company. Nonetheless, users may represent a very powerful buying influence and one that is important for the seller to identify. This point is made quite well in the now-famous story of 3M's Post-It notes. Initial efforts to sell the stick-on notes to office managers met with little success. It wasn't until 3M gave secretaries and office workers free samples that the notes took off.

Technical Buying Influence

The role of *technical buyers* is to act as "gatekeepers" by screening out products and suppliers that do not meet the needs of the buying organization. Their function is to narrow down the choices to those alternatives that are most likely to fulfill particular organizational objectives. These people can have a powerful influence on the final decision, but by themselves they can't say yes, only no.

These buyers are called technical buyers because they focus on the quantifiable aspects of the product or service as they relate to the product's specifications. A number of people may perform this function, including engineers, legal counsel, and purchasing agents.

In summary, a technical buying influence may:

- Be able to say "no," but needs to get approval before saying "yes"
- Be able to recommend
- Be a key influencer to the decision maker
- Be concerned about product specs and financials
- Be focused on the present
- Ask "What?" and not "Why?"

Advocate

In a complex selling situation involving multiple buying influences, it has been suggested that salespeople need to develop a special relationship with a buying influence referred to as an *advocate*. The role of the advocate is to help guide you in the sale by providing critical information about the organization and the people involved in the purchase decision. These people may be internal or external to the buying organization. They do not necessarily make the sale or make referrals, but they are willing to provide key information about those who influence the sale. They are often able to sell for you when you cannot be there, for example, during purchasing committee meetings. Their motivation for providing this information is that they are convinced that your product is best for the organization, and therefore they have a personal interest in seeing that you get the sale. Some ways in which the advocate may win include the following:

- **Personal.** Wants you to win because he or she knows you, likes you, and wants to see you be successful.
- **Professional.** Wins by doing his or her job better, achieving goals, and helping the companies meet objectives.
- **Recognition.** Wins by receiving recognition from his or her own organization.
- **Negative.** Really wants someone else to lose.[19]

Now that we've discussed why an advocate would want to help you, let's talk about what an advocate can do for you. A good idea of the role of an advocate is captured in this statement from a chief information officer at a health care facility when talking about the help a supplier needs to be successful:

> The customer needs to understand his or her own political landscape and help set a path for the vendor to navigate it. The vendor, on his or her part, needs to participate in the navigation of

this landscape, but needs to be very conscious of when to use the white-gloves, handle-with-care approach and when to use the throttle-ahead approach."[20]

Notice that the advocate and the seller must work together. The advocate does not take over the selling role of the vendor salesperson.

Some, but not all, of the ways that advocates can help include:

- **Recommending selling strategies.** They may clarify key organizational issues, the priority areas of interest for each of the buying influencers, identify the key decision maker, etc.
- **Build a groundswell of interest.** They can encourage discussion among the decision influencers.
- **Refer you to other advocates.** They can identify other people who may be interested in your succeeding in the sale.
- **Review your presentation.** They can ensure you are using the right terms, picking up the subtleties, and prioritizing the right areas, for example.
- **Gain access to decision makers.** They can get you access to the executive suite.

An advocate is obviously critical and must be selected and developed with care. Others in the buying center must feel that the person is trustworthy and competent. Ideally, others will recognize the advocate in the buying center as a group leader and major influence. One way to identify a good advocate, in fact, is to listen for the name of a person whom others in the buying center mention frequently. A strong advocate may be important to the seller's long-term success because people are less likely to change after having established a publicly stated position.

To test your practical understanding of the buying center concept and the perspectives of different people in the center, see the Team Exercise "Different Strokes." How would you suggest addressing each of these people's concerns?

TEAM EXERCISE
"Different Strokes"

You are a salesperson for Midmark Medical, a health care company specializing in developing and marketing products for hospital operating and postoperative recovery rooms. Your company has developed a new product designed to address the postoperative hypothermia that medical research indicates occurs in 60 to 80 percent of patients after surgery. The product consists of a blower that injects air into a very thin, plastic-like blanket. Using nanotechnology, the blanket is able to hold the air inside the blanket and does not allow outside air to penetrate the blanket so that it retains its heat for up to 2 hours.

Today the most commonly used treatment for postoperative hypothermia is warmed hospital blankets. Six to eight heated blankets are placed in succession on top of the patient. Almost all patients require more than one application. The advantage of warmed blankets is that they are simple, safe, and relatively inexpensive compared to your new product. The main disadvantage is that they cool quickly, provide only insulation, and require the patient's own body heat for regenerating warmth.

In preparing to sell this product to the hospitals in your territory, you quickly realize that there are at least three groups of people who are likely to get involved in purchase decision: the operating nurses and especially the chief operating nurse, operating physicians, and hospital administrators. Develop a game plan to address the needs and concerns that each group is likely to have with this new product. Be prepared to role play the interaction with one or more of these people.

EVOLUTION OF RELATIONSHIPS

Most marketers would like to establish a long-term relationship with their customers to ensure a stream of purchases and an upgrading of the equipment a client purchases over time. Many companies are emphasizing to their salespeople the importance of understanding how to build and enhance professional relationships at all levels in the organization.[21] It is helpful in this regard to understand how relationships are likely to evolve over time. According to research in social psychology, growing relationships evolve through five general stages: (1) awareness, (2) exploration, (3) expansion, (4) commitment, and (5) dissolution.[22] Although it may be difficult to determine exactly when a relationship progresses to each stage, each represents a major shift in the nature of the relationship. Consequently, salespeople should be aware of these changes and proceed accordingly. These five stages of *relationship evolution* and the objectives associated with each stage are summarized in Figure 4-5.

All relationships are dynamic, however, not linear in fashion. That is, there is often a recycling through the different general stages shown in Figure 4-5. Recall the Satyam-Caterpillar vignette at the beginning of this chapter. This relationship had already reached a level of commitment, when both parties began exploring new opportunities to create customer value. Exploration in this case led to a higher level of commitment between Satyam and Caterpillar.

Though somewhat unusual, dissolution of a customer relationship may also lead to a stronger relationship commitment. Consider the experience of one large North American petrochemical supplier, when an Asian competitor offering lower prices threatened its market. The supplier, in a carefully calculated move, let go of three of its largest, but most unprofitable customers. The supplier understood what was fundamentally important to its customers as well as the weaknesses of its new competitor. Two of the three defecting customers came back to the supplier after just two months of coping with the competitor's poor logistics and even poorer product quality. Indeed, they accepted higher net prices and longer, guaranteed-volume deals.[23]

Relationship Stage	Description	Key Selling Objectives
Awareness	Recognition that a supplier may be able to satisfy an important need	• Gain customer's attention • Allow customer trial of product/service
Exploration	Tentative initial trial with limited commitments by both parties	• Gain initial acceptance • Build a successful relationship
Expansion	Greater rewards for both parties in the relationship	• Increase customer knowledge • Broaden customer engagement
Commitment	Commitment by both the buyer and seller to an exclusive relationship	• Establish multiple relationships between both firms' hierarchies • Provide early involvement in new product development process • Focus on long-term relationship
Dissolution	Total disengagement from the relationship	• Look for warning signals • Reinitiate the relationship

FIGURE 4-5 Stages in a Buyer-Seller Relationship

RELATIONSHIP BINDERS

Certain factors, called *relationship binders*, drive parties, whether individuals or organizations, to progress to a fully committed relationship. Salespeople should be aware of these factors. This section reviews three important underlying factors necessary for a fully developed relationship, which every salesperson and marketer should know and understand—creating value, meeting expectations, and building trust.[24]

Creating Value

Value refers to the perception that the rewards exceed the costs associated with establishing and/or expanding a relationship. Value to a buyer is not always the lowest list price. It may involve the opportunity to save time and labor, or it may result in higher sales of the customer's products. Value must ultimately reach the customer's customers in the form of better quality or less expensive products, wider choices, and/or quicker access to those choices.

Figure 4-6 illustrates the implications of a supplier's account relationship strategy for how the sales force creates customer value during each phase of the purchasing process. In transactional relationships, the opportunities for creating customer value are highest during the final two phases of the purchase process. Making purchasing easy and hassle-free and preventing post-sale headaches are important opportunities for creating customer value in transactional relationships. Consultative customer relationships create customer value by creatively helping customers solve problems and identify growth opportunities during the first two phases of the purchasing process. Consider Motorola, Inc.'s approach to selling customized pagers. Motorola's pager sales force will use the customer's own specifications to design a pager system perfectly suited to the customer's needs. The specs, put together on a laptop computer by the Motorola sales rep, are sent via modem to the company's factory. This individualized product development, however, requires a considerable investment of time and effort during the needs and evaluation of alternatives phase of the purchasing process. The intent of enterprise relationships, on the other hand, is to create exceptional customer value during all four phases of the purchasing process.

Meeting Expectations

In any relationship, the involved parties develop *expectations*, sometimes referred to as rules or norms, with respect to acceptable conduct and performance. Acceptable behavior varies by individual preferences, company policies, and national cultures.

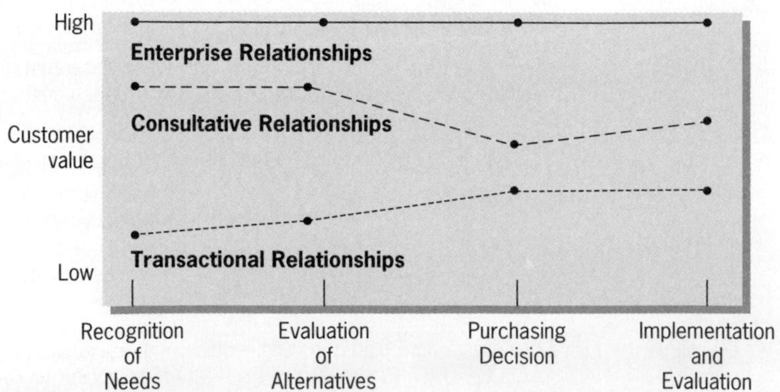

FIGURE 4-6 Customer Value Creation in the Purchasing Process

In some enterprise-type relationships, buyers and sellers derive a mutually agreed-upon set of team values. These values are sometimes put in writing in order to remind all members that these are the accepted standards of conduct of the relationship to which every individual must subscribe. Each may agree, for instance, to be the advocate for the other partner within his or her own company. It is especially important to ensure that new members to the team are aware of and comply with these values.

Salespeople must be careful not to encourage unfavorable buyer expectations as a result of present behaviors. If a salesperson agrees to a special price discount at the buyer's request, for example, the buyer may think this is standard practice and expect some sort of discounting in the future. Because of this behavior, many companies (e.g., IBM and Procter & Gamble) do not give their salespeople the flexibility to discount prices. For an excellent example of an expectations-management issue, see the Team Exercise "A Favor." What would you do in this situation?

TEAM EXERCISE
"A Favor"

Major Contracting has always been one of your biggest accounts—until last year. A downturn in the local economy slowed both construction and renovation projects. As a result, Major Contracting reorganized its management team, including hiring a new CFO. The result? The company has been slow paying its bills for the past six months.

As is customary, your company hired a collection agency to obtain late payments. The agency is now threatening to create credit-rating problems for your account if it doesn't pay within a week. You receive a call from your contact at Major, a friend of fifteen years, pleading with you to intercede on his behalf and promising to be back on track with bill payments. He tells you that Major has bids on a few big projects that should stabilize it financially within the month.

You are now in an awkward position. You know that not all of these projects are firm, so Major may not be able to settle its debt in that time. You want to help your friend, but you also realize that you have a responsibility to your company and yourself—your compensation is based in part on the profitability of your territory. On the other hand, you do not want to risk losing the account and the sales that would come from these projects if they do come through. Do you try to get Major the month it needs to get back on its feet? Do you claim it is out of your hands—which to some degree it is? Is there a better solution?

Expectations also develop with respect to performance. Customer performance expectations include the performance of the product, as well as a number of service activities such as frequency of sales calls, notification of price changes, lead time in delivery, order fill rate, emergency orders, and installation. Studies comparing the performance perceptions of salespeople and buyers in a wide variety of industries show that there is considerable inaccuracy in salespeople's perceptions of buyers' performance expectations. Furthermore, accuracy in identifying the buyer's performance rules is related to high sales performance. Interestingly, the more experienced salespeople are at times less accurate in their buyer performance expectations than younger salespeople.

To encourage accuracy in customer assessment, some companies require their salespeople to provide a yearly written assessment of their key customers. This assessment process involves answering a series of questions. Writing the answers helps to identify key assumptions, inconsistencies, and missing information. Figure 4-7 lists the type of questions that should be answered about an account. The extent of the detail, depth, and complexity of the

Type of Intelligence	Typical Questions to be Answered
Market	• What markets do they serve? • Who are their major competitors?
Financial	• When does annual capital budgeting process begin and end? • What hurdle rate is required to win approval? • What is the projected capital spending for the year?
Organizational	• What are the top business objectives each relevant department manager is expected to achieve in the current year?
Operational	• What are the specific measures of performance for your products or services?
Personnel	• Who are the people having a direct or indirect influence on buying decisions for your products? • What are their formal responsibilities? • What is your relationship with each person?
Competitive	• Which of your competitors are doing business with the account? • What is the account share of each competitor? • Which ones are likely to gain share?

FIGURE 4-7 Account Intelligence

questions will vary according to the type of relationship, that is, transactional, consultative, or enterprise. The objective is to have superior customer intelligence, which means having better information than any competitor has about the account.

Building Trust

Trust refers to the opinion that an individual's word or promise can be believed and that the long-term interests of the customer will be served. Trust in salespeople and their companies is essential to buyers' evaluation of the quality of a relationship and to establishing working partnerships. Indeed, customer surveys often find that it is difficult for customers to distinguish between their feelings toward the supplier and the salesperson.[25] Customer trust in the supplier's salesperson is particularly important in growing the customer-supplier relationship past the exploration phase.[26]

Trust takes time to develop and research indicates that a salesperson's length of experience with an account is important to partnering with customers and to the profitability of customer partner relationships.[27] How does a salesperson earn a buyer's trust? Studies of buyers and sellers have shown that salespeople whom buyers trust possess the following five attributes:

- **Honesty.** Salespeople who tell the truth.
- **Competence.** Salespeople who know what they are talking about.
- **Dependability.** Salespeople who follow through on their promises.
- **Customer orientation.** Salespeople who put buyers' interest ahead of their own.
- **Likability.** Salespeople whom the buyer enjoys knowing.[28]

Studies of buyer's perceptions of salespeople's trustworthiness also indicate that the importance of each of these dimensions to buyers' overall feelings of trust varies according to the stage of the purchasing relationship. Early in the relationship the company's and salesperson's reputation for competence is dominant. As the buyer gains experience with

Relationship Binder	Transactional Relationship	Consultative Relationship	Enterprise Relationship
Create value	A good product that can be conveniently purchased.	A solution to an important problem.	Increase the shareholder value of the organization.
Meet Expectations	Buyer has a clear set of expectations as to the conduct of the relationship.	Buyer knows a problem exists, but is unsure of the solution or what will be involved in addressing the problem.	Buyer's expectations are strategic in nature, though the process for achieving strategic objectives may not be know.
Build Trust	A supplier will do what has been promised.	A supplier will do what is necessary to solve the problem.	A supplier will do everything possible to increase the buyer's competitive advantage in the marketplace.

FIGURE 4-8 Relationship Binders and Account Relationship Strategy

the seller and the particular salesperson, dependability becomes more important. In a fully committed stage of the relationship, customer orientation is most important to the feelings of buyer trust. Honesty and likability are important during all phases of the purchasing relationship.[29]

Trust building is not entirely a matter of being liked, however. There is also evidence that people place greater trust in those whom they feel have good listening skills.[30] Fortunately, good listening skills can be developed by focusing on and not interrupting the speaker, paraphrasing questions, answering at the appropriate time, and using complete sentences instead of saying simply yes or no.

These three relationship binders—creating value, meeting expectations, and building trust—are needed to build lasting relationships with customers. How these relationship binders are achieved, the activities involved, and the skills needed to enhance them will differ depending on the account relationship strategy involved. Figure 4-8 summarizes the differences in each relationship binder according to the three types of account relationship strategies.

SUMMARY

Increasingly, a company's profitability and growth depend on establishing good relationships with the right customers and managing each relationship so as to deliver value to the customer. Skills and concepts important to the successful management of account relationships were discussed in this chapter.

1. **Describe the steps in the professional purchasing process.** We have described four basic steps in the typical purchasing process: recognition of needs, evaluation of options, the purchase decision, and implementation and evaluation of performance. The sales force has the opportunity to create customer value during each of these steps. However, the level of customer value created is likely to depend on the type of buyer-supplier relationship—transactional, consultative, or enterprise.
2. **Identify the different buying influences in the buying center.** A number of people are likely to be involved in most organizational purchasing decisions. These people are collectively referred to as the buying center. It is important that salespeople identify all those involved in the process, as well as the nature of their involvement. Regardless of functional area or level in the organization, people in the buying center will assume one of three roles: economic buyer, technical buyer, or user buyer. In addition, salespeople should choose and cultivate an advocate in the buying center.

3. **Explain how relationships are likely to evolve.** Growing relationships evolve through five general stages: (1) awareness, (2) exploration, (3) expansion, (4) commitment, and (5) dissolution. Because each stage represents a major shift in the nature of the relationship, salespeople should be aware of these changes and proceed accordingly.
4. **Describe factors critical to gaining commitment to a relationship.** Certain factors are important to gaining increasing levels of commitment in relationships. We have reviewed three important factors necessary for a fully developed and productive relationship: creating value, meeting expectations, and building trust. Each factor has been described within a professional account relationship situation, and the means by which to identify and enhance these factors have been described.

KEY TERMS

Accounts
Advocate
Buying center
Complex sales situations
Derived demand
Economic buyer
Expectations
Extranets
Modified rebuy
New buy
Purchasing role
Relationship binders
Relationship evolution
Request for proposal (RFP)
Sales proposal
Straight rebuy
Supplier tiers
Technical buyer
Trust
User buyer
Value
Value analysis
Vendor analysis

DEVELOPING YOUR COMPETENCIES

1. **Technology.** A recent study in the U.S. plastics industry sheds some light on the use of the Internet between suppliers and processors of resin suppliers. Overall, 20 percent of firms were communicating with their suppliers and customers via the Internet. It was also found that contrary to much of the advertising on business Internet use, larger firms are more likely to use the technology than small firms.

   One particularly insightful part of this study was devoted to the content of Internet communications between buying firms and suppliers. Buyers were asked how frequently they personally engaged in communication with resin suppliers via the Internet on each of the following ten factors:

   1. Placing an order
   2. Checking on order/shipping status
   3. Checking on inventory status
   4. Requesting price quotations
   5. Submitting bid requests
   6. Resolving problems/conflicts
   7. Seeing catalog of products
   8. Gaining general information
   9. Receiving technical advice
   10. Sending product specifications

   Responses were in the form of a 5-point scale, with the extremes being never = 1 and very frequently = 5. How frequently do you think the Internet is being used for each of these ten communication reasons? Why do you think the Internet would be especially valuable for the uses you have specified?

2. **Strategic Action.** National Logistics, Inc., provides trucking services to large customers. It has an excellent reputation for reliable scheduling and careful handling. With decreasing regulation, NLI's management decided that they needed more of a marketing orientation. They wanted to build and maintain long-lasting, profitable relationships with their customers. NLI invested time and effort to study customers' shipping needs and were especially effective at helping customers plan for their needs. After two years, NLI's managers were very disappointed with the results. Customers were pleased with the new marketing approach and frequently complimented NLI, but sales were down. Low-cost competitors were particularly bothersome. What went wrong? Why didn't customers want to commit to long-term relationships?
3. **Self-Management.** U.S. business firms and the purchasing managers continue to stress the importance of ethics in purchasing activities. Although such "perks" as the business lunch are common business practice, there is increasing concern about the ethics of such things as free tickets to sporting events and shows. In contrast to the United States, the purchasing function in Mexico is at a relatively early stage in its development as a profession. No professional organization of purchasing agents exists, and the agents are often viewed as necessary evils within their own organizations. Given this discrepancy in their professional development, U.S. and Mexican purchasing agents are likely to disagree on the ethics of particular practices. From the following list of five ethical dilemmas, on which do you think purchasing agents from Mexico and the United States are likely to differ? How would they differ and why?

   1. Accepting free trips from salespeople is okay.
   2. Accepting free entertainment from salespeople is okay.
   3. Making exaggerated statements to a supplier in order to gain a concession is acceptable.
   4. Giving preferential treatment to suppliers who happen to be good customers is sound business practice.
   5. Obtaining information about competitors by asking suppliers for that information is acceptable.

4. **Coaching.** Building successful, long-term customer relationships is a specialty of WESCO International, Inc., the second largest distributor of electrical equipment in the United States. WESCO warehouses and supplies more than a million different products, including fuses, connectors, tools, tape, circuit breakers, transformers, lightbulbs, and data communications products. Customers include manufacturers, contractors, utility companies, and government agencies. WESCO's sales strategy is to profitably expand its relationship with key customers. To get an idea of how it accomplishes this goal, consider the following description of how it established a partnership with an industrial customer in the paper business.

   > Even though we had done relatively little business with this customer before, their headquarters people asked us to compete for their business in November of 1997. We distributed questionnaires to develop details of programs to reduce the customer's inventory and energy costs. We determined that we could serve all but three of their plants. We secured the account in June 1998 after making presentations to their selection committee.
   >
   > As soon as the agreement was signed, we formed an account team and held a national rollout meeting to begin implementation. During the next few months, we moved toward compliance at each customer plant, agreeing to hold monthly meetings to address customer concerns at the customer's various mill sites. As planned, we acquired two distributor branches and opened one new branch. We conducted a complete energy audit and recommended more energy-efficient systems for all their plants. We also reduced inventory and implemented an EDI (Electronic Data Interchange) ordering system.

> By June 1999, the intensive implementation phase was over. Sales had increased tenfold from the year before, reaching $1 million per month. Between transaction cost reductions, energy savings, and inventory reduction, WESCO was able to document over 20 percent cost savings to the customer. This was far more than the customer had expected.

From this description of a successful business expansion effort, what do you think are the keys to successful business expansion? What are the pitfalls? For more on WESCO, see www.wesco.com.

5. **Team Building.** Opportunities to expand sales to customers often result from signing agreements at a customer's headquarters to cover all their product and service needs, similar to the WESCO agreement discussed in the previous question. Implementation of these headquarters-initiated agreements depends on local service and compliance. This is where real teamwork is needed. In the agreement discussed in the previous quote, one of the customer plants, which generated only $50,000 per year in sales, was located 2 hours away from the WESCO branch and demanded semimonthly sales calls. The salesperson responsible for calling on this plant is paid a combination of fixed salary and commissions on sales volume. He offered a blunt opinion on the situation:

> They may be a good customer for WESCO, but from where I stand, they demand a lot of service that is not commensurate with their sales volume—either current or potential. Unless I am ordered to do it, I wouldn't call on this customer, even without the long drive they require. The opportunity costs of serving these customers are way too high. I would rather spend my time selling to other local customers who value my services and from whom I make greater commissions.

If you were this salesperson's branch manager, what would you say to him? If you were the national account manager for this customer, how would you get this salesperson on board the team? If you were the national sales manager for WESCO, what would be your reaction?

6. **Global Perspective.** In business after business, the physical product is no longer enough to create a sustainable competitive advantage. Increasingly, advantage relies on superior after-sale customer service. It has been generally agreed that customer expectations form the basis on which service satisfaction is determined. Expectations are formed from previous experiences and promises made or implied, and are cultural in nature. This presents special problems and requires careful attention from companies competing globally.

To better understand this point, consider the experience of a large Swedish company with nearly fifty years' experience selling engineered industrial products to more than fifty countries. After-sales services such as installation, training, routine maintenance, emergency repair, parts supply, and software services are responsible for about 25 percent of this firm's total revenues and are growing more rapidly than overall product sales. In describing their customers' service expectations across the globe, marketing managers at the Swedish company made the following statements:

- "They want instant service and they want it for free."
- "They are very willing to pay in advance for after-sales services in the form of service contracts."
- "After-sales service was accepted as part of the cost of doing business, but not so well accepted that prepayment on a contract basis could be expected."

Match the service expectation statement with what you think is the appropriate world location: the Far East, Europe, and United States/North America. Be prepared to give the reasons for your choices.

EXPERIENTIAL EXERCISE

1. Make an appointment to interview an industrial purchasing agent. Ask the buyer to explain how parts, raw materials, or equipment are bought at his or her company. Prepare flow diagrams showing all the steps in the purchase process. Write a report comparing your diagrams with the model found in this chapter. Explain how a salesperson could make use of your charts.

FEATURED CASE

SHIELD FINANCIAL: "A CUSTOMER REQUEST"

All Doug Bloom could think was, "Why me?" Doug, sales manager for Shield in Des Moines, had just received the kind of phone call no manager wants—one that pits his salesperson against a customer. The call was from Stella Burns, the new HR manager for Stateline International, the fifth-largest account in the Des Moines area. Burns explained that, although she is happy with Shield's products and pricing, she is uncomfortable with Cathie Simon, the salesperson handling the Stateline account. She finds Simon too informal, too concerned about when they can meet for lunch, a glad-hander who talks far too much and wastes time. Burns asked Bloom to transfer the Stateline account to a salesperson with a more "professional" demeanor, who strictly discusses business problems and solutions. And she wants to meet with that new person in a week, at which time she'd like to discuss some new risk issues. Doug's knee-jerk reaction is that in such a situation he has to comply with an important customer's wishes. At least he knows which salesperson to give the account to: Ray Harley, who fits Burn's request perfectly. Ray has developed nicely and has also enthusiastically embraced the new programs Doug has introduced to the office. The problem is, how does he tell Cathie that he has to take her off her largest account?

Questions

1. Should Doug acquiesce to a customer's request to change salespeople?
2. What are the potential problems with moving Simon from this account?
3. Assuming you decided to move Simon, how would you present the move to her?
4. What alternatives besides moving Simon from the account should be considered?

CUSTOMER INTERACTION MANAGEMENT

> People are more apt to buy when they're talking than when you're talking!
>
> Robert Frost

Chapter Consultants:
S. Keith Hall, Area Manager, Anderson Chemical Company, Inc.
Neil Cronin, Regional Sales Manager, John Wiley & Sons, Inc.
William Evans, President, Evans & Associates

LEARNING OBJECTIVES

After studying this chapter, you should be able to:

- Describe the basic types of selling models.
- State the skills utilized in the preinteraction phase.
- List the skills involved in the interaction phase.
- Explain the skills involved in the postinteraction phase.

A THIRTY-MILLION-DOLLAR SALE

For quite some time, the largest sale in the software industry was the $39 million purchase of Oracle database software by Boeing Aircraft. The Oracle account executive was Jeff Simpson. When asked how he was able to make such a large sale, he shared the following story.

When Boeing Aircraft began the process of building the 777, it recognized that it could not build this aircraft the old way, which involved two-dimensional design systems residing on different machines that could not detect conflicts and interferences until all parts of the aircraft were brought together. This caused a great deal of reengineering to take place to make the pieces fit together. The result was not only delay and expense, but lower quality as well.

Moving to three-dimensional, computer-aided design techniques meant that interferences could be detected early and tolerances could be reduced so that the parts fit the first time they were brought together. The result would be a major saving in time and money. There was also the potential for a strategic benefit to Boeing's customers as well. If airplanes could be made to a high enough quality standard, then an exception might be made to the FAA rule that two-engine, two-pilot aircraft must be flown over land for two years before they could be flown overseas. Such an exception would save Boeing's customers, the airlines, millions of dollars by putting their expensive airplanes into overseas production earlier.

Simpson said, "We were not the strategic design team for the 777. However, we were an enabling technology that was uniquely qualified—because of our scalability of the database system—to build a new aircraft a new way, significantly reduce costs, and gain advantages for Boeing's customers.

"Once we built that value linkage, thirty million dollars was no longer a large number. That's a rounding error to Boeing. This is one part of one aircraft, and they're going to build thousands of them over the next few years. In addition, we became an integral part of the team and gained a measure of insider status."[1]

The Oracle-Boeing sale is indicative of the nature of most business-to-business sales that occur today. A deep understanding of the customer's problems and challenges is needed to drive the sale. Notice that it was also necessary for Oracle to understand the needs of its customer's customers, the airlines. Finally, it is important to note that the sale was not credited to Simpson's giving a great sales presentation or a compelling closing statement, but instead Oracle's ability to identify and meet Boeing's needs with a solution involving a new technology. A strategic customer need in this case resulted in a very large sale.

This chapter continues with our discussion of sales force activities by focusing on customer interactions—in other words, the activities that take place just prior to and following face-to-face customer interactions. While many of the skills involved in performing these activities have not fundamentally changed, some activities have altered due to adjustments in customer relationship strategies, competition, and technology. To help organize this discussion, we have divided the customer interaction process into three phases:

- **Preinteraction.** Actions that are initiated prior to interaction with key decision makers requiring skills in precall planning.
- **Interaction.** Actions initiated while interacting with decision makers, calling on skills in relating, discovery, advocating, handling objections, and closing.
- **Postinteraction.** Activities following a transaction involving supporting skills.

This chapter takes a skills-based approach to selling. The three phases of selling and the skills associated with each phase are specified in Figure 5-1. As we discuss each skill, we will point out its purpose, as well as strategies for achieving one's objectives. In many cases, common mistakes to be avoided are also highlighted. Throughout the discussion, company practices and viewpoints of sales executives have been included to facilitate your learning.

These steps are ordered in a logical sequence for discussion purposes; the actual process may backtrack to earlier phases many times before concluding in a sale. These phases are highly interrelated, in the sense that interaction with one person in an account may help in preparing for interacting with another person. Notice that these phases of the selling process mirror those of the purchasing process described in the previous chapter. This is by design because it is certainly true that the selling process must fit with the customer's purchasing process to be successful.

Basic to any sales force program is a management philosophy about how the selling process is best executed. Following are three types of selling approaches that management may advocate.

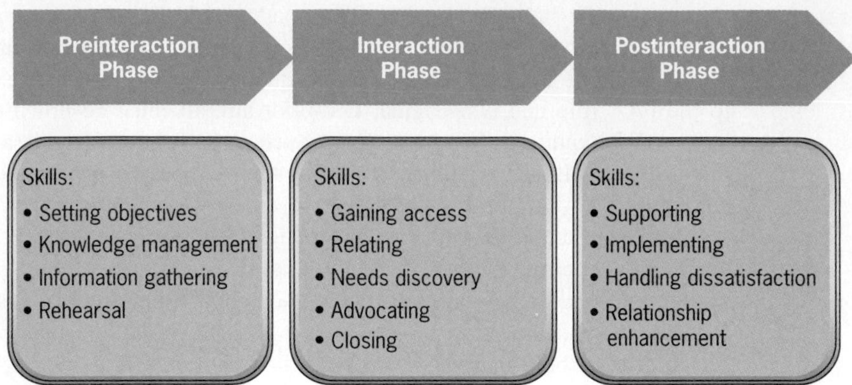

FIGURE 5-1 The Selling Process and Skills

BASIC TYPES OF SELLING MODELS

Sales consultants have devised numerous titles or labels for the selling approaches they teach, but most are based on variations of one of the following basic selling process models: standardized, need-satisfaction, and problem-solution. Each approach is appropriate in certain situations and for different types of account relationships.

Standardized Model

With a *standardized model*, a series of statements are constructed about an offering, so as to stimulate a positive response by the customer. This is often referred to as benefitizing an offering. Benefitizing means translating a product feature in a competitive advantage that is related to a customer benefit. The advantage of a new software package feature, for instance, may be the ease with which employees can learn to use it. The benefits may include fewer employee complaints, greater productivity, and cost savings. At an extreme, specific statements are developed using phrases that tend to elicit a positive response. These may include words such as "user-friendly," "satisfaction guaranteed," "productivity improvement," and "no money down." The sales presentation is highly structured and is often referred to as a *canned presentation* because the same basic presentation is given to each customer. Not much time and effort is put into preparing for any single customer interaction once the basic presentation has been mastered.

The standardized model is most appropriate in situations where a product is standardized or when the benefits are generally the same for all customers. In such a situation, the sales pitch can be studied and refined to such a degree that even voice tone can be studied for its impact on sales.[2] Recalling our discussion in Chapter 2 of different types of account relationships, we see that this type of selling approach would be most appropriate for transactional relationships where customers are concerned about lowest cost and convenience.

Need-Satisfaction Model

The *need-satisfaction model* is oriented to discovering and meeting customers' needs. With this selling model, a salesperson locates a prospective customer and makes some preliminary assumptions about the problems the customer is experiencing and the value his or her company could deliver relative to those problems. The salesperson discusses these assumptions with the customer and determines if the customer is willing to invest the time to prove or disprove the value assumption and discuss the ramifications and potential solutions. If the customer agrees to proceed with the process, the salesperson works with the customer to diagnose the situation in greater depth, determining the extent of the risks and their costs. If the costs or profits are judged to be significant enough, it's time to conduct an inquiry into potential solutions and determine their parameters, alternatives, and costs.

In a needs-satisfaction selling model, the salesperson's goals are (1) to quickly and accurately identify the customer with the highest probability of purchasing the offering; (2) to provide the customer with the incentive to change; (3) to provide the customer with the confidence to invest; and (4) to ensure that the value promises made are fulfilled.[3]

The general line sales forces of most consumer goods and office products companies are trained to use this selling model. Overall, the need-satisfaction type of selling approach is most appropriate for consultative-type customer relationships. Both the customer and the supplier are investing more time and resources in the relationship than is typical of transactional relationships.

Problem-Solution Model

A *problem-solution model* is similar to the need-satisfaction model in that both involve an analysis of each customer's circumstances. The primary difference is that a problem-solution selling process is based on more formal studies of the customer's operations. Instead of identifying the customer's needs on the first sales call, the early selling objective is to get the customer's permission to conduct a formal study. The sales rep or sales team will conduct the study and typically submit a written proposal based on the study. A formal presentation, perhaps by a team including a salesperson, management, and technical personnel, often accompanies the proposal.

This selling model usually involves significant dollar expenditures, and the selling cycle may be quite long. The types of products involved include computer systems, advertising campaigns, telecommunications systems, and information systems. The problem analysis study may be so involved that the customer may be asked to pay to have it performed. EDS's customers, for instance, may be asked to pay several hundred thousand dollars for a study of their computer systems to determine if EDS can help them. It is not unusual for clients to pay several advertising agencies to research and prepare a proposed ad campaign

Standardized Presentation Thinking	Problem-Solution Thinking
All prospects will buy.	Only certain customers will and should buy.
Never take "no" for an answer.	Always be leaving. Give the customer room to breathe.
A good salesperson can sell anything to anybody.	A good salesperson weeds out poor prospects and focuses on high-gain opportunities.
Never walk away when money is on the table.	Always walk away unless you know you can improve your customer's business.
The customer is always right.	The customer requires professional guidance to complete a quality decision.

FIGURE 5-2 Standardized versus Problem-Solution Thinking

before deciding which agency will be awarded the account. As is probably obvious from this description and the EDS example, a problem-solution selling approach is most appropriate for a consultative or enterprise type of relationship where there is a very high investment in the relationship by both the seller and client organizations.

Hopefully, the descriptions of these three selling models have helped you see the differences between the models. The standardized model is very traditional and close to the stereotype of salespeople. The needs-satisfaction and problem-solution models are much more professional and are less about presenting than about connecting. To understand the differences, see Figure 5-2, Standardized versus Problem-Solution Thinking.

The next section of this chapter presents the skills associated with each phase of the customer interaction. These skills are considered to be fundamental to all types of selling models and account relationships, but the level of skill development becomes greater as one moves toward problem-solving selling and enterprise relationships.

THE PREINTERACTION PHASE: PLANNING SKILLS

As the term *planning skills* implies, the *preinteraction phase* occurs when you collect your thoughts and organize your interaction strategy prior to meeting a customer face to face. Many experts believe that it is the preinteraction planning that differentiates the top performers from the average salespeople. This is when you develop an edge over your competition.

Setting Objectives: What Do I Want to Accomplish?

Many selling experts have stated simply that salespeople should not make a call unless they can specify an action that they want the client or prospect to take. The objective should not be vague, such as "to collect information" or "to build a good relationship." Here are some examples of good objectives:

- The client agrees to supply information on historical inventory levels.
- The client tells you who will be involved in the purchase decision.
- The client arranges for a meeting with the chief design engineer.
- The client agrees to a trial run on the system.

Note that each of these examples calls for the customer to take a specific action. Objectives should be stated in terms of client actions so that the salesperson will know whether the objectives have been met. Also, note that the first two objectives involve gathering information.

Knowledge Management: What Do I Know About the Customer?

Preinteraction planning is also a good opportunity to review individual, company, and industry information about clients and their companies. Basic information that may be useful to know about an individual includes exact spelling and pronunciation of her name, title, age, residence, education, buying authority, clubs and memberships, hobbies, and idiosyncrasies. The experience of a medical equipment salesperson illustrates the value of this information. The salesperson was finding it very difficult to persuade doctors at the hospital to allow him to make a presentation. The doctors were usually pressured for time while at the hospital and were concerned about their immediate patients. He found out that many of the doctors belonged to a health club near the hospital and that in this environment they were more relaxed and willing to listen to his sales pitch. He eventually became the top salesperson in his district—and an accomplished racquetball player.

Not only is personal information important, but you should also review what you know or do not know about the client's organization. Apparently, there is a lot of room for improvement in this area even in today's competitive selling environment. According to a recent survey conducted by PepperCom, a consulting firm in New York, 47 percent of salespeople admit to not having a clue about their customer's biggest concerns—in other words what keeps their customers awake at night.[4]

Information Gathering: Where Can I Find the Information?

When you know what information you need to make a successful sales call, you can usually identify a number of sources for obtaining the data. These sources include company records, salespeople, customer employees, published information, and observation. Observation of the prospect's business operations provides a wealth of information to the experienced salesperson. By observing a prospect's retail operations, for instance, a veteran consumer goods salesperson can tell a lot about a client's pricing strategy, merchandising strategy, vendor preferences, and deal proneness.

The Internet is a powerful source of information, ranging from customer information to industry information. Corporate Web sites are an excellent starting point, for they'll give a fairly accurate indication of how a company positions itself, and most contain press releases about changes within the organization. For instance, you can obtain information about industry trade associations and a list of companies in different industries at www.switchboard.com. Some of the leading U.S. business data vendors include Dun & Bradstreet, American Business Information, Database America, IMS, Trinet, R.L. Polk, TRW, Infobase, and Equifax.

Figure 5-3 shows the results of a study comparing the customer interaction techniques of very successful with less successful salespeople in the life insurance industry. One of the biggest differences between the two groups was that more successful salespeople devoted more attention to conducting background research on a prospect before contacting the prospect.

Rehearsal: What Am I Going to Say?

All salespeople should have at least some idea of how they will initially start an interaction, what questions they will ask, and what benefits they plan to present. Salespeople should

Successful Salespeople	Less Successful Salespeople
Research prospect background	Do little background research
Use referrals for prospecting	Use company-generated prospect lists
Open by asking questions	Open with a product statement
Use needs-satisfaction type presentation	Use standard presentation
Focus on customer needs	Focus on product benefits
Let prospect make purchase decision	Close by focusing on the most important customer objection

FIGURE 5-3 Successful versus Less Successful Salespoeple

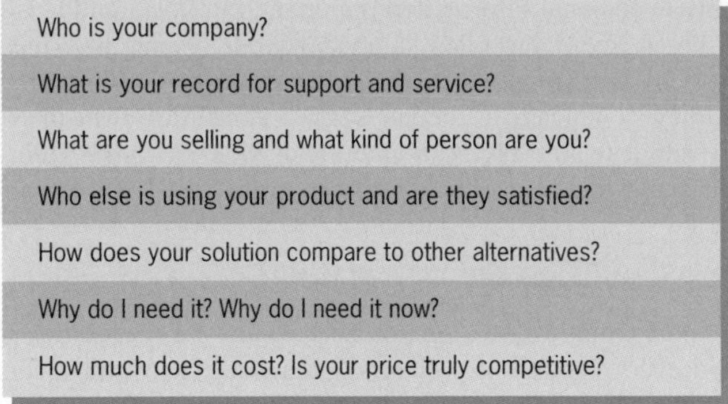

FIGURE 5-4 A Client's Questions

anticipate concerns a customer is likely to raise and should prepare strategies for addressing these concerns.

When preparing to call on clients, it is helpful to put yourself in their position. What would you want to know about your company and its products if you were the customer? If you are prepared to address such questions, you are probably ready for the interaction and have a much better chance of success. Recall from Figure 5-3 that successful people tend to use questions focused on the other person when beginning their interactions. Figure 5-4 shows some of the questions clients may have about you and your company when they have no prior experience with your company. Although these questions may be in the clients' mind, they are often not asked because they expect a good salesperson to address these questions without requiring them to be asked by the customer.

One other suggestion that has proven useful in a variety of situations is to visualize a successful sales encounter. This technique simply means creating a mental picture of the sequence of events that will lead to accomplishing your interaction objective. With practice, this exercise should help you to reduce your anxieties and increase your confidence.

THE INTERACTION PHASE

The *interaction phase* generally refers to what takes place during a face-to-face encounter with a customer. Our discussion of this phase of the selling process focuses on three skills that are important in all business and social interactions: relating, discovering, and advocating. In addition, there are two skills critical to successful selling in certain situations: gaining access and closing. Gaining access to key personnel is very important when calling on prospects (i.e., businesses that have never purchased from your company). Closing the sale is a necessary step in all selling situations but is most problematic during transactional selling and in some stimulus-response type of selling. We start with a discussion of gaining access.

Gaining Access

According to many experts, it is getting increasingly difficult to get "face time" with clients and will be even more so in the future. A study by McKinsey, for instance, found that pharmaceutical salespeople get an opportunity to speak with a physician in only one out of five office visits.[5] Following are four commonly used alternatives for gaining access to decision makers.

Direct Personal Contact. The most difficult approach is the direct personal contact without a prior attempt to communicate with the prospect. This approach is likely to create problems. For example, the person may be busy, so the salesperson must wait. The key is not to waste the time. Use this opportunity to learn more about the prospect from others in the organization, prepare for other scheduled calls, or complete necessary reports. A more difficult problem arises when the client has a negative reaction to being called on without an appointment. Many people do not like to meet with a salesperson who walks in without an appointment. Indeed, many clients simply will not see a salesperson without an appointment.

Phoning Ahead. Using the telephone to approach prospects has a number of advantages. Appointments make better use of the salesperson's time and reduce the hours spent in waiting rooms. Even prospects who are too busy to see anyone often will answer the phone and give salespeople a chance to introduce themselves and set up a future meeting. The major problem with a phone approach is that it is too easy for prospects or their administrative assistants to turn someone down over the telephone. Salespeople, therefore, must develop tactics to secure the cooperation of executive assistants and receptionists. Referring to the person by their first name when talking to the receptionist, for example, often helps to gain access because it implies familiarity with the person.

Personal Letters. Letters are more difficult than phone calls for administrative assistants to screen. In addition, letters allow the person to include brochures that describe the product assortment and benefits, enabling prospects to learn more about a potential supplier than they can over the phone. Approach letters should close by suggesting dates for a meeting. This may also be accomplished by a follow-up phone call. In doing so, the salesperson focuses the prospect's attention on the issue of when to meet rather than whether to meet.

E-mail Messages. An increasingly common method of communications, whether with new or existing clients, is to leave an e-mail message. A recent survey found that 52 percent of companies are using e-mail when prospecting for new customers, while 90 percent are using it for retention of existing customers.[6] E-mail messages have at least two advantages over voice messages. First, it is possible to send the message at very little cost in time or money to a large number of people to whom the same message is applicable. Second, graphics and detailed promotional material may be included with the message as an attachment to the main message. Many of the same guidelines that were mentioned with respect to leaving voice messages also apply to e-mail messages. In particular, the body of the message should be kept as short as possible. It is not unusual for busy executives to receive 80 to 100 e-mail messages a day, and deleting an e-mail message is easier and faster than erasing a voice message.

Referrals. When it comes to getting on a senior executive's calendar, having a referral is by far the most appropriate method. Surveys of senior executives indicate that most of them do not allow salespeople to call on them unless someone inside their company recommends them. In other words, you must first establish relationships with midlevel managers at most large accounts. At the same time, studies show that salespeople who do not gain executive access until late in the selling cycle find their impact to be greatly reduced.[7]

Relating Skills

In most social situations, both of the people meeting for the first time experience a degree of tension. Salespeople have long recognized *call reluctance*, or the fear of making contact with a customer, as a problem. It is estimated that call reluctance will reach intense levels for up to 40 percent of salespeople at some points in their careers.[8] Customers are also likely to feel a form of anxiety, referred to as *relationship anxiety* when meeting a salesperson.[9] This anxiety arises because people don't like to be sold; they like to buy.

In one sense, the role of the salesperson is to help the customer buy wisely. This calls for well-developed *relating skills*, that is, the ability to put the other person at ease in a potentially tense situation. The first few moments of the selling encounter are important because people formulate initial impressions at this time. Impressions of competence, honesty, and likeability all have an important impact on the ultimate outcome of the sales encounter.[10]

To help establish rapport, salespeople should be forthcoming about the purpose of the sales call. Many experts, for example, admonish salespeople to avoid asking, "How are you?" because this question is meaningless and contrary to what the salesperson should be, which is genuinely helpful and direct.[11] Given the time pressures everyone is under today, it is a good idea to first say "Thank you for your time," and then to hand the prospect a business card and introduce yourself. As a result, the prospect can both see and hear the sales-person's name. An introduction might go as follows: "Hello, Mr. Smith, I am Mary Johnson of the Hamilton Company, thank you for seeing me. I am here today to see if we can help you save money on your duplicating budget." Ms. Johnson identifies herself as well as the purpose of the visit and signals that she plans to focus on a possible customer benefit (lower costs). This should be closely followed by laying out an agenda for the meeting, which again relieves the client's anxiety about time. The key here is to quickly and smoothly transition to "Needs Discovery" questions. Continuing with our previous introduction, Mary might say something like, "I've worked with a number of companies who find that they have too much copier capacity, which drives up costs, or too little capacity, which leads to long wait times and less productive employees. Do you have a few moments to explore whether you are experiencing either of these symptoms?"

To better understand the impact of introductory statements on buyer perceptions read Team Exercise "What Does Ms Williams Hear?" How do you think she is interpreting this salesperson's introductory comments?

TEAM EXERCISE
"What Does Ms. Williams Hear?"

Consider the following introduction statement from a salesperson calling on Ms. Williams for the first time.

> "Hello, Ms. Williams, how are you today? My name is Joe James. I'm an account executive with Petro-Safety Technologies. We are a leader in oil rig safety solutions, and we have developed the most advanced safety programs in use by companies like yours. Our programs will improve your safety record and save lives. I would like to get together with you and explain some of the more successful programs that we have created and how they can make your business a better place to work."

The salesperson in this case is trying to create interest, but what does Ms. Williams hear and how does she interpret this call?

In many customer interactions, nonbusiness topics are often discussed initially in the selling process. The psychological foundation for this approach is to relieve tension, to suggest a commonality of perspective, and to limit any negative impact of observable differences between the parties. It is not always necessary, however, to engage in nonbusiness

Propriety	Show buyer respect; dress appropriately.
Competence	Know your product/service; third-party references.
Commonality	Have common interests, views, acquaintances.
Intent	Reveal purpose of call, process, and payoff to the buyer.

FIGURE 5-5 Means of Reducing Relationship Anxiety

bantering. The other person may be more interested in getting down to business, when the discussion is on an important issue and the customer wants to hear what a salesperson has to say.[12] The prospect may also respect the salesperson's time demands. Discussing nonbusiness issues may therefore be seen as a waste of time, and the person may then be judged as someone who cannot provide solutions to the client's business problems.[13]

Much more is involved in demonstrating relating skills than simply getting a dialogue started between you and the other person. Figure 5-5 discusses four strategies by which salespeople can reduce relationship tension. It is critical that salespeople utilize each of these means to reduce tension when meeting with a prospect. With established customers a relationship already exists; thus, many of the rules of the relationship are already set. However, salespeople should constantly strive to reinforce these impressions.[14] Perform the role plays described in Team Exercise "Relating Skills" to see how well you can relate in a sales situation.

TEAM EXERCISE
"Relating Skills"

Develop an opening sales statement as if you are a financial planner. Another team member should take the role of selling sales training services. Another should sell examination tables to physicians. You can select additional product and services so that each team member has a role. After each of you has developed an opening statement, give your opening presentation to the rest of the team members. Critique each statement according to the criteria for reducing client anxiety discussed in this chapter.

Needs Discovery Skills

After establishing initial rapport with the prospect, the salesperson should begin to understand what's on the prospect's mind rather than focusing discussion on the product and its benefits. This may seem counterintuitive, but it's true. See the results of a survey of the top five complaints customers have about salespeople in Figure 5-6. Notice that three of the top four have to do with lack of understanding of the customer's situation and needs.

Remember that customers do not buy products or services; they buy solutions that address their problems or enhance opportunities. Contractors do not want a bulldozer; they want dirt moved quickly and at low cost. Plant managers do not buy computer-controlled milling machines; they are interested in reduced setup time, closer tolerances, and fewer defects. Thus, the salesperson's job is to discover the true needs and then inform the prospect

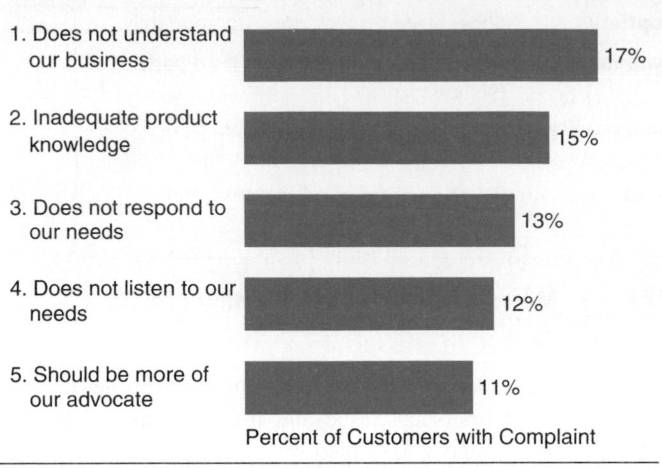

FIGURE 5-6 Top Five Customer Complaints About Salespeople

about the characteristics, capabilities, and availability of goods and services that can address these needs.[15]

Research has shown that there is a direct relationship between the number of needs a salesperson uncovers and selling success. A study by Xerox of more than 500 sales calls revealed that successful sales calls contained three times more identified needs than failed calls. As Larry MacGirr, vice president of sales for North America for CIBA Vision in Duluth, Georgia, says, "Once you get the need well defined and established in both of your minds, the next step is not to present, but to confirm the need. Once that's done, the presentation and close are actually pretty quick."[16]

In today's business environment, 80 percent of the selling process focuses on discovering and matching customer needs.[17] Indeed, this is one of the goals of enterprise relationships—that is, to become intimately knowledgeable about the customer's business, such as knowing the most important organizational opportunities, the customer's opportunities for improvement, and its barriers to change.[18] Achieving this degree of intimacy may go beyond the capabilities of one person, which is why many companies have implemented a team selling structure.

Identifying Motives. In selling to organizations, the situation is complicated because both task and personal motives influence the purchasing decision. *Task motives* can be defined as the logical, practical, or functional reasons for buying; they usually involve either money or productivity. Typical financial motives may include cost savings or profit increases. Productivity motives may focus on increasing output, increasing quality, or reducing effort. In the complex, large-ticket sale situation, it is absolutely critical to uncover the task motive behind the purchasing process. Just knowing the task motive, however, is not enough. This point is raised in the Team Exercise, "Why Beat A Dead Horse?"

The task motive is critical to the purchase decision, but reason that a decision is important today is tied to a personal motive. As shown in Figure 5-7, common personal motives are respect, approval, power, and recognition. It is for one or more of these reasons that people are willing to take on the professional risks associated with making a big purchase decision. Therefore, it is important to identify these personal motives as well as the task motives for a purchase decision.[19]

Many companies have problems getting close enough to the customer to make the necessary inferences concerning buying motives. Anderson Chemical Company, a manufacturer of specialty chemicals and related equipment, has experienced success in what it

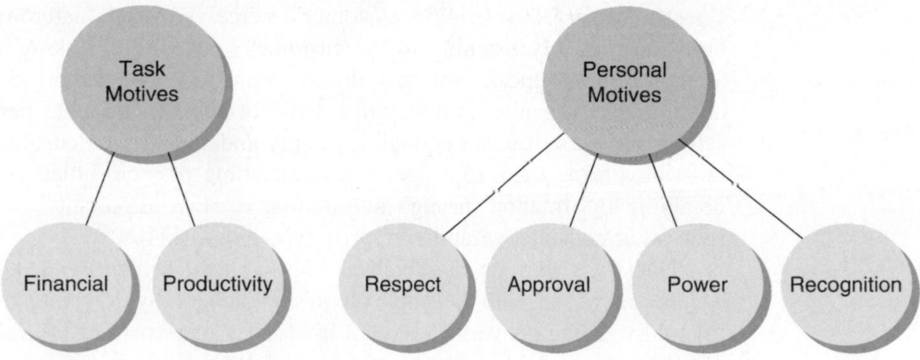

FIGURE 5-7 Types of Motives for Purchasing

TEAM EXERCISE
"Why Beat a Dead Horse?"

Many task motivation discussions lead to something like the following conversation. The salesperson asks, "That sounds as if it is impacting your business quite a lot. How much do you think this problem is costing you?"

"Well, it's hard to say," replies the customer, "but I know it's significant, and I know we need to do something about it. That's why we are talking to you."

End of conversation. The customer knows he's got a bad problem and can't live with the cost. The salesperson knows he can solve the problem and jumps in with both feet. What happens next? After a great presentation, the salesperson gets to the price and pushes the contract across the table.

"We can solve your problem within 90 days for $320,000. We just need you to sign this contract and we can get started on this immediately."

"What?" replies the customer while pushing the unsigned contract back, "No way could we spend that much money."

The salesperson, shocked at the apparent loss of a sure sale, responds, "You seemed quite sure that this was a big problem that had to be solved."

"We know we have a problem," replies the customer, "but it's not *that* big a problem."

What went wrong? Why did the customer retreat into the safer of the two alternatives, spend $320,000 or live with the current situation? What should the salesperson have done or what did he fail to do?

refers to as its Back-up Vendor program. To write a proposal or price quote on a prospect's business, Anderson needs to know the technical data about the plant. The facility engineers, however, must have confidence in Anderson or have other motives for supplying the data. This is where the Back-up Vendor program has worked well. Most prospects see no harm in allowing Anderson to come into their plant sites and perform surveys, tests, and such, and provide information to them free of charge. In effect, Anderson offers a second opinion about their operations. This is done very professionally and without "throwing rocks" at the current vendor. The prospect becomes more familiar with and confident in the Anderson representative over the six- to eighteen-month period the program is in effect. This is a large investment on Anderson's part, but Anderson estimates that its Back-up Vendor program has increased its success rate in converting prospects from 10 percent to approximately 60 percent.

Questioning. Discovering a customer's perceived needs naturally involves asking questions and actively listening to the customer's responses. Asking questions is not as easy as it may first appear. Not only do you want to know perceived needs, but you want to obtain the information in a way that does not alienate the other person. In a more complex selling situation, it is not enough to simply understand your customers and their issues, you must also bring them to a deeper understanding of their situation. Research indicates that obtaining information through questioning is most important in complex sales situations, such as in consultative and enterprise-type relationships.[20]

Questions may be classified as closed-ended or open-ended. *Closed-ended questions* can be answered with a simple "yes" or "no" or by selecting from a list of responses. "Would you like delivery Friday, or is Monday of next week all right?" These questions are often easy to answer and are used to gain feedback and commitment. *Open-ended questions* cannot be answered with a simple "yes" or "no" and are used to identify a topic. "How are the new tax laws affecting your decision regarding the purchase of fleet cars for your salespeople?" These questions are more likely to be used when discovering information about an opportunity.

In addition to closed- and open-ended questions, experts have identified several additional types of questions that may be used in the discovery process. These four types of questions have been found to be effective in discovering motivations, both personal and task focused. They are described in Figure 5-8 along with an example of each type of question.

Discovering a customer's needs usually requires a series of questions. This process generally begins with a permission question and open-ended questions, followed by fact-finding and feeling-finding questions and checking questions.

Advocating Skills

Following the discovery of customer needs, the skill that takes on critical significance is advocating. *Advocating skills* refer to the ability to clearly and fully present a solution that customers can see helps to address their needs. Although the ultimate goal may be to address the customer's needs, advocating is also an opportunity to demonstrate customer

Type of Question	Purpose	Example
Permission	A close-ended question asking the other person's permission to ask questions or probe further into a subject.	"May I ask you a few questions about your current shipping process?"
Fact-Finding	A question focusing on factual information about the business, person, or currect situation.	"Who is your current supplier of sutures? Do you have a JIT arrangement with Ethicon in supplying sutures?"
Feeling-Finding	An open-ended question that tries to uncover feelings about a situation and potential consequences of the situation.	"How do you feel about your current inventory levels in sutures? What effect does this level of inventory have on your operating costs?"
Checking	A question for checking one's understanding and getting agreement concerning the statement.	"If I understand you correctly, you have said that you are happy with the quality of your current supplier, but feel that you may be able to get the same quality of service at a lower price from another supplier. Is that accurate?"

FIGURE 5-8 Discovery Process: Types of Questions

and product knowledge and one's ability to provide solutions that fit the customer's needs. Research has found that successfully demonstrating these qualities is associated with greater customer satisfaction.[21]

In this section, two aspects of advocating are considered: (1) presenting a specific solution to a problem and (2) addressing customer concerns regarding the solution being proposed.

Solution Presentation. The objective of a *solution presentation* is to confirm with customers that the goods and services being offered match their requirements and satisfy their needs. It is very important to remember, however, that the purpose of the solution presentation isn't just for the other person to understand what you are selling. The solution presentation should make them visualize the end-result benefits—how your product or service will satisfy their task and personal needs.

A solution presentation is primarily a discussion of a series of product or service features connected with benefits that the client has already indicated are important, and are followed by evidence that the benefits will in fact be delivered. *Features* are tangible or intangible characteristics of the product or service. For example, a feature of a long-distance telephone service may be that billings are based on one-tenth of a minute rather than the usual full-minute increments. This feature may be emphasized because this person's task motive is cost savings. A *benefit* is a statement about how a product or service can help a customer satisfy an explicit or stated need. Therefore, the salesperson may state the benefit of the previous billing feature in the following terms: "What this means is that on a call of 2 minutes and 6 seconds, you will be billed for only 2.1 minutes. Other companies would bill you for 3 minutes. This will provide you with a significant cost savings on those high monthly telephone bills that are contributing to your operating budget overruns."

Notice that the feature (one-tenth-of-a-minute billings) is connected directly with a stated benefit (billed for 2.1 versus 3 minutes). Also notice that although the feature is product or service centered, the benefit focuses on the client and is related to a task motive (cost savings in this case). The benefit is being sold, not the feature. Research also suggests that benefit statements are most powerful when connected to an explicit need expressed by the customer.

Finally, some *evidence* should be offered to support the claim that one-tenth-of-a-minute billing is a significant savings. Evidence may include presenting the product or a model of the product, showing test results, testimonials from satisfied customers, or trial periods. In the long-distance telephone service example, the salesperson may use testimonials from satisfied customers, as well as actual savings from other installations or test results to show savings.

Presentation skills, like the other skills discussed in this chapter, are related to success regardless of the type of customer relationship being developed. Utilizing these skills, however, is quite different in a transactional relationship than in a consultative or enterprise relationship. Figure 5-9 lists some general differences between the interaction practices in transactional relationships compared to more consultative and enterprise relationships.

Sales Proposals. In today's competitive world, most prospects want to "see it in writing." There is simply too much at stake to make an uninformed decision. Perhaps the most important reason to consider having a sales proposal is that everything is in writing, which means there is less chance of misunderstanding. Sales proposals are also more likely to be used when the purchase decision is made by a committee. It is important to remember, however, that sales proposals must be constructed carefully because they are binding contracts.[22]

It may sound anticlimactic, but a sales proposal should be a document of confirmation. The purpose of a proposal is to document the series of decisions that have already been

Transactional Relationships	*Consultative and Enterprise Relationships*
PRACTICES:	PRACTICES:
Focuses on closing sales	Focuses on customer's bottom line
Makes limited call planning investment	Considers call planning a top priority
Spends most contact time telling account about products	Spends most contact time attempting to build a problem-solving environment
Conducts "product-specific" needs assessment	Conducts discovery in the full scope of the account's operations
Uses "lone wolf" approach to the account	Uses team approach to the account
Makes proposals and presentations based on pricing and product features	Makes proposals and presentations based on profit-impact and on strategic benefits.
Adopts short-term sales followup, focused on product delivery	Adopts long-term sales followup, focuses on long-term relationship enhancement

FIGURE 5-9 Key Differences in Practices Between Types of Relationships

made during the purchasing process. The best proposals support the rationalization of a decision that has already been made.

A sales proposal should consist of a discussion of all the incentives for a customer to change what it is presently doing and confirm the confidence to invest in the solution, which should have already been established with the customer. In short, there should be no surprises. Everything is *us* and *we* in the document if the selling process leading up to the proposal has been complete.

Addressing Customer Concerns. Customer concerns or questions about a proposed solution to a problem are likely to arise in any sales presentation. Ideally, a customer's most fundamental concerns should have been uncovered in the discovery phase before recommending a solution. Because customers are not likely to be aware of all their concerns until faced with making a decision, customer concerns are probably best considered a natural part of any sales presentation and should be viewed by the salesperson as an opportunity rather than an obstacle.

Research on presentations by Xerox salespeople found that successful interactions have 50 percent more objections than failed ones. When prospects raise concerns, they are actually showing interest and are asking for more information. They may be trying to make a clearer connection between their needs and your offering. Instead of being passive, they are actively involved in the buying process. Xerox has also found that failed interactions contain significantly more customer statements of indifference than successful calls. Concerns should be welcomed as a chance to get the prospect involved and to expand the discussion into areas of concern to the client. Most concerns are nothing more than innocent questions and should be viewed as an opportunity for deeper insight into customer needs.

The question remains as to how to handle real concerns that are raised. Wilson Learning Worldwide suggests a method for handling objections that it refers to by the acronym LSCPA. The process involves the following steps:

- **Listen** to the client's feelings.
- **Share** the concerns without judgment.
- **Clarify** the real issue with questions.
- **Problem-solve** by presenting options and solutions.
- **Ask for action** to determine commitment.

These steps are recommended because customers are in no mood to listen to a logical clarification or solution when they are feeling tense. Customer concerns are a signal that they are feeling discomfort with the process. It is a natural part of the process. The listening and sharing steps can reduce tension by helping the customer get objections out in the open and showing that you, the salesperson, care enough to acknowledge and try to understand them. Listen actively and encourage the customer to talk. Don't think about how you will respond while listening to the customer. In the sharing stage, you are trying to demonstrate understanding of the customer's feelings. Listening and sharing take maturity, energy, and patience. Remember that the customer is not attacking you personally, so concentrate on not being defensive.[23]

Closing Skills

Closing occurs when a salesperson asks for a commitment from the customer. In a transactional selling situation, such as in inventory replenishment, the commitment is for an order. A widely quoted figure is that only 10 percent of sales calls in most major business-to-business relationships result in an order. In the other sales calls, the customer is asked to commit to advancing the purchasing process.

Many salespeople find this the most difficult step of the selling process and are very reluctant to close, primarily out of fear of rejection. If salespeople do not ask for the order, they cannot be turned down, and thereby they avoid embarrassment or disappointment. All professional purchasing agents, however, expect a sales representative to attempt to close. It is the job of the salesperson to make the first move. If you have successfully performed the earlier steps in the selling process, the close will follow naturally. In this case, closing is simply asking for a decision when you're fairly certain a person is going to say yes.

When to Close. An often-heard suggestion is to "close early and close often." This advice is not consistent with efforts to build trusting relationships with customers and is inherently adversarial in nature. A client is likely to regard asking for the order before he or she is ready to buy as pushy. In other words, you can be too pushy if you want the sale too badly and become overly aggressive. The client is likely to close up and start pushing back. Once again research supports the idea of not being too pushy when closing the sale.

Does this mean that successful salespeople expect to close only once? No. Often, undisclosed needs still need to be addressed. One of your customer's needs may be to have other people listen to him or her. Salespeople must be prepared to use multiple closes. It is often said that most acceptances are made on the fifth closing attempt.

If undiscovered needs are likely to exist and multiple closes are often required, how does a salesperson avoid being pushy while uncovering hidden needs and making the sale? We suggest the use of *trial closes*. Although closes call for decisions, trial closes are questions that ask for opinions that will serve as indicators of how close the client is to making a purchase decision. You may, for example, ask:

- How does this look to you?
- How important is this to you?
- Is this what you had in mind?
- Will this equipment be consistent with what you have now?

If a prospect makes a positive response to one of these questions, the salesperson can assume that the person is leaning toward buying. The salesperson should be prepared to continue the sales presentation. If the person does not appear ready to make a decision, then one might ask the simple question, "Is there anything I presented that is unclear or doesn't meet your particular needs?" This question will help the salesperson uncover the other person's real needs.[24]

Successful salespeople learn to time their closing remarks on the basis of buying signals given by the customer. These cues can take the form of gestures (the customer nods in agreement, picks up the product and examines it closely, or leans back in his or her chair), or they can be verbal comments. When prospects make comments such as:

- "Shipments must be completed in five months?"
- "We like the speed-control feature."
- "Would we be able to install the custom model within three weeks?"

the salesperson should recognize these as signs of interest and shift to a specific closing routine. Notice that each of these signals suggests an action by the client, not just a problem.

Closing Techniques. Many different closing techniques may be used, and salespeople have personal preferences, depending on the circumstances. This suggests that salespeople need to be familiar with a number of closing techniques so that they can choose methods that are appropriate for each selling situation. Two popular closing techniques are the alternative choice close and the summary close.

Alternative Choice. When the prospect is faced with a variety of colors and models, the *alternative choice close* may be effective. With this technique, the salesperson poses a series of questions designed to narrow the choice and help the prospect make a final selection. For example: "These couplings can be packed in units of 24 or cases of 72. Which is more convenient for you?"

Summary Close. One of the best closes provides a *summary* of the benefits accepted during the call, combined with an action plan requiring the customer's commitment.

SALESPERSON: George, you have said that our word processor has more memory, better graphics, and is easier to use than other machines you have seen. Is that correct?

PROSPECT: Yes.

SALESPERSON: Well, I recommended that you lease one of our machines for three months, and the lease payments will apply to the purchase price if you decide to keep it.

In a Xerox-sponsored study of 500 sales calls, the summary close gave a 75 percent success rate; in only 7 percent of the calls was the summary method a failure.[25]

Myriad other closing techniques have been suggested and can be found in any selling textbook. In fact, some popular business books are devoted entirely to presenting different closing techniques.[26] Although some of the techniques are very creative, in practice, most veteran salespeople prefer one of the more straightforward closes discussed in this section. It is our belief that if the previous steps have been performed correctly, the close may be kept simple. This conclusion is also supported by research on the preferences of industrial buyers, which found that those in a higher level of their organizations much preferred a soft close that allowed them to make the decision compared to either summarizing the benefits or comparing product features with those of a competitor.[27] The point is perhaps best made by a sales consultant who stated: "I've never been a believer in closing, because my objective is to open a relationship."

THE POSTINTERACTION PHASE

A sale only begins the relationship between customer and supplier. Once a salesperson has helped a customer make a purchase, attention shifts to the followup activities, the

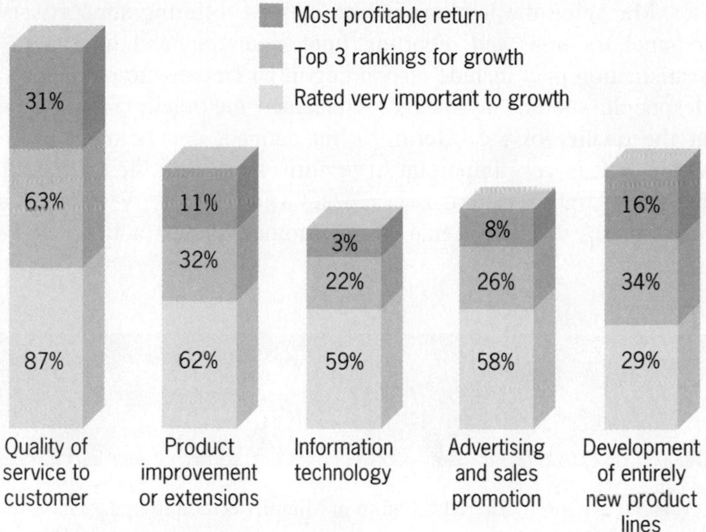

FIGURE 5-10 The Role of Customer Service

postinteraction phase. Followup refers to all the efforts involved in servicing the sale and building a lasting and growing relationship. Customers expect after-sale service, and it is frequently the sales representative's job to make sure that these activities are carried out. PricewaterhouseCoopers measured the importance of this phase in a recent study when it interviewed over 400 CEOs of fast-growing businesses. Executives were asked to rate 25 different strategies with respect to their contribution to profits and growth. As the results shown in Figure 5-10 indicate, quality of customer service was ranked the highest in terms of contributions to growth and profits.

The Wilson Learning Worldwide has identified four pillars of sales support involved in after-sales followup. These are shown in Figure 5-11. Supporting the buying decision means reducing any anxiety that may arise with the purchasing decision. This may be accomplished through a followup sales call or by sending a card or letter thanking the customer for the

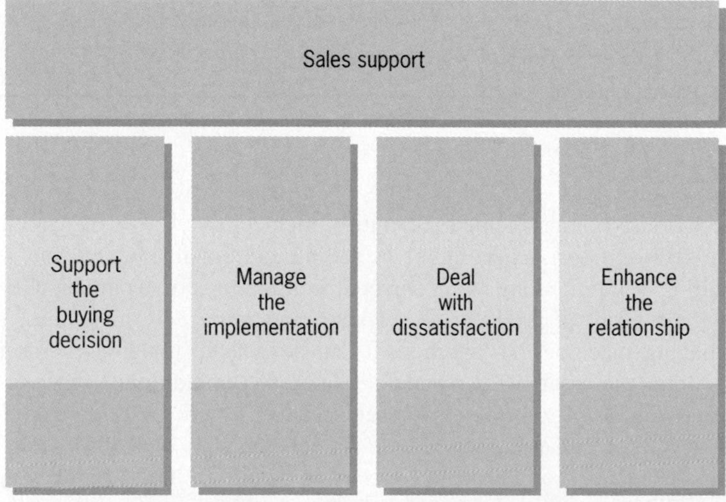

FIGURE 5-11 Servicing the Sale: The Four Pillars of Sales Support

order. Managing the implementation includes offering support services, assisting with any personnel training, and reporting implementation and utilization progress. Dealing with dissatisfaction may include responding in an empathetic manner to any problems that arise. Salespeople should always try to enhance the relationship by being available, ensuring that the quality of the offering is maintained, and being a source of information, help, and ideas. It is very important to perform these activities successfully because the bulk of most salespeople's volume is in repeat business. Team Exercise "Unkept Promise" presents a particularly difficult scenario of customer dissatisfaction. How would you handle this situation?

TEAM EXERCISE
"Unkept Promise"

WHOT, a Latin music radio station in Miami, decided to update its format from Latin standards to new, hip Latin music in an attempt to reach young, upscale Hispanic residents. As part of the changeover, you hired salesperson Rita Vasquez, a 30-year-old Cuban American woman with a master's degree in business, whom you felt embodied the station's new target audience. Vasquez also had a proven track record in advertising sales from her six-year stint with a radio station in Tampa.

Most customers were pleased with the new format and planned to continue advertising on the station. However, one media buyer at an agency that represented three of WHOT's largest accounts was unhappy and planned to cancel his current contract.

You decided to send your new rep to call on the disgruntled media buyer. Having already succeeded in bringing in several new accounts, Vasquez happily accepted the challenge. After an unsuccessful attempt to sway the buyer, Vasquez offered a guarantee that the buyer's clients would get "editorial mentions"—casual comments from the deejay about the client's products and/or services—on the station's popular morning show if the agency agreed to maintain its current media plans. With that, the buyer was sold.

A month later, the buyer calls you to complain that his clients were never mentioned on the morning show as promised by Vasquez. He planned to pull additional advertising if the station didn't meet its promise beginning the following morning. Vasquez has put you in a difficult position. You want to keep the customer, but editorial mentions are strictly against station policy. Worse, Vasquez knew this when she made the promise to the buyer. It is 4:00 P.M. when the customer calls. You need to think quickly. How would you handle the meeting/phone call with the media buyer? How would you handle your meeting with Rita Vasquez? How is each likely to react?

Relationship Enhancement

Relationship enhancement activities include two types of activities: cross selling and up-selling. *Cross-selling* involves selling additional products and services to an account—selling printers along with personal computers, for example. GE Medical Systems sells a large array of products to hospitals, including MRI machines, CT scanners, and x-ray imaging machines. In addition, it can design the imaging rooms for the hospital as well as train the imaging personnel. Selling these additional services is a good example of cross-selling. *Up-selling* is closely related to cross-selling and refers to selling bigger products or enhanced services to an account that typically results in higher margins and greater dollar commitments. Referring again to GE Medical Systems, an example of up-selling would be for GE to offer to provide the personnel needed to run and manage a hospital's imaging department.

Knowledge Management

Whenever salespeople conclude an interaction, they should immediately record what they have learned about the prospect or customer—for example, the prospect's chief concern, who makes the final decision, and the prospect's primary needs. Differences in customers and situations lead to hundreds of natural experiments being carried out every day. The systematic recording of this information helps to encourage learning from these experiments. Sales management should reinforce this type of analysis for both successful and unsuccessful sales calls and help formulate appropriate future behaviors.[28]

Some companies are aggressively adopting technology to facilitate the flow of account information to and from the field. Pfizer not only has equipped its salespeople with laptop computers with wireless internet connections, but also installed broadband access in each salesperson's home along with a wireless router. This allows them to use their laptops in the kitchen or TV room. Pfizer estimates that this saves salespeople up to 38 hours a month that they used to spend sending notes from physician visits to a corporate database via a dial-up connection. Salespeople's laptops are updated at the end of the day with client notes and ordering histories for the next day's appointments.[29]

To facilitate institutional learning, some companies are formalizing the process of collecting customer information. Bergen Brunswig, a pharmaceutical and medical supplies wholesaler, uses a customized interview guide with its customers aimed at collecting meaningful and candid feedback, gaining a better understanding of needs and issues, and building relationships. Between five and ten interviews are completed in every account. No selling is allowed during these sessions. One executive at Bergen Brunswig commented, "We got more information in doing the interviews with one account than we had in our ten years of doing business with the account."[30]

As the previous examples suggest, the collecting, gathering, disseminating, and use of knowledge have become significant for many sales forces. Technology is helping to make this possible, but the gathering and use of this knowledge are important management issues as well.

SUMMARY

Salespeople and sales managers need to understand how to interact with clients in order to properly execute the sales force program. In addition, salespeople respect a sales manager who can help them achieve greater personal success in sales. Sales managers do not need to be the best salesperson in the district, but they must at least have an understanding of the process involved and the skills needed to execute the firm's sales program.

1. **Describe the basic types of selling models.** We have discussed three basic selling process models—standardized, need satisfaction, and problem solution. Each model is appropriate in certain circumstances. A standardized presentation is designed to stimulate a positive customer response. The presentation is well rehearsed and places minimal emphasis on problem discovery. A need-satisfaction type of presentation is oriented toward discovering and meeting customer needs. It relies on well-developed questioning skills to elicit customer-buying needs. A problem-solution selling approach also involves an analysis of the customer's circumstances, but the analysis is more extensive and is based on formal studies of the customer's operations.
2. **State the skills utilized in the preinteraction phase.** The preinteraction phase takes place prior to meeting with the customer. The planning skills involved in this phase focus on setting a good objective for the sales call, obtaining relevant information about the customer, and deciding how to open the conversation with the customer.

3. **List the skills involved in the interaction phase.** The interaction phase includes all face-to-face interactions with the customer prior to arriving at the sale. Our discussion of this phase of the selling process focused on three skills important to all business situations: relating skills, discovery skills, and advocating skills. In addition, we described two skills more critical to success in transactional-type selling situations: gaining access and closing skills.
4. **Explain the skills involved in the postinteraction phase.** The postinteraction phase takes place following the purchase and involves the servicing of the sale and building a lasting and growing customer relationship. Four skills were described in this phase: supporting the buying decision, managing the implementation, dealing with dissatisfaction, and enhancing the relationship.

KEY TERMS

Advocating skills
Alternative choice close
Benefits
Call reluctance
Canned presentation
Checking questions
Closed-ended questions
Closing skills
Cross-selling
Dealing with dissatisfaction
Enhance the Relationship
Evidence
Fact-finding questions
Features
Feeling-finding questions
Followup
Interaction phase
Managing the implementation
Need-satisfaction model
Open-ended questions
Permission questions
Planning skills
Postinteraction phase
Precall planning
Preinteraction phase
Problem-solution model
Relating skills
Relationship anxiety
Solution presentation
Standardized model
Summary close
Supporting the buying decision
Task motives
Trial close
Up-selling

DEVELOPING YOUR COMPETENCIES

1. **Coaching.** Most salespeople are very comfortable with one-on-one interactions with clients. But put some of them in front of an audience of executives and suddenly they can't even remember the product's name. Nervousness can make otherwise competent individuals look like novices. And it's easy for potential clients to mistake a salesperson's public speaking anxiety for a lack of confidence in the product being sold. Salespeople aren't alone in this fear. A recent Gallup Poll shows that more people fear public speaking than fear of heights, spiders, needles, or thunderstorms. How can managers help salespeople put this phobia aside? Develop three specific recommendations by which managers can help coach salespeople to make better group presentations.
2. **Self-Management.** A better understanding of the role of personal selling can be obtained by traveling with a field salesperson for a day. Contact a salesperson and arrange to observe his or her activities for a day. Keep a log of how much of the salesperson's time is spent on meetings, travel, and waiting and how much is spent talking to customers. Write a report describing your experience and the salesperson's activities. The Yellow Pages and your college placement office can be used to identify firms with salespeople in your area. Local chapters of Sales and Marketing Executives clubs and the American Marketing Association are also good sources of salespeople for this assignment.
3. **Strategic Action.** The problem is "biting the bullet." It's the end of the quarter, and you really need a strong finish to make your numbers. You ask your top district manager to move a bit lower than usual on price for his clients, perhaps be a bit more flexible on payment terms, waive the fees for a few value-adds, and beef up the service at a lower cost. What harm can there be in biting the bullet . . . just once?

4. **Global Awareness.** Expanding into foreign markets often involves a healthy dose of research and development. Experts recommend that companies set a specific goal to be achieved in a twelve-month time period and to make sure that a significant portion of business is coming from these new markets, instead of just seeing it as a way to dump product in a new place. A good example of a company that needs to thoroughly research and understand its goals when entering a new market is Speech Works International Inc., which sells conversational speech recognition technology and other products used for telesales. Before opening a new overseas office, the company relies on experts at local universities who understand the nuances of a local language. The technology needs to translate such expressions as, "I want to fly from Singapore to Hong Kong next Tuesday afternoon," into a language the computer will understand. Besides getting the language translated correctly, what additional information would you gather if you worked for Speech Works and what additional actions would you take to ensure a successful expansion into a city such as Mexico City or Singapore? www.speechworks.com
5. **Technology.** Sales force automation (SFA), according to recent reports, represents the fastest growing segment of the computer software business. Unfortunately, many of these efforts face the prospect of failure. To date, more than 60 percent of all SFA projects have been unsuccessful according to industry reports. Given this prospect, the results of a recent study by Mark Rivers and Jack Dart on the factors related to success in SFA are particularly interesting. First, recall that SFA involves converting manual sales activities to electronic processes through the use of various combinations of hardware and software applications. This means that an SFA project may be as simple as substituting electronic equivalents for paper daytimers or as complex as developing advanced systems relying on computer-telephone integration to allow salespeople to enter orders electronically, create their own presentations, correspond via e-mail, and do their own pricing. Which of the following factors do you think were related to achieving SFA success among the 210 manufacturing firms participating in the study?
   - The extent to which top management was involved in the purchase decision.
   - The extent to which sales force management was involved in the purchase decision.
   - Sales management's predisposition toward the SFA concept.
   - Management's difficulty in assessing sales force performance.
   - The resistance of the sales force to adoption of SFA.
6. **Team Building.** Making a presentation is usually difficult enough when you're on your own; when you're part of a group making a team pitch, the stakes go skyward. Group presentations require all the skills of solo flight, plus the ability to handle the tricky dynamics of a public teamwork. What's more, any missteps have an expanded audience and perhaps angry teammates. How can you avoid group presentation blunders? What tips would you offer?

FEATURED CASE SHIELD FINANCIAL: "A VENDOR PROBLEM"

Doug Bloom has always loved technology and is very excited about the opportunities to gather, store, and share market knowledge and information. Six months ago he signed a deal with a vendor, Primary Software, that would provide a comprehensive, custom software package for his sales force. Among the package's features are a database, a contact and schedule manager, a proposal generator, a GPS (global positioning system), and a price and specification estimator. Doug wants to tie his sales force to every other department in the office and eventually the company, allowing everyone to operate more efficiently by having realtime access to customer activities, product information, and other necessary information.

When he called Primary today, however, he learned that the project had fallen behind schedule and that the beta version wouldn't be ready for at least three months (it had been promised to him in one month). The vendor apologized, saying, "It's the best we can do." Doug was aghast. He had already purchased laptops for his salespeople, expecting the software to be running internally by the time the shipment of laptops arrived. He had also based year-end sales projections on the increased productivity and sales he expected as a result of automating the company's sales process.

Coincidentally, a salesperson from another vendor, AllBright Software, called Doug to discuss some industry information he thought Doug would find useful. After a few minutes, the conversation turned to Doug's software problem. The vendor offered his company's services, promising to complete the project within two months, and offering extensive training and support that surpassed what the current vendor was offering. The price would be about the same, but Doug had already paid $12,000 in unrecoverable dollars to Primary. Doug said he needed time to consider the offer.

Questions

1. Should Doug be patient and wait for Primary to complete the job or should he risk going with All-Bright?
2. What other options does Doug have?
3. Are ethical issues involved?

SALES FORCE ORGANIZATION

> The same old way doesn't work any more.
>
> Anonymous

Chapter Consultants:
Russel Donnelly, Sales Manager, Central Region, Ericsson Inc.
B. J. Polk, Customer Business Development Manager, Procter & Gamble

LEARNING OBJECTIVES

After studying this chapter, you should be able to:

- Explain the various ways by which sales forces can be organized.
- Explain what a strategic accounts management program means.
- State the reasons for the growth in telemarketing and its implementation issues.
- Tell why and when sales agents are utilized.
- Describe evolving trends in sales force organization.

XEROX REORGANIZES

During the mid-1980s, Xerox Corporation's dominant position in the office equipment market was in jeopardy. It was being challenged by lower priced Japanese firms, while new electronic workplace technology was threatening to make Xerox's flagship product, the plain-paper copier, obsolete.

In response to these market changes, Xerox management implemented an aggressive strategy aimed at repositioning the company as a leader in office automation. A key element of this strategy was an increase in its customer focus. Xerox's 4,000-plus member sales force was at the center of this customer focus strategy. Historically, Xerox had maintained separate sales forces for each of its major product lines. The largest sales force was dedicated to selling copier equipment, while several smaller sales forces sold information processing systems, printing systems, office systems, and sales engineering. As a result, many customers interacted with several Xerox salespeople.

In 1985, the sales force was reorganized into a single full-line sales force assigned by customer segment and geography. Five market segments were defined including customer system users, standard commercial accounts, small businesses, third parties, and institutional customers such as government and educational institutions. A separate sales force sold the full line of Xerox products to each customer segment within a designated geographic area. One benefit of the reorganization was to increase productivity. The new structure also allowed customers to work with a single Xerox salesperson, thereby improving Xerox's customer focus.

The 1985 reorganization at Xerox was an immediate success; the company experienced steady revenue growth in the years following that reorganization. The sales force was recognized by *Sales and Marketing Management* magazine as one of "America's Best Sales Forces" and the company was lauded for its excellent reputation among customers and its ability to retain and grow existing accounts.

Xerox continued to enjoy success throughout the 1990s, with its stock hitting a record high of $64 in 1999. Despite this success, trouble was brewing for the company. The market for high-tech stocks was weakening, and competitors continued to eat away at Xerox's market share. Xerox decided that changes were needed if it was to meet its aggressive revenue targets.

Xerox management decided to implement a new, two-part business strategy consisting of increased focus on large global customers and smaller independent customers. For large customers, the Xerox strategy was to help these customers create new ways to use documents more effectively and creatively. Xerox salespeople were asked to sell industry-specific bundled packages of products, including copiers, software, consulting, and outsourcing contracts. For small businesses, the Xerox strategy was to reach a broader base of customers by increasing its network of indirect channels such as office superstores, value-added resellers, agents, telemarketing, and the Internet. This would also reduce costs due to the lower overhead associated with these indirect channels.

The 4,300-member Xerox sales force played a critical role in the implementation of the strategy and was realigned twice during 1999 to shift greater effort toward the largest global customers and to create separate industry-specific selling teams. In the first reorganization, four industry sectors were established: financial services and health care, graphic arts, manufacturing/industrial, and the public sector. Several months later, two more sectors were added: retail/wholesale and professional services. Product specialists were provided and were called on when needed to help close a sale. Indirect channels took on even greater significance and were assigned many of the medium-sized accounts formerly covered by direct salespeople.

Unlike the 1985 reorganization, the 1999 sales force restructuring was not initially successful, perhaps due to a series of internal tensions at the time involving bad accounting practices and mismanaged implementations that sent the company's share price plummeting. Having a debt load of $14 billion didn't help either.

By mid-2001, Xerox found itself in serious financial trouble with bankruptcy a real possibility. Nevertheless, new CEO Anne Mulcahy, who began her career as a Xerox salesperson, was optimistic about the company's future and believed that the turnaround at Xerox would depend largely on the success of its sales force.

While it took time, Anne's faith in the sales force was not misplaced. Xerox returned to full-year profitability in 2002, its stock rose 22 percent in 2004 compared with 9 percent for the Standard & Poor's 500-stock index, and Mulcahy expects new products to drive a sales increase in 2005—the first for Xerox since 1999.[1]

As the Xerox example illustrates, sales forces must confront a wide variety of change pressures. From a customer's perspective, sales force organization determines the number of salespeople the customer sees, how responsive the salespeople can be to the customer's needs, and how knowledgeable the salespeople are about the products they sell and the customers to whom they sell. From the sales force perspective, the sales organization defines the job. It determines the type of customers they call on, the breadth of products and services they have to sell, and the activities in which they engage.

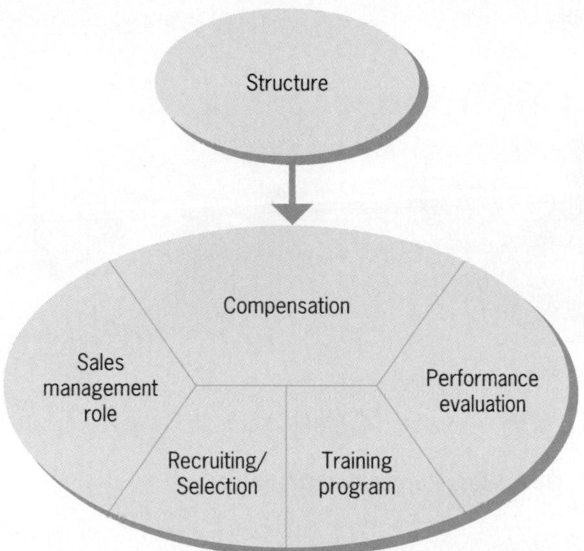

FIGURE 6-1 Decisions Affected by Sales Force Organization

Similarly, the sales force organization defines the sales manager's role and reporting relationships, which is why we examine sales organization before discussing the other management decisions, as shown in Figure 6-1. Since sales organization specifies the salesperson's job description, it affects the type of people selected for sales and management positions, as well as the territory alignment, training programs, compensation plan, and performance evaluation systems.

The discussion in this chapter is organized as follows. First, the questions of sales force specialization and strategic accounts are addressed. This is followed by a discussion of the advantages and pitfalls of telemarketing and independent agents, alternatives to the traditional field sales force. The chapter closes with a discussion of emerging sales organization issues such as accessing global markets, working with sales partners, and sales teams.

GENERALIST VERSUS SPECIALIST STRUCTURES

Sales force organizational structures vary from generalist structures, where each salesperson sells all products to all customers within a particular geographic area, to highly specialized sales forces, where teams of salespeople focus on specific products, markets, or functions.

Figure 6-2 presents the results of a recent survey indicating how sales forces are organized today and in the future. Notice that sales managers are expecting big changes, with many anticipating their sales force to be organized around type of customers. At the same time, fewer organizations are expecting to be generalists calling on all customers within a geographic area. Specialization, however, presents important challenges in terms of coordination, integration, and, most important, higher expenses.

In general, companies attempt to develop a sales force organization that is adaptable, efficient, and effective. A sales organization is adaptive if the company can react quickly to

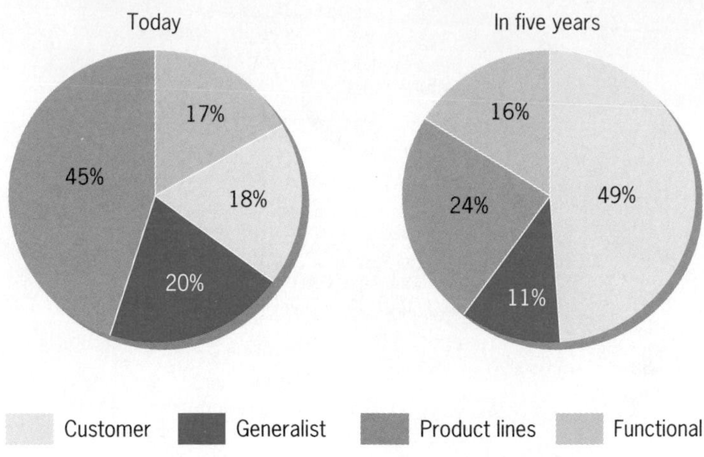

FIGURE 6-2 How Sales Forces Are Organized

product and market changes without a major structural overhaul. Efficiency reflects the rate at which key sales activities, such as calls, demonstrations, and proposals, are performed. Effectiveness represents the buyer's favorable reaction to the sales effort, for example, the customer's positive response to H-P's sales calls is due to the salesperson's superior customer knowledge.

Four fundamental structures for organizing a sales force are generalist, product specialized, customer specialized, and functional specialized. The advantages and issues associated with each of these structures are discussed in this section.

Generalist Structure

The least complicated sales force organization is a *generalist structure*, also referred to as a geographic organization, in which each salesperson sells the firm's entire product line to all accounts and prospects, usually within a specific geographic area. For example, Figure 6-3 shows the Eastern region of the United States divided into eighteen sales territories, where each salesperson sells to all customers and prospects located within a designated state.

Generalist salespeople typically have geographically small sales territories and minimal travel time and spend a high percentage of their time face-to-face with customers. Thus, they tend to be the highly efficient sales structures. A generalist organization works best when the product line consists of related products or services that appeal to a rather homogeneous group of buyers.[2] Salespeople also have a greater opportunity to gain in-depth knowledge of the local culture, economic, and competitive conditions.[3]

Serious shortcomings may arise, however, when salespeople sell a broad line of products to a diverse set of customers. First, when salespeople sell many products, they tend to focus their attention on the lines with which they are comfortable, neglecting the lines that are newer, more difficult to sell, but possibly more profitable. With so many products to sell, it is difficult to develop the expertise needed to develop creative solutions for customers' problems. Second, salespeople may find themselves at a competitive disadvantage if they are asked to sell to customers with problems and needs that are diverse and complex. There is also the risk that salespeople will spend too much time with customers who are easy to sell, but who are not necessarily profitable or high-growth opportunities. As a result, the territory is not developed to its full potential.

With more mergers and acquisitions resulting in customer consolidation, a problem arises in coordinating the selling effort across different geographic areas. For example, a

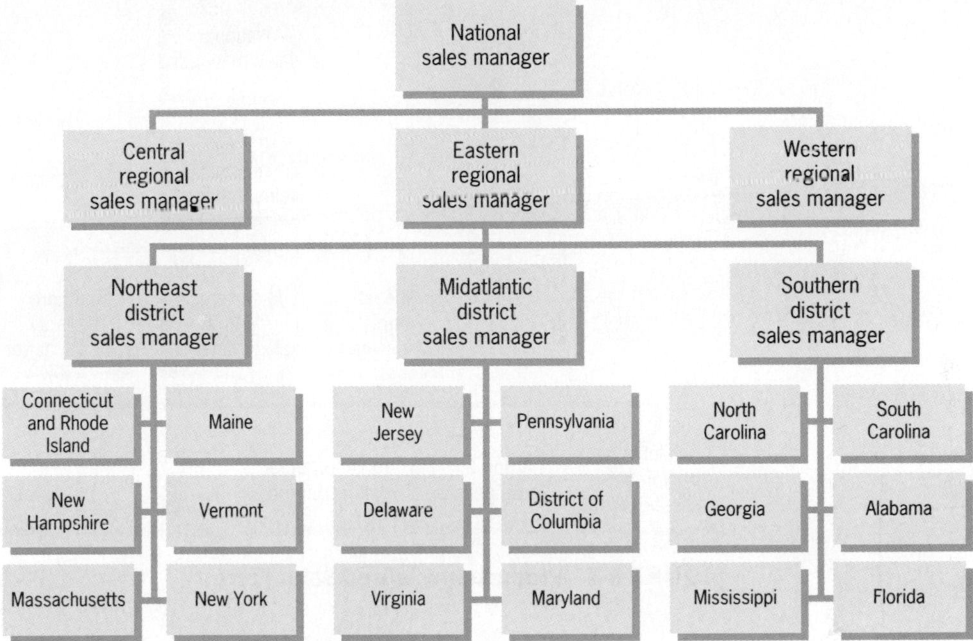

FIGURE 6-3 Generalist Sales Organization

customer's regional headquarters may be located in one territory, but it may purchase product for stores or plants located in other territories. In-store merchandising support or inplant installation support may be needed for the sale. How would you achieve the coordination needed to fully service this customer? How would you split sales credit among the salesperson who calls on the headquarters and the other salespeople who service the local stores in their territories? Many organizations have decided that they need to specialize beyond simple geography. In many cases, firms will focus on one of three areas: products, customers, or activities. We turn our attention to these forms of specialization.

Product Specialization

A product-based specialization is most appropriate when a firm has a large, diverse, and complex line of products. This complexity may happen as a result of new products, mergers, or acquisitions. There are 164 operating companies at Johnson & Johnson producing and selling products such as orthopedic implants, pharmaceuticals, and sutures. How could one person know enough about each product line? The answer is they couldn't, so J&J has organized its sales force around defined product lines.

A product-specialized sales force structure is shown in Figure 6-4. In this organizational structure, each salesperson specializes by selling only a few of the products in the organization's total product portfolio and reports to a management structure that is also focused on the same limited number of product lines. Each product-based sales force calls on its own customers, sets its own goals, and rewards its own salespeople. Coordination occurs only at the highest levels in the organization.

A product-based specialization is probably the most effective way to ensure that a product or product line receives the desired level of selling effort. If, for instance, a product line needs twenty people to sell into a market effectively, then the only way to ensure that this amount of effort is actually devoted to the product line is to establish a sales force of

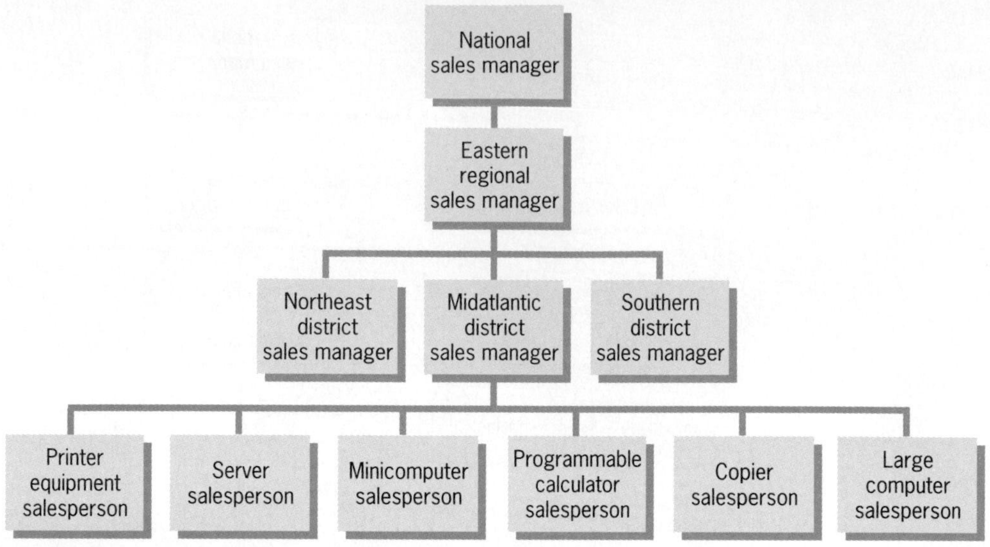

FIGURE 6-4 Product-Specialized Sales Force

twenty people. Training, coaching, and compensation programs can also be used to achieve desired sales effort levels, but their success is not guaranteed.

Unfortunately, product specialization also has a number of limitations. It has low geographic efficiency, meaning that each product specialist must usually cover a large geographic area. This situation increases travel expenses and reduces the amount of face-to-face time with customers; it may also create confusion on the part of customers. A Hyatt Hotel sales situation represents an extreme example of this customer confusion. It was discovered that 63 Hyatt salespeople called on one customer. This happened because each Hyatt resort property had its own sales force. Hyatt has since reorganized into central sales offices with assigned customer accounts. The Hyatt example also points out another potential drawback of product specialization, which is excessive internal competition—in Hyatt's case, too many salespeople competing against each other.

One way that organizations can achieve proper coordination of effort is to organize around markets or customers.

Customer Specialization

In a *customer specialization*-type sales force organization, also referred to as *vertical marketing*, each salesperson or sales team sells the entire product line to select types of buyers. Thus, the six salespeople in Figure 6-5 are assigned to banks, retailers, and other types of customers instead of to geographic regions or product lines, as before. In general, this type of sales organization is becoming more and more popular with companies as they attempt to become more market focused.[4]

IBM's sales force of around 35,000 people is a good example of a company that has organized its sales force around customers. The sales force is organized according to customer size, industry, and location. Salespeople are part of a team that serves three main customer groups: large, integrated accounts; clusters of aligned accounts; and small and medium-sized accounts. The critical factor leading IBM to adopt this type of sales organization is that 82 percent of the IT costs an organization incurs are in services needed to support its IT equipment. In this environment, delivering a great product is not enough,

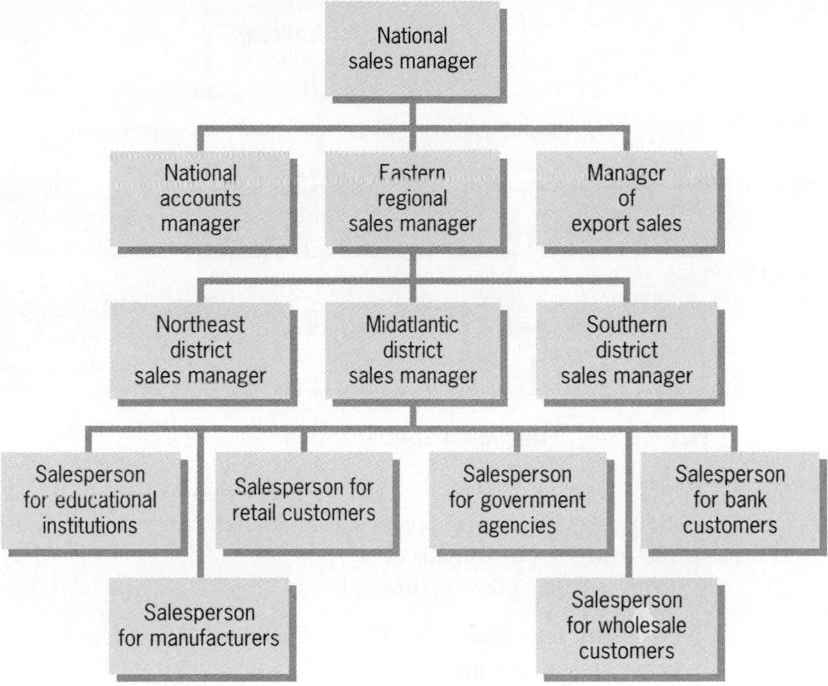

FIGURE 6-5 Customer Specialized Sales Force

and providing solutions to customer needs requires a deep understanding of the customer and its market situation. In such conditions, specializing by customers is highly effective.[5]

The most important advantage of customer specialization is that it allows salespeople to gain a better understanding of the customer's special needs and problems and become experts in a particular customer or industry. Customer-based sales organizations are very adaptive as well to changes in customer needs and buying behavior. Thus, a customer specialization organization may result in an important selling advantage when an organization wishes to execute a consultative or enterprise-level relationship strategy with its customers.

This type of sales organization has an additional benefit in that the sales force can be organized so that each customer or market receives the appropriate level of selling resources. Neither a generalist nor a product-based sales organization can make this guarantee.

A customer-based sales organization also has several downsides. First, it can lead to conflict with the marketing organization, which is usually organized around products. In this case, a product manager will have to work with multiple sales organizations to implement a product's marketing strategy. Another problem arises when in-depth product expertise is critical to solving a customer's problems. Salespeople may not have the necessary product expertise to answer a customer's product questions. To address this shortcoming, organizations with diverse and complex product lines may have technical product specialists that the customer team can call on when needed.

Functional Specialization

A fourth type of specialization in sales organizations, *functional specialization* focuses on the activities or functions performed by customer contact people (Figure 6-6). Product and market heterogeneity and complexity may require a diverse set of skills and knowledge. This increasingly characterizes the situation of many large global organizations. In such

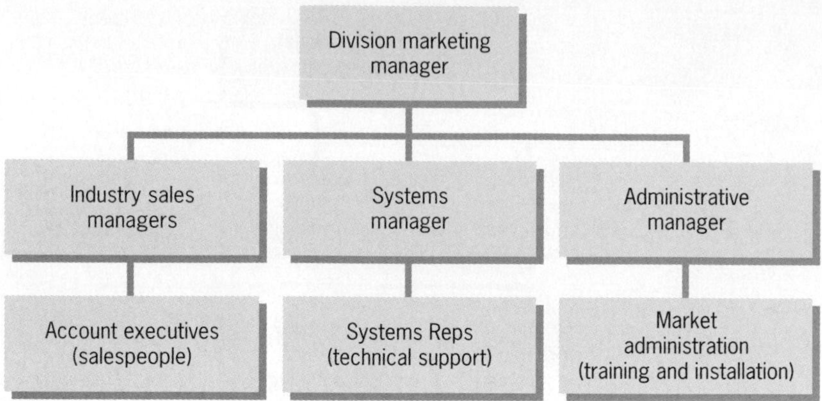

FIGURE 6-6 Functional Specialization

situations, the sales force gains considerable efficiency and effectiveness by specializing in specific functions or activities.

Consider the following examples:

- **New customer specialists.** These people are charged with gaining new customers. The type of person and the skills needed to successfully call on prospects are believed to be quite different from those needed to service existing accounts. American Express is an example of a company that has profited from this type of sales specialty. This type of specialization also helps to ensure that an appropriate amount of effort is dedicated to new customer acquisition.
- **Retention specialists.** Between 80 and 90 percent of most companies' annual revenue is from current customers. Retaining customers and, more importantly, realizing revenue growth are critical to profitability. Browning-Ferris Industries, a large waste services company, recently created a position titled Core Account Retention Specialist. People in this position are responsible for retaining current revenue from current customers.
- **End-user specialists.** Companies that sell through distributors face the challenge of creating demand among end-users. Lexmark International, which manufactures keyboards, printers, and related supplies, found that it needed to devote more effort to its end-users rather than focusing exclusively on its resellers. To ensure that the majority of sales resources went to end-user selling, Lexmark created a new sales position devoted to selling to end-users. In this way Lexmark redeployed its sales effort to spend 85 percent of its effort on end-users.[6]
- **Sales engineers.** In high-tech companies, such as 3M, a new role has been developed, called sales engineers, who are responsible for developing applications for their products within an existing customer's business. For example, a sales engineer at 3M might be responsible for working with the design engineers in an account to take existing disk drive products and create next-generation models.[7] So, it is a technical sale, focusing on technical issues that are usually beyond the expertise of the general sales force.
- **Service consultants.** It is not uncommon for salespeople to spend 15 to 30 percent of their time in service-related activities: finding the status of orders, answering questions about shipments, resolving billing disputes, and the like. To increase selling time, some or all of these service activities are being assigned to specialists. A service consultant may support three or four sales representatives and address customer issues that the salesperson cannot handle adequately but that are important to creating customer value.

There is no one best way to organize the sales force, and companies are experimenting with many different forms in order to compete profitably. A company should start by

Organizational Structure	Advantages	Disadvantages
Generalist (Geographic)	• Low cost • No geographic overlap • No customer overlap	• Limited product line knowldge • Limited customer knowledge • Lack of management control over product or customer emphasis
Product	• Product knowledge • Control over product emphasis	• Low geographic efficicency • Customer duplication • Geographic duplication
Customer	• Deeper customer knowledge • Control over customer emphasis	• High cost • Less product knowledge • More geographic duplication • Diffcult coordination with product managers
Functional	• Effectiveness in performing selling activities	• Coordination • Geographic duplication • Customer duplication

FIGURE 6-7 Comparing Sales Organization Structures

examining its customers and looking at its organization from the customer's perspective. Research suggests that when superior selling skills are required, some form of specialization works best.[8] In general, specialization produces effectiveness gains, but overspecialization will create efficiency losses. The best sales organization achieves the right balance of the two. The best advice is to present the customer as few selling faces as possible, while achieving the greatest potential effectiveness gains.[9] Put simply, some sales organization structures are better in some selling situations than in others. Figure 6-7 summarizes much of what has been discussed in this section by directly comparing the advantages and disadvantages of each of the basic sales force structures. To help determine your understanding of sales force organization options, you might try addressing the questions posed in Team Exercise "The Optimal Sales Organization."

STRATEGIC ACCOUNT MANAGEMENT PROGRAM

Regardless of whether the sales force consists of specialists or generalists, one of the most significant changes occurring today is that many organizations are finding it necessary to develop a strategic account management program in addition to their regular sales force.[10] In a recent survey upward of three-quarters of North American consumer goods manufacturers have reorganized their sales forces since 2002. The primary reason for over 80 percent of the firms reorganizing their sales force is to increase their focus on key customers.[11] Also known as key, national, major, and global accounts programs, a *strategic account management program* is more than a selling strategy. It is a marketing philosophy directed at a select group of customers that account for a disproportionately large share of the seller's total revenues.

In Chapter 2, we discussed the need for companies to define an account relationship strategy for the sales force. More and more companies are finding it necessary to establish a strategic account program because, although they may have a consultative or transactional

TEAM EXERCISE
"The Optimal Sales Organization"

Ferno-Washing (F-W), an emergency medical products supplier in Wilmington, Ohio, has organized its sales force around broad groups of customers. The company sells to three kinds of clients: ambulance manufacturers, national emergency medical service companies, and medical supply distributors (i.e., wholesalers). Ambulance manufacturers purchase products based on their technical specifications, safety, and the configuration of space within the ambulance. Meanwhile, national emergency medical service companies are in the business of running emergency centers for hospitals. They are most interested in distribution issues such as timely delivery and consistency. Pricing is also important and usually based on a negotiated contract. Finally, the most important success requirement for distributors is to get them to push the F-W product line against F-W's competitors. This means getting your products in front of the distributor's clients and getting your share of their salespeople's selling time.

It has been some time since F-W reviewed its sales organization and you have been asked to look at it to see if it is the best design for its sales force. What are the benefits and shortcomings associated with this type of sales organization and are there any possible alternatives to consider? What information would you need to determine if an alternative type of organization is more appropriate for Ferno-Washing?

relationship with most of their accounts, they need to have an enterprise-type relationship with some of their accounts. The case of U.S. consumer goods companies turning to strategic account organizations was precipitated by the consolidation within the U.S. grocery retailers. The top ten U.S. retailers held 29 percent of the U.S. grocery market in 1995, but their share had increased to 55 percent by 2003.[12]

How do these relationships differ from traditional account relationships? The experience of Diageo a $19 billion company headquartered in London, is typical for many companies.[13] Diageo is a leader in the alcoholic beverage business with well-known brands such as Smirnoff, Bailey's Irish Cream, Jose Cuervo, Guinness Beer, and many more. Diageo found that serving customers' retailers and distributors who crossed multiple business units was challenging and inefficient with its existing processes. Diageo therefore created a new position, titled vice president of strategic accounts, for one who works across each of the company's five business units to coordinate best practices, develop the vision for the group, and ensure consistent execution and similar business process in all business units. Directors reporting to this vice president manage each strategic account. The strategic account relationships at Diageo differ in many ways from the traditional account relationship. Figure 6-8 shows the changes that have taken place in just the account planning aspect of the relationship.

	Previous Approach	*New Strategic Account*
Business Plan Duration	• 3–6 months	• 2–3 years
Structure of Business Plan	• Tactical promotional program	• Strategic business plan focused on growth and profitability
Personnel Involvement	• Sales reps and purchasing agents	• Senior management from both companies

FIGURE 6-8 Changes in Joint Account Planning

Despite the potentially significant benefits of strategic accounts, companies often encounter problems in setting them up. In a recent survey of 221 companies, only 21 percent rated their strategic account program as being fully functional and effective.[14] As a result, researchers are starting to direct attention toward identifying the factors associated with successful strategic account programs.[15] Two issues have been particularly problematic with new strategic account programs—account selection and organizational structure.

Strategic Accounts Selection

Which customers, if any, should be treated as a strategic account? Many companies initially choose too many accounts to participate in the program, resulting in an overworked strategic account sales force and underserviced customers. There is often a tendency to focus on customer size. This focus is understandable since the few largest customers often represent a major portion of a company's sales and losing even one of these customers could be a strategic disaster. A memorable example of this risk occurred for Goodyear-Dunlop in England when the MG Rover Group stopped production in 2005. At the time, Rover represented approximately 20% of Goodyear-Dunlop's revenues. The loss in business was obviously very significant in this case.[16]

On the other hand, size is not a good indicator that a customer wants or desires this special type of relationship. An emerging view is that customers who best qualify for a strategic account program are those who purchase a significant volume and exhibit one or a combination of the following characteristics:

- Involve multiple people in the buying process.
- Purchase centrally.
- Desire a long-term, cooperative working relationship.
- Expect specialized attention and service.
- Align strategic intent.

As with many marketing decisions, deciding which company should be a strategic account depends on learning the customer's needs.

Kinko's Inc., a California-based chain of printing and computer centers, is a good example of how a company might use other factors in addition to size to identify its strategic accounts. When Kinko's Inc. launched its program, the company first attempted to identify large Fortune 500-type accounts. It then looked for companies that had divisions or operations in all fifty states, as well as a large mobile sales force that could be serviced by multiple Kinko's branches. But most important, the accounts had to have characteristics similar to Kinko's—a fast-growing business with a similar entrepreneurial spirit.

Trane, a leading manufacturer of heating and air conditioning, designed a process for selecting strategic accounts, which attempts to assure that Trane clearly understands the account's current and desired situation. The unique aspect of Trane's account selection process is that, throughout the process, both parties sign documented agreements, which outline commitments to meeting the customer's objectives. Trane has found that this process aids in its strategic thinking and planning.

How to Organize?

Companies have taken a variety of approaches to organizing their strategic accounts programs. What works for one company and is appropriate for one situation may not work in another.[17] The major organizational alternatives are as follows.

Existing Sales Force. As an initial effort, companies often rely on their existing sales force to service the national account customer. This strategy has the advantage of being less risky and less expensive than setting up a separate sales force. On the other hand, the relationship with these strategic accounts may not be very different from that with regular accounts, thus raising the question of whether a strategic accounts program is needed or is being executed. These salespeople have a strong tendency to focus on closing orders and securing revenue rather than building relationships. A short-term focus is especially likely when the sales force is under constant quota pressure, such as when a monthly quota target has been set up.

Management. A step up in commitment is to assign strategic account responsibility to top management. Computer Task Group, Inc., an Atlanta-based software services firm, assigns a strategic account to each of the top twenty-five executives in the company. In addition to being relatively inexpensive, executives are likely to have the authority and power to meet special customer needs.

Other companies have taken a different approach when assigning middle managers to key accounts. In this case, a majority of the manager's time is spent on strategic account activities, and they are likely to be located locally, near the customer's headquarters. The Diageo strategic account program described earlier is an example of this approach to strategic account organization.

Separate Sales Force. Where the need for a strategic accounts program is greatest, a separate sales force devoted strictly to strategic accounts often evolves. The Gold Bond Building Products Division of National Gypsum is organized in this manner. Successful field salespeople are promoted to the strategic accounts sales force. These people are usually located near their customers and report to a strategic accounts manager, who in turn reports to the national sales manager. Hewlett-Packard, Xerox, MCI, and other companies have similar arrangements.

Cross-Functional Sales Teams. Where the selling process is very complex, sales teams may be assigned to strategic accounts. AT&T has more than 370 such strategic account teams; an account manager with broad product and account knowledge heads each team. Providing technical support to the team are two or three product specialists and staff technical specialists. IBM, Pitney Bowes, and many other organizations also employ national account teams. Recent research has found that this type of strategic account organization stands out from the others in terms of both sales performance and profitability, although this type of organization can be quite expensive to build and maintain. This points to the need to match the organization structure to the appropriate opportunity.

Strategic account management represents a significant opportunity for many companies to grow through meeting the needs of their customers. We have just noted two of the important problems associated with establishing these programs. In many industries, however, a company has no choice but to play the game if it wants to be one of the big players in the industry. Recent research on the performance of strategic account teams suggests that management needs to consider and debate the following questions:

- To what extent are we able to gain greater customer investment in the relationship, sharing of information, and trust?
- Are we able to proactively respond to changing customer needs? Is top management significantly involved with our strategic account program?
- Is there a high level of esprit de corps within the program?
- Are sufficient marketing and sales resources committed to the program?

A positive answer to each of the above questions was found to be needed to develop a high-performance strategic accounts program.[18]

to provide him or her with additional information instead of having it forced on him or her. The advantage of permission marketing is that it increases the efficiency with which information is broadcast. Instead of sending it out to a large group of people who the marketer thinks will be interested in the information, the customer tells the marketer that he or she is interested. The Internet and telemarketing are ideal media for this process.

Airlines, on the other hand, appear to be pursuing a strategy of replacing telemarketers with the Internet, by encouraging people to make airline reservations over the Internet and by offering discounts to those who do so. Here the emphasis seems to be on reducing labor costs by having the consumer perform part of the labor. It is worth nothing, however, that recently airline reservation websites have a popup box asking if you would like to talk to a telemarketer for help in making the reservation. Regardless of the strategy pursued, the Internet offers companies additional choices as to how to best access their customers.

SOME ADDITIONAL ISSUES

The effectiveness of a sales force structure will depend on a firm's objectives, strategies, capabilities, and external environment. Some additional points to consider when evaluating specialization options are the following:

- If a company's objective is to reduce costs, then full-line salespeople and telemarketing are the best low-cost options.
- If a company's objective is to increase revenue, then specialization (product, customer, functional, and major accounts) supported by telemarketing should be considered.
- Exceptional training capabilities are frequently critical to the success of specialized salespeople. Specialization by itself is rarely sufficient to produce exceptional results; development of specialized skills must be fostered and enhanced by appropriate training programs.
- When specializing, a firm must have the capability of developing new products and modifying existing products for individual product lines and/or markets. Sales force reorganization cannot solve a product problem.
- If your market is susceptible to demand or margin downturns, then specialists may prove too expensive and too difficult to redeploy.

These factors are likely to vary within the products/markets in which an organization competes. Thus, many large companies combine a variety of specialized sales force structures within their overall selling organization. This also suggests that there is no optimal way for all companies to organize.

INDEPENDENT SALES AGENTS

Up to this point, we have focused on how to organize a company sales force in which all the salespeople and managers are employees of the firm. An important alternative is to hire *independent sales agents* (sometimes referred to as manufacturers' reps) to perform the selling function. Sales agents are not employees, but independent businesses given exclusive contracts to perform the selling function within specified geographic areas. They take neither ownership nor physical possession of the products they sell and are always compensated by commission. Agents are often used to develop new markets. They are able to get up to speed quickly in such situations because agents usually handle five to eight noncompeting but related product lines that they know fairly well and sell to similar buyers.

When to Use Sales Agents

The decision to pay sales agents to cover a particular product/market is not easy to make or to implement. Management should consider three factors: (1) economic consequences, (2) level of control, and (3) market environment.

Economic Consequences. The economic issue centers on the fixed-cost nature of a dedicated sales force versus the largely variable cost nature of sales agents. A simplified representation of cost differences between sales agents and a company sales force with a straight salary compensation plan is shown in Figure 6-10. Although some fixed costs may be associated with sales agents, sales administration costs are usually a relatively small proportion of total selling costs.

Agents receive neither salary nor reimbursement for travel and entertainment expenses. Because agents are paid strictly on commission, costs rise as sales volume increases. Consequently, there is a breakeven sales volume below which sales agents are less expensive and above which a company sales force costs less. These economic factors are one reason small companies and secondary markets may use agents.

Suppose that independent sales agents receive a 5 percent commission on sales and that administrative overhead costs \$50,000. Company sales personnel receive a 3 percent commission plus a salary. Total salary and administrative expenses are estimated at \$550,000. At what sales level would the cost of a company sales force equal that of sales agents? This question can be answered by setting the cost equation for both types of sales forces equal to each other and solving for the sales level amount as follows:

$$\frac{\text{Cost of company sales force} = \text{Cost of sales agents}}{0.03x + \$550{,}000 = 0.05x + \$50{,}000}$$

where x is the breakeven sales volume.

Solving for x, we see that breakeven sales volume equals \$25 million. If sales are expected to be below \$25 million, then sales agents are less expensive. The cost of a company sales force is less when sales exceed \$25 million.

Although Figure 6-10 accurately depicts the essential economic relationships when comparing agents with a dedicated sales force, the situation is often more complicated than one might expect. Adding new salespeople to produce greater volume, for instance, results in fixed costs increasing in a stair-step fashion. Thus, there may be multiple breakeven points at ever-increasing levels of sales.

This analysis also assumes that sales volume can be maintained during a switch from agents to a dedicated sales force. If agents are able to quickly pick up a competing line of goods, your sales volume may fall below that which was sold by agents. Sales growth is

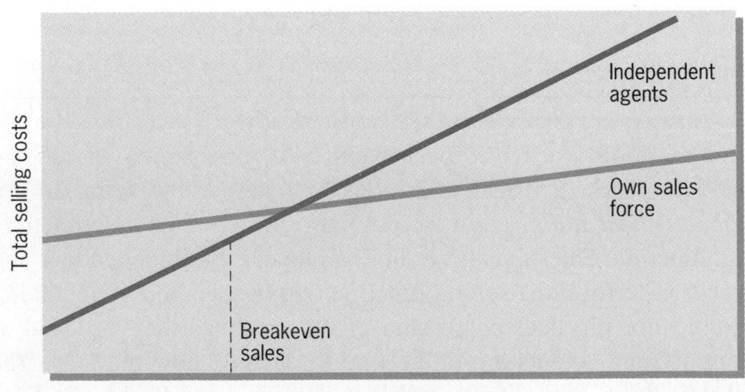

FIGURE 6-10 Total Costs of Independent Agents versus Own Sales Force

driven by loyalty to the sales agent and not loyalty to the supplier company according to a recent study of industrial product sales agents.[21] These and other considerations can make the decision to build a dedicated sales force far less clear-cut than may first appear.

Level of Control. Costs are not the only consideration. Managers can control a company sales force through the selection, training, and supervision of salespeople; establishment of operating policies and procedures; and various evaluation and reward programs. Salespeople who are part of an in-house sales force spend 100 percent of their time on the company's products.

When selling through agents, you face competition at two levels: manufacturers selling competing products and firms selling products through the same agents. In other words, the company competes for the agent's selling time. Although management should try to establish a personal relationship with its agents and sell the agents on the company's marketing program, the primary control mechanism with agents is the commissions paid on sales.[22] This is a market-driven control method, and agents can be expected to spend their time in a manner that will enable them to meet their income objectives. That is, they will evaluate both the amount of commission and the time it will take to earn the commission when deciding how to spend their time.

Market Conditions. Sales agents possess established selling skills, existing client relationships, and general product knowledge. In addition, they represent a largely variable expense, as discussed earlier. These factors combine to favor the use of sales agents in certain market conditions (see Figure 6-11). Notice that these conditions may describe the market conditions that a company faces, or they may be relevant for only certain product lines or markets into which a company sells. As a result, a company may sell all or only some of its products through agents. Large manufacturers such as ITT, Corning, Monsanto, Teledyne, and Mobil Oil supplement their own sales force by contracting with sales agents in secondary markets. Xerox, for instance, sells strictly through agents in rural areas and recently switched to selling smaller metropolitan accounts through agents.

As the above discussion suggests, a company must be very cautious in switching from a sales agent organization to a dedicated field sales organization. A recent example of a company that has successfully made the switch is Sara Lee Corporation, the $4 billion company selling fresh-baked goods, meats, tea, and coffee. Key to its decision to make the switch was the move from a transactional type of relationship to a more consultative relationship with its grocery customers. The consultative relationship is based on data-driven decisions and close customer relationships as opposed to the individual relationships and loyalties that characterized many of its past relationships. The revenue and market share results have been very positive in all of Sara Lee's divisions.[23]

- The market is fragmented, and customers are difficult to find or understand.
- Buying is decentralized.
- Local knowledge and local distribution are important.
- The company is selling only a few products.
- There is a good potential sales agency who has significant marketing expertise in the industry.
- The company is not well known and has little equity in the market.
- The products are easily understood commodities that have been around for a long time.
- The selling cycle is short, and orders are typically small.
- It is not necessary to tightly control the selling effort.
- Ongoing support activities are not important, and the company does not need customer information.

FIGURE 6-11 Market Factors Favoring the Use of Sales Agents

EMERGING SALES FORCE ORGANIZATION ISSUES

Five issues related to sales force organization are getting increasing management attention—marketing-sales disconnect, cross-functional coordination, global account organizations, sales teams, and selling partners.

Marketing-Sales Disconnect

According to the results of a recent survey, aligning sales and market more closely is one of the top three priorities of chief sales executives.[24] This might surprise some because it would seem that sales and marketing would naturally align with their mutual focus on the customer. When sales are disappointing, however, marketing tends to blame the sales force for not executing the marketing plan. The sales team, in turn, attributes the results to marketing setting prices too high and using too much of the budget for advertising instead of hiring more salespeople or paying salespeople higher commissions. More broadly, according to another survey, sales departments tend to believe that marketers are out of touch with what's really going on with the customer, while marketers believe the sales force is myopic—too focused on individual customer experiences while being insufficiently aware of the larger market. In short, each group tends to undervalue the other's contributions.

Figure 6-12 reflects the ways in which marketing and sales influence customer purchasing. There are two sources of friction between sales and marketing. One is economic, and the other is cultural. The economic reason results from the need to divide the total budget between sales and marketing. The budget for each group is likely to reflect the power each department wields within the organization.

The cultural conflict between sales and marketing is even more entrenched than the economic conflict. In part, this is because the two functions attract quite different types of people who spend their time in quite different ways. Marketers tend to be highly analytical, data oriented, and project focused. They are all about building competitive advantage and the future. Often, this does not look like much action to sales because it all takes place behind a desk rather than out in the field. Salespeople, in contrast, spend their time talking to existing and potential customers. They are skilled relationship builders and are also attuned to the product features that customers desire and those that customers don't value.

What can be done to encourage greater alignment between sales and marketing? Experts suggest that the following steps should be considered:[25]

1. **Encourage disciplined communication.** Hold regular meetings between sales and marketing. Make sure the agenda include major opportunities and problems. Focus the discussion on action items.
2. **Create joint assignments and rotate jobs.** Create opportunities for marketing and sales to work together, such as marketers going along on sales calls and salespeople helping to develop marketing plans and sit in on product-planning reviews.
3. **Co-locate marketers and salespeople.** By locating in physical proximity, they will interact more often and are more likely to work better together.

Cross-Functional Coordination

The traditional flow of communications in most organizations has been directed outward from the organization to the customer through the sales force. Although the sales force had some interaction among other functional areas—R&D, production, logistics, and accounting and finance—the need for coordination was limited owing to the mostly one-way flow of communications out to the sales force.

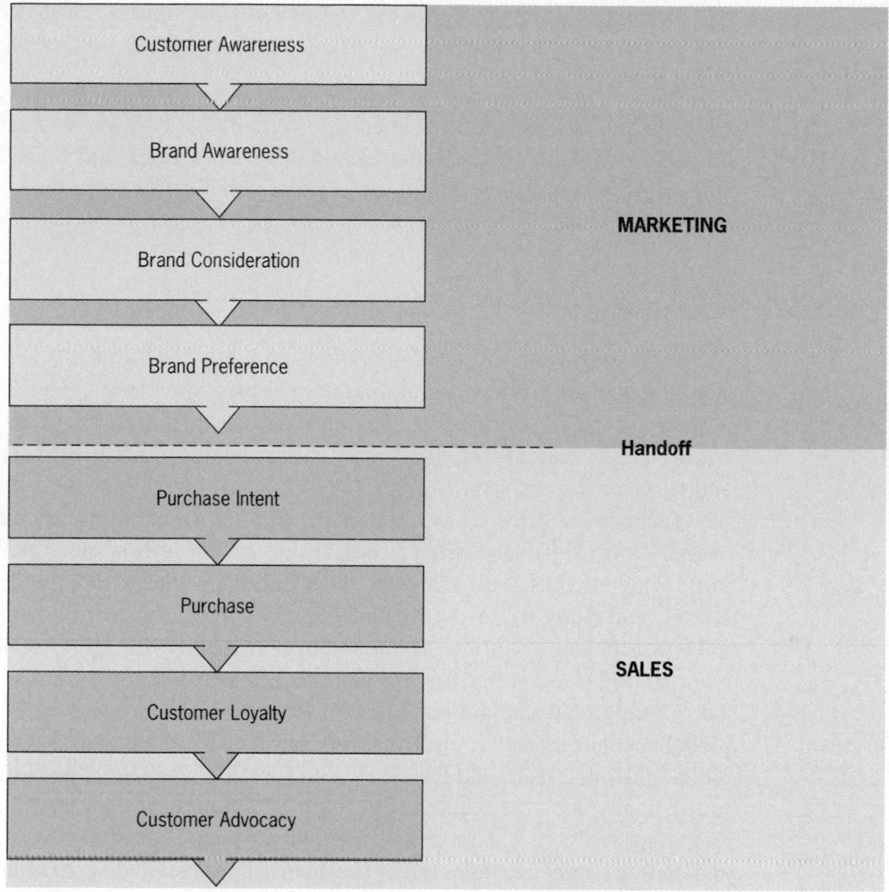

FIGURE 6-12 The Marketing–Sales Handoff

With an increased focus on solving customers' problems, the flow of communications between sales and other departments is becoming more of a two-way communications flow. The sales force now communicates customers' needs and expectations back to the organization. Wal-Mart's and Procter & Gamble's teams have constructed a formal, written code of conduct, for instance, in which each has agreed to be the other's advocate within their respective firms. If both teams agree that a particular type of promotion would work best in Wal-Mart, for example, then the P&G sales team is responsible for selling the program inside P&G. To facilitate more honest and candid exchange of information between functional areas, some companies are turning to networked personal computers to facilitate consensus building and brainstorming[26]

With which functional areas is the sales force most likely to interact? Depending on the organization and situation, sales will often need to work harmoniously with the following departments to successfully address customer needs.

- Engineering—new product and product modification ideas
- Marketing—advertising themes and media, cooperative advertising efforts, development of sales aids, channel issues, competitive pricing, and competitive market information
- Production—product availability, sales forecasting, production scheduling, technical product information, special product features and characteristics, and delivery schedules
- Accounting and finance—special pricing and credit schedules, customer credit information, budgets and quotas, compensation programs, and control of expenses

- Operations/Customer Service—equipment installation, customer training, equipment upgrades, ordering problems, warranty servicing, and emergency needs of customers

According to a recent survey by Accenture, front-line sales are most likely to interact with operations and customer service, followed by product development.[27] Ensuring proper coordination and communications between sales and these functions is often difficult. Nevertheless, the benefits of a coordinated effort to address customer problems are often worthwhile.

Global Account Organizations

Customer expansion to global operations and into new product lines and businesses requires suppliers to have global capabilities and real-time knowledge and responsiveness across businesses and functions. *Global account management* programs treat a customer's operations worldwide as one integrated account with coherent terms for prices, product specifications, and service.[28]

Technology firms were some of the first to utilize global account management (GAM) teams. Typical of these firms is Solectron, an $18 billion electronic manufacturing service firm, which works with many of the technology giants like IBM, Hewlett-Packard, Sun, Nortel, and Sony to design, manufacturer, deliver, repair, and support their product lines. Solectron began its global accounts effort in 1996 with Cisco. Cisco had little interest in manufacturing and relied on providers like Solectron as an essential part of its supply chain. The Cisco global account team began with two members—a global account executive and a global account manager. Over the last six years, Solectron has continued to evolve the Cisco global customer team and has developed fourteen new teams for a total of fifteen global customer teams, which collectively account for 75 percent of Solectron's revenues. The global teams are truly cross-functional, including people in operations, sales, finance, marketing, and new product introductions. The teams are designed around an understanding of customer needs and priorities and are built to reflect specific customer strategies.[29] Despite the increased adoption of GAM programs by suppliers, a recent research study found that only about a third of the suppliers that have adopted GAM programs are happy they did so, and that even for them success can be hard.[30] Many of the successful programs have had over ten years of trial and error to arrive at a place where their gains, a bigger share of the customer's business and a richer sales mix, outweigh the pain of lower prices and a higher cost to serve. The two biggest difficulties with GAM programs are selecting the right global customers for a GAM program and developing the right structure for implementing a GAM program.

The selection question is similar to that of selecting customers for a strategic account management program discussed earlier with the added complexity that there also needs to be a geographic fit as well. Also similar to the discussion of strategic account management programs, the right structure of a GAM program is essentially a tradeoff between tailoring the program for individual customers and minimizing the resources that each program consumes. Additionally, there is a major issue with respect to how much responsibility to give the central GAM group and how much to give the national sales organizations.

Despite the difficulties, market forces are leading more and more companies to adopt GAM programs. Hewlett-Packard has over 200 corporate accounts with global account status. IBM has a similar number of global accounts. For more analysis of global account issues, you should address the issues raised in Team Exercise, "A Global Assignment."

Sales Teams

Today's customers have increasingly customized and complex needs—needs that frequently cannot be met by individual salespeople. In these situations, success depends on the ability to

TEAM EXERCISE
"A Global Assignment"

As Global Sales Director for Access Communications in California, you need to fill a sales slot in Bath, England. You have the perfect candidate for the assignment: Grace Bowens, a strategic account manager in Denver. The problem is, can you convince Grace to take an international assignment given Access's expatriate policy? Access will pay relocation expenses for a contracted two-year-or-more assignment but offers no base pay increase for time abroad. Management believes that an expatriate assignment should be treated the same as any in-country relocation. Otherwise, the company would have to pay too many people a percentage increase because Access has salespeople and managers in more than two dozen countries.

Trying to convince Grace to take the assignment is complicated by the fact that she is married to a successful graphics designer, who probably wouldn't give up his job and lucrative salary. You would like Grace to take the expatriate assignment for three years. If all goes well, you intend to bring her back and promote her as the head of a top-five global account based in the United States. You know you need a creative solution, but what is it? Do you agree with Access's policy for expatriate assignments? What do you recommend? How would you negotiate with Grace? Should Access find an equivalent position for Grace's husband?

marshal resources effectively across a range of buying locations, buying influences, product lines, and internal organizational boundaries. Now, companies such as AT&T, Baxter, Dun and Bradstreet, and Procter & Gamble are discovering that meeting customer procurement requirements and perfecting the overall customer interface require a customer-focused *sales team* consisting of salespeople, customer service, technical specialists, and other functional areas. The objective of these teams is to consolidate greater knowledge and skills to focus on a more creative and complete solution to a customer's needs in order to build stronger customer relationships.

Xerox has used a team approach for some time, utilizing the slogan "Team Xerox." The account team comprises of an account representative, a highspeed duplicating specialist, an electronic printing specialist, an office systems and networking specialist, an electronic keyboard and workstation specialist, a copier specialist, and an account manager.

Figure 6-13 illustrates how part of Ericsson's Key Account sales force is organized. The account manager for a major customer can call on the expertise and support of the account coordinator, a project manager, and a technical support engineer. If the situation is appropriate, the team may also call on the additional technical expertise of the specific product manager. If the customer has international operations, then a global account manager will also work with the team to coordinate their effort worldwide. In Ericsson, Key Account sales teams are responsible for building on existing customer account relationships, while the National Account Team (not shown in Figure 6-13) is responsible for finding new business with totally new customer accounts. Ericsson, as in many large companies, incorporates aspects of different types of sales force organization discussed in this chapter: geographic territories, product specialization, customer specialization, and functional specialization, as well as major accounts and selling teams.

Selling Partners

With the shift to direct channels and the need to customize solutions to individual customers, companies are finding it necessary to market through *selling partners*. These are salespeople who are not on the payroll and who not only sell but also provide technical and

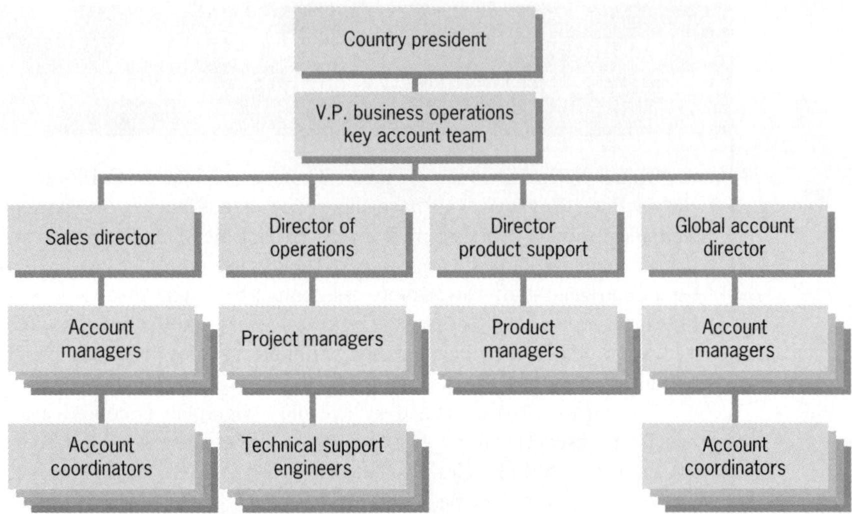

FIGURE 6-13 Sales Team Organization at Ericsson

operating support. An example is Siebel CRM, a division of Oracle Corporation, which uses partner companies to customize its software for large- and medium-size customers. Siebel provides the software code, and the selling partner provides the consulting and systems integration services to install the software in a company. To get the software product to market, Siebel needs value-added selling partners that actually implement the software package. This arrangement raises many strategic issues for Siebel. It does not have to shoulder all the selling costs involved in getting the attention of the final customer, but it also must be creative in attempting to control the selling process. If a conflict arises with its selling partners, will Siebel have the power to influence its resolution?

IBM is another large company that works with selling partners to address the information and technology needs of smaller customers. Worldwide, IBM has relationships with nearly 50,000 "business partners" consisting of independent distributors, value-added resellers, system integrators, and software vendors. The 20 percent of small business customers that account for 80 percent of the dollar sales receive one-on-one attention from the IBM sales force. However, salespeople are responsible for effectively managing the customer relationship by working with their distributors and resellers to present a coordinated and effective message to the customer. To accomplish this coordination, the IBM sales force works closely with its strong telemarketing group. IBM is a good example of a very successful company that has incorporated specialization, sales teams, telemarketing, and selling partners into its sales force organizational design.[31]

SUMMARY

Changes in the competitive environment and in the way your customers want to purchase often require a reorganization of the sales force. Decisions must be made about how many salespeople are needed, how they should work together, and how they should be organized to ensure both efficiency and effectiveness in accessing an identified customer base. These decisions are likely to have a profound effect on the performance of the sales force and the organization as a whole.

1. **Explain the various ways by which sales forces can be organized.** Almost all sales organizations use some sort of geographic breakdown to help control the costs and

activities of field salespeople. Firms with diverse lines of high-technology products often can improve their sales performance by specializing selling efforts by product. Where buyers have special needs, customer specialization can improve efficiency by eliminating duplication of calls and by more effectively identifying and meeting customers' needs. With complex products, the sales organization may be divided along functional lines into initial contact people and account maintenance people.

2. **Explain what a strategic accounts management program means.** This is a marketing philosophy directed at a select group of customers that account for a disproportionately large share of the seller's total revenues and have complex needs and problems. These customers have been selected for special attention because they put more emphasis on value-added options such as education, electronic data interchange, and management information system compatibility.
3. **State the reasons for the growth in telemarketing and its implementation issues.** Telemarketing refers to customer contacts utilizing telecommunications technology for personal selling without direct, face-to-face contact. One reason for the growing popularity of telemarketing is that it allows companies to make cost-effective sales calls, especially on small customers. Another reason for its success is that many customers prefer this method of communications owing to time pressures. The primary obstacles to successful implementation of telemarketing are resistance by field salespeople and the special management issues associated with hiring, motivating, and retaining telemarketers.
4. **Tell why and when sales agents are utilized.** Independent sales agents are not employees, but independent businesses given exclusive contracts to perform the selling function within specified geographic areas. They take neither ownership nor physical possession of the products they sell and are always compensated by commission. Because they are paid on commission and are therefore largely a variable cost, agents are often used to develop new markets or cover geographic areas in which demand is not sufficient to support a company sales force.
5. **Describe evolving trends in sales force organization.** Five sales force organization issues are receiving increasing management attention—centralization versus decentralization, cross-functional coordination, global account organizations, sales teams, and selling partners. These issues are arising due to changes in the technology and the needs of companies' customer bases.

KEY TERMS

Build-up method
Customer specialization
Functional specialization
Generalist structure
Global account management
Independent sales agents
Mapping programs
Permission marketing
Sales teams
Selling partners
Starting points
Strategic account management program
Telemarketing
Territory
Vertical marketing

DEVELOPING YOUR COMPETENCIES

1. **Self-Management.** The world of business-to-business management is changing, radically and permanently. New selling methods, especially national accounts programs and telemarketing, have altered the role of traditional face-to-face selling. The role of the traditional field sales force has shrunk, while telemarketing focuses on small customers and strategic accounts programs sell to the largest customers. How do you think these developments will affect the role of the traditional sales manager and the skills required

for the position? How does the sales manager's role compare with the roles of national accounts managers and telemarketing managers?

2. **Strategic Action.** Corporate restructuring is becoming an everyday occurrence in today's business environment. Such restructuring may happen when one company acquires another company or picks up a new product line. It may also occur in the process of divesting a business or product line or when merging several product lines, each with its own sales and distribution forces, into a single division. Restructuring offers opportunities and also poses threats to sales force management. If, for example, a national company decides to combine its separate housewares and audio business sales forces, what issues must be considered? What kinds of analysis would you do prior to any reorganization? How would you execute a merger between these two sales forces?
3. **Technology.** The 3M Company offers an 800 number to assist its telecommunication equipment customers. The 3M National Service Center, located in St. Paul, Minnesota, is staffed 365 days a year, 24 hours a day, with skilled technicians and coordinators. Through systematic questioning and a variety of facsimile, ASCII communication terminals, the latest monitoring and testing equipment, and a sophisticated on-line computer system, the staff can isolate an equipment problem or operator error. The 3M Center has found that in more than 30 percent of the calls, the equipment failure can be corrected in minutes, without dispatching a service technician. Considering the other possible telemarketing roles besides customer service, what are other possible applications of technology in telemarketing?
4. **Global Perspective.** The goal of Oracle's Global Account Management Program (GAMP) is to dramatically improve international customers' ease and effectiveness of doing business with Oracle. To accomplish this goal, Oracle uses its own database technology to support a worldwide GAMP information networking system. In addition to the customer having access to the database, any Oracle employee supporting an account can access the system. What are the possible risks and uses for such a database? www.oracle.com.
5. **Team Building.** Minneapolis-based ADC Telecommunications strategically uses suppliers as part of its sales team to support its account management efforts. A variety of consulting and training firms serve as resources to address strategic account issues. These firms are brought together on an as-needed basis to address issues collectively rather than independently. By using this approach to address customer needs and issues, ADC has an opportunity to bring additional value to its customers. The practice has been found to improve customer relationships and generate new revenue opportunities. A number of issues are critical to the success of this teamwork effort. For instance, how does ADC ensure the quality of advice given by these outside firms? How does ADC coordinate the efforts of these partners with its own efforts? What are some other issues critical to the success of this program, and how might an organization address these issues? www.adc.com.
6. **Coaching.** A marketing and sales executive for a leading industrial organization who is a relative newcomer to the firm shares the following summary of his initial meeting with one of his larger accounts with whom they do over $10 million in business annually. "While the account is one of our older, more established customers, the account is undergoing some changes that have been difficult for us to put our arms around. Several years ago, they centralized purchasing. It seemed to me at the time that the existing contracts were reasonable and fair. Nevertheless, purchase orders were no longer being placed as frequently from the customer's local plants as in earlier years. When my strategic account team has tried to introduce new product developments, the discussion has quickly transformed itself into requests for price reductions. In addition, the account executive's efforts to bring the latest training concepts to the customer's field team are

being met with a lukewarm reception. The customer's field team seems to be extraordinarily concerned with inventory and delivery issues, not training. As a result, the rate of revenue growth with this account has receded over the last several years, and the opportunity with this account is languishing." What is possibly going on with this account? What advice would you give this executive?

PROBLEMS*

1. Your company currently generates $200 million in revenue selling through 50 independent sales agencies. The agencies are paid a flat 5 percent commission on sales they generated. You are wondering whether it would be less expensive to develop your own dedicated sales force. Your industry's trade association conducts an annual compensation survey, which indicated that the average salary for salespeople is $60,000 including benefits. In addition, an incentive compensation of 0.5 percent (i.e, one-half of 1 percent) of sales was also typical. You estimate that you would need to hire 100 salespeople to replace the sales agents. Given the information provided, which would cost you less at $200 million in revenue—your own dedicated sales force or independent sales agents? What is the breakeven sales volume for your company; that is, when do the two sales force alternatives cost the same?
2. Upon further reflection on the previous problem, you realize that you have neglected to consider several relevant costs in your calculations. You have one national sales manager and a marketing manager who presently interface with the independent sales agents, but additional management levels will be needed to train and manage the number of salespeople you are anticipating hiring.

   First, you have decided to divide the nation into two regions with a regional sales manager in charge of each. According to industry sources, a regional sales manager's average salary is $120,000. Second, a number of district managers will be needed to manage the salespeople directly. A span of control of 10:1 (10 salespeople to 1 manager) is believed to be necessary. Salaries for district managers average $90,000. Incentive pay for managers, both regional and district, is expected to be 0.35 percent of sales. Third, it should cost $12,000 to recruit and train each salesperson. Finally, management wants sales to grow by 10 percent next year to $220 million, so more than 100 salespeople will need to be hired. Average sales per salesperson are expected to be $2 million. Given this new information, which type of sales force will be less expensive? What is the breakeven sales volume now?

FEATURED CASE

SHIELD FINANCIAL "A SPECIAL ASSIGNMENT"

It's been 18 months since he took over the Des Moines office, and Doug Bloom is finally feeling like he has the job under control. His office has exceeded its sales quotas for each of the last five quarters and profits are improving. He also felt as if he understood himself better and had grown as an individual. At dinner the other night, he mentioned to his wife, "You know, as you get involved in this job, your personality changes. Some managers become very people-directed and others are more sales- and

*Excel spreadsheets for working on these problems are available at www.wiley.com/college/cron. Go to "Student Companion Site."

customer-directed. I doubt that you find many people who are perfectly balanced on these dimensions. I think I'm leaning toward the people side now, which surprises me. I always loved the customer contact so much when I was selling."

The next day at work he received a call from Vinny Raccioppi, Vice President of Marketing and Sales for Shield, informing him that as part of his management development he was given a special assignment. Vinny would like to meet with him in New York the following week to discuss this assignment.

In New York, Doug is informed that his special assignment is to plan for the phasing out of independent insurance brokers in the mountain states of Montana, Idaho, Wyoming, Utah, and Colorado. Shield intended to hire full-time salespeople to cover these areas. Among other reasons for the change, the population in these states is growing and the company feels that it can get better penetration of the market with its own dedicated sales force. Vinny also mentions that he believes the sales agents have grown "older and wealthier" and are losing the "energy and drive" of earlier years.

Shield currently has two regional sales managers who supervise the brokers in these states. These regional managers are responsible for recruiting high-quality brokers, working with them to ensure that they understand and know how to sell Shield's products, and producing the sales volumes quotas in these areas. The sales manager will need their help to put together an in-house sales force and undertake damage control when the sales agents are informed of the new organization.

Doug's reaction is one of surprise, followed by a realization of the magnitude of the undertaking. One of Doug's immediate concerns was controlling the damage to customer relationships that may arise when the brokers are told of the new sales organization. Vinny informs Doug that he has two months to complete a plan for starting the new sales force. Doug says that he had better begin right away and suggests that he meet with the two regional sales managers.

The following week, Doug arranges a meeting with the two regional sales managers. Doug informs them of the impending change in organization and the necessity of developing a thorough and thoughtful plan of action. After expressing their surprise, the regional sales managers mention their concern with agents' reactions. They both indicate that there is no way this plan can be kept a secret until it is implemented and that the brokers are likely to be angry about losing the 20 percent commissions they have become used to receiving. During this discussion, possible retaliatory actions by the brokers are discussed. At the conclusion of the meeting, the vice president suggests that they all think about how to "ease out" the 34 agents without suffering undue economic recriminations. They agree to get back together for a meeting the next week to discuss alternative plans.

Questions

1. How would you advise Doug to conduct the meeting with the two regional sales managers?
2. How would you attempt to control the potential economic damage that may occur when switching from brokers to your own sales force?
3. What would you suggest doing if one of the brokers asked you whether it was true that shield was going to release all its brokers and switch to a dedicated sales force?
4. What issues would you have to address in starting your own sales force?

MANAGEMENT RESOURCES

TERRITORY DESIGN

In the previous chapter on sales force structure, we mentioned that one of the most common sales force structures is to assign salespeople all accounts in a particular geographic area. Even when sales forces are organized according to specialties (e.g., products, customers, or functions), salespeople's responsibilities are often restricted to a particular geographic boundary or territory, which is what Xerox has done. So the majority of sales forces have

Resource Consultant: David Pinals, President, TTG, Incorporated some sort of exclusive territory alignment that specifies each salesperson's or sales team's account responsibility and activity mix. The purpose of this chapter is to discuss processes for designing geographic territories and issues that may arise when assigning salespeople to a particular territory.

THREE REASONS WHY PROPER TERRITORY ALIGNMENT IS IMPORTANT

Customers and prospects have a level of activity and coverage that is required to service them properly. Salespeople likewise have an activity capacity. A *territory* is defined as the customers, located in a specified geographic area, that are assigned to an individual salesperson. Thus, although territories are often referenced in geographic terms, the defining element of a territory is the set of customers in the geography.

A properly aligned sales territory is one in which customers receive the proper amount of attention and the workload is balanced across salespeople. Figure MR6-1 illustrates the territory imbalance that existed in a cosmetics firm. According to experts, it is indicative of the imbalance that exists in many sales forces. The vertical axis indicates the amount of workload in a territory, with 1.0 indicating the ideal workload for one salesperson. All 200 territories in the sales force are sorted from highest to lowest, and each territory is represented along the curved line. Territories with indexes above 1.0 have too much workload for one salesperson to properly handle, while those below 1.0 have insufficient work and sales potential. With a tolerance level of +15 and −15 percent, approximately 60 percent of territories have an unacceptable deviation from the ideal workload level. A study of over 4,800 territories indicates that this is not an unusual situation. The study found that well over half of the territories were not the right size. Approximately 25 percent of the territories were too large to be covered effectively, while 31 percent were too small to keep a salesperson sufficiently busy with productive work.[1]

Research on territory alignment suggests that there are at least three reasons for properly aligning sales territories by bringing all territories within a proper workload tolerance level.[2]

- Increased sales
- Cost savings
- Higher morale

Increased Sales

In a properly aligned sales force, work shifts among salespeople so that all customers receive appropriate coverage. A salesperson who has additional time to call on customers is assigned an account that is currently managed by a salesperson who is too busy. This neglected account could turn out to be the best account in a low-workload territory because this salesperson has enough time to work with the customer, while salespeople with too little time are not seeing important customers. Research by ZS Associates indicates that rectifying a workload imbalance can improve sales by between 2 and 7 percent.

Cost Savings Through Reduced Salesperson Travel

Sales territories can be justified economically because they help reduce marketing costs. When only one person covers each geographic area, duplication of sales calls and related travel costs are eliminated. Salespeople in well-designed territories spend less time traveling and more time selling, resulting in lower sales costs as a percentage of sales. For example, a large industrial distributor with over a 1,000 salespeople was able to reduce travel time by 13.7 percent by properly aligning its sales territories. This translated into almost $1 million

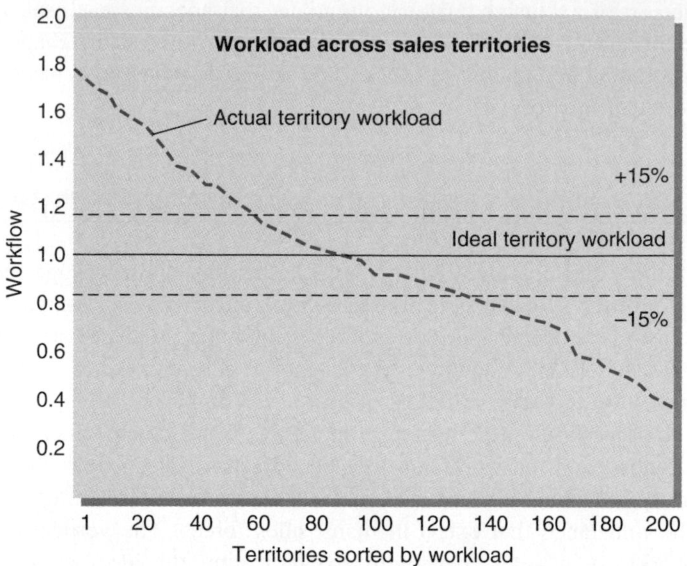

FIGURE MR6-1 Unbalanced Territories for a Cosmetics Company

in savings and increased selling time by 2.7 percent. The company estimated that this increase in selling time resulted in over $15 million in additional sales and over $3 million in additional profits. Another benefit of reduced travel included salespeople having more nights at home and higher morale.

Higher Morale and Reduced Turnover

Studies have consistently shown that sales potential is the single best predictor of territory sales, regardless of any factors related to the salesperson. In other words, high sales potential will lead to high sales, regardless of the sales person's efforts. The reverse is true for low sales potential territories. In a consumer goods company with 250 territories, for instance, the territory ranked fourth highest in sales for the year had been without a salesperson for most of the year. Analysis indicated that the territory had huge sales potential.

The strong sales potential–territory sales relationship suggests that management must be careful to reward the salesperson and not the territory. Inequitable and unfair rewards are likely to result from improper territory alignment. Some very good salespeople may become dissatisfied with the job because they feel they are in a "no-win" situation or because they start questioning their own abilities and career choices. On the other hand, the salesperson who has been going on reward trips for the last ten years may not really deserve the trips. His or her territory may simply have too much sales potential, so that it produced more sales than other territories despite the salesperson's efforts. Compensation systems with a high percentage of incentive pay tend to accentuate the morale and turnover effects of poor territory alignment.

WHEN DO TERRITORIES NEED TO BE REALIGNED?

In a recent survey of 278 sales managers, 62 percent reported that they had had to realign sales territories within the past 12 months.[3] A number of events may require a minor realignment of sales territories. For instance, a large customer may relocate. A new account may need to be shifted from a customer acquisition specialist to an account service and

A change in sales force size
A change in sales force structure
Mergers and acquisitions
Shifts in market opportunities
Demographic shifts
New products
Need to shake things up

FIGURE MR6-2 Reasons for a Major Territory Realignment

maintenance specialist. A salesperson may leave the company, and the uncovered accounts may need to be temporarily assigned to other salespeople.

Major territory realignments usually occur every few years at large U.S. companies. These realignments usually result from a major sales force change or restructuring. Figure MR6-2 lists some of the more likely reasons for a major territory realignment.

On the other hand, management must be careful not to make too many significant changes in territories. Reasons for carefully considering such a change before jumping into it include:

- It disrupts people's lives.
- It disrupts customer relationships.
- It is a cumbersome process.
- It can be costly.
- Data for making realignment decisions are limited.

Despite these reasons for not realigning territories, the costs of a poor alignment are high, as discussed earlier.

TERRITORY DESIGN PROCEDURES

There are many ways to assign accounts to salespeople; in fact, there are more than 1,000 ways to assign ten accounts to two salespeople. The number of solutions rises exponentially as the number of accounts and salespeople increases. Understandably, there are a number of potentially good alignments and an enormous number of poor ones. Fortunately, data and information processing technology advances are facilitating the process.

An effective design of sales territories can be achieved by following the six-step process outlined in Figure MR6-3. The remainder of this Resource focuses on describing these steps.

Select Geographic Control Units

The first step in the process is to select an appropriate geographic control unit, which is a unit of geography that can be combined to form sales territories. Control units must be small enough to allow flexibility in setting boundaries. They must have less area than a territory and clearly recognized boundaries. Examples of commonly used geographic control units are listed in Table MR6-1. At first glance, countries would seem to be too large a unit for designing sales territories. However, a firm that is exporting goods to Europe might combine several small countries such as Holland, Belgium, and Luxembourg into one territory. States or provinces may also appear to be too big for combination into territories. States are most often used as control units when a firm attempts to cover a whole country with a few salespeople. Small states such as Rhode Island, Connecticut, Massachusetts, and New Hampshire are frequently combined to create a single territory.

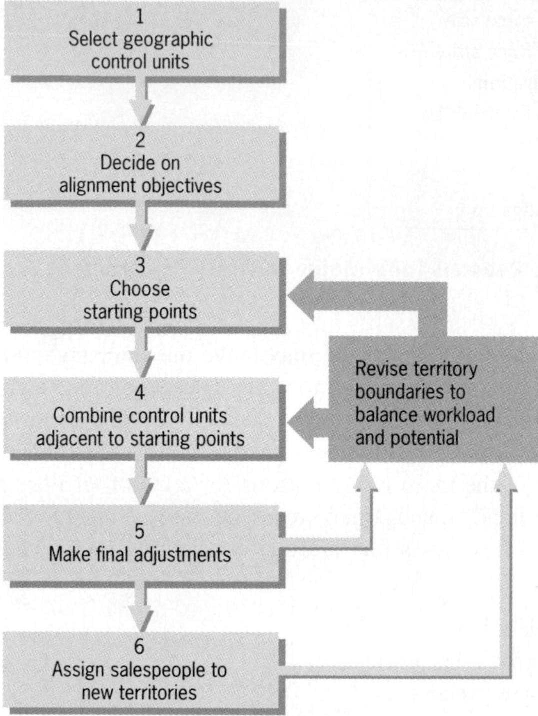

FIGURE MR6-3 Territory Design Process

When a firm has a lot of urban business, cities or metropolitan areas can be desirable control units. Firms that divide up cities into several sales territories often rely on zip codes or census tracts as control units. The smallest control unit might involve building territories by combining individual customers. Only when a company has a very limited number of large customers can accounts serve as territorial design control units. The most common approach in the United States is to build up territories using counties. They are small enough to expedite territory construction, and potential data are routinely published for these units.

Decide on Alignment Objectives

Although a company may choose a variety of objectives when realigning territories, balancing workload and sales potential are usually selected as important alignment goals. Balancing sales potential is particularly important when incentives, such as commissions and bonuses, are a major part of the compensation system. It is important that salespeople have equal earning opportunities for income. Some common measures of sales potential include:

- Total industry sales
- Buying Power Index

TABLE MR6-1 Geographic Control Units Used in Territory Design

Countries	Cities
States or provinces	Zip codes
Counties	Census tracts
Metropolitan areas	Customers

- NAICS Code Information
- Demographic Information (population, number of accounts, etc.)

Balancing company sales is not the same as balancing sales potential. Sales reflect where the sales force is spending its time. Sales potential reflects where the sales force should be spending its time. Territories that are balanced on sales can become inherently unfair, as it punishes salespeople for past success by taking accounts away from high producers.

When the sales force performs a set of well-defined tasks for their customers, then balancing workload should be emphasized. Examples would include many consumer goods sales forces selling to retailers or distributor salespeople who call on existing customers to replenish inventory. In such cases, workload usually can be accurately measured, and a balanced workload should be emphasized to encourage optimal customer coverage.

Measures that could be used to balance workload include:

- Number of accounts
- Number of accounts by segments
- Number of prospects
- Number of hours required to cover accounts and prospects
- Time needed to cover accounts and prospects

Although the measures used to determine sales potential and workload may differ, multiple measures may be considered when designing territories. W. W. Grainger Inc., a $4.8 billion distributor of maintenance and repair supplies, divided its account list among its more than 1,500 salespeople using what it calls an alignment index. An alignment index for each account is based on its revenue history and workload. Workload is measured as the number of service hours devoted to each account. Whether a salesperson manages four small accounts or one large account, the alignment index will total approximately 1,000 points, thereby balancing each territory on both important criteria.

Although balancing sales potential and workload are the most common allocation criteria, a company may also be interested in minimizing travel time and disruption of client relationships. Minimizing travel time is particularly important when it is important to control the number of hours worked, such as when a part-time sales force is employed. In such a case, allocation measures such as square miles and average travel time might be used as allocation criteria. On the other hand, minimizing account disruptions may be important when a consultative and enterprise-type selling is used and in-depth customer knowledge is important. The percentage of accounts and the percentage of dollar sales that have been reassigned would be important allocation criteria.

Choose Starting Points

The third step in territory design is to select geographic locations to serve as *starting points* for new territories. Since geographic control units are combined to form territories, one control unit must be chosen around which to combine the additional control units. This control unit is referred to as the starting point. The starting point that is chosen often determines the geographic boundary of the territories.

A common choice is the salesperson's present home because the cost of relocating salespeople can be avoided and representatives remain near family and friends. Another popular starting point is a large city. Salespeople in urban locations usually have access to a large number of customers, and there is less need for extensive travel. An alternative method is to design the sales territory around the needs of major clients. In this case, the location of the largest customer in an area might be selected as the home base for the salesperson, and other areas might be added to complete the territory. Occasionally, a starting point will

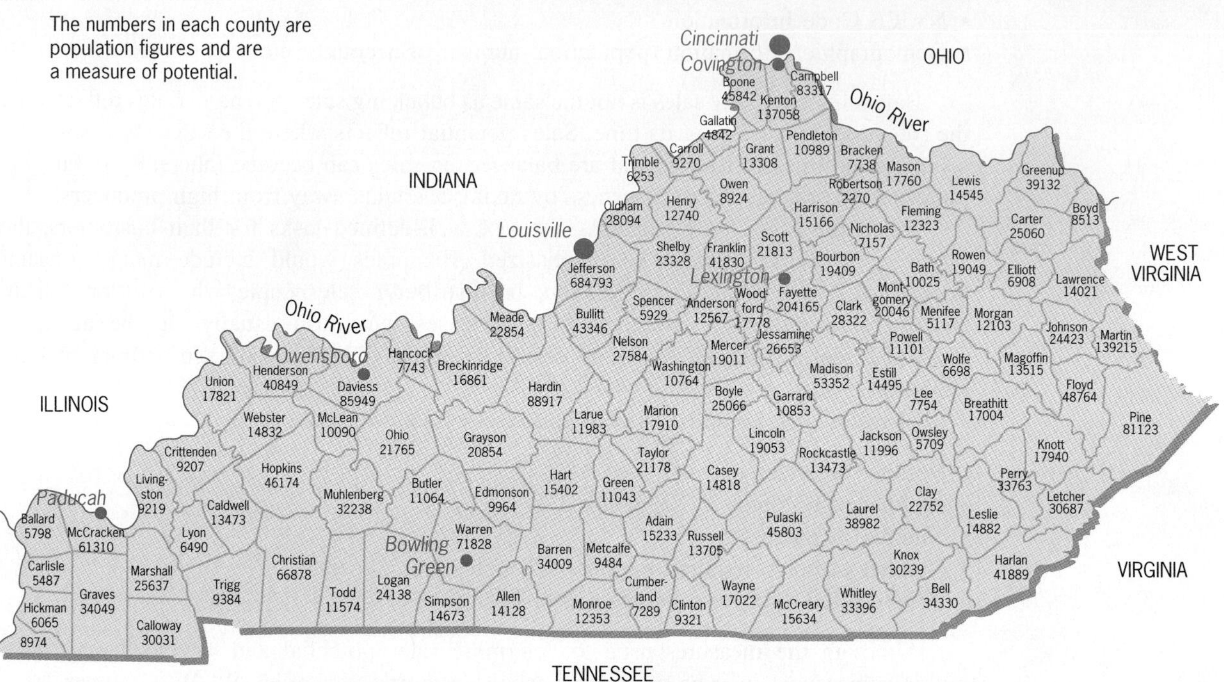

FIGURE MR6-4 Kentucky Counties, Major Cities, and Population Centers

be a central geographic location, and the preference of the salesperson or the presence of a city is disregarded. This approach assumes that a place can be found for the salesperson to live after the territory has been created.

The problems of finding starting points for sales territories can be illustrated by looking at a map of the state of Kentucky (Figure MR6-4). This map shows the location of counties, major cities, and county population as a measure of potential. If two salespeople are placed in Kentucky, one will probably be located in Louisville to cover the western half of the state, and the second will be placed in Lexington to handle the east. Neither location is very good because they are both located in the north-central part of the state. In addition, the Lexington-based salesperson would have to travel to the northern tip of the state to cover Covington, which is across the Ohio River from Cincinnati. The heavy concentration of business in the Cincinnati area would probably lead this salesperson to neglect some of the mountainous areas in the southeastern part of the territory. One possible solution would be to give Boone, Kenton, and Campbell counties to the Cincinnati-based salesperson.

If three salespeople were assigned to Kentucky, then the third territory would be placed in the western part of the state. Possible starting points for this territory would be Bowling Green, Owensboro, and Paducah. Owensboro has the disadvantage of being on the northern edge of the territory, and Paducah is too far to the west. A Paducah location would require extensive travel in an east-west pattern. Also, the north-south orientation of Kentucky Lake and Lake Barkley further complicates travel patterns in the area. One solution would be to carve off the seven most westerly counties and give them to a salesperson in another state. This example shows how difficult it is to find starting points for sales territories when you have an irregularly shaped state bounded by rivers and containing noncentral population clusters. You can also see why some firms use independent agents to cover sparsely populated areas.

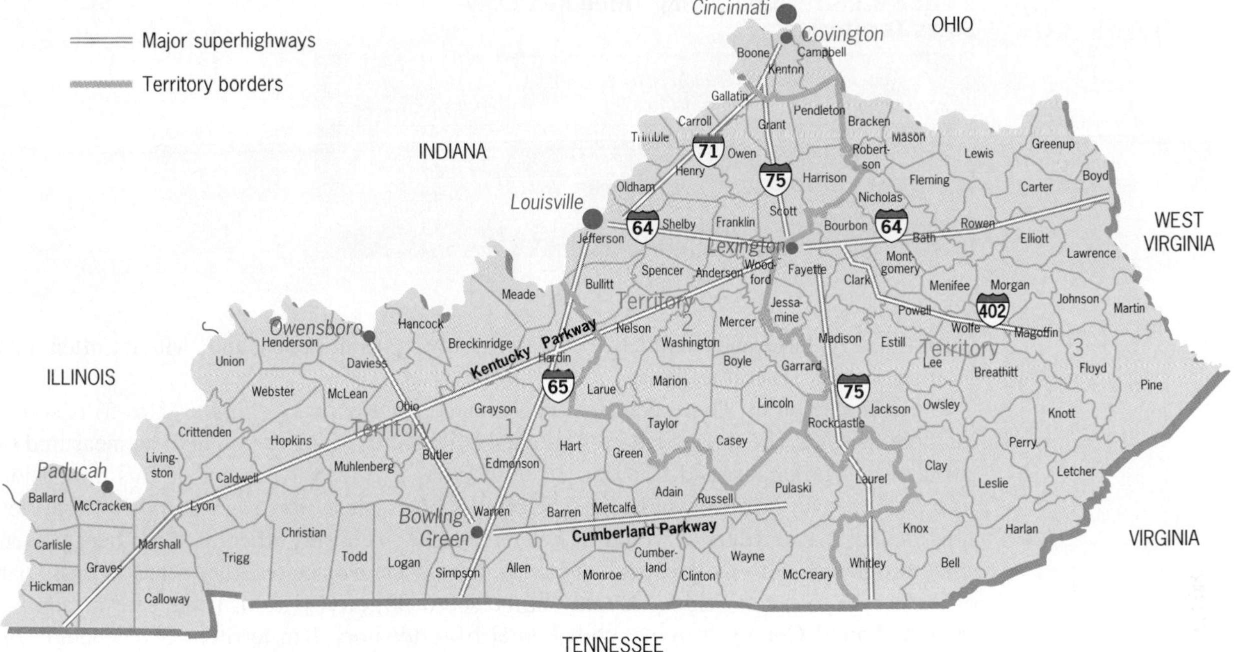

FIGURE MR6-5 Three Kentucky Sales Territories

Combine Control Units Adjacent to Starting Points

Once starting points have been selected, the next step is to begin combining control units. The most popular way of doing this is known as the *build-up method*. To be effective, you need to keep running totals on the allocation criteria for each new territory. If number of customers per county is the criterion, you first combine the counties adjacent to each starting point and keep track of the total number of customers in each territory. Then you assign counties between different starting points to territories to balance the number of customers across the new territories. The process of allocating counties to starting points continues until all control units are assigned to individual salespeople.

An example of three sales territories that were built up around the suggested starting points for Kentucky is shown in Figure MR6-5. The territories were constructed using the country population figures shown in Figure MR6-4. Note that the solution was simplified by including the three northernmost counties in the Cincinnati territory. Territory 2 turned out to be the smallest because of the heavy population concentration in the Louisville–Frankfort area. Territory 1 is large and ungainly, but it can be covered quite well from Bowling Green using Route 64, Cumberland Parkway, Kentucky Parkway, and the Green River Parkway. Routes 64 and 75 are available to travel the northern and western parts of territory 3. However, the rest of territory 3 is mountainous and will be extremely difficult to cover.

Make Final Adjustments

After making an initial allocation of control units on your primary set of allocation criterion, you should compare territories on secondary criteria. For example, after balancing sales potential, you may wish to examine the square miles in each territory to see how the territories compare in size. If there is an imbalance, you may look at counties on the borders of the territories to see if some switching could improve the initial allocation. The solution may be to shift a large county with few customers from the largest to the smallest territory.

TABLE MR6-2 Comparing Three Kentucky Sales Territories

Territory	*Potential as Measured by Population*	*Number of Counties*
1	1,124,897	47
2	1,129,290	27
3	1,131,137	43

Unfortunately, large and small territories are not always contiguous, and switches often must be made across several territories.

A comparison of three sales territories created for Kentucky (Figure MR6-5) is shown in Table MR6-2. The three territories are well matched in terms of potential as measured by population. The largest and smallest territories vary less than 1 percent on this dimension. In terms of size, however, territory 2 is only 60 percent as large as the other territories. This means that territory 2 would be relatively easy to cover, whereas the others present some problems. With the present boundaries, the salesperson in territory 3 has to cross part of territory 1 to get to Whitley County in the south (Figure MR6-5). If the salesperson has to cross Laurel County, why not shift Laurel from territory 1 to territory 3? Although this move would help balance the territories in terms of size, it would lead to greater imbalance on potential. The salesperson in territory 1 would have to give up potential represented by 38,982 people. In this particular case, territory 1 might be willing to give up Laurel County because the Cumberland Parkway stops in neighboring Pulaski County. Given the uneven distribution of potential across Kentucky, there is no way that the three territories can be perfectly balanced on both size and potential.

The problem of designing three territories for Kentucky gets more complicated when you introduce a third allocation factor, such as the number of customers. Because many salespeople receive commission income, it is important to balance territories based on existing customers so that wages do not get out of line. However, keeping track of three allocation variables as you move counties back and forth among territories gets rather confusing. One solution that we will discuss later is to use a computer to help you design sales territories.

Additional Factors. Additional factors to be considered when finalizing sales territories include the location of rivers, lakes, bridges, mountains, and roads. Sales managers often keep relief maps in their offices so that they can see how topographical features will influence sales force travel patterns. The availability of bridges and superhighways often influences how boundaries are drawn for sales territories.

Dividing a Large Territory. A common problem encountered by sales managers is how to divide a territory that has grown to have too many present and/or potential customers for one person to handle. A map of an area to be divided into two sales territories is shown in Figure MR6-6a. The map shows the present number of customers per county for one salesperson working the territory from Brockton. A logical home base for the second salesperson is Hillsdale, located in the west-central part of the territory. If these two cities are used as starting points, two new territories can be constructed by adding and subtracting adjacent counties until all counties are assigned and the number of customers is the same for both territories.

Proposed new territories are shown in Figure MR6-6b. Note that the heavy concentration of customers in the Brockton area has produced one small territory in the eastern region and one very large territory in the west. Although the two new territories have the same

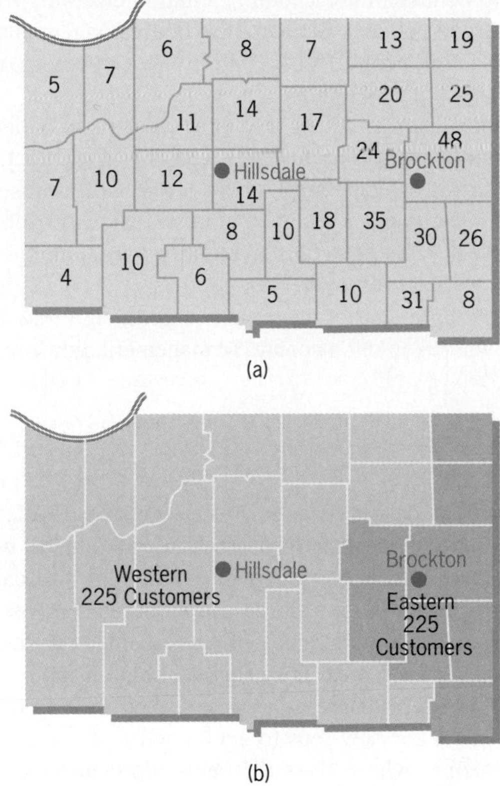

FIGURE MR6-6 Dividing a Large Territory

number of customers (225), the western territory requires considerable travel because the customers are more scattered. This solution may be acceptable if the current salesperson is located in Brockton and has reached an age where a smaller geographic territory would be appreciated. An alternative solution is to divide the area into northern and southern territories, with Brockton located at the boundary between the two. Although the size of the territories, number of customers, and travel time would be equalized, the territories would be wide and narrow. If both salespeople were traveling west from Brockton, travel expenses would be greater than the solution shown in Figure MR6-6b.

You may also wish to consider sales potential figures for each county. The western territory has more undeveloped potential than the eastern region, and the two new territories would be more balanced on size and potential if four or five western counties are shifted to the Brockton territory. Unfortunately, the current workload is then out of balance, since the eastern territory would have about fifty more customers. This example shows that variations in the dispersion of customers and potential across areas make it extremely difficult to construct territories that are equivalent in terms of travel time, number of present customers, and sales potential. Since both the build-up and *workload methods* create territories by combining geographic areas according to a set of rules, computers can be employed to speed the search for the most efficient territory boundaries.

Getting Buy-in. Up to this point, the territory design steps are likely to be, and should be, performed centrally for the company or business unit as a whole. This is the only way to ensure true balancing of territories. It is important to get management and salesperson input into the process before finalizing a new territory design structure for several reasons. First, local conditions need to be taken into account, including customer relationships, salesperson preferences, and local trade patterns. Second, first-line management must take ownership of the alignment. Territory alignment affects people's lives; therefore, it needs to be supported and accepted by the sales organization.

The following quote from a human resources director at a large pharmaceutical firm summarizes the importance of getting buy-in on the new alignment: "A lot of people don't realize this, but after an alignment, most of the dirty work ends up in my office. After we aligned poorly five years ago, I received almost a thousand complaints from the field force. We did it right two years ago. I received only two complaints. We had a minimum of disruptions, relocations, and turnover."[4]

The following quote by a district manager is a good sign that a new alignment will be successful: "My input was taken into account. Management didn't just give me an alignment and say 'go work it.'"[5]

Assign Salespeople to New Territories

The last step in our territory design process is to assign salespeople to individual territories (Figure MR6-1). First-line sales managers, perhaps in consultation with their managers, will usually complete this task. The decisions involve matching the background and needs of salespeople with the opportunities in each geographic area. Factors considered include the present home location, age, and experience of salespeople; the size of the territories; and the customer mix located in each area. For example, some firms initially try to place newly hired young people in territories near areas where they have grown up or have gone to school. This makes it easier for new reps to get started and can reduce first-year turnover.

For existing salespeople whose lives are being affected by a territory realignment, it is important that they understand that every effort has been made to balance territories with respect to sales potential and workload. They must also be assured that they will have the opportunity to maintain or increase their income under the new alignment. Many companies provide a transitional compensation adjustment when a major change in accounts results from territory realignment. These adjustments take the form of some sort of income guarantee for a short period of time while the salesperson gets up to speed in the new territory and with the new list of accounts. Research indicates that transitional compensation plans are very important steps in ensuring salesperson buy-in to the new alignment, as well as promoting overall motivation and morale.[6]

You should realize that territory boundaries do not last forever, and you have to adjust them regularly to resolve local issues (Figure MR6-1). These include situations where salespeople encounter personal problems and are unable to handle all their accounts. Also, you may have a situation where the special needs of a customer require a more experienced rep. Often these problems can be resolved by assigning a few accounts to salespeople in adjacent territories. The idea is to fine-tune territory boundaries without having to go through a complete redesign that may upset everyone.

Having said this, however, you should keep in mind that customization to fit a specific salesperson's strengths should be kept to a minimum. A territory should not be customized too much because territory alignments typically outlast a specific salesperson's assignment to the territory.

Experts advise that the following questions be addressed when considering making a territory change:[7]

- Is this the right thing to do regardless of who the salesperson is?
- Is this right thing to do for the geography and the set of accounts?

A territory is designed to serve the customer. How will customers perceive the coverage? It is important not to forget the customer when realigning territories. Read what one customer had to say after having been assigned a new salesperson following a realignment of territories:

> It would have been helpful to have the company do something in advance of the transition. They could have provided me with a written notice of the change. They could have given me written or verbal indication as to the readiness and qualifications of the new person.[8]

The lesson to be learned here is not to surprise anyone with a change in territories. And don't forget the customer.

DESIGNING TERRITORIES BY COMPUTER

Computer software programs are now routinely used to help design sales territories. Territory design programs function by automating some or all of the design processes shown in Figure MR6-1.

Mapping Programs

Mapping programs include spreadsheet information necessary for territory alignment and a geographic program that displays the control units for a particular geography. The user can allocate control units to any number of territories by a simple click of the mouse and is immediately provided with a visual representation of the new territories. At the same time, the program's spreadsheet automatically tracks the relevant statistics for each territory. Through an interactive process of trial and error, you can reallocate control units to balance the new territories on any criteria for which there is data.

Align Star, published by TTG, Inc., is an example of a commercial mapping program. This software can be purchased for under $1,000 and is used to reallocate territories and draw maps for salespeople. In this program, territory maps are tied in with spreadsheets, which show current potentials, sales, and target number of calls. Any changes made in allocations of control units to territories are automatically reflected in the spreadsheet data. You should be aware that Align Star is an interactive program that helps you create territories, but it does not find an optimum design. To better understand how this type of program really works, data for the Kent Plastics problem that follows has been entered in the Align Star program by TTG, Inc., and can be downloaded from the web site for this book under "Companion Site" at www.wiley.com/college/cron.

Optimization Routines

The most sophisticated design programs balance territories that are financially optimal, using a customer response to selling effort and minimizing driving time. These optimizing programs are quite complicated and must be run on high-powered computers. TerrAlign4 by Metron, Inc., for example, works on a Windows operating system, uses a built-in digital road network for realistic drive time calculations during optimizations, and can override geographic assignments on an account-by-account basis.[9] This type of product and the consulting that accompanies it can be quite expensive. Its use is therefore largely limited to Fortune 1000 companies, which, due to the size of their sales force and the magnitude of their territory realignment problem, can justify the expenditure.

PROBLEMS

Note: Both the Align Star program and an Excel sheet of the data for the Kent Plastics problem that follows are available at www.wiley.com/college/cron. Go to "Companion Site."

FIGURE MR6-7 Current Sales Territories and Location of Indiana Counties and Major Cities

Kent Plastics

The regional sales manager for Kent Plastics, Jill Hayes, was considering how to reorganize the Indiana district. This area had been divided into two sales territories in the past, with Bill Hicks covering the northern half of the state from Kokomo and Sally Hall covering the southern counties from Columbus (Figure MR6-7). However, market growth suggested that four salespeople were now needed. Company policy stated that, when sales in an area exceeded $900,000 per territory, the district had to be divided into smaller segments. Sales in Indiana were currently running $3 million per year.

The Kent Plastics Company began operations as a supplier of plastic parts to manufacturers, but it had expanded into selling plastic bags and meat trays to retailers. Sales personnel were paid a salary plus an annual bonus based on district performance and achievement of territory sales quotas. Travel expenses were paid by Kent, and each salesperson was supplied with a company car.

Jill Hayes wanted to create four compact territories in the state of Indiana that would be similar in terms of sales potential and workload. She felt that equal-opportunity territories would improve morale and make it easier to compare the performance of individual salespersons. Travel expenses would be lower if the territories were designed to minimize the distance from the salespersons' home to different customers' locations. Jill realized, however, that the job of selecting home bases for salespeople was complicated by the heavy concentration of customers located in Marion County in the center of the state.

Counties seemed to be the most logical control units for building new territories, and Jill quickly assembled some statistics for Indiana from secondary sources. She obtained the location of each county and major population centers from maps supplied by the Indiana Highway Department (Figure MR6-7).

As Jill Hayes looked over the available figures, she wondered what factor or factors would make the best allocation criteria. Jill had recently obtained a copy of a territory design program published by TTG. Perhaps it was time to call this program up on her computer to help redesign the Indiana district. She knew she had only a few days left to carve out four new territories from the Indiana district before she presented the plan to the sales force at the annual convention. She also had to decide which of the new territories to assign to Bill and Sally.

RECRUITING AND SELECTING PERSONNEL

> Nothing matters more in winning than getting the right people on the field. All the clever strategies and advanced technologies in the world are nowhere near as effective without great people to put them to work.
>
> Jack Welsh, *Winning*

Chapter Consultants:
Howard Stevens, Chairman, The H. R. Chally Group
John Schreitmueller, Partner, Ray & Berndtson
Jonathan Scarborough, District Marketing Manager, Federated Insurance

LEARNING OBJECTIVES

After studying this chapter, you should be able to:

- Discuss how to plan for recruiting and selection.
- Identify relevant hiring criteria for sales jobs.
- Identify the different sources of recruits.
- Understand the selection and validation process.

FEDERATED INSURANCE'S RECRUITING PROCESS: A MODEL FOR SUCCESS

When it comes to recruiting and hiring salespeople, Federated Insurance has a proven model for success. It all starts with the District Marketing Manager whose number one priority is finding and hiring quality people. An important first step in the recruiting process is to cultivate strategic relationships with influential people such as university faculty and religious and community leaders who can help identify individuals who may have the success qualities Federated is looking for. Once identified, candidates are invited to submit their resumes for an initial review by the District Marketing Manager. If a fit is perceived, the candidate will be invited to a low-key discussion of the career opportunities available at Federated. The purpose of this discussion is to provide candidates with a realistic job preview and to determine if a mutual interest exists.

If a mutual interest is established, the candidate will then complete an online personality profile. The purpose of this step is to match the candidate's profile to the profile of successful Federated salespeople. If a match is not found, the recruiting process is terminated. However, those fitting the success profile will complete a handwritten application. The application is not only checked for completeness and grammar, but also for the length of time to complete—which is an indicator of interest. At this stage all references and past employers are contacted, including past sports coaches and professors. In addition to these phone conversations, Federated managers will conduct face-to-face meetings with at least two of the references.

If no red flags are found, the candidates will then be invited to participate in three patterned interviews with the district manager. In these interviews, the manager will ask questions such as, "Give me an example of how you demonstrated a particular success characteristic." The third interview is an in-home meeting with the candidate's parents, spouse, or significant other. This interview is designed to assess the attitudes and commitment level of the candidate's support system. At the conclusion of the patterned interviews, the candidate is ranked on each of the success characteristics. In between the three interviews, the candidate is required to hold an open forum via phone with ten current Federated salespeople from around the country and summarize the findings in writing. In addition, the candidate will spend one day shadowing two different salespeople. Federated has found that these two assignments help set the candidate's expectations as a new salesperson. A final one-day interview with the Regional Manager and the Director of Field Operations completes the interview process. While the expense of Federated multistep recruiting process is one of the highest in the industry, the investment has more than paid for itself. Federated's turnover rate of first-year salespeople has been lowered to 13 percent, which is tops in the industry.[1]

One reason Federated and many other companies have placed more emphasis on recruiting salespeople is the increased strategic role the sales force has in leveraging customer relationships.[2] This shift requires some companies to continuously upgrade the competency level of the sales force, which enhances the importance of attracting and selecting the "right" person for a particular sales position. Let's face it: Regardless of how well you train, motivate, coach, or counsel your sales staff or develop your sales and marketing strategy, without properly qualified people, you are in the same predicament as a great basketball coach with a team of six-footers who can neither run, jump, shoot, nor rebound.

The costs associated with a poor hiring decision are significant. An often-quoted figure is that out-of-pocket costs associated with recruiting and selection range from 20 to 80 percent of a salesperson's annual salary. Costs go up dramatically, however, when a poor hiring decision is made. Costs associated with a poor hiring include (1) initial training and subsequent training costs needed to overcome deficiencies; (2) costs of absenteeism, poor customer service, and excessive expense account spending associated with gradual withdrawal from the organization; and (3) the opportunity cost associated with lost profits that a qualified person would have generated during the time a poor hire occupies a territory. Experts estimate that the value of the sales lost by a single ineffective salesperson could be as much as $300,000 to several million dollars per year.[3]

In addition to the direct costs, a poor hiring decision can negatively affect a company's culture and productivity. Especially in the case of a termination, the morale among the salespeople who stay on may suffer, since they may be required to pick up the slack caused by the departure of their colleagues. Furthermore, higher turnover leads to a sales force that is low on the productivity and learning curves, thus potentially damaging client relationships. Effective sales managers, therefore, should be especially aware of the total costs, both direct and indirect, of poor hiring decisions.

Selection of good salespeople obviously represents an important opportunity to gain a competitive advantage. However, why is the selection of good salespeople so difficult for many managers? One reason is the pressure to fill open territories. When unemployment is at a historical low, finding and hiring good performers are challenges for managers in every industry. On the other hand, when unemployment is high, managers are vulnerable to making a hiring mistake from the large number of applicants they receive. Recruiting and selecting a successful salesperson is also difficult because many companies fail to provide effective training for sales recruiters and fall prey to the many biases and mistakes of untrained interviewers.

Our discussion of the recruiting and selection process is based on a model that emphasizes proper planning. First, the number of people to be recruited must be determined, together with an analysis of each sales job. A careful review of the activities to be performed by salespeople helps sales managers prepare a list of specific job qualifications, which can then be used to build a profile to guide the search for successful recruits. Next, management must decide where to look for recruits. From a pool of recruits, sales managers then must select job candidates. Finally, a validation of the selection criteria and saleperson success is conducted. We start our discussion with the planning phase of the recruiting process.

PLANNING PROCESS

The recruiting planning process should include a preliminary analysis of personnel needs, company culture, a job analysis, and a job description with the necessary job qualifications. Based on the results of these analyses, sources of sales recruits and selection procedures should be planned. Proper planning will help ensure the success of the recruiting process and provide more time for locating the best candidates.

Personnel Needs

The number of new salespeople needed will depend on several factors, including sales growth targets, distribution strategies, changes in sales force organization, and sales force turnover. For example, open territories should be continually reassessed to determine whether any economic changes have occurred that may have affected previous sales growth estimates. Based on the reassessed growth estimates, a company might combine an open territory into existing territories and not hire a new salesperson, or split the territory and fill it with multiple hires. Additional analyses, therefore, may be necessary when determining the number of new salespeople needed.

Understanding the reasons for salesperson *turnover* is an especially important factor in assessing personnel needs. Examples include resignation because of poor performance, resignation for another job, retirement, or promotion. To calculate an estimate of the rate at which salespeople leave requires an estimate of the sales force turnover rate. The rate is calculated by dividing the number of separations during a year by the average size of the sales force. Thus, if 30 people leave each year and the size of the sales force is 150, the turnover rate would be

$$\text{Turnover rate} = \frac{\text{Separations per year}}{\text{Average size of the sales force}} = \frac{30}{150} = 20\%$$

However, just knowing your turnover rate is 20 percent does not provide a complete picture of the situation and may hide some unpleasant truths. For example, suppose you found out that 15 percent of the 20 percent who left were high performers. Losing top performers could have two or three times the economic impact of losing a bottom performer. Even when replacements are found, it may take months to find them and possibly a full year before they are up to minimum productivity levels. Also, when comparing your turnover rate to

TEAM EXERCISE
"Turnover and Counteroffers"

Your top account executive, Angela Harris, just finished telling you that your best customer, Bernard Wells, president of Sterling Corporation, made her a generous offer to come sell for him. Although Harris hadn't agreed to take the position, she was tempted. She would receive a 15 percent increase in base pay, keep the three weeks vacation she had accumulated working seven years for Austin's ad agency, and could earn a year-end bonus of up to 25 percent of her total compensation. Not to mention that she knows the customer's company as well as she knows your agency (since Sterling has been her client for six years).

You ask Harris to give you a few hours to think about the situation and then you will talk more. She agreed.

As soon as Harris closed the door behind her, you slump into your chair, elbows on your desk, face leaning into your hands, shaking your head. A lot of questions begin racing through your mind. You could wish her well and let her go, but how many accounts would you lose because their key contact at Austin Advertising left (you know too well that advertisers can be a fickle bunch)? Will Sterling leave you for another agency if she stays? Should you counter the offer (you could)—she was well worth it. Is she a loyal employee?

the industry (an average of 10 percent), you realize that you are losing salespeople at twice the rate of the competition. This type of defection may make your customers nervous and eventually harm product sales. These examples demonstrate that simply reporting turnover as a percentage of the workforce should only be used as a starting point for understanding the magnitude of the turnover problem.

Turnover can be too low as well as too high. A well-entrenched sales force may be unable to adjust to a changing environment. While promoting company loyalty, low turnover may also indicate a lack of career growth opportunity by promotion or lateral movement. This suggests that turnover is not something to be minimized or maximized; rather, it is a useful guide for administrative action. The objective is to have enough turnover so that new personnel and enthusiasm can be added to the sales force, yet not so much that sales managers spend all their time recruiting and training new employees.[4] Obviously, you would want to keep your top salespeople from leaving, so what would you do in the team exercise: "Turnover and Counteroffers" to keep Angela Harris, the top salesperson, from taking the new position?

Company Culture

The process of aligning a company's recruiting strategies to its core values should help attract and retain higher performing salespeople as compared with those companies whose recruiting processes are reactive and culturally disconnected.[5] A well-educated, high-energy, articulate candidate, for example, might seem like a superb addition to the sales team. However, if a recruit does not perceive the company's cultural needs and demands as a match with his or her values, the potential for turnover increases dramatically. For instance, some people thrive in a highly competitive environment, while others abhor it. The fact that cultures are likely to vary from one sales branch to another even within the same company makes the task more difficult but even more necessary. Klein Tools, for example, has been a family-run manufacturer of high-quality hand tools since 1857. The firm's success over the past 150 years can be attributed to its focus on quality in all aspects of the business—from making the best hand tools to hiring the right salesperson. Klein's philosophy is to hire a person, not for one or two years, but for an entire career. Klein feels that getting the proper fit with the company's family-friendly culture is a key aspect of its hiring process that keeps turnover low and customers happy.[6]

Job Analysis

Before managers can effectively recruit new salespeople, they must clearly understand the activities, tasks, and responsibilities of their sales representatives. A *job analysis* is a systematic way to describe how a job is to be performed, as well as the tasks that make up the job.

A job analysis should focus on the tasks of high-performing salespeople and compare those with the low-performing salesperson tasks. This can serve as a "reality check" on management's assumptions and can lead to some surprising conclusions. For example, a sales manager might describe a job as the merchandising of sales promotions to store managers. However, if more effective salespeople actually spend their time stocking shelves and checking inventory, those salespeople hired to sell to store managers are likely to be unhappy when they discover that the job entails duties that are similar to a glorified stock clerk. Indeed, research suggests that incongruency between a candidate's job expectations and the actual job activities can lead to increased turnover.[7] In short, job analyses must incorporate the unpleasant as well as the attractive aspects of the job.

A number of different procedures may be used for performing a job analysis. One is the job analysis interview, whereby in-depth interviews are conducted with management and salespeople. Management would be queried, for instance, about the sales and marketing plans of the company so as to clarify the role of the sales force. Salespeople would be interviewed to determine how they see their role and how much time they spend on particular activities. In addition to the interviews, the sales force may be sent questionnaires in which they indicate the frequency of performance as well as the importance of each task in their job.

Another job analysis method is to send an observer into the field. The observer can record the differences in the amount of time higher- and lower-performing salespeople spend talking to customers, traveling, record keeping, setting up displays, and attending meetings. Additional information concerning sales jobs can be obtained by interviewing customers, using daily diaries, and reading sales reports to pinpoint critical incidents that spell the difference between success and failure. Written customer ratings of the sales force are particularly important in identifying salesperson critical success factors.

Job Description. Information from the job analysis should be used to produce a *job description*, which is a written document that spells out the job relationships and requirements that characterize each sales position. A complete job description explains (1) to whom the salesperson reports, (2) how the salesperson interacts with other staff marketing people, (3) the customers to be called on by the salesperson, (4) the specific tasks to be carried out, (5) the mental and physical demands of the job, and (6) the types of products to be sold.

An example of a job description for an entry-level marketing development trainee at Federated Insurance is presented in Figure 7-1. Notice that the job description states that the trainee is expected to develop the necessary product knowledge, communication, and sales skills to successfully fulfill the duties of a Marketing Representative. In this position, the person is expected to master the Marketing Representative competencies in a three-tiered development program with each tier building upon the competencies learned in the previous phase. In the first phase, trainees are expected to understand basic concepts such as equity, integrity, respect, and teamwork in all aspects of the job, whereas in the third phase, trainees will develop specific product and competitive knowledge, selling skills, as well as complete any required licensing prior to taking over a territory.

FEDERATED INSURANCE
SALARIED POSITION DESCRIPTION

Position Title: Marketing Development Trainee
Job Code: 0126
Department: Learning Center Trainee
Status: Exempt
Division: Home Office
Reports to: General Manager-Training & Development

Primary Purpose of Position
Participate in Company-sponsored training programs to gain the level of knowledge required to successfully perform the duties of a Marketing Representative, including using all available time and resources for self-development in product, communication skills, and sales techniques.

Essential Job Functions
The Marketing Development Trainee must have the ability to:

Phase I:

1. Demonstrate the corporate cornerstone of equity, integrity, respect, and teamwork in all aspects of the job, including dealing with employees, policyholders, and others. Treat others in a nondiscriminatory, lawful, and ethical manner, respecting the differences among people, and the value they bring to the company.
2. Attend formal 9-week classroom session covering Personal Auto, Homeowners, Commercial Property and Liability, Group Health and Life insurance.
3. Actively participate in other activities or programs recommended by Federated to raise the level of competence, maturity, and effectiveness as Marketing Representatives through Federated Speakeasy Program, field trips, and self-study courses. These programs continue through all the phases.
4. Establish and maintain good working relations with other Company personnel to facilitate achievement of learning objectives of this position.

Phase II:

5. Actively participate in on-the-job training concentrating on Federated's products, risk identification, programming methods, and marketing philosophy.
6. Acquire and maintain a good working knowledge of underwriting principles, Company policies, and marketing concepts.
7. Begin "How to Master the Art of Selling," "Business Insurance Basics," and "Life Underwriting" courses to build selling skills and life product needs.
8. Complete all necessary assignments and projects, and participate in classroom discussion to further development.

Phase III:

9. Concentrate on programming techniques and coverages for all types of businesses including ability to identify risk and accurately set up a Right Report.
10. Develop and keep current on selling skills through the completion of the "Six Figure Selling" program and participate in role-playing sessions with a trainer.
11. Maintain knowledge of competitors in the marketplace by completed audits on competition's policies and keep abreast of current events through various industry magazines.
12. Successfully handle the responsibilities of an assigned open territory to provide service to clients and prospects.
13. Complete any additional licensing required in assigned territory.

Other Responsibilities
Follow safe practices in all work activities to avoid injuries and accidents.
Perform other duties and responsibilities as assigned.

Supervision of Others
None.

Minimum Position Requirements
Four-year college degree.
Licensed agent for Property/Liability, Life and Health in respective state.
Prefer 1–3 years general business experience. Recent college graduates are acceptable.
Self-motivated, independent, and customer-oriented skills. Occasional travel required. Weekend and extended business hours required.

FIGURE 7-1 Job Description for a Federated Field Sales Representative

Job Qualifications

Whereas a job description focuses on the activities and responsibilities of the job, *job qualifications* refer to the aptitudes, skills, knowledge, and personality traits necessary to perform the job successfully. A statement of job qualifications would typically include education, previous work experience, technical expertise, aptitudes, and interests. These qualifications, based on the job description, not only serve as a set of selection criteria that will help sales managers choose the best prospects from among those who apply, but they also should drive the type of questions asked in the interview. Keep in mind that you should be able to demonstrate to the Equal Employment Opportunity Commission that your job qualifications are required for the job.

Given the increased emphasis on solution selling, customer satisfaction, and building longerterm customer relationships, each company needs to understand its own unique set of success characteristics for adaptive selling, problem solving, and service requirements. One way to do this is to build a profile of success traits by analyzing the specific behaviors, skills, and traits of its own high-performing salespeople. Once all of the success attributes are compiled, the company should then organize these specific success characteristics into a few broad categories. For example, notice that in phase I of Federated's job function (see Figure 7-1) a person is required to possess excellent organization skills, an ability to work in teams, and an aptitude to build relationships of trust inside and outside of the organization. These basic aptitudes and skills were distilled from successful salespeople and are considered essential sales success at Federated.

Desirable Salesperson Qualifications. There is an extensive volume of research investigating the relationship between personal characteristics and sales performance. From this research, two themes emerge that have implications for recruiting. First, certain personality traits have been linked with higher performing salespeople. Recent studies indicate that extraverted, optimistic, and conscientious salespeople, as compared to other personality types, tend to perform better.[8] In addition, these personality traits have been shown to be particularly important in sales jobs that explicitly reward high performance (e.g., commission-based sales positions).[9] Empathy, however, was found not to be related to sales performance because empathetic people have a tendency, when faced with stress, to cope through self-sacrifice.[10] In other words, highly empathetic salespeople are less likely to ask for the order. Note that personality is an enduring characteristic of a person and is impossible for a manager to influence or change. Thus, this research highlights the importance of identifying recruits with desirable traits.

The ability to adjust sales behaviors to a selling situation (i.e., sales adaptiveness) is another desirable trait that research has linked to sales success.[11] However, sales adaptiveness comprises more than one personality characteristic. For example, personality traits such as an internal locus of control (i.e., a tendency to believe that performance is caused by one's own behavior, not luck), high self-monitoring (i.e., the ability to change one's personality in different contexts), and an androgyny trait (i.e., both assertive and yielding) have been associated with sales adaptiveness. Each of these personality traits can be measured using its respective scale, which can be found in academic journals. Thus, this research highlights the importance of proper planning and identifying recruits with desirable traits.

The second theme that emerges is the importance of personal characteristics that are more developmental in nature. A consistent finding across many studies is the direct cause-and-effect relationship between one's ability to plan and organize and job performance. Highly successful salespeople have excellent time and territory management skills that enable them to maximize their time with the most profitable customers. Higher performers also have a better understanding of the selling procedures needed to close a sale as compared to lower performers. They are also better able to recognize critical contingencies as they emerge in a sales call, which enhances the person's adaptability.[12] Other

TABLE 7-1 Individual Traits Linked to Sales Success

Personality Trait	
Optimism	Optimism refers to the tendency to hold positive expectations across time and situations. Optimistic people tend to have a more long-term orientation, more cooperative behavior, and persistence in the face of failure.
Extraversion	Exraverts are people who are sociable, friendly, self-confident, and outgoing. An extraverted salesperson is energized by being around other people and, when given the chance, will talk with someone else rather than sit alone and think. When extravert salespeople are feeling bad, low in energy, or stressed, they are likely to gravitate toward others to find relief.
Sales Adaptiveness	Sales adaptiveness is comprised of a number of personality traits consisting of internal locus of control (a belief that performance is caused by one's own behavior), high self-monitoring (the ability to adapt one's personality to a particular social setting), and an androgyny trait (the tendency to be both assertive and yielding).
Integrity	Integrity refers to basing of one's actions on an internally consistent framework of principles. One is said to have integrity to the extent that everything he or she does and believes is based on the same core set of values. Salesperson integrity has been linked to higher performance because of the higher level of trust buyer–seller trust.
Job Skill	
Time and Territory Skills	Salespeople possessing greater skill in managing their time and territory tend to perform better. Higher performers recognize that business-to-business outside sales is equivalent to running their own business and developing and pursuing professional goals as well as focusing on the most profitable customers leads to greater productivity.
Working Knowledge	Working knowledge refers to the ability to identify customer types and the sequences of selling behaviors that guide the salesperson in interacting with the customer. Salespeople with a greater level of working knowledge are able to negotiate a wider range of sales call contexts and customer types because of more developed patterns of sales call experiences.

developmental characteristics such as specific selling skills, motivation level, and role perceptions can have an impact on performance, depending on the type of customer and the product or service being sold. This evidence, as summarized in Table 7-1, suggests that sales managers can and do have an important influence on the performance of a sales force.

Ultimately, regardless of education, experience, or any other tangible qualification, it is often the hiring manager's impression of "fit" that stacks the deck in favor of a particular candidate. Keep in mind, however, that when forming such impressions, research suggests that sales managers may be predisposed to favor one candidate over another equally qualified candidate.[13] For example, one study found that sales managers who are hiring for their own sales staff would take significantly more risk on a candidate who has a higher performance potential than human resource managers for whom the decision holds less direct impact on their job. This again underscores how sales cultures may differ from other cultures in a company and places a significant burden on the applicant to understand these differences.

Legality of Job Qualifications

Although lists of qualifications are useful in recruiting for sales positions, they must be employed with caution. The main concern is to avoid employment discrimination which is caused when qualifications are used to exclude some individuals from certain jobs.

TABLE 7-2 Legal Issues Affecting Recruitment and Selection

Legislation	*Purpose*
Civil Rights Act (1964)	Prevents employment discrimination based on race, color, religion, national origin, or sex.
Age Discrimination in Employment Act (1967)	Prohibits discrimination against people ages 40 to 70.
Fair Employment Opportunity Act (1972)	Founded the Equal Employment Opportunity Commission to ensure compliance with the Civil Rights Act.
Rehabilitation Act (1973)	Requires affirmative action to hire and promote handicapped persons if the firm employs 50 or more workers and is seeking a federal contract in excess of $50,000.
Vietnam Veterans' Readjustment Assistance Act (1974)	Requires affirmative action to hire Vietnam veterans and disabled veterans of any war by firms holding federal contracts in excess of $25,000.
Americans with Disabilities Act (1990)	Prohibits discrimination based on physical or mental handicaps or disabilities.

The Civil Rights Act of 1964 was the first of several laws designed to prevent illegal employment discrimination. These laws, as summarized in Table 7-2, make it illegal to use as job qualifications any attributes that result in discrimination against persons of a given race, religion, nationality, sex, or age.

A particularly important federal civil rights law is the Americans with Disabilities Act (ADA). This law prohibits employment discrimination against qualified individuals with disabilities. Disabilities covered by the law include visual, speech, and hearing impairment, human immunodeficiency virus infection, cancer, mental retardation, emotional illness, drug addiction, and alcoholism. The law specifies that employers have an obligation to make reasonable accommodation to an individual's known physical or mental limitations. Examples of accommodations include making facilities available, restructuring jobs, reassigning, modifying work schedules, modifying equipment, and providing readers or interpreters. The implications of this law are far-reaching. It is important to point out, however, that employers can take action on an unproductive person and still be in compliance with the ADA. For example, it is well within the employer's right to terminate, or refuse to hire someone, if the employee cannot perform the minimum job requirements, such as having a valid driver's license.

RECRUITING

The goal of *recruiting* is to find and attract the best-qualified applicants for sales positions. The number of applicants needed to meet personnel requirements will be larger than the number of people to be hired. Not every applicant will have the job qualifications, and not everyone offered a job will accept the offer. The number of applicants needed can be determined by using a simple formula based on the company's experience from past recruiting efforts. The number of recruits *(R)* is

$$R = \frac{H}{S \times A}$$

where

H = required number of hires

S = percentage of recruits selected

A = percentage of those selected who accept

Thus, if a company needs to hire 10 people and expects to select 10 percent of those applying, and if 50 percent of those offered a position typically accept, then $R = 10/(0.10 \times 0.50)$ or 200. Therefore, the company needs to plan its recruiting process so as to attract 200 applicants.

Notice that the number of recruits *(R)* can be reduced by either increasing the percentage of people selected *(S)* or increasing the percentage of those selected who accept an offer *(A)*. One way to increase the acceptance rate of those selected *(A)* is to understand that today's sales recruits are looking for more than just a high salary. According to a recent study, candidates for sales positions place more importance on attributes such as job satisfaction, advancement opportunity, employee morale, and job security than salary.[14]

Finding an adequate number of recruits is not as easy as it sounds. Fortunately, sales managers can use a number of sources to find candidates. Each source, however, is likely to produce candidates with somewhat different backgrounds and characteristics. Thus, sources of applicants can vary widely, depending on the job to be filled and past hiring success. For example, referrals and employment agencies tend to be the most popular sources for sales trainees. On the other hand, educational institutions and present employees are good sources for sales candidates who require the ability to learn the technical aspects of the product. Companies rarely rely exclusively on only one source for sales applicants because each source has advantages and limitations. These sources are discussed in the following sections.

Classified and On-line Advertising

Advertisements in newspapers, trade journals, and on the Web are often used to attract salespeople. One advantage of these types of ads is their ability to attract a large number of applicants. The *Wall Street Journal* and employment-related Web sites, such as *Monster.com* and *careerbuilder.com* are full of ads for experienced sales reps, sales managers, and sales executives. These ads have the advantage of reaching a wide audience for relatively little cost and may attract candidates who are not actively looking for a job. Advertising's strength in attracting job applicants may also be its greatest drawback. There is a tendency to overburden the selection process with underqualified applicants, resulting in an extensive and costly screening process, which produces a high cost per hire despite a low cost per applicant.

A company can sharpen its focus and attract higher-quality applicants in several ways. First, an ad should provide enough information to successfully screen unqualified applicants. Information such as the types of products sold, the specific tasks to be carried out, the physical demands (e.g., amount of travel required), and the amount of experience from an ideal candidate could be used as screening devices. It would also be important to include the pay range and type of compensation plan (e.g., commission, salary, etc.). But, keep in mind the legal guidelines discussed earlier in this chapter when developing the hiring qualifications.

For print ads, placing them in industry-specific business publications would help recruit candidates with relevant business experience and help reduce applications from obviously unqualified applicants. Planning is important when considering such ads as the lead time is often much longer than newspapers—typically six to eight weeks.

For Web-based recruiting, there are a number of options available. Internet sites specializing in recruiting and human resources tend to have a large database of sales positions. *Monster.com*, for example, has over 5,000 sales positions listed on its Web site. Sales and Marketing Executives International (*www.smei.org*) is another organization that sponsors sales recruiting resources. Newspapers, such as *The New York Times*, have Web-based versions of their classified sections.

Many companies are also turning to their own Web sites to advertise job openings and allow candidates to apply on-line. A company Web site has an advantage of making a favorable first impression since it can provide ample information about the position and the company. To help organizations automate the review of on-line applications, it may be useful to use Web-based analytic tools, such as PeopleClick (*www.peopleclick.com*) to sort through resumes in looking for specific characteristics.

Recruiting on-line provides several benefits. Posting a job on-line on a national job Web site is relatively inexpensive (from $100 to $300 for 30 days) compared to a local Sunday newspaper ad ($1,000 or more). A one-day full-page color ad in the *Wall Street Journal*, for example, costs approximately $250,000. On-line ads also have the potential for a fast turnaround. Web-based ads can be posted online in one day, while a week may pass before an ad appears in the Sunday paper. A week's delay could be the difference between finding a top recruit and losing the person to a competitor. As more and more people turn to the Web for their job search, having a presence there is critical. However, not all demographics use the Internet equally; therefore, we recommend using other forms of advertising in the recruiting effort so not to exclude portions of the population.

Present Employees

Present employees often make good candidates for sales jobs because they are familiar with the company's products and procedures and do not require as much training as prospects recruited from outside sources. They have established job histories with the firm and can be observed in action when evaluating their potential as sales representatives. People usually consider a transfer to the sales department to be a promotion because of the job's independence and frequently higher earnings potential. This could potentially bolster company morale as employees become aware of the advancement opportunities outside their own department or division. Results of a survey also suggest that salespeople hired from within tend to perform well, as one-third of the top-performing reps surveyed previously held non-sales positions within the same firm.[15]

Candidates for major account sales positions are also most likely to come from company sources. Sources of candidates for these sales positions are likely to differ from those of regular sales positions because of the differences in the responsibilities in major account sales. For example, Banta Corporation, a printing company, has been very successful in hiring its customer service employees for its major account sales force. Banta targets its customer service employees in part because these employees tend to work in cross-functional teams involving logistics, purchasing, and accounts payable, which gives them a basic understanding of how these functions interact to affect the customer. In addition, Banta has found that its customer advocate role has prepared these employees to provide the high level of service and attention a major account requires.[16] While Banta has found success with hiring its customer service employees, the majority of companies tend to recruit their major account salespeople from the regular sales force.

Hiring from within the company, however, can have potential pitfalls. Bad feelings may arise, for example, if managers in other departments think that their best people are being pirated by the sales force. In addition, some companies find that employees may harbor hidden prejudices about sales and rely too heavily on their previous experience. Engineers, for example, may tend to overuse facts and figures, whereas customer service people may find it hard to take a tough negotiating stance.

Referrals/Networking

Another major internal source of recruits is recommendations by present employees. Statistics prove *networking* and *referrals* to be among the top conduits for effective recruiting in today's workplace.[17] Well-informed students and graduates in entry-level positions learn each day the values of networking with other sales professionals, executives, senior executives, faculty members, and others whose daily routines immerse them in the business community. Because informed interviewees have probably gained a significant grasp of the company's cultural, ethical, and business issues, these individuals often make superb candidates for sales representatives and at reduced risk for the company.

References from managers and salespeople are particularly valuable because these people tend to have wide social contacts and often meet individuals who make good prospects for a sales team. They also understand the needs of sales programs and are in a good position to discuss the merits of a sales career. Moreover, they are likely to know when people are looking for new jobs and to have some personal knowledge of their qualifications. A number of companies are also providing financial incentives for employee referrals. Cisco Systems, Inc., for example, has been known to provide a referral fee starting at $500 and a lottery ticket for a free trip to Hawaii for each "friend" who is hired.

Employment Agencies

Employment agencies are a frequently used source of salespeople. Employment agencies are popular because they can save busy sales managers time and money. The agencies advertise, screen resumes, interview prospects, and present successfully prequalified applicants to the client. A private agency is paid only when a person is actually hired. Employment agencies that charge applicants a placement fee must be given a detailed set of specifications because they tend to refer candidates on their current lists. Agencies that charge the employer a fee are more likely to find recruits who match a particular job. Often firms find that the best agencies with which to work are those that specialize in finding sales recruits, such as *IndustrySalesPros.com* and *Findasalesagent.com.*

Colleges and Universities

Perhaps the best source of sales trainees is educational institutions. For many firms, colleges are the focal point of their total hiring process. College placement centers, for example, often provide companies with resumes of applicants, arrange interviews, and provide facilities for interviewing candidates. Many placement centers also provide access to alumni in addition to current students. College campuses are also common sites for career fairs where multiple companies participate in a trade show format to introduce students to sales job opportunities. Merck, a recognized leader for recruiting the best salespeople in the pharmaceutical industry, relies on its college recruiting efforts to fill its entry-level sales positions.

College graduates are an attractive source for entry-level sales positions because graduates tend to be more easily trained and are often more poised and mature than those without college training. Successful college students typically know how to budget their time and, perhaps most important, have the perseverance needed to get jobs done.

College students, however, usually lack sales experience and require considerable training and one-on-one coaching before they become productive salespeople. One way companies are overcoming these issues is by offering sales internships. With an internship, an individual is hired for a limited period of time during which he or she is asked to perform certain tasks as well as work and observe the actions of others in the company. Internships allow the company and the student to preview each other to determine if a match exists. For example, a sales *internship* can not only provide an initial assessment of the person's selling skills, but it also helps determine the person's fit with the company's culture. O'Neal Steel, a Birmingham, Alabama–based steel distributor, has gone so far as to provide a tuition scholarship in addition to an internship as a means to attract the very best students. The scholarship/internship program is a two-year commitment that begins in the student's junior year. The student is rotated throughout the company's departments during the internship as a means of providing experience in all aspects of the company's operations. O'Neal reports an 80 percent success rate in turning the interns into full time employees.[18]

Customers, Suppliers, and Competitors

Customers and suppliers may also be a source of good recruits. They know the business, are familiar with the company, and may know what is expected of a salesperson. Care should be taken to ensure that the customer or supplier is aware of the recruiting process and is willing to cooperate.

Hiring competitors' salespeople is particularly attractive when a firm's training capabilities are limited, when customers are loyal to the salesperson and will therefore buy from the new company, and when new salespeople must be productive in a short period of time. When it decided to sell to large corporate accounts, Apple Computer targeted experienced salespeople currently working at companies such as IBM in its recruiting. Competition is also a common source among insurance firms, stockbrokers, office equipment suppliers, and clothing representatives.

Hiring competitors' salespeople and customers' employees is not without problems. Salespeople from rival companies may find it hard to adjust their selling styles and communication patterns to fit with your company.[19] Indeed, managers often overlook the difficulty in retraining the salesperson to unlearn old practices and adapt their sales practices to the new firm. It also gives rise to ethical and legal issues when the suspicion of divulging company secrets is involved. Retaliation and lawsuits are often the reaction of firms in industries where salesperson raiding is not common. Furthermore, because people rarely leave a job they like strictly for financial reasons, the new company may "buy" an unhappy employee. In fact, the higher costs associated with attracting these people may offset their higher productivity, making this source of sales candidates the least profitable.

SELECTING PROSPECTS

After recruiting a pool of sales candidates, managers must screen out candidates who do not meet the *hiring criteria*. The procedure for selecting prospects is a sequential filtering process, as depicted in Figure 7-2. The recruiter begins the selection process by evaluating application blanks and resumes and proceeds to interviews and background checks. In this way, obviously unsuitable prospects can be eliminated with low-cost methods, and the more expensive testing procedures can be saved for a smaller group of promising candidates. Each of the major selection tools is discussed in this section.

Application Forms

A popular way to gather personal history data is to have candidates fill out an *application blank*. It is easy to administer and requires very little executive time because the information is in a standardized format, as opposed to a resume. The basic purposes of application forms are to (1) provide information, gathered in a standardized manner, that is useful in making a selection decision and (2) to obtain information that may be needed during an individual's employment.

Sales managers are primarily interested in several types of information found on application blanks. First, the sales manager wants information about the candidate's educational background. A second category of information is the past employment record. Sales managers are looking for any employment gaps and prefer candidates whose employment records show a natural progression in job responsibilities and wages. Reasons why a candidate left each previous job can be gathered on the application blank as well.

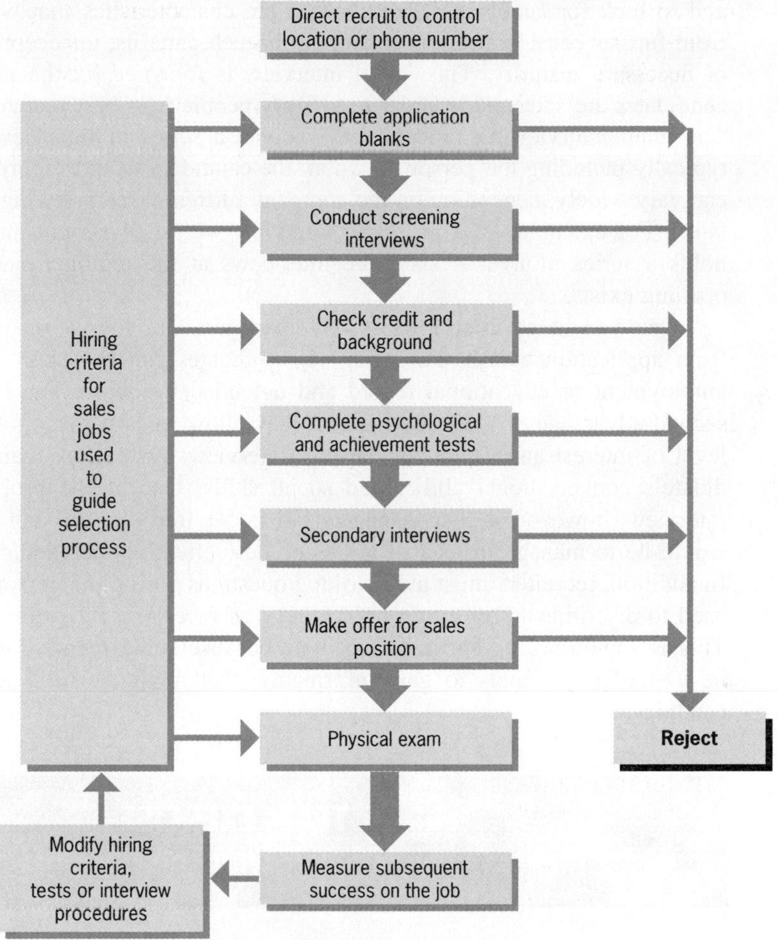

FIGURE 7-2 A Model for Selecting Salespeople

Companies are also interested in the extracurricular activities the candidate may have held in the past. Examples of these activities include offices held in organizations, memberships in social, service, and business organizations as well as hobbies and athletic endeavors. This type of information can be used to gain some understanding about the candidate's leadership potential, interests, and personality.

Questions about marital status, gender, religion, race, handicaps, and age exceeding 18 years are typically not asked. These questions are not included in employment applications for fear that recruiters might use the answers to discriminate against certain candidates. Some applicants may include extraneous information about themselves on an application so that they can later claim they were rejected for unlawful reasons. Thus, all application forms should include a statement indicating that any applications with unrequested information will be automatically rejected.[20] Many application forms ask for data on military service, so that the firm can comply with affirmative action regulations on the employment of veterans.

Personal Interviews

The *personal interview* is a crucial part of the selection process for all sales positions because interpersonal skills are so important in sales. Interviews are typically conducted at two levels. The first interview is used primarily to inform the candidate about the job and to look for *knockout factors*, which are characteristics that would eliminate a person from further consideration, such as poor speech patterns, unacceptable appearance, or lack of necessary maturity. This initial interview is followed by the main interview, in which candidates are screened in order to identify people who best match the job's qualifications. The main interviewing process may include a series of interviews with sales managers, typically including the person to whom the candidate would report. The type of interviews can vary widely, depending on the company (different interviewing styles will be discussed later). For example, after an initial interview with a divisional manager, Hewlett-Packard holds a series of five or six more interviews at the regional sales office where the job opening exists.

One benefit of interviews is that managers can follow up on information obtained from application blanks. For example, candidates can be asked to explain gaps in their employment or educational record and defend decisions to leave previous employers. A second advantage of interviews is that they allow sales managers to assess the applicant's level of interest and desire for the job. Interviews also allow managers to observe a candidate's conversational ability and social skills. One of the problems with the personal interview, however, is that managers fall into a trap of assessing how easy the candidate would be to manage instead of assessing how effective the candidate would be in selling. In addition, recruiters must avoid asking questions during the personal interview that can be used to discriminate by hiring on the basis of race, sex, religion, age, and national origin. This is sometimes easier said than done because some seemingly innocent questions can be viewed as attempts to gain information that might be used to discriminate against a candidate.

TEAM EXERCISE
"Questions About Interviewers"

Throughout this chapter, we suggest that recruiting the "right" salespeople is critical to a firm's success. While there is no guarantee of the perfect hire, the chance of making the wrong decision can be minimized by understanding some biases that can occur in the hiring process. Below are eight questions that research has addressed regarding the interview process. After reading each question, see if you can make an educated guess as to the research findings. How many did you answer correctly?

1. Does extensive interviewing experience help an interviewer to make better judgments?
2. Does pressure to recruit impair the judgment of experienced interviewers less than inexperienced interviewers?
3. When interviewing multiple recruits, do interviewers tend to use previous applicants as the standard of comparison for subsequent applicants?
4. Will the positive effects of good appearance offset an unfavorably rated personal history for a recruit?
5. How much of the factual information presented in an interview will the interviewer remember immediately after a short interview if no notes are taken?
6. How will lack of notes and factual recall affect the interviewer's rating of the recruits interviewed?
7. How reliably can a group of interviewers rate a recruit's qualifications for a job?
8. How reliably can a group of interviewers rate future job performance by a recruit?

Why Should We Hire You?

Regardless of the company and type of sales position for which you may interview, there are some interview questions that are typically asked. Below are just a few of the structured interview questions asked by Federated Insurance managers to sales recruits. You should be prepared to answer these questions.

- You know yourself better than anyone. What do you regard as your major strengths and limitations at this time? Share some experiences that portray each major strength . . . each weakness.
- What have you accomplished or achieved in life that you are most proud of?
- Success means different things to people. What does it mean to you?
- If there was a job that had everything you are looking for, what kind of a job would it be?
- What goals have you established for yourself in the short and long term?

FIGURE 7-3 Typical Interview Questions

Figure 7-3 includes some structured interview questions used by Federated Insurance. It is interesting to note that the questions require candidates to be able to successfully, but effectively articulate how they might add value to an organization. The candidates for any professional selling position should be prepared to present their background and career goals in a capsulation of approximately 2 minutes. This is often referred to as a "Two-Minute Drill," and responds to the question most typically asked at the beginning of the interview cycle, "Tell me about yourself."

Interviewing is a subjective process, so there are bound to be a few mistakes. Substantial evidence indicates that applicant ratings based on personal interviews vary dramatically among interviewers because the interviewer stressed unimportant job attributes during the face-to-face interviews. A recent study found that interviewers have a poor understanding of what job characteristics are important to candidates.[21] Thus, top candidates may be turned off by a particular job because of the way the job was described by the recruiter. Worse yet, studies have found that unstructured personal interviews are not a good predictor of subsequent job success. However, the interview is a useful technique in evaluating a candidate's social skills.[22]

Because of the personal nature of selling, the interview has remained the preferred selection tool of most sales managers. One way to minimize selection mistakes is to train sales managers on what questions to ask, how to ask each question, and how to rate applicants. SmithKline recruiters, for example, are required to be certified by their internal recruiting program so they can consistently apply their standard process around the world.[23] Another, more informal way to improve the interviewing process is to inform recruiters on a regular basis about the progress of candidates previously hired. Feedback on successes and failures can be a tremendous help in refining or improving interviewing techniques.

Patterned Interviews. There are several types of interviewing styles from which to choose. One type of interview is a *patterned interview*, in which the sales manager asks each prospect a set of questions and records the responses on a form. The primary advantage of such structured interviews is that they facilitate comparison of candidates when more than one person is conducting screening interviews. When different questions are asked of each candidate, a comparison of candidates is often based on impressions rather than on recall of relevant information. Indeed, the most consistent finding is that interviews are improved by using a structured approach. The patterned interview is also good to use when the interviewer is inexperienced at evaluating candidates.

Semistructured Interviews. A completely structured interview may not always be appropriate for choosing among candidates. When interviewing veteran salespeople for a major account sales position, an interviewer may be looking for someone who will take control of the situation because this is expected of the individual. In such a situation, it may be more appropriate to use a *semistructured interview* that is intended to gather critical pieces of information, but the questions are not repeated word for word, and the candidate is expected to take a more active role in the direction an interview takes.

Field Observation. A special kind of interview that has proven effective for some organizations is *field observation*, which includes taking candidates out to observe a day of field sales work. The prospect travels with a salesperson, making calls on regular customers. The major benefit of the field interview is that prospects are shown exactly what the job entails, and those who feel they aren't likely to meet the challenge can eliminate themselves before being hired.

Followup

The interview does not end when the face-to-face discussion has ended. The interviewer should rate his or her impressions of each candidate following the interview process. An example of Federated Insurance's candidate evaluation form is shown in Figure 7-4. Note that the form summarizes every piece of information gathered about the candidate. This includes an evaluation of the candidate in the screening interview, the written interview, the patterned interview, and the home interview. An evaluation is also made of the information gathered from the candidate's personal references. All of these inputs are rated using a scale of 1 to 5 (1 = outstanding, 5 = quite low) on ten different criteria. The form also provides room for comments to help the evaluator remember the candidate's pros and cons at each stage of the interview process. Recruiters should also track the timely response of candidates for sales positions by their responses in the form of letters, notes, or other means. This tends to correlate to on-the-job accountabilities, where the most successful sales professionals typically have penchants for following up on their telephone and face-to-face encounters with customers, suppliers, and other key contacts.

Background and Credit Checks

How honest are people about their educational and employment histories? In a recent survey by the Society of Human Resource Management, 90 percent of human resource professionals said that they encountered candidates who had falsified their salaries and time at previous jobs. In addition, 78 percent of those surveyed said that they had detected applicants who had lied about their college degrees.[24] The message is clear: Don't assume that people are telling the truth. While an in-depth probe of a large number of references can be time-consuming and costly, failure to check resumes may result in hiring overpaid and unqualified salespeople. Web-based search tools allow firms to investigate an applicant's job history and criminal record within 4 to 8 hours at a very reasonable cost.

Credit checks are also commonly used to assess the financial responsibility of applicants, since financial responsibility goes hand in hand with job responsibility. Although no research has verified this relationship, Equifax, Inc., of Atlanta, claims it sold 350,000 of its credit reports to 15,000 employers in one year. Under the Credit Reporting Act of 1971, applicants must be told that a credit check is being conducted, and they must be given the name and address of the source if the check results in the rejection of a candidate.

EVALUATION SUMMARY
PROSPECTIVE MARKETING REPRESENTATIVE

Name ______________________ **District Marketing Manager** ______________

Has the applicant reviewed the position description? Yes No

Are any accommodations necessary for the applicant to perform the Marketing Representative position? Yes No

If yes, has the Division Office been contacted regarding accomplishing the accommondations? Yes No

	Screening Interview	Written Interview	References	Patterned Interview	Home Interview
I. ACHIEVEMENT ORIENTATION	*	*	*	*	*
A. Goal and Results Orientation B. Energetic and Industrious C. Work Ethic D. Economic Drive E. Competitive Drive F. Desire for Status and Recognition G. Enterpreneurial & Sales Recognition	Comments:				
II. INTERPERSONAL SKILLS	*	*		*	
A. Sociability B. Service Orientation C. Positive Image D. Assertiveness & Impact	Comments:				
III. COMMUNICATION SKILLS	*	*		*	
A. Oral Presentation & Persuasiveness B. Questioning/Listening Skills C. Written Presentation Skills	Comments:				
IV. SELF-CONFIDENCE & OPTIMISM	*	*		*	
A. Self-Confidence B. Enthusiasm & Optimism	Comments:				
V. SELF-RELIANCE & INDEPENDENCE	*	*	*	*	
A. Self-Reliance B. Coachable C. Team Player	Comments:				
VI. ADMINISTRATIVE & TIME MGT.SKILLS		*	*	*	*
A. Organized & Efficient B. Coping with Papework/Detail C. Computer Literacy	Comments:				
VII. MENTAL ABILITY & PROBLEM SOLVING		*		*	
A. Intelligence to Learn the Business B. Problem Solving Orientation	Comments:				
VIII. MATURITY & STABILITY	*	*	*	*	*
A. Assuming Responsibility for Actions B. Flexibility & Adaptability C. Loyalty & Stability	Comments:				

FIGURE 7-4 Federated Insurance Interview Evaluation Form

IX. ETHICAL & PROFESSIONAL BEHAVIOR			*	*	
A. Ethical & Moral Standards B. Conveying Integrity and Honesty C. Act on Customers' Best Interest	Comments:				
X. ENVIRONMENT & CIRCUMSTANCES	*	*	*	*	*
A. Education & Experience B. Support/Encouragement of Family C. Personal Financial Circumstances D. Geographic Location Desirable E. Appreciate Business Plan	Comments:				

INSTRUCTIONS: Complete each section as that step is completed. Write positive and negative comments to help you remember pros and cons at that stage. Be alert to "contrary evidence" seek it out.
Ratings are: 5-outstanding; 4-well above average; 3-average; 2-below average and of concern; 1-quite low. Fell free to allow new information to increase or lower your rating as you learn more.
Use outline of Building Blocks as a guide in making ratings.

Strong Points for This Position:

Weak Points for This Position:

Overall Rating [5] [4] [3] [2] [1] Recommendation to Employ [Yes] [No]

Do not add or average these dimensions in making the overall rating.
Match the overall qualifications of the applicant against the requirements of Federated Marketing Representative.

District Marketing Manager ____________________ Date ____________

Regional Marketing Manager ____________________ Date ____________

FIGURE 7-4 (continued)

Testing

Today some form of testing is being used more often than in the past to help select field salespeople. Tests often provide more objective information than can be obtained from subjective conversation. Interviewers frequently reject prospects on the basis of personal biases and whims. Candidates have been rejected after interviews for such minor matters as speech accents or wearing short-sleeved shirts, short socks, or light-colored suits. These biases can be offset by the use of valid and reliable tests. Testing was found to be one of the most reliable predictors of entry-level job success.

Three types of tests are being used in sales force selection: (1) intelligence, (2) personality, and (3) aptitude tests.

Intelligence Tests. *Intelligence tests* measure the degree to which a candidate has the minimum mental capabilities to perform the job. Cognitive ability tests have been shown to be the most valid predictor of job success as compared to personality and aptitude tests. As such, the test is used as a knockout factor; that is, not meeting a minimum level will eliminate a candidate, but scores beyond the minimum will not determine the final candidate selection. The *Wonderlic Personnel Test* is a widely used general intelligence test because it is short and it has been extensively validated. It consists of 50 items and requires only about 12 minutes to complete.

Personality Tests. General *personality tests*, such as the *Edwards Personal Preference Schedule*, evaluate an individual on numerous personality traits. Unfortunately, such generalized tests may provide some traits that are irrelevant for evaluating future salesperson success. However, some companies develop specialized tests designed to measure specific personality traits felt to be important in a particular sales position, such as team building. Such tests are generally thought to be a weaker approach than the others mentioned here, but they could provide useful information about candidates if properly validated by careful job analysis.

Aptitude Tests. *Aptitude tests* are designed to determine whether a candidate has an interest in certain tasks and activities. The *Strong Vocational Interest Blank*, for example, asks respondents to indicate whether they like or dislike a variety of situations and activities. Creating or tailoring tests to a company's specific requirements is also recommended. It is possible that top performers selling different product lines within the same company may have different critical success skills. Responses can be compared with those of successful people in a certain type of sales position to determine whether the candidate will be successful in the position.

Assessment Center. An *assessment center* is an additional selection tool to help choose the best candidate by having him or her participate in job-related exercises. The basic way an assessment center works is that candidates are given simulated exercises that they must perform as if they were in a real organization. The types of exercises can vary from individual presentations, role-playing, and case analyses to business games and team-based assignments. Merrill Lynch, for example, has used sales simulation exercises in its selection of account executives. At one brokerage house, candidates were asked to sell a particular stock to a prospect, who is really a psychologist hired by the firm. The prospect greets the telephone caller saying how busy he is at the moment. In this simulation, the employer is assessing the candidate's persistence, an important attribute in this type of sales position. The wide spread use of this tool has been limited duc to its high cost.

Recommendations. One common error made by recruiters is to adopt some readily available intelligence or psychological test that may be inappropriate for selecting field salespeople. Better results are achieved when tests are tailor-made by testing experts and human resource specialists for the needs of a particular firm or industry. It is also important to base the test on an analysis of the job in question and to validate the relationship between test scores and subsequent job performance. Comparing scores of the most successful and least successful salespeople currently employed by the firm is a frequently used validation method. A word of caution is recommended, however. Such tests should only be used as a part of the selection process, not as the sole decision criterion. There is little statistical evidence that these tests successfully discriminate between future high- and low-performing salespeople. One reason may be that candidates provide responses they think management wants, and thus their answers may not be an accurate reflection of the person's feelings or behaviors.

Physical Examination

Traditionally, the last step in the selection process for salespeople has been a routine physical examination (which typically includes testing for illegal drugs). Field selling is strenuous, often involving extensive travel and hauling sample cases into and out of customers' offices. Because salespeople typically must endure a lot of stress and frustration, the sales manager wants to be certain that the candidate has the stamina needed for the job, as well as to avoid costly medical bills.

Although preemployment medical examinations are prohibited, such examinations are permitted once an employment offer is made and prior to commencement of the job. An employer could therefore make a job offer contingent on successful completion of the physical. However, questions about whether the person has a disability, and the nature and severity of the disability, are prohibited.

An Issue of Integrating Diversity

It should come as little surprise that the United States is becoming more diverse. According to the U.S. Census Bureau, one-half of the U.S. population will be African American, Hispanic American, Native American, and Asian American by 2050, and the median age of the U.S. population is projected to rise from the current 36 years to 39 years by 2010. While these statistics suggest significant changes in the future U.S. workforce, future problems could emerge as some companies find it difficult to integrate and utilize a truly heterogeneous workforce at all levels in the organization. Companies that attempt to address diversity issues by meeting hiring quotas are unlikely to be successful. Changes must be made in the way corporations work. Although the solutions are not clear, some of the problems companies are grappling with include the following:

- Identifying and eliminating discrimination in hiring and managing people based on ethnicity, age, and gender.
- Developing creative ways to encourage productive people to stay in the workforce longer by offering part-time, flexible schedules and retraining to upgrade skills.
- Recognizing the concerns of men and women with different family structures and family responsibilities by addressing the issue of family care.

It is important for corporate America to address these concerns because, unless employee differences are taken into account, companies may be unable to attract a sufficient number of qualified people to meet their needs. Another reason is that the markets for products are becoming more diverse, and it is necessary to have an in-depth understanding of those markets that may be facilitated by employee diversity. As a result, managers are faced with a number of challenges in leading newly diversified sales organizations to optimal performance. Not only are we faced with challenges at home, but throughout this text there are examples of how global companies must recognize and adjust to cultural differences in other countries.

VALIDATING THE HIRING PROCESS

The last step in the hiring process involves validating the relationship between the selection criteria used by the firm and job success. *Validation* is generally most useful in large samples where information is collected on the progress of sales personnel and is fed back into the system to modify the factors considered in the hiring process. Validation requires that managers specify exactly what distinguishes top performers from poor performers.

A new insurance salesperson, for instance, might have to meet the following criteria by the end of the first year of work: sales premiums of $120,000; renewal of policies at a rate of 60 percent or more; and submitting orders, reports, and paperwork that are legible, accurate, and timely. Those who achieve the standard will be examined carefully to see what common traits they share. The common traits of those who fail to meet the standard will also be examined to determine differences. The objective of the validation process is to build a profile of the successful performer that can be used to select additional salespeople.

Suppose that an analysis of fifty first-year insurance salespeople reveals that the typical successful salesperson has more than six months' prior sales experience, a score of 65 or better on the Selling Aptitude Test, and a college degree. These results can then be used to help standardize the hiring criteria to screen applicants. Persons who do not have a college degree or six months' sales experience can be weeded out on the basis of information supplied on their application forms. Those who survive the initial screening hurdles would have to take the Sales Aptitude Test. Candidates who score below 65 on the test would be dropped before the final interviews.

Validation seeks to build a set of hiring criteria that filters out poor prospects and makes offers to those who have a high probability of success. No system can be 100 percent correct, but a carefully designed program can improve the ratio of successful hires to failures. The stringency of the hiring criteria will depend on the type of sales job for which the person is being recruited. For some routine sales jobs, a set of fairly easy hiring criteria may be adequate. In more specialized industrial selling jobs where a heavy investment in training is required, a more rigorous set of experience and educational criteria may be justified. The goal of validation is to learn what factors are related to success so that they can be used to select new additions to the sales force.

SUMMARY

The recruitment and selection of salespeople constitutes one of the primary responsibilities of field sales management. A poor hiring decision will not only increase out-of-pocket costs but, in some instances, will damage employee morale, productivity, and client relationships. After reading the concepts discussed in this chapter, you should be able to:

1. **Discuss how to plan for recruiting and selection.** Proper planning for recruiting is essential. To aid in planning, a multistage model for recruiting and selecting salespeople is presented. First, the number of people to be recruited is determined. The sales manager then prepares a thorough analysis of each sales job. A careful review of the activities to be performed by salespeople helps the sales manager in preparing a list of specific job qualifications. These job qualifications can then be used to build a profile to guide the search for successful recruits. Next, management must decide where it will look for recruits. From a pool of recruits, sales managers then must select job candidates. Finally, validating the hiring process helps to modify the hiring process for continued success.
2. **Identify relevant hiring criteria for sales jobs.** Job qualifications refer to the aptitudes, skills, and knowledge necessary to perform the job successfully. These qualifications should be the basis for the posted job opening and serve as a set of criteria that will help limit the number of applicants and help sales managers choose the best prospects from among those who apply. Research suggests that there is no natural-born salesperson, so an important criterion should include customer-focused selling abilities, such as a willingness to follow through for the customer and the ability to adapt to the selling situation.
3. **Identify the different sources of recruits.** Depending on the type of job to be filled and company policy, the sales manager should seek applicants through various sources—educational institutions, other departments within the firm, present employees, employment agencies, classified advertising, competing or customer firms, and even Internet-based sources.
4. **Understand the selection and validation process.** Managers must evaluate the pool of applicants in order to select the most promising candidates. The selection process

involves the use of application blanks, interviews, background and credit checks, and examinations in order to identify those persons who meet the job qualifications. Then the sales manager must decide which, if any, of the candidates should be offered selling positions. Hiring criteria should be validated by identifying traits associated with success on the job and including these traits as screening criteria for new candidates.

KEY TERMS

Application blanks
Aptitude tests
Assessment center
Classified advertisements
Credit checks
Drug testing
Employment agencies
Field observation
Hiring criteria
Intelligence tests
Internship
Job analysis
Job description
Job qualifications
Knockout factors
Networking
Patterned interview
Personal interview
Personality tests
Recruiting
Referrals
Semistructured interview
Turnover
Validation

DEVELOPING YOUR COMPETENCIES

1. **Strategic Action.** Representatives in the pharmaceutical sales industry deal with two distinct groups. They call on physicians, attempting to convince them of the product's superior quality, and they call on pharmacists, who must be persuaded to stock the product instead of a competitor's products. In recruiting salespeople, some firms hire only pharmacy school graduates, whereas others hire business or liberal arts majors and put them through an intense training program. What are the advantages and disadvantages of each method? What implications might this have for sales management? Will there be a difference in the number or type of persons moving into middle and upper management?
2. **Coaching.** The first few days on the job can be very important in determining how quickly the new salesperson gets started in the territory. How would you answer the following questions about the initial socialization of salespeople into the company? Should new people set their own pace during their first week on the job? Should new salespeople be asked to assess their territory before taking it over?
3. **Team Building.** SmithKline's "team interview" process requires that each candidate meet with a team of managers, including a sales manager, service manager, sales director, and technical director. To make an offer of employment, the team must approve an applicant. What are the advantages of using the team approach to interviewing? What types of problems could occur by using such a team?
4. **Self-Management.** The pressure to fill an open sales position frequently leads to situations in ethically gray areas. Earnings potentials may be slightly inflated, or optimistic three-year predictions may be based on one high performer, whereas the average earnings are much lower. Relating how one person was promoted in only eighteen months, even though this was highly unusual, may lead the candidate to believe that quick promotion is very probable. What if your company is in a changing industry in which the role of the salesperson is likely to be quite different in the near future and the earnings potential limited? What if you, the interviewer, are thinking of quitting? Should you let the candidate know? Should candidates be informed when it is likely the organization will go through a downsizing event sometime in the foreseeable future?

5. **Global Perspective.** The Czech economy is booming, and many U.S. companies with facilities there are hiring. The challenge is that the local workforce is steeped in the traditions of socialism, and no one has a track record in selling and servicing in a free market economy. Companies such as Warner Lambert, Kmart, and Amway have turned to Caliper Corporation, a recruiting firm, for help. How should Caliper choose the right person for the job?
6. **Technology.** Peoria Resin and Plastics is a regional manufacturer of special grade plastics that are used as a key component in manufacturing a wide assortment of molded plastic products. The company is located in the three Midwestern states of Illinois, Indiana, and Michigan but is planning to expand its current regional focus to include the adjoining states of Ohio on the east, Kentucky to the south, and Missouri to the southwest. You have been asked to develop an estimate of the number of additional salespeople who will be required to support this expansion. In carrying out your assignment, you have elected to use the "workload approach." Analysis of your sales management database provides you with the following information:

   (a) On average, each one of Peoria Resin and Plastics salespeople can make 500 sales calls annually.
   (b) Each prospect/customer account served requires an average of 25 sales calls over the course of any given 12-month period.
   (c) The company's sales force turnover has averaged 18 percent over each of the previous five years.

   Access the Big Yellow Pages Web site at the URL: www.superpages.com and search for the number of firms in each of the three new states that are active in the manufacture of molded plastic products. In order to do this, type in "molded plastics" in the "Category" box, select one of the states of interest, and click on <Find It>. Do this for each of the three states of interest and record the number of plastic molding firms active in each state. Sum these individual state figures to determine the total number of firms actively involved as manufacturers of molded plastics products in the three new states. Using the workload approach, incorporate this total number of firms in the three states with the previous information produced from the company's sales management database to derive an estimate of the number of new salespeople who will be required to support the expansion.

FEATURED CASE SHIELD FINANCIAL: "HIRING PRESSURES"

Doug Bloom, the newly appointed branch sales manager of the Des Moines location of Shield Financial, recently had to fire his assistant sales manager because of consistently underperforming accounts. In seeking to fill the position, he wanted to promote from within and put on a list three reps who have solid sales performance and the skills and personality traits necessary to succeed as assistant manager. However, before he could arrange to meet with those reps to discuss the situation, the company CEO, George Treadgold, gave Bloom an order: Do whatever it takes to rehire Susan Kelleher. While an assistant sales manager at Shield, Kelleher had increased the revenue and profitability of her accounts by 47 percent. Two years ago she left the company to move to a competitor. Treadgold's mandate was so firm it implied that Bloom's own job would be in jeopardy if he couldn't convince Kelleher to rejoin the firm.

During the next few days, as Bloom prepared an offer to woo back Kelleher, two of the reps he was initially considering approached him to apply for the job. Now he was feeling the pressure.

Questions

1. What do you think Bloom should do?
2. If he didn't at least meet with these reps, would he lose them—either physically (to the competition) or mentally (the reps might be disappointed because they were not considered for the spot)?
3. If he does meet with them, how does he conduct the interviews when he knows that he has only one true choice to fill the spot?
4. Should Bloom take a huge risk and confront Treadgold with a solid explanation of why he should promote from within rather than rehire Kelleher?

SALES TRAINING

> When you are through changing, you are through.
>
> Bruce Barton

Chapter Consultants:
George Pettegrew, Senior Sales Training Manager, Johnson & Johnson Medical
Jerry Willett, National Sales Manager, Software Spectran

LEARNING OBJECTIVES

After studying this chapter, you should be able to:

- → Understand the benefits of sales force training.
- → Determine specific training needs for a sales force.
- → Discuss the topics to include in a training program.
- → Describe the advantages of centralized and decentralized training.
- → Understand the use of line, staff, and outside trainers.
- → Recognize the value of alternative training methods.
- → Describe the different methods for evaluating training results.

SALES TRAINING PAYS OFF

Micros Systems, Inc., the world's leading developer of hardware and software applications for hotel and retail industries, had a problem: Margins were being squeezed and salesperson confidence was on the skids. Management was convinced that a complete overhaul of its sales training was needed. It was decided that even before Micros hires a new salesperson to tout its point-of-sale hardware and software to restaurants, sales managers needed to assess a candidate's potential for consultative selling. All applicants for sales positions are asked to read and report on one of six pre-selected books as the first step in the recruiting process. The purpose is to assess the candidates' writing, thinking, logic, and storytelling skills, which are some of the fundamental skills needed in consultative sales. The task is also an indication of the person's motivation to work for Micros. The fact that four out of six applicants opted out of the assignment helped reduce the pool to highly motivated candidates.

In the first 90 days on the job, sales hires complete a three-part, six-day "Sales 101" course. The first part covers the marketplace, the second introduces the product, and the third teaches a basic strategic selling approach. Upon graduation, each salesperson is provided a customized sales development plan. The plan includes activities such as books to read, additional product training, and personal milestone goals. Dan Interlandi, Executive Vice

President of North American sales, says, "Salespeople by nature want to take the shortest distance to the goal line, and we know that a winning person takes the appropriate steps." Sales managers are instructed to review progress weekly to ensure that reps don't skip any steps or activities.

Micros takes the perspective that sales training is an ongoing developmental process of knowledge, skills, and ability. From year one through year four of employment, salespeople take a weeklong "Sales 201" course that reinforces the strategic selling concepts as well as teaches reps how to handle customer objections and craft sales opportunities. More education on restaurants follows. After four years at Micros, salespeople take an annual three-day "Sales 301" course that's not only focused on strategic relationship selling but also includes a full-day refresher of the basics. Has this investment in training paid off? Salesperson confidence is at an all-time high and sales per salesperson have increased over 20 percent while cost of systems has dropped by 30 percent.[1]

Micros Systems, along with many other companies, adheres to the philosophy that good salespeople are made, not born. Research results also indicate that characteristics that can be developed—such as selling skills, motivation, and role perceptions—are more closely related to sales performance than enduring traits such as appearance, aptitude, and personality.[2] This is one reason why sales training is such a booming business today with U.S. companies spending over $8 billion annually.[3]

Training requirements and spending are closely related to other management decisions such as recruiting and selection procedures. If a firm believes it needs to hire young, aggressive people with little prior sales experience, then training of new recruits takes on special significance. For example, nearly every one of Armstrong World Industries' salespeople has been recruited right out of college. Initial training is conducted at Lancaster, Pennsylvania, near company headquarters. Trainees live in a dormitory-style building called The Manor. Although the total cost of recruiting and training is quite high, Armstrong believes that the benefits of hiring people without industry-related biases and conflicting opinions are worth the cost.

If a firm hires mostly veteran salespeople from within its industry, then training of new salespeople is less expensive and generally focuses on company procedures. DuPont usually hires people with technical backgrounds, and although their compensation is higher than that of trainees with a nontechnical background, the training period is shorter (only a couple of weeks) and focuses on "people sensitivity." There are also obvious differences in the type and level of compensation plans that are appropriate for each situation. The point is that the various management decisions are related and must be compatible. Spending less in one area often means spending more in another area.

The main sales training issues covered in this chapter are highlighted in Figure 8-1. As shown in Figure 8-1, successful training programs consist of four phases: planning, program development, evaluation, and followup actions. In each phase, managers need to make a number of decisions that require time and money. Our goal in this chapter is to provide you with the tools to maximize the return on those decisions. First, we begin by examining the benefits of sales training in more detail, then we discuss the training process model.

WHY TRAIN SALESPEOPLE?

Effective selling is a learned, intellectual process that requires developing sophisticated persuasive, product, and customer relationship skills. Such knowledge enables salespeople to recognize, analyze, interpret, evaluate, and remember effective and appropriate sales strategies and tactics and how to adapt them to fit any sales call contingency. Unfortunately, sales executives and purchasing agents generally agree that most salespeople are not adequately equipped with this type of sophisticated knowledge. In fact, when asked what

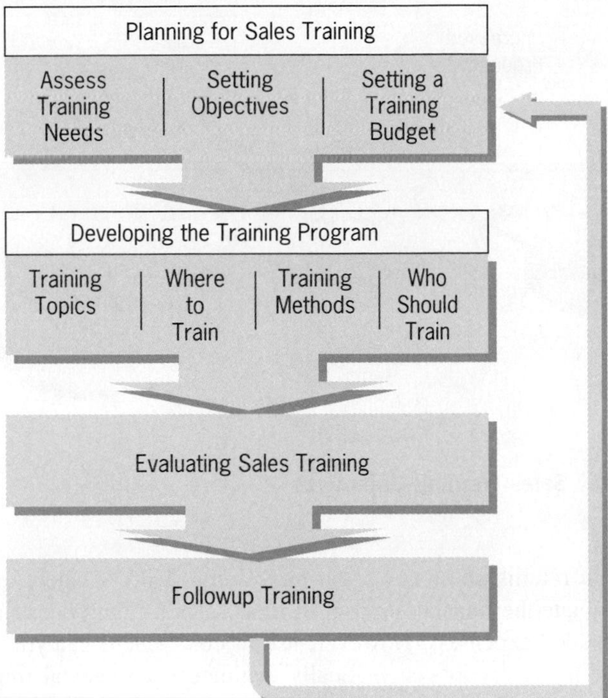

FIGURE 8-1 Sales Training Process

qualities make a top salesperson, purchasing agents frequently mention qualities that can be influenced by training, such as a salesperson's selling skills, ability to understand customer needs, and product knowledge. Indeed, research has shown that sales training can enhance selling effectiveness, improve customer relationships, and improve organizational effectiveness and retention.[4] This is why some of the most respected companies are willing to spend a great deal on sales training. The average new hire for a business-to-business sales job will cost a company a lot of time and money; some estimates are in excess of $100,000 per salesperson.[5] When you add in the costs of pulling in experienced salespeople from the field and lost productivity of the entire sales-force, the costs for larger firms can escalate into the millions. Most of the best sales organizations, however, consider training costs as an investment in the future success of the firm rather than simply as a current expense. Given this investment mentality, what, then, are some of the returns these organizations hope to realize from their sales training programs? Figure 8-2 illustrates some of the common sales training objectives.

Increased Productivity

The ultimate objective of any training program is to produce profitable results. Allstate Insurance Company, for example, realized a 29 percent increase in production on an on-line training program for IRA products. By tracking the 1,633 participants who completed the training over a twelve-month period, it became clear that within the first six months following the training, the agents who accessed an on-line course sold significantly more IRA products than agents who had not accessed the course.[6] A pharmaceutical company also found that just by bringing the bottom half of the sales force up to average through proper training increased sales by 9 percent.[7] Although money spent on poorly conceived and executed training programs is largely wasted, these examples illustrate the potential

FIGURE 8-2 Sales Training Objectives

for significant returns on money spent on training. Unfortunately, most firms today do not formally evaluate the financial impact of their sales training because of the perceived difficulties and added expenses.[8] However, useful cost-benefit analytical models are becoming available for managers to systematically evaluate the financial impact of a sales training program.[9] One benefit of these models is that they allow managers to translate the skills and knowledge gained in a specific training context into a dollar-based estimate of the resulting revenues. Sales trainers report that companies are increasingly requiring this type of justification from training investments.

Reduced Turnover

As discussed in the previous chapter, *turnover* is the ratio of the number of people who leave to the average size of the sales team. Salespeople who go into the field without adequate training typically find it difficult to see buyers, answer questions, or close orders. The resulting confusion and disappointment often cause novices to quit before they have a chance to learn how to sell effectively. Although this may not surprise you, the question remains, does training really help with turnover? The results of one study found that sales training will help keep a new salesperson focused and less affected by the successes and failures that can take an emotional toll on an untrained salesperson. The study also showed that proper training reduces salesperson role ambiguity.[10] These are important factors to control in reducing a person's intention to quit.

Improved Customer Relations

Industrial buyers, in particular, complain that too much of their time is wasted in dealing with untrained salespeople. Buyers do not like to spend their time counseling salespeople on market conditions and product needs. They prefer to work with trained salespeople who have a thorough knowledge of the industry, their firm's business, and their own product lines. Companies are attempting to respond to these concerns. For example, companies such as Caterpillar are teaching their salespeople how to leverage their customer knowledge to gain more share of the customer's business. As a result, prefered vendors are now relied on to provide complete solutions.

With more and more buyers requiring vendors to provide a total business solution, the number of a sales rep's contact points within the buying firm is also increasing. Today's sales training programs are responding by providing information about the buying motives for other potential key influencers, such as finance executives, operating officers, and accountants. Tellabs salespeople, for example, are now trained to discuss strategic growth and capitalization requirements with a prospect's senior executives.[11]

Better Morale

The majority of sales training is designed to increase product knowledge and improve selling skills; one by-product of acquiring these skills is increased self-confidence and enthusiasm among the sales force. When salespeople know what is expected of them, they are in a better position to withstand the disappointments and meet the challenges of a sales career. Trained salespeople start producing orders faster, and the increased earnings help boost morale. In fact, in our personal experiences with sales training over the years, we consistently find sales trainees listing a positive attitude most frequently when asked to describe the characteristics of a successful salesperson. When brought together for training, people get a sense of belonging to a team in which they can exchange successful selling techniques and ideas.

When Lucent Technologies, a large telecommunications company, was hit by the communications slump in 2003, its stock price fell over 95 percent. To increase morale and refocus its sales force, Lucent doubled the amount spent on sales training. Salespeople felt more valued and as a result became a harder-working and more dedicated group.[12]

Improved Time and Territory Efficiency

Enhancing salesperson time and territory management skills is important for all sales organizations. Salespeople are constantly faced with time pressures that make it difficult to effectively allocate resources. A recent study of 289 salespeople, for example, reported that 32 percent of the respondents spent fewer than 5 hours per week with customers.[13] Frequently, it is difficult to determine what is really important and what only seems important. Understanding the difference, however, is often what separates the stellar from the average performer.

PLANNING FOR SALES TRAINING

Planning for sales training involves three related processes: (1) assessing sales training needs, (2) establishing specific objectives for the training program, and (3) setting a budget for the program.

Assessing Sales Training Needs

Without oversimplifying the issue, sales force productivity needs generally break down into one of three elements. The sales force either does not know what to do, or how to do it, or why they should do it. A *training needs analysis* is a process for determining where problems and opportunities exist and whether training can best address the issues. A complete training needs analysis includes a review of the firm's strategic objectives, management observation and survey of salespeople, customer input, and a review of company records.

Strategic Objectives. An organization's strategic programs frequently involve changes in the types of products sold, the customers called on, and the type of customer relationships developed. For example, Pfizer, a New York–based pharmaceutical firm, recently acquired

TEAM EXERCISE
"Sales Training for Profits"

You just came on as vice president of sales for General Industries, overseeing 150 salespeople and 10 sales managers. General's sales were solid, but profit margins were abysmal. General's president charged you with fixing the situation.

During your first few months on the job, you spent much of your time on the road with your salespeople visiting customers. Your mission was twofold: introduce yourself to General's customers and observe the selling styles of your reps. What you discovered was that price cutting was rampant. Your predecessor, you learned, had managed with the credo "sales at any cost." Unfortunately for General, the practice cost the company profits.

You have to devise a turnaround strategy. Your biggest challenge will be to get 150 salespeople to drastically adjust the way they have been selling for the past four years under the former sales VP. And you have to get his ten sales managers to support and encourage the change. You know that your toughest challenge will be managing the drop in sales that may result from your new mandate of "sell on value, not on price cuts." But you're also worried that many of your reps will leave the company over fears that their commissions will be reduced in the short term. How can you introduce your new policy without creating resentment among the reps? What would you focus on in the "retraining" program? What could you do to minimize the financial impact to the sales force when it loses accounts due to the increased prices?

Pharmacia to expand its market coverage. Pfizer quickly realized that a massive training program was needed for the Pharmacia sales reps that it acquired. The company had to rapidly train the Pharmacia's sales reps on Pfizer's products, sales strategies, and culture. In addition to mergers and acquisitions, changing markets, products, customers, and customer relationship strategies will often trigger additional training. DuPont's salespeople, for example, are taking more courses in international areas, in addition to technical and product-oriented courses, as a result of changes to its marketplace. These examples illustrate the necessity of identifying training needs as a result of changes in strategy, market environment, and competitive environment. How would you deal with the changes the vice president of sales was planning to implement in the Team Exercise "Sales Training For Profits"?

Sales Force Observation and Survey. Observation of salespeople is an excellent way to identify shortcomings to target for future training. Managers could observe the macro-level strategies that salespeople use in their approach to conducting business as well as interactions with customers. Observation is especially useful when comparing the superstars with the lower performing salespeople. Observation of the sales calls of a company selling auto parts, for example, revealed that the discussion during successful sales calls focused on which products the customer should order. Less successful salespeople spent far more time waiting or talking about nonbusiness subjects. This type of assessment often identifies a number of areas that need improvement.

Customer Information. Sending customers questionnaires can also be quite revealing. Questions to be asked may include: What do you expect from a salesperson in this industry? How do salespeople disappoint you? Which company in the industry does the best job? In what ways are its salespeople better? An alternative to surveys is to conduct a series of focus group sessions with six to ten customers. A focus group is essentially a meeting with a group of customers to elicit specific information, in this case information on training needs. O'Neal

TABLE 8-1 Cross-Tabulations from Company Records

	Average Order Size per Salesperson	*New Customers per Salesperson*	*Total Customers per Salesperson*
Experience			
Less than 2 years	392	21	86
3–5 years	593	29	145
6–10 years	565	5	152
Over 10 years	470	8	139
Regions			
Northeast	528	6	140
Southeast	520	8	161
Midwest	512	18	111
Southwest	421	26	107
West	544	21	131

Steel, a Birmingham, Alabama–based steel distributor, for example, incorporates customer assessments of its salespeople to help develop advanced training programs for its veterans. It has been O'Neal's experience that its salespeople pay more attention in training when the customer says there's a problem than when the problems come from management.[14]

Company Records. Companies with a degree of computer sophistication may have a great deal of useful data for analyzing training needs, especially if call reports are available. Cross-tabulating performance records may also be helpful in identifying which salespeople need what type of training. *Cross-tabulation* involves examining performance by certain sales force characteristics, such as years of experience, geographic area, or area of specialization.

Table 8-1 illustrates how a cross-tabulation may be useful in identifying specific training needs. Three intermediate measures of performance are crossed with two characteristics of the sales force—years of experience and geographic region. Experience was chosen as a characteristic based on management concerns that both new and senior salespeople were thought to be having difficulties. Regional differences were also of interest because managers had considerable latitude in the training of salespeople and complete responsibility after the initial six-week training of new salespeople.

The results in Table 8-1 suggest that there may be a problem with both new and senior salespeople. New salespeople have the lowest average order size and lowest total number of customers, which may suggest that new salespeople need more training in how to increase business with existing customers. At the same time, salespeople with more than six years experience appear to have reduced their efforts in prospecting for new customers. There also seem to be difficulties with the Southwest region because it has the lowest average order size and total customers per salesperson.

What's the next step? Design a training program on prospecting for senior salespeople? Implement a whole set of training programs for the Southwest region? The answer is no because we have not yet investigated the needs of the sales force in sufficient depth. Cross-tabulating experience with regions may reveal that the Southwest region has mostly new salespeople. There may be competitive reasons for the results. There may be demand and economic differences between the various regions. In short, the needs analysis should return to a dialogue with salespeople and sales managers to identify the causes of the problems. This hypothetical situation points out an important principle when investigating training needs: Use multiple sources of information and cross-validate the information whenever possible.

Setting Objectives

After assessing the training needs of the sales force, specific sales training objectives should be established and put in writing. Like all good objectives, training objectives should be specific enough and measurable so that the extent to which they have been met can be evaluated following the training program. This will also help prioritize various training needs, which makes it easier to properly sequence the training. Written objectives are also helpful in gaining top management's commitment and willingness to provide budget support for training. In fact, a lack of management commitment is often cited as one of the major reasons why sales training fails to produce meaningful results.[15] With top management involved, accountability for quantifiable results tends to become a higher priority.

Setting a Training Budget

The costs of training new salespeople typically include salary, benefits, and sometimes lodging and meal expenses if the training is conducted out of town. For veteran salespeople, the costs also include lost sales while the rep is out of the field. These costs will vary by industry and by company; however, the objectives, location, and number of trainees are typical factors that have the most immediate budget impact. For example, a program with the objective of improving relationship strategies for experienced salespeople may require between two to four days, while a program designed to teach the basics in selling to inexperienced recruits could last as long as six months. It should come as no surprise that the more technically oriented industries spend more money and take more time to train new salespeople. A.G. Edwards, a financial services firm, for example, spends $58,000 per trainee. The total cost to train its 750 new salespeople in one year came at a total cost of $43.5 million. A.G. Edwards, however, views this cost as a five-year investment given what it takes for a new financial consultant to build a successful business.[16]

Some companies are trying different approaches to hold down their training costs. The use of technology, such as Webinars, podcasts, and conference calls allow salespeople to participate in a training program without the travel costs.

FileNet, an e-commerce service provider with 400 salespeople in Costa Mesa, California, saved over $500,000 on travel costs alone when it put its new-product training on-line. Although the majority of companies (52 percent) in a recent survey indicated that they currently do not use on-line training, approximately 60 percent of those companies stated that they would consider using it in the near future.[17] Of course the use of technology has its drawbacks, as we discuss later in the chapter.

DEVELOPING THE TRAINING PROGRAM

After determining the needs of the sales force and setting specific objectives and a budget for training, a number of decisions critical to the success of the individual training program must be addressed. These decisions include (1) what topics to cover, (2) where to conduct the training, (3) what training methods to use, and (4) who should do the training. These four decisions are interrelated so that one decision will impact the others.

Training Topics

The choice of subjects to be covered in a sales training program depends on the products to be sold, the purpose of the training, and the background of those being trained. Firms that sell highly technical products, such as medical equipment, typically include more product-related material in their programs than firms selling less complex products or services (e.g., radio advertising). The purpose of training may be to provide initial training for new hires, continuing development of veteran salespeople, or training for a specialized situation. The most effective training managers also consider the background of those being trained. For example, the Novartis Group, a manufacturer of pharmaceutical products, changed its training program to offer different programs based on skill set and performance level. Results showed that physicians preferred the salespeople who participated in the program more than twice as much to those who did not.[18] Now let's take a look at the topics typically included in training programs.

Product Knowledge. A common misconception is that sales training is designed primarily to improve the selling skills of sales representatives. Although selling skills are important, many companies devote a significant amount of time presenting product information. The amount of time devoted to product knowledge is frequently related to the complexity of the offering or to the introduction of new products. For example, Merck, a multi-billion-dollar pharmaceutical company, has a short time to bring a new product to market following FDA approval. In just one week, Merck's 3,000 salespeople will attend an off-site training session where—with the help of physicians and computerized product information—they learn about the new product and become familiar with the disorder it treats. Six weeks after product introduction, salespeople are brought together once more to solidify their product knowledge. For Merck, product understanding is considered essential if sales representatives are to communicate effectively and address customer needs.

Technology has enabled many salespeople to access detailed product information using the Internet. With the use of portable devices, such as laptops and PDAs, salespeople can access specific product information any time, even during sales calls. This type of support can be a tremendous help to newer salespeople who face a steep learning curve in terms of customer, selling, and product knowledge.

Selling. New recruits must be familiar with how the sales process works before they can be effective and productive field representatives. Even recruits with previous selling experience need this training because selling approaches may differ from one company to the next. Veteran salespeople will also benefit from training in how to sell in specific situations and when presenting new products.

Supporting this notion that even experienced salespeople can benefit from learning new selling skills is research on *cognitive selling scripts*. A script is the knowledge an expert, such as an effective salesperson, possesses based on remembered similar experiences. Experts are said to possess two types of knowledge. The first type of knowledge, referred to as *declarative knowledge*, permits them to recognize a selling situation requiring a somewhat unique selling process. The other type of knowledge is called *procedural knowledge*. This knowledge consists of the process or sequence of behaviors that are necessary to achieve a successful conclusion in a particular sales situation. Research has determined that higher-performing salespeople have more elaborate if-then contingencies stored in memory than lower-performing salespeople. In other words, the amount of selling knowledge a salesperson has is not as important as how that information is stored and indexed in memory for retrieval when needed. The implications of this finding for sales training are significant. For example, we do not recommend teaching novices a body of knowledge gained by high performers in a few training sessions (we believe this is doomed to fail); instead we recommend adopting a long-term approach toward training and retraining that includes elaborating on prior knowledge by teaching pattern recognition through discrimination tasks and explanations.[19]

Improving Teamwork. As sales organizations focus on developing more enterprise relationships (as discussed in Chapter 4), sales training has also begun to focus on training salespeople as members of cross-functional sales teams. Sales teams are generally composed of a group of specialists, each of whom contributes different skills to deliver a system-oriented solution to customer problems. In these situations, a salesperson may be responsible not only for maintaining the customer relationship, but also for motivating and coordinating the sales team. Working in teams, therefore, requires new competencies from people who are used to working independently of other employees. Procter & Gamble, for instance, found that its salespeople needed to be trained in such skills as how to evaluate other team members, coordinate projects, arrive at mutually agreed-upon objectives, settle disputes within the team, and provide feedback to team members. Notice that many of these topics were once the concern of management personnel only.

Customer demands are also requiring salespeople to work more effectively across functional areas within their own firms. The increased interaction across functional areas means a change in training methods. Many companies are now requiring salespeople to know how their products are made. Extended stints in the production and operation facilities, for example, enable salespeople to communicate customer problems more effectively with their own technical and production people. If managed properly, these types of cross-functional training programs tend to strengthen a sense of "team" within a firm.

Customer and Market Information. Training time is also devoted to giving recruits customer information and the general background on the market for the goods and services produced by the firm. Sales recruits are typically given facts about the size and location of present customers, their buying patterns, needs, and technical processes. For example, specific account-level information such as profit potential can be used to identify prospects who are ripe for developing a long-term relationship. Training salespeople to manage the account for long-term profitability rather than the short-term sale requires engaging the customer at multiple levels of the organization as well as a great deal of commitment, openeness, and trust.

Company Orientation. Since salespeople are boundary spanners between the company and its customers, they must be well-versed in the company's history, organization, and policies, as well as having an understanding of corporate citizenship and workplace competencies. As a result, company orientation topics tend to be very broad. Typical organizational training sessions include policy discussions on returns and warranties, credit arrangements, production sources, sequencing of orders, and how to expedite an order. Trainees must know about exclusive merchandise, price guarantees, discounts, and latitude on pricing. It also helps to understand the reasons behind the policies and how noncompliance will negatively affect the company. Salespeople will then be better able to explain the policies to customers who are looking for special deals. Dow Chemical Company's initial sales training program, for example, aims to produce a fully balanced seller, not just someone trained in product knowledge. During its year-long program, trainees work on three related training projects involving such things as working in Dow's customer service center taking customers' calls and orders or producing an in-depth marketing study involving customers or new markets.

Technology-Based Selling Skills. Changes in technology and the marketing environment are driving new sales force automation (SFA) products and, as a result, new sales training topics. These systems are designed to provide company-wide access to customer information that previously was the sole possession of the salesperson. As a result, winning sales force commitment to SFA can be difficult. Unless sales reps are shown how SFA increases productivity and how it fits into the overall marketing strategy, they will resist using it. Many firms are overcoming this resistance by revamping their SFA training to include the "whys," "wheres," and "whos" of the entire business process along with the technical aspects of the software program.[20]

Other Topics. Other topics where salespeople typically receive training includes time and territory management and, as we discuss in Chapter 10, how to resolve legal and ethical issues. In terms of time and territory management, most salespeople are provided a great deal of latitude in how they manage their time and territory. Training salespeople how to allocate their time among the selling, service, and administrative responsibilities can significantly increase their productivity. Some of the more exotic training topics include reading body language, understanding eye movement, and identifying people's decision-making styles. Some research in nonverbal communication has shown a link between salesperson effectiveness and the ability to read a person's body language.[21]

Where to Train

Having determined training topics, a company must still decide where and how training will be conducted and who will lead the training sessions. Although the decisions are interrelated, we discuss alternative locations for training salespeople in this section. First, we look at whether training should be centralized or decentralized.

Centralized Versus Decentralized Training. One of the recurring controversies in sales management is whether sales training should be centralized or decentralized. Some managers contend that centralized training leads to greater efficiency, whereas others insist that training should be done in the field where skills are used.

Centralized training occurs when all the salespeople to be trained are brought to one central location—a plant, the home office, or a training facility. A major advantage of centralized training is the quality and consistency of training. Quality is enhanced through the use of specially trained instructors, custom-designed materials, and audiovisual equipment such as closed-circuit television systems. Furthermore, communications and coordination are enhanced when everyone receives the same training. It is also possible to give trainees exposure to top-level managers and other specialists, which can help boost morale and provide valuable insights into sales procedures and customers' needs.

On the negative side, centralized training is very costly and time consuming. Because training facilities and equipment are expensive, and trainees have to be reimbursed for travel to the central site and for lodging, managers usually attempt to keep these sessions fairly short. Some companies are attempting to reduce the cost while preserving the advantages of centralized facilities by broadcasting training sessions, either using the Internet or videoconferencing from headquarters' facilities. Cisco Systems developed an internal on-line learning portal called Field E-Learning Connection. The portal provides salespeople access to thousands of different training modules without having to lose valuable time in the field. The system cut training-associated travel by 60 percent.[22] We will discuss additional advantages and disadvantages of Internet-based training in the "Training Methods" section of this chapter.

Decentralized training of salespeople is usually done in field or regional sales offices, which moves the learning process closer to the customers and directly involves field sales management. New recruits are able to observe top salespeople selling to customers similar to those they will encounter in their own nearby territories. Location of the training at sales branches also reduces travel and instructional expenses. At Allegiance Healthcare, for example, regional and branch offices share ongoing sales training responsibilities. New hires spend time in the region office to understand how the business works, what role that office plays, and the administrative requirements. The branch level puts together programs on its marketplace with a major focus on specific products, systems, or services required for customers within that particular territory.[23]

Despite these advantages, there are a number of potential problems. Perhaps the most common one is that sales managers are so busy supervising the existing sales force that they fail to take the time needed to train new recruits. Sales managers whose income is based on a percentage of their salespeople's commissions (called *commission overrides*) are likely to be most concerned about current income and may give training of new employees a low priority. As a result, the content and quality of the training process may vary widely across the branches. Additional limitations associated with using field sales managers are discussed in the section titled "Who Should Train."

A common resolution of the centralized versus decentralized training issue is to use some combination of the two approaches. Xerox, for example, brings new recruits into the branch offices for a few weeks of familiarization with company procedures and products. With this background orientation, the novice salespeople are then sent to a central facility for a short session of intensive training. This program allows those who are not committed to the company to drop out before the expensive portion of the program begins. After completing the centralized training, Xerox salespeople go back to the field for more practical experience and coaching by their sales managers. At the end of six months of sales experience, the new salespeople return to the central facility for another week of advanced training.

Field Training. Field or *on-the-job training (OJT)* is the most widely used method of sales training for new recruits. Small companies especially rely on this method of training new salespeople because of the high cost of developing alternative training methods when only a few people need to be trained.

The basic idea of on-the-job-training is that every time salespeople call on customers, they should learn from the experience. To facilitate and encourage learning, new salespeople are often paired with successful veterans. Georgia Pacific and Ortho Pharmaceutical's Biotech Division, for instance, take this approach to OJT. Another alternative is to have the immediate supervisor travel with the new salesperson and observe sales calls.[24]

Although this experience is important and people should be taught to learn from their experiences, OJT should not be relied on as the sole means of learning. First, experience is costly; while salespeople are gaining experience, sales are lost and relationships may be strained. Second, the quality of training is likely to be uneven; some people are simply better trainers than others. More important, the new salesperson may pick up the bad habits of the veteran salesperson, resulting in a lack of consistency in how salespeople are going to market. It was precisely for this reason that Johnson Controls, Inc. established a six-month training program for new salespeople. Johnson's management decided that best means of development is not experience alone, but experience in combination with a planned program.

Training Methods

Companies make use of a variety of methods for sales training. Cost reductions in technology are making it possible to use alternative media, regardless of the training location. Although many people are quite familiar with the classroom and workbook methods of learning, the use of role-plays, CDs, podcasts, audiotapes, and the Internet as instructional media may not be as familiar.

Role-Playing. *Role-playing*, typically of simulated sales presentations, is quite common in sales training. This technique is effective when used to reinforce information presented in videos and lectures by requiring active participation and practice. Role-playing helps to determine if the trainee can apply the information. Video cameras are often employed to capture role-plays on tape so that they can be reviewed for critique and self-observation.

Despite its wide use, role-playing has some pitfalls. The biggest concern is the stress caused by the videotaping. People may be unable to focus on the subject to be learned when they are under too much stress. One way to reduce the stress is to conduct a critique immediately following the role-play, emphasizing positive points and encouraging self-analysis: What did I do right? What will I do differently next time?

Another way to reduce stress in role-playing is to use it in a business game situation in which trainees assume a specified role in a situation. Companies such as Chase Manhattan Bank, BMW's Motorcycle Division, and Johnson & Johnson regularly use games to encourage the learning of product knowledge and selling skills. These companies recognize the value of "edutainment" in adult learning. Taking people out of their comfort zones using fun exercises is an effective technique for teaching important sales skills such as creativity and adaptability.[25]

CDs, Podcasts, and Audiotapes. CDs and podcasts are popular training media because of their portability and storage capabilities. CDs and podcasts are typically used as information sources for products and market intelligence, but they have also been used for more interactive sales training. IBM, for example, developed an interactive self-study system called Info Window to aid in the redeployment of 11,800 employees in the field as marketing representatives and system engineers. Info Window's onscreen actor is programmed to portray a customer in a particular industry whose response depends on the sales trainee's behavior. Trainees can also film themselves as they interact with the actor. Some of the latest computer-based sales training programs include Nintendo-like graphics. Reuters salespeople, for example, train with customized computer programs of football players and race-car drivers in a video-game format to role-play effective and ineffective customer calls.

Audiotapes are also an effective way to present and reinforce selling and product information because of the time salespeople spend traveling and waiting. The fact that more than 500 exhibitors of audiocassette training material attended a recent national meeting for the American Society of Training and Development suggests that there is a large demand for training tapes. Tape Rental Library (www.trlonline.com), for example, has over 2,000 titles for sales training, which it offers to clients such as Pfizer Labs, GE, Scott Paper, Johnson & Johnson, and Gillette. The biggest limitation to audiotapes as a training medium is their inability to get and hold the listener's attention for a significant period of time, which is why audiotapes are frequently used in conjunction with other training media and to reinforce previous training information.

Internet. As changing economic conditions have forced companies to seek cost-effective sales training, more and more are turning to on-line solutions. Many companies have moved a portion of their sales training on-line. IBM, for example, has an "on-demand" learning initiative where salespeople and others can take training courses, share and learn about best practices, and even set up their own blogs about their learning experiences.[26] By using Internet- or Intranet-based technology, managers also ensure their salespeople have access to the necessary information as soon as it's available without leaving their territories or customers. It's that flexibility that's fueling the growth of Internet training in the United States.

Of course, no new technology is without its drawbacks. For example, initial startup costs of e-learning Web sites are high, and distractions at the rep's location could affect learning and retention. Also, many companies have discovered that on-line courses are not as effective as traditional learning environments when teaching advanced skills. This is because adults are better able to master difficult concepts when they can ask questions and role-play to reinforce concepts. Experts recommend a good mix of on-line and classroom training to be 80 percent on-line and 20 percent classroom.[27]

Who Should Train

The three most popular types of sales trainers are staff specialists, outside specialists, and line executives. Because each has certain advantages, it is not unusual to find organizations using all three types. The selection of trainers for individual firms depends on where the sessions are held, the size of the firm, the characteristics of the product line, and the focus of the training.

Staff Specialists. When centralized sales training is used, companies often have staff specialists prepare the materials and conduct the classes. Staff trainers must not only be good teachers but also experts in selecting the proper methods and audiovisual equipment needed to meet program objectives. If sales training is conducted on a decentralized basis, staff specialists in the central office usually prepare the program materials, and the instruction is carried out by line managers.

There are some disadvantages to using staff trainers. One complaint is that despite their teaching skills, they often lack experience in realistic field-selling situations, making it difficult for trainees to apply the classroom instruction to realistic customer situations. In addition, a staff trainer's salary is simply too expensive for many small firms.

Outside Specialists. The employment of outside specialists to conduct sales training is a fairly common business practice. Outside consultants may be entirely responsible for the training programs or may be brought in to conduct specific sessions within a total training program. More effective sales consultants usually tailor their training programs to meet the special needs of individual firms and industries. The main attraction of outside trainers is the variety, inspiration, and excitement they can bring to the training program.

The potential problems with outside specialists are similar to those of staff specialists. In addition, outside trainers may be unfamiliar with a company's selling situation (lack of familiarity with industry jargon, customers, and competitors). For example, a trainer may discuss price discounting in a presentation when the company is emphasizing value-added selling to avoid price discounting. Salespeople may disregard the training altogether as a result or, even worse, may be misled.

Line Executives. Using line executives (usually sales managers and top performing salespeople) as sales trainers lends credibility to the program because these people have successful sales backgrounds and trainees are more likely to recognize their knowledge base. They know how to sell to and they know what skills trainees need in order to perform well in the field. The scheduling of line executives for sales training sessions also enables these managers to become better acquainted with the entire sales force. When sales managers who actually supervise the salespeople do the training, or use the methods themselves, new recruits are more likely to put the ideas into practice.

Line executives are not always asked to lead sales training for a variety of reasons. Although line managers know a great deal about selling, they may not be trained in how to communicate the information to a group of people in a classroom setting. Furthermore, line executives are usually preoccupied with current sales problems and may not have time to do a good job of training. Solutions to these problems include offering "release time" so that they can prepare for their training classes and instructing the managers in better teaching techniques. Smaller firms, in particular, must deal with these problems because many cannot afford staff trainers and are forced to use line executives or outside specialists.

EVALUATING SALES TRAINING

As the costs of sales training continues to rise, sales managers must find ways to determine whether this investment is paying off. One of the most popular training evaluation methods over the past forty years has been Kirkpatrick's four-stage framework.[28] One reason for the model's popularity is its simplicity and practicality. Figure 8-3 illustrates the four levels of the framework and briefly describes how the model could be used for assessing sales training.

Level 1:	Reactions	Are trainees satisfied with the training? This also provides information so that the parts they don't like can be improved.
Level 2:	Learning	Did the training change attitudes, increase knowledge, or improve the skills of the trainees? This usually requires testing before and after training.
Level 3:	Behavior	Are salespeople using their knowledge and skills on the job? This may be measured in a variety of ways: asking salespeople, the sales manager observing salespeople, and questioning customers.
Level 4:	Results	What effect does the training have on the company? The bottom line results of training can include increased sales; higher profits; more new customers; and reduced costs.

FIGURE 8-3 The Four Levels of Training Evaluation

As shown in Figure 8-3, level 1 measures trainee's reactions or feelings about various aspects of a sales training program. Despite the emphasis on showing demonstrable results from training, most companies are likely to use trainee reactions to evaluate training programs, as presented in Table 8-2. However, one study found very little correlation between Level 1 evaluations and how well the people performed in the field. The study actually found that one trainer, who was rated in the bottom third of all trainers by his students in Level 1 satisfaction evaluations, was actually one of the most effective in terms of how his students performed during the first three months after they graduated.[29]

Training evaluation at the second level assesses the acquisition and retention of declarative knowledge (i.e., know what), procedural knowledge (i.e., know how), and/or attitude change, depending on the objectives of the training. Measures can include pencil-and-paper examination instruments along with behavioral evaluations (e.g., role plays, customer evaluations). Behavior change assessments are the third level of evaluating training and measure the extent to which salespeople modify their job-related behavior as a result of the training. Sales manager's appraisal of a trainee's behavior following the training is often used as an assessment tool, as is a salesperson's evaluation of his or her own behavior. Level 4 evaluations measure the extent to which a training program has reached the objectives set forth by the organization.

Bottom-line measures of performance (e.g., sales and profits) were ranked only fourth in frequency of use. One survey found that approximately 60 percent of firms do not measure the value or impact of training on sales performance.[30] A potential problem with using sales as a performance measure is that sales may change as a result of factors outside the salespeople's control. One way to overcome this problem is to compare the results of those who completed a training program with those who did not, but who are in otherwise similar situations (i.e., develop a field experiment). A.G. Edwards tracked a sample group and compared the results to salespeople who did not go through the training. The company found a 205 percent return of investment in the salesperson's second year. After five years, the total revenue generated from this sample group reached more than $290 million, providing an ROI of 667 percent.[31]

TABLE 8-2 Sales Training Evaluation Practices

Measure	*Criteria Type*	*Importance Rank*
Trainee feedback	Reaction	1
Supervisory appraisal	Behavior	2
Self-appraisal	Behavior	3
Bottom-line measures	Results	4
Customer appraisal	Behavior	5

Field experiments to control for outside influences on sales are not easily designed or conducted. People with similar experiences, previous performance, and other characteristics, for instance, should be assigned to both the control group (salespeople not given training) and the group of salespeople given training. Results must usually be measured shortly after training, as well as several months later, to enable comparison between short-term and long-term effects. Similarly, outcomes should be measured before training to determine the extent of the change that can be attributed to training. These are just some of the issues that must be considered.

FOLLOWUP

Regardless of management's philosophy toward the training issues discussed in this chapter, one of the biggest mistakes management can make is failure to follow up on training. One-shot training is a proven formula for failure and a big waste of company money. No one can train salespeople once a year at the annual sales meeting. According to a frequently cited study at Xerox, 82 percent of skills learned in a training session are lost if not reinforced. Training efforts are most successful when training is scheduled at regular intervals throughout the year. At American Bankers Insurance Group, for instance, the sales force goes to Miami twice a year for a weeklong training session. Also, salespeople meet for a full day once every two weeks with their regional managers to review what was taught in the training sessions. Consistent, ongoing training and reinforcement lead to development and improvement as part of an organization's culture. This obviously must start with top management's support and participation. American Bankers demonstrates this commitment when the chairman, vice chairman, or national sales manager holds quarterly meetings with each salesperson.

Additional Sales Training Issues

Developing Salespeople. *Salesperson development* involves helping people develop goals, skills, and habits beyond those necessary for the present job. Many experts feel that developing personnel is the most important and most difficult responsibility of first- and second-line sales managers. This process, sometimes referred to as career planning, often involves retraining salespeople to expand their responsibilities. As companies move toward flatter organizational structures, career planning for salespeople can become even more difficult because of fewer advancement opportunities.

Being stuck in a job in which there is little or no opportunity for further personal development can be very demotivating. Most people are stimulated by new challenges and the possibility of having an important impact on the performance of the organization. Salespeople who face a future of no new responsibilities beyond their present territory are likely to be less motivated and less committed to the organization than those who have these prospects. Their sales performance may also level off or decline.

What can first- and second-line sales managers do to help salespeople develop their full capabilities and prevent career stagnation? Here are a few suggestions:

1. Help salespeople gain a realistic understanding of the process and of their chances of getting promoted. This should begin with the initial socialization of the new salesperson into the organization and continue with veteran salespeople.
2. Give people opportunities to develop new skills within their present job. For example, a veteran salesperson with the appropriate skills and desire may be asked to train a new salesperson or to open a new territory.
3. Be creative in letting veteran salespeople know that they are successful and important to the company even if they are not in management. Recognition is particularly effective

in this regard. For example, an expensive gift for achieving a particular sales level may be very motivating when presented as part of a formal ceremony.

4. Be constantly alert for salespeople with the skills and desire for management or other advanced sales positions. Watching how other salespeople react to the individual in an informal setting is particularly important. Periodic checking of the person's career aspirations is also necessary because these may change, especially as an individual's family situation changes.
5. Design a program for developing salespeople for their next assignment either in management or in an advanced sales position. Similar to a sales training program, this program should begin with the tasks to be performed in the next position that can be practiced and modeled in the current position. For example, a salesperson could be given responsibility for designing and conducting part of the next district sales meeting.

For a career development system to be effective, a company must reward managers for developing its employees. In some companies, this is part of the regular evaluation process of sales managers. Without such rewards, managers often tend to hold on to good representatives rather than develop them for their next position.

SUMMARY

Initial and refresher training sessions are vital to the success of any field sales organization. Sales personnel must understand their products, their customers, and the marketing program of the firm. This chapter has introduced a number of sales force training issues, and so you can now:

1. **Understand the benefits of sales force training.** Sales training should be considered an investment in the sales force. If conducted properly, sales training should pay off in a number of ways. Some of the more common benefits include: increased productivity, reduced turnover, improved customer relations, better morale, and improved time and territory efficiencies.
2. **Determine specific training needs for a sales force.** A training needs analysis is a process for determining where problems and opportunities exist and whether training can best address the issues. A complete training needs analysis includes a review of management objectives, surveys and observation of the sales force, customer input, and a review of company records. Each of these sources of information should be cross-validated whenever possible.
3. **Discuss the topics to include in a training program.** The choice of subjects to be covered in a sales training program depends on the products sold, training purpose, and personnel background. However, the topics typically covered in training programs include product knowledge, selling skills, teamwork, customer and market information, and company orientation, among others. Some recent training developments include sales force automation and Web-based topics.
4. **Describe the advantages of centralized and decentralized training.** An advantage of centralized training is the high quality and consistency of the training. In addition, communications and coordination are enhanced when everyone receives the same training. It can also boost salesperson morale by giving trainees exposure to top-level managers and other specialists. Decentralized training, on the other hand, provides a learning environment closer to the salesperson's customer base. Trainees participate in programs that incorporate customer issues similar to those they will encounter in their own nearby territories. It also tends to reduce travel and instructional expenses.
5. **Understand the use of line, staff, and outside trainers.** Training can be conducted by staff specialists, line managers, or outside consultants. Staff specialists are usually

involved with centralized training activities and the preparation of classroom materials. First-line sales managers are more likely to conduct one-on-one training. This method allows sales managers to take immediate corrective action to improve the skills of those working under their supervision. Outside consultants provide a degree of variety, inspiration, and excitement to the training program.

6. **Recognize the value of alternative training methods.** Company-run training programs generally are the best way to instill the necessary knowledge; a variety of teaching methods can be used, including lecturers, case studies, videotapes, and programmed instruction. Role-playing exercises and one-on-one coaching are also good ways to teach sales skills. Filming and videotaping of trial presentations help to increase participation and to polish skills during training sessions.
7. **Describe the different methods for evaluating training results.** Sales training requires substantial investment in facilities and materials, and sales managers must continually justify these expenditures. Training programs should be evaluated on a regular basis to measure their impact on sales force turnover, morale, product knowledge, and sales revenues. Knowing the results of training efforts can help managers refine these programs for maximum efficiency and effectiveness. Remember: A firm must follow up on training in the field, where sales occur.

KEY TERMS

Centralized training
Cognitive selling scripts
Commission overrides
Cross-tabulation
Decentralized training
Declarative knowledge
On-the-job training (OJT)
Procedural knowledge
Role-playing
Salesperson development
Training needs analysis
Turnover

DEVELOPING YOUR COMPETENCIES

1. **Strategic Action.** As the marketing manager, you are very excited about a new product that R&D has developed that will eventually take your company in a new strategic direction. You know it will sell because you have tons of market research data to back it up. You are also painfully aware that the product and its benefits are complex to the customer, so that it will take significant sales force backing to make it successful. No matter how often you tell the sales department how great this product is, you know that their instinct for selling won't automatically translate into a passion for selling this product. You decide to present your product to the sales force at the next sales training meeting. You are nervous because you realize that sales support is absolutely critical if the product is to succeed. The sales force must put significant time behind it. What directions would you give the marketing manager in preparing for the training session? What are the alternative training approaches (e.g., lecture) that you could use in this training session? What will salespeople want to know about the new product?
2. **Team Building.** It is estimated that about one-third of the nation's major firms have formal mentoring programs, with senior managers providing personal counseling and career guidance for younger employees. However, a mentoring program is difficult for salespeople who spend a lot of time on the road. Georgia Pacific has tried to resolve this problem by using the salesperson's immediate superior as the mentor for the new salesperson. The company has also created some literature that offers advice that is sent directly to the field reps. What do you think of this program? Do you see any problems? Would you like to see anyone else in the mentoring position? For more information about Georgia Pacific, see its Web site at www.gp.com.

3. **Technology.** Westvaco uses the computer to augment its sales training program. Sales managers are given data on costs, profit, volume, and other information and are asked to make recommendations on business alternatives. The computer responds with estimated results for sales dollars, profits, and inventories. The simulation is set up as a game, with managers competing against other managers. List the possible benefits of this unique program. To learn more about Westvaco, visit its Web site at: www.westvaco.com.
4. **Coaching.** As the sales manager for a medium-sized industrial firm, you have just finished reading an article in a business journal that praised the benefits of providing field sales training for experienced salespeople as a refresher. The author claimed that a sales manager observing the calls of veteran salespeople spotted and eliminated bad habits and techniques. When you suggested doing the same thing, your sales force strongly objected. One salesperson feared it would look bad to have the manager come along on calls. Another said that after ten years on the job, he didn't need any further training. You are still convinced that there would be some benefits to this type of training. Would you go ahead with the program, despite the objections? If you do, how do you plan to convince the sales force that there is a need for such a program?
5. **Self-Management.** As discussed in the chapter, the sales manager plays an integral part in the training process. However, one aspect of sales training is to take charge of one's own self-development process. One popular method is the use of audiocassettes. Using audiocassettes as a sales training tool has attracted sales trainers for many years because of the amount of time salespeople spend traveling between accounts. (The history of recorded sales materials can be traced back to 1959, when Bob Stone and Don Reaser started The Business Man's Record Club.) Most companies, however, have been unable to sustain a regular schedule of tapes to the field beyond a few months or, in some cases, only three or four basic tapes. The greatest difficulty has been to produce material that salespeople will find worthwhile and to which they will be willing to listen. Reflect on what would be necessary for you to listen to a tape, enjoy it, and learn from it. What would you recommend to someone producing sales training tapes for a field sales force to ensure that the salespeople will listen to and learn from the tapes?
6. **Global Perspective.** Computer Associates trains its international sales force using weekly conference telephone calls. It may have as many as 3,000 reps worldwide on one conference call. For example, it would not be unusual for one person in France to dial in and have as many as sixty people listening in the room. One benefit is that a phone call isn't as expensive as pulling everyone out of the field and training them for four days. Do you see any problems with this international training program? What would you do differently? To find out more about Computer Associates, visit its Web site: www.cai.com.

FEATURED CASE SHIELD FINANCIAL: "TRAINING WOES"

It was the first day of Shield Financial's Des Moines office three-day sales training meeting. The company's twenty-five salespeople talked excitedly during breakfast about the upcoming events: a few rounds of golf, some whitewater rafting, and an awards dinner at which the annual incentive contest winners would be announced. They even looked forward to the three 5-hour intensive training sessions (one each day) that had been billed as unique and transforming. Also attending the meeting were two recently appointed assistant managers and Doug Bloom, all quietly listening to the reps' banter.

At 7:45 A.M., the salespeople got up from their tables and walked down the resort's hallway to its meeting rooms. The reps took their seats, and at 8 A.M. sharp, their instructor, Tom Baker, walked in and began the session. Five hours later the salespeople emerged and reconvened in the café for lunch. They were soon joined by the two assistant managers who had attended leadership training conducted by the same company.

The moment they sat down, the reps' ranting began: "This was the worst training I've ever attended." "It was tedious." "I could've learned more in my sleep." The assistant managers were surprised because their session was excellent. The reps, however, were so perturbed that they didn't want to sit through the two remaining sessions. "Ten more hours would be pure torture," one salesperson insisted.

Bloom suggested to the reps that they focus on enjoying that afternoon's activity, rafting, then excused himself to handle the situation. He said he would have a resolution by the time he rejoined them for dinner. Bloom didn't want this meeting to turn out to be a bust; he also didn't want to squander the company's investment in the sales meeting and training sessions. As he sat in the lobby awaiting the two instructors from the training company, he tried to devise a solution.

Questions

1. What steps should Bloom take to resolve the situation? (Canceling the remaining sessions is not an option.)
2. How can Bloom avoid this situation in the future?

LEADERSHIP

> Leadership is the art of getting someone to do something you want done because he wants to do it.
>
> Dwight Eisenhower

Chapter Consultant:
Carol Caprio, Software Business Unit Executive, IBM

LEARNING OBJECTIVES

After studying this chapter, you should be able to:

- → Explain what is meant by leadership.
- → Understand how leaders manage change.
- → Determine the appropriate leadership styles for a particular situation.
- → Know when and how to coach salespeople.
- → Discuss what is involved in planning and conducting a sales meeting.
- → Recognize common people problems.

LEADING THE INDEPENDENT SPIRIT

Pitney Bowes, Inc., a leading mail and document solutions company, recently installed a multimillion dollar customer relationship management system. Most of the company's salespeople have bought into the advantages of the system and have been using it effectively. However, some top performers haven't been as eager to change their behaviors and start using the system. They think it's a waste of their time. Pitney Bowes' branch managers have had to deal with this dilemma. For example, in one branch, the top rep, Sonny Esperanzo, has never logged into the system. Sonny continues to be a top performer, and his attitude is "I still bring in the numbers without it, so what's the problem?" Sonny is popular and well liked by the rest of the sales team in his branch, but he has not provided the necessary information to understand his customer base. One of your functions as a sales manager is to generate sales and market forecasts, and you can't make accurate predictions about the market without complete information. The usual procedures have been tried, but Sonny goes his own way, merrily or otherwise. Your boss has raised the concern about Sonny's lack of participation, so now is the time to do something about it but you don't want to smother his high energy and performance. You must make him realize that he is part of a team.[1]

You are considering several options. Which is the best choice?

1. Set an exact time and place to meet with Sonny. At this meeting, tell him that he will not leave the office without first entering his customer information into the computer program. Also tell him that you expect to see his customer data in the system from now on. If he does not abide by these rules, you will not consider him a candidate for bonuses.
2. Tell other salespeople about the problem and ask them to try to get Sonny to fall into line with the policy.
3. At the next sales meeting, have a major discussion concerning the need for the information that Sonny has been omitting. Don't mention any names, but be sure that everyone knows the consequences of not using the software. The guilty should get the hint.
4. Tell Sonny that you need to travel with him for a week in order to better critique his methods. Have him prepare the itinerary and include details of the customers he plans to visit in the upcoming trip.

The most important assets of every company walk out the door each day at 5 P.M. Developing and protecting this highly mobile asset is more demanding for sales managers than for other managers. Salespeople may not even come into the office in the morning. They're out in the marketplace every day, and your best salespeople are subject to all sorts of attractive temptations from other companies. An offer of more money by a competitor is certainly one reason salespeople will leave. However, important as money is in ensuring sales force performance, it alone does not inspire loyalty. In fact, results of a recent survey suggest that compensation alone is not sufficient for a complete retention strategy. Sales managers must also consider career-development opportunities and work/life balance issues to keep their salespeople from leaving.[2] This is just one of many reasons why leadership is critical.

Which option do you favor to persuade Sonny Esperanzo to use the software? As we discuss later in this chapter, some options are better than others. As shown in Figure 9-1, this chapter is centered around four essential concepts. Each of these are discussed separately; however, effective managers will use a variety of these skills within a given situation.

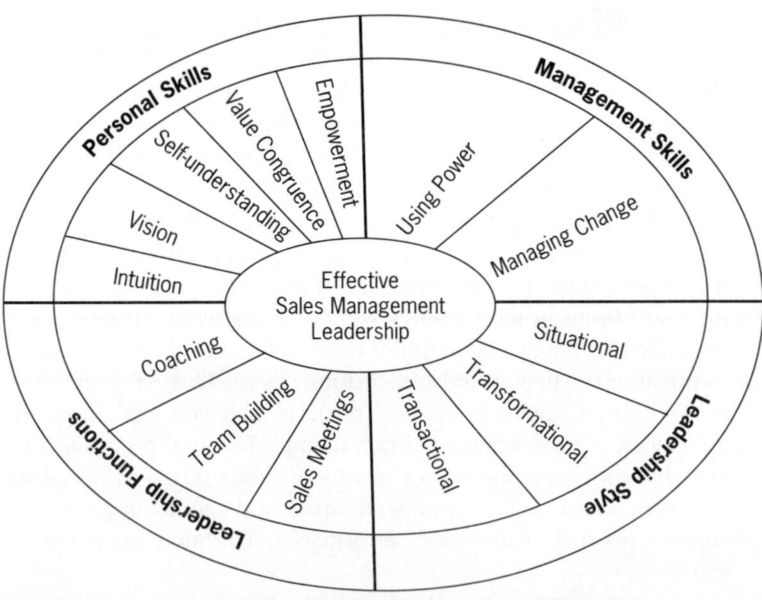

FIGURE 9-1 Effective Sales Management Leadership

TABLE 9-1 Leading Versus Managing

Leaders	*Managers*
Innovate	Administer
Develop	Maintain
Inspire	Control
Ask what and why	Ask how and when
Long-term view	Short-term view
Challenge the status quo	Accept the status quo
Do the right things	Do things right

LEADERSHIP

Leadership is defined as the ability to influence and inspire the actions of people to accomplish worthwhile goals. The terms leadership, management, and supervision are often used interchangeably, but it is important to note that there are important differences between leadership, management, and supervision. Leaders inspire trust and loyalty, and they understand how to direct the talents of others toward achieving important objectives. Sales management and supervision are more concerned with efficiency and "doing things right." Thus, sales leadership requires more intuition and foresight than just supervising the day-to-day activities of the sales force. As illustrated in Table 9-1, effective leaders create and articulate a vision, establish core values and culture, and inspire others to achieve, grow, and develop. It is also incumbent upon leaders to create an atmosphere of change to deal with the realities of the marketplace and provide a realistic vision for the future.[3]

Research on leadership indicates that salespeople have better attitudes toward their jobs, greater commitment, less job stress, more attachment to the job, and improved performance when managers clarify sales roles, demonstrate difficult tasks, and clearly define how salespeople are rewarded for their efforts.[4] In other words, great leaders are able to identify sales force needs and show reps the benefits of accomplishing individual and corporate objectives.

Leadership and management are not mutually exclusive, but rather, they refer to a person's distinctive approach. Two people may approach the same situation differently, one more like a leader, the other more like a manager. Table 9-1 summarizes the key differences in terms of the behaviors associated with leading versus managing.

Skills of Effective Leaders

Liz Crute, Regional Vice President for Pitney Bowes, Inc., has been a highly acclaimed sales manager at her company for over 25 years. She attributes her long-term success to practicing a few basic leadership principles. "My most important task as a manager is to get everyone working toward the goals of the firm while at the same time I try to anticipate the environmental, technological, or other changes that will affect my salespeople. I think I've also been fairly receptive to accepting negative as well as positive feedback from my salespeople over the years. I've found out some surprising things about myself and have been able to grow as a person and manager from this." Liz is also the first one to admit that she needs improvement in some areas. "I have a tendency to take on more work than I need to. I have to remind myself that I've got to let go at times."[5]

Research suggests that the best leaders develop five important skills during their careers (see Table 9-2). As you have may have noticed, Liz's self-description of her leadership principles exemplifies many of the leadership skills in the table. While Liz's experiences, both successes and failures, were instrumental in her development, she also concedes that her company, Pitney Bowes, played an important role in her leadership skill development

TABLE 9-2 Leadership Skills

1. ***Empowerment:*** A leader's ability to share power with others by involving them in setting objectives and planning. This requires spending time with salespeople, particularly top people.
2. ***Intuition:*** The ability to anticipate change and take risks. Although experience helps to develop a sense of intuition, inexperienced sales managers can build a sense of intuition by actively seeking information from customers, salespeople, sales support personnel, company records, and any other source that could serve their ultimate purpose.
3. ***Self-understanding:*** A willingness to receive and understand both positive and negative feedback from others, including subordinates. It also means knowing how it feels to lead and motivate others, especially when there is immense pressure to be more profitable than the previous year.
4. ***Vision:*** The ability to conceive what may affect a business in the future and what changes are needed for it to prosper. A successful vision exists when you can envision where the sales organization needs to go, communicate that belief throughout the organization, get endorsement from all levels, and then execute plans to get there.
5. ***Value congruence:*** A skill achieved when everyone in the organization is striving for the same business objectives. Achieving it requires good communication skills, as well as the ability to convince others that certain ideas are worth implementing. Value congruence allows a leader to delegate to others the authority to run their own operations.

through its many sales management training programs. Unfortunately, managers in many other companies often fail to receive such training.

Using Power Effectively

Power is the ability to influence the behavior of others. All sales managers use power, but effective sales managers know how to use it to get salespeople committed to meeting the manager's expectations. Ineffective use of power may lead to a salesperson who merely complies with a manager's expectations without much enthusiasm. Compliance can quickly lead to abandonment of the request at the first signs of difficulty. Misuse of power may actually lead to resistance by appearing to respond to a manager's requests while not actually doing so or even intentionally delaying or sabotaging plans. Thus, power is critical to leadership because it reveals why subordinates follow leaders. The five sources of power are legitimate, reward, coercive, referent, and expertise.[6] Effective leaders may have to use a combination of all five types of power at different times.

- *Legitimate power* is based on the manager's position in the organization. Salespeople put extra effort behind products that a sales manager has targeted for special promotion because they think the manager has a right to expect this effort. In the case of Sonny Esperanzo, the second option, which asks other salespeople to help solve the problem, undermines your legitimate power as district sales manager. To some degree, you are transferring your role as manager to your salespeople, and this may make you appear weak.
- *Reward power* relies on a leader's ability to reward subordinates for outcomes that they value. For example, salespeople may put extra effort behind a particular product because the sales manager has offered to pay a bonus for each unit sold over a three-month period. This power depends on the size of the bonus and the importance of extra compensation to the salesperson.
- *Coercive power* leads to compliance due to fear of punishment. Salespeople who believe that they could be fired will spend extra time prospecting for new customers. However, if the person is already thinking of quitting, then the power of this threat is minimal. This leadership style is rapidly losing favor, and the role of today's manager is to support the efforts of the team, not to control and direct. The option of setting up a meeting with Sonny Esperanzo and requiring an itinerary is an example of coercive power. This option

is loaded with threats. Keep in mind that withholding bonuses could be illegal, depending on employment contract terms.

- *Referent power* is the leader's influence on others because of friendship with the leader. Salespeople comply because they feel that friends help friends or because they so admire the manager that they want to emulate him or her.
- *Expertise power* is based on the perception that a manager has special knowledge, usually based on past success. Thus, new salespeople may put extra effort into targeted accounts because a sales manager has told them that this is the key to future success and because the manager has a long and distinguished district sales record.

Any of the five power bases can lead to desired behavior by subordinates, but salespeople tend to be more committed to a manager's request when they feel a sales manager is particularly knowledgeable and makes good decisions and suggestions (expert power) and when they identify closely with the sales manager (referent power). Although rewarding salespeople for good performances can be an effective use of power, too much reliance on reward power leads to a mercenary attitude among salespeople rather than a commitment to the overall vision of the organization. A good example of the misuse of reward power is how Oracle, a big database software company, paid its sales commissions. Oracle used a commission structure known as the accelerator: 12 percent commission for a sale made on the last day of a quarter, just 2 percent the day after. This led to false promises, bullying tactics, and deep discounts by the salespeople that damaged the company's long-term position in the marketplace.[7] The use of coercive power can be just as damaging. When coercive power is used, salespeople lack the enthusiasm that accompanies commitment to a course of action. This lack of commitment is usually critical because sales involves more than avoiding mistakes.

Managing Change

As you may have noted in the leadership skills section, an important characteristic that today's sales leaders possess is their ability to deal with change. The dynamic nature of today's competitive environment means that successful sales organizations will have to continuously change their strategies and tactics. For example, markets change—they grow, decline, consolidate, mature, and become more competitive; people change—management decides to increase empowerment or increase control; product lines change—they shrink, broaden, new products emerge, and old products become obsolete; and customer expectations change—for different products, new ways of ordering, and new services. Research suggests that successful organizations will evolve their strategies and tactics with how customers want to conduct business.[8]

Managing change essentially implies changing salesperson behaviors, and although many people thrive on change, others have a low tolerance for the uncertainty and ambiguity of change. How then does a sales manager succeed in getting all salespeople to implement a change initiative? One thing is certain: Salespeople with greater trust in the sales manager will be more accepting of the anticipated changes, especially in the longer run.[9] Effective sales managers today, therefore, not only recognize the need for change but also excel in building trust by communicating how the changes will affect the sales force and the steps involved in implementing the changes.

While leading change is a complex process with many possible avenues for success, research suggests that a successful *change management process* typically has five phases: assessment, redesign, measurement, sales support programs, and implementation.[10] The process is illustrated in Figure 9-2. In the assessment phase of a change management project, sales managers typically engage in reexamining the customer environment(s) in which the company operates. Pharmaceutical manufacturer and marketer, the Upjohn Company

FIGURE 9-2 Sales Force Change Management Process

(a recent acquisition of Pfizer), noticed that the pharmaceutical decision makers were changing, but the company's traditional selling process addressed only prescribing doctors. Upjohn ignored the changes related to managed-care organizations that use different purchase criteria. Based on this assessment, Upjohn's sales force eventually had to develop new skills and new strategies to meet the needs of the large and growing managed-care market.

Once the situation is adequately assessed, the redesign phase typically involves changes in one or all of the following areas: customer orientation, sales strategy, and/or selling processes. To redesign a sales staff's customer orientation, not only do sales managers need to be knowledgeable of their customers needs and wants, but they must align their sales force's selling strategies and tactics with customer buying processes. Many customers, particularly the larger ones, may have new and stringent requirements for suppliers. These include a broader range of salesperson skills, such as financial, communications, and consensus building within and across organizations.

After the customer's buying process is assessed, the next step is to develop a sales strategy that defines how the company deploys its sales resources. One way to do this is to segment the market, which means emphasizing customizing strategic selling approaches to better fit the buying processes and relationship requirements of targeted customer segments or even individual accounts. This approach offers excellent opportunities to grow revenues and increase productivity, since selling efforts are tailored to customer segments with higher potential.

The final step in sales managers' redesign efforts includes implementing changes in the sales processes of the sales force. To accomplish the change initiatives, the sales manager may need to redesign the tactics used in selling present customers, new customers, or both. Often the changes in the sales process include a need to redefine the sales job.

Once the design is in place, it is recommended that managers implement some type of measurement procedure to determine the success of the change initiative. Sales force change management programs typically measure revenue growth in the strategic areas, such as new customer acquisition or new product placements, greater sales productivity, improved customer coverage, or customer retention.

In conjunction with developing an appropriate measurement procedure, managers should also develop a sales support program to help ensure the long-term success of the change initiatives. Sales managers can provide a number of supporting programs to energize and direct continued performance. Examples include advanced training programs, compensation, rewards and recognition, sales automation, and supervision. Allegiance Healthcare's change

TEAM EXERCISE
"Avoiding a Bidding War"

As the new sales manager for a medium-sized manufacturer, you are quickly finding out why you got the job so easily. You've been in the position for only three weeks, but already your salespeople are complaining that the competition is able to outbid you (i.e., cut prices) to the point where they say their current clients are threatening to leave unless the company lowers its prices as well. You could have a major problem on your hands unless you do something. How can you avoid waging a price-bidding war for your client's business?

initiative toward team selling, for example, required its salespeople to enroll in a program designed to sustain the transition to team selling.

How quickly the changes are implemented will be a function of the sales organization's size and complexity. However, one method that has been proven to speed implementation is a pilot test. Many companies undertake a pilot test of their proposed change program so they can experiment with aspects of change in one geographic area or with a particular industry or company type. Upjohn, for example, began its change management program in one state, Minnesota. To sustain sales force morale and motivation, a manager should align compensation incentives with the change initiative and continually update the sales force about the future and the challenges ahead. What would you do as the new sales manager in the Team Exercise "Avoiding a Bidding War"?

EFFECTIVE LEADERSHIP STYLES

When trying to influence and change the behavior of others, your leadership style often determines your success. *Leadership style* is defined as the pattern of behaviors that others perceive you to use when trying to influence their behavior. Every sales manager has his or her own leadership style when dealing with a sales force. Research has shown significant correlations between the type of leadership style employed by first-line field sales managers and salesperson attitudes, role perceptions, and performance.[11] In general, this research suggests that the transformational leadership style tends to be more strongly related to salesperson performance than other styles. However, the consistent use of one type of leadership style in all situations with all types of salespeople is obviously not recommended. There are aspects of a situation and/or needs of a salesperson that may enhance or nullify the effects of a leader's behavior. To this end, we also present the situational leadership model.

Transformational Leadership

The *transformational leadership* style motivates salespeople by appealing to higher ideals and moral values so that they are motivated to exceed performance expectations. Transformational leaders "transform" people by making them more aware of and accepting of the goals of the organization. They are able to change a person's emphasis from focusing on his or her own self interest to focusing on the performance of the team or organization. They do this by listening and responding to the needs of each salesperson using two-way communication. In addition, they are able to create a compelling vision for their organization and encourage the sales force to work toward a common goal. Leaders exhibiting this style have also been called charismatic leaders because they are able to arouse strong emotions and identification from others.

In contrast to transformational leadership is *transactional leadership*. A transactional leader motivates followers by appealing to their self-interest. In other words, they lead by emphasizing fairness and they tend to rely on rewards and punishment to maintain control. A good job such as exceeding quota, for example, is celebrated with praise and accolades, whereas missing quota is cause for reprimand. It is important to note that transactional leaders tend to focus on short-term day-to-day operations and sales force control as compared with transformational leaders who shape others attitudes and actions by appealing to higher-order needs. Research suggests that transformational sales leaders possess many of the personal leadership skills discussed in Table 9-2.[12]

Situational Leadership

A *situational leadership* model with four types of leadership styles is shown in Figure 9-3. These leadership styles are based on two characteristics: directive and supportive behavior. *Directive behavior* is the extent to which a leader engages in one-way communication, spelling out what, where, when, and how to do it. Performance is closely supervised and controlled by the leader. Directing the sales force to use a canned sales presentation is an example of how a manager would implement this leadership behavior. *Supportive behavior*, on the other hand, is the extent to which a leader engages in two-way communication involving listening and providing support and encouragement. With supportive behavior, a sales manager involves the salesperson in the decision process. Participation in quota setting often involves supportive behavior. It is important to note that the situational leadership emphasizes that a leader's style must be flexible to adapt to changing situations and the maturity level of the salesperson. For example, more mature salespeople might appreciate

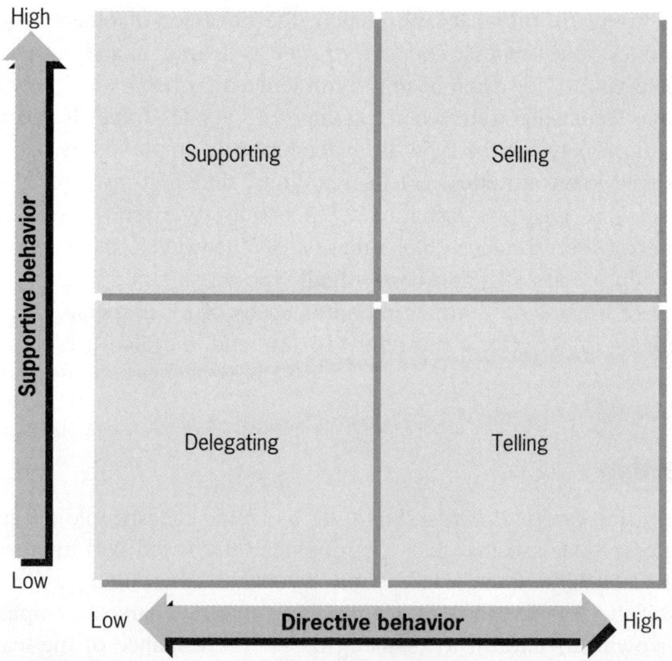

FIGURE 9-3 Four Leadership Styles

supportive leadership behaviors and may not need or want directive behaviors. Indeed, research suggests that more effective managers tend to match their leadership style to the desired leadership behaviors of their salespeople.[13]

Four Leadership Styles

The four leadership styles are referred to as telling, selling, supporting, and delegating. Each style results from a combination of high or low supportive and directive behavior. When the manager provides low supportive behavior, but high directive behavior, he or she is using a *telling style*. In this style of leadership, managers tell a salesperson what, when, how, and where to do various tasks. Identifying the problem and stating how the salesperson will accomplish the goal are initiated by the manager. Communication is largely one way. For example, a sales manager establishes a call frequency pattern for all the customers in a salesperson's territory. No deviations from the pattern are permitted.

In *selling style*, the manager provides high supporting behaviors and also high directive behaviors. Leaders using this style tend to provide a great deal of direction with their own ideas, but they also solicit salespeople's ideas. In this case, the sales manager may ask the salesperson for a reaction to the call frequency schedule and will consider exceptions to the general policy that the salesperson feels are justified.

A *supportive style* is characterized by highly supportive behaviors and low amounts of directive behaviors. Essentially, a supportive style calls for a shift of day-to-day problem solving from the sales manager to the salesperson by allowing the salesperson to share in the decision making. The sales manager's role is to provide recognition, to listen actively, and to facilitate problem solving by supporting the salesperson's efforts to use what they have learned. For example, with a supportive leadership style, management decides that a call schedule is required but allows the salesperson to devise a call plan. The sales manager may provide past call report information and, if necessary, suggest changes in the schedule.

Finally, a manager providing low supportive and low directive behaviors would be using a *delegating style*. The focus of the sales manager-salesperson interaction is to reach agreement on the cause of a problem, but control of how to deal with the problem is left to the salesperson. This discussion is typically held in the salesperson's territory. Decision making is then delegated to the salesperson, who decides how a problem is to be handled. For example, the sales manager and salesperson may agree that there is a problem with small orders in the salesperson's territory. The salesperson may then decide that a revised call pattern would be the best method to fix the problem. Note that the salesperson will manage the details in how, when, and what specific tasks are needed to fix the problem. Thus, the delegating style is appropriate for salespeople who are both competent and motivated to resolve the problem.

We now turn our attention to three key leadership functions that will affect the success of the sales organization: providing one-on-one coaching, developing sales teams, and conducting effective sales meetings.

IMPORTANT LEADERSHIP FUNCTIONS

Coaching

As discussed in Chapter 1, an important function of first-line sales managers is to develop the skills of the sales team through coaching. Given the uncertainty associated with a field sales job, managers are often needed to define and clarify the salesperson's role. Poor coaching can seriously affect job attitudes, role perceptions, and performance; in contrast, good coaching can have a profound effect on these same outcomes.[14] Unfortunately, sales mangers seem to be inconsistent when it comes to coaching their salespeople to success. A recent global study of senior sales executives with strong sales organizations gave their sales forces an average grade of just C- when rating their capabilities.[15] While there may have been a number of factors that contributed to the poor rating, you can be sure that the lack of coaching likely played an important role.

Coaching is essentially a sequence of conversations and activities that provides ongoing feedback and encouragement to a salesperson or sales team member with the goal of improving that person's performance. Coaching sessions may take place in the office, but most sales coaching is done in the field during visits by sales managers. It consists of three basic components: (1) feedback, (2) role-modeling, and (3) trust. Although the three components are interrelated, we will discuss each in turn.

Feedback. While feedback is provided in all facets of a salesperson's job, we will focus on how feedback is used to increase selling effectiveness. To provide effective and useful feedback, it is important to be aware of sales force behaviors that detract from sales effectiveness. Questions or statements dealing with a salesperson's planning, attitude, knowledge, and selling skills of a particular customer, or group of customers, can be particularly effective. Examples used to elicit this information are as follows.

- **Planning.** Includes setting territory and call objectives, routing of sales calls, and use of time. "Before we go in, what is your objective for this call? What do you specifically want to achieve?"
- **Attitude.** Includes the attitude toward products, specific customers, the company, the salesperson's career, company programs, and company policies. "I have the feeling you didn't care for that assistant buyer. Your attitude is pretty evident."
- **Knowledge.** Includes product-related, customer business and specific industry issues, competition, territory, company, and policies. "I liked the angle you took on describing the product benefits, but let me ask you, what other approach could you have taken with this product?"
- **Selling skills.** Includes prospecting, selling steps, handling objectives, buying-center roles, negotiating skills, including helping set customer expectations for investment returns. "Let's talk about the timing when you ask for the order." "Who else do you know at this account who is in a key buying position?"

The best time for feedback is just prior to and following a sales call. This takes advantage of the important learning principle of recency, which suggests that feedback should be given immediately after the behavior. The type of feedback also matters. Research suggests that positive feedback provides both information and motivation, whereas negative feedback communicates only information. It is not surprising that positive feedback has a greater impact on performance and job satisfaction than negative feedback.[16] The key to effective sales coaching, therefore, is not in negative feedback, but in discussions of why the behavior was not correct, how a better response could have been made, and why this response would lead to the desired outcome.

When a manager accompanies a salesperson to a sales call, the manager must remember to let the salesperson control the situation. At times, a manager may be called on to address a particular issue, but should keep his or her remarks focused on that issue while giving the salesperson responsibility for the overall call. Otherwise, the salesperson will turn sales calls over to the manager whenever a tough issue arises. When coaching is the reason for being together, sales calls should not become a team selling effort. The manager is there to observe the salesperson's selling skills. Prior to the call, the manager should make it clear that the salesperson is making the call and that the manager will not interfere with the selling process.

Another important factor to consider when providing feedback is the maturity level of the salesperson. With mature, experienced salespeople, it is probably most useful for managers to use the post–sales call phase of coaching to identify strengths, build on them, and challenge these salespeople to excel in the areas where they do their best work. Any correcting may be accomplished prior to the next call, using the methods described earlier. For less mature salespeople, the post–sales call phase of coaching may be best used to establish and reinforce self-evaluation of the performance. Questions that may be asked include: "How do you think it went?" "What went well?" "What could you have done differently?"

Role-Modeling. The second component of effective coaching is role-modeling. *Role-modeling* is achieved when a salesperson perceives a sales manager's behavior as being consistent with both the sales manager's values and the organization's goals. Although role-modeling can take many different forms, one study suggests that positive role-modeling for sales managers includes such behaviors as personally demonstrating proper selling techniques to salespeople; being on time to meetings and appointments; conducting oneself in an honest, moral manner; always presenting a professional image through appropriate dress and grooming; listening to salespeople (so salespeople will listen to customers); being a team player; and never asking salespeople to do things that the manager would not do.[17] The following quote illustrates the importance of role modeling and its link with building trust.

> [Sales managers] . . . need to be respected. Part of that respect is being a role model. The conduct of being a "role model" garners respect and enhances a manager's leadership status. If as a leader you don't set a good example, you are never in a position to earn the respect of your team. Without respect you cannot get the job done.[18]

Trust. The final component of sales coaching is a salesperson's trust in, and respect for, a manager. In order for a sales force to trust a sales coach, they must respect and have confidence in the manager's integrity, reliability, and competency. Indeed, research suggests that, without trust, role-modeling has no effect on salesperson job satisfaction or performance.[19] Although a recent study suggests that trust in the sales manager does not directly affect salesperson performance, the same study also reported that a manager who sets challenging goals and expresses confidence in the salesperson's ability to meet those goals will strengthen the impact of manager trust on salesperson performance.[20] It appears that setting challenging goals while at the same time instilling salesperson confidence through coaching will increase commitment to the organization, which, in turn, will affect job satisfaction and performance.[21] Although more research is needed in this area, the bottom line is that a salesperson is likely to listen and respond to a sales manager's coaching attempts, but only if the manager is respected and trusted.

By now you may have recognized that the last option in the Sonny Esperanzo case is an example of coaching. Because coaching takes place one-on-one, Sonny is not as likely to be defensive as in a more social situation. By instructing Sonny in preparing an itinerary and a call report, you are giving him an important and specific demonstration of the importance of using the sales automation software. This is a positive approach with a high probability that the lessons learned will be retained. Coaching is the option with the highest probability of success.

Team Building

Teamwork in sales organizations has become much more important in recent years because of changing customer environments and requirements, changing technology, globalization of customers and competitors, as well as an increased emphasis on relationship marketing. One large wireless communications company, for example, recently instituted a team selling approach to meet the increased product and market knowledge demands of larger accounts. Their salespeople became leaders of a team of industry and application specialists designed to enhance the selling process of specific accounts.[22]

Despite the fact that teamwork has become more important for effective selling, companies have difficulties maintaining productive sales teams. One study found that a mere 13 percent of selling teams were rated as highly effective.[23] The most common reasons cited for a lack of sales team cooperation include such things as rewards and compensation that focus on individual performance rather than team efforts. Also information systems often do not keep team members supplied with pertinent data. Another problem is that organizational structures foster internal competition rather than cooperation. Finally, the mindset of some people makes them unwilling to set aside position and power for mutual gains.

The job of the sales manager is to help break down these barriers and reduce destructive competition among reps. Some experts in team selling suggest empowering the members of the selling team and implementing a shared leadership process. According to this model, empowering team members and sharing leadership will increase the collective ability of the team, which, in turn, increases the team's effectiveness. To develop these team attributes, managers should take great care in designing the composition of the team to include people with the right mix of selling task-related skills and leadership skills. There also has to be good chemistry among those selected for a team. Obviously, a sales manager would need a good understanding of the personality and leadership characteristics of the people in the sales force in order to successfully develop such teams.

Factors Affecting Team Success. The job of getting individual members of a sales organization to work together to form a functioning and supportive team is made easier when you have a better understanding of the factors that affect team success. Figure 9-4 provides a graphic illustration of the five key factors that impact sales team effectiveness.[24]

Individual team members. Successful teams share information, resources, and rewards. As a result, individuals working in sales teams require close working relationships with other team members. When selecting individuals to work in sales teams, managers should consider the profiles of the individuals and select those who are able to function effectively within a team. Research also suggests that trust is an important driver of team success. Successful teams tend to have a high level of trust that every team member is committed to the success of the team.

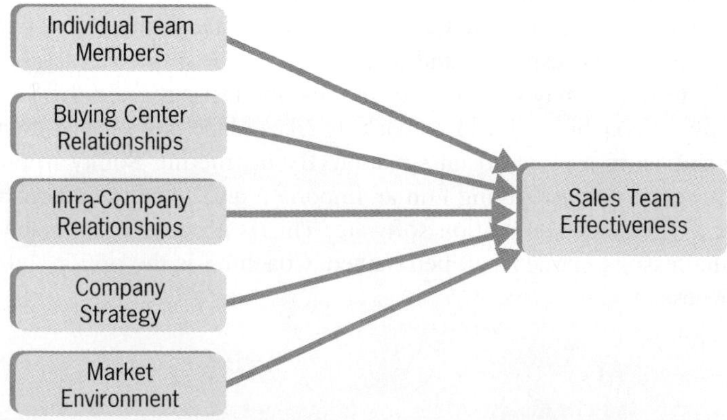

FIGURE 9-4 Factors Affecting Sales Team Effectiveness

The selling team and buying center. Individual salespeople are not knowledgeable enough or influential enough to implement complex selling programs. Selling teams offer improved interfacing with individual members of buying organizations across functions and levels. Essentially, effective selling teams provide a pooling of knowledge across a number of areas to better meet a particular customer's needs. A team learning orientation, therefore, is necessary for understanding and responding to a buying center's needs.

The selling team and intra-company relationships. Customized solutions often require team members to work effectively with engineers, R & D, and marketing personnel. It is also common for sales teams to work with other divisions or business units within a company to co-create new and different solutions for customers. Effective sales teams know how to marshal the necessary resources to champion new ideas from conceptualization to reality.

The selling team and company strategy. A sales team's approach to customers must be driven by corporate strategy. Corporate strategy provides norms for behavior and responsiveness to market information and can have important implications for the sales team. Some emerging research, for example, suggests that a sales team working for a company employing a "defender" strategy (i.e., protect its customer base from eroding) would perceive a particular type of market information much differently than a sales team working for a company with a "prospector" strategy (i.e., aggressively attract new customers).[25]

The selling team and the market environment. External forces, such as the competitive landscape and the changes in technology, will affect the design and success of sales teams. Competitive environments, for example, give customers a variety of suppliers to choose from. As a result, sales teams need to be able to be keenly aware of the benefits and deficiencies of competitor products as well as their own. When working in turbulent environments, sales team members need to be able to anticipate change and be able to respond proactively. Under these conditions, team members who are receptive to change would likely enhance team effectiveness.

Sales Meetings

Coaching is best suited to individual training and motivational issues. When a sales team needs information about a new product, for example, it is often better to address the need in a group setting. A common method for motivating and communicating with the sales team is the sales meeting. Companies hold sales meetings in part because the sales manager can be sure that everyone is exposed to the same message. However, keep in mind that meetings eat into selling time and hurt short-term sales revenues. Meetings perceived as ineffective tend to have a large negative impact on how an employee feels at the end of the workday as well as on overall job satisfaction. One study suggested that employees who attend a rash of bad meetings are stressed, dissatisfied with their jobs, and more predisposed to leave.[26] Considering that some companies have found that fully half of all their scheduled meetings were considered a waste of time by participants, sales managers should always ask, "Do we need to meet at all? Could this information be effectively communicated through a memo or by e-mail?" If so, a meeting may not be necessary.

If you need to organize a *sales meeting*, however, plan to organize around three key factors: meeting objectives, budgets, and location and timing. Planning a sales meeting without proper attention to these factors could cause some headaches, as illustrated by a quote from a frustrated sales manager:

> Planning a sales meeting [was] a horror show. You're hounded for weeks by countless phone calls and faxes. You battle constant budget headaches. What's more, you have to coordinate farflung reps, who dread being taken out of the field. And then, when the meeting starts, a host of potential disasters await. Is this what [I] became a manager for?[27]

Let's see how we can avoid these problems.

Meeting Objectives. Every sales meeting should have a set of meaningful objectives that are relevant to all salespeople. In other words, don't meet just because a certain meeting is a weekly habit. The most common objectives deal with communication, rewards, encouragement, and technical training. Examples of specific meeting objectives might include one or more of the following:

- Present restyled, redesigned, or new products.
- Explain new marketing and advertising programs.
- Train salespeople in advanced selling methods.
- Provide training for new software.
- Recognize contest winners or superior performers.
- Elicit sales force feedback.

A popular objective of sales meetings—eliciting sales force feedback—may come as a surprise to many readers. Meetings are usually thought of as a way to provide information, but effective sales managers also consider them a good opportunity to learn about conditions in the field.

In the case of Sonny Esperanzo, one option was to hold a sales meeting, and in this situation, the topic of using the software was an issue only with Sonny. It is helpful to review the importance of the software with the sales team, but it may not be wise to state the dire results one can expect for not fulfilling the requirements in a sales meeting. People who already use it are likely to wonder why the manager is being so negative, and veiled threats could ultimately lower the productivity of the sales team.

Meeting Budgets. The yearly budget for corporate meeting planners is usually between 0.5 and 1 percent of gross annual sales.[28] For many companies sales force meeting budgets run into the millions of dollars. To illustrate how the costs can add up, one company needed a face-to-face meeting in Dallas for four of its salespeople located in different parts of the country. The total cost for this one 4-hour meeting was over $8,000.[29] To reduce unnecessary costs, companies are now holding more meetings on-line or are using teleconferencing. It is important to remember, however, that sales managers need to control expenses without sacrificing effectiveness.

Locations and Timing. Pulling salespeople away from their territories for meetings means that some sales opportunities will be lost, but this problem can be minimized by careful scheduling. Sales meetings are usually held during slack times so that they will not interfere with normal customer contacts. For sales meetings that require travel of more than a few days, common sense should be used. Some experts recommend the first quarter of the calendar year as a good time to meet. Late second- or third-quarter meetings often conflict with vacation schedules, and late fourth-quarter meetings overlap the holiday season.[30] Although a variety of sales meeting locations are used, they are typically classified as local, regional, or national.

Local sales meetings are usually run by field managers and are held frequently, perhaps as often as every week, month, or quarter. These meetings are informal and take place in a conference room at the branch sales office or in a nearby motel. One advantage about holding local, as compared to regional or national, meetings is that they offer a chance for the salespeople to discuss issues that are unique to that office or branch. However, one drawback of local sales meetings is that field sales managers, who typically run the meeting, may not be adequately trained to provide an energizing, thought-provoking event.

Regional sales meetings include salespeople from several states and are usually held quarterly or less often. These meetings are more structured and often feature presentations by sales executives and training specialists from headquarters. With regional meetings, personnel from the head office do most of the traveling, which can save time and reduce expenses for salespeople.

National sales meetings bring the entire sales force together at a central location and usually occur once a year or less. These meetings require higher travel expenditures and firms tend to stage more elaborate speeches, presentations, and entertainment at these events. A typical objective of national meetings is to boost the sales force's morale and promote "psychic bonding" among salespeople so that they feel more like a team.

Common Problems.

Interest. The most damning outcome of a sales meeting is when participants find it boring and a waste of time. A recent survey indicates that 91 percent of executives admit to daydreaming, and 39 percent say they've actually snoozed during meetings.[31] With statistics like these, it's no wonder why many believe that unproductive meetings are demoralizing and worse than no meeting at all. Successful sales meetings should make good use of the time available and be exciting and fast-paced. Providing information about new products or services through the use of a well-designed theme, for example, is a good way to set expectations and minimize the lack-of-interest problem.

Participation. Another common complaint about sales meetings is that salespeople spend most of their time listening and do not get a chance to participate and interact with management. Encourage audience participation by keeping the meeting groups small so that each speaker leads a discussion rather than presents a formal talk. Automotive-retailer services firm, Reynolds & Reynolds in Dayton, Ohio, encourages participation by asking salespeople to share a new fact or bit of marketing intelligence that pertains to the topics to be discussed in the following week's breakout sessions. This motivates the salespeople to do research during the week, culminating in a fun, information-sharing session that encourages group participation.[32]

Followup. Problems can also result from a failure to determine whether salespeople have actually learned the information provided during the multi-day sales meeting. For example, the use of exams to test reps in the meeting's final session could be are used to determine if a followup session is needed. There should also be reminder letters and checks by local managers to ensure that the information is being used by salespeople.

SALES FORCE PERSONNEL ISSUES

Sales managers face difficult personnel issues in their development of effective selling teams. Several of these problem areas are reviewed, and suggestions are made on ways to manage these situations.

Plateauing

Plateauing occurs when people stop growing as sales professionals. They reach a stage where they are just holding their own or are underperforming. Perhaps they have even stopped showing an interest in the job itself. While most salespeople plateau in mid-career (e.g., in their forties), it is important to remember that plateauing may occur earlier.

TABLE 9-3 Sales Managers' Rankings of the Causes of Plateauing Among Salespeople

	Overall	*Mostly Women*	*Commission Only*
No clear career path	1	2	4
Not managed adequately	2	4	1
Bored	3	3	5
Burned out	4	1	2
Economic needs met	5	7	3
Discouraged with company	6	5	6
Overlooked for promotion	7	6	8
Lack of ability	8	9	7
Avoiding risk of management job	9	10	9
Reluctance to be transferred	10	8	10

Causes of Plateauing. The primary causes of plateauing among salespeople are shown in Table 9-3. Notice that the number-one reason for plateauing is the lack of a clear career path for salespeople. This reinforces our discussion of the benefits of developing a career path for salespeople who do not want to go into management. It also reinforces the suggestion made in the recruiting chapter that a realistic picture of the sales position and future opportunities is presented to all recruits.

Sales managers believe there are some differences among sales forces in terms of the causes of plateauing. The most important reason for women is burnout (Table 9-3). Burnout is also an important cause of plateauing among salespeople on commission. Other common reasons for commission salespeople to plateau is that their economic needs have been met or that they have not been managed adequately. These results suggest that there are limitations to compensation plans and that people want more from their jobs once their basic compensation needs are satisfied.

Signals of the early stages of plateauing should warn managers that this process is happening. Sales managers say the most important early signal is when salespeople do not prospect hard enough. Other signals are a lack of follow through in customer servicing and working fewer hours.

Solutions to Plateauing. Managers need to respect the experience that plateaued salespeople have and at the same time find ways to get them to try new approaches to serving customers. It is important to discuss the situation with the salesperson as soon as indicators suggest that it may be occurring. At the first sign of plateauing, sales managers should look for ways to enrich that person's current sales position. For example, plateaued salespeople could be trained to help coach new salespeople, to help introduce new products, or to develop key customer accounts. Another alternative is to give these salespeople responsibility for gathering competitive intelligence. Tough-to-crack new accounts could be reassigned, together with the award of valuable and unusual prerequisites if the salesperson is successful (e.g., vacations and bonuses). The number of job-enrichment solutions is limited only by the sales manager's imagination.

Termination of Employment

Termination of salespeople should be considered an option of last resort. At some point in their career, managers will find it necessary to terminate a rep. After this decision has been made, termination should be performed in a humane manner, with concern both for preserving human feelings and avoiding lawsuits.

Court dockets today are crowded with wrongful termination suits charging broken promises, invasion of privacy, violation of public policy, and failure of good faith. Former employees are suing—and winning—millions of dollars in damages. Awards are high because a company may have to pay for past and future wages and lost benefits, as well as mental and emotional suffering. In this environment, one misstep by a small company could drive it out of business.

There is no way to eliminate the chance of a lawsuit, but several steps should be followed prior to terminating a salesperson. The first step is to establish a paper trail. The trail should begin with employee manuals that spell out specific company policies and procedures. Performance reviews should occur on a regular basis, be documented in writing, and include both positive and negative elements. The written reviews should be accompanied by a candid discussion between the manager and the salesperson in unambiguous language.

Legal aspects of termination are important, but humanitarian issues are of major concern. One suggestion for softening the blow is to offer an attractive benefit package to terminated employees. This may include an outplacement service to help the person focus on the future and a sizable severance pay, which may range from one to four weeks of pay for each year of employment.

Firing sessions should be brief because neither side gains from a lengthy discussion. Some recommend that the firing session should take place at the beginning of the week—never on a Friday. This allows people to get an immediate start on their future rather than spending the weekend reflecting on the past. Others suggest that a Friday termination provides the weekend to allow the salesperson to recover somewhat. Never terminate anyone over the phone, and always do it in a way that preserves the person's dignity.

Sexual Harassment

Women occupy about 24 percent of all sales positions (Table 9-4). In some industries, such as educational services, the majority of the salespeople are women. Thus, managers need to be aware of the potential for *sexual harassment*. The Equal Employment Opportunity Commission defines sexual harassment as:

> Unwelcome sexual advances, requests for sexual favors, and other verbal or physical conduct of a sexual nature constitute sexual harassment when (1) submission to such conduct is made either explicitly or implicitly a term or condition of an individual's employment; (2) submission to, or rejection of, such conduct by an individual is used as the basis for employment decisions affecting such individual; or (3) such conduct has the purpose or effect of substantially interfering with an individual's work performance or creating an intimidating, hostile or offensive working environment.

Workplace sexual harassment is a form of discrimination and is prohibited by Title VII of the 1964 Civil Rights Act. Although sexual harassment is against the law and higher penalties are being awarded, salespeople still may encounter it. Salespeople are particularly vulnerable to what is known as third-party harassment, which is harassment by someone outside the boundaries of the firm, such as a customer, vendor, or service person. A typical situation could involve a male buyer at a key account asking a female salesperson for sexual favors in exchange for an order. In this case, the salesperson may want the order to help make her quota and fear the contract will be given to a competitor if she refuses. She may also believe that if she complains to her boss, she will be seen as lacking the selling skills needed to resolve the harassment problem. Another worry is that efforts to reform the buyer could sour relations between the two firms. Unfortunately, many managers are unaware that not only is third-party harassment prohibited, but their own firm could be held liable for such behavior.[33]

TABLE 9-4 Women in Sales: Percentages by Industry

Industry	*Percent of Women in Sales Force*
Banking	24.7
Business services	30.3
Chemicals	9.1
Communications	34.7
Educational services	50.4
Electronics	19.6
Food products	28.5
Health services	45.1
Insurance	27.4
Miscellaneous manufacturing	17.6
Office equipment	24.1
Printing/publishing	38.9
Retail	20.0
Rubber/plastics	17.7
Transportation equipment	23.9
Wholesale (consumer)	19.5
Average	24.3

As a sales manager, what should you do to help salespeople deal with harassment? An important first step is to ensure that the formal policies on harassment include procedures on how to deal with third-party harassment. The policies should include the kind of behavior that constitutes sexual harassment, the procedures a victim should follow, and the consequences of offensive behavior.[34] It is important to note that many salespeople may not report an incident because they are embarrassed and may feel that they are taking a risk by going to the boss. Signs to watch for include asking to drop a particular account, requesting a transfer within the company, or asking for general advice on how to handle such situations. As a manager, you should not dismiss or minimize any problems brought to your attention. According to the law, if managers have knowledge of an alleged incident, they must investigate and resolve the matter, or liability could fall on them. Once salesperson identifies a customer as a harasser, however, the sales manager should take corrective actions such as requesting the customer stop the inappropriate behaviors, reassigning the salesperson to a new customer or territory, or closing the account altogether.

Other steps to reduce the chances of sexual harassment situations include creating a culture of professionalism within your own firm. Several specific suggestions to give to your salespeople might include:

Conduct your self professionally.
Dress appropriately.
Be cautious in drinking at business functions.
Don't listen to sob stories.
Avoid being alone in one-to-one situations when possible.
Use independent transportation.

In sum, sales managers have in important role in preventing sexual harassment. An important first step is that the manager understands these policies and is proactive in creating and sustaining a culture that does not tolerate any inappropriate behaviors.

Alcohol and Chemical Abuse

There is no evidence that alcohol and chemical abuse are more prevalent among salespeople than among people in other occupations. However, alcohol and chemical abuse is a national concern, and it is probably no less prevalent among salespeople. Estimates suggest that nearly 18 million people in the United States—1 in every 13 adults—abuse alcohol or are alcoholic.[35] Salespeople spend a lot of time on the road, which is conducive to escape behaviors, including alcohol and drug abuse. In a recent study of legal cases where salesperson's misuse of alcohol resulted in either workers' compensation or company liability, the authors noted two areas of concern for sales managers: salesperson overnight travel and use of a company car.[36] This study also indicated that a significant number of cases in these two areas were settled in favor of the salesperson, and many with large punitive damages.

Most sales managers realize that salespeople will drink socially with some of their customers as part of the personal relationship-building process. Although this is generally considered an acceptable activity, managers know that salespeople are exposed to the potential of alcohol abuse. It is often difficult to detect when a salesperson is a social drinker or has a problem. Alcohol problems are generally detected through personal observation or information from fellow salespeople. Although companies can fire a person for using illegal drugs, very few firms have a company or a division-wide policy for dealing with alcohol abuse. The most common reaction of sales managers is to engage in informal counseling with the abuser. Another is to refer the salesperson to an alcohol abuse program and to terminate, either after a warning or immediately.

In most cases, the responsibility for determining alcohol and chemical abuse (including the abuse of legal drugs) rests with the sales manager. Where there is no formal company policy, a sales manager is advised to develop one and ensure that all salespeople understand exactly what the policy is. You should not ignore or tolerate the signs of abuse among your salespeople. It is also advisable to resist the temptation to engage in informal counseling with the problem drinker or chemical abuser. Alcohol and chemical abuse is a complicated psychological and physical problem that requires the intervention of trained professionals. Finally, sales managers must lead by example. They should ensure that they are sending the right signal by carefully watching their own alcohol consumption, both on and off thc job.

SUMMARY

Leadership is essential to maintaining a high-performing sales force. A sales manager's leadership responsibility is multifaceted and affects every aspect of a salesperson's job. This chapter has introduced you to a number of topics and issues facing sales leaders. You should now be able to do the following:

1. **Explain what is meant by leadership.** Leadership is defined as the ability to influence the behavior of other people. Research suggests that there are five skills that the best leaders develop during their careers: empowerment, intuition, self-understanding, vision, and value congruence. Leaders also rely on five types of power to exert influence: legitimate, reward, coercive, referent, and expert. The most effective use of power results in salespeople who are committed to the manager's goals. Although combination of power types may be appropriate at certain times, salespeople tend to be more satisfied with supervision when they feel a sales manager is particularly knowledgeable and makes good decisions and suggestions (expert power), and when they identify closely with the sales manager (referent power).
2. **Understand how leaders manage change.** Effective sales force change management programs tend to use a five-step process: assessment, redesign, measurement, sales support programs, and implementation. Assessment is the examination of the customer environment in which the company operates. Redesign change initiatives are made in

three areas: (a) customer orientation, (b) sales strategy, and (c) selling processes. Measurement involves measuring indicators of successful change. Sales support programs energize and direct performance for the long term. Finally, the implementation process will be function of the size and complexity of the organization.

3. **Determine the appropriate leadership style for a particular situation.** Based on the combination of two behavior characteristics (directive and supportive), we discuss four leadership styles: telling, selling, supporting, and delegating. In telling style (low supportive/high directive), managers tell a salesperson what, when, how, and where to do various tasks. In selling style (high supportive/high directive), leaders provide a great deal of guidance with their own ideas, but salespeople's ideas are solicited. A supportive style (high supportive/low directive) calls for a shift of day-to-day problem solving from the sales manager to the salesperson. A delegating style (low supportive/low directive) has the sales manager discussing problems in the territory with the salesperson. An important concept of the situational leadership model is that a leader's style should be flexible in order to adapt to changing situations.
4. **Know when and how to coach salespeople.** Coaching consists of three components: (1) positive feedback, (2) role-modeling, and (3) trust. The best time for coaching is before and after actual sales calls. Immediate comments on the salesperson's behavior can be effective in improving the selling and territory management skills of the salespeople. Managers must be careful, however, to always emphasize the things salespeople do well and to praise them for their accomplishments.
5. **Discuss what is involved in planning and conducting a sales meeting.** High performance depends on cooperation between salespeople and others within the company. One of the responsibilities of a sales manager is to develop a team effort emphasizing mutual support and respect. In order to develop effective teams, sales managers must understand how groups function. One of the most commonly used methods for influencing the sales team is through sales meetings. Planning effective sales meetings is based on three key factors: meeting objectives, budgets, and location and timing.
6. **Recognize common people problems.** In today's environment, sales managers are likely to encounter a number of personnel issues that can reduce the effectiveness of selling teams. Chief among these issues are plateaued salespeople, management development problems, termination practices, sexual harassment, and alcohol and chemical abuse. Managers must develop policies to handle them when and if they arise.

KEY TERMS

Coaching
Coercive power
Change management process
Delegating style
Directive behavior
Expertise power
Leadership
Leadership style
Legitimate power
Local sales meetings
National sales meetings
Plateauing
Power
Referent power
Regional sales meetings
Reward power
Role-modeling
Sales meeting
Selling style
Sexual harassment
Situational leadership
Supportive behavior
Supportive style
Telling style
Transactional leadership
Transformational leadership

DEVELOPING YOUR COMPETENCIES

1. **Strategic Action.** Effective leaders make sure that they inspire vision and instill confidence about the organization's ability to achieve that vision. Many corporate annual reports include a vision or mission statement. Look at the annual reports of three

companies you would like to work for upon graduation. Based on the vision statement and any other information contained in the annual report, what type of leadership style does the CEO of the company seem to have? Would you want to work for this person? Why, or why not?

2. **Technology.** Two years ago, reps at AMF Bowling Products had good reason to shudder at the very mention of sales force automation (SFA). Only half the sales force updated the Lotus Notes-based system religiously, and as time went on usage fell. Reps couldn't take their laptops into bowling centers and enter customer data without looking like spies to the alley owners with whom they were trying to establish trusting relationships. So instead, they'd scribble notes on paper. But after schlepping through four to six bowling centers, the last thing reps wanted to do when they got to their hotel at night was fire up their laptop and spend up to an hour logging their sales calls into one database and entering data on what kind of equipment each center had into another database. Because it took as much as two hours to replicate their notes, most reps gave up in frustration. In what ways would a SFA system help AMF Bowling Products? If you were the national sales manager for AMF, and you felt that a centralized customer database was vital to your continued growth, what would you do?
3. **Coaching.** Julie has the talent and experience to greatly improve sales in her territory. A veteran fifteen-year salesperson with the company, Julie has been a top performer in the past but just gets by now. Her husband is a doctor and their children are on their own, so Julie's financial needs are fully met. Julie's sales volume is third in the district of five people, so it's not that she doesn't sell, it's just that her sales volume has not increased much in the past three years, and you believe there is opportunity for greater sales out of her territory. Your company has recently downsized and budgets are tight. It's time to do something about Julie. How would you address this situation without losing a strong salesperson?
4. **Team Building.** As companies recognize that sales involves the ability to work in teams, more and more companies are seeking salespeople with demonstrated leadership capabilities. Choose an industry of interest to you and explore the job announcements. Are companies looking for salespeople who can demonstrate their effectiveness as leaders? Does leadership seem to be more important for some companies than others? Several Web sites provide extensive listings of job openings, including job listings from classified newspaper ads, which can be found at:

   www.monster.com

   jobs posted by hundreds of companies at:

   www.jobfind.com

   and the job seekers Web site of the National Association of Colleges and Employers at:

   www.jobweb.org
5. **Global Perspective.** The Global Leadership and Organizational Behavior Effectiveness Research Program (GLOBE) is a comprehensive worldwide study of leadership. The GLOBE project seeks to address several interesting questions about the nature of leadership in organizations throughout the world. One key question under investigation is whether some leader behaviors are considered effective by managers worldwide. While preliminary research results suggest some leadership patterns are universally considered positive or universally considered negative, there are important cultural-based differences with some leadership behaviors. Japanese leaders, for example, tend to be more effective using a supportive style. Assume that you are working for a company that has recently begun selling in the Japanese market. You have been asked to travel to Japan and work with their sales force. Up to now you have been successful using the telling leadership style with U.S. salespeople. What types of behavior changes would you need to make to be effective in dealing with the Japanese salespeople?

6. **Self-Management.** Consider the following situation described by an executive with the Aurora-Baxter Corporation, a company that makes construction materials:

   A couple of years ago, following a scandal in the awarding of highway contracts, the state legislature enacted some very stiff laws forbidding state purchasing officers from accepting any gifts—even free lunches. This can be a little awkward in certain respects. When our marketing guys are in the middle of negotiations with them, it's natural to go out with the buyers for drinks and a nice meal. Everybody knows that each person there is supposed to pay for his or her own meal. Our guys are told that they have to make that clear. So at some point one of them will say, "Okay, everybody, chip in. You know the rule." Maybe there are five of them and three of us and say the bill is $300. When the meal's over, they've put in $2 each and we pick up the rest of the tab.

   If you were the sales manager in charge of this situation, what would you do?

FEATURED CASE SHIELD FINANCIAL: "CONFIDENTIAL DOCUMENTS"

Doug Bloom recently hired Mark Martin as a sales rep to replace Bill Johnson, who'd just resigned. Martin was a top rep at AllSafe, the company's biggest competitor. With Martin's performance, AllSafe's midwestern region grew about 35 percent annually over the past three years; Shield's midwestern region has grown only about 12 percent annually during that same time.

Bloom thought that hiring Martin was a tremendous coup. He's well known in the industry, has an invaluable contact list, and easily ingratiated himself with his team at Shield. Best of all, within his first three months, Shield's midwestern region sales jumped 25 percent.

Now Bloom was wondering if indeed he made the right choice. Earlier today, when Bloom left a proposal on Martin's desk (Martin was out on a sales call), Bloom noticed some partially hidden papers with the AllSafe logo on them. Curiosity getting the best of him, Bloom took a peek. The papers were confidential AllSafe sales information: pricing, marketing strategies, forecasts, and more. Bloom assumed that Martin used this information to formulate his current tactics with Shield, to Shield's benefit.

Bloom was torn. On the one hand, sales are way up, and he was never meant to see those documents. On the other hand, using a competitor's confidential documents has both ethical and legal ramifications. What's more, if Bloom confronted Martin, would Martin leave and take Shield's confidential information to the next competitor? Bloom was unsure how to proceed.

Question

1. What should Bloom do? Should he forget what he saw? Confront Martin? Is there another solution?

ETHICAL LEADERSHIP

> Act as if what you do makes a difference. It does.
>
> William James

Chapter Consultant:
Georges Michaud, Director of Environment/Health Safety & Ethics, Northern Telecom

LEARNING OBJECTIVES

After studying this chapter, you should be able to:

- Explain why ethics are important.
- Explain the moral bases for business ethics.
- Understand how to make decisions that involve ethical problems.
- Recognize the issues of common sales ethics.
- Discuss how to build a sales ethics program.

WHY ETHICS ARE IMPORTANT

In the post–WorldCom, post–Enron, and post–Tyco era, ethics has become one of the hottest topics in the business world. Companies have instituted more rigorous ethics policies and set up global ethics offices. Business schools have entire courses dedicated to the topic. Despite the increased emphasis on playing by the rules, news stories continue to feature more and more ethical scandals by corporations and their executives. Many of these scandals are the result of unethical and often illegal actions of the top executives; however, there are a number of examples where the unwise actions of even one salesperson or sales manager can bring a corporation to its knees.

Ethical dilemmas are particularly common in selling because salespeople often have to make decisions in the field in response to customers' demands and competitive offers. How a salesperson deals with these dilemmas reflects not only a person's character, but also the company's culture and leadership. Indeed, sales manager decisions and actions quite often reveal and shape the moral character of the sales team. And sometimes these managerial decisions will raise difficult and deeply personal questions. In these situations, sales managers find themselves wondering: Do I have a different set of values at work as compared to home? How much do I have to sacrifice of myself to get ahead? Am I a different person at work? Answers to questions like these are often matters of right versus right, not right versus wrong.[1] In other words, a manager must choose between two ways of resolving a difficult issue where each alternative is the right thing to do, but it is impossible to do both. Managers and the business community typically rely on a code of moral behavior called *business ethics* to guide their behaviors; however, there are some ethical situations that can test a manager's personal values.

Take for example, the situation that Bo Smith, regional sales manager of a medical equipment and supplies company, finds himself in. Stacy, one of Bo's branch managers, wants to fire Kathy, a salesperson who was hired last year by Bo, because she has been underperforming lately relative to her peers in the firm. Stacy, a single woman in her late twenties, was recently promoted to manager because of her success as a salesperson. She typically works longer hours than most other managers and has a serious, down-to-business personality. Stacy wants Bo to allow her to fire Kathy because she feels that Kathy has not fully developed her territory. Kathy is a devoted mother with full custody of her 5-year-old daughter and no child support or other assistance from her ex-husband. Stacy believes that Kathy's responsibilities at home have been keeping her from fully realizing the territory's revenue potential for the branch. Since most of the other salespeople in the firm are in their early twenties and unmarried, the long hours had not raised work-family issues in the past. What do you think Bo should do?

On the one hand, Bo could allow Stacy to fire Kathy because everyone else was working longer hours with no letup in sight, and she has not shown signs that she would be able to handle the competitive pressures the company is now facing. At the same time, however, Bo has serious reservations about firing Kathy. The company executives said they believed in creating a "family-friendly" organization, and Bo now has an opportunity to do something tangible to support this culture. Above all, Bo felt that it was simply wrong to fire someone, especially a single parent, who was working diligently at her job.

Bo's dilemma illustrates the idea that sales managers' decisions are sometimes not choices between right and wrong, but between right and right. For a manager who struggles with these types of decisions, the stakes are very high. In this case, Bo's decision will likely reveal his basic values and, at the same time, provide a strong signal to the other employees. In one sense, Bo's decision could be considered a "defining moment" in his management career.

Similarly, salespeople may find themselves in a "defining moment" when the lure of an easy commission tests their ethical resolve. And there are plenty of examples of how bad ethical decisions by the sales force have resulted in significant penalties to the company. For example, Prudential Insurance Company of America had to take a $2.6 billion charge against earnings to pay policyholders damages after the company allowed its salespeople to use *deceptive sales practices* that encouraged customers to trade in old life insurance policies for new ones.[2] Salespeople told clients that the new policies were no more expensive than policies they replaced when in fact the new policies cost more and could not be paid for with future dividends. In the meltdown of the housing industry in 2007, many of the problems were attributed to salespeople in the housing and banking industries who sold houses and loans to unqualified customers. Salespeople either failed to adequately qualify customers or look the other way when credit issues popped up on customers' credit history. Customers in these inherently risky loans, dubbed "subprime mortgages" couldn't afford the payments when the interest rates in these adjustable rate mortgages moved higher. This, along with some additional market factors, resulted in widespread loan defaults and a surplus of empty houses for sale.[3]

In addition to these specific examples, academic research also provides evidence that the sales force is highly influenced by a company's ethical climate. Indeed, the effects of company's ethical climate have been documented across a variety of outcomes. For example, a company's ethical climate can influence a salesperson's customer orientation, commitment to quality, and organizational commitment.[4] These studies suggest that not only can an ethical climate enhance the customer experience through better salesperson interactions, but it can potentially reduce turnover through enhanced commitment to the organization. Consistent with this rationale, other studies suggest that a positive ethical climate can increase salesperson trust in the sales manager, reduce a salesperson's role ambiguity, and increase job satisfaction—all of which are important in keeping your best salespeople from leaving.[5] One study even found that happier salespeople are more likely to act more ethically than others.[6]

The consistent theme across all of these studies is the competitive advantage gained by creating and maintaining high ethical standards with your sales force. Thus, sales managers must not only train reps in how to recognize and respond to an ethical situation, but also maintain a positive moral culture. This chapter focuses on the ethical problems faced by sales managers and salespeople and provides a set of guidelines to improve one's ethical decision-making skills. We begin by discussing some important ethical perspectives relevant to framing sales manager decision making.

PRINCIPLES OF ETHICAL DECISION MAKING

Recall in the opening vignette that Bo was faced with a difficult decision: to allow or not allow Stacy to replace Kathy. If Bo allows Stacy to fire Kathy, he will be making a personal commitment to a particular set of values. This decision would likely support the interests of the company's shareholders and customers, as well as define fairness as expecting the same effort from each salesperson. In other words, Bo would align his moral compass with the *shareholder view* so as to earn the highest profits he can for the company's owners. But if he does not allow Stacy to fire Kathy, he will accept the *stakeholder view* by possibly reducing company profits to protect employee welfare. This decision would send a very different signal to the other salespeople about the basic values of the company.

At first glance, the shareholder view appears to provide the most practical decision. This approach, however, may not help Bo resolve all the issues at hand. For example, a replacement who had the same sales skills as Kathy, but worked longer hours, would likely add to profits. But how much of this gain would be offset by the added costs of searching for and training a replacement in addition to the severance pay Kathy receives? Any grumbling from other salespeople about Kathy's lack of work ethic would likely stop, thus temporarily improving morale and productivity. But by how much? And how costly would the continuation of the company's high-intensity, "churn-and-burn" personnel practices be in the long run? Also, what are the costs of limiting the future talent pool by discouraging talented people like Kathy from seeking jobs with such a company? As we can see, invoking the grand principle of maximizing profits adds little to the practical issues Bo would face as he tried to make his decision.

Typically, there are no laws or court decisions to guide people in specific situations, so actions must be taken in the "twilight zone" between the clearly right and the clearly wrong. Obviously, many ethical problems are due to the poor decisions made by individual managers and salespeople. Even the best salesperson can go wrong if forced to operate under policies that promote misdeeds.

Role Morality

The moral philosophies held by sales managers are important to maintaining an ethical sales force because managers are the ethics teachers of their organizations. They select field salespeople, provide ethical training, and enforce the moral codes of the firm. Their actions send moral signals, while at the same time, their omissions send signals—almost everything does. In describing the moral philosophies of individuals, scholars have labeled two patterns of moral reasoning as *relativism* and *idealism*. A relativistic manager tends to reject universal moral rules and makes decisions on the basis of personal values and the ramifications of each situation. Such managers place a high value on a personal perspective and will be less inclined from making a harsh judgment on a questionable situation until they understand the situational information that may have led to the behavior. Idealistic managers, on the other hand, accept moral codes and believe that positive outcomes for all can be achieved by morally correct actions. These managers will quickly perceive questionable behaviors as violations of ethical standards and will label such behavior as unethical.

How then do the moral philosophies of relativism and idealism affect sales manager decision making? One study found that these differences would result in significantly different hiring tendencies. A highly idealistic manager would be much less likely to hire an ethically questionable sales candidate as compared to a relativistic manager.[7] Another study reported that idealistic sales managers were more sensitive to moral problems in unethical sales situations than relativistic managers. It also showed that relativism declines with age and that idealism increases with age. Female idealism scores were also significantly higher than those for males. Interestingly, the sales managers in this study were not significantly higher on relativism or lower on idealism than other marketing personnel. This finding calls into question the popular myth that sales personnel have lower ethical standards than those in other business occupations.[8] Together these studies suggest that basic moral philosophies, such as relativism and idealism, may influence how sales managers build and maintain an ethical sales force. Two other moral philosophies having implications for sales personnel are Machiavellianism and conventional morality.

Machiavellianism

Niccolò Machiavelli, secretary of state in the Florentine Republic in the sixteenth century, is best known for his observations on human behavior and the workings of power. Many consider him to have been basically a realist—a person who focused on what is rather than on what ought to be. Machiavelli's political doctrine denied the relevancy of morality in public life and regarded expediency as the guiding principle. He was prepared to manipulate people and bend the laws of business to achieve his own goals. The opportunism that characterized Machiavelli's philosophy is reflected in the following quotation:

> Any person who decides in every situation to act as a good man is bound to be destroyed in the company of so many men who are not good. Wherefore, if a Prince desires to stay in power, he must learn how to be not as good as the occasion requires.[9]

Applying *Machiavellianism* to Bo's dilemma discussed in the opening vignette would lead him in a completely different direction than what has been presented thus far. Machiavelli's advice to Bo would focus on how he could advance his own career with the decision to fire or not fire Kathy, or at the very least, keep Stacy from taking power from him if she went over his head to higher executives. Thus, Machiavelli's question to managers facing such dilemmas is this: Are you playing to win?

While dictionaries define Machiavellianism as the principles and methods of craftiness, duplicity, and deceit, Machiavelli himself would only employ such practices for self-preservation. Unfortunately, some sales executives still employ such practices to achieve personal or corporate goals. It should come as no surprise that a common finding in management studies that include salespeople shows that those with Machiavellian tendencies are less ethical than others. These results suggest that sales managers should think twice about hiring people who score high on Machiavellian surveys and should teach their current salespeople how Machiavellian tendencies could influence ethical decisions in the field.

Conventional Morality

Another ethical standard that can guide the actions of executives is known as *conventional morality* or *situation ethics*. This philosophy is reflected in the familiar phrase "When in

Rome, do as the Romans do." The emphasis shifts from the individual to what society thinks about the ethical issue; that is, the standard of morality becomes what is acceptable to others at a particular time and place. Thus, social approval is the ultimate test of right and wrong. With conventional morality, relationships with others are more important than end results.

The conventional morality approach has no absolute ethical standards to guide the actions of executives. Morality is based on social convention and group consensus. If Bo used this philosophy to guide his decision, the decision to fire Kathy would be based on a consensus of opinions of others within the company. Notice that with this approach Bo's own reluctance to fire Kathy would not be as important to his decision. As we can see, the problem with this approach is that the majority might conflict with either your personal moral standards, as in the case with Bo, or with company policy. For example, salespeople and sales managers sometimes justify cheating on expense accounts with the argument that "everybody does it" or "it's a way to reward salespeople with tax-free dollars." However, these may not be personally acceptable reasons for you to violate organizational policy.

Another problem with conventional morality is that it is difficult for managers to adapt to changing contexts or cultures. Ten dollars given to a headwaiter is a tip, but $10 given to a customs official to get a perishable product moving is a bribe. Although both transactions represent payment for extra services rendered, one is socially acceptable and the other is not—in the United States at least. Often, in fact, what is moral, ethical, or common in one country is unacceptable—or even illegal—in another. For example, the hiring of relatives is called nepotism in the United States; in South America, it is viewed as an honorable family duty.

MAKING DECISIONS ON ETHICAL PROBLEMS

As you could probably surmise by now, ethics are concerned with the effect of actions on the individual, the firm, the business community, and society as a whole. A hierarchical diagram showing the order in which ethical decisions evolve is given in Figure 10-1. Notice that the ethical values and standards of the business firm are derived from the general values

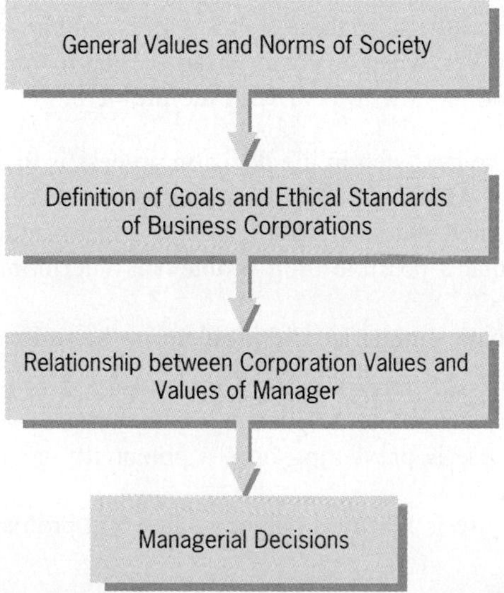

FIGURE 10-1 Making Decisions on Ethical Problems

and norms of society, and that business decisions represent a synthesis of the moral and ethical principles embraced by the various entities. Conflict is common because the values of the firm, as interpreted by its executives, may not match the values held by the individual. The difficult choice for managers in solving problems is whether they should adhere to their own moral standards, rely on company policy, or do what is expedient to maximize the short-run profits of the firm.

When faced with ethical problems, executives too frequently choose what is expedient rather than what is morally correct. Almost half of the 316 sales managers who participated in an ethics survey reported that they have heard their salespeople lie about promised delivery times to secure a deal.[10] This tendency to sell out personal ethical standards for a chance at corporate glory means that organizations need to foster a business climate that reinforces ethical behavior and to establish ombudsmen who train and provide salespeople with guidance on ethical dilemmas. A good starting point is to develop an ethical checklist that includes some basic steps to making ethical decisions.

Ethical Checklist

Managers and salespeople often need practical guidelines when making difficult moral decisions. Some companies suggest using a simple checklist when confronted with an ethical dilemma. One such checklist, used by managers at General Dynamics, is as follows:

1. Recognize the dilemma.
2. Get the facts.
3. List your options.
   - Are they legal?
   - Are they right?
   - Are they beneficial?
4. Make your decision.

Applying this checklist to a salesperson performing below expectations will help explain how it works.

The Case of the Drug-Using Salesperson

Recognizing the Dilemma. Suppose sales manager Smith is concerned about Jones, who used to be the star member of the sales force, Jones's sales volume is slipping. At first, Smith ignores the problem. However, when customers start calling to complain about service, she can no longer put off deciding how to deal with the problem.

Assembling the Facts. The next step in the decision process is to assemble all the relevant facts. Smith could start by asking questions of the other members of the sales force and of customers who can be trusted to tell the truth. Suppose these inquiries reveal that Jones's family life is stable but that a possible drug problem is interfering with normal sales-call patterns.

The sales manager could summarize the problem in the following manner:

1. Jones had an excellent sales record in the past, and the firm is having trouble finding good replacements for salespeople who leave.
2. Jones's apparent drug use is preventing him, a potentially good salesperson, from performing up to standard.
3. Jones's apparent drug use is hurting company sales and profits, and the situation must be corrected.

Any solution should deal with all the facts. If some of the pertinent information is ignored, the sales manager is unlikely to find the best way to resolve the problem.

Making an Ethical Decision. Alternative plans that deal with all aspects of the problem include the following:

1. Smith could have a talk with Jones and indicate her concerns about sales in Jones's territory. The two could agree on an acceptable quota, and Jones could prepare a plan to achieve the new goals. Smith could explain that she does not believe in telling people how to lead their personal lives, but she does not allow personal problems to detract from job performance.
2. Smith could call Jones in and state that she is unhappy with Jones's poor sales and has heard rumors that Jones has a drug problem. Smith could give Jones an ultimatum that unless he submits to a drug test and resolves the problem if the test is positive, his employment will be terminated. Smith would agree to set a reasonable sales quota and express confidence in Jones's ability to meet the goal.
3. Smith could tell Jones that she is concerned with the dual problems of poor sales and possible drug use. Jones could be offered a three-month furlough at half pay to find a way to overcome his problem and be told that a reinstatement or termination decision would be made at the end of the furlough. Smith could suggest that Jones start seeing the company psychologist, explaining that the firm would like to keep Jones because of his impressive record of past successes. Temporary salespeople would be hired to cover Jones's territory during the furlough.
4. Smith could call Jones in and express her displeasure with Jones's poor sales and his possible drug problem. Jones could then be offered a choice of taking a drug test and going to a drug rehabilitation center for a month at company expense or of being terminated. Temporary salespeople would be hired to cover Jones's territory during his absence.

The first of these solutions is a step in the right direction, but it may not be sufficient. Smith alludes to the drug problem but stops short of offering any help. The second plan faces the sales and drug problems squarely. However, it is not clear that Jones would be able to handle the pressure of the "reform or get fired" threat made by the sales manager. The third plan takes some of the pressure off Jones and offers help for the drug problem. But Jones may be unable or unwilling to stop using drugs, and this plan may simply postpone the inevitable decision to dismiss him.

The last solution to the possible drug problem is attractive because it offers advantages for all participants. The sales manager gains because Jones is removed from the territory and customers are handled by experienced reps. In addition, company sales volume in the territory should recover with the added attention. Furthermore, Jones is forced to confront his possible drug problem in a professional environment where chances for recovery are enhanced. The main risk with this approach is that Jones may refuse the treatment and his potential contributions to the firm will be lost forever. As you can see, there is no easy solution. What types of solutions would you have in the ethical dilemma shown in Team Exercise: "Customer Gifts Versus Company Policy"?

COMMON SALES ETHICS ISSUES

Sales managers must make decisions in a wide variety of situations that have ethical dimensions. These include relations with superiors, salespeople, customers, competitors, dealers, and issues such as sexual harassment. As discussed earlier, there are no well-defined guidelines for moral conduct in each of the situations because what is right so often depends on the particular circumstances. Our objective is to raise some questions about business ethics and to point out potential problem areas.

TEAM EXERCISE
"Customer Gifts versus Company Policy"

George Freitag, a salesperson at Steel International, is a professional at relationship building. His customers are the grateful recipients of cards for every occasion, tickets to sporting and entertainment events, even trinkets from Freitag's road trips. Any time he sees "the perfect gift" for one of his customers—whether it is a book on their favorite subject or some nifty gadget that's made just for their hobby—Freitag buys and sends it. Freitag's manager, Jesse Webster, enjoys seeing the pleasure Freitag and his customers get from the gifts—especially since Freitag always makes his quota and the prices of the gifts are always low enough to squeeze into his Travel and Expense (T&E) budget. Unfortunately, Steel's new CEO has recently introduced a strict "No Gifts" policy—right before the holiday season. Webster has learned through the grapevine that Freitag plans to send holiday gifts to his customers anyway and work them into his T&E budget as other expenses, such as "breakfast meetings." Webster is in a tough situation. He wants to keep Freitag and his customers happy, but he knows that he should follow the CEO's policy.

1. What should Webster do now?
   - Should he pretend that he didn't hear the rumor and let Freitag send his gifts?
   - Should he discuss the situation with the CEO?
   - Should he simply tell Freitag, "Sorry, but this is now the policy"?
   - Which option is best, or is there another, better choice?

2. If you were the sales manager, what would you do about the following:
   - Handling the rumor that Freitag plans to disregard the new company policy.
   - Keeping Freitag motivated despite the new policy.
   - Teaching Freitag alternative methods of building customer loyalty.

3. Is there a high probability of Freitag's losing customers because of the new policy?

4. What are the possible reactions from Freitag's customers?

5. Given the precedent that Freitag has set with his customers by supplying them with a continuous flow of gifts, what is going to happen when Freitag stops giving gifts and his competition continues?

Hiring and Firing

Various federal and state laws prohibit discrimination in hiring practices. Thus, firms that hire only white male Christians between the ages of 25 and 30 are breaking the law rather than operating unethically. An ethical problem, in contrast, usually requires considerable judgment as to the proper course of action—for example, in hiring candidates who are relatives of officers of the firm. Suppose a sales manager must choose between a man and a woman for a field representative position. Both candidates are well trained, but the man has somewhat more experience. Assume further that the woman is the daughter of a vice president of the company. If the decision is based strictly on qualifications, the man would get the position. However, the firm is under pressure from the federal government to hire women, so maybe she should get the position even though she has somewhat lower qualifications. Although nothing has been said, the sales manager knows there could be personal advantages in hiring the vice president's daughter. Some would contend that hiring the woman instead of the man would be reverse discrimination and unethical. In this example, the sales manager must make a moral choice between what is best for the firm and what might enhance his or her own position in the firm.

Another sticky ethical question relates to hiring salespeople from competitors. The main advantages are that these people are trained and are likely to bring along some customers from their former employer. However, securing salespeople from competitors can increase selling costs and may lead to lawsuits if trade secrets are involved. Despite these risks, raiding competitors is common in the insurance, real estate, and stock brokerage fields. These firms operate on the premise that it is easier to hire successful agents than it is to train them. To prevent such practices, some firms have unwritten agreements that local competitors will not hire salespeople from each other. Although this arrangement helps to control selling costs, it often precludes salespeople from improving their positions by moving to another firm in the local area.

With so many firms concerned about salesperson productivity, which typically leads to a need to reduce selling costs, some companies are tempted to eliminate the lowest producing salespeople. However, there have been numerous lawsuits by salespeople over wrongful termination. One way to protect yourself from these lawsuits is to have salesperson's duties and responsibilities defined in *job description*, which is a detailed definition of the specific role of an employee. It serves as an important document that specifies matters such as role performance, hours on the job, and goal attainment requirements. If an employee's performance fails to meet the conditions of a job description, there would be grounds for dismissal. When an accurate and complete job description is available, employees are also in a better position to resolve ethical problems when they occur. In looking back at the opening vignette, if Kathy's job description did not indicate that grounds for dismissal include maximizing a territory's revenue potential or working nights and weekends, then Bo could be partly to blame for his dilemma. Bo needs to hold more candid discussions with upper management about the resolve to uphold the company's "family-friendly" policies when faced with the possibility of sacrificing revenues and profits.

There are also situations where firms fire older salespeople who are paid high wages and replace them with younger people who earn less. This approach is clearly illegal if it is part of a general plan to discriminate against older employees. However, the courts have ruled that it is legal to fire older employees if the decision is based solely on the need to reduce costs and/or improve productivity.

House Accounts

A touchy problem for sales managers is how to handle large and important customers. These larger accounts often require special attention that exceeds the time and skills available from the salesperson assigned to the territory. In some companies, these accounts are labeled *house accounts* and are taken over by some manager in the company. Generally, no commissions are paid to the district salespeople for these accounts. Should these accounts be left with the district salesperson or shifted to headquarters as house accounts? This is not an easy decision because the accounts often generate high commission income. The designation of a customer as a house account is usually defended on the grounds that it results in better service. However, the district salesperson that developed the account is likely to feel a proprietary interest because of the historical relationship with the client. Thus, a transfer to house account status is sure to be viewed as unfair by the salesperson losing the account. House accounts are clearly one area where firms need a specific and well-publicized policy in order to avoid misunderstandings and resentment.

Expense Accounts

Most ethical abuse in a sales organization takes place with expense accounts. Salespeople are expected to spend money contacting customers and are then reimbursed for their expenses. Those who abuse the reimbursement policy often claim higher expenditures than the amounts spent, keep the difference, and then don't report it to the Internal Revenue Service. In one survey, 58 percent of the managers surveyed reported catching a salesperson falsifying an expense report.[11]

Sales managers must decide how tight controls on expense accounts should be. For example, if all salespeople who pad their expense accounts were fired, there would be few people left in the sales organization. Tight control on expense accounts could result in salespeople not traveling to contact out-of-the-way customers. However, liberal repayment for expenses invites investigations by the IRS and results in selling expense ratios that are higher than they should be.

A good solution to this problem is to monitor the actual expenses of some reliable salespeople for a month each year and then use these figures to set reimbursement amounts for all field reps. This approach greatly reduces the costs of processing expense accounts and keeps expense payments in line with actual experiences.

Gifts for Buyers

U.S. business has a tradition of giving small *gifts for buyers* to express appreciation for past and future business. Salespeople typically give novelties and samples as well as seasonal gifts (e.g., gift-wrapped bottles of liquor at Christmas). The problem is that the gift giving may start out with a pair of hockey tickets and end up as a portable television set for the customer's den. So how can a gift be distinguished from a bribe?

A recent survey of sales executives revealed that 64 percent of those surveyed felt that a bribe was considered to be a personal gift to a buyer over $100.[12] In the same survey, however, 89 percent of the sales executives had witnessed colleagues offering potential clients personal gifts valued at more than $100 in exchange for their business. Apparently, sales executives understand the cutoff point between a gift and a bribe, but bending the rules in specific situations appears to be a fairly widespread practice. One way to differentiate a gift from a bribe is when the item is unexpected (gift) rather than as part of an agreed-upon payment for business (bribe).

In today's moral and ethical climate, the practice of giving gifts to customers is more scrutinized than ever. Some firms have dealt with this by enforcing policies prohibiting buyers from accepting any gifts. Wal-Mart, for example, has always forbidden buyers from accepting even a can of Coke from a supplier. Although this policy seems to work for Wal-Mart, many companies are not as strict and allow an "appropriate" gift within specific dollar guidelines. The Internal Revenue Service ruling that only $25 can be deducted each year for company business gifts to any one person is one such limitation that many companies adhere to. Other firms use a general policy that prohibits accepting any gifts, meals, or favors that might compromise integrity. In the absence of explicit rules, it becomes incumbent on the salesperson to judge what is a reasonable gift and what others could interpret as a bribe. We recommend using some basic guidelines such as (1) Follow your company's policy on gift giving; (2) keep the gift value low to avoid the appearance of undue influence; (3) never give a gift prior to closing the deal; and (4) be prepared to walk away from the deal if the customer pushes for something excessive.

Bribes

As discussed above, the use of *bribes* to obtain business is not uncommon, so you must know what to do when you feel pressured to engage in this practice. Bribery is fairly easy to spot in its most blatant forms. If a customer says that an order will be placed if a $20,000 commission is paid to a third party, then the salesperson can be sure that someone is being paid off. In a recent federal court case, the president and top marketing executive of United Gunite Corporation have pleaded guilty to offering bribes to city officials throughout

TEAM EXERCISE
"Special Support"

Assume you have taken over the territory of Henry Perkins, who has retired after thirty years with your firm. Henry was well liked by everyone and earned $60,000 in commissions on printing sales in his last year. You are having dinner with one of the best customers in the territory, Mary Stevens. Mary bought $100,000 in printing services from your company in the past year, and this business earned Henry $6,000 in commissions. You have been emphasizing to Mary how you plan to continue to provide the same high-quality service that Henry supplied. Mary responds that she has recently talked to several other quality printers who also offer good service, and she wonders if you intend to continue Henry's special support activities. You say that you are not sure what special support Henry has been providing. Mary indicates that Henry paid $2,000 for a "medical" trip to Jamaica each winter to help relieve her arthritis. How would you respond in this situation?

New Jersey for contract work worth millions of dollars. According to the executives, city officials expected "gifts" in exchange for their influence in getting lucrative contracts. These gifts ranged from furniture, designer suits, trips to Rio, and, in one case, a custom-designed waterfall for a backyard pool.[13] These types of bribes are not only unethical, but also illegal. Unfortunately, much of the bribery and extortion in business dealings is disguised to make it even more difficult for the businessperson to choose right from wrong. Take a look at the Team Exercise "Special Support" and think how you might respond to Mary's request for assistance in her "medical" expenses.

Foreign payoffs are so common that the U.S. Congress passed the *Foreign Corrupt Practices Act* in 1977, making it a criminal offense to offer a payment to a foreign government official to obtain or retain foreign business. However, other industrialized nations have been slow to follow. France, Italy, Belgium, and the Netherlands have yet to pass laws prohibiting bribery and the deduction of bribes as a business expense for tax purposes, which has resulted in billions of dollars of lost international contracts.

Because of the difficulties caused by the Foreign Corrupt Practices Act in bidding on overseas contracts, the law has been amended so that now U.S. companies break the law only if they knowingly make an illegal payment. Also, "grease payments" are now permitted to facilitate a routine matter such as getting a visa or a permit. In addition, it is proper to make payments allowed under the written laws of a foreign country. Although these changes have helped, U.S. firms can't engage in many of the activities their local competitors carry out every day.

Entertainment

Providing entertainment for customers and potential customers is standard practice in U.S. business, but it can lead to ethical problems. The issue is often "How much is too much?" Most would agree that taking a customer to lunch is fair, reasonable, and expected. Few would argue against occasionally taking a client and spouse to dinner and a nightclub. But what about the use of a company car or a weekend on the company yacht? On big orders, it is not unusual to fly personnel from the customer's plant to the supplier's headquarters in order to include plant tours and introductions to corporate executives as part of the sales presentation. Should the expenses of spouses taken on such trips be covered? Is it ethical to offer customers free use of the company hunting lodge in Canada? What legitimately and ethically constitutes business "entertainment"?

We recommend that the entertainment should be a complementary part of a salesperson's relationship strategy, not the sole selling strategy for one particular order. In other words, an entertainment event should be used as a tool to develop a long-term business relationship. In planning an event, we also recommend that you consider the particular customer's tastes as well as the size of the account. It is important to keep the level of entertainment in line with the size of the account.

GOVERNMENT REGULATION

When business fails to operate in an ethical manner, there is usually a public outcry for more *government regulation*. Thus, one of the basic roles of government is to set minimum standards of business morality and then to enforce the rules. The judicial branch of government settles disputes over the interpretation of the regulations, and Congress writes new rules as they are needed. Some of the first government regulations in the United States affecting business were designed to protect the public from noncompetitive activities and ensure businesses the ability to compete in an open marketplace. While it is beyond the scope of this book to cover all legal issues that may affect salespeople, the next section discusses some of the antitrust laws that may affect sales executives.

Consumer Protection

A number of federal laws have also been passed to set ethical standards for transactions between manufacturers and the consumer. ***The Clayton Antitrust Act***, for example, prohibits price discrimination, certain exclusive dealing arrangements, and mergers that may substantially reduce competition or create a monopoly. This Act has a number of implications for sales executives. As but one example of how the Clayton Act might work, suppose a purchasing agent, in collusion with a favored supplier, develops a set of restrictive specifications for the purchase of all the janitorial supplies needed by a particular government agency. The specifications essentially exclude all but the current supplier. As a result, the agency only receives a single bid (from the favored supplier). The primary reason many competitors did not bid is that the bid specifications were so restrictive as to discourage participation. The supplier who wrote the specifications submits an apparent low bid for most of the products, and of course meets all specifications. This subversion of the bidding process is an unreasonable restraint of trade.

The ***Magnuson-Moss Warranty Act*** makes it illegal for salespeople to coerce customers into purchasing replacement components from the salesperson's firm at higher prices than a third party could provide by threatening the buyer that such action would void the product's warranty. To illustrate how this law might work, suppose you overheard a computer system manufacturer's sales representative tell a customer that if the customer uses third party memory in the system manufacturer's computer system (which could be purchased at much lower prices), then the system manufacturer's warranty would be voided. This act essentially requires full disclosure of warranty terms and makes it illegal to use warranties as tie-ins to price gouging.

More recently, the ***Federal Sentencing Commission for Organizations*** established a law that holds both the employee *and* the employee's company responsible for compliance with federal regulations. This means that the government can hold a company responsible for misdeeds of its employees if its standards of behaviors are not established, communicated, and monitored. In addition, companies must allow employees to report criminal activity, punish those who violate the standards, and take proactive steps in preventing further criminal activity. This law essentially places responsibility on sales managers for training salespeople on their legal responsibilities.

Deceptive packaging has been attacked with the ***Fair Packaging and Labeling Act***, which calls for standard package sizes and disclosure of the manufacturer's or distributor's name. Attempts by loan companies and retailers to mislead consumers on interest rates have led to the enactment of the ***Consumer Credit Protection Act***. Truth-in-lending laws require full disclosure of annual interest rates and other charges on loans and credit sales.

Why Are Regulations Needed?

Government often gets involved in business ethics when the problem is too big for individual firms to handle. For example, automobile exhaust is a major cause of air pollution, but it is difficult for an individual firm to solve the problem. If one company feels it is morally correct to install air pollution equipment on its cars, its costs will be higher than those of the competition. Thus, the cars of the ethically lazy firm will be cheaper and more powerful, and they will literally run off with the market. In this situation, government regulation allows the well-intentioned business to be the good citizen it wants to be.

Although many arguments have been advanced for a minimum of government regulation of business, there are also other problems with regulation. Businesspeople generally dislike government controls because they rob them of the flexibility needed to respond to changing conditions. Government rules established to solve problems in one decade are often obsolete by the next decade. For instance, the federal government got into the regulation of natural gas prices because gas is often shipped through interstate pipelines. As might be expected, the government tended to set low gas prices for maximum political gain. However, the drillers were more rational, and they slowed their search for new gas. As a result, the supply of natural gas declined until the price controls were removed.

We believe there should be a balance between too little government ("yield burning" in muni-bond underwriting) and too much regulation (as occurred in the natural gas industry) where business was strangled by endless rules and red tape.

BUILDING A SALES ETHICS PROGRAM

The moral climate of a business reflects the words and actions of its top executives. If management tolerates unethical behavior in the sales force, then there is little a member of the organization can do about it. Superiors set the moral climate and provide the constraints within which business decisions are made. Thus, the best way for a manager to build a strong sales ethics program is to get the backing of the board chairperson and the president of the company (Table 10-1). When this support is not available, there are certain to be ethical violations.

Code of Ethics

Once a sales manager gains the support of top management, the next step is to prepare a written sales *ethics policy statement* that indicates to the sales force that the company believes in playing fair with customers and competitors. Research has shown that salespeople employed in organizations with *codes of ethics* perceived their work environments to have more positive ethical values than did other sales professionals.[14] Another survey indicated that field reps *want* written policies that help them perform their jobs ethically.[15] To be effective, however, the policies need to be monitored on a regular basis to make sure that they are germane to the current selling arena. The advantage of a written ethics policy is that it allows the firm to be explicit about what activities are permissible and what actions

TABLE 10-1 Eight Ways to Keep Your Sales Force Honest

1. Get support from top management showing that they expect you to follow the spirit and letter of the law.
2. Develop and distribute a sales ethics policy.
3. Establish the proper moral climate. If the bosses follow the rules, then the troops are apt to do likewise.
4. Assign realistic sales goals. People who try to meet an unfair quota are more likely to rationalize their way to a kickback scheme.
5. Set up controls when needed. Watch people who live beyond their income.
6. Suggest that salespeople call for help when they face unethical demands.
7. Get together with your competition if payoffs are an industry problem.
8. Blow the whistle if necessary.

violate company standards. This can be useful when customers, suppliers, or your boss ask you to participate in some unethical activities. If your company has a code of ethics, you can reply, "I'm sorry, but company policy forbids that," and graciously end a conversation about a shady deal. The vast majority of firms that were involved in foreign payoff scandals had no written policies on commercial bribery.

An example of what a written code of ethics should look like is provided by General Motors. GM's policy is a twelve-page document complete with instructional scenarios featuring fictional characters.[16] One scenario has a purchasing employee visiting the home office of a possible supplier where he was offered a ticket to a professional football game and a chance to mingle with top executives. This opportunity should be turned down. In another scenario, an investment banking firm that helped with an acquisition for GM invites several GM employees to New York for a dinner and the gift of a mantel clock. In this case, the dinner and the clock should be refused. GM's policy provides some wiggle room for employees outside the United States. Workers in certain countries may accept meals, gifts, or outings to comply with local business practices and to avoid being placed in a competitive disadvantage. Also, GM employees can continue providing gifts and meals to their customers, but only within limits. The most expensive restaurant in town is no longer appropriate. GM's policy requires GM employees to avoid violating the customer's gift policy.

Sales managers should also be prepared to enforce company policies on bribery. This means it pays to keep tabs on salespeople who appear to live beyond their income. It also means setting reasonable sales goals so that salespeople will not be tempted to cheat to reach an unfair quota. Salespeople should be encouraged to ask for assistance when they encounter unethical situations.

If the salesperson has observed unethical behavior and has exhausted all the internal channels for dissent, then he or she should resort to whistle-blowing. *Whistle-blowing* is a last-resort action where an employee informs the public about an employer's or supervisor's immoral or illegal behavior. One test of whistle-blowing is that the evidence should be strong enough to convince the average person that a violation is taking place. Second, the observed ethical or legal violation should be serious enough to require immediate attention. Third, the act of telling the public must have some chance for success. Whistle-blowing is not taken lightly by employers, and employees will likely suffer some repercussion if they "go public" with a moral problem.

Why are whistle-blowers treated so badly for simply following high personal moral standards? The problem seems to be that by speaking up, they violate the *role morality* that demands that employees be loyal and keep their mouths shut. Management can be embarrassed by whistle-blowing, so they often try to get rid of people they feel can't be trusted. To help encourage whistle-blowers to come forward, federal laws have been modified to pay rewards of 15 to 25 percent of any recovery, plus attorneys' fees. As a result of this change, whistle-blowers received an average of $1 million in recent cases. In one case, a whistle-blower won $77 million for exposing to federal prosecutors a scheme to bribe doctors to prescribe their company's drugs over the competition.[17]

Whistle-blowing displays the classic conflict between the high ethical standards of individuals and the often lower morality found in the business world. The ultimate answer may occur when more firms set up formal internal mechanisms so that employees with moral problems to report are not ignored or punished.

Ethics Training

Our discussion has shown that field salespeople are involved in a variety of competitive situations that may tempt reps to engage in unethical behavior to reach company or personal goals. Unfortunately, many companies are not adequately addressing how to deal with ethical issues. In fact, one study reported that 42 percent of respondents felt that their companies either ignored ethical conduct to meet business objectives, or even worse, that their companies *encouraged* unethical practices.[18] This suggests that more attention to ethics training is needed to help salespeople function in today's business environment.

You should remember that simply publishing a sales ethics code does not guarantee that field sales representatives will follow it. Companies should offer classes to make sure employees know what to do in morally ambiguous situations. At one training session a salesperson asked, "When I check in at a motel, I get a coupon for a free drink; can I use it?" The correct answer was that it would be acceptable to use the coupon, but it would be wrong to accept $50 to stay there in the first place. The point here is that effective ethical training should include role-playing using realistic moral dilemmas that salespeople may encounter in the field. By walking through the steps to resolve such issues, managers will help salespeople develop their own moral reasoning capabilities. This type of training, along with a clearly written ethics policy, should provide a strong foundation for ethical decision making.

Research has also confirmed that younger sales managers are less idealistic and more relativistic in their ethical decision making.[19] These findings suggest the importance of adjusting training program content to meet the needs of different age groups. New hires and younger managers, for example, should be given material that emphasizes the importance of company ethical norms and values, as well as examples of specific behaviors to avoid. For example, Honeywell recently replaced its vague employee policy manual with a detailed handbook. Some of the unacceptable practices spelled out in the handbook include catcalls and sexual jokes.

In addition to general sales ethics training, many companies have also provided training to prevent sexual harassment. This type of training can be used to find solutions to simulated moral dilemmas. By working through a number of scenarios, salespeople can learn how to recognize problems, assemble facts, consider alternatives, and make decisions. For example, what should women do when a male customer makes a pass and puts his hand on a saleswoman's knee? In this case she should firmly remove his hand and say, "Let's pretend this didn't happen." Men are also offered advice on how to avoid crude jokes and other forms of intimidation when dealing with women buyers. The idea behind ethics and sexual-harassment training is to make sure employees are equipped to handle real-world issues they are likely to encounter when calling on customers.

SUMMARY

Sales ethics provides a moral framework to guide salespeople in their daily contacts with customers. Ethical dilemmas are common in selling because salespeople often have to make decisions in the field in response to customers' demands and competitive offers. This chapter has attempted to equip you with the following skills:

1. **Explain why ethics are important.** Salespeople often look to the sales manager for cues about the company's ethical stance to help guide their behaviors. When managers exhibit a low standard of moral behavior, the sales force will often exhibit these types of behaviors in front of their customers. As demonstrated in a number of recent salesperson scandals, such behaviors can do irreparable harm to a company.
2. **Explain the moral bases for business ethics.** Sales ethics forms a code of moral conduct that guides sales managers and salespeople in their everyday activities. Ethical decisions can be based on different moral rules, including the stakeholder and shareholder views, idealism, relativism, the self-interest of Machiavellianism, or conventional morality.
3. **Understand how to make decisions that involve ethical problems.** Managers who score high on idealism tend to make the most ethical decisions. Perhaps the best way to solve ethical problems is the pragmatic approach, which involves an objective analysis of relevant facts and leads to more rational decisions.
4. **Recognize the issues of common sales ethics.** Areas in which the sales manager is likely to confront difficult ethical situations involve hiring, house accounts, whistle-blowing, expense accounts, requests for payoffs, and customer gifts and entertainment.
5. **Discuss how to build a sales ethics program.** Building a good company sales ethics program would include the following: getting support from top management, developing and distributing a sales ethics policy, establishing a proper moral climate, assigning realistic sales goals, setting up controls when needed, suggesting that salespeople call for help when faced with unethical demands, and blowing the whistle when necessary.

KEY TERMS

Bribes
Business ethics
Clayton Antitrust Act
Code of ethics
Consumer Credit Protection Act
Conventional morality
Deceptive sales practices
Ethics policy statement
Fair Packaging and Labeling Act
Federal Sentencing Commission for Organizations
Foreign Corrupt Practices Act
Gifts for buyers
Government regulation
House accounts
Idealism
Job description
Machiavellianism
Magnuson-Moss Warranty Act
Relativism
Role morality
Shareholder view
Situation ethics
Stakeholder view
Whistle-blowing

DEVELOPING YOUR COMPETENCIES

1. **Strategic Action.** A report prepared by insurance regulators from thirty states revealed that management at Prudential Insurance Company of America knew of sales abuses by agents and in many cases failed to adequately investigate and impose effective discipline. The report cited cases where agents with "significant complaint histories" were promoted to sales and general managers, with supervisory and training responsibility over agents. Prudential's negligence in its accountability for its agents was particularly noticeable with regard to "churning." This is a practice whereby agents withhold information or use deceptive sales pitches to persuade customers to use the built-up cash value of older policies to finance new, more expensive ones. As a result of Prudential's lack of control over its sales force, the company was forced to pay hundreds of millions of dollars in fines and restitution to its customers. In addition, a new chairman had to clean house and fire hundreds of agents and sales managers. The insurance regulator's report

suggests that Prudential was following an unwritten strategy of allowing its agents to engage in activities that helped the company at the expense of its customers. Why did Prudential permit and even encourage its agents to employ unethical sales practices? What actions should Prudential take to prevent its agents from using these practices in the future?

2. **Self-Management.** A stockbroker pleaded guilty to conspiracy charges in San Diego for accepting $500,000 in bribes to promote the sale of certain stocks. The bribes amounted to 15 percent of the value of stock sold to clients and were paid in cash. In this case, the stocks were recommended to customers regardless of whether they fit the client's investment needs. How should firms structure their self-management programs so that employees will be better able to resist bribes when they are offered? Can employees be trained to refuse payments for unethical conduct?
3. **Technology.** The Internet has proved to be extremely helpful to field salespeople who use e-mail to communicate with customers and their corporate colleagues. Also, Web sites on the Internet allow customers to check product availability and place routine reorders. Although the Internet is a technological marvel, some employees use it to further their own unethical activities. At one company, an employee set up a fake Web site and posted false information on the firm. The Web site was so professional that many outsiders used the false information in buying and selling the company's stock. It appeared that the fake Web site was set up to help the employee make money for his own brokerage account by selling when false rumors drove up the price of company stock. At another firm, an employee sent out phony e-mail messages concerning alleged racial discrimination to enhance the chances for a bigger settlement from the firm. What should companies do to make sure that technological innovations are used ethically and not for personal gain?
4. **Global Perspective.** A United Technologies employee has charged that the company's Sikorsky division offered two Saudi princes a "bonus" of 3 to 5 percent of a $130 million portion of a $6 billion potential Blackhawk helicopter order. Payments to foreign intermediaries to gain orders are illegal under the U.S. Foreign Corrupt Practices Act. The employee is seeking $100 million in damages from United Technologies. Under the U.S. False Claims Act, whistle-blowers are also entitled to 25 percent of any money the government recovers from defendants in cases of fraud. What seems to be the employee's motive in this case, and why are such "commissions" so common in foreign sales agreements? How should the company handle these demands for special favors?
5. **Team Building.** A stockbroker at Merrill Lynch & Company's office in Cape Coral, Florida, complained to the company that a branch manager was soliciting business and making trades before his license had been transferred to the firm. Later, a replacement branch manager asked the broker to oversee things while the new manager was on vacation. The manager had made no arrangements to distribute holiday paychecks, so the broker opened a letter addressed to the manager to get some information on employee pay levels. He then matched this information against the checks and handed them out. For this, the broker was fired and told to pack his things and leave. As soon as the broker left the office, the manager divided up the broker's $82 million of accounts among himself and other brokers in the office. The manager and the brokers stayed late at the office so they could immediately call all the customers to say their broker was no longer with the firm and urging them to stay with Merrill Lynch. The largest portion of the broker's accounts went to the manager, who would now receive commissions on all trades made for these accounts. The unethical practice of firing successful stockbrokers so managers can increase the assets under their own control is more widespread than the industry acknowledges. What can brokerage firms do to encourage more teamwork at their branch offices? Should successful brokers be dismissed for minor offenses so branch managers can make more money?

FEATURED CASE

SHIELD FINANCIAL: "OVERHEARD TRADE SECRETS"

Ken Rowland, a salesperson for Shield Financial in Des Moines, was leaning comfortably back in his airplane seat. He was returning from an industry conference. His head was full of new sales strategies, so instead of napping, he pulled out his laptop and started jotting notes to himself. A short while later there was a break from the hum of the airplane. "I think it's time for a price cut," the man in front of him said to his seatmate. Rowland paused; he listened for what would come next.

As it turns out, the two men seated in front of Rowland were the vice president of sales and the president of Shield's largest competitor, AllSafe. They were flying from the conference to a customer meeting in Rowland's territory. They spent an hour discussing an upcoming pricing strategy, with Rowland feverishly taking notes the entire time. Rowland couldn't believe his luck. Not only did he make a significant number of contacts at the show, he now had at his fingertips the competition's entire pricing strategy for the second quarter of the year. This is too good to be true, he thought.

The next morning in his Des Moines office, Rowland wrote a memo outlining all of the key points of the competition's pricing strategy. He sent the memo via e-mail to all of Shield's sales managers and regional managers, the vice president of sales, and the company president. Bloom, Rowland's manager, was dumbstruck when he read the e-mail. He was shocked that Rowland would send the e-mail without first consulting him on the appropriate action. Rowland's decision to e-mail sensitive information without checking with him first could have any number of repercussions.

Questions

1. What are the ethical issues involved in this case?
2. What are the possible actions Bloom could take?
3. What are the possible reactions from the field (i.e., customers) to Rowland's information?
4. What is an "ideal" course of action given all of the issues involved?

MOTIVATING SALESPEOPLE

> It's not who you think you are that holds you back, it's who you think you are not.
>
> Author Unknown

Chapter Consultants:
Liz Crute, Vice President, Pitney Bowes Credit Corporation
Michael Mahar, Team Leader, IBM Global Services

LEARNING OBJECTIVES

After studying this chapter, you should be able to:

- Define motivation and explain sales managers' concerns with motivation.
- Tell how and why individual needs may differ.
- Describe a basic model of the motivation process.
- Discuss the different types of quotas and the administrative issues involved in using quotas.
- Describe how to design incentive and recognition programs and their limitations.

THE DRIVE TO EXCEL

Robby Armstrong began his career at Eaton Corporation, a leading diversified industrial manufacturer, immediately after graduating from the Industrial Distribution program at the University of Alabama at Birmingham (UAB). After finishing Eaton's training program, Robby worked in a variety of positions, including inside and outside sales positions as well as industry manager. After a few years in his respective assignments, Robby was promoted to Area Manager in the Birmingham Alabama, district.

As an Area Manager, Robby's primary responsibility is to make sure his team achieves quota. A big source of motivation for Robby is knowing that the success or failure of his group can have a big impact on the entire division within Eaton. Robby's personal goal, however, isn't to make quota, it's to exceed it. Says Robby, "Some people may shoot for 100 percent of quota, but I'm always striving to exceed it. I use my quota as a target for minimum accomplishment; anything below that is unacceptable."

Although metrics and incentives can provide short-term motivation, sustained success in a corporate environment often comes down to personal motivation and lots of hard work. According to Robby, "You need a desire to work harder and smarter than your competitors

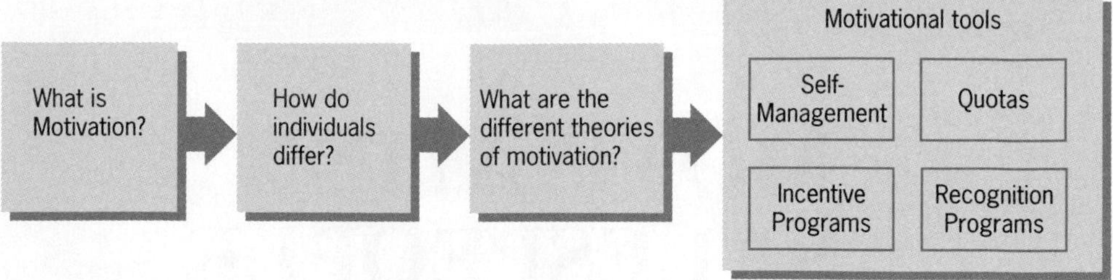

FIGURE 11-1 Sales Force Motivation Model

each day. There are a lot of companies that are satisfied with being good; at Eaton we are striving to be great."

What does Robby Armstrong feel it takes to be a high performer? "The highest performers—the people who really succeed—have tremendous discipline and tenacious follow through. People can always find a reason not to follow through with a customer and go home early. But, doing the little things and going the extra mile for someone is what has made me successful. I try to live by the principle of not promising what you can't deliver, but always delivering what you promise."[1]

Robby provides us with several important points about sales force motivation. First, he illustrates the importance of having the opportunity to succeed. Eaton provides industry-leading products and services to enable its sales force to compete and win in the marketplace. Second, Robby has the ability to succeed. However, he is quick to attribute some of his success to his education at UAB and Eaton's excellent sales training programs. Finally, the vignette demonstrates that Robby has the motivation to succeed. It's likely that Robby's career path would have been entirely different if he were not self-motivated to focus on the critical success factors. The challenge for sales managers, therefore, is to provide the opportunity for success, ensure each salesperson has the ability to succeed, and channel a person's efforts to be consistent with the overall strategic role of the sales force within the firm.

This chapter is concerned with motivation and will follow the topical outline shown in Figure 11-1. First, we define motivation and discuss why sales managers are concerned with sales force motivation. Next, we discuss individual needs and how people's needs differ. This is followed by a model of motivation that identifies the factors that enhance salesperson satisfaction. Finally, we explain how to develop effective quota, incentive, and recognition programs. Although these programs are widely used to motivate salespeople, their limitations are also discussed.

WHAT IS MOTIVATION?

Sales force motivation is a hot topic with sales managers. If the product or service is right and sales force selection, organization, and training are right, then motivation becomes the critical determinant of success. The unique and often demanding nature of the sales profession can have a profound effect on a person's motivation level. Field salespeople are continually going from the exhilaration of making a sale to the disappointment of being turned down. Salespeople frequently must talk with strangers who are not always ready or willing to buy what they have to sell; others must routinely spend long hours on the road away from their families and friends. Faced with these conditions, it is understandable that salespeople may need extra support to do an effective job.

A second reason why motivation is critical is that most salespeople are not under direct supervision in the physical presence of their manager. Veteran salespeople often meet with their immediate sales managers fewer than six times a year. In the absence of direct supervision, self-motivation is critical.

Third, motivation affects not only what activities salespeople perform but also their enthusiasm and the quality of their work. A salesperson's conviction that a product or service is best for the customer will have a profound influence on a customer's purchasing decision. Customers are unlikely to purchase if they feel the salesperson is not really motivated to help them.

Motivation has been studied for decades and is typically defined as an individual's willingness to exert effort to achieve the organization's goals while satisfying individual needs. Inherent in this definition are three components: effort, individual needs, and organizational goals. We have discussed typical sales force related organizational goals—sales volume, market share, profits, customer retention, and so on—and will return to these goals when describing quotas later in this chapter. Let's focus for a moment on effort and individual needs.

Effort

More than thirty years ago in a classic article on motivation, Frederick Herzberg noted that a KITP, which he coyly explained stood for "kick in the pants," may produce compliance, but it never produces motivation.[2] When describing someone as being motivated, sales managers are talking about three characteristics of effort:

1. **The drive to initiate action on a task.** For example, a common concern among sales managers is to get salespeople to call on targeted prospects. Typically, high-performing salespeople, such as Robby Armstrong, concentrate their efforts on high-potential prospects.
2. **The quality of effort on a task.** It's not enough to get people to call on prospects; they must also be motivated to put forth the effort to prospect properly and call on qualified prospects. High-performing salespeople tend to use pre-call planning for more efficient prospecting.
3. **The persistence to expend effort over a period of time sufficient to meet or exceed objectives.** It is not enough to make the effort some of the time; high performers show up to win every time. Robby Armstrong's discussion of what it takes to be a high performer is an excellent example of this drive.

Notice that all three of these dimensions of effort originate within the person. No one can motivate a salesperson to do anything, but a good sales manager can help salespeople to motivate themselves. How then does a manager help a salesperson internalize the drive, quality of effort, and persistence necessary to succeed in selling? In addressing this question, it is important to remember that people have different strengths, weaknesses, and career goals, which affect how they respond to a particular motivation attempt. Thus, understanding salesperson needs before developing motivational programs is an important first step. In the next section, we summarize some classic motivation theories that focus on differences in individual needs. We then explore a typical salesperson's career stage and suggest ways to develop a career-stage perspective in developing a motivational program.

Individual Needs

In sales, the future of the business—and possibly even the sales manager's job—depends on managers' ability to understand the psychology of their salespeople. A good sales manager knows what his or her salespeople want—what drives them. If a sales manager feels that the need for status, control, respect, and routine are most important, a number of actions can be taken to motivate a sales force, as shown in Figure 11-2.

Sales Force Needs	*Company Actions to Fill Needs*
Status	Change title from "salesperson" to "area manager." Buy salespeople more luxurious cars to drive.
Control	Allow salespeople to help plan sales quotas and sequences of calls.
Respect	Invite salespeople to gatherings of top executives. Put pictures of top salespeople in company ads and newsletters.
Routine	Assign each salesperson a core of loyal customers that are called on regularly.
Accomplishment	Set reasonable goals for the number of calls and sales.
Stimulation	Run short-term sales contests. Schedule sales meetings in exotic locations.
Honesty	Deliver promptly all rewards and benefits promised.

FIGURE 11-2 Sales Force Needs and Ways to Fill Them

A number of formal theories have been developed to understand differences in individual needs. Some of the classic theories include Maslow's *hierarchy of needs*, Alderfer's ERG theory, Herzberg's *motivation-hygiene theory*, and McClelland's theory of learned needs. Because you have undoubtedly reviewed these theories in earlier courses, we assume you're familiar with them. Nonetheless, we've summarized them briefly in Figure 11-3.

These classic motivation theories are concerned with unique individual needs. Although each individual is unique, motivational and personality profiles of salespeople's wants and patterns of behavior have been identified. After interviewing more than half a million salespeople, the Gallup Management Consulting Group's research has revealed that high

Theory	*Author*	*Description*
Hierarchy of needs	Abraham Maslow	Physiological, safety, belonging, esteem, and self-actualization needs are ranked in a hierarchy from lowest to highest. An individual moves up the hierarchy as a need is substantially realized.
ERG theory	Clayton P. Alderfer	Hierarchically classifies needs as existence, relatedness, and growth needs. Like Maslow, suggests that people will focus on higher needs as lower needs are satisfied but, unlike Maslow, suggests that people will focus on lower needs if their higher needs are not satisfied.
Motivation-hygiene	Frederick Herzberg	Argues that intrinsic job factors (e.g., challenging work, achievement) motivate, whereas extrinsic factors (e.g., pay) only placate employees.
Theory of learned needs	David McClelland	Proposes that there are three major professional needs: achievement, affiliation, and power. A high need for achievement and affiliation has been related to higher sales force performance. A high need for power has been related to higher sales manager performance.
Equity theory	J. Stacy Adams	Proposes that people will evaluate their treatment in comparison to that of "relevant others" and that motivation will suffer if treatment is perceived to be inequitable.

FIGURE 11-3 Summary of Classic Motivation Theories

The Competitor	This type not only wants to win, but derives satisfaction from beating specific rivals—another company or even colleagues. They tend to verbalize what they are going to do, and then do it.
The Ego-Driven	They are not interested in beating specific opponents; they just want to win. They like to be considered experts but are prone to feeling slighted, change jobs frequently, and take things too personally.
The Achiever	This type is almost completely self-motivated. They usually set high goals, and as soon as they hit one goal, they move the bar higher. They like accomplishment, regardless of who receives the credit.
The Service-Oriented	Their strengths lie in building and cultivating relationships.

FIGURE 11-4 Sales Force Needs and Ways to Fill Them

performers tend to exhibit one of four personality types, each with different drives: the competitor, the ego-driven, the achiever, and the service-oriented.[3] (See Figure 11-4.) Although no one is purely one type of personality, you might think about how you would motivate each type of person and identify the potential pitfalls associated with each type of person.

Career Stages

Experienced sales managers have long understood that motivation varies according to the age and experience of the salesperson. Career stages provide a framework to understand how individual salespeople differ and how their approach to work is likely to change over time.

Jolson was the first to note that salespeople's performance resembled the four stages of the classic S-shaped curve of the product life cycle.[4] Later research suggested that, during their careers, salespeople go through four stages during which they focus on certain career concerns, developmental tasks, personal challenges, and psychosocial needs.[5] These stages are summarized in Figure 11-5.

Exploration Stage. Early in one's career, during the *exploration stage*, the overall concern is finding the right occupation—"What do I want to do for the rest of my life?" The stress associated with resolving this tough issue sometimes results in lower performance, especially among those unable to resolve this concern at an early age. The challenge facing management is to help people successfully address this concern. Recruiters should begin by giving realistic job and career opportunity descriptions during job interviews. Managers should also spend time with new people, providing feedback, reinforcing their accomplishments, and pointing out the long-term benefits associated with working for the organization. Finally, it is recommended to offer exploration stage salespeople a compensation package that includes more salary than commission. Research suggests that salespeople compensated with greater levels of salary display higher job satisfaction and lower turnover intentions than their counterparts who are paid under programs using more incentives.[6]

Establishment Stage. Most people eventually change their focus from searching for the "best" occupation to committing themselves to getting ahead in their current jobs. People at the *establishment stage* of their careers are usually willing to put in long hours to improve their performance. For many people, settling down will occur sometime during the late twenties to early thirties.

One management concern is that the highest performers during this stage are most likely to change jobs. This is especially true if the rewards for high performance are not provided by their current organizations. In fact, research suggests that salespeople in the establishment

	Exploration	*Establishment*	*Maintenance*	*Disengagement*
Career Concerns	Finding an appropriate occupational field.	Successfully establishing a career in a certain occupation.	Holding on to what has been achieved; reassessing career, with possible redirection.	Completing one's career.
Motivational Needs Job Related	Learning the skills required to do job well.	Using skills to produce results.	Developing broader view of work and organization.	Establishing a stronger self-identity outside of work.
	Becoming a contributing member of an organization.	Adjusting to working with greater autonomy.	Maintaining a high performance level.	Maintaining an acceptable performance level.
Personal Challenges	Establishing a good initial professional self-concept.	Producing superior results on the job in order to be promoted.	Maintaining motivation, though possible rewards have changed.	Acceptance of career accomplishments.
			Facing concerns about aging.	
Psychological Needs	Support. Peer acceptance. Challenging position.	Achievement. Esteem. Autonomy. Competition.	Reduced competitiveness. Security. Helping younger colleagues.	Detachment from the organization and organizational life.

FIGURE 11-5 Career Stage Characteristics

stage displayed higher levels of job satisfaction and lower turnover rates when compensated with incentive-based as compared to salary-based programs.[7] In sales, a frequently used sign of getting ahead is promotion to sales management. Unfortunately, the downsizing of many organizations and the elimination of management layers to lower costs and get closer to the customer have reduced these opportunities. Also, some salespeople just don't have the skills to succeed as a manager. A manager's challenge in this case is to broaden salespeople's definition of success as something other than promotion to sales management.

Some companies have responded by developing a "sales career path" for salespeople who do not want to pursue a management position. A typical sales career path might progress from sales rep to senior sales rep to executive rep to major accounts rep. This path leads to retaining senior people with higher base pay, healthier commissions, and a solid growth-oriented career path. In essence, a sales manager needs to be able to continually motivate and challenge high-performing salespeople as they progress through the sales career path.

Maintenance Stage. At some point, usually in their late thirties or early forties, people begin to reflect on their past accomplishments and reassess the career choices they have made. For many people, this reflection coincides with the broader reassessment associated with the midlife crisis. Being turned down for promotion and realizing that future promotion opportunities are unlikely may trigger this reflective reaction in others. How people react to this reassessment of their careers is referred to as the *maintenance stage*.

People often have very different reactions when reflecting on their careers. Some people decide to switch occupations or organizations, whereas others choose to stay where they are. Similar to the stay-or-leave decision in the establishment stage, some people decide that sales is the best occupation for them, while others choose to stay in sales out of fear of change or because of other obligations, especially to their families. Still others choose to take a new direction, often pursuing a dream that had been set aside earlier in life.

Maintenance-stage people no longer desire or value promotion to management as much as during establishment. These people are most likely to be the backbone of the sales force and tend to have the highest sales volume. For most people, this stage will last a long time, typically fifteen to twenty years. A recent survey of 300 sales managers rated maintenance-stage salespeople higher than their establishment stage counterparts on almost every front, including ability to meet sales goals, knowledge of product, commitment to serving clients, and creativity in solving problems.[8] For those who start slowing down, however, the challenge for management is to maintain the high motivation and performance levels by encouraging these people to use their knowledge in new ways. This also means introducing significant rewards for meeting new challenges and mastering them.

Disengagement Stage. Everyone inevitably withdraws from his or her job and career. The *disengagement stage* involves giving greater priority to issues other than work and career. For people facing imminent retirement, this transition period helps them to cope with the feeling of loss of focus and to face the fact they will no longer be making a contribution, which has been an important part of their careers.

For others, disengagement may occur as a gradual process, early in life, long before retirement. Some of these people are in their forties and early fifties and will remain on the job for some time to come. On-the-job reactions of these salespeople are quite dramatic. They tend not to be as involved in and challenged by their work and are dissatisfied with many aspects of the job. The sales performance of these people suffers and is often significantly lower than that of people in the maintenance stage.

Attempts to motivate these people to achieve greater performance are often frustrating. Increased pay usually does not lead to sustained effort, and these people place less importance on management recognition than people in other career stages. Although they feel that it is important to meet sales quotas, they are not usually interested in opening new accounts. In short, their approach is one of achieving the minimum necessary to keep management off their backs.

Perhaps the best way for management to overcome this problem is to try to dissuade people from adopting this attitude when retirement is not imminent. When retirement is imminent, however, managers are left with fewer options. One approach is to get the salesperson to visualize his or her legacy to the firm. The lasting memory of a lower-producing salesperson might be enough to motivate the salesperson to finish strong. If results are not forthcoming, more drastic measures may be necessary, including termination.

A MODEL OF MOTIVATION

Sustained, productive effort requires more than offering the best rewards. Studies have shown that the amount of effort an individual will put into an activity depends on the interplay among three factors shown in Figure 11-6: (1) the relationship between effort and performance (expectancy), (2) the relationship between performance and rewards (instrumentality), and (3) the importance of receiving more of a certain reward (valence). This process model of motivation is referred to as *expectancy theory*.[9]

Effort-Performance Relationship

Expectancy refers to the salesperson's belief that greater effort will lead to greater performance. The more certain an individual is of this effort-performance relationship, the more effort will likely be expended.

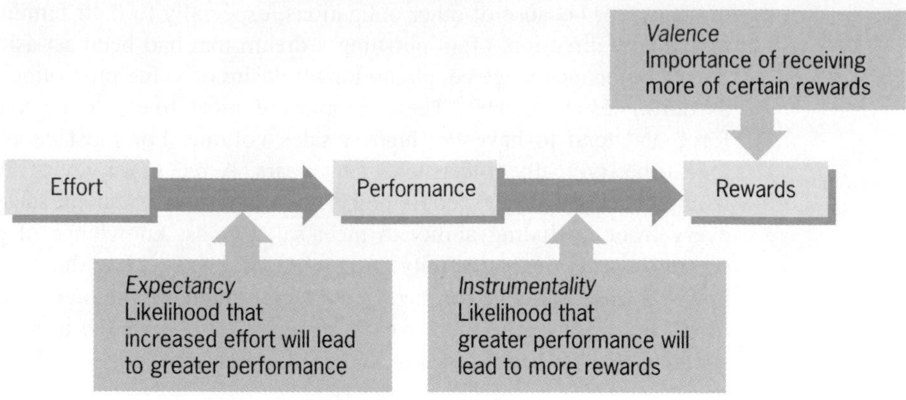

FIGURE 11-6 Model of Motivation

Three aspects of this model are significant to sales management. First, a salesperson's willingness to work hard starts with a belief that the greater the effort, the greater the performance outcome. Managers have an important responsibility in reinforcing the notion that salesperson performance is directly related to one's effort level. Robby Armstrong, for example, sounded very confident in the focused effort it takes to become successful.

Second, management should be concerned with the accuracy of salespeople's role perception. Expending greater effort on the wrong activities will not lead to better performance, and may lead to the conclusion that performance is not related to effort. Some refer to this as "working smarter." If a salesperson consistently uses an inappropriate selling strategy, for instance, sales call objectives are unlikely to be met. The individual may become frustrated, believing that no amount of effort will lead to better performance. This shows the interrelationship that exists among effective sales training, coaching, and motivation. No amount of incentive or cajoling will produce the desired level of performance in the absence of a certain level of skill and confidence in that skill.[10]

Finally, salespeople have a tendency to make attributions about why a certain performance outcome occurred. *Attribution theory* suggests that people are motivated to generate reasons for why an event occurred, especially when the outcome is unexpected (such as an underdog beating a heavy favorite), when the event generates suspicion, or when one fails to achieve something (such as not meeting quota). According to attribution theory, the type of attributions we generate will influence how we respond to the situation. For example, a salesperson may attribute failure to the sales strategy that was used, in which case a search for another sales approach may be undertaken in an effort to make the sale. The theory suggests that salespeople who attribute failure to meet sales quota to their own lack of effort are likely to make adjustments and increase their efforts to make quota in the future. Alternatively, people may attribute failure to factors external to themselves, such as the company, the product available to sell, or the competition. Salespeople who attribute failure to meet quota to circumstances perceived to be beyond their control are unlikely to make these adjustments and will probably decrease their efforts to meet quota in the near future.[11] This reinforces the need for managers to be in the field with the sales force to determine why salespeople believe they performed as they did. It also suggests that sales managers play an important role in coaching and training salespeople to generate performance-related attributions that positively affect expectancies.

Performance-Reward Relationship

The second element of the motivation process is the belief that a higher level of performance will lead to greater personal rewards. This element is referred to as *instrumentality*. When people are certain that their performance will be personally rewarding, their motivation will be higher. This is one of the reasons for the success of commission compensation plans. Salespeople know how much they will be paid for each sale and understand that their incomes will increase as a result of higher sales. This may also explain why limiting the number of winners in a sales contest may not motivate the average salesperson, whose expected performance level is not likely to be high enough to win.

For the past several years, the "pay-for-performance" sales compensation concept has been migrating to other parts of the organization. Marketing, accounting, human resources, virtually all departments, can enjoy additional compensation. Motivating this change in compensation practice, in addition to generating greater performance, is an organization's effort to foster an increased customer and sales orientation among all functional areas.

Importance of Rewards

How much salespeople desire a particular reward will also influence their motivation to perform and is referred to as *reward valence*. Here we can see the connection between the previous need-based theories of motivation and expectancy theory. Both Maslow's and Herzberg's models suggest that there are limits to how much of any reward people will desire. Although many experts believe that salespeople place a high value on pay, this may not reflect a salesperson's day-to-day priorities. Some salespeople may feel that spending an afternoon with the family outweighs the possible financial loss. Wall Data, Inc., for example, has rewarded high performers by donating money to the salesperson's choice of charity or by starting a scholarship in the salesperson's hometown.[12] The managers at Wall Data have found that high performing salespeople value the community recognition from this program as a result of their sales efforts.

People don't simply look at their own rewards; they also make comparisons with other people's rewards. According to *equity theory*, people make inputs (e.g., effort, experience, territories) versus outcomes comparisons with relevant others to determine relative equity. One reaction to an inequitable situation (e.g., Bob puts in less effort but makes more money) is to reduce inputs. In this case, motivation would decrease. Inexperienced sales managers are especially vulnerable to equity problems. In an effort to help one person, they may make exceptions or provide extra help. Other salespeople may see this as unfair unless they are also provided extra help in making the sale. This may eventually result in the sales manager doing the job of the salesperson and lead to lower overall performance.

Our model of motivation provides a framework for managers to understand the internal process by which people are motivated to put forth extra effort. Obviously, helping to motivate salespeople involves more than knowing what they want and need. A breakdown in any of the three dimensions of the motivation process will decrease overall motivation. Therefore, all three aspects of the process must be considered when trying to motivate someone to perform at the desired level. Try applying these concepts to the issues raised in the Team Exercise titled "Expectancy Theory."

How can sales managers put these theories to work? The remainder of this chapter looks at several tools available to sales managers to help salespeople put forth greater effort. Quotas, incentives, and recognition programs have been used successfully in a wide variety of organizations to motivate salespeople. We begin our discussion with self-management, which is embraced by many companies as a response to the freedoms salespeople have from traditional levels of supervisory control and monitoring.

TEAM EXERCISE
"Expectancy Theory"

Assume you are a senior and only have one final exam remaining, and it's worth 100 points. You have done pretty well on the previous tests, but you know you could have aced them if you had studied more.

Suppose you have 360 points accumulated in the class and you need 450 points to get an "A" for your final grade.

Also suppose that if you get an "A" for the course, your total GPA increases so that you are eligible to get an interview with a prestigious firm.

How motivated would you be in this scenario to study hard for the final? How could you change this scenario so that your motivation to study would fall? What component of expectancy theory did you change (valence, expectancies, or instrumentalities)?

SELF-MANAGEMENT

Salespeople typically work independently of direct supervision from their sales managers. In the wake of reengineering and reorganizing, which have eliminated layers of middle management, salespeople in many industries have learned to become even more self-reliant. Sales managers, however, play an important role in self-management by recognizing that people derive considerable rewards in the form of feeling good about themselves and their work. This is referred to as *intrinsic motivation* and is defined as the motivation to engage in an activity for its own sake. Sales managers should do everything possible to reinforce intrinsic motivation when communicating one-on-one with salespeople.[13] One approach used to encourage intrinsic motivation is *behavioral self-management (BSM)*, which consists of a series of steps involving monitoring, goal setting, rehearsal, rewards, and self-contracting. A summary of the techniques used in BSM is presented in Figure 11-7.

To better understand how BSM can be used in sales management, consider a situation in which you are attempting to increase the number of calls made each week on new accounts. Self-monitoring in this situation may mean recording the number of calls made on new customers over a four-week period. Having established the current level of effort, a goal is set for the number of new account calls that should be made each week. Stimulus cues may include such things as a small note placed on the dashboard of the car that says "Have You Met Someone New Today?" Alternatively, it may be a special notebook for recording the number of new-customer calls made each week. Consequence management may include stopping at a nicer place than usual for lunch when the weekly objective is met or skipping lunch if the objective is not met by a certain day of the week. Opening presentations with new accounts may be rehearsed in the car while driving to an account and scheduled for the same time each day. Finally, a contract specifying the criteria for rewarding success and punishing failure should be written and witnessed.

A sales manager can get involved in the BSM process by helping salespeople set challenging, yet achievable, goals and ensuring that they are consistent with the firm's strategic objectives. The manager can also be helpful in rehearsing desired behaviors through one-on-one coaching and can help reinforce rewards through recognition of successes and encouragement. Again, we can see the importance of having sales managers in the field and knowing what is going on in the territory so that they can encourage and facilitate the use of BSM.

Technique	Method	Tools
Self-monitoring	Observe and record behavior.	Can use diaries, counters, tally sheets, charts.
Goal setting	Establish behavior change objectives.	Should be specific and with a short time horizon.
Stimulus control	Modify antecedents to behavior.	May involve introducing or removing cues.
Consequence management	Modify antecedents to behavior.	May involve reinforcement, punishment, or extinction.
Rehearsal	Conduct systematic practice of desired behavior.	May be overt or visualized.
Self-contracting	Specify the relationship between behaviors and their consequences.	May involve public commitment.

FIGURE 11-7 Self-Management Techniques

An important step in BSM is self-set goals. Traditionally, however, management sets goals for salespeople in the form of quotas, which are discussed next.

QUOTAS

Quotas are quantitative goals assigned to individual salespeople for a specified period of time. They are one of the most widely used tools in sales management—approximately 85 percent of U.S. companies use some type of quota system for their salespeople.[14] A sales volume of $150,000 in October is an example of a quantifiable goal for a specific period of time. This is the standard against which performance in October will be compared. Although quotas are often based on sales volume or gross margin, they should not be confused with sales forecasts or sales potential. A sales forecast is an estimate of what a firm expects to sell during a time period using a particular marketing plan. Sales quotas may be set equal to, above, or below the sales forecast. Sales potential, on the other hand, is the maximum demand that a firm can possibly obtain. Potentials are useful for strategic planning and long-range forecasting. Sales quotas are related to sales forecasts and potential, but are used for entirely different purposes.

As illustrated in Figure 11-8, there are five reasons for establishing quotas for salespeople:

1. **To help management motivate salespeople.** Achievement-oriented people want specific and challenging goals, with regular feedback on their performance.
2. **To direct salespeople where to put their efforts.** When companies assign quotas for each product in their total line of products, they are trying to communicate to their sales force which products should be given priority. Often firms will adjust the sales quota according to product profitability or strategic intent. However, too many goals will confuse people and will scatter sales force effort. Limiting the number of quota categories to three or four is recommended. GE Fanuc, a manufacturer of factory automation products, installed a new Web-based quota system that offers its salespeople the ability to track their quota sales numbers for specific product, as well as customer buying patterns of these products in real time.[15] The idea behind this system is to enhance salesperson expectancies and instrumentalities.

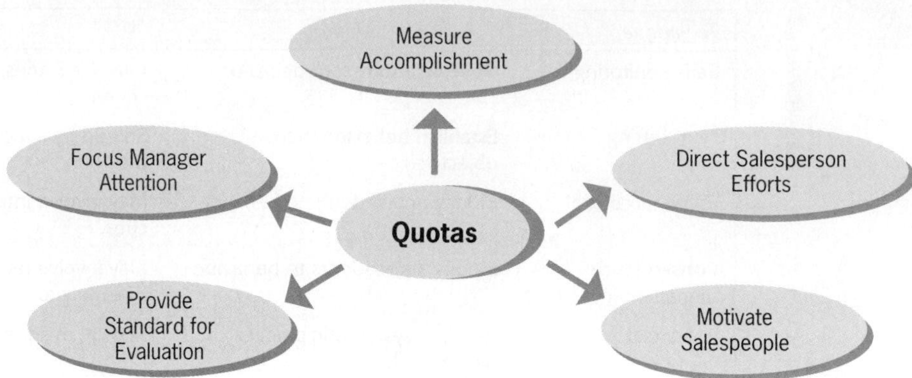

FIGURE 11-8 Impact of Sales Force Quotas

3. **To focus management attention.** Quotas lend themselves to management by exception, that is, focusing management's attention on the performance of people who are exceptionally above or below quota. Time can be spent with people whose performance is poor in order to determine if the salesperson is at fault or whether the poor results are due to factors outside the salesperson's control. At the same time, management may wish to spend time with high performers to identify critical success factors that could be used to improve the performance of other salespeople.
4. **To measure salesperson accomplishment.** Salespeople perceive quota as a barometer for success or failure. Higher-performing salespeople, such as Robby Armstrong, perceive quota as a minimum acceptable standard.
5. **To provide a standard for evaluation.** While quota is the benchmark for success or failure, managers are able to analyze the specific salesperson activities that led to a particular outcome. The activities and behaviors that led to quota attainment should be encouraged and continued. Reasons for not meeting quota can be analyzed and used to develop more successful approaches.

Types of Quotas

Three widely used types of quotas are sales volume, profits, and activity. Figure 11-9 shows the popularity of each type of quota among large and small firms. Sales volume quotas are the most widely used by both large and small companies. Profit-based quotas are used by about 20 percent of all firms, whereas fewer than 10 percent of firms use activity quotas.

Sales Volume Quotas. *Sales volume quotas* are specific volume targets established for each territory, and possibly for each product line, for a specific period of time (usually a month, quarter, or year). The sales volume quota may be stated in a variety of ways, including dollar volume, unit volume, or a point system. A *dollar volume quota* is preferred when there is a large number of similarly priced items to sell (e.g., drugs to wholesalers), when prices reflect management's selling priorities (e.g., higher-priced products are more important than less expensive items), and when prices are relatively stable. With *unit volume quotas*, sales objectives are stated in terms of the number of units of each product to be sold. Unit quotas are more popular in businesses that sell a limited number of high-cost items (e.g., automobiles) and when price changes frequently. By stating quota in units, the effects of inflation are eliminated from the system. With a *point quota system*, the quota is stated as a certain number of points to be earned for selling each product. The point system provides greater management flexibility because points are assigned to the sale of each type

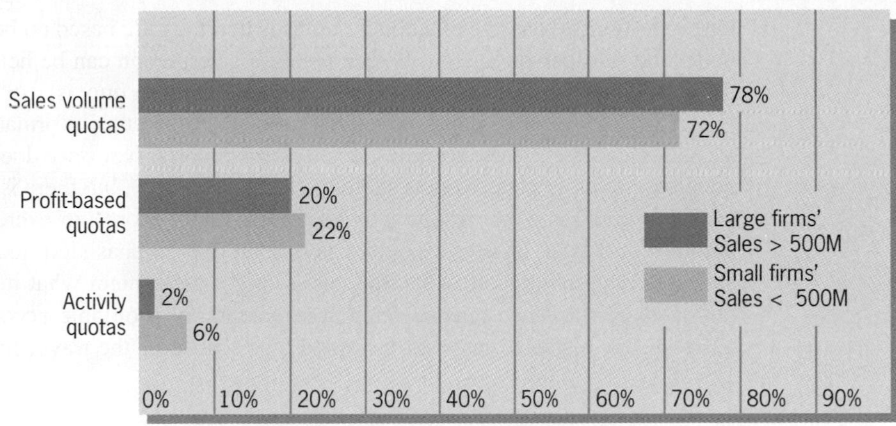

FIGURE 11-9 Use of the Various Types of Quotas

of product. If management wishes to emphasize a new product, for example, it may simply increase the number of points awarded to the sale of the product.

Profit-Based Quotas. *Profit-based quotas* are similar to sales quotas but focus on profits generated instead of just sales volume. Profit quotas are usually not based on bottom-line profits but on gross margin (net sales minus cost of goods sold) or contribution margin (gross margin minus direct selling expenses). As such, they attempt to focus the salesperson's attention on profits as opposed to volume. As one sales manager put it, "There's shipping product, and there's shipping product at the right time to the right customer at the right cost, which is a far bigger idea."

Profit-based quotas are most likely to be used when salespeople make decisions that dramatically affect the profits of the company. For example, salespeople may choose which of many products to recommend, or they may have some flexibility in setting prices. Profit contributions often vary considerably among different products. Unless salespeople are aware of these profit differences and know that they will be held accountable for profits, there is no incentive to sell the more profitable products.

Activity Quotas. Too much emphasis on volume or profit quotas may lead to neglect of important nonselling activities and to lower long-run performance. This problem may be resolved by introducing *activity quotas*. Activity quotas set targets on specific activities that will help meet a firm's sales and profit objectives.

Activity quotas recognize the investment nature of selling; that is, salespeople must often perform activities that have the potential to produce significant sales volume sometime in the future. Firms that use activity quotas, such as Prudential Insurance, believe that success can be achieved by anyone who completes the recommended number of daily or weekly activities. Some typical activity quotas include the following:

- Number of calls per day
- Display racks installed
- Calls on new accounts
- Dealer sales meetings held
- Proposals submitted
- Equipment test sites
- Product demonstrations
- Point-of-purchase displays

One important advantage of activity quotas is that they are based on behaviors that are largely under the salesperson's control. As a result, a salesperson can be held more accountable for the results and will be more motivated to achieve these quotas.

A serious disadvantage of activity quotas is that the information necessary to track activities is obtained from a salesperson's call reports. Not only does this require the salespeople to do more paperwork (usually on their own time), but there is also an opportunity for misrepresentation. As a result, activity reports may become an exercise in creative writing. Another drawback of activity quotas is that an overemphasis on quotas, such as number of calls per day, may result in salespeople giving management what it wants in calls per day, but sales performance may suffer. Large potentially profitable accounts on the fringe of a territory, for instance, may not be called on because of the travel time required.

When Are Quotas Effective?

A good place to start in answering this question is with goal theory. *Goal theory* examines the relationship between goal setting and subsequent performance.[16] This theory proposes that difficult goals, if accepted, will lead to higher performance than moderate or easy goals or no goals, such as "Do your best." This means that management must know what constitutes a difficult goal for a particular salesperson versus one that is easy or impossible. Underscoring the motivational influence of difficult goals is the experience of an electronic equipment manufacturer that had set challenging quotas on its data printer line. Although it took twice as long to sell a data printer compared to the other product lines, the data printer line was considered important to the future of the company. Some salespeople objected to the high quotas, however, so the company relaxed the quotas in six districts to see what the impact would be. A comparison of these six districts with comparable high-quota districts revealed that the high-quota districts outsold those with lower quotas. This led the company to conclude that many salespeople are "quota achieves" and that their motivation decreases if they are given quotas that are too easy to reach.[17]

Since goals appear to motivate sales performance, it is important to understand how salespeople internalize these goals. Recent research results indicate that salespeople internalize performance goals for two basic reasons: First, higher performing salespeople have a need to demonstrate competence and gain favorable judgments from others; and second, they work to avoid negative evaluations (i.e., fear of failure). The study found that working to demonstrate competence and gain favorable judgments leads to higher performance while working to avoid negative evaluations leads to lower performance.[18] Thus, for goal setting to be effective, management must play a much greater role than simply setting specific goals. Management must also be concerned with the following:

1. **Providing feedback.** Feedback, or knowledge of results, is necessary for goals to improve performance. As discussed in the previous chapter, sales manager feedback is a very powerful force in shaping salespeople's performance. Experts suggest that management should give salespeople frequent feedback on their level of sales relative to the quota.[19]
2. **Gaining goal commitment.** Salespeople must consider the goal to be their own. This is what is meant by *goal commitment*—that is, a person's determination to attain a goal. Recall how Robby Armstrong described his quota: "I use my quota as a yardstick for minimum accomplishment; anything below that is unacceptable." Robby has obviously committed himself to meet this objective. There are a number of ways to gain this commitment. One way is through salesperson participation in goal setting. Another approach is to build team spirit and relate individual goals to the greater good of the team. The effectiveness of these approaches will depend on the manager's leadership style, the organization's culture, and the individual salesperson's tendencies.

3. **Building self-confidence.** How people feel about their ability to perform certain behaviors successfully is very important to high performance. Salespeople who are confident in their sales ability typically set higher performance goals and perform better than those who are less confident.[20] This finding points out the considerable benefits of feedback and training, given that one's self-confidence can be enhanced through repeated success, or modeling oneself after successful performers.[21]

Our discussion suggests that it takes more than setting quotas to achieve maximum motivation and performance. Motivation is dependent on the total management system, and, therefore, several issues about quotas remain. The next section examines how to set equitable and fair quotas, how to evaluate performance when multiple quotas are considered, and the relationship between quotas and compensation.

Administering Quotas

Quotas are usually based on one or more of the following: past sales, forecasted sales, sales potential, and individual and salesperson territory adjustments. A "rough" method of determining a sales quota is simply to take sales in a territory for the past year (or an average of several years) and add a percentage based on the company's sales forecast. For example, if sales in territory B are currently $600,000 and the firm wants an 8 percent increase in company sales next year, the new quota will be $648,000. On the surface, this method appears to be equitable and fair. The problem is that past mistakes are likely to be perpetuated. If, in the past, for example, a salesperson has done a poor job covering territory B, then a quota based strictly on past performance will not reflect the true potential that exists in the area. The other problem is that historical sales figures may predate a recent industry slump, a loss of a major account, or they might fail to account for the product's being at a more mature stage in its life cycle, where the opportunities are different. To be realistic, quotas should reflect regional or local conditions.

A better approach is to compute sales potential in each territory and to consider this figure when setting quotas. (Procedures for estimating sales potentials are described in Estimating Potentials and Forecasting Sales in the Sales Management Resource section.) Suppose the Buying Power Index[22] shows that territory B has 5 percent of the total U.S. potential. If the firm plans to sell $17 million in total volume in the next year, then the quota for territory B will be 0.05 × $17 million, or $850,000. Note that the potential-based quota requires the salesperson to realize a sales increase of $250,000 for the year.

Basing quotas strictly on sales potential may not always be workable because it ignores past sales and assumes that all territories are the same with respect to the other factors that will determine the actual sales volume achieved. These include environmental factors (e.g., competition, size of customers), organizational factors (e.g., advertising support, proximity to warehouse and manufacturing facilities), and salesperson factors (e.g., experience, ability). Ignoring these factors may render the quota useless as a performance evaluation tool and for motivating salespeople. Thus, a quota of $850,000 may discourage rather than stimulate a salesperson when current sales in the territory are only $600,000. The best method, therefore, for setting quotas is to consider all three factors: past and forecasted sales, sales potential, and individual territory and salesperson characteristics. Setting quotas, therefore, often requires considerable judgment on management's part. Some sales consultants recommend setting goals realistically so that at least 70 percent of the people achieve the goal.[23] It is easy to see why quotas are a potential bone of contention and why salesperson input can be beneficial. What would you do to resolve the sales force concerns raised in Team Exercise titled "Sales and the Web"?

Another administrative concern of sales managers is how to evaluate performance when salespeople must meet several quotas. For example, Table 11-1 shows sales volume and

TABLE 11-1 Evaluating Quota Performance in Territory B

Quota Factor	*Three-Month Quota*	*Actual*	*Percentage of Quota Attained*
Total sales volume	$83,000	$84,660	102%
Unit sales of Model 75	6	5	82
Point-of-purchase displays	25	17	68
Average calls per day	5	7	140
Percent store distribution	0.75	0.70	93
			Average: 97.2%

activity quotas together with actual results for the salesperson in territory B. Note that although the overall sales goal was achieved, the salesperson was below quota on three of the five factors. Furthermore, only about two-thirds of the allotted displays were achieved. The average quota achievement of 97 percent, however, appears to be good. It would be especially beneficial if all other salespeople in the company reached only 70 to 90 percent of their quotas. What should be this person's overall performance rating?

Although average quota achievement is a convenient summary figure, one potential problem is that "average performance" places equal weight on each element used to arrive at the average. In the example in Table 11-1, for instance, as much value is placed on point-of-purchase displays as on total sales dollar results. Some managers assign different weights to the various quota factors to handle this problem. Quota achievement is weighted by the importance of each quota factor, and the weighted ratings are added together to form an overall performance index. Care should be taken, however, not to create an overly complicated system.

Another important question is how high management should set the bar. Aiming high is laudable, but setting unattainable goals is a sure way to puncture a sales force's morale. Should a quota be set so that all people will likely exceed it, the top half, or only the few best salespeople? There is no clear-cut answer to this question, and practices vary from one company to the next. If bonuses for exceeding the quota are treated as a normal part of the salespeople's income, then achievable quotas should be set. Conversely, some companies try

TEAM EXERCISE

"Sales and the Web"

Your company recently began offering its products and services via its Web site. Since the site features only those products and services that do not require interaction with a sales representative, all communication and documentation are done electronically. After just a few months, more than 100 customers have used the Web site to make purchases.

Although the customers are happy with the site, your reps are not. Reps earn commission on orders from current customers processed via the Web, but orders from new customers have no commission. Reps feel that this cheats them out of commissions and sets up the Web site as competition to their efforts. Your company's CEO feels that the Web is like another rep: The accounts that the site "sells" belong to it.

As a branch sales manager, you are caught in the middle of this situation. Your reps are spending so much time complaining to you (and to each other) about the Web that productivity and morale are suffering. The reps want commissions on sales made via the Web, period. A few have hinted at leaving if the situation persists. Can a compromise be reached? How should the Web-based order entry system be positioned to the sales force?

to challenge their people to greater performance by setting quotas at higher than expected levels and attach substantial and exceptional financial rewards to beating the quota. In this case, financial rewards for quota achievement may be treated as a way to retain top performers. The level at which a quota is set will depend on the role of quota achievement within the overall financial and nonfinancial rewards system of the organization.

When Not to Use Quotas

In certain circumstances, it is probably not advisable to use individual quotas. For example, when a significant portion of sales depends on cooperation between salespeople in different territories, individual quotas may either be unfeasible or discourage cooperation. This is likely to occur when third-party referrals involve prospects in other territories. The referral may not be passed along, especially if quota achievement is evaluated on a relative basis—that is, if bonus quota achievement is evaluated relative to how each salesperson performed.

Another situation not conductive to quotas is when sales are infrequent with a long selling cycle but the dollar value is very high. In this case, no sales may be recorded in a period, followed by extremely high sales volume in a subsequent period. Short-term quota performance is relatively meaningless in such a situation.

INCENTIVE PROGRAMS

Incentive programs are short-term promotional events intended to inspire salespeople to a greater-than-usual performance level and provide them with rewards. Incentives are a proven motivational device with widespread acceptance. It is estimated that two-thirds of all consumer goods companies and more than half of all industrial goods companies have sponsored incentive programs. Incentive budgets can range in size from under $5,000 to more than $1 million. In total, U.S. firms will spend more than $23 billion annually on sales incentive programs.[24] The large budgets and widespread acceptance of sales incentive programs may be explained by referring back to our model of motivation. Greater rewards will usually lead to greater motivation if the rewards are valued by the salesperson. Our model also explains why incentive programs are usually tied to special customer promotion efforts, a special low price, or premium offer, because these should help salespeople understand that their extra efforts will lead to higher performance. Recall that these estimates of success are critical to one's decision to put forth greater effort.

Goals

Incentives are not a giveaway. A generally accepted performance standard is to produce $4 for each $1 put into them. The objectives of a sales incentive program may also include more than just producing overall increases in sales volume. Programs have goals such as finding new customers or boosting the sales of special items, counteracting seasonal slumps in sales, and introducing new items to customers. Other companies have used incentive programs to obtain a better balance across product lines or encourage dealers to build more in-store displays.

In addition to specific quantitative goals, incentive programs may be used to enhance qualitative goals such as team building. Basing rewards on department or team results is especially helpful in this regard.

Prizes

The success or failure of an incentive program often depends on the attractiveness of the awards offered to the participants. There are no firm rules for selecting prizes, except that different prizes should be chosen for each contest and participants should find the prizes attractive. The most frequent award is cash because it offers the greatest flexibility in how to use the prize. On the other hand, travel and merchandise awards can be shown and promoted to the sales force, which may add some glamour and excitement to the contest. Furthermore, merchandise can be purchased at wholesale prices, giving the awards a higher value than they actually cost the company to buy. However, merchandise prizes can lose their attractiveness if they duplicate things salespeople already own. One solution is to have the salespeople accumulate points that can be used to choose items from a catalog.

Administration Issues

Although incentive programs have the potential to be very powerful motivators, they must be properly planned and executed. One of the keys to successful sales incentive programs is choosing a good theme for the contest. The theme is a unifying statement that ties together the business objective of the contest, the prizes, and the individual. Ideally, the theme will be simple, easy to execute, and something about which the participants can get excited. Common sales contest themes include sports (Super Bowl, World Series), travel locations, treasure hunts, gambling, and detective and mystery themes. These themes are used as reminders during the contest and may also be used to display current standings among the contestants.

A successful program should encourage the average salesperson to expend extra effort because superior salespeople produce regardless of the contest, and people at the bottom are less likely to respond to any stimulus. We recommend setting the qualifications and rewards at a level that will motivate the middle 60 percent of the sales force. With this objective in mind, it is often advisable to have many prizes, instead of having one or two grand prizes that are likely to be won by the superstars. A good guideline is that half of the salespeople eligible for sales contests should win some sort of prize.

The incentive program should be highly promoted. Promotion informs salespeople of the incentive program and reminds them of the prizes to be won. A good way to build initial interest is to begin with a kickoff sales meeting in which the sales force can see the prizes and learn the details of the contest. This meeting should be followed by mailings, articles in the company newspaper, and trade advertising to maintain the attention and interest of the field reps. Because sales contests are short lived, it is essential to issue frequent progress reports to let participants know where they stand and what they must do to qualify for an award.

RECOGNITION PROGRAMS

Without a doubt, recognition and prizes push people closer to their potential than envelopes stuffed with money. Indeed, some studies suggest that noncash recognition programs can be more motivating to salespeople than cash prizes.[25] This is why almost all sales managers have some sort of *recognition program.* A recognition program is similar to incentives in that an individual or group of salespeople receives an award for exceptional performance. However, recognition programs differ from incentive programs in several important ways. Although some monetary award may be involved, the primary award is recognition by management for exceptional performance. There are also timing differences. Where incentive programs are usually short in duration, a recognition program can be based on performance over a year or longer. In addition, recognition programs usually focus on overall performance rather than the sale of targeted products.

Pitney Bowes, a leading supplier of mailing equipment and office automation, has one of the most professional and successful sales forces in the world. One key to its success is the company's many recognition programs. These programs are based on two principles: (1) generate enthusiasm and motivation for as many salespeople as possible and (2) get useful feedback from the sales force to improve performance opportunities even more. Three of Pitney Bowes' programs illustrate these principles:

- **Pace-Maker Conference.** This week-long conference is an all-expenses-paid trip to an exotic location for the senior salespeople and their spouses or partners who are in the top 10 percent of sales in the company for the past year. In addition to the recognition award ceremonies and other activities, the salespeople are provided a forum with senior managers, including the CEO, to learn more about the company's strategic plans, express problems or concerns, and ask questions.
- **Top Honors Conference.** This conference is designed to recognize the top new salespeople in the company. While top rookie salespeople are given a vacation trip, the most valued aspect of the trip is the recognition from Pitney Bowes' top executives.
- **Walter Wheeler Award.** This award is given to any person in the company, including salespeople, who has had an extraordinary accomplishment, or exhibited a strong sense of the company's vision over the past year. One person from each country where Pitney Bowes is located can be nominated for this award. Each nominee, including the overall winner, is recognized by top executives and invited to a lavish vacation.[26]

To be successful, recognition programs must become part of the company's culture; that is, they should be long-standing, anticipated, and have lasting value. As you can see, recognition programs focus on one of the three characteristics of effort discussed earlier—the drive to persistently put forth exceptional effort. Successful recognition programs also appeal to the highest of Maslow's needs, self-actualization, which, you may recall, is never fully satisfied.

Why does recognition motivate salespeople? Part of the reason is that most people strive for recognition by management and peers, and most people cannot get enough recognition. For high performance to lead to positive job attitudes and subsequent high performance, individuals should have a positive emotional reaction to their performance.[27] A well-administered recognition program can help foster a strong, positive reaction to high performance.

Ethical Situations

Despite their widespread use, ethical problems may arise with quota systems, contests, and rewards to motivate people on the job. Some people have questioned whether managers should administer rewards in ways that promote desirable behaviors from the organization's point of view and not worry too much about the individual's freedom to choose which behaviors to engage in to satisfy his or her own desires. When does a manager have too much power to manipulate people into doing what they would not otherwise do? There is also the issue of whether promising rewards detracts from the job. Does promising a reward for doing a job they already enjoy doing lead salespeople to view the reward as the motivation for performing the task, thus undermining their enjoyment of the job?

Poorly run or poorly conceived quotas and contests have high potential for fostering unethical behaviors by salespeople. When salespeople know that a contest is imminent, for example, they may withhold orders prior to the contest in order to have greater volume during the contest. During a contest, "soft" orders, which will be totally or partially returned by the customer, may be submitted. If quotas are set on activities, such as calls per day, salespeople may be tempted to falsify call reports to avoid problems with an overzealous manager or to meet end-of-year objectives for which they are rewarded. If salespeople are rewarded for exceeding the quota, they may withhold additional orders during the reporting period in order to make their job easier during the next period. Some people have been known to start their own companies during the time they have available after meeting the quota. If a quota or contest is not designed or administered properly, people may easily justify unethical behavior. A good question to consider is how you would design a program in order to prevent or discourage each of these behaviors.

SUMMARY

Role perceptions, skill levels, aptitude, and motivation all affect a salesperson's on-the-job performance. Salespeople need basic selling skills, but they also must be motivated to put forth the effort needed to achieve their objectives. Given the demanding environment in which salespeople operate, an effective motivator is often the only difference between a salesperson's success or failure. Sales managers who are able to motivate will be rewarded with a sales force that expresses little dissatisfaction and exerts high levels of effort. In order to be effective, however, managers must first understand the many factors that constitute motivation:

1. **Define motivation and explain sales managers' concerns with motivation.** Motivation is an individual's willingness to exert effort to achieve the organization's goals while satisfying individual needs. Sales managers should understand that people have different needs and that these needs change over a salesperson's career. The four basic career stages a salesperson experiences are: exploration, establishment maintenance, and disengagement. Each of these stages has different career concerns, motivational needs, personal challenges, and psychosocial needs.
2. **Tell how and why individual needs may differ.** Sales managers are concerned with motivation because of the demanding environment in which salespeople operate. Also, the lack of direct, day-to-day supervision requires a focus on self-motivation. In addition, motivation is directly related to salesperson success.
3. **Describe a basic model of the motivation process.** Expectancy is the salesperson's belief that greater effort will lead to greater performance. Expectancy theory is based on three interrelated factors: (1) the relationship between effort and performance (expectancies), (2) the relationship between performance and rewards (instrumentalities), and (3) the importance of receiving more of a certain reward (valences). Salespeople estimate the chances that their actions will lead to specific goals and that goal achievement will lead to rewards, and they assess the desirability of the rewards offered for achieving those goals. If the objectives seem reasonable and the rewards sufficiently attractive, then salespeople will be motivated.
4. **Discuss the different types of quotas and the administrative issues involved in using quotas.** Quotas are widely used motivational devices that not only provide goals and direct salesperson efforts, but also set standards for evaluation of individual performance. The common types of quotas are sales volume (which includes dollar volume, unit volume, and point quota systems), profit-based, and activity quotas. Management plays an important role in both setting quotas and ensuring that salespeople accept the goals. Quotas are usually set on one or more of the following: past sales, forecasted sales, sales potential, and individual and salesperson territory adjustments. For salespeople to accept the goals as their own, management should provide frequent feedback, have salespeople committed to the goal, and build salesperson self-confidence.

5. **Describe how to design incentive and recognition programs and their limitations.** Incentive programs are short-run promotional events that can stimulate salespeople to reach their quotas through the offer of prizes such as merchandise, cash, or trips. Recognition awards, such as "Salesperson of the Month" titles, trophies, and certificates, are also effective motivational devices.

KEY TERMS

Activity quota
Attribution theory
Behavioral self-management (BSM)
Disengagement stage
Dollar volume quota
Equity theory
Establishment stage
Expectancy theory
Exploration stage
Goal commitment
Goal theory
Hierarchy of needs
Incentive program
Instrumentality
Intrinsic motivation
Maintenance stage
Motivation
Motivation-hygiene theory
Point quota system
Profit-based quota
Quota
Recognition program
Reward valence
Sales volume quota
Unit volume quota

DEVELOPING YOUR COMPETENCIES

1. **Strategic Action.** Quotas at DSC Technologies are based on the average of sales over the past 2 years plus a 20 percent increase. The reason for the high increase in sales quota is that DSC manufactures and sells telephone switches in the communications industry, where new technologies are frequently introduced and industry growth over the past decade has averaged just over 20 percent a year. Bonuses are paid on the following schedule:

Bonus Percent	*Percent of Quota*
5	100–105
7	106–110
10	111–120

No additional bonus is given for windfall sales over 20 percent of the quota. What are the advantages and disadvantages of this approach? What is likely to happen? How would you change the method?

2. **Team Building.** Select another member of your class and use the expectancy theory of motivation to analyze this course. To what extent does the design of the course influence your expectancy, instrumentality, and valence perceptions? Discuss with each other how various elements of the course affect your perceptions of the three components of motivation.
3. **Global Perspective.** IBM's incentive programs are designed to include its worldwide sales force. A recent program dubbed "You Sell, You Sail" was one of the largest sales incentive contests ever run by a U.S. company. It included 7,000 participants. IBM believed it could communicate program goals, rules, and results directly to the 7,000 participants in 140 countries around the world using e-mail. However, making the contest meaningful and competitive was another challenge. What factors would you need to consider in order to have a meaningful competition for all 7,000 salespeople?
4. **Coaching.** You are a sales manager for an industrial manufacturer. The performance of one of your salespeople, James Weber, has slipped and he has achieved only 75 percent of his quota for the past six months. The average sales quota achievement in your

district was 90 percent. Weber has worked for your firm for six years and has a bachelor's degree in business administration. Jim's territory is above average in potential but requires considerable travel. At the recent company picnic, Weber seemed depressed and spent his time drinking rather than interacting with the other salespeople. Weber is divorced, and his ex-wife lives in another city with their three children. You have decided that it is time to call in Weber for a conference. Develop a script for a meeting with Weber that will motivate him to work up to his potential. Be prepared to play the role of the sales manager or Weber in a meeting to be acted out in front of the class.

5. **Self-Management.** The following series of questions is designed to assess the needs that are important to you. There are no right or wrong answers. The best response to any item is simply the one that best reflects your feelings—either as you have experienced them or as you anticipate that you would experience them—in a work situation. Respond to the 20 statements by indicating the degree to which each is true for you. Use the following key and circle the number that best indicates how true and accurate the statement is.

1 = Not true and accurate.
2 = Slightly true and accurate.
3 = Partly true and accurate.
4 = Mostly true and accurate.
5 = Completely true.

1. I believe that the real rewards for working are good pay, working conditions, and the like.	1	2	3	4	5
2. The most important thing to me in evaluating a job is whether it gives me job security and employee benefts.	1	2	3	4	5
3. I would not want a job in which I had no coworkers to talk to and share work stories with.	1	2	3	4	5
4. I want a job that allows rapid advancement based on my own achievements.	1	2	3	4	5
5. Searching for what will make me happy is most important in my life.	1	2	3	4	5
6. Working conditions (office space, equipment, and basic physical necessities) are important to me.	1	2	3	4	5
7. I would not want a job if the equipment was poor or I was without adequate protection against layoffs.	1	2	3	4	5
8. Whether the people I was going to work with were compatible would affect my decision about whether to take a promotion.	1	2	3	4	5
9. A job should offer tangible rewards and recognition for a person's performance.	1	2	3	4	5
10. I want a job that is challenging and stimulating and has meaningful activities.	1	2	3	4	5
11. If I took a job in which there were strong pressures to rush and little time for lunch, coffee breaks, and the like, my motivation would suffer.	1	2	3	4	5
12. My motivation would suffer if my fellow employees were cold or held grudges toward me.	1	2	3	4	5
13. Being a valued member of the team and enjoying the social aspects of work are important to me.	1	2	3	4	5

14.	I'm likely to work hardest in a situation that offers tangible rewards and recognition for performance.	1	2	3	4	5
15.	Going as far as I can, using my skills and capabilities, and exploring new ideas are what really drive me.	1	2	3	4	5
16.	An important factor for me is that my job pays well enough to satisfy the needs of my family and me.	1	2	3	4	5
17.	Fringe benefits, such as hospitalization insurance, retirement plans, and dental programs, are important to me.	1	2	3	4	5
18.	I would likely work hardest in a job where a group of employees discuss and plan their work as a team.	1	2	3	4	5
19.	My accomplishments give me an important sense of self-respect.	1	2	3	4	5
20.	I would work the hardest in a job where I could see the returns of my work from the standpoint of personal interest and growth.	1	2	3	4	5

Scoring directions: In the following table, insert the number you circled for each of the 20 statements. Then add each column to get your summary scores.

	1. ______	2. ______	3. ______	4. ______	5. ______
	6. ______	7. ______	8. ______	9. ______	10. ______
	11. ______	12. ______	13. ______	14. ______	15. ______
	16. ______	17. ______	18. ______	19. ______	20. ______
Totals:	______	______	______	______	______
Motives:	Basic Creature Comfort	Safety and Security	Social or Affiliation	Self-Esteem	Self-Actualization

Interpretation: For each of the five motives, there is a minimum of 4 and a maximum of 20 points. Scores of 18 or more are quite high and suggest that the motives measured by that scale are very important to you. Scores from 13 to 17 suggest that the motives measured are moderately important to you. Scores from 9 to 12 suggest that the motives are not especially important to you. Scores below 9 are quite low and suggest that the motives measured are not at all important to you.

FEATURED CASE: SHIELD FINANCIAL: "MOTIVATION AND ROLE CONFLICT"

Jonathan MacMillan has worked as a rep for Shield Financial in Des Moines for almost three years. His first year he made 110 percent of quota, generating $750,000 in revenues. In year 2, he hit 120 percent of quota, a hefty $1.25 million. To do this, he worked 14-hour days during the week prospecting and meeting with customers, plus whatever weekend time was necessary to complete reports and write proposals. Keeping this pace, MacMillan was on target to reach this year's quota as well—that is, until he became a first-time father two months ago. He's now working only 40- to 50-hour weeks. The result is, of course, fewer sales.

Doug Bloom is worried. Shield is in the process of introducing the new First-Plus account program and has ambitious growth plans. Bloom also had hoped to make MacMillan a member of the management team. But when talking casually with him about goals and future plans, Bloom discovered that MacMillan is not interested in becoming a manager because at Shield the big money is in sales. Even working fewer hours, MacMillan is earning a fat paycheck.

Bloom is at a loss. He wants to get back the fiery, hard-charging MacMillan he was told of, but he's not sure how.

Questions

1. How can Bloom remotivate MacMillan?
2. How should a manager deal with family role conflict? How can Bloom make MacMillan more efficient?
3. Is MacMillan now a slacker? MacMillan is now only willing to work 50 hours a week and is not interested in changing. Is he going to be deadweight from now on? Is he worth the sales manager's time and effort if he will never work more than 55 hours per week? Should he be reprimanded?
4. Why is Bloom so worried about MacMillan's lack of interest in management? Is this important?

COMPENSATING SALESPEOPLE

> I've always been worried about people who are willing to work for nothing. Sometimes that's all you get from them, nothing.
>
> Sam Ervin

Chapter Consultants:
Randy Cimorelli, President/COO, Massey-Fair Industrial, Inc.
Robert C. Conti Vice President, The Alexander Group, Inc.

LEARNING OBJECTIVES

After studying this chapter, you should be able to:

- ⟶ Explain the need to balance wages against company resources.
- ⟶ Describe the various compensation methods.
- ⟶ Set pay levels.
- ⟶ Assemble a compensation plan.

COMPENSATION OBJECTIVES

Compensation is one of the most important tools for motivating and retaining field salespeople. However, sales force compensation is a cost that can quickly spiral out of control if the compensation plan is designed improperly. Thus, to maintain profitability, managers must design compensation plans that encourage salespeople to work efficiently, which is not easy to do. In fact, salesperson compensation has long been an issue marked by trial and error and many managers struggle to discover just the right formula or approach.[1] The key to a successful plan is to keep the goals as simple as possible. And resist the temptation to harness the compensation system to fix everything wrong with the company. Part of the problem, however, is a tendency to micromanage salesperson compensation in an attempt to drive specific behaviors and product sales. According to David Luke, a principal at sales consultancy Integrative Sales Concepts, in Irvine, California, "If you see a system that says you make ten bucks if you make quota, $10.50 if you make quota and have a happy customer, and $10.75 if you do it all on the first Tuesday of the month and file your expense report on time, that's a system with too many goals at once. Often what you have there are sales managers not doing the management work they ought to be doing, and they're farming it out by connecting the tasks to the sales reps via the compensation system."[2]

A good starting point to develop the optimal pay plan is to understand the company's strategic goals and how the sales force can support those goals. Although the most important goal of senior-level managers is to increase sales and revenues, there are many short- and long-term sales force tactics at a manager's disposal. For example, do you want reps to sell more premium items in certain product lines? Increase long-term customer relationships? Or increase salesperson motivation? After at least ten years of paying its salespeople the same way, E-Z-GO, a manufacturer of golf carts in Augusta, Georgia, changed its compensation plan. Instead of using the number of units sold to determine salesperson commission, E-Z-GO started using profit margins. E-Z-GO realized that customers were making purchasing decisions based solely on cost and prices had either decreased or remained flat over the past five years. The change forced salespeople who were unwilling or unable to maintain a price premium to take a pay cut. Not surprisingly, E-Z-GO's salespeople were less than thrilled with the change. However, their fears never materialized; the sales force earned considerably more under the new plan and the company's profitability skid was reversed.[3]

This example highlights the important balancing act between aligning compensation objectives with overall firm strategy and offering a competitive pay package. It also demonstrates the importance of balancing the natural desire of salespeople to earn more money with the firm's need to control expenses. This means that you have the difficult task of designing compensation programs that motivate salespeople to reach company goals and satisfy customers without bankrupting the firm. And because 20 to 30 percent of all sales reps are unhappy with their compensation plans at any one time, you may be constantly challenged to come up with a better program.

A useful tool to begin translating company objectives and, the desired sales job into an appropriate compensation plan is to consider a Customer-Product Matrix. As shown in Figure 12-1, the Customer-Product Matrix divides sales opportunities into combinations of new and current customers and products. In general, sales positions that focus primarily on New Business Development (upper right-hand quadrant) and Convergence Selling (upper left-hand quadrant) require a greater proportion of incentive (e.g., commissions and bonus) in the compensation plan than those sales jobs in the lower left-hand quadrant (Account Management). Sales jobs consisting primarily of Account Management involve a greater account servicing component and are therefore better suited to a salary form of compensation. Leverage selling jobs should have a combination of salary and incentive. The relative percentage of incentive should be based on the amount of creativity and skill needed to add new products. As you can probably tell from this framework, it is imperative that sale force compensation plans are consistent with corporate strategy because they communicate what is important. How would *you* handle the issues raised in the Team Exercise titled "Changing Sales Compensation Plans"?

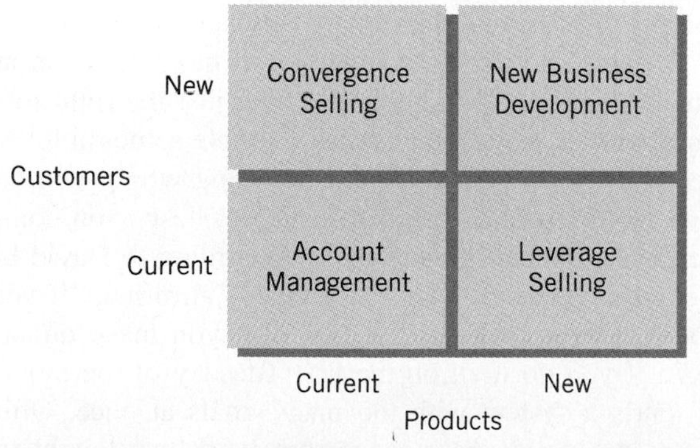

FIGURE 12-1 The Customer-Product Matrix

TEAM EXERCISE
"Changing Sales Compensation Plans"

As the new vice president of sales for Widget Corporation, you have spent two weeks reviewing the company's current compensation plan. After deciding that the plan no longer matched the company's new objectives and attitude, you revamped it. Salespeople's commission would no longer be based solely on revenue generation. Now that the company was trying to be more customer-driven and give better service, 70 percent of the commission would be based on a sales quota, and 30 percent would be based on the quality of service given to current customers (which would be judged by repeat business and surveys). However, sales quotas for bringing in new business were increased to reflect the coming year's projected increase in business.

Three months after implementing the new compensation plan you noticed that sales were falling and that morale was low. When you met with your salespeople to discuss the problem, you found that they felt cheated: How could they meet their quota—necessary to keep their job—and still give the kind of service needed to make the same money they made on their previous plan? You are now thinking: Was the new compensation plan fair or not? Why did the salespeople think it was unfair? How could you redesign the compensation plan so that the sales force will enthusiastically accept it?

COMPENSATION METHODS

Building an effective sales force compensation program boils down to finding the right combination of salary and incentive pay. As shown in Table 12-1, there are three basic methods of compensation plans, straight salary, straight commission, or a combination of fixed pay and incentive. By far the most common compensation plan combines a base salary with some type of incentives. One advantage of the combination plan is that the incentive portion can be used to influence specific salesperson behaviors, such as focusing on a particular segment of customers or product line. A useful guideline for any company thinking of exerting some behavioral control using incentives is to make sure that the incentive component is between 15 and 30 percent of total compensation.[4] However, as we discuss next, there are advantages and disadvantages to each compensation method.

Straight Salary

Although a familiar form of compensation for most nonselling personnel, *straight salary* involves paying a fixed amount each pay period. Straight salary programs were used by

TABLE 12-1 Use of Compensation Plans

	Percentage of Companies Using
Straight salary	18
Straight commission	19
Combination plans (63%)	
Salary plus bonus	24
Salary plus commission	20
Salary plus bonus plus commission	18
Commission plus bonus	1
Total	100%

approximately 18 percent of the firms reported in Table 12-1. A national compensation survey showed that the average salary plan paid midlevel salespeople is 30 percent less per year than salespeople on salary plus incentive programs.[5] This does not necessarily imply that salary plans are inherently lower paying compensation plans but that the sales activities associated with most straight salary plans tend to be lower paying.

Advantages. The major benefits of salary are more control over wage levels and salesperson activities. Salaried employees can be directed to sell particular products, call on certain customers, and perform a variety of account servicing and other nonselling activities. Salary is also helpful when a salesperson is responsible for covering an entire territory as opposed to a specific account list. In these situations, a manager can require a salesperson to call on all the accounts, not just the "best" accounts in a given region. This is an important issue in jobs where "blanket" coverage is expected, such as that of a manufacturer's rep. Because a salesperson's income is not tied to the sales volume of specific customers, it is easier for the sales manager to divide territories and reassign salespeople to new areas. Also, since salary plan wages are a fixed cost to the firm, the proportion of wage expense tends to decrease as sales increase. These plans are also fairly straightforward and tend to be easier to explain to new employees.

Salary plans provide salespeople with security and a steady, predictable monthly income. Trainees, in particular, tend to favor this payment plan because they run the risk of having low incomes if they start out on a commission plan.[6] Salary programs are also often preferred by customers, since they know salespeople are there to help rather than to load them with inventory. However, emerging research is starting to demonstrate boundary conditions to this general notion. One study, for example, found that customer suspicion about salesperson motives is triggered when the customer knows the salesperson is personally benefiting from the sale. However, the negative effects of suspicion on salesperson perceptions depends on the amount of persuasion used in the sales message. The results of two separate experiments showed that customers actually preferred commission-based salespeople over salaried-based salespeople when the salesperson used more balanced (i.e., less persuasive) sales presentations. Conversely, customers preferred salespeople paid on salary (i.e., no suspicion triggered) as compared to commission when the salesperson used more persuasive sales messages.[7]

Limitations. The most frequently heard criticism is that salaries do not provide strong incentives for extra effort. Even though salary adjustments are made to reward performance, these adjustments are usually annual and lack the more immediate reinforcement of alternative plans. As a result, some salespeople may not exert the extra effort to meet the needs of the company. Some experts argue that those who are allowed to "share the wealth" bring the most "help" to the buyer, which is why "account management" still needs to reward growth and discourage flat sales growth. Another problem is that salaried salespeople usually require much closer supervision by sales managers than salespeople who work under commission plans. Also, salary plans often overpay the least productive members of a sales team and cause morale problems when new trainees earn almost as much as experienced salespeople.

Applications. Research has shown that salary is used more often in competitive labor environments, in situations where it is difficult to assess sales force activities and performance, and in companies where salespeople spend a lot of time on service and paperwork.[8] This suggests that salary is most appropriate in sales positions of Account Management when it is difficult to relate the efforts of individual salespeople to the size or timing of a sale. For example, the "detail people" for pharmaceutical companies are engaged primarily in missionary activities with doctors and do not sell directly to most of their customers. For years it was impossible to track drug orders prescribed by particular physicians. However, given the sophistication of today's information systems and the ability to calculate hospital and drugstore profitability across different product lines, the compensation plans of pharmaceutical sales forces are becoming more incentive oriented and salary is a lower percent of total compensation.

Salary is also used when teamwork of other departments is required in the sales process. Salary, for example, is widely used in the sales of complex aerospace products to airlines and the government as well as in nonferrous metals such as aluminum. Salespeople in this industry are technical advisers, and it may take years to convert a customer from one material to another. Salary is also appropriate in situations where the products are presold through advertising and the salesperson primarily takes orders. Liquor, for example, is largely presold through magazines and newspaper ads, and salespeople are mainly responsible for in-store merchandising and displays.

Straight Commission

Salespeople on commission are paid a percentage of the sales or gross profits that they generate. The *straight commission* plan rewards people for their accomplishments rather than their time or efforts. Straight commissions work on the principle that a salesperson will add value above his or her cost. Although this principle should be true for all compensation plans, this type of pay plan is ideal for those who are confident of adding value and want to be equitably rewarded for their efforts with commissions. The potential to earn higher wages tends to attract better qualified applicants and provides a strong incentive to work efficiently. It is interesting to note that straight commission plans are used by a relatively small number of firms. As shown in Table 12-1, about 20 percent of the firms in the study reported using straight commissions.

Advantages. Straight commission plans foster independence of action and provide the maximum possible incentive. They are easy to understand, and it is fairly simple to calculate wages and administer the plan. Because the selling costs are entirely variable, the firm does not pay as much when sales decline or fail to meet growth objectives. When commissions are paid at the time revenues are received, definite cash flow benefits follow. It is also becoming more popular for firms to base commissions on the profitability of sales to motivate the sales force to focus on the most profitable products or customers. In these plans, the sales force would have a variable commission structure where relatively high commissions are paid for sales of the most profitable products or most profitable accounts. In addition, the variable rate plan can also be used to direct the sale force's efforts toward new strategic objectives, such as introducing a new product line.

The advantages of a 10 percent commission plan are shown graphically in Figure 12-2. Notice that when the sales-per-person figure is low, the costs of the commission plan are lower than the *fixed cost* salary plan ($40,000). Figure 12-2 also shows that when sales are less than $400,000 per year, the salary plan is the high-cost method. But when sales exceed $400,000 per year, the straight salary plan results in lower total costs for the company. Thus, small firms often start off using commission plans and then shift to salary when they grow. However, financial risk should not be the sole or even primary basis for choosing between a salary or commission compensation plan. The sales job to be performed should be the most important criterion. Note, for instance, that sales jobs with most new, small companies will fall in the New Business Development quadrant of the Customer-Product Matrix, so compensation should include a significant incentive component.

Limitations. Despite some advantages, straight commission has a number of drawbacks. The major problems are that sales managers have little control over commission salespeople

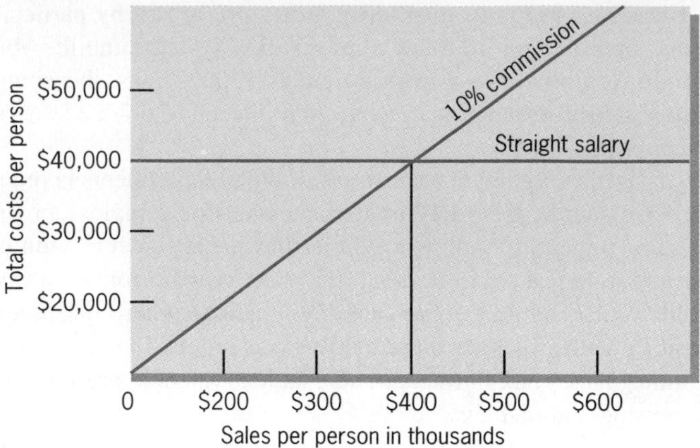

FIGURE 12-2 Comparing Salary and Commission Plans for Field Sales Representatives

and nonselling activities are likely to be neglected. Commission salespeople are tempted to sell themselves rather than the company and to service only the best accounts in their territories. Because salespeople's wages are directly related to sales to particular accounts, salespeople are often reluctant to have their territories changed in any way. Turnover can become excessive among commission salespeople when business conditions are bad, because they often have little company loyalty. Wide variations in pay under commission plans may also lead to poor morale among lower paid personnel, and highly paid salespeople with management potential may be reluctant to move into supervisory or managerial positions.

Applications. Straight commission works best when maximum incentive is needed and when a minimum of after-sale service and missionary work is required. This situation exists for most door-to-door organizations and many car dealerships, although this is changing somewhat as a result of Saturn's success with "no-haggle" pricing. Other types of businesses that use straight commission plans include life insurance, real estate, stock brokerage, printing, and wholesalers in many industries. Commission rates often range from 5 to 14 percent of sales.

Salary Plus Bonus

Salary plus bonus programs are used to provide reps with income security while the bonus gives added incentives to meet company objectives. Bonuses are discretionary payments for reaching specified goals and are usually paid annually. Probably the most widely used basis for determining bonus pay is sales to quota. Another popular basis is average gross margin achieved by the rep. Other bonus factors are the number of new accounts, unit sales, and overall company performance. Salary plus bonus programs were the most preferred plan in Table 12-1, used by 24 percent of firms. In fact, a number of companies are starting to switch to this plan because of its flexibility in rewarding different salesperson activities. Minneapolis-based Carlson Marketing, for example, recently scrapped its commission compensation plan in favor of a salary plus bonus plan. The bonus portion of the plan is designed to foster teamwork by using customer satisfaction and cost to serve its customers as its performance metrics instead of sales volume.[9]

Advantages. This compensation plan has several advantages. The main advantage of salary plus bonus plans is that they balance the need to control selling expenses and provide extra rewards for added results. When products are largely presold by advertising, like many consumer items, it makes no sense to pay a salary plus a commission to get salespeople to push for added volume. Under these conditions, a salary plus a modest bonus is enough to get the job done.

Another possible advantage of salary plus bonus plans is that they may lead to lower turnover among salespeople.[10] This is particularly important when buying cycles are long and reps must invest time to understand how customers do business. The security of a salary allows reps time to both court prospects over a considerable period of time and to service existing customers.

Limitations. One of the potential problems with the salary plus bonus plan is that in some firms the size of the bonus has been arbitrary. Managers review sales results, customer relations, and after-sale service and then decide how much each person should receive. Managers who fail to communicate how bonuses are determined can lose some of their effectiveness as motivational devices. Another limitation of the salary plus bonus plan deals with the relationship between performance and rewards. Since bonuses are typically paid annually, salesperson instrumentality perceptions (i.e., a higher level of performance will lead to greater personal rewards) may be reduced, thus reducing motivation.

Examples. Salary plus bonus plans are commonly used by large food manufacturers, such as Quaker Oats and Procter & Gamble. Some companies have used the salary plus bonus plan to foster teamwork. Principal Financial, for example, uses a bonus plan where all salespeople in a particular branch office receive a year-end bonus if all salespeople meet or exceed a certain threshold of performance. Using this approach, Principal has found that the top performing reps will be more proactive in providing advice and sharing tips to help the lower performers throughout the year.[11]

Salary Plus Commission

Industrial sales reps are frequently paid *salary plus commission* to give them the push needed to sell complex products or services. Twenty percent of the firms in Table 12-1 employ salary plus commission programs. Although most firms start paying commissions on the first dollar of sales, approximately 40 percent establish *commission thresholds* that must be reached before the commissions apply. Often the commission rates vary, depending on sales volume. As an illustration, a salesperson might earn 4 percent on the first $20,000 of sales each month, 5 percent on the next $15,000, and 6 percent on anything over $35,000. These types of *progressive commission rates* are used when sales increases require extra efforts.

Advantages. Commission rates can be adjusted to promote the sale of individual products or to intensify efforts among specific market segments. Many firms vary commission rates according to the profitability of products. Also, it is common for firms to have wage caps on the incentive portion of their compensation plans to prevent windfall earnings as a result of circumstances unrelated to salespeople's efforts.

Commissions are usually paid monthly, providing almost immediate reinforcement for the salesperson's efforts. Some firms spread commissions over several months or years to smooth out the pattern of payments and to ensure that salespeople continue to service their accounts after the initial sale. Spreading commissions over a period of time also discourages a salesperson from leaving the firm once a large sale has been made.

Limitations. The major drawback to salary plus commission plans is that they can be expensive and costly to administer. Annual compensation surveys consistently show that the average wages paid with a salary and commission program are higher relative to the other plans. What this suggests is that either salespeople are more motivated by these plans and sell more, or that commission rates are higher than they need to be. Firms that try to gain some control over the salary plus commission plan expense by imposing commission ceilings, however, could potentially dampen the enthusiasm and motivation of the sales force. In particular, the higher performers could reach the earning maximum early in the year and then take it easy for the remainder of the year.

Applications. Managers who use the salary plus commission plan tend to use the commission part of the plan to motivate certain salesperson behaviors during the year. It's the flexibility that is particularly appealing in industries where business fluctuates with seasonal or economic cycles. Industries that use salary plus commission plans are industrial firms selling building materials, machinery, electrical supplies, and paper products.

Salary Plus Commission Plus Bonus

The most comprehensive payment plans combine the stability of a salary, the incentives of a commission, and the special rewards of a bonus. Table 12-1 indicates that 18 percent of firms surveyed used this plan. A few years ago executives at FedEx Corporation, the shipping and logistics giant based in Memphis, Tennessee, realized they needed a new compensation plan for their sales organization. The sales force was constantly complaining that their current *salary plus commission plus bonus* plan wasn't paying out in a timely manner, and the unpredictability on commissions and bonuses was frustrating. Plus, FedEx needed to focus its salespeople on selling two new additional product lines instead of just one. An important goal of the plan was to make it simple enough so that the sales force understood exactly what levels they had to reach on all three products before they could attain certain bonus and commission levels. After the plan was introduced, FedEx quickly noticed a change in its salespeople. The complaining and negativity was quickly replaced by creative conversations about how to increase revenues on all three product lines. FedEx's sales and stock price quickly took off as a result. This example illustrates that salary plus commission plus bonus plans can be effective when they are simple to understand and consistent with corporate objects.[12]

Advantages. The primary benefit of these plans is they allow the sales manager to reward virtually every activity performed by salespeople. Experts indicate that the salary plus bonus plus commission plan will become more widely used in the future because sales managers will be looking to reward salespeople using a more comprehensive set of behaviors, rather than rewarding solely on revenue. Factors such as teamwork, customer satisfaction, company profits, and sales to certain customer types (e.g., distributors) are just some of the sophisticated mix of activities that reps can be measured against. This plan gives managers maximum flexibility for aligning compensation with these diverse activities. In addition, the three components of salary, commission, and bonus provide the possibility of designing a variety of different plans to appeal to different salesperson needs. According to David Cocks, managing partner of CompensationMaster, based in Charlotte, North Carolina, "When you give people options, you empower them to make work suit their style and the spot they are in within their careers."[13]

Limitations. Despite these advantages, salary plus commission plus bonus plans have some significant drawbacks. One of the major drawbacks with the plan is its complexity. A complex plan provides two challenges. First, administration of the plan becomes more expensive. Significantly more salesperson, sales manager, and human resource personnel time is needed for reporting and managing the different components. Second, complexity of the plan can be confusing to sales reps, as discussed in the FedEx example. As a result, reps might focus on activities that are less difficult to achieve (given their personal strengths) and ignore other important components of the plan. This could result in sales managers having to spend valuable time micro-managing some salespeople.

Applications. Industries such as office equipment, instruments, electronics, and business services tend to use these types of plans. However, as mentioned earlier, more and more companies from a variety of industries are adopting the salary plus commission plus bonus plan because of its flexibility.

Commission Plus Bonus

The *commission plus bonus* plan, although used by only 1 percent of the firms in Table 12-1, combines the incentives of a commission plus special rewards for meeting objectives.

Advantages. Similar to straight commission plans, commission plus bonus plans are easy to understand and are fairly simple to administer. These plans also provide similar cash flow benefits because commissions are paid at the time revenues are received, while the bonus is typically paid out at year end. However, these plans differ from straight commission plans in that the bonus feature provides some additional control over the salesperson's activities. Another unique benefit of the commission plus bonus plans is the added recruiting feature of the bonus package. For example, Logical, an international professional services and network integration company, uses its attractive year-end bonus to recruit the highest performing salespeople in the industry.[14]

Limitations. As with any compensation plan where 100 percent of a person's pay is at risk, there are a number of inherent limitations. While some were mentioned in the straight commission limitation section, other problems arise when the bonus component is added. For example, one limitation is the perceived equity of the year-end bonus. A typical high-performing salesperson could become frustrated and possibly quit when he or she sees another top salesperson receive a significantly larger year-end bonus. It becomes particularly difficult to retain these high producers when they attribute their smaller bonus to something outside of their control (e.g., a bad territory). Also, the recruiting advantage that the bonus package offers could become a liability if you lose your best salespeople to your competitors. Finally, salespeople could develop a mercenary attitude toward year-end to achieve the bonus, which, in turn, could affect customer relationships.

Applications. Commission plus bonus plans are particularly well suited to a company that uses brokers or independent sales reps. They are also widely employed for stockbrokers and bond traders. For example, the financial services industry typically pays its brokers commissions plus cash bonuses and memberships in recognition circles. These clubs reward recipients with trips and deferred compensation worth tens of thousands of dollars each year. To maintain their club membership, brokers must sell a predetermined number of financial products a year. However, trying the receipt of such perks to quotas on particular products doesn't appeal to every salesperson.

Companies are recognizing that compensation plans are more than just a way to pay salespeople for their services, they have become everything from a recruiting tool to a culture driver. Also, companies need to have a cutting-edge program, or risk losing top producers to the competition. It should be no surprise, then, that a recent survey reported approximately 80 percent of companies will change their compensation program from year to year.[15] Communicating the reasoning behind a new compensation plan and the amount that above-average, average, and below-average salespeople can expect to earn is vital to maintaining motivation and increasing acceptance of the new plan. Thus, how you introduce a new compensation plan could spell the difference between a successful or unsuccessful transition.

Customer Satisfaction and Sales Force Compensation

The concept of total quality management focuses on delivering high-quality products to clients and making sure customers are satisfied. However, linking a portion of sales force compensation with customer service is not easy. Part of the problem is that firms have trouble measuring customer satisfaction, and measurability is critical to the success of any incentive-based plan. There is also the possibility that salespeople will manipulate the data to gain an advantage. Despite these problems, there is a growing trend toward tying compensation to customer satisfaction.

One common procedure in tying compensation to buyer satisfaction is to ask buyers to complete customer satisfaction surveys. Companies that use surveys to measure satisfaction typically ask questions on sales force responsiveness and integrity, problem solving, after-sale service, and communication skills. This information is then used to modify some other sales force compensation factor or to calculate a percentage of base salary to award as a bonus. A typical firm assigns about 20 percent of total pay for achievements with customer satisfaction.

At JD Edwards, a global e-business solutions provider, 20 percent of a sales rep's earnings are based on the results of twice-yearly customer satisfaction surveys. Customers are asked questions about software product quality, employee integrity, and overall satisfaction. Salespeople must score at a certain level, from 1 to 10, to receive from 75 to 125 percent of their bonus. Don White, senior vice president for the company's U.S. field operations, says that at first, some sales reps were resistant to the new metric, feeling it was unfair that they would be judged based on things out of their control, such as software quality, but they soon came around. The salespeople are beginning to view their job as less transactional and more project management—doing anything internally that's necessary to make customers happy.[16]

Team-Selling Plans

Customer demands and an increasingly complex business environment are making team selling more common than ever before. In fact, we believe that effective team selling will be the critical determinant to a firm's competitive advantage in the future. Compensating sales teams to accommodate this trend, therefore, will become crucial to firm performance. In its simplest form, *team selling* involves two or more salespeople in separate territories who need to coordinate their activities to complete the sale. For example, the salespeople from different divisions of Maritz, Inc., a professional services firm, were not working together, which stalled growth. Realizing that their current compensation program did not reward a team approach, executives revised the plan so that reps and managers receive commission whether they cross-sell into another division or simply pass on a lead to another sales team. Salespeople now receive redemption points for the first part of the sale and potentially cash, depending on a seller's involvement in closing the deal. Maritz executives say that the different divisions now operate as a cohesive unit.[17] How would *you* deal with the compensation issues raised by the Team Exercise titled, "Incentives for Team Selling"?

A more complicated team-selling scenario has outside salespeople, technical specialists, service reps, and telemarketers all working together to make a sale. Because many firms are emphasizing organizational teamwork to improve sales and profits, compensation programs must be designed to reward other members of the selling team besides the outside salesperson. Since technical reps and service people are typically paid salaries, the usual approach is to share incentive payments with all members of the selling team. Thus, technical reps and service people on sales teams may be rewarded with small commissions but, more likely, group bonuses.

TEAM EXERCISE

"Incentives for Team Selling"

Team selling is becoming more common with technical products, and managers need to find ways to provide incentives for all members of the team. As a regional sales manager, you are assigned the task of developing an incentive program for the two-person teams selling your new software package. This program allows PCs to exchange a wide variety of information and requires considerable initial customer education. The sales teams include a salesperson and a systems engineer to help demonstrate the product, explain its technical details, answer queries, and seek out new applications of the software. How would you compensate the salesperson and the systems engineer? Would they both share in commissions equally? In developing your compensation plan, assume that the system engineers are more security conscious than the salespeople with regard to compensation.

Profit-Based Commissions

As mentioned earlier, the main objective of compensation programs is to provide direction to the sales force to achieve the business's objectives. Unfortunately, this is not an easy task due to the multifaceted nature of the sales job. In fact, research suggests that the greater the role stress (brought on by the many job demands), the lower the performance.[18] It is likely that some salespeople try to compensate for the stress associated with the different job demands by focusing on the products and services that are easiest to sell or carry the highest commissions. Also, when incentive payments are based on a percentage of the revenues each product generates, it is unlikely that a salesperson will sell the mix of items that lead to the highest profits. Thus, managers would do well to tie a salesperson's compensation to those job functions that maximize profits.[19]

One pay plan that ensures a sales force is working to achieve the highest profits possible is the *gross margin commission* plan. Under these plans, commissions are a percentage of the gross margins realized by the salesperson (i.e., sales price − cost of goods = gross margin). With a gross margin commission plan, the company and the salesperson share the same pool of money (realized gross margin); therefore, both are interested in maximizing this amount. Theoretically, when this occurs, the company makes more gross profit so that it can share the increased profitability with the sales force, and the sales reps earn more money. Medical supply and retail automobile salespeople are typically paid a percentage of the gross margin on each sale so that they will attempt to negotiate with customers to obtain the highest possible profit for their employer and themselves.

Gross margin plans have not been successful in all situations. A potential problem with gross margin plans is the implicit incentive to work on larger, lower gross margin orders, instead of smaller, more profitable sales. Certain-Teed Corporation, for example, tried paying its building materials salespeople a commission on gross margin but was forced to shift to a salary plus incentive program because the salespeople were bringing in too many low-margin orders. The problem arose because the salespeople viewed a 10 percent gross margin on a $1 million order as equivalent to a 20 percent gross margin on a $500,000 order (Table 12-2). On both orders, the company makes $100,000 in gross margin, and the salesperson collects $15,000 in commission. But if the selling time is similar, the salesperson is likely to work for the prestige of the $1 million order. However, the company may be better off with the $500,000 sale because the smaller order means lower inventory carrying costs and a reduced drain on raw materials and plant capacity. Perhaps a more appropriate plan would have been to pay commissions on a combination of gross margin and order size. The plan

TABLE 12-2 Comparing Gross Margin Commissions on Two Orders

Order Number	*Percentage Gross Margin on Each Order*	*Size of Order*	*Gross Margin to Company*	*Percentage Commission on Gross Margin*	*Commission Paid to Salesperson*
1	10	$1,000,000	$100,000	15	$15,000
2	20	$ 500,000	$100,000	15	$15,000

could have been designed to pay a lower commission rate when gross margin and the order size were smaller.

EXPENSE ACCOUNTS AND BENEFITS

No discussion of sales force compensation would be complete without mention of expense accounts and other benefits. Almost all firms that pay straight salaries or some combination of salary, commission, and/or bonus cover expenses for salespeople. Typical expenses paid by firms include those for automobiles and other travel, tips, lodging, food, samples, telephone, postage, and tickets for sporting and theater events. Annual expense budgets can run in the tens of thousands of dollars per salesperson per year. It is important, therefore, to have an effective system for reimbursing salespeople for their business expenses.

Expense Reimbursement Programs

Three types of expense plans can be used: (1) unlimited, (2) per diem, and (3) limited repayment.

Unlimited Plans. One type of expense reimbursement plan has salespeople submit itemized forms showing their expenditures, and the firm simply pays all reported expenses. This approach allows salespeople wide discretion on where they travel and how they entertain customers. In addition, an unlimited expense plan is inexpensive to administer because no one regularly spends time checking expense accounts to see if they are overstated.

Unlimited expense plans are often favored by small firms that don't want to bother auditing expense accounts. They are also used by companies that sell expensive products such as airplanes and defense systems, where extensive entertainment of clients is routine. The main problem with these plans is that some salespeople get too greedy and try to profit from their expense accounts. This forces management to occasionally fire reps who get out of line.

Per Diem Plans. A per diem expense plan pays the salesperson a fixed dollar amount for each day or week spent in the field. The amount is designed to cover food, gasoline, lodging, telephone calls, and other expenses. A major benefit of a per diem plan is that it is simple and inexpensive to supervise. However, salespeople may try to profit from the plan by spending less than the allowance, usually by cutting back on travel. Instead of driving to distant customers, salespeople could save money by concentrating on nearby prospects. Also, there is less incentive to entertain customers with a per diem plan than with an unlimited plan. These actions may keep salespeople under their expense allowance, but they may also cost the company sales revenues. Another problem is that per diem allocations have to be revised periodically to reflect inflation. Firms typically use per diem plans for routine reorder selling of standard items.

Limited Repayment Plans. With this approach the firm sets dollar limits on each category of sales expenses. For example, a firm might allow 48 cents a mile for travel, $8 for breakfast, $12 for lunch, $25 for dinner, and $90 for a room. These limits must reflect actual field experience, and they need to be adjusted frequently to reflect inflation. The objective of this plan is to make salespeople aware of what the company will pay and encourage them to control their expenses. The limited expense approach makes it easier to budget for sales costs and should reduce expense-account padding.

One problem with limited reimbursement plans is that salespeople may spend their valuable time juggling expenses from one category to another or from one time period to another to make sure they cover their costs. This time could be better spent solving customers' problems. Another potential drawback with limited repayment plans is that they may be expensive to monitor. One way to cut monitoring costs would be to keep track of a few experienced salespeople's actual expenses for one week a few times a year. The observed expenses would then be used to set repayment rates for all reps. This new plan would require minimal administrative overseeing costs and, at the same time, provide few reporting requirements for the salespeople, which gives more time to sell. Another alternative would be to "spot-check" expense reports by randomly selecting expense reports to be verified.

Selecting Benefits

Benefits can be used to attract and reward salespeople. One study found that salespeople prefer benefits to recognition and incentive awards.[20] Benefit packages include a variety of hospitalization, insurance, and pension plans, as shown in Table 12-3. The recent explosion in medical care costs has made it difficult for many firms to control the expenses of benefit packages. One approach has been to raise the medical deductible levels so that employees pay more of the costs. Another popular solution is to allocate a certain number of benefit dollars to each salesperson and let each one choose from a cafeteria line of possible benefits. This allows reps to select a benefit package that fits their individual needs.

You have to decide how much the salesperson should be required to contribute to the benefit program. If the salesperson is asked to pay a portion of the costs, the firm may give the person extra compensation to cover the contribution. However, this extra money is taxable and may even move the person into a higher income tax bracket. If the firm pays for these benefits directly so that salespeople receive the tax advantage, they may receive lower total wages than those offered by other firms, but they are ahead in the long run.

Another recent trend is the opportunity for salespeople to negotiate stock purchase plans and stock options. Companies are offering salespeople an opportunity to buy stock shares at discounts from market prices, or, better yet, match the investment dollar-for-dollar or more. Of course, market risk is always a factor, but if the company is not high-risk or of

TABLE 12-3 Benefits Offered by Companies

Benefit	*Percentage of Firms Offering*
Hospital costs	90%
Life insurance	77
Dental plan	69
Long-term disability	56
Pension plan	55
Short-term disability	49
Profit sharing	44
Thrift savings	22
Employees stock purchase plan	21

questionable health, such purchase accumulation can be quite lucrative. Stock option plans are more likely to be offered by ambitious, fast-growing companies, or those that have only recently—or are about to—become publicly owned. Because such companies rapidly chew up capital, they often prefer to offer mixed compensation packages of cash and stock purchase opportunities.

Expense accounts and benefit packages amount to a substantial portion of the costs of keeping a salesperson in the field. To some degree, cash wages, expense accounts, and benefits may be substitutes for one another, since they all provide rewards and incentives to salespeople. On the other hand, Maslow's hierarchy of needs theory would suggest that they address different needs.

ASSEMBLING THE PLAN

Sales managers are responsible for combining the various wage elements into an appropriate compensation plan and then predicting its effectiveness. At first glance, this task does not seem difficult, because there are only three *wage level* options. The firm can pay the average prevailing wage, pay a premium, or offer less than the going rate. A premium wage level is appealing because it may attract better salespeople and motivate them to sell high volumes. Paying higher than average wages makes it easier to recruit higher qualified people who can be promoted into managerial positions later on. However, overpaying salespeople could cause resentment and low morale among the firm's other employees and executives when salespeople earn more than even top management. It is also not clear that offering unlimited opportunities to earn higher pay is always an effective method for continual motivation to increase sales effort. The results of one study showed that most salespeople will work toward a "satisfactory" level of compensation rather than to maximize their pay.[21]

Sales managers can obtain guidelines about current pay levels by reviewing surveys published by the Dartnell Corporation, the Conference Board, and trade and industry associations. For example, Figure 12-3 shows the results for *Sales and Marketing Management* magazine's recent compensation survey for companies using combination (salary plus incentives) plans.[22] Note that the highest pay goes to top-performing sales representatives ($161,500) followed by sales managers ($147,800). Sales managers typically earn less than the top rep in their district when sales reps are on an incentive-based plan. Note that having positions such as a key account rep in the middle of the compensation range ($94,800) provides incentives for others, such as trainees and telesales reps to move up the compensation

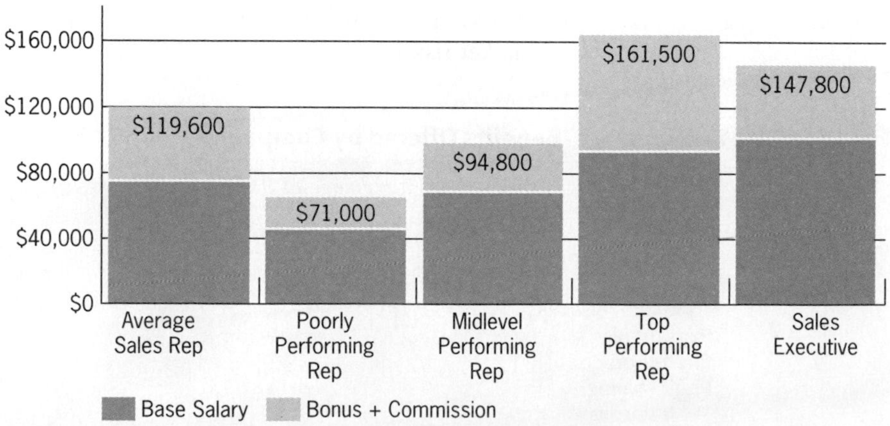

FIGURE 12-3 Compensation Levels for Firms Using Salary Plus Incentives

ladder. Although sales trainees start with a lower base salary than more experienced reps, they are often provided an opportunity to earn commissions or a bonus. In addition, new sales reps are often given a car and an expense account.

To determine a relevant average wage level, another good starting point is to determine the average compensation paid by other firms of the same size in your industry. Other considerations might be the labor market where people are entering and leaving. Assume that comparable firms are paying their first-year salespeople an average annual total compensation of $52,000. The sales manager must now split this total into salary, commissions, and a bonus. Based on an analysis of the sales job to be performed, the breakdown might be $38,000 for salary, $10,000 for commissions, and $4,000 for a bonus. The monthly salary of $3,167 provides stability of income and amounts to 73 percent of the wage package. For this company the commission rates could be set to vary from 1 to 4 percent of sales, depending on the profitability of the various products in the line and the source of the business. The following breakdown shows how the commission portion of the wage would be calculated:

Commission Rate	*Type and Source of Business*	*Sales Achieved*	*Commission Amount*
0.01	Reorders of supplies	$100,000	$ 1,000
0.02	New equipment sales	250,000	5,000
0.04	Sales to new accounts	100,000	4,000
Totals		$450,000	$10,000

Note that the compensation plan pays a fairly low commission rate of 1 percent on reorders of supplies that carry low profit margins. However, a 2 percent commission is paid on sales of the more profitable new equipment. Also, a 4 percent commission is paid on all sales to new accounts to encourage sales force prospecting.

The bonus portion of the plan is set up to pay 8.3 percent of salary and commissions to salespeople who exceed their annual quota for sales achieved. Assuming the salesperson met this quota, the bonus payment would be 8.3 percent of $48,000 ($38,000 in salary + $10,000 in commissions), or $4,000. The actual payment of the $4,000 bonus would be delayed until the end of the year. The total compensation for the salesperson in this case amounts to $52,000, which is about the average total compensation for a beginning sales representative. The following list shows the addition of a car, other expenses, and benefits to the compensation program:

$38,000	Salary
10,000	Commission (1 to 4 percent of sales)
4,000	Bonus (8.3 percent of salary and commissions for exceeding new account quota)
7,500	Benefits
12,000	Car expense (25,000 miles at 48 cents per mile)
20,000	Lodging, food, and entertainment
87,200	Total costs per salesperson

Although car expenses and payments for lodging, food, and entertainment are not part of real wages for salespeople, these expenditures do represent a growing proportion of the cost of keeping a salesperson in the field. Thus, as the price of lodging and entertainment increases, sales managers may have less money available for cash wages. Although a current car expense of $12,000 seems high, this figure represents only 125 miles a day for a person who is on the road 200 days a year. Also, $20,000 a year for food and lodging seems adequate, but it amounts to only $100 a day for salespeople who are on the road four days a week. Unless sales managers can find ways to control escalating entertainment and travel expenses or increase sales volume or profits, they will have trouble keeping cash wages competitive.

EVALUATING THE PLAN

After you have selected an appropriate compensation method and wage level, the plan must be evaluated to see how it will affect salespeople's wages and total costs. This evaluation usually involves taking sales figures from the previous year and calculating expected wages for a group of salespeople under the new program. These calculations are greatly simplified if you have an automated computer program. Your objective is to see how above- and below-average salespeople would fare under the new system. You want to avoid having salespeople reap windfall gains or suffer from unfairly low earnings. Caution should be used when introducing new compensation programs that pay lower wages than the current plan, because this often produces resistance among salespeople and can lead to higher turnover. In some situations, however, turnover may be welcome. Why?

SUMMARY

Compensation is one of the key factors in motivating salespeople to achieve the sales and profit objectives of the firm. However, the spiraling costs of compensating a sales force have made it increasingly important to be able to design a plan that encourages salespeople to work efficiently. After reading this chapter, you should be able to:

1. **Explain the need to balance wages against company resources.** Compensation plans should allow salespeople to reach their own income goals without overstocking customers or ignoring nonselling duties. However, it is difficult to design a compensation program that motivates salespeople to reach company goals and satisfy customers without bankrupting the firm. The Customer-Product Matrix is a useful tool for conceptualizing a compensation plan that matches company objectives with the desired sales job. Sales positions that focus primarily on new business development require a greater proportion of incentive (e.g., commissions and bonus) in the compensation plan than account management sales jobs. Account management-type sales jobs involve a greater account servicing component, which is better suited to a larger component of salary compensation.
2. **Describe the various compensation methods.** Straight salary plans and straight commission plans represent two extremes in compensating salespeople. Straight commission plans offer maximum incentives for performance, but little control over sales force activities. The opposite is true for straight-salary plans. The limitations of both plans have made combination plans the most popular with sales organizations. The combination compensation plans discussed are: salary plus bonus, salary plus commission, salary plus commission plus bonus, and commission plus bonus. It is important that sales managers learn to combine salary, commissions, bonuses, and benefits so that both salespeople and the company benefit.
3. **Set pay levels.** Beyond the issue of what plan to use is the question of how much to pay. To determine the appropriate level of wages to pay salespeople, a sales manager could start with an analysis of competitors' compensation packages. The availability of qualified people in a particular labor market is also a consideration. Field sales reps are sometimes highly paid, and it is the job of the sales manager to balance constantly the costs against the benefits received for sales force expenditures.
4. **Assemble a compensation plan.** When properly conceived and implemented, a pay plan should offer a balance of control and incentive. Important considerations in obtaining such a balance include determining an expense reimbursement program, selecting a level

of benefits to be offered, and evaluating the plan to see how it will affect salespeople's wages and total cost.

KEY TERMS

Benefits
Commission plus bonus
Commission threshold
Fixed cost
Gross margin commissions
Progressive commission rates
Salary plus bonus
Salary plus commission
Salary plus commission plus bonus
Straight commission
Straight salary
Team selling
Wage level

DEVELOPING YOUR COMPETENCIES

1. **Strategic Action.** Assume you are a national sales manager for a large manufacturer of interconnectivity products for the Internet. The sales force is paid on a salary plus bonus arrangement. Currently, salespeople can earn up to 35 percent of their salary in annual bonus once they achieve their yearly sales quota. The current economic situation is very favorable to salespeople at your firm. You expect salespeople to easily exceed quota and earn a large bonus. The total average salesperson compensation next year, in your estimation, will be greater than your competitors'. As a result, you are considering changing the compensation package because of the expected windfall earnings that you believe your salespeople will make. Your plan is to increase quota by 20 percent and cut the annual bonus to a maximum of 20 percent of salary. A few weeks prior to announcing your new compensation plan to the sales force, you overhear the following conversation between two of your salespeople:

   GEORGE: I'm looking forward to this year. I've really struggled the past two years to make only 80 percent of my quota. It's about time we get a break around here.

   LIZ: I agree. If it wasn't for some unbelievable last-minute luck, I wouldn't have made quota last year either. I made it by the skin of my teeth.

   GEORGE: I was thinking about leaving the company if things didn't change and I came up short again. The salary is good enough to make ends meet, but when I get into the third quarter of the year, I realize I will not make quota and I just give up trying. What's the point?

   LIZ The company gives us a very attractive incentive program, but they set quota so high that it's nearly impossible to achieve it. I agree with you, George, this year is going to be different.

   Should you take into consideration this new information? What do you think needs to be done, if anything, about your plans for introducing the new compensation program?
2. **Team Building.** Designing compensation plans for team selling when the sales cycle is long and complicated is a difficult task. One consultant suggests dividing the selling job into parts, such as identifying the lead, qualifying the prospect, performing technical assistance, writing the proposal, and closing the sale. Then if a 20 percent commission was being paid, 4 percent would be allocated to team members who performed each of these tasks. If some tasks are more important than others, the 4 percent allocations could be changed to reflect these differences. What are the advantages and disadvantages of this system?
3. **Global Perspective.** As discussed in previous chapters, culture has a powerful influence on an individual's values. A recent study of salesperson reward valences in the *Journal of*

Personal Selling and Sales Management suggests that Chinese salespeople and their Hong Kong counterparts value rewards differently. The study reported that Chinese salespeople attached the highest importance to managerial encouragement and support, followed by recognition for high performers, work-related factors, and finally individual incentives. Hong Kong salespeople, on the other hand, considered opportunities for career growth to be the most important factor, followed by incentives, support functions, and quotas. Assume you are the new international sales director for a multinational company with sales forces made up of both Hong Kong and Chinese salespeople. Using this new information, what would you do to design different compensation systems for each?

4. **Self-Management.** Different types of compensation plans fit different types of people. Northwestern Mutual Life is a marketer of permanent and term life insurance, disability income insurance, and annuity plans for the personal, business, estate planning, and pension markets. Northwestern's sales agents typically work on 100 percent commission. Visit Northwestern Mutual Life's home page at www.northwesternmutual.com. Once on the home page, click the link "Financial Representative" under the "Careers" tab and explore the information about what Northwestern considers important traits for success. You can even take the on-line sales aptitude test (click on the "Take the first step" tab) to see if you meet Northwestern's requirements to succeed. Would you like to work in this type of entrepreneurial culture? Why or why not?
5. **Technology.** Equity theory introduces the perception of fairness into sales force motivation and should be considered in the design and implementation of sales force compensation and reward plans. One concern regarding the equity of compensation stems from the fact that the cost of living varies from one location to another. Most compensation programs take these differences into consideration, and the calculation of these differences has been made much easier through the use of the Home Buyer's Fair site on the World Wide Web. One of the many popular features of this Web site is its section that calculates the difference in the cost of living between virtually any two cities in North America.

   As the national sales manager for the Big Cyclone Paper Company, headquartered in Kansas City, Kansas, you are designing a compensation system that will take into consideration the different cost-of-living figures for your regional dealer account managers in ten cities across the United States: (1) Kansas City, Kansas; (2) Peoria, Illinois; (3) Louisville, Kentucky; (4) Denver, Colorado; (5) Dallas, Texas; (6) Los Angeles, California; (7) Rochester, New York; (8) Orlando, Florida; (9) Atlanta, Georgia; and (10) Cincinnati, Ohio.

   As designed, your compensation plan is a hybrid system incorporating a mixture of fixed salary plus commission and incentive bonuses. The cost-of-living adjustments will be made through changes in the fixed salary component of the plan. That is, a base salary of $30,000 paid to salespeople in other locations will be increased (or decreased) according to the specific location's cost of living as compared to the Kansas City base figure. In this manner, all salespeople will be on an adjusted base salary equivalent to the $30,000 Kansas City figure.

   Access the Home Buyer's Fair World Wide site at http://www.homefair.com and click on "The Salary Calculator" located on the left column. Determine the fixed salary for each of the locations that would be equivalent to the $30,000 base salary in Kansas City, Kansas:

Kansas City, KS	$30,000	Los Angeles, CA	______
Peoria, IL	______	Rochester, NY	______
Louisville, KY	______	Orlando, FL	______
Denver, CO	______	Atlanta, GA	______
Dallas, TX	______	Cincinnati, OH	______

6. **Coaching.** As regional sales manager, you have to make salary recommendations for six district sales managers whom you supervise. They have just completed their annual appraisal period and are now to be considered for their annual raise. Your company has set aside 10 percent of salary costs for merit increases. Your total current annual salary cost is $297,300, which means that you have $29,730 for salary increases. There are no formal company restrictions on how you may distribute the 10 percent merit increase. All managers have the same job classification, and the salary recommendations are secret. Using the profiles below, indicate the size of the raise that you would like to give each sales manager.

Sales Manager Profile Sheet

- *John Smith* Age 30, three children, current annual salary $59,000, MBA, Harvard. John is married to the daughter of the chairman of the board and has been with the company five years, the last two as sales manager. He has one of the easiest groups to supervise, doesn't impress you as being very bright, but is a hard worker. You rated him as "slightly above average" (68 percent) on his last performance rating. You checked your opinion with others you respect; they, too, felt that he was less effective than other managers who work for you, but they reminded you of his potential influence.
- *Larry Foster* Age 27, single, current annual salary $38,300, BA, University of Maine. Larry has been with the company for four years, the last two as sales manager. He has a difficult group to supervise, is bright, often works overtime, and has "turned around" the group he supervises. You rated him as "an excellent manager with a good future" (89 percent) on his last performance rating.
- *Tim Hall* Age 44, four children, two in college, current annual salary $60,000 (three years of college, no degree). Tim has worked for the company for the past eighteen years and has been in his current position for the past eight years. He is unhappy that you were named regional sales manager because he was hoping to get the job. He is well liked by all the other managers and by his employees. He rarely works on weekends, and he seems to be easygoing with his salespeople. However, his group had the second highest performance of the groups you manage. You rated him as outstanding (85 percent) on his last performance appraisal.
- *Ellen Panza* Age 30, married, two children, current annual salary $45,000, BA, City University of New York. Ellen has been with the company for two years and worked as sales analyst for the one year before being promoted to manager. You feel that she was given the job because she is a woman, and frankly, you resent it. In addition, you feel that her salary is too high compared with the salaries of others in the company. However, you must admit that she has performed in an outstanding manner, since her group went from last to first place in performance this year. Her score on the rating sheet was 90 percent.
- *Otto Lechman* Age 36, married (wife works for the company as assistant personnel director), no children, current salary $55,000, MBA, University of Michigan. Otto has been with the company for nine years, the past six as manager. He is aggressive and hot-tempered, and though at one time you thought he was your best employee, during the past two years, you have found him to be a disappointment. You rated him as "slightly below average" (59 percent) on his last performance rating. You believe that one of the reasons Otto's performance has fallen off is that he has found out about John Smith's and Ellen Panza's salaries.
- *David L. Green III* Age 29, single, current annual salary $40,000, BA, Wayne State University. David has been with the company for six years and became the first black manager in your company five years ago. He has been instrumental in recruiting other blacks into the company and is often called on by the president to represent the company at civic and social events. You have found David's work to be marginal, and although you assigned him to manage the best group five years ago, the group's

performance is not as high now. Based on the drop in performance, you rated David as "below average" (60 percent). Some people would like to get rid of him, but you don't know how you would replace him, given his past success in recruiting minorities.

Your company has a secret pay policy. What information do you plan to share with your employees? What was your decision rule for administering the pay increases?

FEATURED CASE SHIELD FINANCIAL: "THE ELUSIVE COMMISSION–NOW YOU SEE IT, NOW YOU DON'T"

Doug Bloom, the branch sales manager of Shield Financial in Des Moines, is appalled. The district director, Liz Shute, again adjusted one of his sales rep's commissions. When the rep, Nancy Carr, finds out, she'll certainly quit.

Since the introduction of the First-Plus program at Shield, the reps' compensation has changed in accordance with the company CEO's new policy. Now 70 percent of the commission would be based on a sales quota and 30 percent on each sales rep's numbers from the First-Plus activities. Lately, however, on several occasions, once the sale was made, Shute decided that it didn't warrant the original commission and lowered it by whatever she felt was appropriate. In this case, she decreased the commission by $8,000.

Bloom did his best, as usual, to keep the commission as promised, but once Shute's mind is made up, that is that. She feels that the handsome base salary and benefits package are more than enough to compensate for any discrepancies in commissions.

When Bloom tells Carr about the commission change, Carr's response is as Bloom expected: Get my $8,000 back or today's my last day.

Bloom doesn't want to lose one of his top performers.

Questions

1. What could he do to broker a compromise between Shute and Carr?
2. It is obvious that Bloom should try to change Shute's mind about sticking to one standardized commission program. What would you recommend he do?

PROBLEMS*

1. You were recently hired as the new vice president of sales because something needs to be done to increase sales growth—sales have been flat the past two years. You are convinced that the sales force could turn things around for you, if only you could motivate your salespeople. One of your ideas is to change the compensation plan for next year. However, you don't want to "break the bank" in the process.

   Your marketing manager has developed three different compensation plans for your review. Which of these will be the most expensive? Which will be the least expensive? Which plan would you adopt for your sales staff? Why?

   Plan A: Give each salesperson a salary of $40,000. Once a salesperson reaches a sales volume of $400,000 during the year, an incentive bonus of 8 percent of all sales made during the year will be awarded. No bonus will be awarded for annual sales volumes of under $400,000.

*Contributed by Avery Abernethy, Auburn University. Excel spreadsheet templates for these problems are available at www.wiley.com/college/cron. Go to the "Student" companion site.

Plan B: Give each salesperson a salary of $30,000 plus an 8 percent commission on all sales made during the year.

Plan C: Give each salesperson a commission of 15 percent on the first $420,000 of sales made each year and 25 percent commission on all sales made over $420,000.

Below are the forecasted sales for next year. An Excel spreadsheet is available to help you in your analysis (the spreadsheet can be found at www.wiley.com/college/cron).

Salesperson	*Forecasted Sales for Next Year*
Jagger	$ 550,000
Costello	$ 520,000
Keith	$ 500,000
McCartney	$ 475,000
Dylan	$ 450,000
Timberlake	$ 420,000
Clarkson	$ 420,000
Lovett	$ 400,000
Richards	$ 400,000
Cash	$ 360,000
Total	$4,495,000

2. You own the Mayer Electrical Distribution Company, and your goal is to maximize your before-tax profits. You currently pay salespeople a base salary and a flat 4 percent commission on sales. You sell three products. Following this question is an Excel spreadsheet printout titled "Current Situation" that gives the starting information.

Unit Costs do not include sales commission costs. You have 10 salespeople. You pay them $30,000 salary and $10,000 benefits each. This gives you $400,000 fixed sales costs. You have annual fixed costs of $1,400,000 (including fixed sales costs).

Unfortunately, your firm keeps losing the best salespeople. You are considering several options to retain your best salespeople. (1) Increase the commission to 6 percent or (2) alter the commission structure to reflect the profitability of each product. You think that if the total compensation plan is increased for the sales force your sales will increase 10 percent next year due to retaining the best people and increased motivation. Without this increase in sales compensation, you think that sales will increase 4 percent.

You might want to look at the potential financial impact of (a) doing nothing, (b) increasing the commission from a flat 4 percent to a flat 6 percent, or (c) increasing the commissions in a manner that reflects the profitability of each product.

1. What was your total profit before taxes this year?
2. What is your expected total profit before taxes next year if the sales force payment plan remains the same (and sales increase 4 percent)?
3. What is your expected total profit before taxes next year if you increase commissions to 6 percent?
4. If you raise your commissions to 6 percent, sales are expected to increase next year by 10 percent instead of 6 percent. Is this a reasonable expectation? What is the percentage increase in before-tax profit next year for a 6-percent commission compared to a 4 percent commission?
5. What were your unit contributions this year for products 1, 2, and 3?
6. Since your goal is to maximize before-tax profits next year, specifically how should you increase the commission structure to retain your best salespeople? Be sure to explain your answer.

A quick way to complete this exercise is to copy the first spreadsheet and then adjust the copied tables for the new information given above. Note that you will have to change the formulas in the cells titled "Commissions per Unit" and "Sales Commissions" to reflect the new adjustment on the commission increase. For example, to change the commission increase to 6 percent, you just multiply the unit sales by the new increase and change the sales commission percentage. Also, remember to change the units sold formula. The program automatically recomputes all of the other calculations.

EVALUATING PERFORMANCE

> You can't manage what you can't measure.
>
> William Hewlett, co-founder of Hewlett-Packard

Chapter Consultant:
Bob Braasch, Manager Sales Planning, SABRE

LEARNING OBJECTIVES

After studying this chapter, you should be able to:

- Conduct a sales force performance review.
- Describe the criteria used to evaluate salespeople.
- Distinguish between input and output measures of sales performance.
- Discuss the value of behavioral control procedures for salespeople.
- Understand outcome-based evaluation procedures.
- Describe the evaluation models that use both input and output data.

SALES PERFORMANCE REVIEW

At first glance, evaluating a salesperson's performance seems simple: Merely measure sales volume. The thinking behind this theory is that higher volume means increased performance. But the focus on sales volume can be misleading. Consider the following scenario: You are a first-line sales manager for Bear Computer Company, which is a startup computer solutions provider for manufacturers. Because of the unique nature of each customer's solution needs, Bear relies on its field sales force as its primary go-to-market strategy. In other words, salesperson performance is crucial for the young firm's survival. Recently, Brett Williams, Bear's President asked you: "How's your branch been doing?" You reply, "We've been doing great!" Brett follows up with the question: "What do you mean by 'great'?" You quickly respond: "Last year was a tough year for everyone, but our branch made our performance goal. That makes it three years in a row for us."

Does three years of goal attainment make a sales team "great"? One salesperson may generate a high sales volume made up of low profit items. Another may have a high volume with a few customers but make too few calls. Still another high-volume salesperson may spend too much time and money on each call. The point is that a higher volume may not represent a higher level of profit for a business. Properly evaluating sales personnel requires a look at many factors that influence their value to the company.

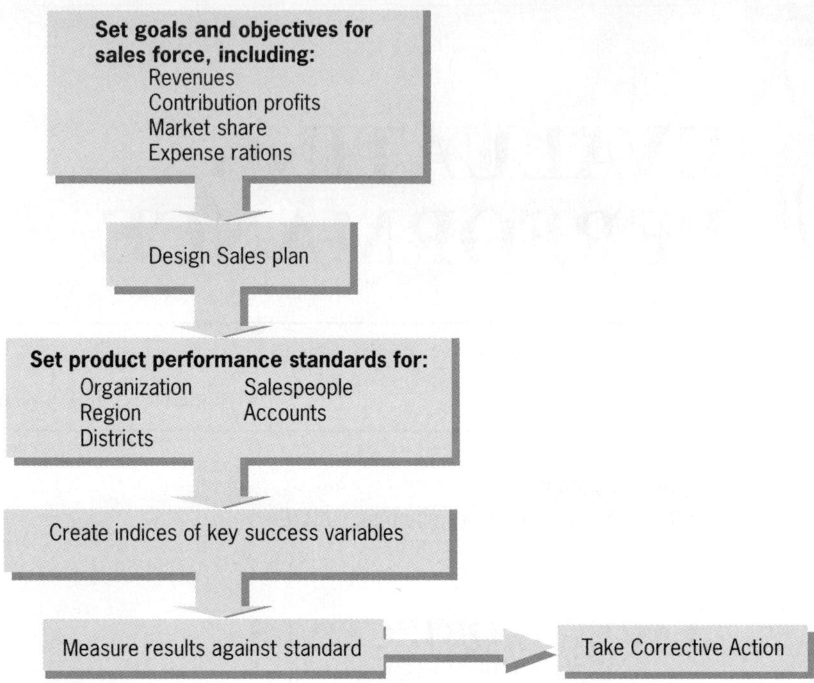

FIGURE 13-1 A Sales Force Evaluation Model

We define *evaluation* as a comparison of sales force goals and objectives with actual achievements in the field. A general model of the evaluation process is shown in Figure 13-1. To begin the evaluation process, management must first decide what it wants the sales force to accomplish. The most common objectives are the attainment of specific sales revenues, contribution profits, market shares, and expense levels. Then, a sales plan must be prepared to show how the goals are to be achieved. The next step is to set performance standards for individual products for different levels in the organization. This typically requires setting goals for total sales, as well as sales by regions, by product, by salesperson, and for each separate account.

Once the sales goals are established, the key indicators of success need to be established. These indicators are the specific measures used to evaluate performance. Care should be taken to make sure these key metrics are aligned with overall firm goals and strategies.[1] For example, the metrics of successful salesperson performance for a prospector strategy where a firm is looking to increase market share will be very different than those of a defender strategy where the firm is looking to retain its market share. Firms with a prospector strategy compete by identifying and taking advantage of emerging marketplace opportunities. Salesperson success for these firms would likely center around indices such as sales growth and the number of new customers attained. Defender firms seek to achieve operational efficiencies and tend to serve stable market segments with a standard set of offerings. These firms are likely to rely morc heavily on contribution margins and expense ratios as important salesperson success indices.[2]

At the conclusion of an evaluation period, differences between the performance standards and the results attained are determined. In this comparison between actual results with budgeted performance goals, a manager will need to determine the specific factors that accounted for the variance in overall performance. Understanding the underlying causes for the above- and below-standard performance for each factor is a critical step in this process.

Once the reasons for the performance variance are understood, then corrective action is taken and modifications are made in the plans for the future.

The sales force evaluation model provides an overview of the steps necessary to fairly and objectively evaluate performance. The remainder of this chapter will explore each of these steps in more depth. We begin our discussion of sales force evaluation by looking at the big picture. In this regard, we focus on the process companies use to understand sales force performance at the organizational level. A good starting point is an examination of *total sales volume*, which is the combined sales of all products and all customers from all salespeople in the firm. To illustrate how to conduct this type of evaluation, we will continue with the Bear Computer Company example introduced in the opening vignette. Next, we provide an overview of how to use sales force expenses in analyzing performance. In this section, we highlight the impact of salesperson efficiency on firm profits. Following our sales force expense and efficiency discussion, we turn to evaluating individual salesperson performance and provide specific methods for creating key success factors. We conclude the chapter with a review of four different sales evaluation models for measuring results against objectives and offer some "best practices" tips for effective sales force evaluation systems.

THE BIG PICTURE

To determine whether a company or division has met its sales goals, the first step is to examine the aggregate sales figures. Some sample sales figures for the Bear Computer Company are provided in Table 13-1. Bear seems to be doing well; sales have increased from $17 million to $26 million in only four years, or 18 percent annually. However, the rate of growth is declining. For some reason, Bear has been unable to maintain the sales increases that it achieved in earlier years. One excuse for such a situation is that slow growth simply reflects general economic conditions. However, industry sales have been expanding rapidly at the same time that Bear's sales gains have fallen off. The resulting impact on market share is shown in column 4. Bear's market position fell from 13.6 percent in 2005 to only 8.6 percent in 2008. Thus, although Bear's sales increased 53 percent, its market share took a disastrous plunge. A sales increase, like the tip of the iceberg, tells only part of the story. The *iceberg principle* encourages managers to search through their data to find out what is really going on.

There could be many reasons for the 37-percent drop in market share at Bear Computer. Competitors may simply be more aggressive and may have attracted the new business from Bear. Another possibility is that the product itself may be deficient in terms of performance or reliability. Because personal selling is the primary method of selling business networking computer solutions, it is a potential problem area. Bear may not have enough salespeople or sales offices, or the sales force may not be calling on the right prospects.

TABLE 13-1 Sales Data for Bear Computer Company

Year	1 *Company Volume ($ millions)*	2 *Percentage Change from Previous Year*	3 *Industry Volume ($ millions)*	4 *Company Market Share (percent)*
2008	26	+8.3	300	8.6
2007	24	+14.3	219	10.9
2006	21	+23.5	165	15.7
2005	17	–	125	13.6

TABLE 13-2 Comparing Dollar and Unit Sales at the Bear Computer Company

	2007			2008		
Products	*Thousands of Dollars*	*Units*	*Avg Price Per Unit*	*Thousands of Dollars*	*Units*	*Avg Price Per Unit*
Computer Solutions	$16,800	560	$30,000	$18,200	520	$35,000
Accessories	4,800	4,000	1,200	5,200	4,727	1,100
Software	2,400	1,200	2,000	2,600	1,280	2,031
Total	$24,000	5,760		$26,000	6,527	

Dollar Versus Unit Sales

Sales can also be broken out in terms of number of solutions sold (Table 13-2). Unit sales can be useful when inflation and other price changes distort dollar sales figures. For example, dollar sales of Bear computer solutions went from $16.8 million in 2007 to $18.2 million in 2008. However, unit sales actually declined from 560 to 520 over the same period, meaning that the average price of a Bear solution went from $30,000 in 2007 to $35,000 in 2008. Although some of the 17 percent increase in computer prices was due to inflation, some other factor is contributing to this change. The data suggest that the sales force is trading customers up to more expensive solutions. Further breakdown of sales by individual installations would tell you what items are being ignored.

A decline in the number of units installed is a serious problem in an expanding market, so adjustments should be made in the wage and quota systems to achieve more balanced growth. Unit sales growth is desirable because it keeps production lines and employees busy.

A somewhat different situation exists with Bear's line of accessory equipment (Table 13-2). Note that both dollar and unit sales increased between 2007 and 2008. However, unit sales grew much more rapidly than dollar sales, and the average unit price dropped from $1,200 in 2007 to $1,100 in 2008. These results suggest that the sales force may be cutting prices to boost unit volume. This push for market share is to be applauded as long as profit margins are not completely destroyed. Bear's software product line also experienced growth in dollar and unit sales. In this case, the sales force was able to sell more units at higher average prices. These efforts are commendable, but Bear's software sales are still far below the levels suggested by industry and company potential figures.

Sales by Customer Type

Another useful approach is to break down sales by individual customers. These reviews often show that you obtain a high percentage of sales from a small-number of customers. When 80 percent of your sales come from only 20 percent of your buyers, you are probably losing money serving small accounts. Some sales managers use the *80–20 principle* to shift low-volume accounts to mail-order, telephone reorder systems, or the Internet. Other firms give small accounts to independent distributors so that the regular sales force can concentrate their efforts on a reduced number of large accounts. Frequently, a policy of providing extra service to large accounts leads to greater total sales for the firm.

EXPENSE ANALYSIS

Although a sales analysis provides useful data on the operation of a field sales force, it does not tell the whole story. Sales figures show trends, but they do not reveal the effects of price-cutting or the differences in selling expenses, potential, and saturation that exist across

TABLE 13-3 Expense Analysis by Product Line, Bear Computer Company, 2008

Products	*2008 Sales (000)*	*CGS and Commission $*	*CGS as a Percentage of Sales*	*Contribution Margin*	*Contribution Margin Percentage*
Computers	$18,200	$12,740	70	$5,460	30
Accessories	5,200	3,120	60	2,080	40
Software	2,600	520	20	2,080	80
Total	$26,000	$16,380	63%	$9,620	37%

products or territories. A more complete picture of sales force efficiency can be obtained by reviewing expense data to show the effects of changes in selling tactics on the profitability of the firm.

What Expenses Are Relevant?

We believe that controllable expenses such as wages and travel are the figures that are relevant to field sales managers. Thus, national advertising and production costs, which are not directly controlled by sales managers, should not be used to judge the efficiency of the sales organization. Of course, cost-of-goods-sold figures are necessary to help measure price-cutting by salespeople.

Product Expenses

A logical first step in an expense analysis is to look at the differences associated with each product line. Table 13-3 shows such an analysis for the Bear Computer Company. Note that the cost-of-goods-sold plus commissions is considerably higher for computer solutions (70 percent) than it is for accessories (60 percent) and software (20 percent). These results can be explained in several ways. One possibility is that Bear is paying too much for parts, with the result that its manufacturing costs are simply higher than those of competitors. Another explanation is that competition has driven down selling prices in the market and raised Bear's cost-of-goods sold as a percentage of sales. A more disturbing possibility is that salespeople are cutting prices to close sales so that they can raise their commission income. If this is the case, then the sales manager may need to place limits on the sales force's authority to negotiate prices. The sales manager could also shift to a gross margin commission system so that there would be less incentive to cut prices. A third approach is to revise the commission structure so that salespeople can earn more by pushing the higher margin accessories and software lines. This discussion shows that a review of the contribution margins produced by different product lines can be very helpful for sales managers.

EVALUATING SALESPEOPLE

One of the most difficult tasks you will face as a sales manager is evaluating the performance of salespeople under your control. Although appraisals are opportunities to motivate salespeople to higher levels of achievement, they also provide evidence for disciplinary action. Thus, performance reviews demand that sales managers play the role of coach and judge. Some experts believe that salesperson evaluation is the single most difficult job of the sales manager because of the difficulty of finding the optimal level of monitoring and the difficulty of eliminating biases in the evaluation process.[3] For example, studies suggest that sales managers may provide inconsistent disciplinary action based on the salesperson's gender and weight.[4]

TEAM EXERCISE
"Evaluating for Profit"

As the new vice president of sales for Beta Corporation, you spent your first month traveling to visit clients with your new sales team. Unfortunately, you don't like what you've seen. You quickly discovered that discounting is the number one way your salespeople close deals. Since a key component of your job at Beta is to increase the company's profitability, you had to stop the price cutting. How would you structure an evaluation system that would help in this effort?

Why Are Performance Reviews Needed?

Performance reviews are usually conducted on an annual basis, although many firms conduct evaluations semiannually or quarterly. While these reviews are difficult to administer, they do provide valuable information for staffing decisions and serve as a basis to improve salesperson performance. The results of performance reviews can be used to answer a number of important questions such as:

- Who should receive raises, bonuses, and prizes?
- Who should be promoted?
- What criteria should be used in hiring?
- Who needs retraining?
- What subjects should be emphasized in training classes?
- Have the company's strategic selling objectives been met?
- How should sales territories be adjusted?
- Who should be terminated?

Each of these decisions requires you to look at a slightly different set of evaluative criteria. For example, performance evaluations used for determining raises, bonuses, and prizes should emphasize activities and results related to the salesperson's current job and situation. Performance evaluations used for the purpose of promoting a salesperson into a sales management position should focus on criteria related to successful sales managers and not just current salesperson performance. Adding to the complexity of the evaluation process is the wide variety of procedures to measure how well salespeople are performing on each dimension. If you were the new vice president of sales at Beta Corporation in the team exercise "Evaluating for Profit," how would you restructure the evaluation system?

Selecting Performance Measures

The task of selecting a set of sales performance measures for a firm is difficult because each unique sales environment can have its own set of evaluation criteria. The basis for any salesperson evaluation, however, is typically comprised of one of the following: outcome controls, behavior controls, or qualitative measures. When using *outcome controls*, managers set performance standards for each salesperson and evaluate the results against the preset standards. Examples of outcome controls are shown in Table 13-4 and include sales, orders, contributions to profit, number of accounts, and so forth. Companies tend to emphasize and track only a few of these results however. Firms with outcome systems typically tie salespeople's compensation closely to two or three key metrics.

Behavior control systems are concerned with keeping track of what happens at each stage of the sales process. Under behavior control, managers measure what the salesperson

TABLE 13-4 Outcome Controls Used in Sales Force Evaluation

Sales	*Profit*
Sales volume dollars	Net profit
Sales volume previous year's growth	Gross margin percentage
Sales to quota	Return on investment
Sales growth	Net profit as a percentage of sales
Sales volume by product	Gross margin dollars
Sales volume by customer	Margin by product category
New account sales	*Accounts*
Sales volume in units	Number of new accounts
Sales volume to potential (market share)	Number of accounts lost
Orders	Number of accounts sold
Number of orders	Number of accounts buying full line
Average order size	
Batting average (orders/calls)	

actually does—prospecting activities, number of sales calls made, number of hours worked, for example. Table 13-5 provides examples of the most frequently used behavior controls. As shown in Table 13-6 *qualitative measures* include attitude, communication skills, product knowledge, among others. Typically, a manager provides a subjective evaluation of the salesperson's performance on each dimension. These indicators are widely used, but are difficult to measure accurately and can often lead to biased evaluations. In addition, they tend to be deemphasized as the managers' span of control increases.

TABLE 13-5 Behavior Controls Used in Sales Force Evaluation

Expenses	*Effort*
Total expenses	Number of calls
Selling expenses to budget	Number of calls per day
Selling expenses as a percentage of sales	Number of calls to quota
Nonselling Activities	Number of days worked
Advertising displays set up	Number of reports turned in
Number of service calls	Number of prospecting phone calls
Number of customer complaints	Selling time vs. nonselling time

TABLE 13-6 Qualitative Bases Used in Sales Force Evaluation

Attitudinal and Personality Factors	*Time Management*
Attitude	*Ability to Plan*
Enthusiasm	*Appearance and Manner*
Cooperation	*Knowledge*
Creativity and resourcefulness	Product knowledge
Initiative and aggressiveness	Pricing knowledge
Motivation	Knowledge of competition
Selling Skills	*Ethical and Moral Behavior*
Communication Skills	*Team Player*

Behavior Versus Output Performance Measures

A great unresolved controversy in sales management is whether outcome or behavior controls are best for evaluating salesperson performance.

TABLE 13-7 Conditions When Outcome Versus Behavioral Systems Are Preferred

Outcome Systems (OS) Preferred When...	*Behavioral Systems (BS) Preferred When...*
Customers need information: When customers require lots of information to make a decision, such as a new buy, or modified rebuy situation, OS ensure salespeople will work to provide the most relevant information.	Salespeople lack experience: Inexperienced salespeople often lack the necessary know how to become successful. BS provide the essential building blocks for developing good sales habits.
Customers trust the salesperson: In markets where salespeople need to forge high levels of trust with customers, such as those in the financial industry, OS afford salespeople the freedom needed to develop deep, trusting relationships.	There is need to protect the brand image: In situations where the firm is building or protecting its brand image, it is critical that the sales force represent the firm and its products and services correctly. BS provide the necessary management control over the sales process.
There are many ways to close the deal: When there are many sales behaviors that can be effective in contributing to performance, OS provide the independence necessary for success in any situation.	Nonselling behaviors are a priority: When companies need their salespeople to contribute to other nonselling functions, such as new product development, BS provide the flexibility for management to reward such behaviors.
The sales environment is competitive: OS provide salespeople the freedom to use their creativity in developing successful sales strategies.	It is difficult to assign sales credit: When the personnel involved in a sales team cannot agree on the appropriate drivers of a successful sale, then BS are recommended to avert endless disputes.

An example of salespeople who are evaluated on behavior measures of performance are those who receive the majority of their compensation in salary, such as pharmaceutical and alcoholic beverage salespeople. For these people, number of calls, demonstrations, and displays erected are key success factors. On the other hand, managers who direct stockbrokers and insurance and real estate agents who are paid on commission tend to emphasize outcome measures. Despite these preferences, neither group relies exclusively on behavior or outcome measures of performance. Sales jobs are multidimensional, and comprehensive evaluation systems must include multiple criteria. Thus, your dilemma is how to select and balance a set of behavior and outcome factors that will achieve the best results for your organization.

Recent research by Anderson and Onyemah, however, provides some guidance as to when a behavior or outcome system should be considered.[5] As a general guideline, when the salesperson has a substantial influence on the results, an outcome system is recommended. Conversely, a behavior-based evaluation system is recommended when the sales force does not have the expertise to conduct the job properly. In other words, a behavior-based system should be considered when your salespeople are not sure how to handle the freedom that comes with the job. The specific conditions for an outcome- versus a behavior-based system are discussed in more detail in Table 13-7. Our discussion of this issue begins with a review of behavioral measures of performance.

BEHAVIOR-BASED EVALUATION

When using *behavioral systems*, managers are concerned with keeping track of what happens at each stage of the sales operations. In some sense, behavioral systems value how people make sales more than the number of sales they make. The idea is that if the salesperson follows the recommended behaviors, the sales results will follow. This means that management must closely monitor sales force activities and direct and intervene to improve customer relations. For example, Swissôtel reviewed the activities of its ten U.S. salespeople to see how they were allocating their time and how many calls they were making per week.[6]

The hotel company found that salespeople were spending too much time in the office preparing proposals and expense accounts instead of talking to customers. Swissôtel set a new goal of six calls per day and expected its people to spend 80 percent of their time in direct customer contact. To help make salespeople more efficient, they equipped them with cellular phones and laptop computers to provide up-to-the-minute inventory of hotel rooms. This provided salespeople with the information needed to close calls on the spot.

Behavior-based systems usually require managers to make some subjective evaluations about individual salespeople. As a result, qualitative factors as illustrated in Table 13-6 are commonly used in these performance evaluations. Note that factors such as communication skills, attitude, team player, and appearance can only be judged using subjective interpretations and rating scales. This may introduce problems of bias, halo effects, and credibility into the evaluation process. Despite these limitations, behavioral systems are thought to produce a number of desirable benefits.

Since behavioral-based evaluations focus on the activities and procedures of successful selling, these systems can enhance salesperson knowledge and commitment. Many companies are now evaluating the sales force not just on the increase in sales, but also on a number of other dimensions such as competitor product knowledge, customer knowledge, and attainment of personal goals.[7] These behavioral measures are designed to encourage salespeople to achieve all-around excellence and better serve the needs of customers.

Management by Objectives

A commonly used behavioral system is *management by objectives (MBO)*—also called development and performance management. With this method, salespeople and sales managers jointly set personal development goals for the subordinate that can be completed within a specific time period. Salespeople then develop an action plan to reach each goal. Written performance appraisals are presented to salespeople during review sessions with sales managers. Reps react favorably to MBO systems because they can see where they stand and know that progress toward their goals will be rewarded.

Although MBO systems work well for some firms, they are not without problems. One issue is that some sales force goals do not lend themselves to expression in quantitative terms. This problem is particularly serious with technical reps when the job often involves problem solving. In addition, MBO goals can sometimes become ceilings that salespeople refuse to exceed. Perhaps the biggest weakness of MBO systems is that they require a lot of the sales manager's time and heavy paperwork. Because implementing an MBO control system takes a few days per subordinate per year, a manager supervising twelve salespeople would spend more than a month every year on this activity alone!

Behavioral Observation Scales

An improvement on MBO is an approach called *behavioral observation scales (BOS)*, which focuses on identifying a list of critical incidents that lead to job success.[8] This approach assumes that some of a salesperson's job requirements are more critical to job success than are others, and the key to evaluating people is to focus on these factors. Salespeople, their superiors, and customers can help identify these important behaviors. Once the key job behaviors are identified, they can then be grouped together to form job dimensions. Next, 5-point scales are attached to each activity. The resulting behavioral scales can be used by regional or district sales managers to measure the frequency with which subordinates engage in critical behaviors.

Scores on scale items are totaled, and categories for adequate, good, excellent, and superior performance are set by management. For example, good people skills are often the difference between success and failure among field sales employees. The use of BOS allows managers to measure the personal interaction skills of their subordinates and identify any problems.

One advantage of the BOS is that this system requires an extensive analysis of the salesperson's job responsibilities that lead to success. Identifying these behaviors is important because they are considered drivers of sales success. Another advantage of this evaluation system is that, once these behaviors are identified, use of BOS is less time-consuming for sales managers than MBO systems.

The main problem with BOS is the expense entailed in preparing reliable and valid rating scales. They require a good deal of time from a number of people. Also, the task-specific nature of the scales they produce suggest they are most reliable in evaluating salespeople performing very similar job functions. Separate job dimensions and critical incidents, therefore, must be developed for each level and type of sales job. For example, BOS would have serious shortcomings if used to compare a territory salesperson against a national account representative because of differences in their job responsibilities.

Using Behavior-Based Systems

Successful implementation of behavioral evaluations requires periodic analysis of data on sales force activities. One widely used way to gather this information is through the completion of daily, weekly, or monthly *call reports* by salespeople. These reports detail who was called on, at what stage the prospect is within the sales cycle, and what followup activities are needed in the future. Some managers use the 10-3-1 rule, meaning that for every 10 qualified prospects, 3 will entertain a proposal and 1 will become a customer. By monitoring three key databases, a lead log, a proposal log, and an order log, managers can see how reps are moving leads through the sales cycle.

Firms that do not monitor sales force activities can create serious evaluation problems. One company gave its salesperson-of-the-year award to a rep who did not close any new accounts and lost 40 percent of his old customers. Although this person produced high sales revenues by closing a few existing customers, he was not positioned for the future because he had no new prospects to move into the proposal stage. He left the company the following year. To avoid similar situations, companies are relying on technology-based programs to help keep track of salesperson activities. Internet-based programs, for example, provide excellent platforms for storing and organizing the details of salesperson activities. Companies such as Salesforce.com and CRMonDemand.com offer Web-based applications designed to help manage salesperson behaviors and customer accounts. In the pharmaceutical industry, salespeople record call data directly on notebook computers using a pen or keyboard. The salespeople have doctors sign their names directly on the screens to request product samples. At the end of the day, reps download the information to central computers for processing. This speeds the collection of field data and simplifies the filling of customer requests for samples, brochures, and merchandise. A side benefit of using notebook computers for call reports is that the machines have built-in clocks that allow managers to monitor field activities to ensure that the reps are actually making the calls they are reporting. If you were the person responsible for changing the sales force evaluation system to include a bevavior-based component as discussed in Team Exercise: "Measuring More Than Sales Quotas," what changes would you recommend?

OUTCOME-BASED EVALUATIONS

In *Outcome-based evaluations*, managers set performance standards for each salesperson and evaluate the results against the preset standards. Outcome-based evaluations have been shown to improve salesperson job attitudes when the salesperson understands what

TABLE 13-8 Measuring Sales Force Output for Bear Computer Company

	1	2	3	4	5	6	7	8
Territory	*Sales '07 Jan-Sept (000)*	*Sales '08 Jan-Sept (000)*	*Dollar Change*	*Sales Growth*	*Market Potential index (percent)*	*Sales Quota (000)*	*Percentage of Quota Achieved*	*Sales Variance (000)*
Jones	$ 750	$ 825	+$75	10.0%	26.0%	$ 943	87.0%	−$118
Smith	500	570	+70	14.0	15	543	105	+27
Brown	1025	1110	+85	8.3	32	1160	96	−50
West	960	1000	+40	4.2	27	977	102	+23
	$3235	$3505	+$270	8.3%	100.0%	$3623		

is expected and is able to modify his or her work strategy to meet the expected goals.[9] An example of a sales results system employed by Bear Computer Company is shown in Table 13-8. The figures are broken out by territory so that the manager can evaluate the performance of individual salespeople. Columns 1 and 2 show year-to-date sales volumes for 2007 and 2008. Note that Brown and West had the highest sales, with Brown also producing the largest dollar increase. When these changes are converted into percentages, we see that Smith had the best sales growth, followed by Jones (column 4). Up to this point, the figures suggest that Brown ranked number one on revenues, and Smith showed the best sales improvement.

Differences in Potential

One problem with the results-based sales figures given in columns 1 through 4 (Table 13-8) is that they do not adequately measure conditions faced by salespeople in the field. Thus, the sales outputs we have observed may simply reflect differences in the size of the territories. This suggests that sales results need to be compared with the potential available in each territory.

Bear's sales potential for the four areas can be estimated from published industry figures, from the *Survey of Industrial Purchasing Power*, or from *Census of Business* data.

TEAM EXERCISE

"Measuring More Than Sale Quotas."

Victoria Knudson, the new vice president of sales for a New York-based telecommunications company, feels that the current salesperson evaluation system is flawed. The company's mission is to offer the best service and value to its customers through its highly responsive and well-trained sales force. Under the current system, salespeople are judged primarily on sales quotas that emphasize gross sales dollars. According to Victoria, "judging salespeople on sales quotas alone isn't always the best solution. In many business-to-business sales forces like ours, less-than-average sales are not necessarily the problem, but more a symptom of a greater problem. It's our responsibility to train the sales force so that all-around excellence can be achieved."

Victoria wants you to change the sales force evaluation system. Instead of measuring—and compensating—its account executives, sales managers, and branch managers on sales quota alone, you need to institute a behavior-based component to the evaluation process. What changes would you recommend? Why?

Once reliable measures of potential are available, the next step is to convert these numbers into sales quotas. For example, Jones has 26 percent of the sales potential in the area (column 5, Table 13-8). Because Bear expected district sales to increase 12 percent to $3,623,000 ($3,235,000 × 1.12 = $3,623,000), the sales quota for Jones would be 0.26 × $3,623,000, or $941,980. Similar calculations can provide sales quotas for each territory that can be compared with actual sales results.

Sales to Quota

Dividing actual territory 1 sales of $825,000 by the quota of $942,812 shows that Jones was only producing 87 percent of company expectations (column 7, Table 13-8). Also, Brown has not achieved his quota even though he has the largest potential of all (32 percent). West, who had the lowest dollar increase, was still able to sell 102 percent of his quota. Thus, two territories with large dollar increases in computer sales actually were the two weakest territories when sales were related to potential. The best performance was achieved by Smith, who had the smallest potential in the division and was third in terms of dollar sales growth. These results suggest that you should consider rewarding Smith with some of the accounts from Brown. This change may increase total sales of the division because Brown is apparently not covering this large market adequately.

The figures in Table 13-8 also indicate that Jones needs further review. Jones achieved a 10 percent sales increase, which is better than the average for the division. However, computer sales are still $118,000 below potential (column 8). One possible explanation is that Jones is new to the territory and has not had time to develop the area properly. Perhaps the area has a history of poor sales because of competitive pressure, or Jones is poorly trained and needs additional coaching from you. These examples suggest that a careful analysis of territorial sales data can help in addressing problems that affect performance results.

Contribution-Based Evaluations

Measuring salespeople on the basis of the *profit contribution* that results from their activities is often a useful exercise for sales managers. An example of a contribution profit review for Bear Computer Company is shown in Table 13-9. The analysis begins with net sales for each territory, from which the cost-of-goods-sold and sales commissions are subtracted. This gives a *dollar contribution margin*. Note that Brown had the highest dollar margin. However, when the dollar contributions are divided by sales to give a *contribution margin percentage*, West had a 34 percent margin, compared with only 32 percent for Brown. Brown is apparently pushing a mix of items with low markups or is possibly cutting prices to gain sales volume.

Trading Profits for Revenues. The disadvantages of trading profits for volume can be clearly seen by comparing Jones's and Smith's performances. Jones appears to be selling high-profit products at list prices to generate an impressive 40 percent margin. On the other hand, Smith is cutting prices, leaving only a 25 percent contribution margin. These results help explain the sales figures reported in Table 13-8. This earlier analysis showed that Smith achieved a 14 percent sales growth and produced 105 percent of quota. The information in Table 13-9 suggests that the results were related to Smith's selling strategy—offering low prices and pushing low-markup items. Conversely, the high prices charged by Jones resulted in slower sales growth, and Jones attained only 87 percent of the planned sales quota.

An analysis of the direct selling expenses in the four computer sales territories provides another view of the results of individual efforts (Table 13-9). Even though West had the

TABLE 13-9 Measuring Territory Profit Output for Bear Computer Company

	Territory Performance (thousands)[a]			
	Jones	*Smith*	*Brown*	*West*
Net Sales	$825	$570	$1100	$1000
Less CGS and Commissions	495	428	744	660
Contribution margin	330	142	356	340
CM as a percentage of sales	40%	25%	32%	34%
Less direct selling costs				
Sales force salaries	55.0	35.0	55.0	65.0
Travel	15.5	4.1	3.5	5.0
Food and lodging	12.5	4.0	3.2	4.5
Entertainment	11.4	0.3	0.5	1.0
Home sales office expense	4.5	2.3	2.0	4.5
Profit contribution	$231.1	$96.3	$291.8	$260.0
PC as a percentage of sales	28%	17%	26%	26%

[a]Sales figures are from Table 13-8.

second-highest contribution margin percentage, he was tied with Brown on net profit contribution as a percentage of sales (26 percent). The reason is that Brown kept direct selling expenses to 6 percent of sales, while these expenses ran to 8 percent of sales in West's territory. Part of the problem was that West was paid more than anyone else. In addition, West's expenses for travel, food, and entertainment were relatively high. If these could be reduced to the level achieved by Brown without hurting sales, West's profits would improve substantially.

Buying Customers. Another profitability issue is raised by the activities of Jones, who produced a contribution margin that was 6 percent higher than that produced by any other territory (Table 13-9). However, the profit contribution of 28 percent was only 2 percent more than that generated by Brown and West. The explanation for the failure to push this advantage through to the bottom line lies in the various expense categories. Although Jones's salary ($55,000) seems reasonable, the amounts spent on travel, food, lodging, and entertainment appear to be excessive. Although salespeople in the other three territories averaged $11,500 for these expenses, Jones spent $43,900. The typical response of a sales manager to expenditures of this size would be to pressure the salesperson to cut back so that the profit contribution would increase. However, the issue of how much control managers should place on sales expenses is a very delicate one. Salespeople need to spend enough to get the sale, but not so much that profits are reduced. Sometimes it pays to entertain customers. For example, one study revealed that the most successful insurance agents were those who exceeded their office expense budgets.[10] Thus, Jones' success may be due to his ability to wine and dine clients. On the other hand, it is possible that Jones is using his expense account to offer customers under-the-table discounts. If these travel, food, and entertainment expenditures are legitimate, the manager might consider asking the other salespeople to spend more on these items.

USING MODELS FOR EVALUATION

As mentioned earlier, most sales managers use both behavioral and outcome-based factors. This combination approach allows them to appraise more effectively the multidimensional nature of the field sales job. Several evaluation models allow you to review different aspects of selling at the same time.

Four-Factor Model

Perhaps the simplest sales force evaluation model includes just four measures of performance. Individual input is gauged by the number of days worked and the total number of calls made. The output of the salesperson is measured by the number and average size of orders. These factors are combined to give the following equation:

$$\$\text{ Sales} = \text{Days worked} \times \frac{\text{Calls}}{\text{Days worked}} \times \frac{\text{Orders}}{\text{Calls}} \times \frac{\text{Sales }\$}{\text{Orders}}$$

The *four-factor model* indicates that sales can be increased by working more days, making more calls per day, closing more sales with customers, and increasing the sales per order. If a salesperson is not generating sufficient volume, then the problem must be a deficiency in one or more of these areas. The model must be used with caution because of the interactions among the factors. Calls, for example, have a positive correlation with sales but often have a negative relationship with sales per order. This means that even though sales increase as you make more calls, at some point the size of the order begins to decline because there is less time to spend with each customer. Thus, there appears to be an optimum number of sales calls for each salesperson that will maximize profits.

An example of the four-factor model is presented in Table 13-10. The data show that Pete's sales were about average for a salesperson in 2008 ($1,400,000), whereas Ann's were a little low. However, Ann worked more days, made more calls, had lower expenses, and landed more orders. As a result, she made one more call per day and had a 50 percent *batting average* (orders per calls). Although Jones closed the sale on only 40 percent of his calls, he had a high *average order size*. Thus, despite lower values for days worked, calls per day, and batting average, Jones obtained larger orders and a higher total sales volume.

In this case, a sales manager might be tempted to encourage Ann Smith to increase the size of her average order. Suggestions of using different selling strategies to account for differences within and across territories are sometimes warranted. A first step to get Ann to focus on larger accounts, for example, could be to direct her smaller, less profitable, accounts to the Internet for reordering. Care must be taken, however, to approach only those customers who would feel comfortable with this new ordering procedure. Although larger orders should increase total sales, Ann would be making fewer and longer sales calls and possibly could be experiencing a reduction in her batting average. Fewer calls per day produced larger orders in Jones' territory, but it is not clear that this strategy would work as well for Smith. It is possible that Ann's average order size is lower than Pete's because her *account opportunity* is lower. For example, Ann's territory may have fewer numbers of large firms. If this is the case, then Ann's overall evaluation would be higher than Pete's.

TABLE 13-10 Evaluating Performance Using Behavior and Outcome Data

Performance factors	*Pete Jones*	*Ann Smith*
Sales (annual)	$1,400,000	$1,100,000
Days worked	210	225
Calls	1,200	1,500
Orders	480	750
Expenses	$19,000	$14,900
Calls per day	5.7	6.7
Batting average (orders per calls)	40%	50%
Sales per order	$2,916	$1,466
Expenses per call	$15.83	$9.93
Expenses per order	$39.58	$19.86
Expenses as % of sales	1.35%	1.35%

Also, Pete's expenses were $3,000 above industry averages in 2008 and Ann's were below average. Jones's expenses are also sharply higher than Smith's when expressed on a per call or order basis. It is important to point out, however, that *expenses as a percentage of sales* were the same for both representatives.

Ranking Procedures

A second way to combine sales force evaluations is to use *ranking procedures*. Rankings can be added up to give an overall measure of efficiency. For example, Table 13-11 shows how five salespeople ranked on ten different *input/output factors*. The first factor used to evaluate performance is sales per person. Although this variable is a good overall measure, it can be deceiving. Note that Ford, for example, had the highest total sales but was last on *sales to potential*, suggesting that this high volume was due to a large territory. Gold, on the other hand, had low volume and high sales to potential, indicating good coverage of a limited market.

Sales to quota shows a salesperson's ability to increase revenue, and Mann was best on this factor. *Sales per order* is important to some firms because they have found that small orders are unprofitable. Ford, for example, achieved a high sales volume by making a large number of calls and selling small amounts to each customer. Gold had the best batting average, ranking first on the ratio of orders to calls. The gross margin percentage achieved by the salespeople shows how well they control prices and sell the right mix of products. The data suggest that Ford's low margins were the result of price-cutting to increase the *number of accounts* and boost sales. Ford was also weak on the behavioral factors measuring the number of reports turned in and expense control.

The performance of the five salespeople varied widely across the ten factors in Table 13-11, and each person ranked first on two criteria and last on at least one factor. When the rankings are added to give an overall measure of performance, Bell, Shaw, and Mann had total scores close to 30, the expected value. However, Ford's score of 36 and Gold's score of 25 suggest that these two representatives require special attention. Although Ford had the best sales volume, he had the lowest scores on four other factors and the weakest overall record. Gold, on the other hand, was doing a good job despite low total sales. The most obvious change suggested is to shift some of Ford's territory to Gold, giving Gold more to do and providing better coverage for some of Ford's customers. Also, Ford should be encouraged to work for larger orders and told to stop cutting prices.

Summing the ranks of the factors in Table 13-11 provides a rough indication of the salespeople's performance levels. Companies such as Ford, General Electric, and Microsoft use rankings because of its supposed objectivity. At General Electric, supervisors use the

TABLE 13-11 Ranking Salespeople on 10 Input/Output Factors

Ranking Factors	*Ford*	*Bell*	*Shaw*	*Mann*	*Gold*
Dollar Sales	1	2	3	4	5
Sales to Potential	5	3	4	2	1
Sales to Quota	5	4	2	1	3
Sales per Order	5	1	4	3	2
Number of Calls	2	5	1	3	4
Orders per call	4	2	5	3	1
Gross Margin Percent	5	1	3	4	2
Direct Selling Costs	4	3	5	1	2
New Accounts	1	4	2	5	3
Number of Reports Turned in	4	3	1	5	2
Total of Ranks	36	28	30	31	25

ranking system to identify the top 20 percent and the bottom 10 percent of their staffs each year. The top 20 percent are richly rewarded, while the bottom 10 percent will likely be fired.[10] Ranking procedures, however, do have some disadvantages. Perhaps the biggest weakness is that it assumes that all 10 criteria are equally important. This is rarely the case, because firms may be looking for sales growth at one point in the business cycle and profits at another. Also, ranking does not eliminate the potential for subjectivity and bias to enter into the process, especially when behavioral data are used.

Performance Matrix

Deficiencies of the four-factor model and ranking procedures have led to the development of a new *performance matrix*[11] shown in Figure 13-2. The diagram was constructed by dividing sales force sales and contribution margin percentages into high and low categories. Then averages were calculated for age, calls, and contribution dollars for salespeople falling into each cell. The four cells of the matrix have been given descriptive names to highlight comparisons among different groups. The stars in the upper-right quadrant produced the highest sales and highest gross margin percentages. Slowpokes in the lower-right cell produced good percentage margins but lower sales. Salespeople who fell into the lower-left quadrant were low on both sales and percentage margins. The compromisers in the upper-left cell had high sales and lower contribution margin percentages.

A performance matrix allows you to review and compare the accomplishments of your sales force along several input/output dimensions at the same time. Note that Figure 13-2 includes data on two input measures (calls and age as a proxy for experience) and three output measures (sales, contribution dollars, and contribution margin percentage). In this case, the matrix shows that the youngest salespeople are either slowpokes or stars and that the oldest are laggards or compromisers. These data suggest that many reps start their careers by selling a high-margin mix of products and end it by sacrificing margins for revenue.

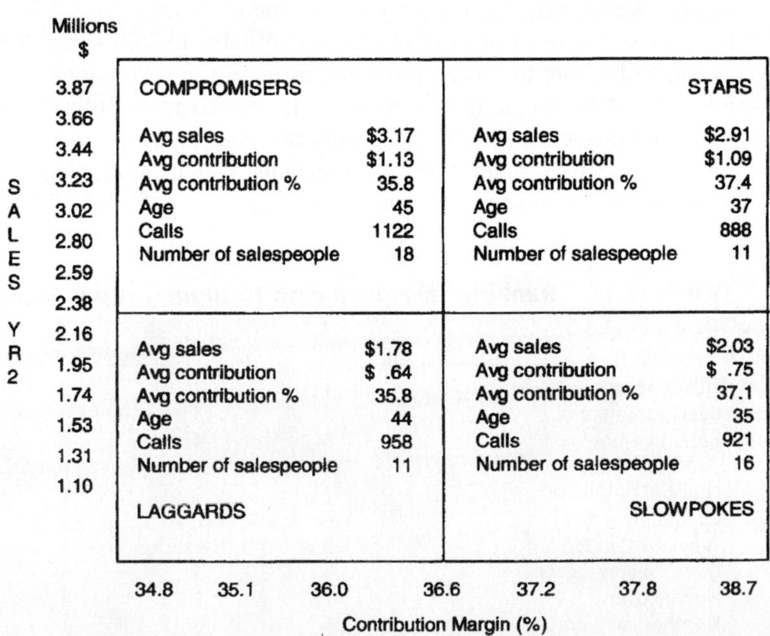

FIGURE 13-2 Performance Matrix for 56 Building Products Salespeople

Data from the performance matrix shown in Figure 13-2 can be used to make a number of managerial recommendations. The eleven laggards represent a plateau problem and, therefore, are ripe for retraining, redeployment, or dismissal. Also, if these salespeople made more calls, they might be able to move up to the compromiser category. A crucial issue for the sales manager is deciding whether to encourage reps to become stars or compromisers. This is a tough choice because although the stars had the highest contribution percentage, the compromisers produced more sales and more contribution dollars. Thus, managers looking for dollars would reward the compromisers, and those seeking a higher net profit percentage would reward the stars. After reviewing the data in Figure 13-2, management of the firm changed the compensation plan from straight commission to a salary plus commission plus bonus program to tie sales efforts more closely to the profitability of the different product lines.

This example shows that a performance matrix can provide a useful way to review behavior and the results achieved by salespeople. The matrix is easy to construct, and it neatly summarizes a variety of sales activities in a readable format. With this procedure, the manager's key task is to select appropriate performance measures for the review process.

Relative Performance Efficiency

Another procedure called the *relative performance efficiency index* uses both inputs and outputs to compare performance to a peer group. This approach employs data envelopment analysis and simulation techniques to prepare a single index of efficiency.[12] Table 13-12 shows a relative performance index of 85 percent calculated for a salesperson selling advertising space to businesses. In this case, rep 22 is compared with three other salespeople who had scores of 100 percent operating in similar conditions. The analysis is based on a comparison of output measured by three variables relative to the size of four input variables. If salesperson 22 had been as efficient as his peers, he would have exceeded his quota by 20 percent, sold $5,500 more advertising, received $2,000 less salary, had one less management support person, and had operated in a smaller territory.

Sales manager can use the results of the analysis to allocate resources and make decisions on retraining. Organizations that pay their salespeople straight commissions to maximize output are rarely concerned with input factors, and relative performance indexes would not be an appropriate evaluation technique. However, some companies are experimenting with relative performance systems to reduce manager time in setting, managing, and adjudicating complaints about quotas.

TABLE 13-12 Relative Performance Efficiency for Sales Rep 22

Variable Type	*Variable Name*	*Value Measured*	*Value if 100% Efficient*	*Slack*
Output	Percent Quota Attained (%)	100	120	20
Output	Supervisor Evaluation	5	5	0
Output	Sales Volume ($)	45,000	50,500	5,500
Input	Sales Training	5	5	0
Input	Salary ($)	20,000	18,000	2,000
Input	Management Ratio	3	2	1
Input	Territory Potential ($)	60,500	50,000	10,500

Reference Set	Influence
Salesperson 7	0.49
Salesperson 20	0.43
Salesperson 45	0.08

Efficiency = 0.85
Iterations = 10

Six Insights for Successful Evaluation and Control Systems

Throughout this chapter, we have focused on the development and management of the sales force evaluation and control systems. However, experts suggest that sales managers are more likely to spend time in the evaluation process and use the results if a similar process is employed to manage their own performance as well as others in the sales organization. The six insights listed below are based on research conducted by Andris Zoltners and his colleagues.[13]

1. **The evaluation system is used at all levels of the company.** Although the focus of this chapter is on developing salesperson evaluation systems, these development processes work at all levels in the sales organization. First-line sales managers (as well as salespeople) are more likely to take the process seriously and use it if a similar process is used to manage their own performance.
2. **A good evaluation system reflects the company's culture.** An evaluation system needs to be consistent with the sales force culture. For example, a results-based evaluation system works well where the culture of the company is informal and the focus of the commissioned-based sales force is to increase its customer base with new accounts. A behavior-based evaluation system in this culture will likely lead to confusion and conflict.
3. **Peer influence is powerful in helping manage performance.** Most evaluation interactions occur between a salesperson and his or her superior. That is, the evaluation system is hierarchical. Some companies that use team selling have discovered a powerful way to influence performance—horizontal (i.e., peer) evaluations. Team selling naturally lends itself to horizontal evaluations because team members expect good performances and encouragement from one another. This system will identify nonperformers relatively quickly.
4. **Evaluation systems must leverage a person's motivators.** It is important to remember that people are motivated by positive feedback, specific and understandable goals, and a compensation system that reinforces these goals. In addition to these factors, the manager must also take the role of a coach by appealing to the achievement, power, ego gratification, social affiliation, and survival needs of the salespeople.
5. **Empowerment and direction—it's not just a question of "either/or"; it's also a question of when.** A person may need to be empowered in one area and directed in another. For example, a salesperson may have excellent prospecting and relationship-building skills but poor closing skills. Thus, an evaluation system that permits the manager to tailor the evaluation procedure to an individual is recommended.
6. **The evaluation system itself must evolve.** As indicated throughout this book, high-performing sales organizations are able to change with the marketplace; and these changes include salesperson success factors. Thus, the evaluation system must also evolve to adapt and reflect these changes.

SUMMARY

Sales force evaluation is a process that compares goals with accomplishments. Our discussion has shown that the evaluation of salespeople is an essential but tricky task. You want to be able to motivate reps to higher levels of achievement while at the same time judge them on their accomplishments. This chapter has introduced you to a number of topics and issues dealing with the sales force evaluation process. You should now be able to:

1. **Conduct a sales force performance review.** The first step is to decide what you want the sales force to accomplish. Once decided, the second step is to prepare a sales plan. The third step is to set performance standards for individual products for different levels

in the organization. Next, measures of success need to be developed. Finally, reasons for above- and below standard performance are analyzed, and modifications are made in future plans.

2. **Describe the criteria used to evaluate salespeople.** The most common criteria used are sales by territories, products, units sold, and customers. However, sales figures do not tell the whole story; you must also evaluate selling expenses and margins. An effective expense analysis could show whether salespeople are wasting company travel funds or cutting prices to boost their commission income.
3. **Distinguish between input and output measures of sales performance.** Input criteria measure important factors that are generally thought to be closely associated with sales, such as number of calls, days worked, and expenses. Output measures, on the other hand, look at those criteria that are direct measurements of salesperson performance, such as sales volume, number of new accounts, margins, and the number of orders. Although selecting a set of sales performance measures for a firm is difficult, one guideline is to use those performance measures that are consistent with the organization's goals and objectives. Most sales managers use both input and output criteria to assess the multidimensional character of sales jobs. Ranking procedures, performance indexes, and performance matrices can be used to combine control factors to show overall effects and interactions more clearly.
4. **Discuss the value of behavioral control procedures for salespeople.** Behavioral systems produce a number of desirable benefits. First, behavior-based evaluation procedures can lead to knowledgeable and expert salespeople who are more committed to the organization. Second, salespeople tend to be self-motivated and react favorably to peer recognition. With behavior systems, salespeople can be expected to spend more time planning their calls and providing sales support activities to their customers. Third, behavioral measures encourage salespeople to achieve company goals and better serve the needs of customers. Commonly used behavioral systems are management by objectives (MBO) and behavioral observation scales (BOS).
5. **Understand outcome-based evaluation procedures.** Results-based evaluation criteria are effective when the salesperson understands what is expected and is able to modify his or her strategy to meet the expected goals. Sales-to-quota and contribution-based evaluation procedures are commonly used. One problem with outcome based measures is that they do not adequately measure the conditions faced by salespeople in the field.
6. **Describe the evaluation models that use both input and output data.** Based on the four-factor model, the individual's input is gauged by the number of days worked and the total number of calls made. The output of the salesperson is measured by the number and average size of orders. Ranking also combines input and output measures of sales force output and are generally added up to give an overall measure of efficiency. The performance matrix is constructed by dividing sales force sales and contribution margin percentages into high and low categories. Then averages are calculated for age, calls, and contribution dollars for salespeople falling into each cell. The four cells of the matrix are given descriptive names to highlight comparisons among different groups. Finally, the relative performance efficiency index uses both inputs and outputs to compare performance to a peer group. The analysis is based on a comparison of output measures relative to the size of the input variables.

KEY TERMS

Account opportunity
Average order size
Batting average
Behavioral observation scales (BOS)
Behavioral systems
Call reports
Contribution margin percentage
Dollar contribution margin
80–20 principle

Evaluation
Expenses as a percentage of sales
Four-factor model
Iceberg principle
Input/output factors
Management by objectives (MBO)
Number of accounts
Outcome controls
Outcome-based evaluation
Performance matrix
Profit contribution
Qualitative measures
Ranking procedures
Relative performance efficiency index
Sales per order
Sales to potential
Sales to quota
Total sales volume

DEVELOPING YOUR COMPETENCIES

1. **Technology.** In order to use salesperson performance information, a sales manager must first correctly interpret problems and causes influencing salesperson performance. Interpretation is often assisted by better understanding the personal values and motives that are primary determinants of the individual salesperson's behavior and performance. One of the more highly accepted personal assessment instruments used for this purpose is the VALS2 survey developed by SRI.

   A version of VALS2 has recently been added to SRI's extensive set of sites on the World Wide Web and can be accessed through the URL: http://www.sric-bi.com/VALS/presurvey.shtml. Access this Web page and complete the VALS2 survey as provided. Immediate feedback is provided to the user regarding their personal values and motivation profile. Additional informational pages provided on this site are designed to give the user more information and discussion of their profile, what it means regarding behaviors, and how it compares with the rest of the population.

   What is your VALS typology? Consider a salesperson with this same typology. What are its implications for evaluating and motivating that individual salesperson's (a) performance and (b) job satisfaction? Why?
2. **Global Perspective.** Richard Smith is the vice president of sales and marketing for Triton Manufacturers, Inc., which manufactures electric motors. For the past seven years, the company has been doing business in Germany and Switzerland. The first three months of the company's fiscal year have ended, and Richard is preparing for the European quarterly sales review meeting.

   The managing director for the German and Switzerland operations is Helmut Schmidt. Sales in Switzerland are currently above projected targets, but sales in Germany are not keeping pace with the rate of industry or competitor growth. What factors would you need to examine to guide your evaluation and feedback to Helmut?
3. **Strategic Action.** The most successful companies reward their salespeople by growing the value of each customer. One metric used to measure customer value is the "share-of-customer." It is calculated using the ration of business the customer gives to your firm divided by the amount of business the customer is doing with the competition. What are the strategic implications for the share-of-customer metric in the evaluation process? How will you know that a rep is on the right track when his or her relationship with the customer is strong, but the share-of-customer is low?

PROBLEMS*

1. You have recently been hired as the new branch sales manager for a distributor of steel products and manage four salespeople. The company has been in business for twenty-five years and has been successful over the years. However, sales revenues have

*Contributed by Avery Abernethy, Auburn University. Excel spreadsheets for working on these problems are available at www.wiley.com/college/cron. Go to "Student Resources."

been relatively flat the past three years. One reason why you took the job was because success of this business is dependent on the success of the sales staff, and you knew you could turn things around. Also, the company's marketing research department had recently discovered a need for prefabricated steel products, which, up to this point, has not been offered by your firm. Fortunately, your company had recently invested in some state-of-the-art fabrication equipment, and you now are able to offer this service. This is exciting news to you because pre-fab processing typically provides a healthy 30 percent contribution margin. Off-the-shelf products, on the other hand, are similar to the competition's product offerings and have lower contribution margin (forged steel = 10 percent; stainless steel = 12 percent). Last year, your sales quota for each product line was $10,000/month for forged steel, $15,000/month for stainless steel, and $10,000/month for prefabricated products.

The year-end evaluation of your four salespeople is due to your immediate boss, the marketing director, next week. She wants to review your written evaluation of each salesperson and your recommendations and ideas for performance improvement of your sales staff, including any recommended changes in quotas for the three product lines.

Below are the net sales revenues for last year. An Excel spreadsheet has been developed to help you in your evaluation. When using the spreadsheet, insert the net sales and the number of sales calls shown below into the appropriate cells. The spreadsheet has the formula necessary to complete the ratios needed to complete this assignment and can be found at www.wiley.com/college/cron.

Net Sales	*Bailey*	*Karr*	*Craig*	*Kennedy*
Forged steel products	$135,000	$115,000	$132,000	$121,000
Stainless steel products	188,000	198,000	205,000	190,000
Prefabricated products	95,000	101,500	105,500	103,000
Total Sales	$418,000	$414,500	$442,000	$414,000
Number of Sales Calls	79	94	81	97
Salary	$ 42,000	$ 50,000	$ 50,000	$ 55,000
Travel	4,560	4,800	5,100	6,750
Food and Lodging	2,200	2,100	2,350	3,500
Entertainment	850	1,100	1,200	1,500
Total Salesperson Expenses	$ 49,610	$ 58,000	$ 58,650	$ 66,750

2. You are the district sales manager for Conglomerate Corporation in the Southeast region. It is January 2009, and you've completed the annual evaluations. You now need to distribute the $60,000 in bonus money and $20,000 in salary increase money to your five-person sales force.

   The company's goal is profits. Sales force pay is salary plus commission. If the firm does well, bonus money is allocated on the basis of merit.

   Your salary as district manager was $94,000 in 2007 ($88,000 in 2006, and you also have a bonus system for meeting district goals that is not discussed here). You received the second biggest percent salary raise last year; it would have been number one except for a failure to turn in paperwork on time, largely due to Ann's being chronically late with her call reports.

   Salespeople have quotas for sales, new accounts, expenses, and average calls per day. They are also expected to turn in paperwork correctly done and on time. District managers are responsible for setting quotas, allocating raise/merit money, and hiring/firing salespeople. As district manager, you are evaluated by your superior on the following criteria:

   - District total sales
   - District sales to quota

- District profit (sales minus expenses)
- Following company policy (e.g., paperwork done, don't violate company rules or federal/state Laws)

Following is a copy of a performance printout that gives the previous two-year performances of your five salespeople (2007 and 2008). Inflation in 2008 was 3.2 percent.

The Excel spreadsheet of this performance data can be downloaded from the student companion Web site for this textbook. The textbook Web site can be found at www.wiley.com/college/cron.

1. Allocate the salary and bonus money.
2. Give a written allocation of your funds.
3. Give a written performance review to each person.
4. Sign each performance evaluation and date it February 1, 2009. *Note:* Contribution margin, attitude, selling skills, product knowledge, and paperwork are all measured on a 1–10 scale with 1 = unacceptable and 10 = excellent; 5 is average.

In May 2008, Mr. McDonald's wife was diagnosed with cancer. She has been through extensive, painful treatments.

2007 Annual Evaluation

	Bob Smith	*Janice Davis*	*Sam Cheek*	*Jeff McDonald*	*Ann White*
Sales	$222,000.00	$191,000.00	$351,000.00	$422,500.00	$895,000.00
Sales/Quota	1.01	1.12	0.95	1.67	2.45
New Accounts	6	9	19	8	26
New Accounts/Quota	1	1.11	1.8	0.75	3
Expense/Quota	0.98	0.96	1.04	1.1	1.01
Avg. Calls/Day	4.5	3.7	4	4.9	4.2
Contribution Margin	8	7	6	5	6
Attitude	5	5	5	7	3
Selling Skills	5	7	4	8	9
Product Knowledge	7	3	5	9	7
Paperwork	7	7	7	9	1
Years with Firm	2	1	4	8	6
2007 Salary	$29,500.00	$29,000.00	$37,800.00	$40,500.00	$49,750.00
2007 Commission	$6,660.00	$5,730.00	$10,530.00	$12,675.00	$26,850.00
Salary (Increase) (1/1/08)	$1,600.00	$2,500.00	$1,400.00	$2,500.00	$4,250.00

2008 Annual Evaluation

	Bob Smith	*Janice Davis*	*Sam Cheek*	*Jeff McDonald*	*Ann White*
Sales	$240,000.00	$250,000.00	$350,000.00	$300,500.00	$960,000.00
Sales/Quota	1.03	1.49	0.94	1.13	2.51
New Accounts	6	15	9	6	20
New Accounts/Quota	1	1.6	0.9	0.65	2.7

2008 Annual Evaluation

	Bob Smith	*Janice Davis*	*Sam Cheek*	*Jeff McDonald*	*Ann White*
Expense/Quota	0.97	0.99	1.06	0.98	1.01
Avg. Calls/Day	4.5	4.3	3.9	4.1	4.2
Contribution Margin	7	6	4	5	6
Attitude	5	7	4	9	4
Selling Skills	6	7	4	8	9
Product Knowledge	6	5	4	9	7
Paperwork	8	8	5	6	4
Years with Firm	3	2	5	9	7
2008 Salary	$31,100.00	$31,500.00	$39,200.00	$43,000.00	$54,000.00
2008 Commission	$7,200.00	$7,500.00	$10,500.00	$9,015.00	$28,800.00
2009 Salary Increase (1/1/09)					

FEATURED CASE SHIELD FINANCIAL: "MISSED QUOTA"

Jon MacAllister has been one of the lowest performer at Shield's Des Moines location. Every month since being hired he has sold 60 or 70 percent of quota, but just can't seem to get any higher. MacAllister keeps saying that he is on the verge of turning things around in his performance and that introduction of a new First-Plus account program would only make things worse if the change was forced on him.

When MacAllister, a two-year insurance sales veteran, joined Shield, he was given the accounts of the rep he replaced. Those accounts are performing well. Doug Bloom went on sales calls to these customers with MacAllister and observed that he's a natural at developing relationships and partnering. The problem is that he is unwilling to change the way he handles his accounts and prospecting activities. Bloom wanted to help MacAllister improve his performance by showing him a more efficient way to organize his work schedule in order to see new prospects. However, MacAllister was angry at Bloom and said that he realizes that he's not the best performer in the company, but he is not incompetent and is close to improvement on his own. MacAllister even turned in his letter of resignation after a heated argument with Bloom regarding his performance. After some time, he reconsidered his decision and wanted to return to Shield. Bloom didn't mind taking MacAllister back, but only if he knew for sure that changes will be made to his performance and attitude.

Bloom could tell that MacAllister was not going to change a thing about his current performance, nor would he accept any changes forced on him. Doug assumed that MacAllister was capable of doing better, but was having a difficult time finding a way to get him to improve.

Questions

1. How should Bloom handle this situation?

- Should Bloom keep investing his time in helping MacAllister to improve?
- Should he let MacAllister try to prove himself on his own?
- Is there a better approach?

NOTES

Chapter 1: Introduction to Selling and Sales Management

1. "Round Table Talk," *Sales & Marketing Management* (January/February 2007), pp. 33–35.
2. Rebecca Aronauer, "What's It All Worth?" *Sales & Marketing Management Magazine* (May 2007), p. 29.
3. This section is based on some excellent discussions of current market and sales force changes, including the following: Gerald Bauer, Mark Baunchalk, Thomas Ingram, and Raymond LaForge, *Emerging Trends in Sales Thought and Practice* (Westport, CT: Quorum Books, 1998); and Neil Rackham, *Rethinking the Sales Force* (New York: McGraw-Hill, 1999).
4. Howard Stevens, "Eight Sales Myth-Breakers," *Repertoire* (October 2002), p. 70.
5. Allen Webb, *Profiting from Proliferation* (New York, NY: McKinsey & Company, 2006), p. 22.
6. Jim Carbone, "Motorola Simplifies to Lower Costs," *Velocity*, 1 (2002), p. 45.
7. Thomas Ingram, Raymond LaForge, and Thomas Leigh, "Selling in the New Millennium: A Joint Agenda," *Industrial Marketing Management*, 31 (2002), pp. 1–9.
8. Joseph Kornik, "Risky Business," *Sales & Sales Management Magazine* (June 2007), p. 32.
9. Kenneth R. Evans, David Good, and Theodore Hellman, "Relationship Selling: New Challenges for Today's Sales Manager," in Bauer, Baunchanet, Ingram, and La Forge (eds.) *Emerging Trends in Sales Thought and Practice*, (Wesport, CONN: Quorum Books), p. 36.
10. Greg Marshall, Danel Goebel, and William Moncrief, "Hiring for Success at the Buyer-Seller Interface," *Journal of Business Research*, 56 (2003), pp. 247–55.
11. Tuba Ustuner and David Godes, "Better Sales Networks," *Harvard Business Review* (July–August 2006), pp. 1–10.
12. See Ken Le Meunier-FitzHugh and Nigel Piercy, "Does Collaboration Between Sales and Marketing Affect Business Performance," *Journal of Personal Selling & Sales Management* 27 (Summer 2007), pp. 207–220; Andrea Dixon, "Successful and Unsuccessful Sales Calls: Measuring Salesperson Attributions and Behavioral Intention," *Journal of Marketing*, 65 (July 2001), pp. 64–79; and Greg Marshall, William Moncrief, and Felicia Lassk, "The Current State of Sales Force Activities," *Industrial Marketing Management*, 28 (1999), pp. 87–98.
13. See Jennifer McFarland, "Behind Every Successful Manager Is a Great Inside Sales Job," *Harvard Management Update* (December 2001); Christopher Plouffe, "Salesperson Navigational Competency: A Conceptualization and Empirical Examination," unpublished doctoral dissertation, 2003, The University of Western Ontario: London, Ontario, Canada; Sanjit Sengupta, Robert Krapfel, and Michael Pusateri, "An Empirical Investigation of Key Account Salesperson Effectiveness," *Journal of Personal Selling & Sales Management*, 20 (Fall 2000), pp. 253–261; and Christian Homburg, John Workman, and Ove Jensen, "Fundamental Changes in Marketing Organization: The Movement Toward a Customer-Focused Organizational Structure," *Journal of of the Academy of Marketing Science*, 28 (2000), pp. 459–478.
14. Linda Hill, *Becoming a Manager* (Boston: Harvard Business School, 1992), p. 88.
15. Our definition of sales management competencies is adapted from the definition for managerial competencies provided in Don Hellriegel, Susan Jackson, and John Slocum, *Management*, 10th ed. (Cincinnati, OH: Southwestern College Publishing, 2006), p. 4.
16. David Cravens, "The Changing Role of the Sales Force," *Marketing Management*, 4 (Fall 1995), pp. 49–57.
17. The discussion in this section and the dimensions of coaching are based on Gregory Rich, "The Constructs of Sales Coaching: Supervisory Feedback, Role Modeling and Trust," *Journal of Personal Selling & Sales Management*, 18 (Winter 1998), pp. 53–63.

18. "Quota Busters," *Sales & Marketing Management* (July 2001), p. 67.
19. Anna Britnor Guest, "Use the GROW Model for Better Coaching," *Sales & Marketing Management Magazine* (June 2007), p. 4.
20. R. Venkatesh, Goutam Challagalla, and Ajay Kohli, "Heterogeneity in Sales Districts: Beyond Individual-Level Predictors of Satisfaction and Performance," *Journal of the Academy of Marketing Science*, 29 (2001), pp. 238–254.
21. Terry Loe, "The Effect of Perceived Ethical Climate on the Search for Sales Excellence," *Journal of Personal Selling & Sales Management* (Summer 2004).
22. Hill, *Becoming a Manager*, p. 171.
23. Mica Douglas, "Selling Peak Performance," *Industrial and Commercial Training*, 34, 5(2002), pp. 188–191.
24. Bonnie Guy and W.E. Patton, "Managing the Effects of Culture Shock and Sojourner Adjustment on the Expatriate Industrial Sales Force," *Industrial Marketing Management*, 25 (1996), pp. 385–393.
25. Paul Greenberg, *CRM: At the Speed of Light* (Berkeley, CA: Osborne/McGraw-Hill, 2001), pp. 69–70.
26. Cheri Speier and Viswanath Venkatesh, "The Hidden Minefields in the Adoption of Sales Force Automation Technology," *Journal of Marketing* (July 2002), p. 98.
27. Devon Johnson and Sundar Bharadwaj, "Digitization of Selling Activity and Sales Force Performance," *Journal of the Academy of Marketing Science* (Winter 2004), pp. 3–18.
28. Alan Dubinsky, "Salesperson Failure: Sales Management Is the Key," *Industrial Marketing Management*, 28 (2000), pp. 7–17.
29. Oranauer, "What's It All Worth," p. 29.
30. Christine Galea, "The 2004 Compensation Survey," *Sales & Marketing Management* (May 2004), p. 29.
31. "So You Wanna Be a CEO," *Sales & Marketing Management* (January 2002), pp. 31–32.

Chapter 2: Strategy and Sales Program Planning

1. Joe Sperry, "2002 SAMA Performance Award," *Velocity* (3rd Quarter 2002), pp. 43–44.
2. Stanley Slater and Eric Olson, "Marketing's Contribution to the Implementation of Business Strategy: An Empirical Analysis," *Strategic Management Journal*, 22 (2001), pp. 1055–1067.
3. "Data Watch," *Velocity* (1st Quarter 2002), p. 5.
4. Michael Porter, *Competitive Strategy* (New York: Free Press, 1980).
5. Stanley Slater and Eric Olson, "Strategy Type and Performance: The Influence of Sales Force Management," *Strategic Management Journal*, 21 (2000), pp. 813–829.
6. For more information on marketing strategy in general and these decisions in particular, see David Cravens, *Marketing Strategy* (Boston: Irwin McGraw-Hill, 1999): Shelby Hunt and Robert Morgan, "The Comparative Advantage Theory of Competition," *Journal of Marketing*, 59 (1995), pp. 1–15: and Charles Lamb, Joseph Hair, and Carl McDaniel, *Marketing*, 6th ed. (Cincinnati, OH: Southwestern Publishing, 2002).
7. Theodore Kinmi, "How Strategic Is Your Sales Strategy?" *Harvard Management Update* (February 2004), p. 5.
8. Kevin Lane Keller, "Building Customer-Based Brand Equity," *Marketing Management* (July/August 2001), p. 15.
9. Tom Mitchell, "Cisco Resellers Add Value," *Industrial Marketing Management*, 30 (2001), pp. 115–118.
10. This section is based on Rajendra Srivastava, Tasdduq Shervani, and Liam Fahey, "Marketing, Business Processes, and Shareholder Value: An Organizationally Embedded View of Marketing Activities and the Discipline of Marketing," *Journal of Marketing*, 63 (1999), pp. 168–179.
11. The discussion in this section draws primarily from Andris Zolners, Prabhakant Sinha, and Greggor Zoltners, *Accelerating Sales Force Performance* (New York: AMACOM, 2001).
12. Per Vagan Freytag and Ann Hojbjerg Clarke, "Business to Business Market Segmentation," *Industrial Marketing Management*, 30 (2001), pp. 473–486.
13. This and other customer contact estimates in this section are based on the Penton Media, PRO Reports No. 303A, 1997.
14. Erin Strout, "Fast Forward," *Sales & Marketing Management* (December 2001), p. 39.
15. Zoltners et al., *Accelerating Sales Force Performance*, p. 22.
16. "IBM to Shift Business to Resellers," *Sales & Marketing Management* (March 1995), p. 36.
17. Rajiv Mehta, Alan Dubinsky, and Rolph Anerson, "Marketing Channel Management and the Sales Manager," *Industrial Marketing Management*, 31 (2002), pp. 429–439.
18. Bob Kearney, "Joining Forces: 3M Puts Stock in Bonding," *3M Today* (January 1995), pp. 2–5.

19. Greg Stevens and James Burley, "3, 000 Raw Ideas = 1 Commercial Success!" *Research-Technology Management* (May–June 1997), pp. 16–27.
20. James Cross, Steven Hartley, William Rudelius, and Michael Vassey, "Sales Force Activities and Marketing Strategies in Industrial Firms: Relationships and Implications," *Journal of Personal Selling & Sales Management*, 21 (Summer 2001), pp. 199–206.
21. Cravens, *Marketing Strategy*, p. 256.
22. Roger Kerin, Steven Hartley, Eric Berkowitz, and William Rudelius, *Marketing*, 8th ed. (New York: Irwin McGraw-Hill, 2006), p. 144.
23. Jim Carbone, "Lucent's Supply Chain Focus Fattens Margins," *Velocity*, 4 (2002), p. 56.
24. Paul Greenberg, *Customer Relationship Management at the Speed of Light* (New York: McGraw-Hill, 2001).
25. Lesley Abery, Colleen Chirsten, and Erin Kriessmann, "Customers Talk, BT Listens," *Velocity* (1st and 2nd Quarter 2002), p. 14.
26. Jeff Golterman, "Strategic Account Management in the Age of the Never Satisfied Customer," *Velocity*, 2 (2000), pp. 13–16.
27. It is certainly beyond the scope of this text to fully describe CRM. Good sources of additional information on CRM include Jay Curry and Adam Curry, *The Customer Marketing Method* (New York: Free Press, 2000); Philip Evans and Thomas Wurster, *Blown to Bits* (Boston: Harvard Business School Press, 2000); Greenberg, *Customer Relationship Management at the Speed of Light*; Don Peppers and Martha Rogers, *One to One B2B* (New York: Currency Doubleday, 2001); and Ronald Swift, *Accelerating Customer Relationships* (Upper Saddle River, NJ: Prentice Hall PTR, 2001).
28. Robert Peterson and George Lucas, "What Buyers Want Most from Salespeople: A View from the Senior Level," *Business Horizons*, 30 (October 2001), pp. 576–586.
29. Much of the discussion in this section is adapted from Neil Rackham and John DeVincentis, *Rethinking the Sales Force* (New York: McGraw-Hill, 1999).
30. For more information on customer-supplier relationships, see Esko Penttinen and Jonathan Palmer, "Improving Firm Positioning through Enhanced Offerings and Buyer-Seller Relationships," *Industrial Marketing Management*, 36, 5 (July 2007) pp. 552–564.
31. Kapil Tuli, Ajay Kohli, and Sundar Bharadwaj, "Rethinking Customer Solutions: From Product Bundles to Relational Processes," *Journal of Marketing*, 71 (July 2007), p. 13.
32. For more on partnering relationships, see Jean Johnson, Raviprett Sohi, and Rajdeep Grewal, "The Role of Relational Knowledge Stores in Interfirm Pertnering," *Journal of Marketing*, 68, 3 (July 2004), pp. 21–36.
33. Nicole Coviello, Roderick Brodie, Peter Danaher, and Wesley Johnston, "How Firms Relate to Their Markets: An Empirical Examination of Contemporary Marketing Practices," *Journal of Marketing*, 66 (July 2002), pp. 33–46.
34. Rackam and DeVincentis, *Rethinking the Sales Force*, p. 146.
35. David Wilson, "Deep Relationships: The Case of the Vanishing Salesperson," *Journal of Personal Selling & Sales Management*, 20 (Winter 2000), p. 53.
36. Gary Frankwick, Stephen Porter, and Lawrence Crosby, "Dynamics of Relationship Selling: A Longitudinal Examination of Changes in Salesperson-Customer Relationship Status," *Journal of Personal Selling & Sales Management*, 21, 2 (Spring 2001), pp. 135–146.
37. Michael Beverland, "Contextual Influences and the Adoption and Practice of Relationship Selling in a Business-to-Business Setting: An Exploratory Study," *Journal of Personal Selling & Sales Management*, 21, 3 (Summer 2001), pp. 207–216.
38. See Barton Weitz and Kevin Bradford, "Personal Selling and Sales Management: A Relationship Marketing Perspective," *Journal of the Academy of Marketing Science*, 27 (Spring 1999), pp. 241–254, for more on conflict management.
39. Joseph Cannon and Christian Homburg, "Buyer-Supplier Relationships and Customer Firm Costs," *Journal of Marketing*, 65 (January 2001), pp. 29–43.

Sales Management Resource: Estimating Potentials and Forecasting Sales

1. Rolph Anderson, Rajiv Mehta, and James Strong, "An Empirical Investigation of Sales Management and Training Programs for Sales Managers," *Journal of Personal Selling & Sales Management*, 17, 3 (Summer 1997), p. 61.
2. "2004 Survey of Buying Power," *Sales & Marketing Management* (September 2004), p. 77.
3. William Keenan, "Numbers Racket," *Sales & Marketing Management* (May 1995), p. 66.
4. The seasonal indexes derived in Table F-4 are easy to explain, but most computer programs use a more sophisticated procedure known as the ratio to moving average method.

Sales Management Resource: Sales Force Investment and Budgeting

1. Andris Zoltners, Prabhakant Sinha, and Greggor Zoltners, *The Complete Guide to Accelerating Sales Force Performance* (New York: AMACOM), 2001.
2. Ibid., p. 77.
3. A word of caution here: most costs are neither purely variable nor fixed, but are actually a combination of the two. Similarly, most operating costs are relatively fixed in the short term, but fixed costs will increase over time as the sales volume increases beyond current capacity limits.
4. Andy Cohen, "Budget Backlash," *Sales & Marketing Management* (September 2002), p. 38.
5. Kathleen Cholewka, "Looking for a Travel Alternative," *Sales & Marketing Management* (December 2001), p. 23.
6. Kathleen Cholewka, "Easy ROI," *Sales & Marketing Management* (May 2002), p. 21.
7. Cohen, "Budget Backlash," p. 38.

Chapter 3: Sales Opportunity Management

1. Ernest Waaser, Marshall Dahneke, Michael Pekkarinen, and Michael Weissel, "Smarter Segmentation for Your Sales Force," *Harvard Business Review* (March 2004), pp, 14–18.
2. Robert Blattberg, Gary Getz, and Jacquelyn Thomas, *Customer Equity* (Cambridge, MA: Harvard Business School Press, 2001), p. 11.
3. Michael Johnson and Fred Selnes, "Customer Portfolio Management: Toward a Dynamic Theory of Exchange Relationships," *Journal of Marketing* (April 2004), pp. 1–17.
4. Michele Marchetti, "Is Cold Calling Worth It?" *Sales & Marketing Management* (August 1997), p. 103.
5. For more information on trade shows, call or write to Trade Show Bureau, 1660 Lincoln Street, Suite 2080. Denver, Colorado 80264–2001 or call 303-860-7626.
6. Sam Whitmore, "Forecasting The Future of Webcasting," *Forbes.com* (December 2003).
7. John Boe, "Sales Training: Six Powerful Prospecting Tips," *Sales & Marketing Management* (October 2007), p. 21.
8. Catherine Arnold, "Reference Programs Keep b-to-b Customers Satisfied," *Marketing News* (August 18, 2003), p. 4.
9. Christine Galea, "2002 Salary Survey," *Sales & Marketing Management* (May 2002), p. 33.
10. Michele Marchetti, "1999 Sales Manager's Budget Planner," *Sales & Marketing Management* (September 1999), pp. 56–57.
11. Raymond LaForge, David Cravens, and Clifford Young, "Improving Salesforce Productivity," *Business Horizons* (September–October 1982), pp. 50–59.
12. Andris Zoltners and Sally Lrimer, "Sales Territory Alignment: An Overlooked Productivity Tool," *Journal of Personal Selling & Sales Management* (Summer 2000), pp. 139–150.
13. This discussion is based on Stephen Heiman, Diane Sanchez, Tad Tuleja, and Robert Miller, *The New Strategic Selling* (New York: Morrow, 1998), pp. 234–269.
14. "Data Watch," *Velocity* (3rd Quarter 2007), p. 8.
15. For more on the development of CLV for valuing customers see Robert Blattberg, Gary Getz, and Jacquelyn Thomas, *Customer Equity: Building and Managing Relationships as Valuable Assets* (Boston: Harvard Business School Press, 2001); Sunil Gupta, Donald Lehmann, and Jennifer Stuart, "Valuing Customers," *Journal of Marketing Research*, 16 (February 2004), pp. 7–18; Roland Rust, Valarie Zeithaml, and Katherine Lemon, *Driving Customer Equity: How Customer Lifetime Value Is Reshaping Corporate Strategy* (New York: The Free Press, 2001).
16. For examples of calculating CLV see Rajkumar Venkatesan and V. Kumar, "A Customer Lifetime Value Framework for Customer Selection and Resource Allocation Strategy," *Journal of Marketing*, 68 (October 2004), pp. 106–125; and Roland Rust, Katherine Lemon, and Valarie Zeithaml, "Return on Marketing: Using Customer Equity to Focus Marketing Strategy," *Journal of Marketing*, 68 (January 2004), pp. 109–127.
17. Martin Elling, Holly Fogle, Charles McKhann, and Chris Simon, "Making More of Pharma's Sales Force," *McKinsey Quarterly*, 3 (2002), p. 5.
18. Jeff Marr and Mark Walker, "Value Mapping for Strategic Accounts," *Velocity* (2nd Quarter 2007), p. 35.
19. For more on time management, see Julie Morgenstern, *Time Management from the Inside Out* (New York: Henry Holt and Company, 2004).
20. Stephen Covey, *The Eighth Habit* (New York: Free Press, 2004).

Chapter 4: Account Relationship Management

1. Joseph Sperry, "Turning Innovative Account Management into Dollars: The Satyam-Caterpillar Story," *Velocity* (4th Quarter 2003), pp. 31–34.
2. Marvin Jolson, "Broadening the Scope of Relationship Selling," *Journal of Personal Selling & Sales Management* (Fall 1997), pp. 75–88.
3. "Looking at the Numbers," *Sales & Marketing Management* (January/February, 2007), p. 39.
4. William Weeks and Lynn Kahle, "Salespeople's Time Use and Performance," *Journal of Personal Selling & Sales Management* (Winter 1990), pp. 29–37.
5. For further development of the purchasing process, see William Moncrief and Greg Marshall, "The Evolution of the Seven Steps of Selling," *Industrial Marketing Management*, 34 (January 2005), pp. 13–22.
6. Weijun Xia and Shiming Wu, "Supplier Selection with Multiple Criteria in Volume Discount Environments," *Omega*, 35 (2007), pp. 494–504.
7. Kapil Tuli, Ajay Kohli, and Sundar Bharadwaj, "Rethinking Customer Solutions: From Product Bundles to Relational Processes," *Journal of Marketing*, 71 (July 2007), 1–17.
8. Tim Minahan, "Chrysler Elects Procurement Team Leader as Its New President," *Purchasing Magazine* (January 1998), pp. 22–25.
9. For more on writing proposals, see Bud Porter-Roth, *Writing Killer Sales Proposals*, (Toroato, Canada: E. P. Entrepreneur, 2004).
10. Mary Shoemaker, "A Framework for Examining IT-enabled Market Relationships," *Journal of Personal Selling & Sales Management*, 21 (Spring 2001), p. 178.
11. James Anderson and James Narus, *Business Market Management* (Upper Saddle River, NJ: Prentice Hall, 2003), pp. 172–173.
12. Tuli et al., "Rethinking Customer Solutions: From Product Bundles to Relational Processes," p. 5.
13. Barton Weitz and Kevin Bradford, "Personal Selling and Sales Management: A Relationship Marketing Perspective," *Journal of the Academy of Marketing Science*, 27, 2 (1999), pp. 241–254.
14. Tuli et al., "Rethinking Customer Solutions: From Product Bundles to Relational Processes," p. 8.
15. Jim Morgan, "Top Execs Pinpoint Six Game-Changing Strategies," *Velocity* (2nd Quarter 2001), p. 48.
16. For more on understanding buyer-seller relationships and interactions, see Gabriel Gonzalez, Douglas Hoffman, and Thomas Ingram, "Improving Relationship Selling Through Failure Analysis and Recovery Efforts: A Framework and Call to Action," *Journal of Personal Selling & Sales Management*, 25 (Winter 2005), pp. 57–65.
17. This discussion is based on concepts presented in Stephen Heiman, Diane Sanchez, Tad Tuleja, and Robert Miller, *The New Strategic Selling* (New York: Morrow, 1998), pp. 81–115.
18. Mark Shonka and Dan Kosch, *Beyond Selling Value* (Chicago: Dearborn Trade Publications, 2002), p. 58.
19. Shonka and Kosch, *Beyond Selling Value*.
20. Tuli et al., "Rethinking Customer Solutions: From Product Bundles to Relational Processes," p. 12.
21. Ben Liu, Nicholas Petruzzi, and D. Sudharshan, "A Service Effort Allocation Model for Assessing Customer Lifetime Value in Service Marketing," *Journal of Services Marketing*, 21 (2007), pp. 24–35.
22. For more on relationship development, see Paul Schurr, "Buyer-Seller Relationship Development Episodes: Theories and Methods," *Journal of Business & Industrial Marketing*, 22 (2007), 161–170.
23. John Abele, Brian Elliott, Ann O'Hara, and Eric Roegner, "Fighting for Your Price," *McKinsey Quarterly*, 4 (2002), p. 21.
24. For more on relationship binders, see Kristof De Wulf, Gaby Oderkerken-Schroeder, and Dawn lacobucci, "Investments in Consumer Relationships: A Cross-Country and Cross-Industry Exploration," *Journal of Marketing*, 65 (October 2001), pp. 33–50.
25. Susan DelVecchio, James Zemanek, Roger McIntyre, and Reid Claxton, "Buyers' Perceptions of Salesperson Tactical Approaches," *Journal of Personal Selling & Sales Management*, 23 (Winter 2003), pp. 39–49.
26. Sandy Jap, "The Strategic Role of the Salesforce in Developing Customer Satisfaction Across the Relationship Lifecycle," *Journal of Personal Selling & Sales Management*, 21 (Spring 2001), pp. 95–108.
27. Douglas Bowman and Das Narayandas, "Linking Customer Management Effort to Customer Profitability in Business Markets," *Journal of Marketing Research*, 41 (November 2004), pp. 433–447.
28. For more on building trust, see Louise Young, "Trust: Looking Forward and Back," *Journal of Business & Industrial Marketing*, 21 (2006), pp. 439–445; Carolyn Nicholson, Larry Compeau, and Rajesh Sethi, "The Role of Interpersonal Liking in Building Trust in Long-Term Channel Relationships," *Journal of the Academy of Marketing Science*, 29 (2001), pp. 3–15.

29. Lan Xia, Kent Monroe, and Jennifer Cox, "The Price is Unfair! A Conceptual Framework of Price Fairness Perceptions," *Journal of Marketing*, 68 (October 2004), pp. 1–151; and Roy Lweicki and Barbara Bunker, "Trust in Relationships: A Model of Development and Decline," in *Conflict, Cooperation, and Justice: Essays Inspired by the Work of Morton Deutsch*, The Jossey-Bass Management Series and The Jossey-Bass Conflict Series, vol. 33.

30. See the work of Erik Rautalinko and Hans-Oluf Lisper, "Effects of Training Reflective Listening in a Corporate Setting," *Journal of Business and Psychology* 18 (Spring 2004), pp. 281–299, and Lucette Comer and Tanya Drollinger, "Active Empathetic Listening and Selling Success: A Conceptual Framework," *Journal of Personal Selling & Sales Management*, 19 (Winter 1999), pp. 15–29.

Chapter 5: Customer Interaction Management

1. Rick Page, *Hope Is Not a Strategy* (New York: Nautilus Press, 2002), p. 45.
2. Robert Peterson, Michael Cannito, and Steven Brown, "An Exploratory Investigation of Voice Characteristics and Selling Effectiveness," *Journal of Personal Selling & Sales Management* (Winter 1995), pp. 1–15.
3. Jeff Thull, *Exceptional Selling*, p. 59.
4. Betsy Cummings, "Wake Up, Salespeople," *Sales & Marketing Management* (June 2002), p. 11.
5. Martin Elling, Holly Fogle, Charles McKhann, and Chris Simon, "Making More of Pharma's Sales Force," *McKinsey Quarterly* (August 2002), pp. 12–13.
6. Kathleen Cholewka, "E-Market Stats," *Sales & Marketing Management* (June 2002), p. 19.
7. Alston Gardner, Stephen Bistritz, and Jay Klompmaker, "Selling to Senior Executives: Part 1," *Marketing Management* (Summer 1998), p. 14.
8. For more on call reluctance, see Willem Verbeke and Richard Bagozzi, "Sales Call Anxiety: Exploring What It Means When Fear Rules a Sales Encounter," *Journal of Marketing*, 64 (July 2000), pp. 88–101.
9. Thomas Stafford, "Conscious and Unconscious Processing of Priming Cues in Selling Encounters," *Journal of Personal Selling & Sales Management* (Spring 1996), pp. 37–44.
10. For more on the impact of first impressions, see Kenneth Evans, Robert Kleine, Timothy Landry, and Lawrence Crosby, "How First Impressions of a Customer Impact Effectiveness in an Initial Sales Encounter," *Journal of the Academy of Marketing Science* (2000), pp. 512–526.
11. John Andy Wood, "NLP Revisited: Nonverbal Communications and Signals of Trustworthiness," *Journal of Personal Selling & Sales Management*, 26 (Spring 2006), pp. 198–204.
12. David Lichtenthal and Thomas Tellefsen, "Toward a Theory of Business Buyer-Seller Similarity," *Journal of Personal Selling & Sales Management*, 21 (Winter 2001), pp. 1–14.
13. There is also research suggesting that buyer and seller nonbusiness disclosures do not affect the quality of the relationship, but that business disclosures have an impact on the quality of the relationship. See Richard Jacobs, Kenneth Evans, Robert Kleine, and Timothy Landry, "Disclosure and Its Reciprocity as Predictors of Key Outcomes of an Initial Sales Encounter," *Journal of Personal Selling & Sales Management*, 21 (Winter 2001), pp. 51–61.
14. Ralph Giacobbe, Donald Jackson, Lawrence Crosby, and Claudia Bridges, "A Contingency Approach to Adaptive Selling Behavior and Sales Performance: Selling Situations and Salesperson Characteristics," *Journal of Personal Selling & Sales Management*, 26 (Spring 2006), pp. 115–142.
15. Lawrence Chonko and Eli Jones, "The Need for Speed. Agility Selling," *Journal of Personal Selling & Sales Management*, 25 (Fall 2006), pp. 372–382.
16. Theodore Kinni, "How Strategic is Your Sales Strategy?" *Harvard Management Update* (February 2004), p. 5.
17. Richard Jacobs, Ken Evans, Robert Kleine, and Timothy Landry, "Disclosure and Its Reciprocity as Predictors of Key Outcomes of an Initial Sales Encounter," *Journal of Personal Selling & Sales Management*, 21 (Winter 2001), pp. 51–61.
18. Roberta Schultz and Kenneth Evans, "Strategic Communication by Key Account Representatives," *Journal of Personal Selling & Sales Management*, 22 (Winter 2002), pp. 23–31.
19. This is not the only way that personal motives have been classified. For alternatives see Lou Quast and Jane Helsing, "Motivating Others as They Would Have You Motivate Them," *Velocity* (1st Quarter 2001), pp. 31–34; LaVon Koerner, "Value Door Relationship Management," *Velocity* (2nd Quarter 2001), pp. 29–34.
20. David Reid, Ellen Pullins, and Richard Plank, "The Impact of Purchase Situation on Salesperson Communication Behaviors in Business Markets," *Industrial Marketing Management*, 31 (2002), pp. 205–213.
21. Annie Liu and Mark Leach, "Developing Loyal Customers with a Value-adding Sales Force: Examining Customer Satisfaction and the Perceived Credibility of Consultative Salespeople," *Journal of Selling & Sales Management*, 21 (Spring 2001), pp. 147–156.

22. For more on the format of successful sales proposals, see Tom Sant, Mark Shonka, and Dan Kosch, "Gaining Competitive Advantage by Integrating Sales Process and Proposal Creation," *Velocity* (3rd Quarter 2000), pp. 25–30.
23. Kim Sydow Campbell, Lenita Davis, and Lauren Skinner, "Rapport Management During the Exploratory Phase of Salesperson-Customer Relationship," *Journal of Personal Selling & Sales Management*, 26 (Fall 2006), pp. 359–370.
24. For more on buyer reactions to selling tactics, see Susan DelVecchio, James Zemanek, Roger McIntyre, and Reid Claxton, "Buyers' Perceptions of Salesperson Tactical Approaches," *Journal of Personal Selling & Sales Management*, 23 (Winter 2003), pp. 39–49.
25. *Exchange*, 17 (Stamford, CT: Xerox Learning Systems, 1990), p. 3.
26. See, for example, Stephen Schiffman, *The 250 Sales Questions to Close the Deal* (Avon, MA: Adams Media, 2005); Brian Tracy, *Be a Sales Superstar* (San Francisco: Berrett-Koehler Publishers, 2002); or Wendy Weiss, *Cold Calling for Women: Opening Doors and Closing Sales* (Philadelphia: D.F.D. Publications, 2000).
27. Richard McFarland, "Crisis of Conscience: The Use of Coercive Sales Tactics and Resultant Felt Stress in the Salesperson," *Journal of Personal Selling & Sales Management*, 23 (Fall 2003), pp. 311–325.
28. Andrea Dixon, Rosann Spiro, and Maqbul Jamil, "Successful and Unsuccessful Sales Calls: Measuring Salesperson Attributions and Behavioral Intentions," *Journal of Marketing*, 65 (July 2001), pp. 64–78.
29. Jennifer Gilbert, "No Strings Attached," *Sales & Sales Management* (July 2004), pp. 22–27.
30. Stacy Dehnel, "Sharing Success Factors," *Velocity* (1st Quarter 2001), p. 21.

Chapter 6: Sales Force Organization

1. Andris Zoltners, Prabhakant Sinha, and Sally Lorimer, *Sales Force Design for Strategic Advantage* (New York: Palgrave Macmillan, 2004), pp. 27–32; and "The Best Managers," *BusinessWeek* (January 10, 2005), p. 62.
2. Andris Zoltners, Prabhakant Sinha, and Greggor Zoltners, *The Complete Guide to Accelerating Sales Force Performance* (New York: AMACOM, 2001), p. 117.
3. George Day, "Managing Market Relationships," *Journal of the Academy of Marketing Science*, 28 (Winter 2000), pp. 24–30.
4. Christian Homburg, John Workman, and Ove Jensen, "Fundamental Changes in Marketing Organization: The Movement Toward a Customer-Focused Organizational Structure," *Journal of the Academy of Marketing Science*, 28 (2000), p. 467.
5. Erin Strout, "Blue Skies Ahead?" *Sales & Marketing Management* (March 2003), pp. 25–29; Spenser Ante, "The New Blue," *Business Week* (March 17, 2003), pp. 80–88; and Daniel Eisenberg, "There's a New Way to Think @ Big Blue," *Time* (January 20, 2003), pp. 49–52.
6. Jerome Colletti and Mary Fiss, *Compensating New Sales Roles*, 2nd ed. (New York: AMACOM, 2001), p. 8.
7. Erika Rasmussen, "3M's Big Strategy for Big Accounts," *Sales & Marketing Management* (September 2002), p. 92.
8. Ravipeet Sohi, Daniel Smith, and Neil Ford, "How Does Sharing a Sales Force Between Multiple Divisions Affect Salespeople?" *Journal of the Academy of Marketing Science* (Summer 1996), pp. 195–207.
9. Zoltners et al., *Accelerating Sales Force Performance*, p. 125.
10. Homburg et al., "Fundamental Changes," p. 463.
11. Jeremy Allen, Sherina Ebrahim, and Gregory Kelly, "Building a Top Consumer Goods Sales Force," *The McKinsey Quarterly* (February 2006), p. 1.
12. Allen et al., "Building a Top Consumer Goods Sales Force," p. 1.
13. Tom Johnson, Larry Killingsworth, and Amy Miller, "Success Is a Marathon, Not a Sprint," *Velocity* (4th Quarter 2001), p. 30.
14. "Data Watch," *Velocity* (3rd Quarter 2003), p. 6.
15. See for example Julian Birkinshaw, Omar Toulan, and David Arnold, "Global Account Management in Multinational Corporations: Theory and Evidence," *Journal of International Business Studies*, 32 (2nd Quarter 2001), pp. 231–248; Sanjit Sengupta, Robert Krapfel, and Michael Pusateri, "An Empirical Investigation of Key Account Salesperson Effectiveness," *Journal of Personal Selling & Sales Management*, 20 (Fall 2000), pp. 253–261; and John Workman, Christian Homburg, and Ove Jensen, "Intraorganizational Determinants of Key Account Management Effectiveness," *Journal of the Academy of Marketing Science*, 31, 1 (2003), pp. 3–21.
16. Based on presentation by Nigel Percy at the M. J. Neeley School of Business, Texas Christian University, February 20, 2008.
17. Christian Homburg, John Workman, and Ove Jensen, "A Configurational Perspective on Key Account Management," *Journal of Marketing*, 66 (April 2002), p. 53.

18. John Workman, Christian Homburg, and Ove Jensen, "Intraorganizational Determinants of Key Account Management Effectiveness," *Journal of the Academy of Marketing Science*, 31 (Winter 2003), p. 15.
19. Connie Bateman and JoAnn Schmidt, "Do Not Call Lists: A Cause for Telemarketing Extinction or Evolution," *Academy of Marketing Studies Journal*, 11 (January 2007), p. 84.
20. Reed Research Group, *Evaluating the Cost of Sales Calls in Business-to-Business Markets* (January 2002). available at www.cahnerscarr.com.
21. Robert Palmatier, Lisa Scheer, and Jan-Bendict Steenkamp, "Customer Loyalty to Whom? Managing the Benefits and Risks of Salesperson-Owned Loyalty," *Journal of Marketing*, 44 (May 2007), pp. 185–199.
22. For more on nonfinancial means of motivating sales agents, see Erin Anderson and Bob Trinkle, *Outsourcing the Sales Function* (Mason, OH: Thomson/Southwestern, 2005).
23. Julia Change, "The Sweet Taste of Sales," *Sales & Marketing Management* (July/August 2007), pp. 20–24.
24. Barry Trailer and Jim Dickie, "Understanding What Your Sales Manager Is Up Against," *Harvard Business Review* (July–August 2006), pp. 48–55.
25. Philip Kotler, Neil Rackham, and Suj Krishnaswamy, "Ending the War Between Sales and Marketing," *Harvard Business Review* (July–August 2006), pp. 68–78.
26. Michael Ahearne, Narasimhan Srinivasan, and Luke Weinstein, "Effect of Technology on Sales Performance: Progressing from Technology Acceptance to Technology Usage and Consequences," *Journal of Personal Selling & Sales Management*, 24 (Fall 2004), pp. 297–310.
27. Economist Intelligence Unit and Andersen Consulting, "A Survey of More than 200 Leading Executives in North America, Europe and Asia," *Velocity* (Summer 1999), p. 3.
28. George Yip and Audrey Bank, "Managing Global Accounts," *Harvard Business Review* (September 2007), p. 103.
29. Julie LaNasa, "Building Customer Teams to Deliver on Your Company's Value Proposition," *Velocity* (1st Quarter 2002), pp. 31–34.
30. Yip and Bank, "Managing Global Accounts," pp. 103–111.
31. Michele Marchetti, "IBM's Marketing Visionary," *Sales & Marketing Management* (September 2000), pp. 52–61.

Management Resource: Territory Design

1. Andris Zoltners and Sally Lorimer, "Sales Territory Alignment: An Overlooked Productivity Tool," *Journal of Personal Selling & Sales Management*, 20 (Summer, 2000), p. 140.
2. This section is based on the discussion in Andris Zoltners, Prabhakant Sinha, and Greggor Zoltners, *Accelerating Sales Force Performance* (New York: AMACOM, 2001), pp. 136–140.
3. Sheree Curry, "Coping with Ever-Enlarging Sales Territory," *Sales & Sales Management* (March 2002), p. 11.
4. Zoltners et al., *Accelerating Sales Force Performance*, p. 154.
5. Ibid.
6. Kirk Smith, Eli Jones, and Edward Blair, "Managing Salesperson Motivation in a Territory Realignment," *Journal of Sales & Sales Management*, 20 (Fall 2000), pp. 215–226.
7. Zoltners et al., *Accelerating Sales Force Performance*, p. 157.
8. Neeli Bendapudi and Rober Leone, "Managing Business-to-Business Customer Relationships Following Key Contact Employee Turnover in a Vendor Firm," *Journal of Marketing*, 66 (April 2002), p. 94.
9. TERRALIGN, Metron, Inc., 11911 Freedom Drive, Suite 800, Reston, VA 20190.

Chapter 7: Recruiting and Selecting Personnel

1. Based on discussions with Jonathan Scarborough, District Manager, Federated Insurance (2007).
2. Thomas N. Ingram, Raymond W. LaForge, and Thomas W. Leigh, "Selling in the New Millennium—A Joint Agenda," *Industrial Marketing Management*, 31 (October 2002), pp. 559–567; Thomas W. Leigh and Greg W. Marshall, "Research Priorities in Sales Strategy and Performance," *Journal of Personal Selling and Sales Management*, 21 (Spring 2001), pp. 283–293.
3. Andris Zoltners, Prabhakant Sinha, and Greggor Zoltners, *The Complete Guide to Accelerating Sales Force Performance* (New York: AMACOM, 2001), p. 167.
4. For more information on the causes of turnover and how to manage turnover, see Eli Jones, Donna Massey Kantak, Charles Futrell, and Mark Johnston, "Leader Behavior, Work-Attitudes, and Turnover of Salespeople: An Integrative Study," *Journal of Personal Selling & Sales Management*, 16 (Spring 1996), pp. 13–23; Pradeep Tyagi and Thomas Wotruba, "An Exploratory Study of Reverse Causality Relationships Among Sales Force Turnover Variables," *Journal of the Academy of Marketing Science*, 21 (Spring 1993), pp. 143–153; and Jeff Sager, "A Longitudinal Assessment of Change in Sales Force Turnover," *Journal of the Academy of Marketing Science*, 19 (Winter 1991), pp. 25–36.

5. Harris and Brannick, *Finding and Keeping Great Employees*, pp. 18–19; and Rick E. Ridnour, Felicia G. Lassk, and C. David Shepard, "An Exploratory Assessment of Sales Culture Variables: Strategic Implications Within the Banking Industry," *Journal of Personal Selling & Sales Management* (Summer 2001), pp. 247–254.
6. Based on discussions with Alan Frakes, Zone Vice President, Klein Tools, Inc. (2008).
7. Earl Naumann, Scott M. Widmier, and Donald W. Jackson, Jr. "Examining the Relationship Between Work Attitudes and Propensity to Leave Among Expatriate Salespeople," *Journal of Personal Selling & Sales Management* (Fall 2000), pp. 227–241.
8. William L. Cron, Greg W. Marshall, Jagdip Singh, Rosann L. Spiro, and Harish Sujan, "Salesperson Selection, Training and Development: Trends, Implications, and Research Opportunities," *Journal of Personal Selling and Sales Management*, 25 (Spring 2005), pp. 123–136; Andrew J. Vinchur, Jeffery S. Schippmann, Fred S. Switzer III, and Philip L. Roth, "A Meta-Analytic Review of Predictors of Job Performance for Salespeople," *Journal of Applied Psychology* (August 1998), pp. 586–597.
9. Murray R. Barrick, Greg L. Stewart, and Mike Piotrowski, "Personality and Job Performance: Test of the Mediating Effects of Motivation Among Sales Representatives," *Journal of Applied Psychology* (February 2002), pp. 43–51.
10. Lyndon E. Dawson, Jr., Barlow Soper, and Charles E. Pettijohn, "The Effects of Empathy on Salesperson Effectiveness," *Psychology & Marketing* (July/August 1992), pp. 297–311.
11. Rosann Sprio and Barton Weitz, "Adaptive Selling: Conceptualization, Measurement, and Nomological Validity," *Journal of Marketing Research*, 27 (February 1990), pp. 61–69.
12. Arun Sharma, Michael Levy, and Heiner Evanschitzky, "The Variance in Sales Performance Explained by the Knowledge Structures of Salespeople," *Journal of Personal Selling and Sales Management*, 2 (Spring 2007), pp. 169–181; Thomas W. Leigh and Patrick F. McGraw, "Mapping the Procedural Knowledge of Industrial Sales Personnel: A Script-Theoretic Analysis," *Journal of Marketing*, 53(1) (1989), pp. 16–34; Leong, Siew Meng, Paul S. Busch and Deborah Roedder John, "Knowledge Bases and Salesperson Effectiveness: A Script-Theoretic Analysis," *Journal of Marketing Research*, 26 (May 1989), pp. 164–178.
13. For more on the biases involved in hiring salespeople, see Greg W. Marshall, Thomas H. Stone, and I. M. Jawahar, "Selection Decision Making by Sales Managers and Human Resource Managers: Decision Impact, Decision Frame and Time of Valuation," *Journal of Personal Selling & Sales Management* (Winter 2001), pp. 19–28; and Greg W. Marshall, Miriam B. Stamps, and Jesse N. Moore, "Preinterview Biases: The Impact of Race, Physical Attractiveness, and Sales Job Type on Preinterew Impressions of Sales Job Applicants," *Journal of Personal Selling & Sales Management* (Fall 1998), pp. 21–38.
14. Michael A. Wiles and Rosann Spiro, "Attracting Graduates to Sales Positions and the Role of Recruiter Knowledge: A Reexamination," *Journal of Personal Selling and Sales Management*, 24 (Winter 2004), pp. 39–48.
15. Tricia Campbell, "Finding Hidden Sales Talent," *Sales & Marketing Management* (March 1999), p. 84.
16. Campbell, "Finding Hidden Sales Talent," p. 85.
17. Andy Cohen, "Hire Power," *Sales & Marketing Management Magazine* (December 2001), p. 13; Zoltners et al., *The Complete Guide to Accelerating Sales Force Performance*, p. 187.
18. Per discussion with Bill Jones, CEO, O'Neal Steel, Inc. (2008).
19. Julia Chang and Andy Cohen, "Should You Raid Your Rival's Sales Force?" *Sales & Marketing Management Magazine* (August 2002), pp. 43–47.
20. Timothy S. Bland and Sue S. Stalcup, "Build a Legal Employment Application," *HR Magazine*, 44 (March 1999), p. 129.
21. Michael A. Wiles and Rosann Spiro, "Attracting Graduates to Sales Positions and the Role of Recruiter knowledge: A Reexamination," *Journal of Personal Selling and Sales Management*, 24 (Winter 2004), pp. 39–48.
22. William L. Cron, Greg W. Marshall, Jagdip Singh, Rosann L. Spiro, and Harish Sujan, "Salesperson Selection, Training and Development: Trends, Implications, and Research Opportunities," *Journal of Personal Selling and Sales Management*, 25 (Spring 2005), pp. 123–136.
23. Harris and Brannick, *Finding and Keeping Great Employees*, p. 74.
24. See Zoltners et al., *The Complete Guide to Accelerating Sales Force Performance* for more information about this study.

Chapter 8: Sales Training

1. Kelly Shermach, "Shifting the IT Sales Game: Increased Competition Has Changed Sales Processes," www.salesandmarketing.com (September 6, 2006), accessed August 17, 2008.
2. William L. Cron, Greg W. Marshall, Jagdip Singh, Rosann L. Spiro, and Harish Sujan, "Salesperson Selection, Training and Development: Trends, Implications, and Research Opportunities," *Journal of Personal Selling and Sales Management*, 25 (Spring 2005), pp. 126–136.

3. Cron et al., "Salesperson Selection, Training and Development: Trends, Implications, and Research Opportunities," p. 124.
4. Mark P. Leach and Annie H. Liu, "Investigating Relationships Among Sales Training Evaluation Methods," *Journal of Personal Selling and Sales Management* (Fall 2003), pp. 327–339; Seonaid Farrell and A. Ralph Hakstain, "Improving Salesperson Performance, A Meta-Analytic Investigation of the Effectiveness and Utility of Personnel Selection Procedures, and Training Interventions," *Psychology & Marketing* (March 2001), pp. 281–316.
5. Mark P. Leach and Annie H. Liu, "Investigating Relationships Among Sales Training Evaluation Methods," p. 327.
6. Tammy Galvin, "The 2004 Top 100," *Training* (October 2004), pp. 40–48.
7. Andris Zoltners, Prabhakant Sinha, and Greggor Zoltners, *The Complete Guide to Accelerating Sales Force Performance* (New York: AMACOM, 2001), p. 167.
8. For more information about the difficulties in evaluating sales training, see Ashraf M. Attia, Earl D. Honeycutt, and Magdy Mohamed Attia, "The Difficulties of Evaluating Sales Training," *Industrial Marketing Management*, 31 (2002), pp. 253–259.
9. Earl D. Honeycutt, Jr., Kiran Karande, Ashraf Attia, and Steven D. Maurer, "A Utility Based Framework for Evaluating the Financial Impact of Sales Force Training Programs," *Journal of Personal Selling & Sales Management* (Summer 2001), pp. 229–238.
10. Mark P. Leach, Annie H. Liu, and Wesley J. Johnston, "The Role of Self-Regulation Training in Developing the Motivation Management Capabilities of Salespeople, *Journal of Personal Selling and Sales Management*, 25 (Summer 2006), pp. 270–281.
11. Based on conversations with William J. Bartholomew, former Director of Sales, Tellabs, Inc.
12. Andris Zoltners, Prabhakant Sinha, and Sally E. Lorimer, *Sales Force Design for Strategic Advantage* (New York: Palgrave Macmillan, 2004), p. 336.
13. Erin Strout, "Prisoners of Paperwork," *Sales & Marketing Management* (December 2002), pp. 41–45.
14. Based on conversations with John Campo, Vice President of Sales, O'Neal Steel, Inc. (February 2008).
15. Mark McMaster, "Is Your Training a Waste of Money?" *Sales & Marketing Management* (January 2001), pp. 40–48.
16. Tammy Galvin, "The 2004 Top 100," *Training* (October 2004), pp. 40–48.
17. Carl Wiens, "2002 Sales Training Survey," *Sales & Marketing Management* (July 2002), pp. 34–37.
18. Zoltners et al., *Sales Force Design for Strategic Advantage*, p. 333.
19. For more information on salespeople's knowledge structures, see Thomas W. Leigh, Thomas E. DeCarlo, David Allbright, James Lollar, and Kay Keck, "Persuasion Knowledge Distinctions Among Higher and Lower Performing Sales Agents" (Working Paper, 2008); Thomas W. Leigh and Patrick McGraw, "Mapping the Procedural Knowledge of Industrial Sales Personnel: A Script-Theoretic Investigation," *Journal of Marketing*, 53 (January 1989), pp. 16–34; and Thomas Ainscough, Thomas E. DeCarlo, and Thomas W. Leigh, "Building Expert Systems for Novice Salespeople from the Selling Scripts of Multiple Experts," *Journal of Services Marketing*, 10 (1996), pp. 23–40.
20. Malcolm Wheatley, "ERP Training Stinks," *CIO Magazine* (June 1, 2000).
21. Thomas W. Leigh and John O. Summers, "An Initial Evaluation of Industrial Buyers' Impressions of Salespersons' Nonverbal Cues," *Journal of Personal Selling and Sales Management*, 25 (Winter 2002), pp. 41–53.
22. Zoltners et al., *Sales Force Design for Strategic Advantage*, p. 335.
23. The H. R. Chally Group, *The Customer Selected World Class Sales Excellence Research Report*, p. 52.
24. For more on mentoring, see Ellen Pullins, Leslie Fine, and Wendy Warren, "Identifying Peer Mentors in the Sales Force: An Exploratory Investigation of Willingness and Ability," *Journal of the Academy of Marketing Science*, 24 (Spring 1996), pp. 125–136.
25. Julia Chang, "Born to Sell?" *Sales & Marketing Management* (July 2003), 34–37.
26. Chris Lee, "IBM Takes the Top Spot," Sales & Marketing Management.com (March 1, 2005).
27. Mark McMaster, "Express Train," *Sales & Marketing Management* (May 2002), pp. 46–54.
28. For an interesting application of Kirkpatrick's framework in assessing sales training effectiveness, see Mark P. Leach and Annie H. Liu, "Investigating Interrelationships Among Sales Training Evaluation Methods," *Journal of Personal Selling & Sales Management*, 23 (Fall 2003), pp. 327–329; Donald L. Kirkpatrick, "Techniques for Evaluating Training Programs," *Journal of the American Society for Training and Development*, 13 (1959), pp. 3–9.
29. Sarah Boehle, "Are You Too Nice to Train?" *Sales & Marketing Management* (August 1, 2006). Retrieved March 1, 2008, www.smm.com

30. Christine Galea and Carl Wiens, "2002 Sales Training Survey," *Sales & Marketing Management* (July 2002), pp. 34–37.
31. Tammy Galvin, "The 2004 Top 100," *Training* (October 2004), pp. 40–48.

Chapter 9: Leadership

1. Per conversation with Liz Crute, Divisional Vice President of Pitney Bowes, Inc. (August 2007). The name of the sales rep was changed for confidentiality purposes.
2. Society for Human Resource Management's *2006 U.S. Job Retention Poll* (http://www.shrm.org/press_published/CMS_019635.asp). Accessed April 20, 2008.
3. See Thomas N. Ingram, Raymond W. LaForge, William B. Locander, Scott B. MacKenzie, and Philip M. Podsakoff, "New Directions in Sales Leadership Research," *Journal of Personal Selling & Sales Management* (Spring 2005), pp. 137–54; and Scott B. MacKenzie, Phillip M. Podsakoff, and Gregory A. Rich, "Transformational and Transactional Leadership and Salesperson Performance," *Journal of the Academy of Marketing Science* (Spring 2001), pp. 115–34.
4. For a review of sales leadership studies, see Artur Baldauf, David W. Cravens, and Nigel F. Piercy, "Sales Management Control Research-Synthesis and an Agenda for Future Research," *Journal of Personal Selling and Sales Management* (Winter 2005), pp. 7–26; and Thomas N. Ingram, Raymond W. LaForge, William B. Locander, Scott B. MacKenzie, and Philip M. Podsakoff, "New Directions in Sales Leadership Research," *Journal of Personal Selling & Sales Management* (Spring 2005), pp. 137–54.
5. Per conversation with Liz Crute, Divisional Vice President, Pitney Bowes, Inc. (August 2007).
6. Based on John French, Jr. and Bertram Raven, "The Bases of Social Power," in *Studies in Social Power*, D. Cartwright, ed. (Ann Arbor: University of Michigan Press, 1959).
7. Michael Weinreb, "A Fine Line," *Sales & Marketing Management* (October 2002), pp. 49–54.
8. For more on organizational change see: Lawrence B. Chonko, Eli Jones, and Alan J. Dubinsky, "The Role of Environmental Turbulence, Readiness for Change, and Salesperson Learning in the Success of Sales Force Change," *Journal of Personal Selling & Sales Management* (Fall 2004), p. 227–245.
9. See William A. Weeks, James Roberts, Lawrence B. Chonko, and Eli Jones, "Organizational Readiness for Change, Individual Fear of Change, and Sales Manager Performance. An Empirical Investigation," *Journal of Personal Selling & Sales Management* (Winter 2002), pp. 7–17; and Karen E. Flaherty and James M. Pappas, "The Role of Trust in Salesperson-Sales Manager Relationships," *Journal of Personal Selling & Sales Management*, 20 (Fall 2000), pp. 271–278.
10. This section is based on Jerome A. Colletti and Lawrence B. Chonko, "Change Management Initiatives: Moving Sales Organizations from Obsolescence to High Performance," *Journal of Personal Selling & Sales Management*, 17, No. 2 (Spring 1997), pp. 1–30; and Gerald Bauer, Mark Baunchalk, Thomas Ingram, and Raymond LaForge, eds. *Emerging Trends in Sales Thought and Practice* (Westport, CT: Quorum Books, 1998).
11. Thomas N. Ingram, Raymond W. LaForge, William B. Locander, Scott B. MacKenzie, and Philip M. Podsakoff, "New Directions in Sales Leadership Research," *Journal of Personal Selling & Sales Management* (Spring 2005), pp. 137–154.
12. This section is largely based on Gary A. Yukl, *Leadership in Organizations*, 6th ed. (Englewood Cliffs, NJ: Prentice Hall, 2006); and Scott B. MacKenzie, Phillip M. Podsakoff, and Gregory A. Rich, "Transformational and Transactional Leadership and Salesperson Performance," *Journal of the Academy of Marketing Science* (Spring 2001), pp. 115–134.
13. For an international perspective on matching desired sales styles, see Thomas E. DeCarlo, Raymond C. Rody, and James E. DeCarlo, "A Cross National Example of Supervisory Management Practices in the Sales Force," *Journal of Personal Selling & Sales Management*, 19, No. 1 (Winter 1999), pp. 1–14.
14. Bernard Jaworski and Ajay Kohli, "Supervisory Feedback: Alternative Types and Their Impact on Salespeople's Performance and Satisfaction," *Journal of Marketing Research*, 28 (May 1991), pp. 190–201.
15. Tom Atkinson and Ron Koprowski, "Finding the Weak Links," *Harvard Business Review* (July-August 2006), pp. 22.
16. Atkinson, "Finding the Weak Links," p. 22. Jaworski and Kohli, "Supervisory Feedback: Alternative Types and Their Impact on Salespeople's Performance and Satisfaction," pp. 190–201.
17. Gregory A. Rich, "The Constructs of Sales Coaching: Supervisory Feedback, Role Modeling and Trust," *Journal of Personal Selling & Sales Management*, 18, No. 1 (Winter 1998), pp. 53–63.
18. Ibid.
19. Gregory A. Rich, "The Sales Manager as a Role Model: Effects on Trust Job Satisfaction, and Performance of Salespeople," *Journal of the Academy of Marketing Science*, 25 (October 1997), pp. 319–328.

20. Kwaku Atuahene-Gima and Haiyang Li, "When Does Trust Matter? Antecedents and Contingent Effects of Supervise Trust on Performance in Selling New Products in China and the United States," *Journal of Marketing* (July 2002), pp. 61–81.
21. Karen E. Flaherty and James M. Pappas, "The Role of Trust in Salesperson-Sales Manager Relationships," *Journal of Personal Selling & Sales Management* (Fall 2000), pp. 271–278.
22. Andris Zoltners, Prabhakant Sinha, and Sally E. Lorimer, *Sales Force Design for Strategic Advantage* (New York: Palgrave Macmillan, 2004), p. 38.
23. Michele Marchetti "Why Teams Fail," *Sales & Marketing Management* (June 1997), pp. 91–92.
24. This section is based on: Eli Jones, Andrea L. Dixon, Lawrence B. Chonko, and Joseph P. Cannon, "Key Accounts and Team Selling: A Review, Framework and Agenda," *Journal of Personal Selling & Sales Management* (Spring 2005), pp. 181–198.
25. Michael J. Barone and Thomas E. DeCarlo, "Trend Effects in Managerial Decision Making," Working Paper (July, 2007).
26. Steven G. Rogelberg, Cliff Scott and John Kello, "The Science and Fiction of Meetings," *MIT Sloan Management Review* (Winter 2007), pp. 17–21.
27. John Ueland, "Meetings," *Sales & Marketing Management* (August 1998), p. 49.
28. Erin Strout, "Masterful Meetings," *Sales & Marketing Management* (May 2000), pp. 68–76.
29. Brian Moskal, "Easy ROI: Three Areas Where It Pays to Get Technical," *Sales & Marketing Management* (May 2002), p. 21.
30. Harry J. Abramson, "The Perfect Sales Meeting in the Eye of the Rep," *Agency Sales* (February 2002), pp. 55–60.
31. Jennifer Gilbert, "Become a Meeting Master," *Sales & Marketing Management* (December 2002), pp. 46–51.
32. Julia Chang, "A Bore No More," *Sales & Marketing Management* (August 2002), p. 55.
33. Leslie M. Fine, C. David Shepherd, and Susan L. Josephs, "Insights into Sexual Harassments of Salespeople by Customers: The Role of Gender and Customer Power," *Journal of Personal Selling & Sales Management*, 19 (Spring 1999), pp. 19–34.
34. See Wendy L. Kosanovich, Jill L. Rosenberg, and Lisa Swanson, "Preventing and Correcting Sexual Harassment: A Guide to the Ellerth/Faragher Affirmative Defense," *Employee Relations Law Journal* (Summer 2002), pp. 79–99 for more information about developing sexual harassment policies.
35. As reported on the National Institute on Alcohol Abuse and Alcoholism's Web page (http://www.niaaa.nih.gov), August 2007.
36. Judith Spain and Rosemary Ramsey, "Workers' Compensation and Superior Liability Legal Cases Involving Salespersons' Misuse of Alcohol," *Journal of Personal Selling & Sales Management* (Fall 2000), pp. 263–269.

Chapter 10: Ethical Leadership

1. This section is based on Joseph L. Badaracco, Jr., *Defining Moments: When Managers Must Choose Between Right and Right* (Boston: Harvard Business School Press), 1997.
2. Bridget O'Brian, "Prudential Fined $20 Million by NASD over Its Sales of Variable Life Insurance," *The Wall Street Journal* (July 9, 1999), pp. C1, C11.
3. Mara Der Hovanesian, "Markets in Turmoil: Bonfire of the Builders," *Business Week* (August 13, 2007), pp. 26–30.
4. Charles H. Schwepker, Jr. and David J. Good, "Marketing Control and Sales Force Customer Orientation," *Journal of Personal Selling & Sales Management*, 24 (Summer 2004), pp. 167–179. See also William A. Weeks, Terry W. Loe, Lawrence B. Chonko, and Kirk Wakefield, "The Effect of Perceived Ethical Climate on the Search for Sales Force Excellence," *Journal of Personal Selling & Sales Management*, 24 (Summer 2004), pp. 199–214.
5. Jay Prakash Mulki, Fernando Jaramillo, William B. Locander, "Effects of Ethical Climate and Supervisory Trust on Salesperson's Job Attitudes and Intentions to Quit," *Journal of Personal Selling & Sales Management*, 26 (Winter 2006), pp. 19–26. See also, Fernando Jaramillo, Jay Prakash Mulki, Paul Solomon, "The Role of Ethical Climate on Salesperson's Role Stress, Job Attitudes, Turnover Intention, and Job Performance," *Journal of Personal Selling & Sales Management*, 26 (Summer 2006), pp. 272–282.
6. Susan Powell Mantel, "Choice or Perception: How Affect Influences Ethical Choices Among Salespeople," *Journal of Personal Selling & Sales Management*, 25 (Winter 2005), pp. 43–55.
7. Eugene Sivadas, Susan Bardi Kleiser, James Kellaris, and Robert Dahlstrom, "Moral Philosophy, Ethical Evaluations, and Sales Manager Hiring Intentions," *Journal of Personal Selling & Sales Management*, 23 (Winter 2003), pp. 7–21.
8. Ken Bass, Tim Barnett, and Gene Brown, "The Moral Philosophy of Sales Managers and Its Influence on Ethical Decision Making," *Journal of Personal Selling & Sales Management*, 18 (Spring 1998), pp. 1–17.

9. Niccolò Machiavelli, *The Prince* (New York: Mentor Classics, 1952).
10. Eric Strout, "To Tell the Truth," *Sales & Marketing Management* (July 2002), pp. 40–47.
11. Erin Strout, "Are Your Salespeople Ripping You Off?" *Sales & Marketing Management* (March 2001), p. 59.
12. Melinda Ligos, "Are Your Reps Bribing Customers?" *Sales & Marketing Management* (March 2002), pp. 33–40.
13. Ibid.
14. Sean Valentine and Tim Barnett, "Ethics Codes and Sales Professionals' Perceptions of Their Organizations' Ethical Values." *Journal of Business Ethics* (October 2002), pp. 191–200.
15. Alan J. Dubinsky, Marvin A. Jolson, Ronald E. Michaels, Masaaki Kotabe, and Chae Un Lim, "Ethical Perceptions of Field Sales Personnel: An Empirical Assessment," *Journal of Sales & Marketing Management* (Fall 1992), p. 18.
16. Gabriella Stern and Joann S. Lublin, "New GM Rules Curb Wining and Dining," *The Wall Street Journal* (May 5, 1996), p. B1.
17. Charles Haddad and Amy Barrett, "A Whistle-Blower Rocks an Industry," *Business Week* (June 24, 2002), pp. 126–130.
18. Charles H. Schwepker Jr., "Ethical Climate's Relationship to Job Satisfaction, Organizational Commitment, and Turnover Intention in the Sales Force," *Journal of Business Research* (October 2001), p. 39.
19. Ken Bass, Tim Barnett, and Gene Brown, "The Moral Philosophy of Sales Managers and Its Influence on Ethical Decision Making," *Journal of Personal Selling & Sales Management*, 18 (Spring 1998), pp. 1–17.

Chapter 11: Motivating Salespeople

1. Based on discussions with Robby Armstrong, Area Manager, Eaton Corporation (October 2007).
2. Frederick Herzberg, "One More Time: How Do You Motivate Employees?" *Harvard Business Review*, 46 (January–February 1968), pp. 53–62.
3. Geoffrey Brewer, "What Makes Great Salespeople?" *Sales & Marketing Management* (May 1994), pp. 82–92.
4. Marvin Jolson, "The Salesman's Career Cycle," *Journal of Marketing*, 38 (July 1974), pp. 39–46.
5. The discussion in this section is based on the following studies: Karen E. Flaherty and James M. Pappas, "The Influence of Career Stage on Job Attitudes: Toward a Contingency Perspective," *Journal of Personal Selling & Sales Management*, 22 (Summer 2002), pp. 135–143; William L. Cron and John W. Slocum, "The Influence of Career Stages on Salespeople's Job Attitudes, Work Perceptions and Performance," *Journal of Marketing Research* (May 1986), pp. 119–129.
6. Karen E. Flaherty and James M. Pappas, "The Influence of Career Stage on Job Attitudes: Toward a Contingency Perspective," *Journal of Personal Selling & Sales Management*, 22 (Summer 2002), pp. 135–143.
7. Ibid.
8. Katharine Kaplan, "Better With Age," *Sales & Marketing Management* (July 2001), pp. 58–62.
9. For further discussion of expectancy theory, see Gordon T. Gray and Stacia Wert-Gray, "Research Note: Decision-Making Processes and Formation of Salespeople's Expectancies, Instrumentalities, and Valences," *Journal of Personal Selling & Sales Management* (Summer 1999), pp. 53–59; Thomas E. DeCarlo, R. Kenneth Teas, and James C. McElroy, "Salesperson Performance Attribution Processes and the Formation of Expectancy Estimates," *Journal of Personal Selling & Sales Management*, 27 (Summer 1997), pp. 1–17; and Wesley J. Johnston and Keysuk Kim, "Performance Attribution and Expectancy Linkages in Personal Selling," *Journal of Marketing*, 58 (October 1994), pp. 68–81.
10. For a detailed discussion of role perceptions, see Jeffrey Sager, "A Structural Model Depicting Salespeople's Job Stress," *Journal of the Academy of Marketing Science*, 22 (January 1994), pp. 74–84.
11. See Andrea L. Dixon, Rosann L. Spiro, and Maqbul Jamil, "Successful and Unsuccessful Sales Calls: Measuring Salesperson Attributions and Behavioral Intentions," *Journal of Marketing* (July 2001), pp. 64–78; and Thomas E. DeCarlo, R. Kenneth Teas, and James C. McElroy, "Salesperson Performance Attribution Processes and the Formation of Expectancy Estimates," *Journal of Personal Selling & Sales Management*, 27 (Summer 1997).
12. Andris Zoltners, Prabhakant Sinha, and Greggor Zoltners, *The Complete Guide to Accelerating Sales Force Performance* (New York: AMACOM, 2001), p. 277.
13. For more on this subject, see C. Fred Miao and Kenneth R. Evans, "The Impact of Salesperson Motivation on Role Perceptions and Job Performance: A Cognitive and Affective Perspective." *Journal of Personal Selling & Sales Management*, 27 (Winter 2006), 89–101: Steven Brown and Robert Peterson, "The Effect of Effort on Sales Performance and Job Satisfaction," *Journal of Marketing*, 58 (April 1994), pp. 70–80.
14. Zoltners et al., *The Complete Guide to Accelerating Sales Force Performance*, p. 329.
15. Michele Marchetti, "The Art of Setting Sales Quotas," *Sales & Marketing Management* (April 2000), p. 4.

16. For more information on goal theory and its application to sales management, see Lawrence S. Silver, Sean Dwyer, and Bruce Alford, "Learning and Performance Goal Orientation of Salespeople Revisited: The Role of Performance-Approach and Performance-Avoidance Orientations," *Journal of Personal Selling & Sales Management* (Winter 2006); pp. 27–39; Thomas Wotruba, "The Effect of Goal-Setting on the Performance of Independent Sales Agents in Direct Selling," *Journal of Personal Selling & Sales Management*, 9 (Fall 1989), pp. 22–29.
17. See William Ross, "Performance Against Quota and the Call Selection Decision," *Journal of Marketing Research*, 28 (August 1991), pp. 296–306, for more information on how quota difficulty may influence salespeople's strategies for achieving the quota.
18. Silver, Dwyer, and Alford, "Learning and Performance Goal Orientation of Salespeople Revisited: The Role of Performance-Approach and Performance-Avoidance Orientations," pp. 27–39.
19. Zoltners et al., *The Complete Guide to Accelerating Sales Force Performance*, p. 359; see also Bernard Jaworski and Ajay Kohli, "Supervisory Feedback: Alternative Types and Their Impact on Salespeople's Performance and Satisfaction," *Journal of Marketing Research*, 28 (May 1991), pp. 190–201; and Ajay Kohli and Bernard Jaworski, "The Influence of Coworker Feedback on Salespeople," *Journal of Marketing*, 58 (October 1994), pp. 82–94.
20. Steven P. Brown, William L. Cron, and John W. Slocum Jr., "Effects of Trait Competitiveness and Perceived Intraorganizational Competition on Salesperson Goal Setting and Performance," *Journal of Marketing*, 62 (October 1998), pp. 88–98.
21. AnJanette A. Nease, Brad O. Mudgett, and Miguel A. Quinones, "Relationships Among Feedback Sign, Self-Efficacy, and Acceptance of Performance Feedback," *Journal of Applied Psychology* (October 1999), pp. 806–814.
22. The Buying Power Index is reported by cities, countries, and states each July by *Sales & Marketing Management* magazine.
23. Zoltners et al., *The Complete Guide to Accelerating Sales Force Performance*, p. 265.
24. Kathleen Cholewka, "Tech Tools: Online Incentives," *Sales & Marketing Management* (July 2001), p. 24.
25. Julia Chang, "Trophy Value," *Sales & Marketing Management* (October 2004), pp. 24–29.
26. Based on discussions with Liz Crute, Vice President, Pitney Bowes' Credit Corporation (October 2007).
27. Steven Brown, William Cron, and Thomas Leigh, "Do Feelings of Success Mediate Sales Performance-Work Attitude Relationships?" *Journal of the Academy of Marketing Science*, 21 (Spring 1993), pp. 91–100.

Chapter 12: Compensating Salespeople

1. Joseph Kornik, Maggie Rauch, Rebecca Aronauer, "What's It All Worth? 2007 Compensation Survey," *Sales & Marketing Management* (May 2007), pp. 27–39.
2. Ellen Neuborne, "A Compensation Plan Checkup," *Sales & Marketing Management* (May 2003), pp. 38–41.
3. Michele Marchetti, "Rethinking Compensation Plans," *Sales & Marketing Management* (September 2007), p. 14.
4. Andris Zoltners, Prabhakant Sinha, and Greggor Zoltners, *The Complete Guide to Accelerating Sales Force Performance* (New York: AMACOM, 2001), p. 301.
5. Ibid., p. 50.
6. For more information on how salesperson career stages attect compensation perceptions, see Karen E. Flaherty and James M. Pappas, "The Influence of Career Stage on Job Attitudes: Toward a Contingency Perspective," *Journal of Personal Selling and Sales Management*, 22 (Summer 2002), pp. 135–143.
7. Thomas E. DeCarlo, "The Effects of Suspicion of Ulterior Motives and Sales Message on Salesperson Evaluation," *Journal of Consumer Psychology*, 15 (2005), pp. 238–249.
8. George John and Barton Weitz, "Salesforce Compensation: An Empirical Investigation of Factors Related to Use of Salary Versus Incentive Compensation," *Journal of Marketing Research*, 26 (February 1989), p. 9.
9. Leo Jakobson, "The Leader of The Band," *Incentive* (January 2007), pp. 12–17.
10. Kissan Joseph and Manohar U. Kalwani, "The Role of Bonus Pay in Salesforce Compensation Plans," *Industrial Marketing Management*, 27 (March 1998), pp. 147–159.
11. Based on conversations with John Burns, Branch Sales Manager, Des Moines, IA (2005).
12. Andy Cohen, Jennifer Gilbert, Melinda Ligos, "Extreme Makeovers," *Sales & Marketing Management* (May 2004), pp. 36–43.
13. Christine Galea, "Third Annual Compensation Survey," *Sales & Marketing Management* (May 2003), p. 39.
14. Based on conversations with Mike Cox, President and CEO of Logical (Spring 2003).
15. Christine Galea, "Third Annual Compensation Survey," *Sales & Marketing Management* (May 2003), pp. 32–36.

16. Eilene Zimmerman, "Quota Busters," *Sales & Marketing Management* (January 2001), pp. 59–63.

17. Betsy Cummings, "Breaking Down Boundaries," *Sales & Marketing Management* (October, 2004). Retrieved November 1, 2007, from www.salesandmarketingmanagement.com.

18. For more on salesperson stress and performance, see George J. Avlonitis and Nikolaos G. Panagopoulos, "Role Stress, Attitudes, and Job Outcomes in Business-to-Business Selling: Does the Type of Selling Situation Matter?" *Journal of Personal Selling & Sales Management*, 26 (Winter 2006), pp. 67–77; Fernando Jaramillo, Jay Prakash Mulki, and Paul Solomon, "The Role of Ethical Climate on Salesperson's Role Stress, Job Attitudes, Turnover Intention, and Job Performance," *Journal of Personal Selling & Sales Management*, 26 (Summer 2006), pp. 272–282.

19. Suni Erevelles, Indranil Dutta, and Carolyn Galantine, "Sales Force Compensation Plans Incorporating Multidimensional Sales Effort and Salesperson Efficiency," *Journal of Personal Selling & Sales Management*, 24 (Spring 2004), pp. 101–112.

20. Lawrence B. Chonko, John F. Tanner, and William A. Weeks, "Selling and Sales Management in Action: Reward Preferences of Salespeople," *Journal of Personal Selling & Sales Management* (Summer 1992), p. 69.

21. Rene Y. Darmon, "Salesmen's Responses to Financial Incentives," *Journal of Marketing Research* (July 1974), pp. 39–46.

22. Joseph Kornik, Maggie Rauch, and Rebecca Aronauer, "What's It All Worth? 2007 Compensation Survey," *Sales & Marketing Management* (May 2007), pp. 27–39.

Chapter 13: Evaluating Performance

1. Erin Anderson and Vincent Onyemah, "How Right Should the Customer Be?" *Harvard Business Review* (July-August 2006), pp. 59–67.

2. For more information on business strategy and sales force management, see Stanley Slater and Eric Olson, "Strategy Type and Performance: The Influence of Sales Force Management," *Strategic Management Journal*, 21 (August 2000), pp. 813–829.

3. Donald W. Jackson, John L. Schlacter, and William G. Wolfe, "Examining the Bases Utilized for Evaluating Salespeoples' Performance," *Journal of Personal Selling & Sales Management*, 15, No. 4. (Fall 1995), p. 65.

4. Joseph A. Bellizzi and Ronald W. Hasty, "The Effects of a Stated Organizational Policy on Inconsistent Action Based on Salesperson Gender and Weight," *Journal of Personal Selling & Sales Management*, 21 (Summer 2001), pp. 189–198; for related findings, see Nigel F. Piercy, David W. Cravens, and Nikala Lane, "Sales Manager Behavior Control Strategy and Consequences: The Impact of Gender Differences," *Journal of Personal Selling & Sales Management*, 21 (Winter 2001), pp. 39–49.

5. Anderson and Onyemah, "How Right Should the Customer Be?" pp. 59–67.

6. Andy Cohen, "Movin' Out," *Sales & Marketing Management* (January 1996), pp. 24–25.

7. William L. Cron, Greg W. Marshall, Jadip Singh, Rosann L. Spiro, and Harish Sujan, "Salesperson Selection, Training, and Development; Trends, Implications, and Research Opportunities," *Journal of Personal Selling & Sales Management*, 25 (Spring 2005), pp. 123–136.

8. Sanjeev Agarwal, "Impact of Job Formalization and Administrative Controls on Attitude of Industrial Sales-persons," *Industrial Marketing Management*, 28 (1999), pp. 359–368.

9. Kay L. Keck, Thomas W. Leigh, and James G. Lollar, "Critical Success Factors in Captive, Multi-Line Insurance Agency Sales," *Journal of Personal Selling & Sales Management*, 14, No. 1 (Winter 1995), pp. 17–33.

10. Mark McMaster, "Should You Rank Your Salespeople?" *Sales & Marketing Management* (August 2001), p. 13.

11. Douglas J. Datrymple and William M. Strable, "Career Path Charting: Frameworks for Sales Force Evaluation," *Journal of Personal Selling & Sales Management*, 10, No. 203 (Summer 1990), pp. 59–68.

12. James S. Boles, Naveen Donthu, and Ritu Lohtia, "Salesperson Evaluation Using Relative Performance Efficiency: The Application of Data Envelopment Analysis," *Journal of Personal Selling & Sales Management*, 15, No. 3 (Summer 1995), pp. 31–49; to compute relative efficiency by adjusting for territory considerations, see Bruce K. Pilling, Naveen Donthu, and Steve Henson, "Accounting for the Impact of Territory Characteristics on Sales Performance: Relative Efficiency as a Measure of Salesperson Performance," *Journal of Personal Selling & Sales Management* (Spring 1999), pp. 35–45.

13. Andris Zoltners, Prabhakant Sinha, and Greggor Zoltners, *The Complete Guide to Accelerating Sales Force Performance* (New York: AMACOM, 2001), pp. 430–431.

CASES ANALYSIS

	CASE	CHAPTERS
1	The Case Method	
2	Adams Brands	7
3	Arapahoe Pharmaceutical Company	1, 7, 9, 13
4	Atomic Company	2, 6, 12
5	Conner Labs	4, 5
6	Crestfield Furniture (A)	2, MR: Budgeting
7	Crestfield Furniture (B)	2, 6, MR: Budgeting
8	Dave MacDonald's Ethical Dilemmas	4, 8, 10
9	Erekson Industrial Supply	MR: Forecasting
10	First National Bank	7, 9, 13
11	General Electric Appliances	2, 11, 12
12	Hanover-Bates Chemical Corporation	1, 2, 13
13	Hyde-Phillip Appliances	MR: Forecasting
14	Inject Plastics	2, 10, 12
15	Milligan Pharmaceuticals	2, 6, 11, 13
16	National Mutual Funds	2, 5, 6, 8
17	Power and Motion Industrial Supply	7, 12, 13
18	Quado Systems Group	2, 3, 5
19	Romano Pitesti	9, 13
20	Skata, Inc.	11, 12, 13
21	Tekspan Corporation	2, 6, 8, 12
22	The Sullivan Group (A)	5
23	The Sullivan Group (B)	5
24	Venture Insurance Corporation	10, 11, 13
25	White Electronics	13, MR: Territory Design
26	Winston Liu, Bookman	4, 10

THE CASE METHOD

The objective of the case method is to introduce a measure of realism into business education. A case approach forces you to deal with problems as they actually occur in a for profit or a not-for-profit organization. Each case is simply a written description of the facts surrounding a particular business situation. With the case approach, it is your responsibility to develop solutions to the problem. Instructors, for example, may set the stage for the case discussion by providing background material or by helping you gain insight into the problem. They may also act as devil's advocates and as critics to test arguments and proposals that you put forth. Finally, they evaluate your performance, assign grades, and make suggestions for improvement.

BENEFITS AND LIMITATIONS

The case method becomes an effective teaching device when students are encouraged to analyze the data presented and to formulate their own sets of recommendations. Because each case is different, the solution that is developed for one case cannot be randomly applied to another. This raises the question of what you actually learn by working with business cases. One obvious benefit is that preparation and discussion of case studies helps you improve your skills in oral and written expression. In addition, the case method provides an easy way to learn about current business practices. Perhaps the most important advantage of the case method is the experience it provides in thinking logically about different sets of data. The development of your analytical ability and judgment is the most valuable and lasting benefit derived from working with business cases.

Most cases, including those in this book, are drawn from the experiences of real firms. The names and locations may be disguised to protect the interests of the companies involved. In addition, final decisions are usually omitted to enhance the problem-solving orientation of the cases, thus permitting you to reach your own conclusions without being forced to criticize the actions taken by others. The case method departs from the typical business situation in that the business executive usually does not have the facts presented as clearly and as neatly as they are in casebooks. Problem solving in business usually involves extensive data collection, something that has been essentially completed for you.

A FRAMEWORK FOR ANALYSIS

You can approach the analysis of business cases in many different ways. Each instructor has his or her own ideas on the number and nature of the steps involved. We believe the following six-step procedure is a logical and practical way to begin.

1. Define the problem.
2. Formulate the alternatives.
3. Analyze the alternatives.
4. Recommend a solution.
5. Specify a plan of action.
6. Prepare contingency plans.

Defining the Problem

Once you are familiar with the facts of the case, you should isolate the central problem. Until this is done, it is usually impossible to proceed with an effective analysis. Sometimes instructors provide questions to help you start your analysis. You should look at questions as guides for action rather than as specific issues to be resolved. All cases should be considered as problems in the management of the marketing mix, not as specific issues concerned only with some narrow phase of management.

We use the term *problem* loosely and employ it to indicate a state of nature that may involve either a negative situation possibly requiring corrective action or simply a situation needing opportunity assessment. You must distinguish between problems and symptoms of problems. Declining sales, market share, or the size of the sales force are symptoms of more fundamental underlying problems that are their cause. Any business situation may pose multiple problems. The key to solving unstructured problems is to identify the one that must be solved first, the one whose solution will either

This case was prepared by Professor Richard C. Leventhal of Regis University in Denver, Colorado. Reproduced by permission.

eliminate other problems or permit their solution. We are usually interested in solving the most immediate critical problem. For example, we may have problems maintaining the size of our field sales force, problems that have been created by a poor recruiting and selection process. Our immediate concern, however, is with finding ways to get new salespeople quickly into unfilled sales territories. We may well recommend an evaluation of the firm's recruitment process, but we will leave that for future study. Note that the central problem is a state of nature. A statement of it should not contain any action verbs (i.e., *to do* is part of the plan of action). Nor should it contain the words *or* and *and,* which are, respectively, part of the statement of alternatives, and an indication of compound problems and lack of identification of *the* central problem.

Selecting the Alternatives

The second step is to define possible alternatives available to resolve the problem. Some of these alternatives may be obvious from the material supplied in the case and from the statement of the main issue. Others may have to be supplied from your own review of the situation. You should be careful to limit your analysis to a reasonable number of alternatives. Three or four alternatives are usually sufficient for a typical case. One alternative that should always be considered is the maintenance of the status quo. Sometimes doing what you have been doing is the best course of action.

Analyzing the Alternatives

The heart of the case method is the analysis of alternatives. To analyze is to separate into parts so as to find out the nature, proportion, function, and underlying relationships among a set of variables. Thus, to analyze is to dig into, and work with, the facts to uncover associations that may be used to evaluate possible courses of action. Your analysis should begin with a careful evaluation of the facts presented in the case. You should be sensitive to the problem of sorting relevant material from that which is peripheral or irrelevant. In reviewing a case, you must be careful to distinguish between fact and opinion. You must also make sure that the facts are consistent and reliable. Some cases may contain errors, and the instructor may prefer to remain silent.

You are expected to base your analysis on the evidence presented in the case, but this does not mean that other information cannot be used. You should utilize facts that are available to the trade and information that is general or public knowledge. You should incorporate relevant concepts from other disciplines, such as accounting, statistics, economics, psychology, and sociology. The criterion in using outside material is that it must be appropriate to the particular situation. For example, do not use census data for 2000 to make decisions in a case dated 1995. For this book we have attempted to select cases that provide you with enough information to complete the analysis. In some situations, however, you may wish to collect additional materials from other sources.

Sometimes the most important facts in the case are buried in some chance remark or seemingly minor statistical exhibit. Be careful to sift through the data to uncover all the relationships that apply to the alternatives being considered. This means that the quantitative information must be examined using a variety of ratios, graphs, tables, or other forms of analysis. Rarely are the data supplied in the case in the form most appropriate to finding a solution, and instructors expect students to work out the numbers.

Marketing analyses are usually based on incomplete information. Assumptions must be made.[1] However, they should be made only when necessary and must be clearly labeled as such. Moreover, a rationale should be given for any assumption made. For example, a retail chain stops carrying one of your product lines but continues carrying another. You are interested in what your sales of the dropped product line would have been. You might note that over the past few years the ratio of the sales of the two product lines had been relatively constant. You could assume that the ratio would have remained the same for the current year as well, and multiply this ratio by the current year's sales of the continuing product line to estimate sales of the discontinued line in that chain. Or perhaps you would calculate the lowest and highest ratios over recent history to calculate conservative and optimistic estimates of lost sales. In any case, at the end of any decision-making exercise, you always want to review your assumptions to see how dependent your conclusions are on the assumptions made. (At one extreme, you could assume away the problem!) You should make contingency plans in the event that major assumptions do not hold.

You should realize that a complete analysis is not one-sided. A review of a business situation is not sound unless both sides of important issues are examined.

[1] In most large companies, a corporate planning group provides certain forecasts, assumptions, and planning premises so that everyone in the company is using the same numbers, for instance, on future inflation rates. These tend to be long documents and are not included in casebooks.

This does not necessarily mean that every point must be mentioned, but major opposing arguments should be addressed where possible. You will find it helpful to explicitly list the pros and cons or advantages and disadvantages of each alternative.

Making Recommendations

After you have carefully analyzed the data and alternatives, you are in a position to make recommendations. Sometimes more than one course of action will look attractive. This is not an unusual situation, as most cases do not have a single right answer. Still, you must come up with a concrete proposal. To arrive at a solution, you should judge the relative risks and opportunities offered by the various alternatives. The optimum choice is the one that provides the best balance between profit opportunities and the risks and costs of failure. Make a clear-cut decision, and avoid qualifications and other obvious hedges. Instructors are much more concerned with how a particular decision was reached than with what alternative was selected.

Students sometimes review the facts and decide that they do not have enough information to reach a decision. They recommend that the decision be postponed pending the results of further research. Usually, "get more information" is not an acceptable solution to a business case. Decisions cannot wait the length of time necessary to conduct good research. In addition, it is unlikely that you will ever have all the information you think you need. Because of the cost of research and the penalties of delay, business decisions are almost always made under conditions of uncertainty.

Specifying a Plan of Action

Having made your decision, how are you going to implement it? You should suggest, in as much detail as the case allows, what actions you would take, when they would be taken, and how much they would cost. You may want to provide pro forma income statements, and other relevant supporting material. Once you have proposed your actions, you would do well to reflect on the potential market reactions to them, especially competitive reactions. These possible reactions might lead you to modify your actions.

If you judge that collecting additional information is the only feasible means of solving a case, you must provide support for this decision. First, you should state exactly what the research will show and how this information will be used. In addition, you should indicate the research methodology to be followed and the anticipated cost of the study. After you have completed these tasks, you will be in a better position to decide whether additional research is needed. Remember, managers should have a predisposition to act and then adapt, rather than to procrastinate.

Preparing Contingency Plans

When you make a decision, it is based on the facts at hand, as well as on your expectations about the future that you hold at that point in time. Since the future does not always unfold as we expect or wish, we must be prepared for any significant alternative future scenario. You must ask yourself what you will do if the market does not respond to your marketing actions as you anticipate, if competitors take actions that deviate from their usual behavior, if the economy is different than economists have forecasted, and so on.

Writing the Report

We believe that students who prepare written reports do a better job of analyzing business problems. Writing a good report takes a certain skill, and we would like to suggest a few ideas that may be of help.

When instructors read reports, they check to see whether students fully understand the situation and whether student interpretations of the facts are reasonable. They also like to see papers that are objective, balanced, consistent, and decisive. Perhaps the most common error made by students in writing case reports is to repeat the facts that have been provided. Instead of analyzing the data in light of alternatives, students frequently repeat statements that appear in the cases, with no clear objective in mind. Nothing upsets an instructor more than reading a paper that devotes several pages to explaining what he or she already knows about the case.

Another deficiency often observed in writing reports is lack of organization. Students who make this error begin with the first thought that enters their minds and continue, in almost random fashion, until they run out of ideas. The end result is a paper that has no beginning and no end, and often consists of one long paragraph. To avoid this problem, some instructors require that reports be presented in outline form. However, the condensed nature of such reports sometimes makes them hard to follow. Therefore, we prefer the more readable narrative approach.

There is no optimal length for a written case analysis. It depends on the amount of data provided, the preferences of the instructor, and the number of case reports the student turns in during the course. The report should be long enough to cover the subject adequately. It is fairly obvious that written reports must be neat, legible, and free of grammatical and spelling errors. Business professors are not hired to teach English composition, but they do expect certain minimal standards of performance in written expression. Their standards for written work reflect what the business community expects from college graduates.

SUMMARY

Case analysis is designed to give you an opportunity to develop a productive and meaningful way of thinking about business problems. The case method helps train you to use logic to solve realistic business issues. Remember, however, that solutions are worthless unless they can be sold to those who are in a position to act on the recommendations. The case approach provides you with practical experience in convincing others of the soundness of your reasoning.

ADAMS BRANDS

Ken Bannister, Ontario regional manager for Adams Brands, was faced with the decision of which of three candidates he should hire as the key account supervisor for the Ontario region. This salesperson would be responsible for working with eight major accounts in the Toronto area. Bannister had narrowed the list to the three applicants and began reviewing their files.

COMPANY

Warner-Lambert, Inc., a large, diversified U.S. multinational, manufactured and marketed a wide range of health care and consumer products. Warner-Lambert Canada Ltd., the largest subsidiary, had annual sales exceeding $200 million. Over one-half of the Canadian sales were generated by Adams Brands, which focused on the confectionery business. The major product lines carried by Adams were:

1. Chewing gum, with brands such as Chiclets, Dentyne, and Trident.
2. Portable breath fresheners including Certs and Clorets.
3. Cough tablets and antacids such as Halls and Rolaids.
4. Several other products, including Blue Diamond Almonds and Sparkies Mini-Fruits.

In these product categories, Adams Brands was usually the market leader or had a substantial market share.

The division was a stable unit for Warner-Lambert Canada, with profits being used for investments throughout the company. Success of the Adams Brands was built on the following:

1. Quality products.
2. Strong marketing management.
3. Sales force efforts in distribution, display, and merchandising.
4. Excellent customer service.

Adams was organized on a regional basis. The Ontario region, which also included the Atlantic provinces, had forty-six sales representatives whose responsibilities were to service individual stores. Five district managers coordinated the activities of the sales representatives. As well, three key account supervisors worked with the large retail chains (e.g., supermarkets) in Ontario and the Atlantic area. The key account supervisor in the Toronto area had recently resigned his position and joined one of Adams's major competitors.

THE MARKET

The confectionery industry comprised six major competitors that manufactured chocolate bars, chewing gum, mints, cough drops, chewy candy, and other products. The market shares of these six companies are provided in Exhibit 1.

In the past few years, total industry sales in the confectionery category had been flat to marginally

This case was prepared by Gordon McDougall, Wilfrid Laurier University, and Douglas Snetsinger, University of Toronto.

EXHIBIT 1 Major Competitors in the Confectionery Industry

Company	*Market Share (%)*	*Major Product Lines*	*Major Brands*
Adams	23	Gum, portable breath fresheners, cough drops	Trident, Chiclets, Dentyne, Certs, Halls
Nielsen/Cadbury	22	Chocolate bars	Caramilk, Crunchie, Dairy Milk, Crispy Crunch
Nestlé Canada	15	Chocolate bars	Coffee Crisp, Kit-Kat, Smarties, Turtles
Hershey	14	Gum, chocolate bars, chewy candy	Glossette, Oh Henry, Reese's Pieces, Lifesavers
Effem Foods	11	Chocolate bars, chewy candy	Mars, Snickers, M&M's, Skittles
Wrigley's	9	Gum	Hubba Bubba, Extra, Doublemint
Richardson-Vicks	2	Cough drops	Vicks
Others	4		

Source: Company records and industry data.

declining in unit volume. This sales decline was attributed to the changing age distribution of the population (i.e., fewer young people). As consumers grew older, their consumption of confectionery products tended to decline. While units sales were flat or declining, dollar sales were increasing at a rate of 10 percent per annum as a result of price increases.

In the confectionery business, it was critical to obtain extensive distribution in as many stores as possible and, within each store, to obtain as much prominent shelf space as possible. Most confectionery products were purchased on impulse. In one study it was found that up to 85 percent of chewing gum and 70 percent of chocolate bar purchases were unplanned. While chocolate bars could be viewed as an indirect competitor to gum and mints, they were direct competitors for retail space and were usually merchandised on the same display. Retailers earned similar margins from all confectionery products (25–36 percent of the retail selling price) and often sought the best-selling brands to generate those revenues. Some industry executives felt that catering to the retailers' needs was even more important than understanding the ultimate consumers' needs.

Adams Brands had always provided store display racks for merchandising all confectionery items, including competitive products and chocolate bars. The advantage of supplying the displays was that the manufacturer could influence the number of prelabeled slots that contained brand logos and the proportion of the display devoted to various product groups such as chewing gum versus chocolate bars. The displays were usually customized to the unique requirements of a retailer, such as the height and width of the display.

Recently, a competitor, Effem, had become more competitive in the design and display of merchandising systems. Effem was regarded as an innovator in the industry, in part because of its limited product line and its new approach to the retail trade. The company had only eight fast-turnover products in its line. Effem had developed its own sales force, consisting of over 100 part-time merchandising salespeople and eight full-time sales personnel, and focused on the head offices of "A" accounts. "A" accounts were large retail chains such as 7-Eleven, Beckers, Loblaws, A&P, Food City, Shopper's Drug Mart, K-Mart, Towers, and Zellers. Other than Adams, Effem was one of the few companies that conducted considerable research on racking systems and merchandising.

THE RETAIL TRADE

Within Adams Brands, over two-thirds of confectionery volume flowed through wholesalers. The remaining balance was split between direct sales and drop shipments to retailers. Wholesalers were necessary because, with over 66,000 outlets in food, drug, and variety stores alone, the sales force could not adequately cover a large proportion of the retailers. The percentage of Adams sales through the various channels is provided in Exhibit 2.

The volume of all consumer packaged goods sold in Canada was increasingly dominated by fewer and larger retail chains. This increased retail concentration resulted in retailers becoming more influential in trade promotion decisions, including dictating the size, timing, and number of allowance, distribution, and coop advertising events. The new power of the retailers had not yet been fully wielded against the confectionery business. Confectionery lines were some of the most profitable lines for the retailer. Further, the manufactures were not as reliant on listings from any given retailer as were other food and household product manufacturers.

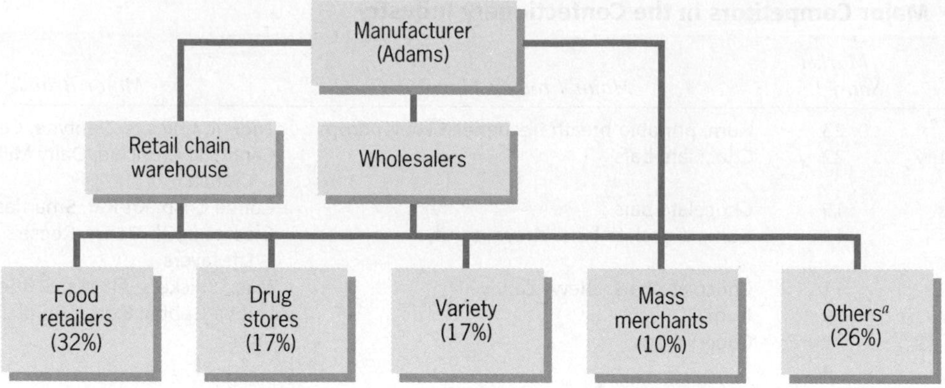

[a]Consists of a wide variety of locations, including vending machines, restaurants, cafeterias, bowling alleys, and resorts.

EXHIBIT 2 Adams Brands Sales by Distribution Channel

The increased size of some retail chains also changed the degree of management sophistication at all levels, including that of the retail buyers—those individuals responsible for deciding what products were carried by the retail stores. At one time, the relationship between manufacturers' sales representatives and retail buyers was largely based on long-term, personal associations. Usually the sales representative had strong social skills, and an important task was to get along well with the buyers. Often when the representatives and buyers met to discuss various promotions or listings, part of the conversation dealt with making plans for dinner or going to a hockey game. The sales representative was the host for these social events.

More recently, a new breed of buyer had been emerging in the retail chains. Typically, the new retail managers and buyers had been trained in business schools. They often had product management experience, relied on analytical skills, and used state-of-the-art, computer-supported planning systems. In some instances, the buyer was more sophisticated than the sales representative with respect to analytical approaches to display and inventory management. The buyers frequently requested detailed plan-o-grams with strong analytical support for expected sales, profits, and inventory turns. The buyer would also at times become the salesperson. After listening to a sales presentation and giving an initial indication of interest, the buyer would attempt to sell space, both on the store floor and in the weekly advertising supplements. For example, the buyer for Shopper's Drug Mart offered a dump bin location in every store in the chain for a week. In some instances, both the buyer and the representative had the authority to conclude such a deal at that meeting. At other times, both had to wait for approval from their respective companies.

The interesting aspect of the key account supervisor's position was that the individual had to feel comfortable dealing with both the old and new schools of retail management. The task for Bannister was to select the right candidate for this position. The salary for the position ranged from $54,000 to $74,200, depending on qualifications and experience. Bannister expected that the candidate selected would probably be paid somewhere between $56,000 and $70,000. An expense allowance would also be included in the compensation package.

THE KEY ACCOUNTS SUPERVISOR

The main responsibility of the key accounts supervisor was to establish and maintain a close working relationship with the buyers of eight A accounts whose head offices were located in the Toronto area. An important task was to make presentations (15 to 30 minutes in length) to the retail buyers of these key accounts every three to six weeks. At these meetings, promotions or deals for up to five brands would be presented. The supervisor was responsible for all Adams brands. The buyer might have to take the promotions to the buying committee, where the final decision would be made. In addition, the representative used these meetings to hear about and inform the buyer of any merchandising problems occurring at the store level.

Midyear reviews were undertaken with each account. These reviews, lasting for 1 hour, focused on reviewing sales trends and tying them into merchandising programs, listings, service, and new payment terms. Another important and time-consuming responsibility of the key account supervisor was to devise and present plan-o-grams and be involved with the installation of the displays. The key account representative also conducted store checks and spent time on competitive intelligence. Working with the field staff was a further requirement of the position.

Bannister reflected on what he felt were the attributes of the ideal candidate. First, the individual should have selling and merchandising experience in the retail business in order to understand the language and dynamics of the situation. On the merchandising side, the individual would be required to initiate and coordinate the design of customized display systems for individual stores, a task that involved a certain amount of creativity. Second, strong interpersonal skills were needed. The individual had to establish rapport and make effective sales presentations to the buyers. Because of the wide range of buyer sophistication, these skills were particularly important. Bannister made a mental note to recommend that whoever was hired would be sent on the Professional Selling Skills course, a one-week program designed to enhance listening, selling, and presentation skills. Finally, the candidate should possess analytic skills because many of the sales and performance reports (from both manufacturers and retailers) were or would be computerized. Thus, the individual should feel comfortable working with computers. Bannister hoped that he could find a candidate who would be willing to spend a minimum of three years on the job in order to establish a personal relationship with the buyers.

Ideally, the candidate selected would have a blend of all three skills because of the mix of buyers he or she would contact. Bannister felt it was most likely that these characteristics would be found in a business school graduate. He had advertised the job internally (through the company's newsletter) and externally (in the *Toronto Star*). A total of twenty applications were received. After an initial screening, three possible candidates for the position were identified. None were from Warner-Lambert (Exhibit 3).

Bannister and a member of the personnel department interviewed each of the candidates. After completing the interviews, brief fact sheets were prepared. Bannister began reviewing the sheets prior to making the decision.

EXHIBIT 3

Lydia Cohen

Personal:	Born 1974, 168 cm; 64 kg; Single
Education:	B.B.A. (1996), Wilfrid Laurier University, Active in Marketing Club and intramural sports
Work:	2003–2005 Rowntree Macintosh Canada, Inc.–District Manager
	Responsible for sales staff of three in Ottawa and Eastern Ontario region. Establish annual sales plan and ensure that district meets its quota.
	1996–2002 Rowntree Macintosh Canada, Inc.–Confectionary Sales Representative
	Responsible for selling a full line of confectionary and grocery products to key accounts in Toronto (2001–2002) and Ottawa (1998–2000). 2002 Sales Representative of the Year for highest volume growth.
Interests:	Racquet sports
Candidate's Comments:	I am interested in working in the Toronto area, and I would look forward to concentrating on the sales task. My best years at Rowntree were in sales in the Toronto region.
Interviewer's Comments:	Lydia presents herself very well and has a strong background in confectionary sales. Her record at Rowntree is very good. Rowntree paid for her to take an Introductory course in data analysis, but she has not had much opportunity to develop these skills. She does not seem to be overly ambitious or aggressive. She stated that personal reasons were preeminent in seeking a job in Toronto.

John Fisher

Personal:	Born 1978, 190 cm; 88 kg; Single
Education:	B.A. (Phys. Ed.) (1992), University of British Columbia
	While at UBC, played 4 years of varsity basketball (team captain for 2 years). Assistant Coach, Senior Basketball, at University Hill High School, 1999–2003. Developed and ran a 2-week summer basketball camp at UBC for 3 years. Profits from the camp were donated to the Varsity Basketball Fund.

EXHIBIT 3 (*continued*)

Work:	1998–2004 Jacobs Suchard Canada, Inc. (Nabob Foods) Six years' experience (full-time 2003–2004, and 5 years part-time, 1998–2003, during school terms and full-time during the summers) in coffee and chocolates distribution and sales; two years on the loading docks, 1 year driving truck, and 3 years as a sales representative. Sales tasks included calling on regular customers, order taking, rack jobbing and customer relations development. 2004–2005 Scavolini (Professional Basketball) One year after completing studies at UBC, traveled to Western Europe and Northern Africa. Travel was financed by playing professional basketball in the Italian First Division.
Candidate's Comments:	I feel the combination of educational preparation, work experience, and my demonstrated ability as a team player and leader make me well suited for this job. I am particularly interested in a job, such as sales, that rewards personal initiative.
Interviewer's Comments:	A very ambitious and engaging individual with a good record of achievements. Strong management potential is evident, but interest in sales as a career is questionable. Minored in computer science at UBC. Has a standing offer to return to a sales management position at Nabob.

Barry Moore

Personal:	Born 1975, 180 cm; 84 kg; Married with two children
Education:	Business Administration Diploma (1990), Humber College While at school, was active participant in a number of clubs and political organizations. President of the Young Liberals (1989–1990).
Work:	2002–2005 Barrigans Food Markets–Merchandising Analyst Developed merchandising plans for a wide variety of product categories. Negotiated merchandising programs and trade deals with manufacturers and brokers. Managed a staff of four. 1999–2002 Dominion Stores Ltd.–Assistant Merchandise Manager Liaison responsibilities between stores and head office merchandise planning. Responsible for execution of merchandising plans for several food categories. 1998–Robin Hood Multifoods, Inc.–Assistant Product Manager Responsible for the analysis and development of promotion planning for Robin Hood Flour. 1993–1998 Nestlé Enterprises Ltd.–Camation Division Sales Representative. Major responsibilities were developing and maintaining sales and distribution to wholesale and retail accounts. 1990–1993 McCain Foods Ltd.–Inventory Analyst Worked with sales staff and head office planning to ensure the quality and timing of shipments to brokers and stores.
Activities:	Board of Directors, Richview Community Club Board of Directors, Volunteer Centre of Etobicoke Paste President of Etobicoke Big Brothers Active in United Way Yachting–CC 34 Canadian Champion
Candidate's Comments:	It would be a great challenge and joy to work with a progressive industry leader such as Adams Brands.
Interviewer's Comments:	Very articulate and professionally groomed. Dominated the interview with a variety of anecdotes and humorous stories, some of which were relevant to the job. Likes to read popular books on management, particularly books that champion the bold, gut-feel entrepreneur. He would probably earn more money at Adams if hired.

ARAPAHOE PHARMACEUTICAL COMPANY

Note: An Excel file with the data for this case is available at www.wiley.com/college/cron. Go to "Students Companion Site."

As he reread the annual report that he had prepared for Phil Jackson, his regional sales manager, John Ziegler, shook his head and kept repeating to himself, "What a year!"

He could not forget the surge of pride he felt when his district sales manager asked him to call Phil Jackson to let him know whether he wanted to accept a promotion to district sales manager for the Dallas area. As he remembered, he couldn't get to the telephone quickly enough, and it was only after Phil had asked him how his wife had taken the news that he realized that he had forgotten to ask her. He immediately telephoned Lynn and found that she was thrilled both with his promotion and the move to Dallas, even though neither one of them had been there before. Lynn was particularly pleased that her company had a sales opening in Dallas, and she felt that she could obtain a transfer to that city. John once again expressed his appreciation to his sales manager, Betsy Warner, for all of the help that she had given him so that he could qualify for the promotion.

John had joined Arapahoe Pharmaceuticals as a sales rep immediately after graduating from San Francisco State University. While he had been interested in science in high school, and he had taken one course in chemistry and another course in biology at San Francisco State, he was more interested in marketing communications. When Arapahoe Pharmaceuticals recruited at the college in his junior year and again in the spring of his senior year, John decided that he might combine the interests in science and marketing communications as a sales representative. He was interviewed, hired, and assigned to a territory near Omaha in Betsy Warner's district. John's willingness, personality, and communications skills, plus Betsy's encouragement and guidance, helped him to quickly achieve above-average productivity and allowed him to win a transfer to a territory in the greater metropolitan Denver area. The new territory offered him additional experience in working with food and drug chain headquarters, large hospitals, and drug wholesalers. John reviewed these experiences with considerable pleasure as he recalled the events of the past year. Betsy worked regularly with him and delegated to him some of the training of new sales reps, which he found both challenging and rewarding, especially when the new sales trainee did well. His selling skills flourished as did his income and the recognition of his achievements by Betsy and the regional sales manager. A year later he was selected to attend his company's leadership training program, which was a milestone in his career.

Even before his first trip to Dallas, John was asked by Tom Boyle, the general sales manager, to spend a couple of days at the corporate headquarters in Philadelphia with him and various department heads in marketing, legal, and human resources. They were all very complimentary about his past performance and how much he deserved his promotion. However, each of them in a different way seemed to repeat the same message: "Managing people is different from selling products." How well the events of the past year were to bear that out! The thrust of Boyle's message was a bit different. He wanted John to realize that he had full confidence in his ability, that John had earned his promotion, and that although John was a sales rep one day and a district sales manager the next, the company recognized the change wouldn't take place overnight, and it would provide him with further training. In the meantime, Boyle advised John that the Dallas district was productive, operating efficiently, and staffed with well-trained sales reps, and that he was not expecting John to "sweep the district clean" and make radical changes. He also emphasized that (1) John should give the sales reps in Dallas time to get to know him and he them; (2) he would be surprised and disappointed to discover that all the reps didn't operate with the same level of efficiency that he did nor use the same methods he used when he was a rep; (3) he shouldn't try to correct too many deficiencies at one time; (4) telling someone to do something doesn't necessarily get it done; (5) everyone doesn't remember hearing something the same way; and (6) it's better to have three sales reps working with you than ten working for you.

One year later, John realized that at the time he and Boyle talked, he didn't understand or appreciate the full

This case was prepared by Professor Richard C. Leventhal of Regis University in Denver, Colorado. Reproduced by permission.

meaning of that advice. The legal department wanted him to be aware of his increased responsibilities as a manager in speaking or acting for the company. The various departments in sales, marketing, and human resources emphasized the importance of his new role and his support in administering the company's promotional programs and gaining the compliance of his sales reps. Increasingly, he realized the duality of his role as a member of management and of the field sales force. The sales management training programs he attended during the succeeding months reinforced these points and helped prepare him for the types of problems he was to encounter.

His introduction to the ten sales reps in the Dallas district went quite well. His predecessor, Chuck Morgan, who was retiring after thirty years with Arapahoe, fully reviewed all of the sales statistics for the district and the human resource records of the sales reps. He also gave him the benefit of his thoughts for the future and what John's immediate concerns should be. John had inherited a district that was operating on target both for sales and expenses and appeared to have no major personnel problems other than one territory that had been open for four weeks. Chuck even had two resumes on promising candidates who needed processing.

John telephoned both applicants and scheduled interviews for the following week, along with trips of two days each with two of his sales reps. The interviews seemed to go well, but they took almost a full day. On his first day at his office the following week, John called the references and previous employers of both applicants, scheduled a second interview several days later with Larry Palmer, the most promising applicant, and, in accordance with the company's interviewing procedure, set up an information session with Larry and his wife for the following evening. Since this was John's first session of this type, he was pleased that it went well. Jean Palmer, Larry's wife, had numerous questions about transferring, the amount of travel, and how much extra time that her husband would have to spend responding to e-mail and other computer-type reports. John was glad that he was able to address her concerns. The telephone conversations with the other applicant's references and previous employers had been an interesting experience and tended to confirm what the applicant had said, except in two instances. A previous employer and one reference were guardedly enthusiastic about the applicant. When John pressed the issue, the reference refused to say more, while the previous employer provided specifics that confirmed an earlier impression John had noted at the initial interview. Comments about Larry Palmer all emphasized the great personality he had and what a terrific job they thought he would do in sales. Following the second interview with Larry Palmer and the spouse information session, John completed the company's applicant appraisal reports on both applicants and decided that Larry was the better of the two. He telephoned his regional sales manager, Phil Jackson, to set up a final interview for Larry. Then he faxed Phil his applicant appraisal reports and wrote the other applicant a polite turndown letter.

The day following Larry's interview, Phil Jackson called to say that while he had some misgivings, he had hired Larry to begin training in a class at the regional office the first of the month. John's reaction was a sigh of relief because of all of the time he had put into the screening and the hope that he wouldn't have to do that too often. The reports that he completed on his first field trips with his reps took longer to prepare than he anticipated. Coupled with the correspondence and appraisal reports on the applicants, John realized that communications were going to be a bigger part of the job than he had realized. He would have to learn how to use the computerized information system in a more effective and efficient manner if he were to have the necessary time for his other responsibilities.

John's relationship with his sales reps seemed to go well during the first few months on the job, with the exception of Dick McClure, an above-average producer, aged 50, with twelve years experience, and the senior man in the district. Dick had been described by Chuck Morgan as a friendly, outgoing individual with a good sense of humor and a highly individualistic style of selling. As John worked with Dick, he was able to confirm in Dick's interaction with his customers, the general description Chuck had given him. However, Dick was curt with John, relatively subdued, and at other times almost hostile. For the next several working trips, John tried to ignore Dick's conduct and concentrated on the calls that they were making and the objectives that they were trying to achieve. At a recent sales meeting, Dick seemed to take delight in being argumentative and disruptive until John jokingly asked him if he would like to take over the sales meeting. After that, Dick settled down but made almost no contribution to the discussions for the rest of the meeting.

The situation came to a head immediately following a physician call, during which Dick introduced John without indicating who he was or his purpose for being there. The physician's reaction was: "Oh a new rep, eh?" and to Dick, "Are you being promoted?" This forced Dick, somewhat embarrassed, to indicate that John was his new district sales manager. As they left the office, it was clear that Dick was furious, as he muttered in a sarcastic manner, "Are you being promoted?" John decided that it was time to take action, whereupon he said emphatically, "Dick, I don't know what is eating you, but I think that it's time that we get it out in the open. You've been complaining from the day that I arrived. You're sarcastic, uncooperative, and just as cool as ice. If you and I are going to continue to work together, things had better change. I don't know what I have done that has upset you, but whatever it is or whatever I've said, it certainly wasn't intentional and I'm sorry. You're too good a person to go around perpetually angry. What the heck is bothering you?"

Dick's reaction was an angry, somewhat subdued and embarrassed, "I just guess it's not really your fault or anything that you did. I've been here twelve years and I'm the best rep in this district. Chuck even told me so. And bam—you get promoted and I'm left hung out to dry. Man, that's gratitude for you!"

Now that the problem was out in the open, John realized how long Dick had been carrying his anger locked up inside himself and felt sorry for him. With that, he said, "Dick, I've sure been blind. Let's knock off and sit down somewhere to talk this thing out." Three hours later they shook hands and parted on a much better understanding. Their relationship improved steadily, and now as John reflected on the district's productivity for the past year, he realized that Dick's support had been of paramount importance in terms of the district's overall success.

Thinking about the successful year reminded him of Peggy Doyle, the sales trainee who was doing such a terrific job. She was the one who had taken Larry Palmer's place. When he thought of Larry Palmer, he winced thinking about the mistake that he had made. Larry was the first sales rep that he had recruited. He had completed the basic sales training class, but just barely. The report from the sales training manager was anything but encouraging. Larry had difficulty acquiring the necessary product knowledge, and his scientific communication skills were marginal at best. The qualities that saved him from being dropped from the sales training class were his desire, his willingness to work, and the fact that he was such a great guy—everybody loved him! Notwithstanding Larry's shortcomings, John was convinced he could turn Larry around. He worked with him every opportunity he had, quizzed him, coached him, and drilled him in an effort to improve his knowledge and skills so that Larry could be able to capitalize on his sincerity and personality.

As the months wore on, John became increasingly aware that while Larry's customers liked him, he couldn't sell, and his sales showed it. It was a tough decision John had to make to let Larry go, and an even tougher decision to implement, but John realized it really was in everyone's best interests. As he looked back on all the time and effort he had put into Larry's ultimate failure, John realized that it was at the expense of the time and effort he should have spent with his more productive sales reps. He also realized that in spite of the overwhelming evidence, he had carried Larry much longer than he probably should have and was thankful that Phil Jackson did not remind him of it. Sometimes, however, events have a bright side. As much as John regretted the amount of time that it took to recruit Larry's replacement, he felt that he had lucked out with Peggy Doyle. She seemed to do everything right. In the four months since she'd been in the territory, sales had taken a noticeable increase, and her enthusiasm was infecting the other sales reps in the district. John hoped her progress and productivity would continue on in this manner for a long time to come. Some performance data for Peggy and the other reps are shown in Exhibits 1 and 2.

EXHIBIT 1 Performance Data for Sales Reps in the Dallas/Ft. Worth District

Sales Rep	*Last Year's Sales*	*This Year's Sales*	*Sales Quota Current Year*
Larry Palmer[a]	$ 180,000	$ 181,000	$ 275,000
Dick McClure	450,000	583,000	535,000
Peggy Doyle[b]	-	120,000	150,000
Tom Jones	445,000	555,000	550,000
Bill Morrison	465,000	560,000	550,000
Sam Hanna	435,000	535,000	525,000
Jared Murphy	365,000	370,000	420,000
Marty Nakai	475,000	625,000	575,000
TOTALS	$2,815,000	$3,529,000	$3,580,000

[a]Sales and quota figures are for eight months.

[b]Peggy Doyle has been in her territory for only four months; there is no sales figure for the previous year. This year's sales and quota are for four months.

EXHIBIT 2 Input Factors Affecting Territory Coverage in the Dallas/Ft. Worth District

Sales Rep	*Number of Sales Calls*	*Annual Expenses ($)*	*Physicians in Territory*
Larry Palmer[a]	800	$ 6,300	1,600
Dick McClure	1,500	9,300	2,100
Peggy Doyle[b]	400	2,500	1,650
Tom Jones	1,300	8,000	1,850
Bill Morrison	1,350	8,300	1,800
Sam Hanna	1,350	8,500	1,900
Jared Murphy	1,050	7,800	2,000
Marty Nakai	1,550	9,800	2,200
TOTALS	9,300	$60,500	15,100

[a]Number of sales calls and expenses are for an 8-month period.
[b]Number of sales calls and expenses are for a 4-month period.

Peggy's performance, however, did not eliminate the logjam that recruiting her had created in John's other activities. Her interviews, reference checking, early sales orientation, and training, plus the extra time he had spent over the last few months helping Larry try to succeed, extended the intervals since he last worked in the field with his above-average sales reps, to the extent that several were beginning to make humorously sarcastic comments about being "orphans." John tried to explain that they were practically self-sufficient, while others needed his help more urgently. While they were willing to listen, John could see that they weren't buying into his excuse.

To further compound the problem, he received an e-mail that his semiannual appraisal interviews were to begin within 30 days. This would be the second time he would be holding these performance reviews, but it would be the first time alone since Phil Jackson had helped him. As John began to review the trip reports and correspondence in each sales rep's file, along with sales performance data generated from the company's computerized database (Exhibits 1 and 2), he realized the files of the above-average producers were relatively thin. If it hadn't been for performance data, John would have been at a serious loss to justify his appraisal of their productivity.

Preparing for and conducting the performance reviews took a lot of time, and this was when he really earned his salary. When the reps and John had different evaluations, the differences were resolved and then it became a matter of jointly agreeing on a plan of action to close the gap between actual and desired performance. As difficult as it was to achieve the agreement at times, and harder still to implement the agreed-upon plan, John felt that it was at this point that he was making a significant contribution to the success of the company and the growth and development of the individual sales reps in the district.

The second appraisal and counseling session of the year had its peaks and valleys. It had been a pleasure to provide several with the recognition their performances merited and to help them to further define the goals they would achieve for the forthcoming year. The case of Jared Murphy was another matter. Jared had been in the training class at the time John was hired. He had done reasonably well but hadn't really lived up to his potential. Lately, Jared seemed to have lost interest. When John challenged Jared's own evaluation of his performance, Jared sheepishly commented that he "wondered whether you'd let it pass." When John pressed him for an explanation of his performance in view of the potential in his territory, Jared quickly replied: "I didn't know you cared that much."

John also stated he felt that Jared had sufficient experience and intelligence to exert the necessary self-discipline to do what was required without a lot of personal attention from him. At this point, John said: "Jared, I think that it's time to decide whether you really have a future with Arapahoe. You definitely have the capabilities to be an above-average performer. If you really want to do a better job, I'll make every effort to help you to do a better job, but you will have to help me and really want to work at it. So what I want you to do is to go home, think about what I said, talk it over with your wife, and we will get together next Wednesday and make a plan for your future."

The problem John faced with Marty Nakai was almost the opposite. Marty was a young, single sales rep who had three years' experience in a territory that required quite a bit of travel in the Texas panhandle. He had about every good quality anyone could want in a salesperson, except maturity and self-control. He was smart, eager, highly motivated, and extremely ambitious. His favorite question of John was: "What else do I have to do to get promoted?" and he posed that question on every field trip and frequently at sales meetings. In addition, John could count on Marty calling him at home on weekends. In a way, John wished he had more sales reps who were as productive and as eagerly cooperative, but he also wished that Marty would develop more patience and self-discipline. While John certainly didn't want to do anything to dampen Marty's enthusiasm, he was running out of ways to help Marty grow up.

As he thought about the challenges he had with his reps and the logjam he had created as a result of his recruiting activities, he realized that he had to formalize a set of objectives and specific plans for the coming year to discuss with Phil Jackson during his own coming appraisal session. Although the year had been a successful one, performance on a couple of major products could have been at a higher level, and he would have to figure out some kind of action plan to correct that situation. And then there were the territory revisions to be done to take advantage of the growth potential in the Ft. Worth area. Not the least important or urgent matter he needed to address was to evaluate his own performance during the past year and to set some personal objectives.

In addition, John had to prepare some written comments on the performance of each of his reps for the past year to put in their personal files. He thought he should calculate some ratios from the data in Exhibits 1 and 2 such as sales growth, sales to quota, sales per call, sales per physician, expenses per call, and selling expenses as a percent of sales to include in his report on each rep. Also he had to decide what to do about Jared and Marty. Overall, John saw his problems were really people problems and people opportunities, and their interaction and interdependence were what made his job both challenging and fun.

CASE 4 ATOMIC COMPANY

Roger Post, an executive at Atomic Company, was humming a happy tune as he reviewed the sales figures for Tiger Pants. Tiger Pants had already generated a personal $20,000 bonus for him for beating the 2002 sales quota of $5 million in sales. Better yet, it was only March 8, 2002, and there were still three weeks to go in the first quarter. He might end up getting a total bonus of $80,000 for the year, which would be the biggest bonus he had ever gotten for the sales of just one product. Beth Clinton, the CEO of Atomic Company, had just purchased a new luxury boat and had invited all of Atomic's key managers to a party Saturday to show it off.

BACKGROUND

The Atomic Company was founded in 1946 with a focus on manufacturing and selling men's casual and leisure wear clothing. Although sales were steady, it remained a very tiny company with only 0.3 percent market share in 2000 for the men's casual and leisure clothes market. Even though the market share was small, Atomic had benefited from the trend toward business casual clothing in the 1990s. Although Atomic's clothes were distributed throughout the United States and Canada, sales came primarily from the Southeastern part of the United States.

Atomic had originally owned several textile mills in Alabama, Georgia, and South Carolina, with the first plant purchased in 1946 just after World War II. By 1976, Atomic had grown to nine textile mills, which were all located in rural areas with inexpensive labor. However, rising costs and the influx of lower cost textiles from Southeast Asia started eroding margins and greatly harmed Atomic's profits in the late 1970s. Atomic shifted its manufacturing strategy and opened plants in Taiwan while starting to close plants in the United States. In 1983, the last manufacturing plant in the United States was sold. Manufacturing operations were eventually shifted from Taiwan to China as China

This case was prepared by Avery Abernethy, Professor of Marketing, Auburn University.

opened its markets to foreign investment and liberalized trade policies.

China had a large textile industry and also produced large quantities of cotton, the primary raw material for Atomic's line of men's clothing. Atomic's headquarters were in Atlanta and consisted of fewer than twenty employees. Dolly Green, the vice president of production and logistics, spent much of her time in China making sure that subcontractors in China maintained quality manufacturing standards. After the Taiwan plants were sold, Atomic no longer owned manufacturing facilities.

Dolly was very good with languages and after a couple of years of hard work had become fluent in Chinese. She also handled the logistics of getting the finished clothing collected at Chinese ports and then shipped to San Diego in the United States. From San Diego, the clothes were shipped by truck to warehouses in Atlanta.

Ramon Fernandez, the vice president of finance, also had his duties split between the United States and China. Ramon made sure that funds were transferred to China to pay for the purchase of raw materials, manufacturing, and the export of clothing by containerized cargo shipped out of Chinese ports. Ramon was an expert in letters of credit. He was also skilled in using currency options to help protect Atomic from large swings in the exchange rate between the U.S. and Chinese currencies. Because most of Ramon's job mandated working with large banks and the international currency markets, he was able to stay in the United States most of the time, although a few trips to China were necessary every year.

The president and CEO of Atomic was Beth Clinton. Beth is 52 and has an MBA from Yale. She had worked for an international shipping company in Los Angeles prior to her employment with Atomic. Atomic hired Beth as vice president of production and logistics in 1992. She was the driving force in selling Atomic's manufacturing plants in Taiwan and using Chinese subcontractors for all manufacturing. Because of her successful manufacturing and logistics strategy, she was promoted to CEO of Atomic in 1992 upon the retirement of her predecessor.

ATOMIC'S FINANCIAL PERFORMANCE

Under Beth Clinton's leadership, sales of Atomic had continued to increase, with about 3 percent annual growth from 1992 to 2000. Atomic's net profit before income taxes had increased from 5 percent in 1992 to 12 percent in 2000. Much of the increase in profits was due to favorable exchange rates, with the strong dollar in the 1990s coupled with lower manufacturing and materials costs from the shift in operations from Taiwan to China. This was accomplished in spite of a 10 percent decrease in average prices to retailers between 1992 and 2000 caused by competitive pressures.

Atomic Company's total sales were $14 million in 2000. Due to a huge increase in the sales of Tiger Pants, Atomic's sales jumped to $22 million in 2001. The profit picture was even brighter. Atomic's profits were $1,680,000 in the year 2000 but jumped to $4,400,000 in 2001, with most of the profit increase coming from Tiger Pants.

The profit increases were due to two factors: (1) the tremendous increase in sales of Tiger Pants and (2) the unexpected popularity of Tiger Pants, which allowed Atomic to increase prices to retailers by 15 percent on the Tiger Pants line. Although costs increased somewhat for Tiger Pants because of the need to contract for expanded production on short notice and the need to pay for expedited shipping from China, the 15 percent price increase both covered the increase in costs and allowed for increased margins.

Quarterly Sales of Tiger Pants

	2000	*2001*	*2002*
Quarter 1	$100,000	$90,000	$5,680,000 (3 weeks left in the quarter)
Quarter 2	120,000	150,000	
Quarter 3	280,000	2,350,000	
Quarter 4	100,000	4,100,000	

SALES STRATEGY FOR TIGER PANTS

Roger Post was promoted to vice president of sales for Atomic Company in 1995. Roger is 55 years old. Prior to being named national sales manager, he was in charge of training, selecting new styles for the year, and coordinating advertising to the retailers carrying Atomic Company's product lines. Although Atomic used trade shows, trade advertising, direct mail, and independent reps to persuade retailers to carry Atomic's men's clothing lines, the company did not have the funds to engage in direct-to-consumer advertising.

Bonus Clothes and Celebrity Clothes

When faced with little in the way of consumer marketing funds, Roger tried to use the product itself to market the brand. One of the first things he attempted upon becoming vice president of sales was to set up sales contests for participating retailers. Store managers whose sales of Atomic's clothing lines increased by 10 percent over the previous year were given vouchers for $200 (in wholesale prices) for Atomic clothing. In terms of consumers' retail price, this worked out to about $425 worth of merchandise. If sales increased 25 percent, then $400 in merchandise (in wholesale prices) was awarded. When sales increased 100 percent over the previous year, $1,000 in merchandise was provided.

Although some managers just sold the additional free clothing to consumers to increase their store profits, most managers either kept the clothing for themselves or awarded the clothes to top salespeople within their stores. Roger encouraged store managers to give at least part of the clothing to top salespeople, but he was also happy when the store managers decided to keep the bonus clothing for themselves. In 2000, the "Bonus Clothes for Bonus Performance" program cost about $10,000. However, in 2001 the total cost for "Bonus Clothes" totaled a whopping $75,000.

In addition to the "Bonus Clothes" program, Roger gave free merchandise to celebrities in hopes that they would wear Atomic's clothing line. In 1999, $8,000 (wholesale value) worth of merchandise was given away; in 2000, it rose to $9,000 and in 2001 to $35,000. The celebrity merchandise was given away to college coaches, television reporters and newscasters, and music and movie personalities. Some of the headquarters staff jokingly accused Roger of giving away clothes just so he could "schmooze with people he saw on TV."

During the midyear business meeting of 2001, Ramon Fernandez had asked Roger to justify the programs to the rest of the management team. Roger got angry and asked if the company was going to audit all of Ramon's submitted expenses to visit banks and financial companies in New York City. It got down to the point where Ramon pointedly discussed the need to control marketing expenses and the need for far closer oversight of these sales programs by the management team. At this point Roger lost his temper and told Ramon: "You know nothing about marketing. You think that all of this company's sales are generated with a wave of the hand. These clothes don't sell themselves, and we have to have some way to convince retailers to stock and push our lines."

At Ramon's urging, the "celebrity clothing" and "bonus clothes" projects were audited to ensure that all of the expenses were justified. Dolly backed up Ramon, and Beth seemed to reluctantly agree to Ramon's idea just to move the meeting forward.

Beth set up a lunch meeting with Roger two days later. Roger told Beth that he felt Ramon was accusing him of embezzling merchandise at worst or misusing company money at best. Beth admitted that Ramon could be blunt about cost control, but she also reminded Roger that all company expenditures were subject to review by the management team. She also reminded Roger that Ramon had convinced the management team to audit the new manufacturing contracts when she had just completed switching manufacturing from Taiwan to China.

She summed up by saying: "Look, I know that Ramon can be a real jerk sometimes. He really does care about company profits, and his financial skills are essential to the management team. He is also 60 years old and approaching retirement. He has told me that company profits could really take off, and points out that most of the increase in profits from the last ten years were due to cost control and not increasing the units sold. Remember, Roger, I have confidence in your abilities and feel sure that the review of these two programs will show that you are running the sales team in an outstanding fashion."

Personal Selling Strategy for Tiger Pants

All of Atomic's clothing lines were sold by independent reps, and the Tiger Pants line was no different. One rep covered the Southeastern part of the United States. The second rep sold to New England, the upper Midwest, and Canada. The territory of the third rep was the United States west of the Mississippi.

The reps were paid a flat 15 percent commission on all sales. Payments were made quarterly, and the checks were issued only after the retailer's payment was received. Roger used different independent reps to sell each line of clothes to retailers in their region. He thought that using different reps for each line of clothing would spark competition and innovation between the different sales teams. It also allowed him to reward top-selling reps with a more profitable line of clothing if they turned out to be outstanding salespeople.

Each independent rep was treated as an independent contractor for tax purposes. This allowed each rep unlimited potential for commissions but prevented the company from having to pay salaries or benefits. In the past, Atomic had never had the financial strength that would have allowed it to have an internal company sales force.

Two of the salespeople for Tigers had high school diplomas, while the third rep had never completed high school. All three reps had more than fifteen years of experience selling clothing to the channel of distribution. However, all three had been hired in the last five years, with the most junior representative hired only nine months ago. Roger had a lot of confidence in the Tiger sales team. Tigers had been a fairly minor line, but the current team of independent reps had sales of Tiger Pants growing faster than almost all of the other clothing lines marketed by Atomic in 1999 and 2000.

The contract with each rep allowed Atomic to cancel the reps services with two weeks' notice. Several times in the past, Roger had been forced to fire reps who failed to produce. However, Atomic's turnover in independent reps averaged about 8 percent annually, which was pretty low for the industry. He tended to cancel contracts for poor sales performance more frequently when the sales of the clothing line were strong in the overall market. He had never let a rep go without first having a replacement sales representative lined up. This helped to maintain customer relations and avoid gaps in customer service. Roger felt that one of the reasons he had been able to grow Atomic's sales was his good track record in getting better-than-average reps under contract with Atomic.

Punk Rock Academy

In April 2001, Roger Post's 17-year-old daughter Lonnie asked him for four pairs of Tiger Pants for a local band called "Punk Rock Academy." Lonnie said the band was really hot and had just signed a contract with Epitaph records. One of the band members had seen Lonnie wearing a pair of old, beat-up Tiger Pants at a concert at the Echo Lounge. Lonnie had taken a red marker and had given the tiger symbol on the back of the pants blood-red eyes and had also drawn on blood dripping from the tiger's fangs.

Although Roger thought that Lonnie was a good kid who made excellent grades, he knew she was always a little weird and was really interested in music. Roger and his wife had demanded that Lonnie not get pierced or tattooed, but that agreement did not stop her from wearing some pretty odd clothes and dyeing her hair strange colors. Roger briefly shuddered when he recalled that horrid purple hair with bright red highlights that Lonnie came up with one month. Lonnie did ask really nicely for the pants and showed two compact disks and a couple of posters of Punk Rock Academy to show that they really were an upcoming band. Although he had more than a few reservations, Roger gave Lonnie the four pairs of pants she asked for and filled out the paperwork showing who the pants had been given to.

Roger could not believe what happened next. On July 24, he came home late to find Lonnie more excited than he had ever seen her. MTV had picked up Punk Rock Academy's video for "Fight Song." Lonnie had taped the video from the TV. She was in the video for about 20 seconds wearing her beat-up Tiger Pants, thrashing around on the dance floor while the band played.

The video for "Fight Song" told a story of the four tattooed, nose-pierced band members going to their first day of high school and getting a notice that they would have to follow the school dress code (khaki pants and a button-down white shirt) or be expelled. Next, the band members have Tiger Pants, which they knock the knees out of and mark up with red eyes and bloody fangs like Lonnie had done. They go back to school the next day dressed in the ripped up Tigers. The principal has a nervous breakdown when the band plays at the high school dance that night dressed in the ripped up Tigers. The band finishes up by setting the drum kit on fire and throwing their button-down white shirts on the flames.

Roger saw the video for the first time only three weeks after the ugly midyear business meeting. The audit of the "bonus clothes" and "celebrity clothes" programs would start next Monday. After seeing the video, Roger felt sick to his stomach and knew that Ramon would jump on his giving the band members four free pairs of pants. Roger was happy that he ended up being very, very wrong.

"Fight Song" went into MTVs heavy rotation. Punk Rock Academy opened for the Green Day/Blink 182 summer tour, and the album went gold. Sales exploded. More than 2 million Tigers were sold in the third quarter of 2001. There were $4 million in sales for the fourth quarter of 2001 and a whopping $5,680,000 in sales for the first quarter of 2002 alone!

Retailers had great difficulty keeping Tiger Pants in stock, especially in the third quarter of 2001. The three Tiger Pants reps made a killing and even had to prioritize the orders of their old customers since it was difficult for enough pants to reach the United States from China quickly enough to meet the surging demand. One of the reps even told Roger that "she just had to answer her cell phone and write down orders" instead of really hustling to drum up sales. Roger ended up getting a $40,000 bonus check for the 2001 sales of Tigers just before Christmas of 2001. In a nod of thanks for Lonnie's help, Roger flew Lonnie and her Mom to New York to see Punk Rock Academy play in MTV's New Year's Eve concert. Even better, that jerk Ramon had been shown that Roger really understood marketing and that there was nothing unprofessional about the "bonus clothes" and the "celebrity clothes" programs.

THE MARCH 9, 2002, ATOMIC MANAGERS MEETING

Beth asked Roger to start the meeting off by giving actual and projected sales for Tiger Pants for the first quarter. Roger smiled as he reported $5,680,000 in paid sales, with an estimate of an additional $400,000 in sales of Tigers for the last three weeks of the quarter. Roger also reported on the end of the year totals for the bonus clothing and celebrity clothing programs. Beth asked for a breakdown for the Tiger Pants line alone for the entire year of 2001. Roger responded that the celebrity clothing costs for Tiger Pants were $25,000; $60,000 in bonus clothes; and sales commissions to the three independent reps of $1,003,500. He followed up by mentioning that, although these figures might seem a bit high, they were caused by the huge sales increase for Tigers. Sales cost as a percentage of total sales, he said, had remained flat in 2001 for the Tiger line despite the huge sales increase.

Ramon asked for estimated sales for Tiger Pants for 2002. Roger admitted that "it was going to be very difficult to estimate. Was the boom in sales just a fad? Would sales plateau at the $10-million level? Sales could even be as high as $25 million before expenses." "I have never seen anything like this sales jump, and I do not think that it will last. Sales will be at a higher level than the $600,000 in 2000, but 2003 sales may be as low as $3 million. The company has benefited from the celebrity program, but I do not think current sales levels will continue when the fad dies down. We all know that kids go from one new thing to another."

Dolly pointed out that "this uncertainty is making my job very hard. I don't know if I should sign long-run production contracts for Tigers at the current sales level. I can get production discounts of as much as 20 percent, but I need to give a firm annual sales figure to get this kind of discount. The way we have been operating, with all of the short-run rush orders, has caused our manufacturing and logistics costs to increase by a full 10 percent. Roger, surely you can do better than a three-quarter sales estimate for 2002 of between $5 and $20 million. This uncertainty is killing cost control!"

Roger answered: "You know, all of us have made a lot of bonus money, and the value of our stock options has gone sky high. Sure, all of this may not continue. But even if it does not last, we have all made a lot of money. I'm looking forward to seeing how Beth has spent some of her money on that new boat!"

Ramon jumped in stating that "more than $1 million in sales commissions for 2001 for one line of clothing is just nuts." None of the salespeople, he pointed out, even had a college degree and yet they were "living like kings." "You know, for the first quarter those three have already pulled in $852,000 in commissions that we will have to cut a check for. This is more than four times the money that I made in salary and bonus for all of 2001."

Ramon followed up by asking Roger if the company could not just fire the three reps and hire company salespeople. Roger responded that they could probably get three people to cover the territories for $40,000 salary, the standard $15,000 benefits package that all of the headquarters staff received, plus perhaps a 0.5 percent sales commission. Roger pointed out that he did not have anyone lined up and that the company had never fired a rep for performing "way over expectations." What sort of message would they be sending to the other independent reps who were responsible for the sales of all of Atomic's other lines of clothing?

Beth spoke up for the first time. "Roger, it is your masterful marketing efforts that gave Atomic this huge sales boost for Tiger Pants. I promise never to crack a joke about your daughter's hair ever again," which was followed by warm laughter from all four managers. Dolly chimed in with "Roger, it is your good idea that got us all of these great results. We could hire anyone off the street to push Tiger Pants." Roger reminded everyone that without the effort of the independent reps, Atomic would not be generating any sales at all.

At this point, Beth told Roger to prepare a sales cost comparison between keeping the current sales structure for Tiger Pants versus going to a company sales force. She also expressed confidence that Roger would be able to get some "quality salespeople" in two weeks time with the generous compensation package of $40,000 salary plus benefits and a small commission. Besides, people "like the security of a salary," and "some bright college kid would jump at the chance to sign up with Atomic and sell Tigers."

Beth finished up by taking up a point that Ramon had made earlier. "You know, these three salespeople are not well educated, and all of these sales for Tigers basically fell into their laps with their making very little effort. The salespeople basically just sat back and let the orders roll in. Atomic paid them more than $1 million in commissions last year—far more than they really deserved. Roger, we all know that the core management team is responsible for Atomic's success. According to the contract, we can fire the reps with two weeks' notice. If we fire them and then cancel the orders placed for the quarter, we can get the retailers who have already paid up for the quarter new purchase orders. This will allow us to take the $852,000 in commissions for the first quarter of 2002 and use them as a bonus pool for top management. Each of us would get a bonus of more than $200,000."

Beth ended the meeting by thanking them for all of their great decisions over the last three quarters. "I want everyone to have a great time on my new boat on Saturday. On Tuesday of next week, we need to meet again and decide what direction we want the sales force to take. Roger, we will need the figures from you for all of the options at our next meeting. See all of you and your spouses tomorrow on my new boat!"

CONNER LABS

While at the Chicago airport, I was awaiting a flight to Los Angeles. I checked my e-mail and there was another message from Bill Short, who is vice president of strategic planning. He was concerned over the apparent loss of Joysco Technological Surgeries (JTS). The message was:

"Please call me tomorrow at 7:00 A.M. to discuss the loss of JTS. I am extremely disturbed at losing this account. I have reviewed your records on this account through the last quarter. The records do not have third-quarter profiles." He continued, "Be prepared to discuss how you approached this strategic account and why we lost the business. As the most senior sales representative for Conner, I am discouraged that you have not called before now to discuss this matter."

Each quarter, the field sales force downloads all account profiles and sales activities from their laptops to home office computers. Current-quarter records are due next week, containing information that Bill Short has not yet examined. I decided it would be a good idea to look over all of the information on this account that had been logged on my laptop for the last eight months. If I could discover why this account was lost, obviously I could make some changes in my selling strategy.

It was only a week ago that I had caught a flight to Cincinnati on a sales call to JTS, only to be frustrated by this account. I was certain that prior to my arrival, everything was in order to close this sale. I was shocked that JTS had purchased what I believed to be a substantially inferior surgical system for performing cataract surgery from Bayson Laboratories. Bayson Labs is a relative newcomer in the medical supplies field, and JTS always had dealt with vendors who have an established reputation. I was given no indication that any other vendor was being seriously considered for this purchase.

As I reflected on the situation, I wondered how much the loss of the JTS sale would affect my division in the upcoming budget for the year. I also wondered how the loss would impact my own position.

THE CATARACT SURGERY MARKET

The cataract surgery market has grown tremendously over the last twenty years. Much of this growth occurred as a result of Medicaid and Medicare reimbursement for the procedure. In 2004, there were 2.7 million cataract surgeries performed in the United States, of which almost 65 percent were covered by government Medicare and Medicaid programs. Cataracts typically occur in patients after 45 years of age. When patients develop cataracts, the lens of their eye forms an opaque mass and light rays are unable to pass to the back of the eye. With the diminishing ability of the lens to pass light, patients will eventually go totally blind. Estimates indicate that 35 percent of the population will develop cataracts. Approximately

This case was prepared by John Cheneler and Professor William Cron of Texas Christian University. Neither names nor financial data are intended to reference anyone or a particular business. All cataract surgery information is accurate; however, competitive and product information has been modified for reasons of company security.

40 percent of all Medicare and Medicaid patients can be certified as needing cataract surgery.[1]

Cataract surgery is a procedure requiring superb skills, yet it is not time-consuming; the surgery can be performed in 20 to 30 minutes. Patients feel little, if any, discomfort, and the surgery is usually performed on an outpatient basis. In 2004, the cost for the procedure was typically about $1,500 per eye. Today, surgeons typically operate two days a week, averaging twenty surgeries weekly.

Patients are typically asked to arrive at the surgery center about an hour prior to surgery. Prior to surgery, a number of eye drop medications are applied to the eye to prevent pain, to reduce inflammation and the risk of infection, and to fully dilate the pupil. The surgery is typically performed under local or topical anesthesia. With local anesthesia, the entire eye and eye muscles are numbed to prevent discomfort. With topical anesthesia, just the front of the eye is numbed. The type of anesthesia chosen depends mostly on the surgeon's preference.

During surgery, most patients remain fully awake; however, mild sedation may be used depending on the physician and patient wishes. Once the surgery is complete the patient is briefly monitored, post-op instructions given, and in most cases, the patient is discharged to go home within an hour.

Cataract surgeons are most commonly general ophthalmologists who specialize in the removal of cataracts and the implantation of intraocular lens implants. General ophthalmologists typically treat the broadest range of eye conditions and may perform a large variety of procedures in addition to cataract surgery.

With increased competition and better equipment, many hospitals are fighting to maintain market share by having the latest equipment available. In the early stages of the cataract surgery market, all surgery was performed at hospitals. Soon off-site surgery centers began to compete actively with hospitals for the patients of large surgical group practices.[2] Now some large group practices are even soliciting other surgeons to use the group's facilities for performing cataract surgeries, rather than going to either hospitals or offsite surgery centers.

EQUIPMENT

Diagnostic Units

Diagnostic units are used to determine the relative focal ability of an eye. Even though a physician can determine that a patient suffers from eye degeneration with a routine examination, there is still a need to quantify eyesight to justify the need for cataract surgery.

While a patient places his or her chin on a leather strap, a laser beam is projected into the eye. The patient reads a series of randomly generated letters or numbers. The diagnostic unit predicts how much eyesight will be regained by the patient after surgery. When cataract surgery is completed, patients will see as well as they did using the diagnostic unit. An examination can be performed in less than 5 minutes.

Conner introduced the first diagnostic unit in 1990 and offers the highest priced diagnostic unit on the market at $20,000. Competitors have attempted either to continue to sell the Snellen Chart method, using dilation, or to use a variation of the Centrust diagnostic unit, though with limited success.[3] Competitors' products range in price from $2,500 to $27,000. Surgeons considered Conner's diagnostic unit as the only one currently on the market in which they could have 100 percent confidence in diagnosis. The U.S. government had ruled only the Conner unit as acceptable in confirming the need for cataract surgery for Medicaid and Medicare patients without a second medical opinion. No other competitor is currently able to offer a product that can duplicate this process with as much reliability. Conner was quite successful in selling this unit by emphasizing that it lasts for the life of a medical practice and, further, that no dilation drops are needed. Conner was the only vendor offering lifetime warranties on diagnostic products for eye care.

Surgical Units

The price for a surgical unit used in cataract surgery varied between $100,000 and $300,000. This price differential was due solely to the name recognition of the vendor and the number of modifications needed to adapt the unit to other equipment in the operating room as opposed to distinguishable product difference.

[1] Information on the profiles of cataract surgeons and the number of procedures supplied by the U.S. Office of Medical Statistics. Washington, DC.

[2] Off-site surgery centers are conveniently located centers for performing a variety of surgeries in which the patient needs to stay for less than a day. Surgeries that can be performed at these centers include removal of gallbladders, cosmetic surgery, liposuction, and cataract surgery.

[3] The chart consists of rows of letters or numbers that decrease in size with each row. One major concern of a physician is that patients will often memorize the letters after repeated examinations.

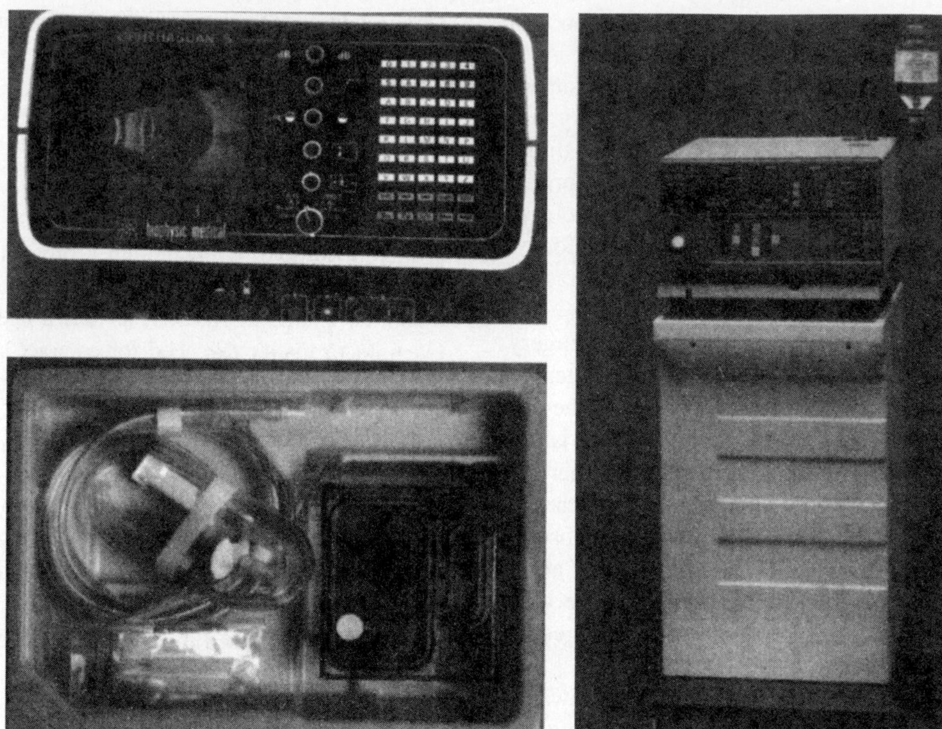

EXHIBIT 1 A Diagnostic Unit, a Surgical Unit, and a Disposable Instruments Pack (clockwise from top left)

Modifications can be as simple as adapting electrical outlets or as complex as writing computer programs to link the unit to other surgical units.[4]

The surgical unit is a large console, usually 4 feet long by 2 feet wide by 5 feet tall. It consists of a computer that sends an electric impulse to handheld cutting tools, tubing for flowing fluid into the surgery area and suctioning the fluid back, and several aspirating tubes to remove the lens of the eye after incision. The minuscule pieces of material around the lens must be removed without damaging the surrounding area. The surgery site is smaller than the size of a period on a piece of paper. Most units offered by manufacturers appear to have similar capabilities; therefore, surgeons and hospitals often shopped vendors on price. Seldom would surgeons be aware of the difference in vendors' products. In the past, surgeons always purchased the highest priced unit, believing that quality and price were absolutely related. As their surgical techniques improved, surgeons were less willing to pay higher prices unless they observed a distinct difference in product quality. Hospital surgery management viewed a surgical unit, however, as much more critical for their success in attracting doctors and patients than a diagnostic unit.

Disposable Instruments

Disposable cutting instruments used in cataract surgery typically cost $125. Every surgical procedure requires a new set of disposable surgical hand pieces each time an incision is made. Disposable hand pieces are plugged into surgical units that supply electrical current, along with proper irrigation and aspiration.[5] After completion of the surgery, disposable cutting tools and gauze patches must be discarded. Little difference exists among the disposable products of various vendors; therefore, most disposable instruments were purchased primarily based on the lowest price

[4] Conner was not aggressive in requiring the purchaser to share the costs of modifying surgical units, in which extensive modifications could add up to 50 percent to the cost of the unit. In 1990 Conner made major modifications to 11 percent of its units; in 1993 the percentage of units requiring adjustments soared to 38 percent.

[5] The handheld piece makes a quite thin incision along the lens of the eye, and the surgeon removes the lens and extraneous materials with suction tubes supplied via the unit. The cleaner the incision, the quicker the recovery of the patient.

EXHIBIT 2 Conner Labs: Income Statement and Statement of Retained Earnings for the Year Ending December 31, 2004 (in Millions)

	2001	2002	2003	2004
Sales revenues	$436.6	$515.5	$558.5	$456.1
Cost of sales	330.6	372.7	385.4	345.8
Gross margin	106.0	142.8	173.1	110.3
Expenses				
Depreciation	$24.0	$24.1	$24.4	$24.6
Sales expenses	28.1	30.3	32.5	34.1
Other expenses	10.9	10.7	10.3	10.2
Income taxes	18.9	35.0	48.7	19.1
Total expenses	81.9	100.1	$115.9	88.0
Net Income	$24.1	$42.7	$57.2	$22.4
Less: Cash dividends	7.2	12.8	17.2	6.7
Net retained earnings	$16.9	$29.9	$40.0	$15.7

available through distributors. Pictures of a diagnostic unit, a surgical unit, and a disposable instruments pack are shown in Exhibit 1.

CONNER LABS

Conner has been a pioneer in the development of digital/laser technology in the medical field. It started almost exclusively as a fledgling medical manufacturer in New York City, with a limited product line. However, in the last few years with the introduction of new diagnostic products, Conner had grown to a leadership position in medical diagnostics and surgical products for cataract eye surgery. See Exhibit 2 for financial information on Conner. Few medical companies enjoy Conner's reputation for quality.

Although the technology for the diagnostic unit is protected by patents, the cataract surgery units and disposable instruments are not. With its superior manufacturing processes, however, R&D was able to modify slightly its line of surgical units to fit the needs of off-site surgery centers and other medical specialities. The delicate aspirating capabilities of the surgical unit, for instance, have been modified for use by vascular surgeons in nerve and vascular reattachment. The success of product extensions depends on both the identification of viable extension opportunities and the manufacturer's reputation. Most successful vendors develop a strong association with a particular specialty and use this relationship for product line extensions. Due to Conner's success in the cataract area and resulting selling time demands, the sales force has not been aggressive in promoting Conner's products to other specialities.

Conner's marketing strategy had been to establish its reputation through aggressive promotion of its high-quality products. The margins on cataract equipment had been high, but with increased competition and product maturity, they had declined. After 1992, numerous competitors for Conner's digital/laser products appeared. This was not unusual, as typically a break-through product could hold market share for only three years or less.

With its reputation and high margins, Conner was able to attract extraordinarily skilled and established sales representatives plus similarly qualified sales managers. The sales force consisted of six sales representatives, three sales managers, and one national sales director. There had been no turnover in the sales force in the last two years. The average sales representative had over ten years' industry experience and covered a large territory.

Market Purchasing Behavior

Conner had watched its market share dwindle from 70 percent in 1990 to 22 percent in 2004. Although much of the market share loss was due to successful imitation and maturing of the market, some of the market share loss was also felt to be due to the quality of selling effort put behind the equipment. This is clearly a complex selling process and a New Account Planning Program (NAPP) was developed to help guide Conner's sales force through the process and to keep management informed of the selling progress (Exhibit 3).

To complete the selling cycle for a surgical system, sales representatives need to work through several layers of approval. Sales representatives typically meet

EXHIBIT 3 National Account Planning Program (NAPP)

NAPP is an effort by Conner to change the selling behavior of the sales force to a more consultative approach, emphasizing account relationship building, value-added selling, identification of product line extension opportunities, an account tracking system, and coordination with management. Following is a brief description of this program.

1. Relationship Building: With all important members of the buying center, build a relationship based on trust, rapport, and meeting each member's concerns and expectations. Backgrounds on people who may be involved in the purchase include the following:

Marketing Manager:	Promotes the hospital and is often involved in its strategic planning.
Hospital Administrator:	Acts as CEO of the hospital. Concerned with financial matters and the strategic direction of the hospital. Usually does not have a technical background in medicine.
Purchasing:	Establishes and maintains vendor relationships and ensures continuous supply at the lowest price. Usually a business or liberal arts education.
Reimbursement Officer:	Determines and tracks billing of patients and third parties (e.g., insurance and government) to meet government guidelines. Usually has some medical background.
Head of Nursing:	Primary user of many medical supplies; acts as a budget director for surgery and is highly influential in deciding which products will be used in surgery.
Safety Director:	Concerned with government safety regulations compliance and exposure to lawsuits. Frequently a highly technical individual; often an engineer.
Head of Surgery:	Usually a senior, well-respected surgeon who is highly influential in the hospital. Would have worked solely with one hospital in the past; this is not necessarily the case today.

2. Value-Added Selling: With hospitals' recent emphasis on low price, emphasis should focus on nonprice benefits, such as demonstrating technical superiority of equipment and instruments, fewer complications following surgery, lower cost per surgery due to greater speed, value in hospital's marketing to doctors, and exceeding government-mandated safety specifications.

3. Product Line Extension Opportunities: In an effort to expand sales opportunities for current cataract equipment, salespeople should be on constant alert for opportunities to apply cataract technology to other medical specialties.

4. Opportunity Tracking System: In order to better track the current selling situation, salespeople are to classify all sales opportunities into one of the following classifications:

"Unqualified"	When salesperson thinks there may be an opportunity but has not identified all buying influences.
"Qualified"	When a need has been verified, there is a confirmed intention to buy, and funding is available within a defined time frame.
"Best"	All influencers have been identified and concerns addressed, and there is a 90 percent probability of a sale.

5. Management Coordination: Salespeople are to update management quarterly on the status of all opportunities. In addition, management is to be personally involved in all "Best Opportunities" valued at more than $500,000, must approve all equipment discounts, and should be notified of all line extension opportunities by completing Form LEO-2000.

with several individuals to identify their needs and to demonstrate the product's advantages. This process becomes quite confusing if the sales representative tries to sidestep anyone influential in the decision-making process. The commitment to buy medical products is seldom impulsive; therefore, sales representatives who try to complete the sale without total buyer commitment to the product will become frustrated. A successful sales representative must be prepared to allot several months to gain the endorsement and commitment of everyone involved in the process.

To keep the selling process flowing, effective sales representatives must find a champion, either inside or outside the hospital, to help promote their products and to identify potential roadblocks hindering completion of the sale. The purchasing agent, for instance, may not be the most influential individual in the decision process. The head nurse, rather than the surgeon, most often purchases disposable surgical products and determines the budget. Hospital management may desire a particular surgical unit based on low price, but surgeons in many specialties may influence the decision in another direction by demonstrating that the slightly higher-priced unit has more applications. Each purchase decision is unique, though multiple people are always involved.

The medical community has come under greater scrutiny in the last few years concerning the purchase and costs of medical care. With the impending government legislation, purchasing agents have been instructed to acquire products at the lowest possible price. Often, the value of products and services is not readily apparent. Very seldom are vendors able to sell a purchasing agent on any point other than price without first establishing strong relationships with everyone influential in the decision process.

Laptop Records of Account Activities. The following notes appear in their original grammatical form as copied from laptop notes. The sales representative is required to input daily activities on all accounts.

Business Practices at JTS

JTS is a rather large surgical hospital that has a solid business reputation. It performed the most surgical procedures in a three-county region that served 7 million residents. In an effort to retain the most skilled surgeons, JTS had one of the highest compensation programs in the industry and its turnover rate was low throughout the hospital. JTS had published several brochures recently that indicated it was establishing total quality management (TQM) programs this year. I thought it might be advantageous to link this to Conner.

TIMELINE

January 6

JTS had been targeted as being an account that had tremendous profit potential by our Strategic Analysis Department. During a scheduled appointment with B. J. Avery, JTS Director of Purchasing, we examined the new product lines that Conner is offering. I assessed the potential purchases of this account as 4 diagnostic units, 16 surgical units, and around 4,000 disposable surgical instruments for the first year. The total potential is $10.5 million.

Spent the day doing informational interviews at the JTS facility. Developed a list of people who I think will be influential in the purchasing decision. The buyers assured me that Conner had maintained a positive relationship in the past with delivery, service, and quality. Spent two hours looking around to obtain information about the business. I noticed that there was a business services unit that actually marketed medical services and products.[6] Made an appointment to see Avery's boss, the Vice President of Purchasing, for the morning of January 22 and the Head of Surgery for the afternoon of January 22.

January 22

Met with Sandy Adams, who has been the Vice President of Purchasing for three years. In the past I had been able to sell at JTS without needing to meet Sandy Adams. I was informed that all bids must be at the lowest market price. I must find users of the products to champion the full price. Dropped off the proper brochures to show Sandy Adams the features of our products that fit perfectly into their existing surgical protocols. I have classified JTS as a "Qualified Opportunity."

I met with Dr. Stenz (a leading surgeon who works with JTS) to discuss the technical aspects of Conner products. He appeared more comfortable with Conner after understanding the surgical benefits of our products over our competitors' products. He seemed to be impressed by our products.

I asked if any other competitor had established solid relationships with JTS, and I was guaranteed that we were in the "driver's seat." It was even suggested that I stop by the office of Dr. Stenz and speak with his four associates. We also discussed the delivery process and training. The order for $10.5 million from JTS should be coming soon, and we are in a position to hold full price. Stenz does not feel that we will need to discount very much to JTS. He also indicated that he would be purchasing for his office seven diagnostic units; an unusually large order for an established practice. I wonder?

January 24

Stopped by to see the associates of Dr. Stenz. I was surprised that no one was aware that I was coming. Stenz had seemed so enthusiastic and promised that he would arrange my visit with his associates and pass along the brochures I gave him. Even though I was disappointed that they were unprepared for my visit, I used this as an opportunity to speak with the office manager, whom I found was influential in the office's buying process.

One interesting development is that I found out during the meeting with the office manager that there were two other competitors who had spoken with the hospital and other surgeons during the last month. Dr. Stenz had assured me that there was no real competition. I am not worried too much since I know from the December Vendors Trade Show in New Orleans that there is no threat for upcoming products from any other vendor.

[6] Even though hospitals are traditionally thought of as nonprofit, they will often have marketing and promotion departments that are extremely aggressive.

February 3

Called on JTS to check on the Purchasing Department's progress concerning the order. Took the Purchasing Vice President's Assistant to lunch to find new information. The discussion centered around the politics of the organization. Learned that they felt we are being too aggressive and need to slow down. I took this as an opportunity to discuss our company and try to establish a rapport rather than focus on selling product. After lunch I stopped by surgery to see if any competitors' products were being used. It seemed like a smorgasbord of products with no one vendor in dominance.

Made an appointment to see the Nursing Head of Surgery on the 14th. It's interesting. When I mentioned this to the Purchasing Assistant, he said, "Go ahead and do that, but remember we are the ones who sign all the purchasing orders."

February 14

It's Valentines Day so I stopped by with candy and flowers for the Surgical Nursing Department. This has always paid off well. The atmosphere was light and everyone was very receptive to listening to benefits of our products. They seemed to be pleased with what I told them. Looks as though the "ducks are being lined up." Look for the order soon!

March 16

Called Stenz to schedule an appointment since I will be in the area in April. He said that I needed to talk to H. M. Jones over at JTS. Found out that Jones was the Head of Safety at JTS. Made an appointment for April 23 and sent a followup letter and brochures on every product that we could possibly offer. I am not sure who this individual is, but I am sure his role will be explained at our meeting.

April 23

I arrived at JTS and initiated a discussion with H. M. Jones concerning purchases on the original "bid." I was surprised to find that Jones was rather unsophisticated and appeared confused by both the literature and our conversation. Conner had hired the finest ad agency in the city to prepare these brochures for a high school level education. Jones may actually understand the material and is simply testing me. I'm sure I passed the test. The last question I asked was, "If this is all clear, do you have any other questions?" The reply I got was "nope"—another duck lined up!!!! I have moved JTS's classification up to a "Best Few Opportunity."

May 15

Received a phone message from Stenz stating that our prices on the diagnostic units for his office are too high, and I need to come down on price immediately. I called and was unable to reach him, but I did speak with an associate who told me that they were actually looking for an order that might be twice as large as my original estimate, but the problem is that we are too high on price. I asked him if they were basing this opinion on a price relative to someone else or if our price was too high in general. They assured me that their business could not support our prices. I set an appointment on May 18 to speak in person with everyone in their office.

May 18

I had prepared new proposals in accordance with the practices of Conner. There had been an offer by our Vice President of Sales to attend the meeting, but I felt comfortable that I would finalize this sale in 90 days so I rejected the suggestion. I proposed to the Strategic Analysis Department that we offer a new pricing structure for Dr. Stenz and his associates if they are able to help us get the JTS contract. After some arm twisting, I was given the authority to discount Stenz's order by 25 percent on the condition that they help us obtain the JTS order. All I need now is the JTS account. The shipment of diagnostic units to Stenz's office is scheduled for July 1, with some modification of mounting devices to fit on their examination equipment. Stenz wants this order rushed, but modifications always require a minimum of 30 days from R&D. I am sure he will negotiate on our behalf to JTS. Stenz said he would set an appointment with B. J. Avery at JTS for June 16.

June 16

I was shocked to find that Stenz was not present for the meeting at JTS. When I called Stenz's office, they said they were nervous about meetings with JTS. For the first time, I found out that they now compete with JTS over some surgical business.[7] Avery was very pleasant, but informed us that our prices appeared to be quite high. I explained that this was due to the "state-of-the-art technology" and that the price is actually reasonable. He asked if I might supply him with technology specifications to verify this statement. While this may not be standard protocol, I agreed to

[7] It is becoming very competitive for the cataract business, with the ability of cataract surgeons to perform surgery in their offices. The U.S. Food and Drug Administration has been quite liberal on the restrictions of in-office surgery for this field.

share the information I had with him. I also stated that we would share anything else that they needed after the order was delivered. I again mentioned to Avery that in an earlier meeting everyone had agreed that pricing would not be an issue. He asked me to return on July 7 and meet with the purchasing board. I asked why it was necessary to meet with this board. He said that it was a formality that was rarely used; however, with the size of this order he wanted another opinion. I asked if there was anything else we needed to cover and he said, "No, I am comfortable for now. I am also looking forward to finalizing this transaction."

July 7 morning

Tried to see Dr. Stenz before heading to JTS. The delivery of the seven diagnostic units had occurred and training was complete. The staff was not using the system, and I am concerned about this. I'll bring this up with Dr. Stenz at the meeting with JTS this afternoon. With the discount I had given them, they must be happy. Normally, this discount is reserved for long-term accounts. All in all everything appeared to be in control.

July 7 afternoon

My meeting with the purchasing board took only 3 minutes. They were totally unaware of what we were to discuss. Since Avery had been so concerned about my meeting them, I was frustrated that they were not prepared for the meeting. Once again, Avery assured me that everything was OK and that we will meet on August 1 to finalize the sale.

August 1

When I arrived for my scheduled meeting with Sandy Adams and B. J. Avery, there was a note left for me at the front desk from Sandy Adams. It read:

> Sorry to miss you this time around. We are busy with R&D helping with the installation of new diagnostic and surgical equipment. Again, sorry you lost this business. Better luck next time. Sandy Adams

I stopped by Adams' office and found a helpful secretary who informed me that Bayson Laboratories had won the business. They had apparently had a price similar to Conner's.

Next, I proceeded to Avery's office and had the following conversation:

B. J. AVERY: Oh Hi! I was unaware that you were stopping by today. Did we have an appointment?

(I didn't let on that I had read the note and acted as though all was still in order. I wanted to see if I could gain some information as to what had happened.)

ME: No, I was in the area and wanted to see if you were close to arriving at your decision. Is there anything more that I can supply you with?

B. J.: No, I received the new brochures that you sent and passed them along to everyone that you indicated in your letter. I believe that everyone was quite impressed with them. The videos that you sent were very professional too. All in all, I would say that you have done an excellent job of presenting your company and your products.

ME: I am happy that you feel that way, and I hope that we will soon be engaging in a long-term relationship. As I indicated to you in one of our last meetings, we will also be able to offer substantial discounts with multiple units installed.

B. J.: This was a hard decision, but we have decided to purchase all of our surgical products from Bayson Laboratories. There was no real reason other than that was the decision by all parties. We do want to thank you for your trouble. I have a meeting in 5 minutes, so I hope you will forgive me. Here is a note I was about to send you.

There was nothing different in this note from the one left by Sandy Adams. It appeared that they both wrote these together.

CRESTFIELD FURNITURE (A)

Late in the evening of January 6, 2004, Charlton Bates, President of Crestfield Furniture, called Dr. Thomas Berry, a marketing professor at a private university in the Northeast and a consultant to the company. The conversation went as follows:

BATES: Hello, Tom. This is Chuck Bates. I'm sorry to call you this late, but I wanted to get your thoughts on the tentative 2004 advertising program proposed by Mike Hervey of Hervey and Bernham, our ad agency.

BERRY: No problem, Chuck. What did they propose?

BATES: The crux of their proposal is that we should increase our advertising expenditures by $225,000. They suggested that we put the entire amount into our consumer advertising program for ads in several shelter magazines.[1] Hervey noted that the National Home Furnishings Foundation has recommended that furniture manufacturers spend 1 percent of their sales exclusively on consumer advertising.

BERRY: That increase appears to be slightly out of line with your policy of budgeting 5 percent of expected sales for total promotion expenditures, doesn't it? Hasn't John Bott [Vice President of Sales] emphasized the need for more sales representatives?

BATES: Yes, John has requested additional funds. You're right about the 5 percent figure too, and I'm not sure if our sales forecast isn't too optimistic. Your research has shown that our sales historically follow industry sales almost perfectly, and trade economists are predicting about a 6 percent increase for 2004. Yet, I'm not too sure.

BERRY: Well, Chuck, you can't expect forecasts to be always on the button. The money is one thing, but what else can you tell me about Hervey's rationale for putting more dollars into consumer advertising?

BATES: He contends that we can increase our exposure and tell our quality and styling story to the buying public—increase brand awareness, enhance our image, that sort of thing. He also cited industry research data that showed that as baby boomers [consumers born between 1946 and 1964] age they are becoming more home oriented and are replacing older, cheaper furniture with more expensive, longer lasting pieces. Baby boomers make up 44 percent of all U.S. households. All I know is that my contribution margin will fall to 25 percent next year.

BERRY: I appreciate your concern. Give me a few days to think about the proposal. I'll get back to you soon.

After hanging up, Berry began to think about Bate's summary of the proposal, Crestfield's present position, and the furniture industry in general. He knew that Bates expected a well-thought-out recommendation on such issues and a step-by-step description of the logic used to arrive at that recommendation.

[1] Shelter magazines feature home improvement ideas, new ideas in home decorating, and so on. *Better Homes and Gardens* is an example of a shelter magazine.

This case was prepared by Professor Roger A. Kerin, of the Edwin L. Cox School of Business, Southern Methodist University, as a basis for class discussion and is not designed to illustrate effective or ineffective handling of an administrative situation. All names and data have been disguised.

THE COMPANY

Crestfield Furniture is a manufacturer of medium- to high-priced wood bedroom, living room, and dining room furniture. The company was formed at the turn of the century by Charlton Bates's grandfather. Bates assumed the presidency of the company upon his father's retirement. Year-end net sales in 2003 were $75 million with a before-tax profit of $3.7 million.

Crestfield sells its furniture through 1,000 high-quality department stores and independent furniture specialty stores nationwide, but all stores do not carry the company's entire line. The company is very selective in choosing retail outlets. According to Bates, "Our distribution policy, hence our retailers, should mirror the high quality of our products." As a matter of policy, Crestfield does not sell to furniture chain stores or discount outlets.

The company employs ten full-time salespeople and two regional sales managers. Sales personnel receive a base salary and a small commission on sales. A company sales force is atypical in the furniture industry; most furniture manufacturers use sales agents or representatives who carry a wide assortment of noncompeting furniture lines and receive a commission on sales. "Having our own sales group is a policy my father established years ago," noted Bates, "and we've been quite successful in having people who are committed to our company. Our people don't just take furniture orders. They are expected to motivate retail salespeople to sell our line, assist in setting up displays in stores, and give advice on a variety of matters to our retailers and their salespeople." He added, "It seems that my father was ahead of his time. I was just reading in the *Standard & Poor's Industry Surveys* for household furniture that the competition for retail floor space will require even more support, including store personnel sales training, innovative merchandising, inventory management, and advertising."

In early 2003, Crestfield allocated $3,675,000 for total promotional expenditures for the 2002 operating year, excluding the salary of the Vice President of Sales. Promotion expenditures were categorized into four groups: (1) sales expense and administration, (2) cooperative advertising programs with retailers, (3) trade promotion, and (4) consumer advertising. Sales costs included salaries for sales personnel and sales managers, selling-expense reimbursements, fringe benefits, and clerical/office assistance but did not include salespersons' commissions. Commissions were deducted from sales in the calculation of gross profit. The cooperative advertising budget is usually spent on newspaper advertising in a retailer's city. Cooperative

EXHIBIT 1 Allocation of Crestfield Promotion Dollars, 2002

Sales expense and administration	995,500
Cooperative advertising allowance	1,650,000
Trade advertising	467,000
Consumer advertising	562,500
	$3,675,000

Source: Company records.

advertising allowances are matched by funds provided by retailers on a dollar-for-dollar basis. Trade promotion is directed toward retailers and takes the form of catalogs, trade magazine advertisements, booklets for consumers, and point-of-purchase materials, such as displays, for use in retail stores. Also included in this category is the expense of participating in trade shows. Crestfield is represented at two shows per year. Consumer advertising is directed at potential consumers through shelter magazines. The typical format used in consumer advertising is to highlight new furniture and different bedroom, living room, and dining room arrangements. The dollar allocation for each of these programs in 2002 is shown in Exhibit 1.

THE HOUSEHOLD FURNITURE INDUSTRY

The household furniture industry is divided into three general categories: wood, upholstered, and other (ready-to-assemble furniture and casual furniture). Total furniture industry sales in 2003 were estimated to be $23.9 billion at manufacturers' prices.

Household wood furniture sales represent 48 percent of total household furniture sales, followed by upholstered furniture (42 percent) and other forms (10 percent), according to the American Furniture Manufacturers Association (AFMA). The principal types of wood furniture are dressers, tables, and dining room suites. Bedroom and dining room furniture accounts for the majority of wood furniture sales.

In recent years, wood furniture manufacturers have increased their emphasis on quality by monitoring the entire production process from the raw materials used, to construction, finishes, and packaging. In addition to improving quality controls, companies also stress price points and basic styling features, and are trying to improve shipping schedules. Wood furniture manufacturers' sales rose 5 percent in 2003 but are expected to rise by 6 percent in 2004, according to the AFMA.

More than 1,000 furniture manufacturers operate in the United States. Two manufacturers have annual sales of more than $2 billion and represent about 20 percent of industry sales. These are Furniture Brands International, Inc. (owner of the Drexel Heritage, Maitland-Smith, Henredon, Broyhill, Lane, and Thomasville brands) and La-Z-Boy, Inc. Other well-known manufacturers include Ethan Allen, Bassett, and Sherrill. The top 25 manufacturers account for about 50 percent of U.S. furniture sales. Exports are not a major factor in the U.S. household wood furniture industry.

Consumer Expenditures for Furniture

Consumer spending for wood furniture is highly cyclical and closely linked to the incidence of new housing starts, consumer confidence, and disposable personal income. Because wood furniture is expensive and often sold in sets, such as a dining room table and chairs, consumers consider these purchases deferrable.

Expenditures for furniture of all kinds have fluctuated as a percentage of consumer disposable personal income since 1979. It has been estimated that about 1 percent of a U.S. household's disposable income is spent for household furniture and home furnishings. Forecasted retail sales for 2003 are about $70 billion. Exhibit 2 shows annual furniture sales at retail prices from 1992 through 2002.

Furniture Buying Behavior

Even though industry research indicates many consumers consider the furniture shopping process to be enjoyable, consumers acknowledge that they lack the confidence to assess furniture construction, make judgments about quality, and accurately evaluate the price of furniture. Consumers also find it difficult to choose among the many styles available, fearing they will not like their choice several years later or that their selection will not be appropriate for their home and they will be unable to return it. According to a recent summary of furniture-buying behavior published in Standard & Poor's Industry Surveys:

> Consumers are quite finicky when it comes to buying furniture—a procedure fraught with concerns that are often not associated with buying other consumer durables, such as appliances and cars. With appliances and cars, consumers may have a more limited selection, they can do their own research, and they know what they are buying and what to expect. On the other hand, most consumers know little about evaluating the price or quality of furniture. It is also difficult for consumers to imagine how furniture will look in their homes, or whether they will still like their purchase in several years. Furthermore, there are questions about delivery—as in whether the item will arrive on time

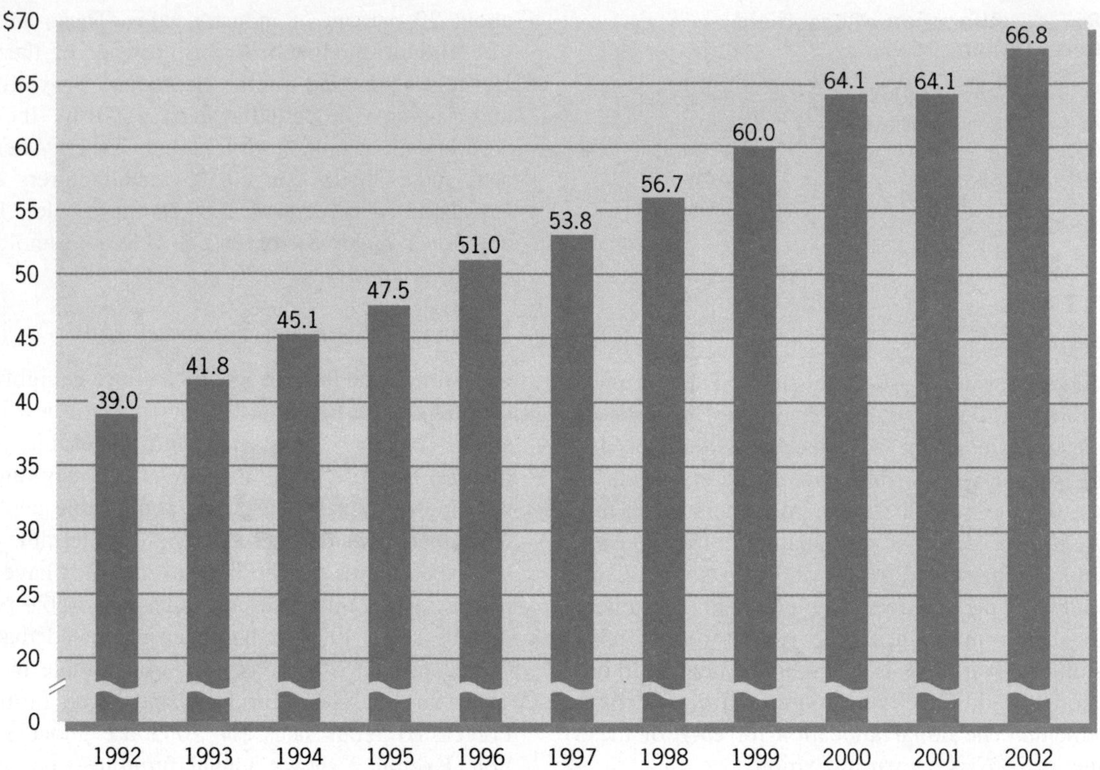

EXHIBIT 2 Total Retail Furniture Sales in the United States, 1992–2002 (In billions of dollars at retail prices)

Source: U.S. Department of Commerce, Bureau of Economic Analysis.

and in good condition and whether it can be returned for a full refund.

The furniture industry's efforts to educate consumers over the past years have failed for the most part. These efforts have included in-depth market studies to learn what consumers look for when they buy furniture, improved distribution, and new programs for training sales personnel. Despite these efforts, consumers still find the quality of furniture difficult to discern, and tend to base their furniture choice on price.

Results of a consumer panel sponsored by *Better Homes and Gardens* and composed of its subscribers provide the most comprehensive information available on furniture-buying behavior. Selected findings from the *Better Homes and Gardens* survey are reproduced in the appendix following this case. Other findings arising from this research are as follows:

- 94 percent of the subscribers enjoy buying furniture somewhat or very much.
- 84 percent of the subscribers believe "the higher the price, the higher the quality" when buying home furnishings.
- 72 percent of the subscribers browse or window-shop furniture stores even if they don't need furniture.
- 85 percent read furniture ads before they actually need furniture.
- 99 percent of the subscribers agree with the statement "When shopping for furniture and home furnishings, I like the salesperson to show me what alternatives are available, answer my questions, and let me alone so I can think about it and maybe browse around."
- 95 percent of the subscribers say they get redecorating ideas or guidance from magazines.
- 41 percent of the subscribers have requested a manufacturer's booklet.
- 63 percent of the subscribers say they need decorating advice to "put it all together."

Consumer research data have prompted both furniture retailers and manufacturers to stress the need for well-informed retail sales personnel to work with customers. For example, many manufacturers have established education centers where they train retail salespersons in the qualitative and construction details of the furniture they sell. Some manufacturers also distribute product literature to customers via retailers. Drexel Heritage, for instance, provides a series of books, titled *Living with Drexel Heritage*, to its authorized retailers, who then give them to customers.

Distribution

Furniture is sold through over 100,000 specialty furniture and home furnishing stores, department stores, and mass-merchandise stores in the United States. Industry trends indicate that the number of independently owned furniture stores has declined while furniture store chains have grown. The top ten furniture retailers in the United States captured approximately 19 percent of total U.S. furniture retail sales. Ethan Allen is the largest furniture retailer in terms of retail sales.

Furniture manufacturers have eschewed the Internet as a sales channel for the most part. Smaller manufacturers consider the up-front cost to build a Web site coupled with the ongoing cost to maintain a furniture Web site to be prohibitive. Also the costs of delivering and returning heavy items are a concern. These costs, plus the limited success of Internet furniture retailers, has led some larger manufacturers to instead build and operate promotional Web sites at roughly half the cost. These Web sites feature new styles and list retailer locations that sell their products. Examples of these Web sites are *drexelheritage.com* and *thomasville.com*. Ethan Allen is an exception. As a vertically integrated furniture manufacturer that sells exclusively through company-owned and franchised stores, Ethan Allen sells selected furniture and accessories at its ethanallen.com Web site.

A significant trend among furniture retailers is the movement toward the "gallery concept"—the practice of dedicating an amount of space and sometimes an entire freestanding retail outlet to one furniture manufacturer. There are currently 11,000 galleries, and it is estimated this number will reach 12,500 by 2004. Commenting on the gallery concept, Charlton Bates said:

> The gallery concept has great appeal for a furniture manufacturer, since product is displayed in a unique and comfortable setting without the lure of competitive brands. We have galleries in a small number of our furniture stores. The fact that we are not getting our full line in all of our retailers galls me because the opportunity to even discuss the gallery concept with many of our retailers doesn't exist.

Bates added: "Galleries and upscale furniture and department stores attract and serve our target customer, the 38- to 56-year-old home owner with an annual

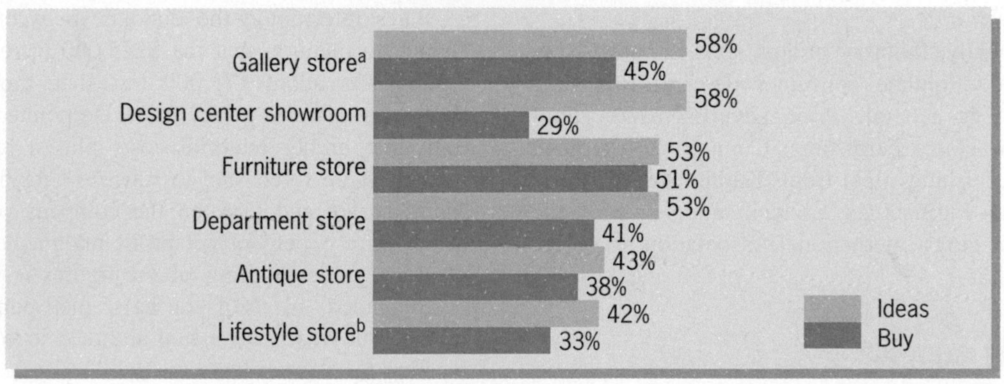

[a] Furniture from single company
[b] Crate & Barrel, Pottery Barn, Ikea, etc.

EXHIBIT 3 Furniture Retailers That Upscale Shoppers (Household Income $100,000 and Up) Have Used for Ideas and Where They Buy

household income over $100,000. That's where our customers get ideas and buy the quality furniture we sell" (see Exhibit 3).

The selling of furniture to retail outlets centers on manufacturers' expositions held at selected times and places around the country. The major expositions occur in High Point, North Carolina, in October and April. Regional expositions are also scheduled during the June-August period in locations such as Los Angeles, New York, and Boston. At these *marts,* as they are called in the furniture industry, retail buyers view manufacturers' lines and often make buying commitments for their stores. However, Crestfield's experience has shown that sales efforts in the retail store by company representatives account for as much as one-half of the company's sales in any given year.

Advertising Practices

Manufacturers of household furniture spend approximately 3.5 percent of annual net sales for advertising of all types (consumer, trade, and cooperative advertising). This percentage has remained constant for many years. The typical vehicles used for consumer advertising are shelter magazines such as *Better Homes and Gardens, House Beautiful,* and *Southern Living.* Trade advertising directed primarily toward retailers includes brochures, point-of-purchase materials to be displayed on a retailer's sales floor, and technical booklets describing methods of construction and materials. Cooperative advertising, shared with retailers, usually appears in newspapers, but there are also some television and radio spots featuring the brands carried by retailers.

Occasionally, industry groups sponsor advertising designed to stimulate consumer demand for home furnishings in general. Print advertisements sponsored by the Home Furnishings Council, for example, featured furnishing tips from Kathie Lee Gifford. (The Home Furnishings Council merged with the Home Furnishings International Association in August 2002.)

THE BUDGET MEETING

At the January 6 meeting attended by Hervey and Bernham executives and Crestfield executives, Michael Hervey proposed that the expenditure for consumer advertising be increased by $225,000 in 2003. Cooperative advertising and trade advertising allowances would remain at 2003 levels. Hervey further recommended that shelter magazines account for the bulk of the incremental expenditure for consumer advertising.

John Bott, Crestfield's Vice President of Sales, disagreed with the budget allocation and noted that sales expenses and administration costs were expected to rise by $65,000 in 2004. Moreover, Bott believed that an additional sales representative was needed to service Crestfield accounts because fifty new accounts were being added. He estimated that the cost of the additional representative, including salary and expenses, would be at least $70,000 in 2004. That's about $135,000 in additional sales expenses that have to be added into our promotional budget for 2004," Bott noted. He continued:

> We recorded sales of $75 million in 2003. If we assume a 6 percent increase in sales in 2004, that means our total budget will be $3,975,000, if my figures are right—a $300,000 increase over our previous budget. And I need $135,000 of that. In other words, $165,000 is available for other kinds of promotion, some of which should go to trade promotion to assist our salespeople servicing new accounts.

Hervey's reply to Bott noted that the company planned to introduce several new styles of living room and dining room furniture in 2004 and that these new items would require consumer advertising in shelter magazines to be launched successfully. He agreed with Bott that increased funding of the sales effort might be necessary and thought that Crestfield might draw funds from cooperative advertising allowances and trade promotion.

Bates interrupted the dialogue between Bott and Hervey to mention that the $225,000 increase in promotion was about $75,000 less than the 5 percent percentage-of-sales policy limit. He pointed out, however, that higher material costs plus a recent wage increase were forecasted to squeeze Crestfield's gross profit margin and threaten the company objective of achieving a 5 percent net profit margin before taxes. "Perhaps some juggling of the figures is necessary," he concluded. "Both of you have good points. Let me think about what's been said and then let's schedule a meeting for a week from today."

As Bates reviewed his notes from the meeting, he realized that the funds allocated to promotion were only part of the question. How the funds would be allocated within the budget was also crucial. A call to Tom Berry might be helpful in this regard, too.

APPENDIX: SELECTED FINDINGS FROM THE *BETTER HOMES AND GARDENS*® CONSUMER PANEL REPORT–HOME FURNISHINGS[2]

Question: If you were going to buy furniture in the near future, how important would the following factors be in selecting the store to buy furniture? (Respondents: 449)

Factor	*Very Important*	*Somewhat Important*	*Not Too Important*	*Not at All Important*	*No Answer*
Sells high-quality furnishings	62.6%	31.0%	3.8%	1.1%	1.5%
Has a wide range of different furniture styles	58.8	29.2	8.2	2.9	0.9
Gives you personal service	60.1	29.9	7.8	0.9	1.3
Is a highly dependable store	85.1	12.7	1.1	–	1.1
Offers decorating help from experienced home planners	26.5	35.9	25.4	10.9	1.3
Lets you "browse" all you want	77.1	17.8	3.3	0.7	1.1
Sells merchandise that's a good value for the money	82.0	15.6	0.9	0.2	1.3
Displays furniture in individual room settings	36.3	41.2	18.7	2.4	1.3
Has a relaxed, no-pressure atmosphere	80.0	17.1	1.6	–	1.3
Has well-informed salespeople	77.5	19.8	1.6	–	1.1
Has a very friendly atmosphere	68.2	28.1	2.4	–	1.3
Carries the style of furniture you like	88.0	10.0	0.9	–	1.1

Question: Please rate the following factors as to their importance to you when you purchase or shop for case-goods furniture, such as a dining room or living room suite, *1* being the most important factor, *2* being second most important, and so on, until all factors have been rated. (Respondents: 449)

Factor	*1*	*2*	*3*	*4*	*5*	*6*	*7*	*8*	*9*	*10*	*No Answer*
Construction of item	24.1%	16.0%	18.5%	13.1%	10.5%	6.9%	4.9%	1.6%	0.2%	1.1%	3.1%
Comfort	13.6	14.7	12.9	12.3	12.7	10.9	8.2	4.5	4.0	2.4	3.8
Styling and design	33.6	19.8	11.1	9.6	4.7	7.3	4.5	1.6	2.9	1.6	3.3
Durability of fabric	2.2	7.6	9.8	14.5	15.1	14.7	12.9	5.6	5.8	7.8	4.0
Type and quality of wood	10.9	17.8	16.3	15.8	14.7	5.8	5.3	3.1	4.9	2.0	3.4
Guarantee or warranty	1.6	3.8	1.6	5.3	8.7	10.0	13.8	25.2	14.5	11.1	4.4
Price	9.4	6.2	8.7	8.5	10.0	12.5	14.2	11.8	6.9	8.0	3.8
Reputation of manufacturer or brand name	6.2	3.6	4.7	5.6	6.2	6.2	12.7	17.1	22.7	11.6	3.4
Reputation of retailer	1.6	1.8	1.6	2.4	4.0	7.3	7.4	13.6	22.0	34.5	3.8
Finish, color of wood	4.7	7.6	10.2	8.0	8.9	13.4	10.7	10.0	10.2	12.7	3.6

Question: Below is a list of 15 criteria that may influence what furniture you buy. Please rate them from *1* as most important to *5* as least important. (Respondents: 449)

Criterion	*1*	*2*	*3*	*4*	*5*	*No Answer*
Guarantee or warranty	11.4%	11.1%	26.3%	16.9%	5.3%	29.0%
Brand name	9.1	6.5	14.3	25.6	11.6	32.9
Comfort	34.7	27.8	14.5	8.5	4.7	9.8
Decorator suggestion	4.0	2.4	2.7	8.2	44.8	37.9
Material used	14.9	24.1	14.9	13.4	6.2	26.5
Delivery time	0.7	0.5	1.3	2.9	55.2	39.4
Size	7.6	10.7	13.6	30.9	4.0	33.2
Styling and design	33.4	17.8	21.8	13.6	2.2	11.2
Construction	34.3	23.6	13.1	11.4	2.9	14.7
Fabric	4.0	25.6	24.9	14.0	4.5	27.0

(*Continued*)

[2] Reprinted courtesy of the *Better Homes and Gardens*® Consumer Panel.

Criterion	1	2	3	4	5	No Answer
Durability	37.0	19.4	13.6	6.9	4.9	18.2
Finish on wooden parts	5.8	14.7	16.7	10.7	16.7	35.4
Price	19.4	21.8	16.0	10.9	15.4	16.5
Manufacturer's reputation	4.2	9.1	15.4	22.9	14.3	34.1
Retailer's reputation	2.2	4.7	10.5	21.2	26.5	34.9

Question: Listed below are some statements others have made about shopping for furniture. Please indicate how much you agree or disagree with each one. (Respondents: 449)

Statement	Agree Completely	Agree Somewhat	Neither Agree nor Disagree	Disagree Somewhat	Disagree Completely	No Answer
I wish there were some way to be really sure of getting good quality in furniture	61.9%	24.7%	4.7%	4.2%	3.6%	0.9%
I really enjoy shopping for furniture	49.2	28.3	7.6	9.8	4.2	0.9
I would never buy any furniture without my husband's/wife's approval	47.0	23.0	10.9	9.8	7.1	2.2
I like all pieces in the master bedroom to be exactly the same style	35.9	30.7	12.7	11.1	7.6	2.0
Once I find something I like in furniture, I wish it would last forever so I'd never have to buy again	36.8	24.3	10.0	18.9	9.1	0.9
I wish I had more confidence in my ability to decorate my home attractively	23.1	32.3	12.5	11.6	18.7	1.8
I wish I knew more about furniture styles and what looks good	20.0	31.0	17.1	13.4	16.7	1.8
My husband/wife doesn't take much interest and what looks good	6.5	18.0	12.3	17.8	41.4	4.0
I like to collect a number of different styles in the dining room	3.3	10.5	15.2	29.8	38.3	2.9
Shopping for furniture is very distressing to me	2.4	11.6	14.3	18.0	51.9	1.8

Question: Listed below are some factors that may influence your choice of furnishings. Please rate them with *1* being most important, *2* being second most important, and so on, until all factors have been rated. (Respondents: 449)

Factor	1	2	3	4	5	No Answer
Friends and/or neighbors	1.3%	16.9%	15.8%	22.1%	41.7%	2.2%
Family or spouse	62.8	9.4	14.3	9.8	2.0	1.7
Magazine advertising	16.3	30.3	29.6	17.6	4.2	2.0
Television advertising	1.1	6.7	14.7	32.5	42.3	2.7
Store displays	18.9	37.2	22.1	14.0	5.6	2.2

Question: When you go shopping for a *major piece* of furniture or smaller pieces of furniture, who, if anyone, do you usually go with? (Respondents: 449—multiple responses)

Person	Major Pieces	Other Pieces
Husband	82.4%	59.5%
Mother or mother-in-law	6.2	9.1
Friend	12.0	18.9
Decorator	4.2	1.6
Other relative	15.6	15.4
Other person	2.9	3.3
No one else	5.1	22.3
No answer	0.9	3.1

Question: When the time comes to purchase a *major* item of furniture or other smaller pieces of furniture, who, if anyone, helps you make the final decision about which piece to buy? (Respondents: 449—multiple responses)

Person	Major Pieces	Other Pieces
Husband	86.0%	63.5%
Mother or mother-in-law	2.4	4.5
Friend	3.6	8.0
Decorator	3.1	2.7
Other relative	10.0	12.9
Other person	1.6	1.8
No one else	7.1	24.3
No answer	0.9	2.2[2]

CRESTFIELD FURNITURE, INC. (B)

In April 2004, Crestfield Furniture, Inc. merged with Lea-Meadows, Inc., a manufacturer of upholstered furniture for living and family rooms. The merger was not planned in a conventional sense. Charlton Bates's father-in-law died suddenly in early February 2004, leaving his daughter with controlling interest in Lea-Meadows. The merger proceeded smoothly, since the two firms were located on adjacent properties and the general consensus was that the two firms would maintain as much autonomy as was economically justified. Moreover, the upholstery line filled a gap in the Crestfield product mix, even though it would retain its own identity and brand names.

The only real issue that continued to plague Bates was merging the selling effort. Crestfield had its own sales force, but Lea-Meadows relied on sales agents to represent it. The question was straightforward, in his opinion: "Do we give the upholstery line of chairs and sofas to our sales force, or do we continue using the sales agents?" John Bott, Crestfield's Vice President of Sales, said the line should be given to his sales group; Martin Moorman, National Sales Manager at Lea-Meadows, said the upholstery line should remain with sales agents.

LEA-MEADOWS, INC.

Lea-Meadows, Inc. is a small, privately owned manufacturer of upholstered furniture for use in living and family rooms. The firm is more than seventy-five years old. The company uses some of the finest fabrics and frame construction in the industry, according to trade sources. Net sales in 2003 were $5 million. Total industry sales of upholstered furniture manufacturers in 2002 were $10 billion. Forecasted 2003 industry sales for upholstered furniture were $10.4 billion. Company sales had increased 7 percent annually over the past five years, and company executives believed this growth rate would continue for the foreseeable future.

Lea-Meadows employed fifteen sales agents to represent its products. These sales agents also represented several manufacturers of noncompeting furniture and home furnishings. Often, a sales agent found it necessary to deal with several buyers in a store in order to represent all the lines carried. On a typical sales call, a sales agent first visited buyers to discuss new lines, in addition to any promotions being offered by manufacturers. New orders were sought where and when it was appropriate. The sales agent then visited the selling floor to check displays, inspect furniture, and inform salespeople about furniture styles and construction. Lea-Meadows paid an agent commission of 5 percent of net company sales for these services. Moorman thought sales agents spent 10 to 15 percent of their instore time on Lea-Meadows products.

The company did not attempt to influence the type of retailers that agents contacted, although it was implicit in the agency agreement that agents would not sell to discount houses. Sales records indicated that agents were calling on specialty furniture and department stores. An estimated 1,000 retail accounts were called on in 2002 and 2003. All agents had established relationships with their retail accounts and worked closely with them.

CRESTFIELD FURNITURE, INC.

Crestfield Furniture,Inc. is a manufacturer of medium-to high-priced wood bedroom, living room, and dining room furniture.[1] Net sales in 2003 were $75 million; before-tax profit was $3.7 million. Industry sales of wood furniture in 2003 were $11.5 billion at manufacturers' prices. Projected industry sales for 2003 were $12.2 billion.

The company employed ten full-time sales representatives, who called on 1,000 retail accounts. These individuals performed the same function as sales agents but were paid a salary plus a small commission. In 2003, the average sales representative received an annual salary of $70,000 (plus expenses) and a commission of 0.5 percent on net company sales. Total sales administration costs were $130,000.

Crestfield's salespeople were highly regarded in the industry. They were known particularly for their knowledge of wood furniture and willingness to work with buyers and retail sales personnel. Despite these advantages, Bates knew that all retail accounts did not carry the complete Crestfield furniture line. He had therefore instructed Bott to "push the group a little harder." At present, sales representatives were making ten sales calls per week, with the average sales call running three hours. Salespersons' remaining time was accounted for by administrative activities and travel. Bates recommended that the call frequency be increased to seven calls per account per year, which was consistent with what he thought was the industry norm.

MERGING THE SALES EFFORTS

Through separate meetings with Bott and Moorman, Bates was able to piece together a variety of data and perspectives on the question of merging the sales efforts. These meetings also made it clear that Bott and Moorman differed dramatically in their views.

John Bott had no doubts about assigning the line to the Crestfield sales force. Among the reasons he gave for this view were the following. First, Crestfield had developed one of the most well-respected, professional sales forces in the industry. The representatives could easily learn the fabric jargon, and they already knew personally many of the buyers who were responsible for upholstered furniture. Second, selling the Lea-Meadows line would require only about 15 percent of present sales call time. Thus, he thought that the new line would not be a major burden. Third, more control over sales efforts was possible. Bott noted that Charlton Bates's father had created the sales group thirty years earlier because of the commitment it engendered and the service "only our own people are able and willing to give." Moreover, the company salespeople have the Crestfield "look" and presentation style, which is instilled in every one of them. Fourth, Bott said that it wouldn't look right if both representatives and agents called on the same stores and buyers. He noted that Crestfield and Lea-Meadows overlapped on all their accounts. He said, "We'd be paying a commission on sales to these accounts when we would have gotten them anyway. The difference in commission percentages would not be good for morale."

Martin Moorman advocated keeping sales agents for the Lea-Meadows line. His arguments were as follows. First, all sales agents had established contacts and were highly regarded by store buyers, and most had represented the line in a professional manner for many years. He, too, had a good working relationship with all fifteen agents. Second, sales agents represented little, if any, cost beyond commissions. Moorman noted, "Agents get paid when we get paid." Third, sales agents were committed to the Lea-Meadows line: "The agents earn a part of their living representing us. They have to service retail accounts to get the repeat business." Fourth, sales agents were calling on buyers not contacted by the Crestfield sales force. Moorman noted, "If we let Crestfield people handle the line, we might lose these accounts, have to hire more sales personnel, or take away 25 percent of the present time given to Crestfield product lines." Finally, Moorman took issue with Bott's view that Crestfield salespeople could easily learn about upholstered furniture. He said, "Lea-Meadows has some 1,000 different frames for sofas and upholstered chairs. If all combinations of fabric, skirts, pillow, springs, and fringes are considered, a sales rep would need to be conversant in no fewer than 1 billion possibilities."

As Bates reflected on the meetings, he felt that a broader perspective was necessary beyond the views expressed by Bott and Moorman. One factor was

[1] Additional background information on the company and industry can be found in the case titled "Crestfield Furniture, Inc. (A)."

profitability. Existing Crestfield furniture lines typically had gross margins that were 5 percent higher than those for Lea-Meadows upholstered lines. Another factor was the "us and them" references apparent in the meetings with Bott and Moorman. Would merging the sales effort overcome this, or would it cause more problems? The idea of increasing the sales force to incorporate the Lea-Meadows line did not sit well with him. Adding new salespeople would require restructuring of sales territories, involve potential loss of commissions by existing salespeople, and be "a big headache." Still, it had been Crestfield's policy for many years to have its own sales force and not use sales agents. In addition, there was the subtle issue of Moorman's future. Moorman, who was 55 years old, had worked for Lea-Meadows for twenty-five years and was a family friend and godfather to Bates's youngest child. If the Lea-Meadows line was represented by the Crestfield sales force, Moorman's position would be eliminated. Given these circumstances, Bates also thought his wife's views had to be considered. He could bring up the topic on their way to the High Point, North Carolina, furniture exposition early next week.

CASE 8 DAVE MacDONALD'S ETHICAL DILEMMAS

The following situations are real events experienced by the case writer. Only the names have been changed.

HALCO MANUFACTURING

Dave MacDonald was excited when he got the unexpected phone call from Nicki Steele, a senior buyer from Halco Manufacturing.

"I know it's a year since we bought that prototype reel from you, but we just got a contract from the government to build ten more 'bear traps' and we desperately need to hold our price on these units. Could you possibly sell us ten new reels at the same price you charged last year?" Nicki inquired.

"I'll see what I can do and call you back today," Dave replied.

Dave immediately retrieved the file from the previous year and saw that they had supplied the reel for $6,990.00 F.O.B. the customer's warehouse. There was a breakdown of the pricing on the file:

Manufacturer's list price	$4,000.00
Special engineering charge (25%)	1,000.00
Total list price	5,000.00
Distributor discount (20%)	1,000.00
Distributor net cost	4,000.00
Estimated currency exchange (8%)	320.00
Estimated duty ($22\frac{1}{2}$%)	972.00
Estimated freight	245.00
Estimated brokerage	55.00
Estimated distributor cost, F.O.B. destination	5,592.00
Markup (25%)	1,398.00
Selling price, F.O.B. destination	$6,990.00

There were some notes on the file that Dave reviewed. The reel was designed as part of a "bear trap" on Canadian navy ships. These bear traps would hook onto helicopters in rough weather and haul them safely onto landing pads on the ship decks. The reel was really a model SM heavy-duty steel mill reel, except that some of the exposed parts were to be made of stainless steel to provide longer life in the saltwater atmosphere. There was a special engineering charge on the reel, as it was a nonstandard item that had to be specially engineered. The manufacturer had suggested at the time it quoted that Dave could keep the full 20 percent discount, as the person thought there was only one other manufacturer capable of building this unit, and its price would likely be much higher.

When Dave got a price from the manufacturer on the ten new units, he was surprised that the quoted price was only $3,200.00 each, less 40/10 percent. When he asked that the price be verified, the order desk clarified the pricing. First, there had been a 20 percent reduction in all SM series reels. That made the manufacturer's list price only $3,200.00. Then, because there was a large quantity, the distributor discount was increased to less 40/10 percent instead of the 20 percent that was given on the original reel.

As Dave estimated his cost, things got better. The original reel was imported from the United States at $22\frac{1}{2}$ percent duty as "not otherwise provided for manufacturers of iron or steel, tariff item 44603-1." In the interim, the company Dave worked for had gotten a duty remission on series SM steel mill reels as "machinery of a class or kind not manufactured in Canada, tariff item 42700-1," and the duty was remitted (and the savings supposedly passed on to the end customer). The currency exchange rate also improved in Dave's favor, and the estimated freight and brokerage charges per unit dropped considerably because of the increased shipment size. Dave estimated his new cost as follows:

Manufacturer's list price	$3,200.00
Distributor discount (40/10%)	1,472.00
Distributor net cost	1,728.00
Estimated currency exchange (2%)	35.00
Estimated duty (remitted)	0.00
Estimated freight	85.00
Estimated brokerage	14.50
Estimated distributor cost, F.O.B. destination	$1,862.50

Now that he had all the figures, Dave had to decide what the selling price should be to his customer.

CROWN PULP AND PAPER LTD.

Bill Siddall had been promoted to the position of salesperson, and he was pleased when he received an order for nearly $10,000 for stainless steel fittings from the new pulp mill being built in his territory. Unfortunately, he quoted a price that was 40 percent below his cost.

"We have to honor the price quoted," Bill insisted.

"I know if you let me talk to Rory, he'll let us raise the price," replied Dave MacDonald, the Sales Manager. "Rory used to be the purchasing agent at one of my best accounts before he came to the mill."

"No. You gave me responsibility for this account, and I want to build a good relationship with Rory myself. He gave us the order over two weeks ago. He can't change suppliers now because he needs the material next week, and I don't want to put him on the spot now because it would be unfair. Since this is our first order, I would like to supply it without any problems. We'll get back the money we lost on this order many times if we can get their future business. This material is needed for a small construction job, and they haven't even started to consider their stores inventory yet."

After much discussion, it was agreed that the order would stand, but Dave would call the fitting manufacturer's sales manager, Chuck Knowles, as the two men were good friends.

"We need some help on that last order we placed with you. Bill sold it at 40 percent below our cost," said Dave.

"How could that happen?" Chuck seemed amazed.

"Well," replied Dave, "you give us a 25-percent distributor discount, and we gave 10 percent to the customer due to the size of the order. What we forgot was to double the list price because the customer wanted schedule 80 wall thickness on the fittings instead of standard schedule 40. This was Bill's first large inquiry, and he made an honest mistake. He doesn't want me to get involved with the customer, and I don't want to force the issue with him, so I'm hoping you can help us on this one order. We expect to get a lot of business from this account over the next few years."

"I'll split the difference with you. What you're selling now for $0.90, you're paying $1.50 for, and if I give you an additional 20 percent discount, your cost will come down to $1.20. Can you live with that?" Chuck asked.

"It's a help. We appreciate it. We'll see you on your next trip to our territory, and I'll buy lunch."

"A deal. See you next month." The conversation ended.

When it was over, Dave was feeling reasonably satisfied with himself, but he still felt somewhat uneasy. He promised not to call Rory, and he promised not to interfere with the account, but he still thought something could be done.

On Saturday morning, Dave went to the Brae Shore Golf Club. He was confident that Rory would be there. Sure enough, at 8:00 A.M., Rory was scheduled to tee off. Dave sat on the bench at the first tee and waited for Rory to appear. Promptly, Rory arrived with Bob Arnold, one of his senior buyers. The three men greeted each other pleasantly, and Rory asked who Dave was waiting for.

"Just one of my neighbors. He was supposed to be here an hour ago, but I guess he won't show."

"Join us. We don't mind. Besides, we might need a donation this fall when we have our company golf tournament. We'll invite you, of course, and we'll invite Bill if he plays golf."

"He doesn't play often, but he's pretty good. Beat me the last time we played. How is he doing at your mill? Is everything okay?" Dave asked.

"Checking up on him? Sure. He's fine. He made a mistake the other day when he went to see our mill-wright foreman without clearing it through my office first, but he'll learn. He'll do a lot of business with us because we want to buy locally where possible, and you have a lot of good product lines. I think he'll get along well with all of us as well. He seems a bit serious, but we'll break him in before long. We just gave him a big order for stainless fittings a few weeks ago, but we told him to visit at ten o'clock next time and to bring the doughnuts."

"I know," replied Dave. "Unfortunately, we lost a lot of money on that order."

"Your price was very low. I couldn't understand it because I knew your material wasn't manufactured offshore. Did you quote the cheaper T304 grade of stainless instead of the T316 we use?"

"No. We quoted schedule 40 prices instead of schedule 80. The wall thickness for schedule 80 is twice as thick, and the price should have been double as well."

"Heck. Double the price. We'll pay it. I'll make a note on the file Monday. I know you're not trying to take us, and I can appreciate an honest mistake. At double the price, you might be a bit high, but you know we want to place the order with you anyway because you're local. Eventually, we'll want you to carry some inventory for us, so we might just as well make sure we're both happy with this business."

STRAIT STRUCTURAL STEEL LTD.

Dave MacDonald was sitting in the outer office waiting to see Stan Hope, the purchasing agent for Strait Structural Steel, a new account that had just begun operations in a remote coastal location about 40 miles from the nearest city. Stan had telephoned Dave the previous week and had an urgent request for four large exhaust fans that were required to exhaust welding fumes from enclosed spaces where welders were at work. The union had threatened to stop the project unless working conditions were improved quickly, and although Dave didn't sell fans at the time, he found a line of fans and negotiated a discount from the manufacturer, along with an agreement to discuss the further possibility of representing the fan manufacturer on a national basis.

When Stan gave the order to Dave for the fans, the two men discussed other products that Dave sold. Dave sold products for a company that was both a general-line and specialty-line industrial distributor. Included in the general-line products were such items as hand and power tools, cutting tools (drills, taps, dies), safety equipment, wire rope and slings, fasteners (nuts, bolts), and fittings (stainless steel, bronze, and carbon steel flanges, elbows, tees). Included in the specialty-line products were such items as electric motors and generators, motor controls, hydraulic and pneumatic valves and cylinders, rubber dock fenders, and overhead cranes. When the men finally met, they were almost instantly friends, and it was obvious that the opportunities for them to do further business were great. "One item that really interests me," said Stan, "is PTFE tape. We need some, and we will be using a lot of it."

"We have the largest stock of PTFE tape in the country," replied Dave. "We import it directly from Italy, but it's high quality and is the same standard size as all others on the market; $\frac{1}{2}$ inch wide, .003 inch thick, and 480 inches long. How much are you interested in?"

"Let's start with 400 rolls," Stan suggested.

PTFE tape was a white, nonadhesive tape that was used as a pipe thread sealant. It was wrapped around the threads of pipe or fittings before they were screwed together to make a leakproof seal. The tape first came on the market in the late 1960s at prices as high as \$3.60 per roll, but since then prices had dropped considerably. North American manufacturers were still selling the tape for list prices near \$1.80 and were offering dealer discounts of between 25 and 50 percent, depending on the quantities that dealers bought. Dave was importing the tape from Italy at a landed cost of \$0.17 per roll.

"We have a standard price of \$1.00 per roll as long as you buy 200 rolls," Dave offered.

"No question. You have an excellent price. How much would you charge M H Sales?"

"I don't know. Who is M H Sales?" asked Dave.

"A small industrial supply company located in my basement. The 'H' is for Hope. I share the company with Bruce Malcolm, the 'M,' and he's in purchasing at Central Power Corporation. M H Sales is a small company, and we are looking for additional products to sell. Between Strait Structural and Central Power, we could sell several thousand rolls of PTFE tape each year."

MCCORMICK GLEASON LIMITED

Dave MacDonald telephoned Clarey Stanley, a Senior Buyer at McCormick Gleason Limited. "Clarey, I'm calling about that quote we made on Lufkin tapes. Can we have your order?"

"Sorry. Your price was high. I gave the order to Ken Stafford. You need a sharper pencil."

"How much sharper?" Dave asked.

"I can't tell you that. But you were close," Clarey replied. "By the way, Kenny called me from the stores department this morning, and he has a large shipment of electric relays that was delivered yesterday. They weren't properly marked, and he can't identify the ones with normally open contacts from the ones with normally closed contacts. Do you want them returned, or can someone see him and straighten it out here?"

"Tell him I'll see him immediately after lunch. I can tell them apart, and I'll see they get properly identified."

When the conversation ended, Dave made a note to see Clarey about the tapes. There was a problem somewhere. Dave knew his cost on Lufkin tapes was the lowest available, and he quoted 12 percent on cost because he really wanted the order. The order was less than $1,500, but it meant that Dave could place a multiple-case order on the manufacture and get the lowest possible cost for all replacement inventory. That would increase the margin on sales to other customers who bought smaller quantities. There was no possibility that Stafford Industrial, a local, one-person, "out-of-the-basement" operation that bought Lufkin tapes as a jobber, not as a distributor, could match his price.

That afternoon, while waiting to see Ken MacKay, the store's manager, Dave noticed a carton from Stafford Industrial Sales being unloaded from a local delivery van. Although he knew that Stafford supplied quite a few maintenance, repair, and operating (MRO) supplies to this customer, Dave decided to play ignorant.

"What do you buy from Stafford Industrial?" he asked the young stores clerk who was handling the package.

Opening the carton, the clerk read the packing slip. "It says here we ordered 144 measuring tapes, $\frac{3}{4}$ inches wide by 25 feet long."

"Are those things expensive?" Dave asked.

"Don't know. There's no price on the packing slip. Clarey Stanley in purchasing ordered them. You could talk to him." The clerk continued to unpack the shipment. As he did, Dave noticed that the tapes were manufactured offshore and were poor in quality compared to the Lufkin tapes that he sold and that he quoted to Clarey Stanley the previous day.

"Aren't those supposed to be Lufkin tapes?" Dave asked.

"Not that I know. The packing slip just says tapes. Wait, and I'll haul our copy of the purchase order." The clerk went to a filing cabinet next to his desk and returned with a carbon copy of the purchase order. "No, it just says tapes. It doesn't specify any brand."

There was something wrong, and Dave was determined to get an answer.

CASE 9 EREKSON INDUSTRIAL SUPPLY

Note: An Excel file with the data for this case is available at www.wiley.com/college/cron. Go to "Students Companion Site."

Phil Harper had been recently appointed marketing manager for Erekson Industrial Supply. Bates was a regional wholesaler of industrial cleaners and related chemicals. Phil directed the field sales force and was in charge of reordering stock for the warehouse. Recently, the company had been having trouble balancing orders against inventory. Customers were complaining about late shipments and items being

This case was prepared by Douglas J. Dalrymple of Indiana University.

EXHIBIT 1 Monthly Sales of Four Industrial Cleansers

Time Period	*SH60*	*PN25*	*SX80*	*TL75*	*Time Period*	*SH60*	*PN25*	*SX80*	*TL75*
1	3848	362	5666	885	19	4667	1132	6104	884
2	4024	346	5405	870	20	3555	1360	6812	878
3	3416	382	5001	866	21	3101	1589	8367	874
4	3671	526	4688	859	22	3507	1137	8130	865
5	3762	675	5492	862	23	3131	1739	7525	868
6	4444	440	5231	855	24	3639	1380	6918	855
7	5375	547	4813	857	25	2762	1366	6737	857
8	3752	655	4780	839	26	2929	915	6900	865
9	2884	313	4611	847	27	3137	1651	6112	861
10	3324	555	5201	836	28	2975	1282	6717	853
11	3133	806	5136	876	29	3274	1128	7937	860
12	3048	678	5124	873	30	3422	1397	7647	863
13	3163	568	6149	865	31	4507	1102	6993	882
14	3217	741	6202	860	32	4054	769	8089	876
15	3106	631	5808	846	33	4426	1412	9279	883
16	3196	1006	5572	839	34	4083	1161	9547	875
17	3118	1216	7069	852	35	3924	1210	8064	861
18	3305	862	6839	864	36	4274	1133	8188	864

short on delivery. The company president asked Harper to look into the problem and come up with some recommendations.

Phil realized that establishing direct computer links with manufacturers who supplied them with chemicals could reduce their out-of-stock problem. However, it would take months to buy the necessary equipment and debug the programs. Anticipated costs for direct computer links would be several hundred thousand dollars. A simpler approach would be to study the variations in sales of inventoried items to see if improved demand forecasts would help. Phil decided to call up some sales figures for four popular industrial cleaners on his desktop computer (Exhibit 1). The numbers on the screen represented three years of monthly sales for the four items. Several series seemed to exhibit seasonal patterns, and others were dominated by trends and unknown components. Bates normally prepared forecasts for each inventoried item twelve months into the future so that purchase discounts could be taken and delivery charges minimized. The usual procedure was to use simple projection methods to obtain the forecasts.

Computer forecasting offered several advantages over the current methods. First, the computer would make it easier to seasonally adjust the data to help improve forecasting accuracy. Also the computer would make it simpler to calculate MAPEs to see which techniques worked best. Computers were fast, and they would allow Phil to try out more forecasting procedures.

Phil thought he should run naive, moving average, exponential smoothing, and simple regression forecasting techniques on his four time series. Since regression required five periods of data to get started, forecasts for all of his methods should start in period 6 and run through period 36. This would make it easier to compare the MAPE values for each method because they would all be based on forecasts for the same time periods.

Phil decided to start with the sales data from SH60 to see if he could find the best forecasting technique for this series. Then the computer could be used to project sales for periods 37 through 48. One issue Phil was not sure about was whether the technique that worked best for SH60 could be used to forecast sales of the other chemicals. Certainly, it would save him a lot of time if he used the same forecasting procedure for all the products. He also wondered whether seasonal adjustments were worth the bother. Once he had some results for the four chemicals, he would be in a better position to decide whether improved forecasting procedures would solve the out-of-stock problem. Since it was getting late, Phil decided he better get started.

FIRST NATIONAL BANK

"I'm concerned about Karen," said Margaret Costanzo to David Reeves. The two bank officers were seated in Costanzo's office at the First National Bank's branch in Federal Square.

Costanzo was a vice president of the bank and manager of the Federal Square branch, the third largest in First National's 92-branch network. She was having an employee appraisal meeting with Reeves, customer service director at the branch. Reeves was responsible for the Customer Service Department, which coordinated the activities of the customer service representatives (CSRs, formerly known as tellers) and the customer assistance representatives (CARs, formerly known as new accounts assistants).

Costanzo and Reeves were discussing Karen Mitchell, a 24-year-old customer service rep, who had applied for the soon-to-be-vacant position of head CSR. Mitchell had been with the bank since graduating from junior college with an associate in arts degree three and a half years earlier. She had applied for the position of what had then been called head teller a year earlier, but the job had gone to a candidate with more seniority. Now that individual was leaving—his wife had been transferred to a new job in another city—and the position was once again open. Two other candidates had applied for the job.

Both Costanzo and Reeves were agreed that, against all criteria used in the past, Karen Mitchell would have been the obvious choice for head teller. She was both fast and accurate in her work, presented a smart and professional appearance, and was well liked by customers and her fellow CSRs.

However, the nature of the teller's job had been significantly revised nine months earlier to add a stronger marketing component. (Exhibit 1 shows the previous job description for teller; Exhibit 2 shows the new job

EXHIBIT 1 First National Bank: Position Description for Teller

FUNCTION
Provides customer services by receiving, paying out, and keeping accurate records of all monies involved in paying and receiving transactions. Promotes the Bank's services.

RESPONSIBILITIES

1. Serves customers
   Accepts deposits, verifies cash and endorsements, and gives customers their receipts.
   Cashes checks within the limits assigned or refers customers to supervisor for authorization.
   Accepts savings deposits and withdrawals, verifies signatures, posts interest, and balances as necessary.
   Accepts loan, credit card, utility, and other payments.
   Issues money orders, cashier's checks, traveler's checks, and foreign currency and issues or redeems U.S. savings bonds.
   Reconciles customer statements and confers with bookkeeping personnel regarding the discrepancies in balances or other problems.
   Issues credit card advances.
2. Prepares individual daily settlement of teller cash and proof transactions.
3. Prepares branch daily journal and general ledger.
4. Promotes the Bank's services:
   Cross-sells other bank services appropriate to customers' needs.
   Answers inquiries regarding bank matters.
   Directs customers to other departments for specialized services.
5. Assists with other branch duties:
   Receipts night and mail deposits.
   Reconciles ATM transactions.
   Provides safe deposit services.
   Performs secretarial duties.

description for customer service representative.) CSRs were now expected to offer polite suggestions that customers use automatic teller machines for simple transactions. They were also required to stimulate customer interest in the broadening array of financial services offered by the bank. "The problem with Karen," as Reeves put it, "is that she simply refuses to sell."

THE NEW FOCUS ON CUSTOMER SERVICE AT THE FIRST

Although it was the largest bank in the state, the "First" had historically focused on corporate business, and its share of the retail consumer banking business had declined in the face of aggressive competition from other financial institutions. Three years earlier, the Board of Directors had appointed a new CEO and given him the mandate of developing a stronger consumer orientation at the retail level. The goal was to seize the initiative in marketing the ever-increasing array of financial services now available to retail customers. The new CEO's strategy, after putting in place a new management team, was to begin by ordering an expansion and speed-up of the First's investment in electronic delivery systems. The bank had tripled the number of automatic teller machines in its branches during the past eighteen months and was engaged in an active branch renovation program. One year ago, the First had also joined a regional ATM network, which boasted freestanding 24-hour booths at shopping centers, airports, and other high-traffic locations.

These actions seemed to be bearing fruit. In the most recent six months, the First had seen a significant increase in the number of new accounts opened, as compared to the same period of the previous year. And quarterly data released by the Federal Reserve Bank showed that the First was steadily increasing its share of new deposits in the state.

Customer Service Issues

New financial products had been introduced at a rapid rate. But the bank found that existing platform staff—known as new accounts assistants—were ill-equipped to sell these services because of lack of product knowledge and inadequate training in selling skills. Recalled Costanzo:

> The problem was that they were so used to waiting for a customer to approach them with a specific request, such as a mortgage or car loan, that it was hard to get them to take a more proactive approach that involved actively probing for customer needs. Their whole job seemed to revolve around filling out forms.

As the automation program proceeded, the mix of activities performed by the tellers started to change. A growing number of customers began to use automatic teller machines for cash withdrawals and deposits, as well as for requesting account balances. The ATMs at the Federal Square branch had the highest utilization of any of the First's branches, reflecting the large number of students and young professionals served at that location. Costanzo noted that customers who were older or less well educated seemed to prefer being served by "a real person, rather than a machine."

A year earlier, the head office had selected three branches, including Federal Square, as test sites for a new customer service program. The Federal Square branch was in a busy urban location, about one mile from the central business district and three blocks from the campus of the state university. The branch was surrounded by retail stores and close to commercial and professional offices. The other two branches were among the bank's larger suburban offices and were located in a shopping center and next to a big hospital, respectively. As part of the branch renovation program, each of these three branches had previously been remodeled to include no fewer than four ATMs (Federal Square had five), a customer service desk near the entrance, and two electronic information terminals that customers could activate to obtain information on a variety of bank services. The teller stations were redesigned to provide two levels of service: an express station for simple deposits and for cashing of approved checks, and regular stations for the full array of services provided by tellers. The number of stations open at a given time was varied to reflect the volume of anticipated business. Finally, the platform area in each branch was reconstructed to create what the architect described as "a friendly, yet professional, appearance."

HUMAN RESOURCES

With the new environment came new training programs for the staff of these three branches and new job descriptions and job titles: customer assistance representatives (for the platform staff), customer service representatives (for the tellers), and customer service director (instead of assistant branch manager). The head teller position was renamed head CSR. Position descriptions for all these jobs are reproduced in Exhibits 2, 3, 4, and 5. The training programs for each group included sessions designed to develop improved knowledge of both new and existing retail products. (CARs received more extensive training in this area than did CSRs.) The CARs also attended a 15-hour

EXHIBIT 2 First National Bank: Position Description for Customer Service Representative

FUNCTION

Provides customers with the highest quality services, with special emphasis on recognizing customer needs and cross-selling appropriate bank services. Plays an active role in developing and maintaining good customer relations.

RESPONSIBILITIES

1. Presents and communicates the best possible customer service.
   - Greets all customers with a courteous, friendly attitude.
   - Provides fast, accurate, friendly service.
   - Uses customer's name whenever possible.
2. Sells bank services and maintains customer relations.
   - Cross-sells retail services by identifying and referring valid prospects to the customer assistance representative or customer service director. When time permits (no other customers waiting in line), should actively cross-sell retail services.
   - Develops new business by acquainting noncustomers with bank services and existing customers with additional services that they are not currently using.
3. Provides a prompt and efficient operation on a professional level.
   - Receives cash and/or checks for checking accounts, saving accounts, taxes withheld, loan payments, Master Card/Visa, mortgage payments, Christmas clubs, money orders, traveler's checks, cashier's checks, premium promotions.
   - Verifies amount of cash and/or checks received, being alert for counterfeit or fraudulent items.
   - Accepts deposits and withdrawals, verifying signatures where required by policy.
   - Cashes checks in accordance with bank policy. Identifies payees; verifies signatures; checks dates and endorsements; compares written dollar and figure amounts; ensures that numbers are included on all counter checks, deposit slips and savings withdrawal and deposit slips; watches for stop payments and holds funds per bank policy.
   - Where applicable, pays credit card cash advances and savings withdrawals. Accepts credit merchant deposits. Receives payment for collection items, safe deposit rentals, and other miscellaneous items.
   - Confers with head CSR or customer service director on nonroutine situations.
   - Sells traveler's checks, money orders, and cashier's checks and may redeem coupons and sell or redeem foreign currency.
   - Handles sale and redemption of U.S. savings bonds.
   - Sells monthly transit passes.
   - Ensures timely batching and preparation of work for transmittal to proof department.
   - Prepares coin and currency orders as necessary.
   - Services, maintains, and settles automatic teller machines as required.
   - Ensures that only minimum cash exposure necessary for efficient operation is kept in cash drawer; removes excess cash immediately to secured location. Ensures maximum control over cash drawers and other valuables on hand throughout daily operation.
   - Prepares accurate and timely daily settlement of work.
   - Performs bookkeeping and operational functions as assigned by customer service director.

course, offered in three separate sessions, on basic selling skills. This program covered key steps in the sales process, including building a relationship, exploring customer needs, determining a solution, and overcoming objections. The sales training program for CSRs, by contrast, consisted of just two 2-hour sessions designed to develop skills in recognizing and probing customer needs, presenting product features and benefits, overcoming objections, and referring customers to CARs.

All staff members in customer service positions participated in sessions designed to improve their communication skills and professional image: clothing and personal grooming and interactions with customers were all discussed. Said the trainer, "Remember, people's money is too important to entrust to someone who doesn't look and act the part!" CARs were instructed to rise from their seats and shake hands with customers. Both CARs and CSRs were given exercises designed to improve their listening skills and their powers of observation. All employees working where they could be seen by customers were ordered to refrain from smoking, drinking soda, and chewing gum on the job.

Although First National management anticipated that most of the increased emphasis on selling would fall to the CARs, they also foresaw a limited selling role for the customer service reps, who would be expected to mention various products and facilities offered by the bank as they served customers at the teller window.

For instance, if a customer happened to mention a vacation, the CSR was supposed to mention traveler's checks; if the customer complained about bounced

EXHIBIT 3 First National Bank: Position Description for Head Customer Service Representative

FUNCTION

Supervises the customer service representatives in the designated branch office, ensuring efficient operations and the highest quality service to customers. Plays an active role in developing and maintaining good customer relations. Assists other branch personnel on request.

RESPONSIBILITIES

1. Supervises the CSRs in the branch.
   Allocates work, coordinates work flow, reviews and revises work procedures.
   Ensures that teller area is adequately and efficiently staffed with well-trained, qualified personnel.
   Assists CSRs with more complex transactions.
   Resolves routine personnel problems, referring more complex situations to the customer service director.
   Participates in decisions concerning performance appraisal, promotions, wage changes, transfers, and terminations of subordinate CSR staff.
2. Assumes responsibility for CSRs' money.
   Buys and sells money in the vault, ensuring adequacy of branch currency and coin supply.
   Ensures that CSRs and cash sheets are in balance.
   Maintains necessary records, including daily branch journal and general ledger.
3. Accepts deposits and withdrawals by business customers at commercial window.
4. Operates teller window to provide customer services (see Responsibilities for Customer Service Representative).

EXHIBIT 4 First National Bank: Position Description for Customer Assistance Representative

FUNCTION

Provides services and guidance to customers/prospects seeking banking relationships or related information. Promotes and sells needed products and responds to special requests by existing customers.

RESPONSIBILITIES

1. Provides prompt, efficient, and friendly service to all customers and prospective customers.
   Describes and sells bank services to customers/prospects who approach directly or via referral from customer service reps or other bank personnel.
   Answers customers' questions regarding bank services, hours, etc.
2. Identifies and responds to customers' needs.
   Promotes and sells retail services and identifies any existing cross-sell opportunities.
   Opens new accounts for individuals, businesses, and private organizations.
   Prepares temporary checks and deposit slips for new checking/NOW accounts.
   Sells checks and deposit slips.
   Interviews and takes applications for and pays out on installment/charge card accounts and other credit-related products.
   Certifies checks.
   Handles stop payment requests.
   Responds to telephone mail inquiries from customers or bank personnel.
   Receives notification of name or address changes and takes necessary action.
   Takes action on notification of lost passbooks, credit cards, ATM cards, collateral, and all other lost or stolen valuables.
   Demonstrates automatic teller machines to customers and assists with problems.
   Coordinates closing of accounts and ascertains reasons.
3. Sells and services all retail products.
   Advises customers and processes their applications for all products covered in CAR training programs and updates.
   Initiates referrals to the appropriate department when a trust or corporate business need is identified.

checks, the CSR should suggest speaking to a CAR about opening a personal line of credit that would provide automatic overdraft protection; or if the customer mentioned investments, the CSR should refer him or her to a CAR who could provide information on money market accounts, certificates of deposit, or the First's discount brokerage service. All CSRs were supplied with their own business cards. When making a referral, they were expected to write the customer's name and the product of interest on the back of a card, give it to

EXHIBIT 5 First National Bank: Position Description for Customer Service Director

FUNCTION

Supervises customer service representatives, customer assistance representatives, and other staff as assigned to provide the most effective and profitable retail banking delivery system in the local marketplace. Supervises sales efforts and provides feedback to management concerning response to products and services by current and prospective banking customers. Communicates goals and results to those supervised and ensures operational standards are met in order to achieve outstanding customer service.

RESPONSIBILITIES

1. Supervises effective delivery of retail products.
   - Selects, trains, and manages the customer service representatives and customer assistance representatives.
   - Assigns duties and work schedules.
   - Completes performance reviews.
2. Personally, and through those supervised, renders the highest level of professional and efficient customer service available in the local marketplace.
   - Provides high level of service while implementing most efficient and customer-sensitive staffing schedules.
   - Supervises all on-the-job programs within office.
   - Ensures that outstanding customer service standards are achieved.
   - Directs remedial programs for CSRs and CARs as necessary.
3. Develops retail sales effectiveness to the degree necessary to achieve market share objectives.
   - Ensures that all CSRs and CARs possess comprehensive product knowledge.
   - Directs coordinated cross-sell program within office at all times.
   - Reports staff training needs to branch manager and/or regional training director.
4. Maintains operational adherence to standards.
   - Oversees preparation of daily and monthly operational and sales reports.
   - Estimates, approves, and coordinates branch cash needs in advance.
   - Oversees ATM processing function.
   - Handles or consults with CSRs/CARs on more complex transactions.
   - Ensures clean and businesslike appearance of the branch facility.
5. Informs branch manager of customer response to products.
   - Reports customer complaints and types of sales resistance encountered.
   - Describes and summarizes reasons for account closings.
6. Communicates effectively the goals and results of the bank to those under supervision.
   - Reduces office goals into format that translates to goals for each CSR or CAR.
   - Reports sales and cross-sell results to all CSRs and CARs.
   - Conducts sales- and service-oriented staff meetings with CSRs/CARs on a regular basis.
   - Attends all scheduled customer service management meetings organized by regional office.

the customer, and send that individual to the customer assistance desks.

In an effort to motivate CSRs at the three test branches to sell specific financial products, the bank experimented with various incentive programs. The first involved cash bonuses for referrals to CARs that resulted in the sale of specific products. During a one-month period, CSRs were offered a $50 bonus for each referral leading to a customer's opening a personal line of credit account: the CARs received a $20 bonus for each account they opened, regardless of whether it came as a referral or simply a walk-in. Eight such bonuses were paid to CSRs at Federal Square, with three each going to just two of the seven full-time CSRs, Jean Warshawksi and Bruce Greenfield. Karen Mitchell was not among the recipients. However, this program was not renewed, since it was felt that there were other, more cost-effective means of marketing this product. In addition, Reeves, the customer service director, had reason to believe that Bruce Greenfield had colluded with one of the CARs, his girlfriend, to claim referrals that he had not, in fact, made. Another test branch reported similar suspicions of two of its CSRs.

A second promotion followed and was based upon allocating credits to the CSRs for successful referrals. The value of the credit varied according to the nature of the product—for instance, a cash machine card was worth 500 credits—and accumulated credits could be exchanged for merchandise gifts. This program was deemed ineffective and discontinued after three months. The basic problem seemed to be that the value of the gifts was too low in relation to the amount of effort required.

Other problems with these promotional schemes included lack of product knowledge on the part of the

CSRs and time pressures when many customers were waiting in line to be served.

The bank had next turned to an approach that, in David Reeves' words, "used the stick rather than the carrot." All CSRs had traditionally been evaluated half-yearly on a variety of criteria, including accuracy, speed, quality of interactions with customers, punctuality of arrival for work, job attitudes, cooperation with other employees, and professional image. The evaluation process assigned a number of points to each criterion, with accuracy and speed being the most heavily weighted. In addition to appraisals by the customer service director and the branch manager, with input from the head CSR, the First had recently instituted a program of anonymous visits by what was popularly known as the "mystery client." Each CSR was visited at least once a quarter by a professional evaluator posing as a customer. This individual's appraisal of the CSR's appearance, performance, and attitude was included in the overall evaluation. The number of points scored by each CSR had a direct impact on merit pay raises and on selection for promotion to the head CSR position or to platform jobs.

To encourage improved product knowledge and "consultative selling" by CSRs, the evaluation process was revised to include points assigned for each individual's success in sales referrals. Under the new evaluation scheme, the maximum number of points assignable for effectiveness in making sales—directly or through referrals to CARs—amounted to 30 percent of the potential total score. Although CSR-initiated sales had risen significantly in the most recent half-year, Reeves sensed that morale had dropped among this group, in contrast to the CARs, whose enthusiasm and commitment had risen significantly. He had also noticed an increase in CSR errors. One CSR had quit, complaining about too much pressure.

Karen Mitchell

Under the old scoring system, Karen Mitchell had been the highest scoring teller/CSR for four consecutive half-years. But after two half-years under the new system, her ranking had dropped to fourth out of the seven full-time tellers. The top-ranking CSR, Mary Bell, had been with First for sixteen years but had declined repeated invitations to apply for a head teller position, saying that she was happy where she was, earning at the top of the CSR scale and did not want "the extra worry and responsibility." Mitchell ranked first on all but one of the operationally related criteria (interactions with customers, where she ranked second) but sixth on selling effectiveness (Exhibit 6).

Costanzo and Reeves had spoken to Mitchell about her performance and expressed disappointment. Mitchell had told them, respectfully but firmly, that she saw the most important aspect of her job as giving customers fast, accurate, and courteous service.

> I did try this selling thing [she told the two bank officers], but it seemed to annoy people. Some said they were in a hurry and couldn't talk now; others looked at me as if I were slightly crazy to bring up the subject of a different bank service than the one they were currently transacting. And then, when you got the odd person who seemed interested, you could hear the other customers in the line grumbling about the slow service.
>
> Really, the last straw was when I noticed on the computer that this woman had several thousand in her savings account, so I suggested to her, just as the trainer had told us, that she could earn more interest if she opened a money market account. Well, she told me it was none of my business what she did with her money and stomped off. Don't get me wrong, I love being able to help customers, and if they ask for my advice, I'll gladly tell them about what the bank has to offer.

Selecting a New Head CSR

Two weeks after this meeting, it was announced that the head CSR was leaving. The job entailed some supervision of the other CSRs (including allocation of work assignments and scheduling of part-time CSRs at busy periods or during employee vacations), consultation on—and, where possible, resolution of—any problems occurring at the teller stations, and handling of large cash deposits and withdrawals by local retailers (see position description in Exhibit 3). When not engaged in such tasks, the head CSR was expected to operate a regular teller window.

The pay scale for a head CSR ranged from \$12.00 to \$17.00 per hour, depending on qualifications, seniority, and branch size, as compared to a range of \$8.00 to \$13.00 per hour for CSRs. The pay scale for CARs ranged from \$7.50 to \$14.00. Full-time employees (who were not unionized) worked a 40-hour week, including some evenings until 6:00 P.M. and certain Saturday mornings. Costanzo indicated that the pay scales were typical for banks in the Midwest, although the average CSR at the First was better qualified than those at smaller banks and therefore higher on the scale. Karen Mitchell was currently earning \$7.80 per hour, reflecting her associate's degree, $3\frac{1}{2}$ years' experience, and significant past merit increases. If promoted to head CSR, she would qualify for an initial rate of \$5.00 an hour.

EXHIBIT 6 First National Bank: Summary of Performance Evaluation Scores for Customer Service Representatives at Federal Square Branch for Two Half-Year Periods

CSR Name[a]	*Length of Full-Time Bank Service*	*Operational Criteria*[b] *(max: 70 points)* 1st Half	2nd Half	*Selling Effectiveness*[c] *(max: 30 points)* 1st Half	2nd Half	*Total Score* 1st Half	2nd Half
Mary Bell	16 years, 10 mos.	65	64	16	20	81	84
Richard Dubois	2 years, 3 mos.	63	61	15	19	78	80
Bruce Greenfield	1 year, 0 mos.	48	42	20	26	68	68
Karen Mitchell	3 years, 7 mos.	67	67	13	12	80	79
Sharon Ronsky	1 year, 4 mos.	53	55	8	9	61	64
Naomi Rubin	7 mos.	–	50	–	22	–	72
Jean Warshawski	2 years, 1 mo.	57	55	21	28	79	83

[a]Full-time CSRs only (part-time CSRs were evaluated separately).

[b]Totals based on sum of ratings against various criteria, including accuracy, work production, attendance and punctually, personal appearance, organization of work, initiative, cooperation with others, problem-solving ability, and quality of interaction with customers.

[c]Points awarded for both direct sales by CSR (e.g., traveler's checks) and referral selling by CSR to CAR (e.g., ATM card, certificates of deposit, personal line of credit).

When applications for the positions closed, Mitchell was one of three candidates. The other two candidates were Jean Warshawski, 42, another CSR at the Federal Square branch, and Curtis Richter, 24, the head CSR of one of the First National Bank's smaller suburban branches, who was seeking more responsibility.

Warshawski was married and had two sons in high school. She had started working as a part-time teller at Federal Square three years previously, switching to full-time work a year later in order, as she said, to put away some money for her boys' college education. Warshawski was a cheerful woman with a jolly laugh. She had a wonderful memory for people's names, and Reeves had often seen her greeting customers on the street or in a restaurant during the lunch hour. Reviewing her evaluations over the past three years, Reeves noted that she had initially performed poorly on accuracy and at one point, while still a part-timer, had been put on probation because of frequent inaccuracies in the balance in her cash drawer at the end of the day. Although Reeves considered her much improved on this score, he still saw room for improvement. The customer service director had also had occasion to reprimand her for tardiness during the past year. Warshawski attributed this to health problems with her elder son who, she said, was now responding to treatment.

Both Reeves and Costanzo had observed Warshawski at work and agreed that her interactions with customers were exceptionally good, although she tended to be overly chatty and was not as fast as Karen Mitchell. She seemed to have a natural ability to size up customers and to decide which ones were good prospects for a quick sales pitch on a specific financial product. Although slightly untidy in her personal appearance, she was very well organized in her work and was quick to help her fellow CSRs, especially new hires. She was currently earning $10.00 per hour as a CSR and would qualify for a rate of $14.50 as head CSR. In the most recent six months, Warshawski had ranked ahead of Mitchell as a result of being very successful in consultative selling (Exhibit 6).

Richter, the third candidate, was not working in one of the three test branches and so had not been exposed to the consultative selling program and its corresponding evaluation scheme. However, he had received excellent evaluations for his work in the First's small Longmeadow branch, where he had been employed for three years. A move to Federal Square would increase his earnings from $11.00 to $14.50 per hour. Reeves and Costanzo had interviewed Richter and considered him intelligent and personable. He had joined the bank after dropping out of college midway through his junior year but had recently started taking evening courses in order to complete his degree. The Longmeadow branch was located in an older part of town, where commercial and retail activity was rather stagnant. The branch had not yet been renovated and had no ATMs, although there was an ATM accessible to First National customers one block away. Richter supervised three CSRs and reported directly to the branch manager, who spoke very highly of him. Since there were no CARs in this branch, Richter and another experienced CSR took turns handling new accounts and loan or mortgage applications.

Costanzo and Reeves were troubled by the decision that faced them. Prior to the bank's shift in focus, Mitchell would have been the natural choice for the head CSR job, which, in turn, could be a stepping stone to further promotions, including customer assistance representative, customer service director, and, eventually, manager of a small branch or a management position in the head office. Mitchell had told her superiors that she was interested in making a career in banking and that she was eager to take on further responsibilities.

Compounding the problem was the fact that the three branches testing the new customer service program had just completed a full year of the test. Costanzo knew that sales and profits were up significantly at all three branches relative to the bank's performance as a whole. She anticipated that top management would want to extend the program systemwide after making any modifications that seemed desirable.

GENERAL ELECTRIC APPLIANCES

Larry Barr had recently been promoted to the position of District Sales Manager (B.C.) for G.E. Appliances, a division of Canadian Appliance Manufacturing Co. Ltd. (CAMCO). One of his more important duties in that position was the allocation of his district's sales quota among his five salespeople. Barr received his quota for next year in October of the previous year. His immediate task was to determine an equitable allocation of that quota. This was important because the company's incentive pay plan was based on the salespeople's attainment of quota. A portion of Barr's remuneration was also based on the degree to which his sales force met their quotas.

Barr graduated from the University of British Columbia with the degree of Bachelor of Commerce. He was immediately hired as a product manager for a mining equipment manufacturing firm because of his summer job experience with that firm. Three years later he joined Canadian General Electric (C.G.E.) in Montreal as a product manager for refrigerators. There he was responsible for creating and merchandising a product line, as well as developing product and marketing plans. Two years later he was transferred to Coburg, Ontario, as a sales manager for industrial plastics. The next year he became Administrative Manager (Western Region) and when the position of District Sales Manager became available, Barr was promoted to it. There his duties included development of sales strategies, supervision of salespeople, and budgeting.

BACKGROUND

Canadian Appliance Manufacturing Co. Ltd. (CAMCO) was created under the joint ownership of Canadian General Electric Ltd. and General Steel Wares Ltd. (G.S.W.). CAMCO then purchased the production facilities of Westinghouse Canada Ltd. Under the purchase agreement the Westinghouse brand name was transferred to White Consolidated Industries Ltd., where it became White-Westinghouse. Appliances manufactured by CAMCO in the former Westinghouse plant were branded Hotpoint.

The G.E., G.S.W., and Hotpoint major appliance plants became divisions of CAMCO. These divisions operated independently and had their own separate management staff, although they were all ultimately accountable to CAMCO management. The divisions competed for sales, although not directly, because they each produced product lines for different price segments (Exhibit 1).

COMPETITION

Competition in the appliance industry was vigorous. CAMCO was the largest firm in the industry, with

---

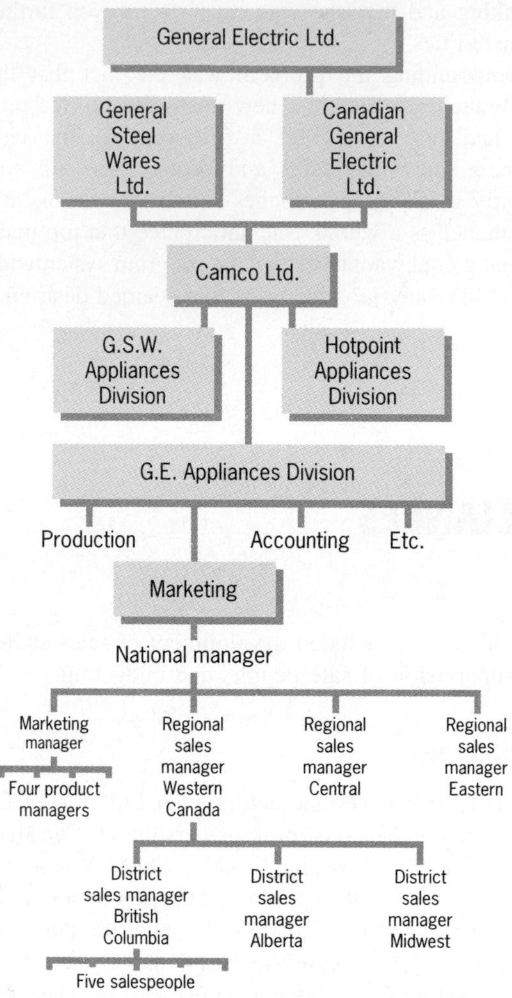

EXHIBIT 1 Organization Chart

approximately 45 percent market share, split between G.E., G.S.W. (Moffatt & McClary brands), and Hotpoint. The following three firms each had 10 to 15 percent market shares: Inglis (washers and dryers only), W.C.I. (makers of White-Westinghouse, Kelvinator, and Gibson), and Admiral. These firms also produced appliances under department store brand names such as Viking, Baycrest, and Kenmore, which accounted for an additional 15 percent of the market. The remainder of the market was divided among brands such as Maytag, Roper Dishwasher, Gurney, Tappan, and Danby.

G.E. marketed a full major appliance product line, including refrigerators, ranges, washers, dryers, dishwashers, and television sets. G.E. appliances generally had many features and were priced at the upper end of the price range. Their major competition came from Maytag and Westinghouse.

THE BUDGETING PROCESS

G.E. Appliances was one of the most advanced firms in the consumer goods industry in terms of sales budgeting. Budgeting received careful analysis at all levels of management.

The budgetary process began in June of each year. The management of G.E. Appliances division assessed the economic outlook, growth trends in the industry, competitive activity, population growth, and so forth in order to determine a reasonable sales target for the next year. The president of CAMCO received this estimate, checked and revised it as necessary, and submitted it to the president of G.E. Canada. Final authorization rested with G.E. Ltd., which had a definite minimum growth target for the G.E. branch of CAMCO. G.E. Appliances was considered an "invest and grow" division, which meant that it was expected to produce a healthy sales growth each year, regardless of the state of the economy. As Barr observed. "This is difficult, but meeting challenges is the job of management."

The approved budget was expressed as a desired percentage increase in sales. Once the figure had been decided, it was not subject to change. The quota was communicated back through G.E. Canada Ltd., CAMCO, and G.E. Appliances, where it was available to the District Sales Managers in October. Each district was then required to meet an overall growth figure (quota) but each sales territory was not automatically expected to achieve that same growth. Barr was required to assess the situation in each territory, determine where growth potential was highest, and allocate his quota accordingly.

THE SALES INCENTIVE PLAN

The sales incentive plan was a critical part of General Electric's sales force plan and an important consideration in the quota allocation of Barr. Each salesperson had a portion of earnings dependent upon performance with respect to quota. Also, Barr was awarded a bonus based on the sales performance of his district, making it advantageous to Barr and good for staff morale for all his salespeople to attain their quotas.

The sales force incentive plan was relatively simple. A bonus system is fairly typical for salespeople in any field. With G.E., each salesperson agreed to a basic salary figure called "planned earnings." The planned salary varied according to experience, education, past performance, and competitive salaries. A salesperson was paid 75 percent of planned earnings

EXHIBIT 2 Sales Incentive Earnings Schedule: Major Appliances and Home Entertainment Products

Sales Quota Realization Percent	*Incentive Percent of Base Salary Total*	*Sales Quota Realization Percent*	*Incentive Percent of Base Salary Total*
70	0	106	37.00
71	0.75	107	39.00
72	1.50	108	41.00
73	2.25	109	43.00
74	3.00	110	45.00
75	3.75	111	46.00
76	4.50	112	47.00
77	5.25	113	48.00
78	6.00	114	49.00
79	6.75	115	50.00
80	7.50	116	51.00
81	8.25	117	52.00
82	9.00	118	53.00
83	9.75	119	54.00
84	10.50	120	55.00
85	11.25	121	56.00
86	12.00	122	57.00
87	12.75	123	58.00
88	13.50	124	59.00
89	14.25	125	60.00
90	15.00	126	61.00
91	16.00	127	62.00
92	17.00	128	63.00
93	18.00	129	64.00
94	19.00	130	65.00
95	20.00	131	66.00
96	21.00	132	67.00
97	22.00	133	68.00
98	23.00	134	69.00
99	24.00	135	70.00
100	25.00	136	71.00
101	27.00	137	72.00
102	29.00	138	73.00
103	31.00	139	74.00
104	33.00	140	75.00
105	35.00		

on a guaranteed regular basis. The remaining 25 percent of salary was at risk, dependent upon the person's sales record. There was also the possibility of earning substantially more money by selling more than quota (Exhibit 2).

The bonus was awarded such that total salary (base plus bonus) equaled planned earnings when the quota was just met. The greatest increase in bonus came between 101 and 110 percent of quota. The bonus was paid quarterly on the cumulative total quota. A holdback system ensured that a salesperson was never required to pay back a previously earned bonus by reason of a poor quarter. Because of this system, it was critical that each salesperson's quota be fair in relation to those of the other salespeople. Nothing was worse for morale than one person earning large bonuses while the others struggled.

Quota attainment was not the sole basis for evaluating the salespeople. They were required to fulfill a wide range of duties including service, franchising of new dealers, maintaining good relations with dealers, and maintaining a balance of sales among the different product lines. Because the bonus system was based on sales only, Barr had to ensure that the salespeople did not neglect their other duties.

A formal salary review was held each year for each salesperson. However, Barr preferred to give his salespeople continuous feedback on their performances. Through human relations skills, he hoped to avoid problems that could lead to dismissal of a salesperson and loss of sales for the company.

Barr's incentive bonus plan was more complex than the salespeople's. He was awarded a maximum of 75 annual bonus points broken down as follows: market share, 15; total sales performance, 30; sales representative balance, 30. Each point had a specific money value. The system ensured that Barr allocated his quota carefully. For instance, if one quota was so difficult that the salesperson sold only 80 percent of it, while the other salespeople exceeded quota, Barr's bonus would be reduced, even if the overall area sales exceeded the quota (Exhibit 3).

QUOTA ALLOCATION

The total sales budget for G.E. Appliances division for next year was about $100 million, a 14 percent sales increase over the current year. Barr's share of the $33 million Western region quota was $13.3 million, also a 14 percent increase over the previous year. Barr had two weeks to allocate the quota among his five territories. He needed to consider factors such as historical allocation, economic outlook, dealer changes, personnel changes, untapped potential, new franchises or store openings, and buying group activity (volume purchases by associations of independent dealers).

SALES FORCE

There were five sales territories within British Columbia (Exhibit 4). Territories were determined on the basis of number of customers, sales volume of customers, geographic size, and experience of the

EXHIBIT 3 Development of a Sales Commission Plan

A series of steps are required to establish the foundation upon which a sales commission plan can be built. These steps are as follows:

Determine Specific Sales Objectives of Positions to Be Included in Plan

For a sales commission plan to succeed, it must be designed to encourage the attainment of the business objectives of the component division. Before deciding on the dimensions of a commission plan, you have to decide on which of the following objectives are important.

1. Increase sales volume
2. Do an effective, balanced selling job in a variety of product lines
3. Improve market share
4. Reduce selling expense to sales ratios
5. Develop new accounts or territories
6. Introduce new products

Although it is probably neither desirable nor necessary to include all such objectives as specific measures of performance in the plan, they should be kept in mind, at least to the extent that the performance measures chosen for the plan are compatible with and do not work against the overall accomplishment of the component's business objectives.

Also, the *relative* current importance or ranking of these objectives will provide guidance in selecting the number and type of performance measures to be included in the plan.

Determine Quantitative Performance Measures to Be Used

Although it may be possible to include a number of measures in a particular plan, there is a drawback to using so many as to overly complicate it and fragment the impact of any one measure on the participants. A plan that is difficult to understand will lose a great deal of its motivating force, as well as being costly to administer properly.

For components that currently have a variable sales compensation plan(s) for their sales, a good starting point would be to consider the measures used in those plans. Although the measurements used for sales managers need not be identical, they should at least be compatible with those used to determine commissions.

However, keep in mind that a performance measure that may not be appropriate for individual salespeople may be a good one to apply to their manager. Measurements involving attainment of a share of a defined market, balanced selling for a variety of products, and control of district or region expenses might well fall into this category.

The accompanying table lists a variety of measurements that might be used to emphasize specific sales objectives. For most components, all or most of these objectives will be desirable to some extent. The point is to select those of greatest importance where it will be possible to establish measures of standard or normal performance for individuals, or at least small groups of individuals working as a team.

If more than one performance measurement is to be used, the relative weighting of each measurement must be determined. If a measure is to be effective, it must carry enough weight to have at least some noticeable effect on the commission earnings of an individual.

As a general guide, it would be unusual for a plan to include more than two or three quantitative measures with a minimum weighting of 15 to 20 percent of planned commissions for any one measurement.

Establish Commission Payment Schedule for Each Performance Measure

Determine Appropriate Range of Performance for Each Measurement. The performance range for a measurement defines the percent of standard performance (R%) at which commission earnings start to the point where they reach maximum.

The minimum point of the performance range for a given measurement should be set so that a majority of the participants can earn at least some incentive pay, and the maximum set at a point that is possible for some participants to obtain. These points will vary with the type of measure used and with the degree of predictability of individual budgets or other forms of measurement. In a period where overall performance is close to standard, 90 to 95 percent of the participants should fall within the performance range.

For the commission plan to be effective, most of the participants should be operating within the performance range most of the time. If a participant is either far below the minimum of this range or has reached the maximum, further improvement will not affect his commission earnings, and the plan will be largely inoperative as far as he is concerned.

Actual past experience of R%'s attained by participants is obviously the best indicator of what this range should be for each measure used. Lacking this, it is better to err on the side of having a wider range than one that proves to be too narrow. If some form of group measure is used, the variation from standard performance is likely to be less for the group in total than for individuals within it. For example, the performance range for total district performance would probably be narrower than the range established for individual sales within a district.

Determine Appropriate Reward:Risk Ratio for Commission Earnings. This refers to the relationship of commission earned at standard performance, to maximum commission earnings available under the plan. A plan that pays 10 percent of base salary for normal or standard performance and pays 30 percent as a maximum commission would have a 2:1 ratio. In other words, participants can earn twice as much (20 percent) for above-standard performance as they stand to lose for below-standard performance (10 percent).

Reward under a sales commission plan should be related to the effort involved to produce a given result. To adequately encourage above-standard results, the *reward:risk ratio* should generally be at least 2:1. The proper control of incentive plan payments lies in the proper setting of performance standards, not in the setting of a

EXHIBIT 3 (Continued)

low maximum payment for outstanding results that provides a minimum variation in individual earnings. Generally, a higher percentage of base salary should be paid for each 1%R above 100 percent than has been paid for each 1%R up to 100%R to reflect the relative difficulty involved in producing above-standard results.

Once the performance range and reward:risk ratios have been determined, the schedule of payments for each performance measure can then be calculated. This will show the percentage of the participant's base salary earned for various performance results (R%) from the point at which commissions start to maximum performance.

Example: For measurement paying 20 percent of salary for standard performance:

Percent of Base Salary Earned	
1% of base salary for each + 1%R	0%
	20%
1.33% of base salary for each + 1%R	60%
Percent of Sales Quota	
80% or below	
100% (standard performance)	
130% or above	

Prepare Draft of Sales Commission Plan

After completing the above steps, a draft of a sales commission plan should be prepared using the accompanying outline as a guide.

Keys to Effective Commission Plans

1. *Get the understanding and acceptance of the commission plan by the managers who will be involved in carrying it out.* They must be convinced of its effectiveness in order to properly explain and "sell" the plan to the salespeople.
2. *In turn, be sure the plan is presented clearly to the salespeople* so that they have a good understanding of how the plan will work. We find that good acceptance of a sales commission plan on the part of salespeople correlates closely with how well they understood the plan and its effect on their compensation. The salespeople must be convinced that the measurements used are factors which they can control by their selling efforts.
3. *Be sure the measurements used in the commission plan encourage the salespeople to achieve the marketing goals of your operation.* For example, if sales volume is the only performance measure, the salespeople will concentrate on producing as much dollar volume as possible by spending most of their time on products with high volume potential. It will be difficult to get them to spend much time on introducing new products with relatively low volume, handling customer complaints, etc. Even though a good portion of their compensation may still be in salary, you can be sure they will wind up doing the things they feel will maximize their commission earnings.
4. One solution to maintaining good sales direction is to put at least a portion of the commission earnings in an "incentive pool" to be distributed by the sales manager according to his judgment. This "pool" can vary in size according to some qualitative measure of the sales group's performance, but the manager can set individual measurements for each salesperson and reward people according to how well they fulfill their goals.
5. If at all possible, you should test the plan for a period of time, perhaps in one or two sales areas or districts. To make it a real test, you should actually pay commission earnings to the participants, but the potential risk and rewards can be limited. No matter how well a plan has been conceived, not all the potential pitfalls will be apparent until you've actually operated the plan for a period of time. The test period is a relatively painless way to get some experience.
6. Finally, after the plan is in operation, take time to analyze the results. Is the plan accomplishing what you want it to do, both in terms of business results produced and in realistically compensating salespeople for their efforts?

Tailoring Commission Plan Measurements to Fit Component Objectives

Objectives	*Possible Plan Measurements*
1. Increase sales/order volume	Net sales billed or orders received against quota
2. Increase sales of particular lines	Sales against product line quotas with weighted sales credits on individual lines
3. Increase market share	Percent realization (%R) of shares bogey
4. Do balanced selling job	%R of product line quotas, with commissions increasing in proportion to number of lines up to quota
5. Increase profitability	Margin realized from sales Vary sales credits to emphasize profitable product lines Vary sales credit in relation to amount of price discount
6. Increase dealer sales	Pay distributor salespeople or sales manager in relation to realization of sales quotas of assigned dealers
7. Increase sales calls	%R of targeted calls per district or region
8. Introduce new product	Additional sales credits on new line for limited period
9. Control expense	%R of expense to sales or margin ratio Adjust sales credit in proportion to variance from expense budget
10. Sales teamwork	Share of incentive based upon group results

EXHIBIT 4 G.E. Appliances–Sales Territories

Territory Designation	*Description*
9961 Greater Vancouver (Garth Rizzuto)	Hudson's Bay, Firestone, K-Mart, McDonald Supply, plus seven independent dealers
9962 Interior (Dan Seguin)	All customers from Quesnel to Nelson, including contract sales (50 customers)
9963 Coastal (Ken Block)	Eatons, Woodwards, plus Vancouver Island north of Duncan and upper Fraser Valley (east of Clearbrook) (20 customers)
9964 Independent and Northern (Fred Speck)	All independents in lower mainland and South Vancouver Island, plus northern B.C. and Yukon (30 customers)
9967 Contract (Jim Wiste)	Contract sales Vancouver, Victoria. All contract sales outside 9962 (50–60 customers)

salesperson. Territories were altered periodically in order to deal with changed circumstances.

One territory was composed entirely of contract customers. Contract sales were sales in bulk lots to builders and developers who used the appliances in housing units. Because the appliances were not resold at retail, G.E. took a lower profit margin on such sales.

G.E. Appliances recruited M.B.A. graduates for its sales force. It sought bright, educated people who were willing to relocate anywhere in Canada. The company intended that these people would ultimately be promoted to managerial positions. The company also hired experienced career salespeople in order to get a blend of experience in the sales force. However, the typical salesperson was under age 30, aggressive, and upwardly mobile. G.E.'s sales training program covered only product knowledge. It was not felt necessary to train recruits in sales techniques.

Allocation Procedure

At the time Barr assumed the job of DSM, he had a meeting with the former sales manager, Ken Philips. Philips described to Barr the method he had used in the past to allocate the quota. As Barr understood it, the procedure was as follows:

The quota was received in October in the form of a desired percentage sales increase. The first step was to project current sales to the end of the year. This gave a base to which the increase was added for an estimation of the next year's quota. From this quota, the value of contract sales was allocated. Contract sales were allocated first because the market was considered the easiest to forecast. The amount of contract sales in the sales mix was constrained by the lower profit margin on such sales.

The next step was to make a preliminary allocation by simply adding the budgeted percentage increase to the year-end estimates for each territory. Although this allocation seemed fair on the surface, it did not take into account the differing situations in the territories or the difficulty of attaining such an increase.

The next step was examination of the sales data compiled by G.E. weekly sales reports from all regions were fed into a central computer, which compiled them and printed out sales totals by product line for each customer, as well as other information. This information enabled the sales manager to check the reasonableness of his initial allocation through a careful analysis of the growth potential for each customer.

The analysis began with the largest accounts such as Firestone, Hudson's Bay, and Eatons, which each bought over $1 million in appliances annually. Accounts that size were expected to achieve at least the budgeted growth. The main reason for this was that a shortfall of a few percentage points on such a large account would be difficult to make up elsewhere.

Next, the growth potential for medium-sized accounts was estimated. These accounts included McDonald Supply, K-Mart, Federated Cooperative, and buying groups such as Volume Independent Purchasers (V.I.P.). Management expected the majority of sales growth to come from such accounts, which had annual sales of between $150,000 and $1 million.

At that point, about 70 percent of the accounts had been analyzed. The small accounts were estimated last. These had generally lower growth potential but were an important part of the company's distribution system.

Once all the accounts had been analyzed, the growth estimates were summed and the total compared to the budget. Usually, the growth estimates were well below the budget.

The next step was to gather more information. The salespeople were usually consulted to ensure that no potential trouble areas or good opportunities had been overlooked. The manager continued to revise and adjust the figures until the total estimate matched

EXHIBIT 5 Sales Results

Territory	Previous Budget (× 1,000)	Percent of Total Budget	Previous Actual (× 1,000)	Variance from Quota (V%)
9967 (Contract)	$2,440	26.5	$ 2,267	(7)
9961 (Greater Vancouver)	1,790	19.4	1,824	2
9962 (Interior)	1,624	17.7	1,433	(11)
9963 (Coastal)	2,111	23.0	2,364	12
9965 (Independent dealers)	1,131	12.3	1,176	4
House	84	1.1	235	-
Total	$9,180	100.0	$ 9,299	1

Territory	Following Year Budget (× 1,000)	Percent of Total Budget	Following Year Actual (× 1,000)	Variance from Quota (V%)
9967 (Contract)	$2,587	26.2	$ 2,845	10
9961 (Greater Vancouver)	2,005	20.3	2,165	8
9962 (Interior)	1,465	14.8	1,450	(1)
9963 (Coastal)	2,405	24.4	2,358	(2)
9965 (Independent dealers)	1,334	13.5	1,494	12
House	52	.8	86	-
Total	$9,848	100.0	$10,398	5

the budget. These projections were then summed by territory and compared to the preliminary territorial allocation.

Frequently, there were substantial differences between the two allocations. Historical allocations were then examined, and the manager used his or her judgment in adjusting the figures until he was satisfied that the allocation was both equitable and attainable. Some factors that were considered at this stage included experience of the salesperson, competitive activities, potential store closures or openings, potential labor disputes in areas, and so forth.

The completed allocation was passed on to the Regional Sales Manager for his approval. The process had usually taken one week or longer by this stage. Once the allocations had been approved, the district Sales Manager then divided them into sales quotas by product line. Often, the resulting average price did not match the expected mix between higher and lower priced units. Therefore, some additional adjusting of figures was necessary. The house account (used for sales to employees of the company) was used as the adjustment factor.

Once this breakdown had been completed, the numbers were printed on a budget sheet, and given to the Regional Sales Manager (RSM). He or she forwarded all the sheets for the region to the central computer, which printed out sales numbers for each product line by salesperson by month. These figures were used as the salesperson's quotas for the next year.

Current Situation

Barr recognized that he faced a difficult task. He felt that he was too new to the job and the area to confidently undertake an account by account growth analysis. However, due to his previous experience with sales budgets, he did have some sound general ideas. He also had the records of past allocation and quota attainment (Exhibit 5), as well as the assistance of the RSM, Anthony Foyt.

Barr's first step was to project the current sales figures to end-of-year totals. This task was facilitated because the former manager, Philips, had been making successive projections monthly since June. Barr then made a preliminary quota allocation by adding the budgeted sales increase of 14 percent to each territory's total (Exhibit 6).

Barr then began to assess circumstances which could cause him to alter that allocation. One major problem was the resignation, effective at the end of the year, of one of the company's top salesmen, Ken Block. His territory had traditionally been one of the most difficult, and Barr felt that it would be unwise to replace Block with a novice salesperson.

Barr considered shifting one of the more experienced salespeople into that area. However, that would have involved a disruption of service in an additional territory, which was undesirable because it took several months for a salesperson to build up a good rapport with customers. Barr's decision would affect his quota

EXHIBIT 6 Sales Projections and Quotas

Projected Sales Results, Current Year

Territory	Current Year October Year to Date (× 1000)	Current Projected Total (× 1000)	Current Budget (× 1000)	% of Total Budget	Projected Variance from Quota (V%)
9967	$2,447	$3,002	$2,859	25.0	5
9961	2,057	2,545	2,401	21.0	6
9962	1,318	1,623	1,727	15.1	(6)
9963	2,124	2,625	2,734	23.9	(4)
9965	1,394	1,720	1,578	13.8	9
House	132	162	139	1.2	–
Total	$9,474	$11,677	$11,438	100.0	2

Preliminary Allocation, Next Year

Territory	Current Projection (× 1000)	Next Year Budget[a] (× 1000)	% of Total Budget
9967	$ 3,002	$ 3,422	25.7
9961	2,545	2,901	21.8
9962	1,623	1,854	13.9
9963	2,625	2,992	22.5
9965	1,720	1,961	14.7
House	162	185	1.4
Total	$11,677	$13,315	100.0

[a]Next budget = current territory projections + 14% = $13,315.

allocation because a salesperson new to a territory could not be expected to sell immediately as well as the incumbent, and a novice salesperson would require an even longer period of adaptation.

Barr was also concerned about territory 9961. The territory comprised two large national accounts and seven major independent dealers. The buying decisions for the national accounts were made at their head offices, where G.E.'s regional sales had no control over the decisions. Recently, Barr had heard rumors that one of the national accounts was reviewing its purchase of G.E. appliances. If they were to delist even some product lines, it would be a major blow to the salesman, Rizzuto, whose potential sales would be greatly reduced. Barr was unsure how to deal with that situation.

Another concern for Barr was the wide variance in buying of some accounts. Woodwards, Eatons, and McDonald Supply had large fluctuations from year to year. Also, Eatons, Hudson's Bay, and Woodwards had plans to open new stores in the Vancouver area sometime during the year. The sales increase to be generated by these events was hard to estimate.

The general economic outlook was poor. The Canadian dollar had fallen to 92 cents U.S., and unemployment was about 8 percent. The government's anti-inflation program, which was scheduled to end next year, had managed to keep inflation to the 8 percent level, but economists expected higher inflation and increased labor unrest during the postcontrol period.

The economic outlook was not the same in all areas. For instance, the Okanagan (9962) was a very depressed area. Tourism was down, and fruit farmers were doing poorly despite good weather and record prices. Vancouver Island was still recovering from a 200 percent increase in ferry fares, while the lower mainland appeared to be in a relatively better position.

In the contract segment, construction had shown an increase recently. However, labor unrest was common. There had been a crippling eight-week strike recently, and there was a strong possibility of another strike next year.

With all of this in mind, Barr was very concerned that he allocate the quota properly because of the bonus system implications. How should he proceed? To help him in his decision, he reviewed a note on development of a sales commission plan that he had obtained while attending a seminar on sales management the previous year (Exhibit 3).

HANOVER-BATES CHEMICAL CORPORATION

Note: An Excel file with the data for this case is available at www.wiley.com/college/cron. Go to "Students Companion Site."

James Sprague, newly appointed Northeast district sales manager for Hanover-Bates Chemical Corporation, leaned back in his chair as the door to his office slammed shut. "Great beginning," he thought. "Three days in my new job and the district's most experienced sales representative is threatening to quit."

On the previous night, James Sprague, Hank Carver (the district's most experienced sales representative), and John Follett, another senior member of the district sales staff, had met for dinner at Jim's suggestion. During dinner, Jim had mentioned that one of his top priorities would be to conduct a sales and profit analysis of the district's business in order to identify opportunities to improve the district's performance. Jim had stated that he was confident that the analysis would indicate opportunities to reallocate district sales efforts in a manner that would increase profits. As Jim had indicated during the conversation, "My experience in analyzing district sales performance data for the national sales manager has convinced me that any district's allocation of sales effort to products and customer categories can be improved." Both Carver and Follett had nodded as Jim discussed his plans.

Hank Carver was waiting when Jim arrived at the district sales office the next morning. It soon became apparent that Carver was very upset by what he perceived as Jim's criticism of how he and the other district sales representatives were doing their jobs—and more particularly, how they were allocating their time in terms of customers and products. As he concluded his heated comments, Carver had said:

> This company has made it damned clear that thirty-four years of experience don't count for anything... and now someone with not much more than two years of selling experience and two years of pushing paper for the national sales manager at corporate headquarters tells me I'm not doing my job.... Maybe it's time for me to look for a new job... and since Trumbull Chemical (Hanover-Bates's major competitor) is hiring, maybe that's where I should start looking... and I'm not the only one who feels this way.

As Jim reflected on the scene that had just occurred, he wondered what he should do. It had been made clear to him when he had been promoted to manager of the Northeast sales district that one of his top priorities should be improvement of the district's performance. As the national sales manager had said, "The Northeast sales district may rank third in dollar sales but it's our worst district in terms of profit performance."

Prior to assuming his new position, Jim had assembled the data presented in Exhibits 1 through 7 to assist him in his work. The data had been compiled from records maintained in the national sales manager's office. Although he believed that the data would provide a sound basis for a preliminary analysis of district performance. Jim had recognized that additional data would probably have to be collected when he arrived in the Northeast district (District 3). To provide himself with a frame of reference, Jim had also requested data on the north-central sales district (District 7). This district was generally considered to be one of the best, if not the best, in the company. Furthermore, the north-central district sales manager, who was only three years older than Jim, was highly regarded by the national sales manager.

THE COMPANY AND INDUSTRY

The Hanover-Bates Chemical Corporation was a leading producer of processing chemicals for the chemical plating industry. The company's production process was, in essence, a mixing operation. Chemicals purchased from a broad range of suppliers were mixed according to a variety of user-based formulas. Company sales in 2003 had reached a new high of $47,780,000, up from $43,780,000 in 2002. Net pretax profit in 2003 had been $7,644,000, up from $6,338,000 in 2002. Hanover-Bates had a strong balance sheet and the company enjoyed a favorable price-earnings ratio on its stock, which was traded on the over-the-counter market.

Although Hanover Bates did not produce commodity-type chemicals (e.g., sulfuric acid and

This case was prepared by Professor Robert W. Witt of the University of Texas, Austin. Reproduced by permission.

EXHIBIT 1 Summary Income Statements (thousands), 1999 to 2003

	1999	2000	2001	2002	2003
Sales	$39,780	$43,420	$38,120	$43,960	$47,780
Production expenses	23,868	26,994	24,396	27,224	29,126
Gross profit	15,912	16,426	13,724	16,736	18,654
Administrative expenses	5,212	5,774	5,584	5,850	6,212
Selling expenses	4,048	4,482	4,268	4,548	4,798
Pretax profit	6,652	6,170	3,872	6,338	7,644
Taxes	3,024	2,776	1,580	2,852	3,436
Net profit	$ 3,628	$ 3,394	$ 2,292	$ 3,486	$ 4,208

EXHIBIT 2 District Sales and Gross Profit Quota Performance (thousands), 2003

District	Number of Sales Reps	Sales Quota	Sales Actual	Gross Profit Quota[a]	Gross Profit Actual
1	7	$ 7,661	$ 7,812	$ 3,104	$ 3,178
2	6	7,500	7,480	3,000	3,058
3	6	7,300	6,812	2,920	2,478
4	6	6,740	6,636	2,696	2,590
5	5	6,600	6,420	2,620	2,372
6	5	6,240	6,410	2,504	2,358
7	5	5,440	6,210	2,176	2,260
		$47,600	$47,780	$19,040	$18,654

[a]District gross profit quotas were developed by the national sales manager in consultation with the district managers and took into account price competition in the respective districts.

EXHIBIT 3 District Selling Expenses, 2003

District	Sales Rep Salaries[a]	Sales Rep Commissions	Sales Rep Expenses	District Office	District Manager's Salary	District Manager's Expenses	Sales Support	Total Selling Expenses
1	$354,200	$38,852	$112,560	$42,300	$67,000	$22,920	$139,000	$ 776,832
2	286,440	37,400	101,520	42,624	68,000	24,068	142,640	702,692
3	314,760	34,060	108,872	44,246	70,000[b]	24,764	140,000	736,722
4	300,960	33,180	98,208	44,008	65,000	22,010	132,940	696,306
5	251,900	32,100	85,440	42,230	66,000	22,246	153,200	653,116
6	249,700	32,530	83,040	41,984	67,000	22,856	134,200	631,310
7	229,700	35,060	89,400	44,970	63,000	23,286	117,500	602,916
								$4,797,830

[a]Includes cost of fringe benefit program, which was 10 percent of base salary.

[b]Salary of Jim Sprague's predecessor.

EXHIBIT 4 District Contribution to Corporate Administrative Expenses and Profit, 2003

District	Sales (thousands)	Gross Profit (thousands)	Selling Expenses	Contribution
1	$ 7,812	3,178	$ 776,832	$ 2,401,168
2	7,480	3,058	702,692	2,355,308
3	6,812	2,478	737,058	1,740,942
4	6,636	2,590	696,306	1,893,694
5	6,420	2,372	653,116	1,718,884
6	6,410	2,358	630,752	1,727,248
7	6,210	2,620	600,516	2,019,484
	$47,780	$18,654	4,797,272	$13,856,648

EXHIBIT 5 District Sales and Gross Profit Performance by Account Category, 2003

	Sales by Account Category (thousands)			
District	*(A)*	*(B)*	*(C)*	*Total*
Northeast	$1,830	$3,362	$1,620	$6,812
North-Central	1,502	3,404	1,304	6,210

	Gross Profit by Account Category (thousands)			
District	*(A)*	*(B)*	*(C)*	*Total*
Northeast	$712	$1,246	$520	$2,478
North-Central	660	1,450	510	2,620

EXHIBIT 6 Potential Accounts, Active Accounts, and Account Call Coverage, 2003

	Potential Accounts			*Active Accounts*			*Account Coverage (total calls)*		
District	*(A)*	*(B)*	*(C)*	*(A)*	*(B)*	*(C)*	*(A)*	*(B)*	*(C)*
Northeast	90	381	635	53	210	313	1297	3051	2118
North-Central	60	286	499	42	182	216	1030	2618	1299

EXHIBIT 7 Product Line Data

Product	*Container*	*List Price*	*Gross Margin*	*Sales (000)*
SPX	400 lb drum	$160	$56	$7,128
ZBX	50 lb drum	152	68	8,244
CBX	50 lb drum	152	68	7,576
NBX	50 lb drum	160	70	9,060
CHX	100 lb drum	440	180	8,820
BUX	400 lb drum	240	88	6,952

others), industry customers tended to perceive minimal quality differences among the products produced by Hanover-Bates and its competitors. Given the lack of a variation in product quality and the industry-wide practice of limited advertising expenditures, field sales efforts were of major importance in the marketing programs of all firms in the industry.

Hanover-Bates's market consisted of several thousand job-shop and captive (i.e., in-house) plating operations. Chemical platers process a wide variety of materials including industrial fasteners (e.g., screws, rivets, bolts, washers), industrial components (e.g., clamps, casings, couplings), and miscellaneous items (e.g., umbrella frames, eyelets, decorative items). The chemical plating process involves the electrolytic application of metallic coatings such as zinc, cadmium, nickel, and brass.

Regardless of the degree of plating precision involved, quality control is of critical concern to all chemical platers. Extensive variation in the condition of materials received for plating requires a high level of service from the firms supplying chemicals to platers. This service is normally provided by the sales representatives of the firm(s) which supply the plater with processing chemicals.

Hanover-Bates and the majority of the firms in its industry produced the same line of basic processing chemicals for the chemical plating industry. The line consisted of a trisodium phosphate cleaner (SPX), anesic aldehyde brightening agents for zinc plating (ZBX), cadmium plating (CBX), and nickel plating (NBX), a protective postplating chromate dip (CHX), and a protective burnishing compound (BUX). The company's product line is detailed in Exhibit 7.

COMPANY SALES ORGANIZATION

The sales organization consisted of forty sales representatives operating in seven sales districts. Sales representatives' salaries ranged from $28,000 to $48,000 with fringe-benefit costs amounting to an additional 10 percent of salary. In addition to their salaries, Hanover-Bates's representatives received commissions of 0.5 percent of their dollar sales volume on all sales up to their sales quotas. The commission on sales in excess of quota was 1 percent.

In 2002, the national sales manager of Hanover-Bates had developed a sales program based on selling the full line of Hanover-Bates products. Anticipated benefits included the following: (1) Sales volume per account would be greater and selling costs as a percentage of sales would decrease; (2) a Hanover-Bates sales representative could justify spending more time with such an account, thus becoming more knowledgeable about the account's business and better able to provide technical assistance and identify selling opportunities; (3) full-line sales would strengthen Hanover-Bates's competitive position by reducing the likelihood of account loss to other plating chemical suppliers (a problem that existed in multiple-supplier situations).

The national sales manager's 2002 sales program had also included the following account call frequency guidelines: A accounts (major accounts generating $24,000 or more in yearly sales)—two calls per month; B accounts (medium-size accounts generating $12,000 to $23,999 in yearly sales)—one call per month; C accounts (small accounts generating less than $12,000 yearly in sales)—one call every two months. The account call frequency guidelines were developed by the national sales manager after discussions with the district managers. The national sales manager had been concerned about the optimum allocation of sales efforts to accounts and felt that the guidelines would increase the efficiency of the company's sales force, although not all of the district sales managers agreed with this conclusion.

It was common knowledge in Hanover-Bates' corporate sales office that Jim Sprague's predecessor as Northeast district sales manager had not been one of the company's better district sales managers. His attitude toward the sales plans and programs of the national sales manager had been one of reluctant compliance rather than acceptance and support. When the national sales manager succeeded in persuading Jim Sprague's predecessor to take early retirement, he had been faced with the lack of an available qualified replacement.

Hank Carver, who most of the sales representatives had assumed would get the district manager's job, had been passed over in part because he would be 65 in three years. The national sales manager had not wanted to face the same replacement problem again in three years and had wanted someone in the position who would be more likely to be responsive to the company's sales plans and policies. The appointment of Jim Sprague as district manager had caused considerable talk, not only in the district but also at corporate headquarters. In fact, the national sales manager had warned Jim that "a lot of people are expecting you to fall on your face. They don't think you have the experience to handle the job, in particular, and to manage and motivate a group of sales representatives most of whom are considerably older and more experienced than you." The national sales manager had concluded by saying, "I think you can handle the job, Jim. I think you can manage those sales reps and improve the district's profit performance, and I'm depending on you to do both."

HYDE-PHILLIP APPLIANCES

Note: An Excel file with the data for this case is available at www.wiley.com/college/cron. Go to "Students Companion Site."

Two engineers, Bill Parks and Anne Smith, founded Hyde-Phillip in 1990. The company specialized in the manufacture of high-end outdoor kitchen appliances. Bill was chairman of the board, and Anne was director of research and development. For the first ten years of its life,

This case was prepared by Douglas J. Dalrymple of Indiana University.

EXHIBIT 1 Quarterly Sales for the PC220 and PC440

	2001		*2002*		*2003*	
Quarter	*PC220*	*PC440*	*PC220*	*PC440*	*PC220*	*PC440*
1	1950	770	3150	545	2924	350
2	2920	620	2600	450	3380	420
3	2560	623	3002	400	2554	310
4	3330	830	4250	639	2800	775

Hyde-Phillip enjoyed steady growth in sales and profits. Hyde-Phillip's success was based on providing customers with superior performance at prices slightly above average. However, in 2000 aggressive price cutting by large competitors began to erode sales growth. Hyde-Phillip's revenue peaked in 2002 at $75 million.

SOLVING HYDE-PHILLIP'S PROBLEMS

Although customers were willing to pay for high-quality outdoor appliances in the 1990s, this strategy did not attract many buyers in the cost-conscious 2000s. Bill Parks realized that the company had to do a better job of both marketing and cost reduction. The company currently employed a small sales force but relied primarily on a network of local dealers to sell its appliances. Bill knew that the company needed a stronger customer focus, so he hired a CEO with a marketing background. As a result, the company started to pay more attention to marketing activities and began to prepare detailed marketing plans for each product line. Jane Austin, a recent business graduate, was hired as a marketing assistant to help with the planning.

Part of Jane's responsibility was to estimate sales for the PC220 and PC440 outdoor grills for the next year. In the past, these forecasts had been developed using judgmental procedures. Jane knew that the CEO expected a more thorough analysis of sales trends for the 2004 marketing plan. When she was in school, Jane had become familiar with the use of computers to predict future sales. This seemed to be a good time to make use of her computer expertise.

ENTERING THE DATA

Jane entered the quarterly sales data for PC220 from Exhibit 1 in the first twelve spaces on her spreadsheet. Sales for 2001 were entered as observations 1 through 4, sales for 2002 were entered as observations 5 through 8, and sales for 2003 were entered as observations 9 through 12. Sales figures for PC440 were entered in a separate column.

As a first step in analyzing the data, Jane thought she would plot the sales figures to see what trends were evident. Sales were placed on the Y axis and time was plotted on the X axis. Next she decided to calculate some quarterly seasonal indexes for the two products to see if seasonal adjustments were needed.

SELECTING FORECASTING METHODS

The first method Jane tried with the outdoor grill sales data was the naive approach. Sales in quarter 1 were used to predict sales in quarter 2, then sales in quarter 2 were used to predict sales in quarter 3 and so on until all the periods had been predicted. Once she had forecasts for 11 periods, she could calculate the average forecasting error for the naive method using the formula for MAPE.

The second method Jane decided to use was the moving average. With this technique, sales in several periods are averaged to give a forecast of sales in the next period. To use this method, she had to decide how many periods to include in her forecast. She decided to start with a two-period moving average and compare her results with those from three- and four-period moving averages. Her decision on the length of moving average would then be made on which method produced the lowest average forecasting error.

Jane knew that a variation of the moving average known as exponential smoothing would sometimes produce lower forecasting errors than the moving average procedure. However, with this method she would have to select an appropriate value for the smoothing constant. These constants could vary in size from 0.01 to 1.0 with low values giving forecasts that lagged the data and high values that were similar to naive forecasts. She decided to try out smoothing constants of different sizes to see which one gave the lowest MAPE.

The fourth method Jane selected was simple regression. This approach calculates a trend line equation that can be used to forecast the four quarters of 2004. While this method does well when there is a trend in the sales data, it can lead to large forecasting errors when there are changes of direction. The *R* statistic printed out by her computer program would give her some idea of how well the regression equation fit the computer sales data.

Once Jane had run her four methods through the historical sales data in Exhibit 1, the MAPE values that she had calculated would help her select a method to predict outdoor grill sales in 2004. This choice was complicated by the need to decide whether to seasonally adjust the sales data for either the PC220 or PC440 grills.

Another issue that Jane was concerned about was whether to report one set of quarterly forecasts for 2004 for each grill line or to average the forecasts of the best two methods. Although her software program allowed Jane to try many different forecasting techniques, it did not tell her which forecasts to include in her report.

CASE 14 INJECT PLASTICS

Note: An Excel file with the data for this case is available at www.wiley.com/college/cron. Go to "Students Companion Site."

Roger Zelazny, the sales manager for the Southeast District of Inject Plastics, was shaken after attending the December sales executive meeting in Louisiana. Although Inject Plastics had increased sales 12 percent last year compared to 2 percent industry sales growth, Mr. Brand, Vice President of Marketing, had ordered every district sales manager to cut staff by 30 percent on January 16th! The notice to the fired employees would have to go out on January 2nd. Roger would have to determine who was going to be fired and then let them know they were without a job. Thinking about having to notify three people on his staff that they were terminated was going to make the holidays very grim indeed.

INJECT PLASTICS

Inject Plastics is a plastics molding and manufacturing company with plants in Louisiana, Texas, and New Jersey. One of the company's unique advantages is its flexibility in manufacturing; it can shape everything from delicate medical devices to car parts and toothbrush handles. Inject Plastics created molds, made plastic of the appropriate strength and flexibility out of petroleum products, and then created the plastic part for its buyers. The finished parts are shipped to customers, who handle final product assembly and sales.

Due to raw material needs, Inject Plastic's manufacturing plants are located near major oil refineries. The sales staff had to discover customers, coordinate manufacturing and logistics needs, and service accounts. Because of the huge number of applications of plastic parts in the U.S. economy, the individual salespeople called on a wide variety of manufacturers across many industries.

Last year Inject Plastics generated $200 million in sales, a 12 percent increase from last year. The plastics molding and manufacturing industry was quite mature. Because of the huge number of plastics applications, industry sales tended to follow the trends in the overall U.S. economy. Although Inject Plastics was relatively small for the industry, its manufacturing and sales expertise had generated sales growth higher than industry averages as well as higher profit margins over the last ten years.

The plastics molding and manufacturing business was highly competitive. Sales were generated by having the lowest unit costs along with flexible delivery. Most large purchasers used just-in-time inventory systems, which meant that Inject Plastics had to have highly flexible manufacturing and logistics systems. Even small cost savings could shave prices, which could mean the difference between getting and losing an order.

THE CUSTOM WEB SITE INITIATIVE

Nine months ago the logistics manager suggested that Inject develop a customized Web strategy. Inject would build an individual, password-protected Web site for each customer. An individual site was necessary to protect customer trade secrets. The customer could log into

This case was prepared by Avery Abernethy, Professor of Marketing, Auburn University.

the site and check the status of orders and shipments. The customer would also be able to make new orders, adjust previous orders, and ask questions of the manufacturing, logistics, or sales staff. Each salesperson would be responsible for answering the customer sales questions from the Web site for customers in his or her territory. The manufacturing and logistics manager would answer other questions.

Inject accepted this proposal and spent $200,000 setting up the customized customer Web strategy. Inject also hired a new technology staffer to maintain the site, coordinate customer questions, and ensure that a prompt and accurate response is given to each customer question. The new technology staffer's pay is $60,000, including benefits.

The district sales managers were concerned that the customized Web strategy would be resisted by the sales force, if change lowered commissions. After thinking it through, Mr. Brand decided that the 1 percent commission would apply to both Web sales and sales processed by the salesperson for firms located in their territory.

The salespeople were very enthusiastic about the customized Web site initiative when it started on July 1. Because a lot of routine order taking, inventory management, and logistics issues would be communicated directly to the relevant Inject manager, the customized Web initiative freed up a lot of salesperson time. The salespeople used this time to generate a record number of new customers. Sales to new customers were a major factor behind the 12 percent increase in sales. Existing customers were also impressed with the service improvements and increased their orders.

By December, approximately 25 percent of all orders were being placed through the individual customer Web sites. Much of the routine communication between customers and Impact no longer went through the salespeople and instead often went directly to logistics and manufacturing.

DECEMBER MEETING WITH MR. BRAND

Mr. Brand started off the sales executive meeting by lavishing praise on the four sales managers. He noted that average sales per district had increased to $50 million. Customer complaints were down and the sales growth for Inject greatly exceeded the industry average.

Mr. Caine, the logistics manager, added additional good news. Raw materials and work-in-process inventory levels were down. Turnaround on orders had improved. The number of manufacturing mistakes were also down, primarily due to cutting down on miscommunication between Inject and its customers. Overall, manufacturing and logistics costs per dollar of sales had declined, which had padded Inject's profit margins. After answering a few questions, Mr. Caine left the meeting.

Mr. Brand then started a new PowerPoint presentation. The presentation focused on salesperson efficiency. Because the customized Web program had improved customer communication and handled an increasing amount of routine sales tasks, the efficiency of the sales staff had decreased. "Our new technology has improved productivity everywhere but the sales staff. Salespeople continue to get large commissions, even though an ever larger proportion of sales efforts are being automated through the custom web initiative. I think that by this time next year 50 percent of routine orders and customer contacts will be through the Web."

"We need to change our sales incentive program," Brand continued, "and make the sales force more efficient. Inject is going to do this through a number of changes. First, the commission rate for sales to existing customers would be cut from 1 percent to 0.1 percent. Second, the commission rate for the first twelve months of sales to new customers would be 2 percent. We really want the salespeople to generate new business. With all of the sales time freed up with the Web program, the salespeople can concentrate on getting new customers. Third, the annual salary of salespeople would increase from $25,000 to $60,000. We are doing this to retain our best salespeople. Average total compensation in the industry is $75,000 per salesperson, we want to remain competitive in retaining our best salespeople. Fourth, each district will terminate three salespeople. This would cut the total number of salespeople from 40 to 28."

Brand went on to inform them that salespeople being laid off would be notified on January 2nd and that their last day of work would be January 16th.

"Before we make any final decisions and notify the salespeople," Brand stated, "each district sales manager needs to get some information to me. First, identify the three salespeople that will be laid off. I also need the criteria you used to select the salespeople for termination. Second, estimate the total sales costs in your district next year. I don't think that the number of new customers or sales generated from new customers will drop. The two-week salary of the fired salespeople can also be disregarded because it is not a reoccurring cost."

"Third, send a copy of your draft letter terminating each employee. I want to review them before they are sent. Last, let me know how you are going to communicate the changes in the compensation plan to the

EXHIBIT 1 Salesperson Performance and Compensation Last Year: Southeast District

Salesperson	*Sex*	*Age*	*Years with Company*	*Total Sales Last Year*	*Salary*	*Commission*	*New Customers Generated*	*Total Sales By New Customers*
Bret	M	62	32	$6,000,000	$25,000	$60,000	9	$700,000
Cathy	F	35	7	$6,250,000	$25,000	$62,500	6	$500,000
Ethan	M	42	15	$4,900,000	$25,000	$49,000	5	$300,000
Gretchen	F	28	2	$4,300,000	$25,000	$43,000	5	$330,000
Mark	M	63	41	$4,850,000	$25,000	$48,500	4	$220,000
Matthew	M	50	5	$4,900,000	$25,000	$49,000	4	$600,000
Sam	M	45	10	$4,750,000	$25,000	$47,000	6	$270,000
Susan	F	48	22	$5,300,000	$25,000	$53,000	5	$300,000
Trey	M	48	17	$5,000,000	$25,000	$50,000	5	$340,000
Wally	M	26	1	$3,700,000	$25,000	$37,000	2	$75,000

Note: New customers and sales generated by new customers is for the entire year. Sales by new customers is part of the total sales last year. For example, Bret had sales of $5,300,000 from existing customers and $700,000 from new customers.

salespeople we are retaining. We want to maintain a high morale level with the people who are the future of the company."

At this point, Jeff Corwin pointed out that both he and the company had promised the salespeople that the custom Web site initiative would not affect sales pay. "How do we know that these staffing changes will not harm the growth in sales. If it is not broke, why fix it?"

Mr. Brand seemed a bit taken back by Jeff's comment. Brand off-handedly said that, "If you think that my strategic change will hurt sales, put your objections in writing along with specific estimates of how you think your suggestion will affect both sales costs and revenue generation. Remember, we are in a highly competitive industry. We must keep striving to lower costs if we want to survive."

Brand then wrapped up the meeting. He said, "Each of you has a week to get all of the information to me. After I get your reports, I will make a final decision on Inject's sales strategy. You are not to communicate any information about this potential strategic change to anyone on your staff."

Roger was in a state of shock. Since sales performance had been so good last year, he was expecting to be able to tell his salespeople that the senior executives were proud of them and supported all of their hard work. Exhibit 1 provides information on the ten people in Roger's district, along with their sales performance and compensation last year. Instead of praise, he had to fire three salespeople and tell the rest that their compensation package had been radically changed. Roger wondered if the new plan would cut the pay of his remaining staff. If that happened, he might lose his best people. He would also have to restructure the sales territories to cover the customers from the laid off salespeople. This would add further turmoil to his sales staff.

Roger wondered if Mr. Oberon, the company president, was aware of Brand's plan to fire one-third of the sales force. Oberon has an "open-door policy," so it would be possible to drop in and alert him to the proposed strategy. As his stomach churned, Roger wondered if he should follow up on that job feeler for a sales management position he got from a competitor two weeks ago.

MILLIGAN PHARMACEUTICALS

On February 1, 2008 Mark Reid celebrated twenty years as CEO and chairman of the board of Milligan Pharmaceuticals, a global pharmaceutical company. The company's major revenue

This case was prepared by Gouri Gupte, Ph.D. student in Health Professions, and Thomas E. DeCarlo of the University of Alabama at Birmingham.

streams come from the development of pharmaceutical drugs and biotechnology products. Milligan is organized into four business units: branded drugs, generics, "me-too" drugs, and over-the-counter (OTC) drugs. The company has a strong reputation as a leader in the pharmaceutical industry.

Over the past twenty years, Reid's leadership style has been described as a benevolent dictator. His structured, top-down management style has given Reid an unusually high level of control over the company relative to other firms in the industry. His vision and uncanny ability to recognize underdeveloped opportunities have produced some very profitable years for Milligan. However, the last five years (2003–2007), Milligan's revenue growth has not met expectations. While some of the blame can be attributed to Reid's recent misses in developing the next big drug, other factors such as recent drug legislation, the acceleration in generic drug introductions, and new blockbuster drugs by other companies have also contributed to the company's lackluster growth in revenues and earnings. In addition, Milligan's organizational culture has evolved from one of innovation to maintaining the status quo. This has resulted in a slow down of innovation and research and development initiatives.

A NEW MANAGEMENT TEAM

At the Annual Meeting held in March 2007, Reid expressed his concerns about the change in culture and stagnant growth to the Board and his decision of adding new marketing personnel. The Board agreed there was a need for a new aggressive style of marketing and embraced Reid's decision to make changes to its management team. The first hire was Christopher Roper, the new Executive Vice President of Marketing. Prior to joining Milligan in June 2007, Roper had been the Vice President of Wellcare Pharmaceuticals for eight years. He had also served as the Vice President of Cure-All and Vice President of Georgia Pharmaceuticals, the parent company of both Cure-All and Wellcare Pharmaceuticals.

Roper was known for his efficient organizational and leadership skills, as well as his leadership abilities in growing sales revenues. Roper knew that he needed to adopt some aggressive marketing strategies to grow sales and marketshare and the only way to do that was to surround himself with outstanding management talent. With that in mind, he appointed the first team member, Katrina Graham, as the Vice President of Marketing. She had more than fifteen years of marketing and executive management experience as the Director of Marketing for LifeCare Pharmaceuticals, with specialization in marketing at the physician level. Graham subsequently asked Candice Griffin, who had worked with her at LifeCare, to join Milligan as Director of Marketing. Griffin had eight years' experience in marketing and field sales management. Roper also promoted Kimberly Lathan to Associate Director of Marketing; they would manage the regional directors. Lathan had been with Milligan since 1995 and had overseen the sales recruiting function for the On-Call agency since 1998. The On-Call agency had consistently been the most profitable unit in the company.

A STRATEGIC REVIEW

Mark Reid had high expectations for this new team because his concern for the flat revenues demanded quick action. Roper, after assembling the team, asked for a complete strategic marketing review from an independent marketing research company that specialized in working with pharmaceutical companies. In September 2008, the team met at a conference room at Pinehurst, North Carolina, away from the company's offices, to hear and analyze the consultants' report. This report would provide a foundation for the strategic change in direction needed to meet the Board's, Reid's, and the shareholders' expectations. The managers were aware that crucial discussions would revolve around the development of a new sales force strategy because only a sharp growth in pharmaceutical sales would result in a significant increase in corporate-wide revenues.

MILLIGAN'S SALES FORCE

Similar to many pharmaceutical companies, Milligan distributed its drugs primarily through independent medical representatives (MR). At the beginning of 2007, there were approximately 2,000 independent medical representatives distributing Milligan products. These MRs typically represented two to three pharmaceutical companies, and although the MRs did not work directly for Milligan, they were given extensive training and support and were responsible for selling the entire line of Milligan products. In addition to providing widespread geographic market coverage throughout the United States, MRs managed all hospital contracts in their territory. Hospitals liked working with the MRs because they represented a variety of other pharmaceutical companies, which enabled them the flexibility to provide better deals to physicians and pharmacies. First-year gross margin commission rates for the drugs sold by the MRs were in the 50 to 60 percent range.

The MRs are managed by independent sales companies specializing in the pharmaceutical industry. Milligan's policy is that any sales company employing Milligan MRs must have one sales manager for every ten MRs it has on staff. Thus, there are approximately 200 sales managers who oversee the 2,000 "Milligan" MRs. Not only do the managers motivate and lead the MRs in their sales tasks, but they work directly with the twenty Milligan Regional Directors who oversee the sales and distribution function of these independent companies. Because of the unique requirements of Milligan, the managers are provided specialized training and administrative support. The managers are paid a small salary subsidy during the training period, but then it is converted to a commission-only basis. The managers earn commission overrides based on the sales of Milligan products by their MRs in their territory. Milligan has always paid competitive commission rates and, as a result, the sales companies have many long-time loyal MRs and managers. One of the negatives of the position was a lack of upward career potential as an MR and, more important, the high commission rate made it an expensive strategy for Milligan.

THE CONSULTANTS' PRESENTATION

Christopher Roper convened the meeting in one of the conference rooms at Pinehurst with his new team members. Never one to waste time, he started, "Well, team, I am pleased to introduce to you Jocelyn Stewart and Tony Pirom from Austin Notes, the marketing research company assisting us in our project."

Pirom began, "Ladies and gentleman, last week we emailed you the documents and the complete report. I am sure you have them in front of you on your laptops. But we are here today to give a summary of the key points and issues and answer any questions you may have. As you are aware, apart from conducting an overall market analysis and survey, we also interviewed several Milligan executives. This helped us better understand the major issues that need to be addressed. The number one concern has been the modest annual revenue growth for the past five years, as compared to your competitors. Milligan has always been among the top pharmaceutical companies and has an excellent workforce. But, there are areas where immediate action needs to be taken. These have been highlighted in our analysis."

COMPETITIVE ANALYSIS

"While conducting the analysis, we compared your company to thirteen other pharmaceutical companies. Seven of these we refer to as 'indirect competitors' and six of them are what we call 'direct competitors.' As the name implies, direct competitors are those you compete with on a day-to-day basis for drug sales and new agents. In other words, these companies directly compete with Milligan on strategically important drugs. And then we also have the 'indirect competitors,' which are pharmaceutical companies that sell drugs but do not have a strong brand presence in Milligan's strategic focal areas. All of the rating services we have cited rate Milligan's MRs as the highest in terms of product selling ability. Only five of the thirteen peer companies in our report had similar ratings. Financial strength of the company is considered as the competitive advantage by a few, while the others commented about the conservativeness of the company's approach."

PERFORMANCE ANALYSIS

"This slide (Exhibit 1) is a comparison of your operating performance over the 2002–2007 periods with the other thirteen peer pharmaceutical companies. We can clearly see in the annual percent change data that drug sales have grown more slowly than the direct and indirect competitors. The low growth in the productivity of your MRs as compared to competitors appears to be a strong reason. We'll discuss the possible reasons for this later in our presentation. However, it's not all bad news. As you can see from the same annual percent change data, the net gain before pharmacy contract discounts is greater than the indirect competitors but less than your direct competitors. On further analysis, we found that your revenue stream from North and South Carolina and Virginia is larger than any other states."

"So, why do you think our drug sales are lower than those of the competitors?" Katrina Graham asked.

"Katrina, that is a good question," Jocelyn Stewart replied. "Our analysis validates our earlier assumptions that Milligan has been concentrating too much in the Southeast, where the physician number can be lower than in the Northeast. A number of peer companies have a strong footprint in the Northeast. Also, we have a feeling that some of the agents have not capitalized on the opportunities in their markets, but the regional difference remains the most important concern."

PRODUCT COMPARISON

"Katrina, I hope we answered your question. We now move on to discuss the sales trends of Milligan products." Tony Pirom resumed, "The next

EXHIBIT 1 Milligan's Summary of Operations 2003–2007 (Dollar Amounts in Millions)

	2003	*2004*	*2005*	*2006*	*2007*
Drug Sales	$648.1	$718.0	$716.3	$727.2	$768.9
Net investment income	250.1	295.3	313.0	326.6	338.7
Other income	32.0	25.8	24.1	28.0	26.8
Total income	930.2	1039.1	1053.4	1081.8	1134.4
Total expenses	802.3	916.8	890.0	896.9	930.6
Net gain before pharmacy contract discounts	127.9	122.3	163.4	184.9	203.8
Discounts to pharmacy contracts	18.8	25.3	24.7	23.8	22.5
Net gain after discounts	109.1	97.0	138.7	161.1	181.3

	Change from 2003–2007			*Average Annual Percent Change*		
	MP	*Direct Competitor Average*	*Indirect Competitor Average*	*MP*	*Direct Competitor Average*	*Indirect Competitor Average*
Drug Sales	$120.8	$850.9	$3,182.0	4.4%	7.5%	11.7%
Net investment income	88.6	3717.7	723.4	7.9%	9.1%	6.2%
Total income	204.2	796.5	3,590.10	5.1%	4.7%	8.6%
Total expenses	(128.3)	(528.9)	(3337.8)	−3.8%	−3.5%	−8.8%
Net gain before pharmacy contract discounts	75.9	267.6	252.30	12.4%	14.4%	6.3%

EXHIBIT 2 Product Mix Trends (Percent of First-Year Commission)

	2005	*2006*	*2007*
MILLIGAN PHARMACEUTICALS			
Branded drugs	76%	70%	63%
Generics	7	11	12
Me-too drugs	13	14	17
OTC	4	5	7
Group	0	0	0
Total	100%	100%	100%
DIRECT COMPETITORS			
Branded drugs	78%	75%	75%
Generics	7	6	6
Me-too drugs	4	6	7
OTC	5	6	8
Group	7	7	5
Total	100%	100%	100%
INDIRECT COMPETITORS			
Branded drugs	76%	78%	77%
Generics	5	5	5
Me-too drugs	8	9	9
OTC	3	3	4
Group	7	6	4
Total	100%	100%	100%

slide (Exhibit 2) presents a competitive analysis of Milligan's product mix, based on first-year commissions. As the exhibit illustrates, Milligan has had a steady decline in drug sales, down from 76 percent, based on the first-year commissions, to 63 percent since 2005. The other pharmaceutical companies have shown a relative consistency over the same time period. The MRs are selling more generic drugs, OTC drugs, and "me-too" drugs."

"That's interesting. Why would do you think our MRs are selling more generics and OTC?" Chris Roper asked.

"Our consultants have always observed that selling these drugs is easier than selling branded drugs," Tony Pirom answered. "Because of the new review systems by managed care organizations, physicians buy these easily, and the salespeople find them easier to explain. As a result, generic drugs are more supported in the general market even by the sales force and, since generics never have expiring patent issues, the contracts can be renewed more easily. Thus, at the end of the day, the easier job gets done."

SALES FORCE COMPARISON

"How do our MRs feel about the products we give them to sell?" Kimberly Lathan questioned.

Jocelyn Stewart explained, "If we move to the next slide (Exhibit 3), I think it would help answer your question. As you can see, in comparison with other companies, Milligan's MRs had a lower satisfaction level with the variety of drugs you have to offer and also a lower satisfaction level with new drugs being developed. They felt that the company was not as market driven as it should be."

EXHIBIT 3 Sales Force Ratings of Milligan's Products (Percent of Agents Agreeing)

Agents' Overall Assessment of Company's Products	*Milligan Pharmaceuticals*	*Norm*
I am pleased with the variety of products our company offers	68%	79%
I am satisfied with our company's development of new products	34	67
Our company is market driven, responding to the needs of its target market with appropriate products and services	27	68

"Jocelyn, as we are discussing the subject of how MRs feel, how has Milligan stacked up in relation to the recruitment and retention level of the sales force as compared to our competitors?" Candice Griffin pondered. "I know that we don't technically hire our MRs, but we play a big role in helping to recruit and train them. So in a sense, our performance here can be attributed to our efforts."

"Well, another important question, Candice. Our study demonstrates that only 35 percent of new MRs whom you helped recruit and train made it through the first year, which is 15 percentage points below the direct competitor's average. At the same time, only 15 percent are making it through the first two years. And those who stay for more than four years comprise only 5 percent.

"The next slide (Exhibit 4) summarizes the situation pretty well. The first part of the overhead shows that in 2007, recruits represented 48 percent of the base sales force, as compared with 29 percent and 38 percent for the two peer groups. At the same time, an important point worth noticing is the declining Milligan's MR numbers and the stable or increasing competitor's numbers. Likewise, Milligan's MR turnover rates have been higher than other competitors. Finally, the slide shows that only 35 percent of your MR sales reps have been with you more than five years as compared with 40 percent and 46 percent for the two comparison groups. And this is a serious issue when we consider that in most marketing cycles, salespeople are most productive after five years."

"Tony, what is your analysis on Milligan's MR productivity compared with the peer groups?" Chris Roper asked.

"We did analyze the issue of productivity closely. We found that Milligan MRs earned, on average, lower first-year commissions (not including renewal commissions) in each year as compared with their peers. Your base sales force had average first-year commissions of about \$44,000 versus \$49,000 for the direct competitors and almost \$45,000 for the indirect competitor peer group.

"Were you able to confirm why our productivity is lower, Tony?"

"Yes, Chris. Although there are many factors that affect productivity, our team felt that Milligan's product variety was lower than the competitors. This may have resulted in fewer productive senior MRs selling fewer of your products. It seems that the MRs may be meeting their performance goals with you, but they then place other business with other pharmaceuticals in order to meet goals there.

"We did not find any evidence that the managers overseeing the MRs consider the sales levels of Milligan as being too low. In fact, the managers believe that they have been setting high but attainable goals for the MRs. However, while studying the performance standards the first-year MRs must meet, 69 percent of the MRs believed they were modest or too low. Finally, we noted that the managers had considerably fewer relationship management activities with physicians than the managers of other peer companies. It is no surprise that many managers, while very capable, seemed to be too busy to perform these important relationship management activities."

"Milligan's Regional Directors and managers also seem to have a contrasting opinion on what is required of MRs. We've determined that over 90 percent of your managers felt that they give a realistic preview of the job activities to a recruit, yet only 32 percent of the new MRs agreed with it. Moreover, when the managers were questioned about the activities that they expected from an MR prior to signing a contract with them, we received a contrary response from the new MRs who were asked the same question. Seventy-three percent of your new hires have not worked as full-time MRs previously, so it is likely that they may not be completely aware of the requirements of being a pharmaceutical industry rep."

"Chris, I think that we have covered all the points that we thought would be relevant to your planning process. We will, of course, be available to answer

EXHIBIT 4 Sales Force Recruitment and Retention

RECRUITS AS A PERCENT OF BASE FORCE				
	Milligan Pharmaceuticals			
	Rate	*No. of Recruits*	*Direct Competitors*	*Indirect Competitors*
2007	48%	280	29%	38%
2006	58	378	31	41
2005	34	316	30	40
2004	40	459	30	45
2003	42	501	33	41

PERCENT CHANGE IN BASE FORCE			
	Milligan Pharmaceuticals	*Direct Competitors*	*Indirect Competitors*
2007	−6%	−1%	−1%
2006	−11	−2	2
2005	−31	−3	1
2004	−2	1	9
2003	−2	1	6
TURNOVER RATE			
2007	36%	24%	28%
2006	44	24	28
2005	48	23	28
2004	30	23	25
2003	31	24	25
DISTRIBUTION OF SALES AGENTS BY YEARS OF SERVICE			
Years of Service			
1	35%	50%	53%
2	15	14	15
3	10	9	9
4	5	7	7
5+	35	46	40

additional questions you have as you proceed with your planning," Tony concluded.

"Thank you, Jocelyn and Tony. We appreciate all the assistance you have provided us. We'll let you go now and continue with our discussion. But we'll be in touch if we need more information."

OPTIONS

"Well, I think we would all agree that all these findings were certainly very sobering." Chris began, "Obviously, there is a lot of work to be done. The Board and Mark Reid expect us to achieve substantial growth and profitability within a few years. The target is to grow earnings per share by 10 percent per annum and achieve above average returns on capital. Katrina, what do you think our strategy should be?"

"Chris, at this point, we need a change in our marketing efforts. We have been focused on using MRs to sell our products, but there seems to be some clarification needed of what we expect from them. Having an ineffective sale force means less business, less growth, and less profits. As a result, we have fewer resources to innovate and develop new competitive drugs. It is a vicious cycle.... I am sure, Candice, that you have something to say."

"I absolutely agree," Candice joined in. "We are aware that our MRs and managers are very important to the whole system. Our core base of customers, physicians and pharmacists, has been acquired through this channel. We have many long-term, loyal managers. As you all know, my father worked here too and helped oversee the agencies that recruited the managers and MRs. The appropriate strategy at this point would be to improve the quality of new recruits, provide better training, and enhance their loyalty and commitment to selling our products. If we can do these things, we will grow faster and there will be an increase in profitability."

"I second that, Candice," Kim agreed, "but as we look to the future I think we need to make more drastic changes. The report very clearly shows that the independent MRs are not as productive as we would like. I propose a new idea. We should contract with the best of the 200 managers to sell exclusively for us. In other words, we should consider hiring the top managers to become exclusive Milligan sales representatives, which is something we've never had. Also, since we will be hiring experienced people, it would provide us dedicated reps who would make an immediate impact on our bottom line. We would continue with our current strategy of using MRs to sell our products, but we supplement this effort with enough of our dedicated reps to cover the largest markets. This would ensure that we have adequate market coverage. Instead of using all twenty regional directors in the oversight and recruiting capacity as we do now, we could outsource the recruiting function to independent marketing organizations and have the directors oversee the managers. We could provide the directors with an override commission on sales made in their territory."

"Candice, I know you used this kind of system at LifeCare, but wouldn't this be a radical transition for Milligan?" Katrina responded, "My experience makes me feel that the MRs would be terribly threatened. And imagine the problems that might arise if our managers run into the independent MR trying to sell the same drug to a physician or pharmacist! However, I also know the MRs don't have enough of an incentive to be loyal to our products. I am also worried about the lack of control we currently have over what they sell and over the quality of their work with physicians. Something needs to be changed."

"Chris, you asked about various options," Katrina continued. "I guess this discussion highlights that both of the options, maintaining status quo or making the changes Kim suggested, carry concerns that we will have to address. A final growth option is acquisition of some other small drug company. We definitely have the financial strength to do that, but even then we are going to have to address the issue of how we distribute, how we sell our products to our customers."

"Yes, Katrina, distribution is the primary issue," Chris responded. "We would all agree that before making a decision, we will have to deal with a number of issues. Here's what I would like you all to do. I'd like each of you to individually analyze our situation and develop recommendations as to how we should proceed. We could all meet in two weeks with your presentations. I will check my calendar and send you all an e-mail to confirm the specific time and venue for our discussions."

NATIONAL MUTUAL FUNDS: RETAIL SERVICES DIVISION

Harry Smallwood, president of National Mutual Funds (NMF) Retail Services, pondered the future of his department and operating unit. NMF had spent most of the 1990s building its brokerage stock trading business to accompany its core mutual fund business. However, because of the market slowdown of 2001, trading volume at its call centers had substantially slowed and profit margins were being squeezed.

Top management at NMF responded to this business challenge with a set of directives. NMF had built a culture of strong commitment to its people and believed that the stock market would bounce back in 2002. So instead of laying off people, as many competitors had done, senior executives chose to invest in the company's future. One directive was to reorganize the call centers in the Retail Services Division in an effort to grow its asset base in the face of a tough market. The reorganization called for traders, people responsible for placing the more complex transactions, to take on more of a selling function by proactively calling current clients to determine their interest in purchasing additional stock instruments. If they detected sufficient buying interest, the client would be forwarded

Brian Robb, Professor Daniel Goebel, and Professor William Cron prepared this case as the basis for class discussion rather than to illustrate either effective or ineffective handling of an administrative situation. Certain names and numbers have been disguised.

to sales representatives. To generate increased business, it would be very important that the clients were "hot" prospects for an immediate selling effort. This change in the trader's job description would require more interaction and cooperation between traders and sales representatives at NMF's call centers.

Smallwood had just come from a planning meeting with his vice presidents. It was obvious from the meeting that there were a lot of issues involved in implementing the reorganization directive. Training and retraining would be needed. Team building and change management would be critical. The success of the program would depend on a smooth handoff of the selling process between traders and sales representatives.

It was also clear from the meeting that the reorganization would be an emotionally charged situation. Traders would be concerned about being subservient to the salespeople. Salespeople would be concerned about traders becoming too involved in the selling process and potentially costing them sales and, more important, bonus money. In short, Smallwood knew the program for implementing the reorganization directive would need to foster coordination, trust, and team spirit. To add more pressure, Smallwood's management team needed to design and implement a successful reorganization plan within two months. One thing of which he was now fully aware was that the whole program would be much more involved and complex than it first appeared.

THE BROKERAGE SERVICE INDUSTRY

Brokerage service firms can be distinguished from each other based on their participation in three key industry sectors: full-service trading of stocks and bonds, mutual funds, and discount trading. Merrill Lynch, one of the largest financial services firms in the world, focuses primarily on full-service trading of stocks and bonds. Merrill does not offer its own line of mutual funds, as does NMF, but makes the majority of its profits from actively managing customer accounts and charging commissions. Commissions at Merrill run from $75 to $150 on average because of the additional services offered to investors. Brokers at Merrill can place discretionary trades in customer accounts, for instance, as market conditions dictate. The value proposition of a full-service broker is that the extra money paid in commissions will generate higher returns because the broker is armed with exceptional market information, the skills to understand the meaning and significance of the information, and attention to the needs of individual investors.

Mutual funds allow individuals to buy shares in a fund, which a fund manager in turn invests in various types of securities. This allows individual investors to diversify their risk across a number of securities without spending the time to investigate individual stocks. While the Massachusetts Investors Trust introduced the first modern mutual fund in March 1924, mutual funds really began to grow in popularity in the 1940s and 1950s. In 1940, there were fewer than 80 funds with total assets of $500 million. Twenty years later, there were 160 funds with $17 billion in assets. Today there are more mutual funds available than individual stocks, and fund assets exceed $4 trillion.[1] A typical sales charge, or load, on a mutual fund transaction could be anywhere from 0 to 7.0 percent of the amount invested. This is a one-time charge either when a fund is purchased or sold, depending on the type of load. In addition to this one-time load, mutual funds also carry a management fee, which is typically a 0.5 to 1.5 percent charge on the entire assets of the mutual fund, usually assessed yearly. While investors directly see loads that are charged, they don't see management fees because they are incorporated into the share price. Equity funds were particularly profitable as most of these funds carry a 1 percent management fee. There is a much smaller management fee on money market funds, which generate very little profit for the investment firm. In addition to NMF, other major mutual fund companies in the United States include Janus, Putnam, Schwab, and Vanguard.

One of the newest and fastest growing segments in the financial services industry today is the discount broker segment.[2] This sector's growth is closely tied to the development of the Internet. Investors can now access information and analytical tools on a variety of Web sites that help them make their own investment decisions without the need to pay high commissions for a full-service broker. As a result, broker commissions range from $5 to $75. Schwab is one of the biggest players in this arena.

The Internet has also led to a number of specialty boutiques in the discount trade business, such

[1] Robert C. Pozen, *The Mutual Fund Business* (Cambridge, MA: MIT Press, 2000).

[2] A discount broker is referred to in the industry as a "directed broker," meaning that he will only move money (e.g., take money one mutual fund to another, from one stock to another, or from a cash account to either a mutual fund or a stock, etc.) as directed by the customer.

EXHIBIT 1 Summary of Options for Customer Financial Stability

Product/Service	*Description*	*Potential Benefit*
Mutual Fund	An actively managed account where clients pool their assets, which are invested in a financial vehicles depending on the objective of the fund	• Reduced risk due to the investments being spread over a large number of financial vehicles • Active management by an expert
Stock	Share of ownership in a company	• Appreciation in value • Dividend payouts
Bond	Debt vehicle where a company borrows from you and promises to pay back the amount, plus interest, at some point in the future	• More stability than stocks • A steady stream of interest payments
Insurance product	Contract to pay a stated beneficiary a certain value in the case of the account holder's death	• Income to heirs • Tax benefits to the account holder
Planning tools	Calculators and worksheets that can help investors determine the right amount to save for major life needs, such as college or retirement	• Easy to use and self-paced • Valuable information on financial planning

as E-trade and Ameritrade. In exchange for extremely low commissions, less than $10 per trade in some cases, customers conduct trades on-line with little or no human interaction. While enormously successful in attracting customers, these companies have found it increasingly difficult to keep customers. In relying on technology to handle most of the business, these companies offer very little in the way of customer service. Many customers are discovering that it is worth the price to pay a little more for the opportunity to interact when necessary with well-trained representatives.

NATIONAL MUTUAL FUNDS

Company Background

NMF has built an enviable track record of performance, becoming one of the most important mutual fund companies in the United States. It has created over 220 mutual funds. Founded in the 1940s, NMF has succeeded through its emphasis on excellence and people. Its managers believe that how people are treated—and how they treat each other and the customer—are critical to their success. It has built a reputation of being unwilling to compromise on these principles. To support its people and to provide exceptional customer service, NMF has invested heavily in information technology, having spent $1.5 billion on technology in 1999 alone. Some would argue that NMF is more investment than marketing focused.

Though still primarily known for its mutual funds, NMF has developed a strategy of diversification in an effort to satisfy all the investment needs of its clients. In the words of NMF's chairman, "NMF has shifted from a mutual fund company to a supermarket of financial services products where investors can meet a multitude of financial needs in one place." NMF is now fully diversified into all major market segments offering mutual funds, brokerage products including stocks and bonds, insurance products, and a variety of planning tools to help customers save for major life needs (see Exhibit 1). More recently, NMF has become an important player in the discount brokerage business.

MARKETING PROGRAM

NMF's marketing program has evolved as a major presence in the company. A variety of media and marketing tools are used to communicate to prospective customers. For instance, databases with investor information are purchased so that direct mail can be sent to prospective clients. Service offerings are tailored to their unique investment needs based on the database information.

Television advertising takes up a large percentage of the advertising budget. Most of it is targeted to cable networks such as MSNBC and CNBC airing during shows discussing the market, such as CNBC's *Squawk Box* and CNNFN's *Market Call*. The ads focus on getting prospects to call AMF to place a trade or request additional information.

Technology is playing a bigger role in reaching and communicating with prospective investors. Promotional e-mails or banner ads are sent to people who have recently conducted a Web search on financial service providers. Referral programs using the Internet allow people who have Palm or other PDAs to receive "push messages" consisting of promotional offers that are sent via e-mail. Partnerships with pager providers, such as Skytel, are creating customized quote lists that can be automatically sent to clients throughout the day.

One of the cornerstones of NMF's new marketing strategy is to increase its share of customer spending on financial services (i.e., "share of wallet"). The typical household in the United States has relationships with three or more financial institutions. They place their money in an average of ten financial accounts, ranging from mutual fund investments to credit cards. As a result, the potential lifetime value of a customer is quite high—certainly much higher than most broker-age houses had estimated in the past. Based on the logic that the more relationships you have with a customer, the more secure is the relationship, firms are adding more services to their offerings. NMF, for instance, added estate planning and private banking services to retain its wealthier clients. It also started programs designed to encourage people to think of NMF for all their financial and investing needs. Funds Universe, for instance, allows investors to choose among more than 4,400 mutual funds managed by hundreds of different companies. This program has the added advantage for customers of consolidating their funds statements. The average mutual fund investor owns five funds; this program allows them to consolidate their statements to one account. Assets in this program have tripled since its inception.

To help direct their resources and provide the best mix of products and services to their customers, NMF segments their customer base according to investment behavior and value. Clients are identified as being in one of four segments:

- **The basic segment.** This segment makes up approximately 52 percent of NMF's clients and includes less affluent customers who trade infrequently, typically two to three times a year. Because these clients are less profitable, they do not receive specialized services offered to other customers.
- **The frequent investor segment.** These clients trade securities often and receive discounts on trading commissions. They make up approximately 9 percent of clients.
- **The high net worth segment.** These more affluent clients, 17 percent of NMF's customers, are offered personalized services such as estate planning, tax planning, and a dedicated representative.
- **The high-value segment.** This segment, 22 percent of all customers, consists of very active traders, regardless of asset level. These clients typically pay the lowest commissions and receive customized market information such as a monthly newsletter that tracks individual company performance.

NMF RETAIL SERVICES

The retail services division of NMF is responsible for selling mutual funds and providing customer service to individual investors. NMF retail services is organized into four call centers as shown in Exhibit 2. Each call center included approximately 200 traders reporting to 10 trading managers and 90 sales representatives reporting to 10 sales managers. Customers may call a variety of 800 numbers to have financial questions and transactions handled. For instance, a customer who wished to place a trade would speak with a phone trader. Approximately 42 percent of all trades are initiated by a phone call to a call center, while the rest are conducted over the Internet. A new customer who wanted to open an account or learn more about mutual funds would speak with a sales representative. Typical of the questions people might ask included: What is the yield on your money-market fund? What is the average annual return on your most popular equity growth fund? What is the best vehicle for me to invest my IRA account in? What is the average maturity of the bonds in your GNMA fund?

SALES DEPARTMENT OVERVIEW

The sales department is responsible for developing and retaining assets. An important part of the job is assisting current and prospective customers in determining the best mix of investment products to meet their own unique needs. Unlike full-service brokers, however, NMF's sales representatives do not cold call prospective clients. They respond to only inbound calls. A

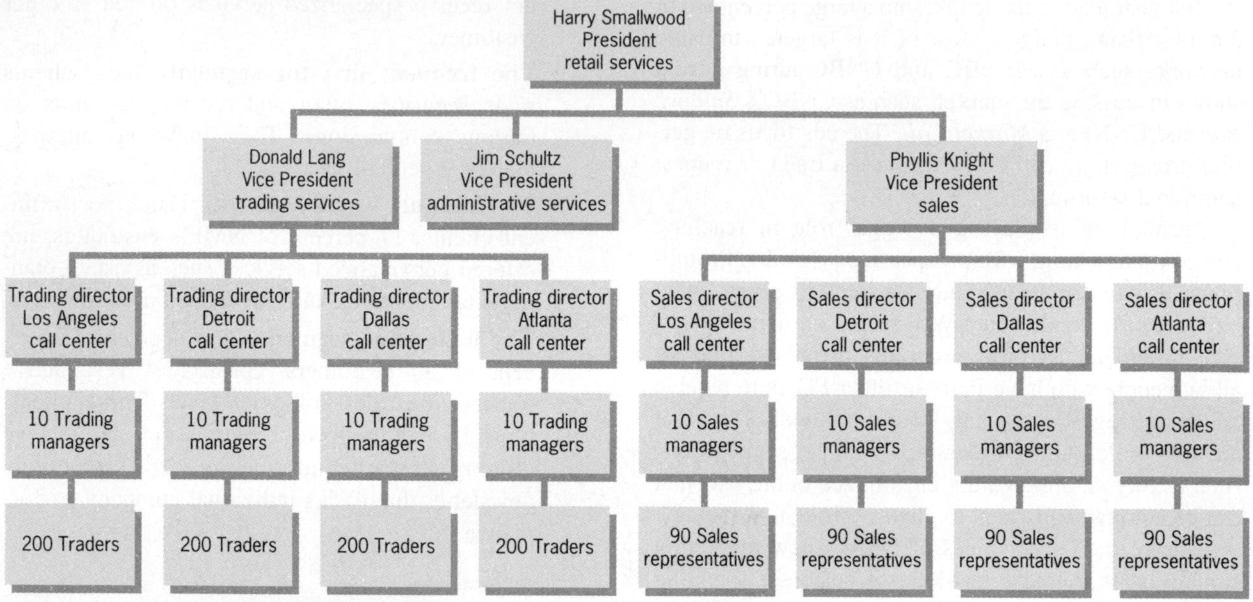

EXHIBIT 2 NMF Retail Services

typical sales representative-client conversation is found in Appendix A.

Sales representatives are recruited by placing ads in local papers, the Internet, and an extensive referral program. A typical applicant is a recent college graduate looking for a start in the finance industry; however, NMF also hires many professionals looking for a career change. Usually, qualified applicants are not hard to find, and positions are quickly filled.

The initial interview is usually held over the phone. During this initial interview, candidates are assessed to determine if they will be a good fit for NMF. Candidates are asked questions that are situational in nature and focus on their professional drive, and general customer service and financial aptitudes. See Exhibit 3 for typical questions asked in the initial interview.

Candidates passing the first interview and judged to have the aptitude and communication skills for a sales position at NMF are interviewed in person at a local hotel or conference center by a manager from the sales department. The questions asked in the second interview focus on relationship-building aptitudes (see Exhibit 4 for sample questions).

Candidates who are successful in the second interview are asked to take an intelligence test to determine the likelihood of an applicant passing the securities licensing tests required of both sales representatives and traders. Following an offer of employment, an extensive background check is conducted, including credit and criminal checks, work history, education, salary history, and references.

EXHIBIT 3 Initial Interview: Sample Questions

1. Tell me about a time when you set a specific performance goal for yourself? What was the goal, and what steps did you take to accomplish it?
2. Give me an example of when you went out of your way to help a customer. Why did you go out of your way? What did you learn?
3. What would you consider to be a recent major event occurring in the financial markets? What makes this a major event?

New employees go through a vigorous initial training program consisting of two months of internal training on NMF systems, products, and services. Following this, trainees are given another six weeks of training in preparation for their licensing exams. All employees go through this standardized training. After passing the licensing exam, sales representatives receive additional training during their first year of employment. They learn effective questioning strategies, followed by training at addressing customer objections. Toward

EXHIBIT 4 Sales Representative Candidate Second Interview: Sample Questions

1. Tell me about a time when a customer relationship that was important to you and your company was in trouble. What did you do to resolve the issue? What did you learn from the experience?
2. Give me an example of when you were the expert in something and had to show this to someone else. What did you find to be the pitfalls? Assuming you were successful in communicating your knowledge of the subject, why were you successful?
3. Please tell me about a time when you had to convince someone to do something they didn't know would be good for them to do. What was the situation? Were you successful?

EXHIBIT 5 Quarterly Bonus Schedule

Stack in the Team	*Rank*	*Quarterly Bonus*
Top	5%	$8,000
Next	5%	$6,500
Next	5%	$4,500
Next	10%	$3,500
Next	10%	$2,500
Next	15%	$1,500
Next	15%	$1,000
Next	15%	$750
Bottom	20%	$0

the end of the first year of employment, advanced sales skills training is offered. Recruiting and training during a sales representative's first year costs NMF between $42,000 and $52,000.

Sales representatives are paid a base salary and a quarterly bonus, based on a stack rank of the sales results posted by all the sales representatives in each phone center. Top representatives make up to $8,000 in bonuses each quarter, with the lowest performing representatives earning no bonuses. (See Exhibit 5 for the quarterly bonus schedule.) The average salary for a first year salesperson is $75,000 and is anticipated to increase 5 percent per year.

TRADING DEPARTMENT OVERVIEW

The trading representatives at NMF are responsible for helping customers place trades in a variety of investment vehicles. Traders are organized into teams of fifteen to twenty-five people who report to a trading

EXHIBIT 6 Trader Candidate Second Interview: Sample Questions

1. Tell me about a time when you were required to gather and synthesize a large amount of information. Why were you gathering it? How did you synthesize the information?
2. Would you give me an example of when you really had to listen to someone to understand what he or she was trying to tell you? Why was the person having a difficult time communicating their message? How did you figure out his or her true concerns?
3. Tell me about a very difficult task you had to accomplish on the job or at school. What made it so difficult? How did you accomplish the task?

manager, who in turn report to the trading director. The trading department focuses primarily on buying and selling securities. Traders are generally detail-oriented, like lots of activity, prefer to develop a deep understanding of a few job tasks, and then perform those tasks very well. They thrive in a fast-paced environment. The average trader made 50 to 70 trades a day.

Candidates for trading positions go through a similar set of two interview sessions and take an intelligence test to determine their likelihood of passing the securities licensing test. The first interview is usually conducted over the phone, while a trading manager conducts the second interview in person. Questions asked in the second interview attempt to gain a better understanding of a candidate's attention to detail, ability to handle multiple tasks at once, and ability to listen. Sample questions from the second interview are listed in Exhibit 6.

Following the standard initial training and after passing the licensing exam, all new traders receive additional mutual fund training and equity trading training. At around the end of the first year, they receive training on options and fixed income trading. During their second year, traders attend sessions on helping customers make financial decisions. For example, they learn how to help a customer who wants to know the background on a company before investing.

During a typical day, an NMF trader receives inbound calls from clients interested in placing mutual fund, stock, bond, or option trades, or who have basic questions on investing. See Appendix B for a typical trader–customer conversation. Traders' compensation package includes a base salary and a quarterly bonus,

EXHIBIT 7 Bonus Payment Schedule for Trackers

Stack in the Team	*Rank*	*Quarterly Bonus*
Top	5%	$2,200
Next	5%	$1,800
Next	5%	$1,400
Next	10%	$1,000
Next	10%	$1,600
Next	15%	$1,200
Next	15%	$800
Next	15%	$400
Bottom	20%	$0

depending on where they rank among their peers in customer service skills and in efficiently placing trades. The two rankings are combined to derive an overall performance ranking for each trader. Trading managers monitor customer service skills during customer phone calls. Rankings are based on a trader's ability to answer questions, maintain a professional demeanor, help customers solve problems, and level of courteousness. Trading efficiency is based on how quickly a trader places trades and how many errors are made, such as buying the wrong security or too many shares. Employees are ranked from highest to lowest based on their overall performance ranking. In the case of ties, the trader with the most trades is ranked highest. A quarterly bonus is paid based on a trader's overall ranking in a team. Bonuses range from $2,200 per quarter for the highest ranked traders to no bonus for the lowest performing traders. See Exhibit 7 for the bonus payment schedule for traders.

A MARKET DOWNTURN

While the stock markets enjoyed tremendous growth for most of the 1990s, late 2000 signaled a major market slowdown that worsened in the first part of 2001 (see Exhibit 8). As the new economy stock-bubble burst and the old economy slowed to a crawl, $1.6 trillion were lost in the stock market (i.e., price times number of shares) in the last half of 2000. The downturn worsened in 2001, as stock trading plunged by 50 percent. The Nasdaq Composite index shed 27 percent of its value, and even the larger stocks of the Standard & Poor's 500 index declined 14 percent. With earnings reports continuing to show a decline in profits, no sign of a return to strong market growth was in sight.

Many of the largest on-line brokerage and mutual fund houses reacted by making severe cuts in their labor forces as a result of the slowdown in trading. Schwab reduced its head count in 2001 by 25 percent. Putnam Investments in Boston terminated 4 percent of its workforce in April, and Merrill eliminated 15,000 positions. Other financial giants making significant staff cuts were Morgan Stanley, Goldman Sachs Group, and Citigroup's Salomon Smith Barney.

The market slowdown had a significant impact on NMF's profits and operations as well. NMF clients transferred over $5.2 billion from equity funds to less volatile money market funds. In addition, trading and customer call volume were down significantly in 2001 from forecasted levels. While the company had forecast average daily trades to be 130,000 in 2001, by February this average was only 68,000 per day. NMF was only receiving 64,000 phone calls per day, versus a forecast of 110,000 calls. Traders, used to spend their days taking calls almost back-to-back, now waited up to 30 minutes for a customer call. Something had to be done.

NMF'S RESPONSE

In an emergency meeting in March 2001, NMF's top management met to decide on their response to the market in light of the market downturn and prospects of continued lower volumes and activity in the market through 2001 and possibly into 2002. Its operating expenses were clearly out of line with the company's near-term revenue prospects. Having built the company on principles of commitment, continuous improvement of operations, and development of people, however, management simply did not feel that it could respond, as had other securities firms, by laying off a significant number of its people.

EXHIBIT 8 Stock Market Growth and Decline

Market Indicators	*1998*	*1999*	*2000*	*2001*
Dow Jones Industrial Average % change	16%	25%	−6%	−7%
NASDAQ % Change	40%	86%	−39%	−42%
NYSE Average Daily Volume	667	800	1,061	1,166
NASDAQ Average Daily Volume	786	1,046	1,665	1,811

After a number of long and challenging meetings, top management decided on a three-pronged response to the present difficult environment. First, merit raises in 2001 were eliminated for employees who earned more than $90,000. Second, a hiring freeze was ordered in nonrevenue-generating units of the company. Third, and most significant for the NMF Retail Services Division, management decided to redirect excess human capacity toward revenue generation efforts. It was felt that in this tough environment everyone should focus on revenue generation. After all, NMF was known for its selling and customer service; management felt that this was the time to rely on these competencies and to take this opportunity to develop them even further. This approach had the further advantage, they felt, of putting NMF in a position to benefit handsomely when the market finally turned around. The security investment companies that had laid off people would eventually need to ramp up and would be in danger of missing out on an important window of opportunity.

A key element of management's human resources redirection plan called for NMF Retail Services to reorganize its four retail services call centers. While not changing the reporting lines within the call centers, the reorganization plan called for traders to take on more of a selling function and to coordinate their activities with the sales force. Traditionally, salespeople were responsible for assisting existing customers in determining the best mix of investment products to meet their own unique needs, while traders were responsible for assisting customers who phoned in to the call center in placing more complex transactions. Under the reorganization plan, traders would be asked to proactively call on current clients instead of just receiving inbound calls. Sales representatives would be expected to close the sale. NMF Retail Services' management team was asked to design a plan for executing the reorganization and was expected to implement the plan by the beginning of the third quarter of 2001.

PLANNING MEETING

In late March 2001, Harry Smallwood called a meeting with Phyllis Knight, Vice President of Sales, Donald Lang, Vice President of Trading, and Jim Schultz, Vice President of Administrative Services, to begin developing a plan for implementing the reorganization directive for Retail Services.

HARRY SMALLWOOD: We have been given the opportunity to make a real difference at NMF. Most important, management has not taken the easy way out and asked us to cut head count in this division. Underlying this decision is a belief that we are part of the solution, not the problem. Understandably, it is very important that we deliver on the faith that has been shown in us. What do we need to do to make this reorganization successful? What do you see as the key issues we need to address to put together a first-rate program?

DONALD LANG: The problem we face and the key to the success of this program is apparent—my traders don't have the training and support that they need to do the job that we're asking of them. We've never had goals focusing on bringing in revenue to the firm. They just aren't used to doing a job like this. Not to mention, when the economy picks up and we start increasing our trading volume, I'll need to reduce the time that they spend calling on clients so they can handle their first priority—making trades.

HARRY SMALLWOOD: Don, we'll have to let the future take care of itself on this one. This is too important to lose our focus on today. Donald, tell me more about what you would see as the training your traders would need to be successful.

DONALD LANG: They will need a week of training, at least. They need to be trained in how to ask questions in order to identify a potential prospect. They should also be trained in how to make a professional and informative presentation of our various offerings. And they should also be comfortable in how to answer customer questions and objections. We already have a good program in place for the sales representatives, so we should just take that and condense it into something that will work for us.

PHYLLIS KNIGHT: I agree with Donald that the training can be compressed into a week, but you have to be careful not to overload the program and the traders with information. For instance, I don't think that they need training in presentation and objection handling skills. What we need to do is let the experts do what they do best. When the traders call a client, they can transfer them to a sales representative who is better trained to answer questions and is better able to attempt to bring in additional assets. We should form a partnership between the trading and sales departments. We need to work as allies to reach our revenue goals, instead of competing with each other.

JIM SCHULTZ: I agree with Phyllis. We already spend three weeks training our sales representatives on how to bring more money to NMF; we shouldn't have to do the same thing for the traders.

DONALD LANG: I don't think I like where this is going. Exactly what role would you have my traders play in this process? Would they simply make a lot of telephone calls and when they find someone willing to talk to them, tell the prospect, "I'm going to pass you on to someone who knows what they're talking about. Bye."? That isn't a partnership; it's servitude. Who would look forward to a

Monday morning in which this would be the highlight of the day? If you think today's 25 percent is a high turnover rate among first-year traders, wait till you see what happens if this is what we ask traders to do with half of their time.

HARRY SMALLWOOD: Donald, no one is trying to crowd your people out. However, you do raise some important issues. First, at what point in the selling process should the handoff take place between traders and sales? I think this is absolutely critical to the program's success and fundamental to everything else we do in this program. Don, I want you and Phyllis to put your heads together and come up with a clear resolution to this issue. You should give this priority one.

The second issue that you raise is also a good one—turnover. We will undoubtedly be hiring traders due to attrition. Should this change our recruiting and selection processes? What do you think, Jim?

JIM SCHULTZ: We will need to start determining if the traders we hire will be good at selling as well as trading. I don't think this means we'll need to change our recruiting of candidates since we are already able to hire salespeople successfully. However, it will be harder to find someone who is really good at both trading and sales. I've already talked with some of my people, and I'm sure we can draw up some new questions to ask during the second interview for trader candidates.

HARRY SMALLWOOD: Jim, will you and Donald get together and lay out a plan for the changes you see in our selection process as a result of this reorganization?

Let's talk about how much resistance there will be to this change. I'm not naïve enough to think that everyone will embrace the program because it is the right thing to do. Just how much pushback do you feel we will get?

DONALD LANG: I think it all depends. Everyone wants to be productive and successful. With the slowdown in trading calls, the job is getting real boring for some of my people, and they are looking for ways to fill their day. If this is seen as a challenge, a growth opportunity, and one in which they are equipped with the tools to succeed, then I think our best people will jump on board. If they are having the phone slammed in their faces all the time and see themselves as gofers for the sales boys, then you are going to lose some very, very good people. Worse yet, you may lose the motivation and commitment of people who stay here. We all know these are tough times, but it really depends on the program we put together.

PHYLLIS KNIGHT: I think the main issue we have here is how to get the entire company more focused on selling—marketing, trading, human resources, everybody. The competition is not going to go away, and I'm sure this won't be the last downturn in the market. Unless we have a solid plan on how to handle these contingencies in the future, we're going to be searching for answers every time our business slows down. What we need to do is evaluate our entire program.

JIM SCHULTZ: My department is ready to help in any way we can. I think the training and selection aspects are going to be very important to the success of this program. At the same time, Harry, I think that we need to come up with a program to promote teamwork between sales and traders. In other words, how do we get them to emotionally feel like a team? This has to come from above. It has to come from you.

HARRY SMALLWOOD: Well. Looks like we have our work cut out for us. You've all raised some excellent points. Donald, will you and Joe get together to lay out a plan for changes in the selection and training of new traders? You should also come up with a plan for the ongoing training and development of veteran traders.

Phyllis, you and Donald need to get together to develop a plan for the handoff between traders and sales. By the end of the week I need a memo outlining the handoff between traders and sales. It needs to be specific. You will need to include enough implementation details to help me make a decision on your plan. Whatever you come up with has to work for all parties concerned, and most important, must get us to our revenue target of $400 million. This is critical. It's the centerpiece of the program.

Jim, you and I need to set down and come up with a program to minimize resistance to this program and to promote teamwork within the call centers. We want to get everyone behind this program, 100 percent.

There is some real time pressure here. We need to implement the reorganization this quarter. That gives us less than two months to put it in place. At the same time, we have to do this right. Our jobs depend on it.

APPENDIX A

Sales Representative–Customer Conversation

Salesperson: "Thank you for calling NMF; this is Pat, how may I help you?"

Customer: "Hi, I saw your ad on the news and I was wondering if I could get some information on your mutual funds."

Salesperson: "Sure—we can certainly help you with that. Let me ask you, do you currently have an account with us?"

Customer: "Uh, no, not currently. But my wife used to invest with you through her job."

Salesperson: "OK—no problem. Why don't you let me get a little information so I can get you exactly what you're looking for? To start with, can I get your name?"

Customer: "This is Leonard Cross. I'm calling from Orlando."

Salesperson: "Great. Sounds like a nice place to live this time of year. Let me ask you—which advertisement did you see us on?"

Customer: "It was the one with the kid who is going off to college for the first time."

Salesperson: "Yes, that one talks about some of the new college savings plans that were passed into law last year. The new 529 plans must be what you're calling about."

Customer: "Yeah, I've got an 8-year-old daughter who I need to start saving for, but I really want to find out about your funds as well."

Salesperson: "No problem. Why don't we determine which plan best fits your needs first; then I can tell you about some of the investment vehicles you can think about. First of all, are you just thinking about investing for your daughter's college, or would you also like to discuss some of your other goals?"

Customer: "Right now I just want to talk about my daughter since I'm getting a late start. I do have some other small accounts, mostly IRAs, that are with a few other places."

Salesperson: "OK, we can start with your daughter and then see if we can help you with your other investments as well. I know you may not have a lot of time to discuss that today, but keep in mind we're here until 10:00 P.M. your time, or I can always call you back tomorrow or the next day. But to start out with, there are a few ways you can save for her education. Not too long ago, most parents just put money in the bank and earned a small amount of interest. But with skyrocketing higher education costs, some other options like UTMAs and the new 529 plans are becoming pretty popular. The UTMA account lets you put away money that is taxed at your daughter's tax rate in most cases, so you don't need to worry about paying too much in taxes. However, the nice thing about the new 529 plans is that money grows tax-free, so you can really save a lot on taxes over ten years."

Customer: "I heard that from the ad. Can you send me anything on that so I can read it over?"

Salesperson: "Sure—I can mail you some information, but you can also take a look at our Web site which has a ton of information on 529s, including some graphs that show the difference these plans can make over a simple savings account. Do you have Web access, or would you prefer me to mail you some information?"

Customer: "I'm actually on your Web site right now. Can you show me where to go?

A dialogue about the Web site follows, with instructions on how to download an application for a new account.

Salesperson: "Now that we've picked out a pretty good plan for your daughter, you have an important decision to make regarding how to invest her savings. As you might know, we offer pretty much everything under the sun to invest in, including stocks, bonds, and money market instruments. There are a couple of different ways to invest, so tell me a little about your investing experience in the past."

Customer: "Well, I know a little bit. My IRAs are currently in some stock mutual funds, but they haven't grown much in the last few years"

Salesperson: "Its been a rough few years for the market, but the good news is we can help you make the most out of volatile markets. Of course, the most important thing is for you to be comfortable with your investments. Do you like the idea of mutual funds where a professional manages the fund assets, or would you also like to get some exposure to individual stocks, like IBM or AT&T?

The customer and salesperson continue to discuss investment vehicles based on the customer's experience and risk tolerance.

Salesperson: "I'm glad you like the idea of mutual funds. They really are easy and take a lot of worry out of the investing process. Why don't we discuss which funds would be appropriate for your daughter. Tell me, how much are you interested in putting away each year, and what do you think her college expenses will be?

The customer describes how much he is able to put away and also what he expects his daughter's expenses to be. They also discuss the mutual funds that have the potential to generate the type of returns the customer would need to meet with aggressive college savings goals.

Salesperson: "So it sounds like a value mutual fund and a few index funds are what you would be most comfortable with for your daughter's new 529 plan. I know that we've gone over a lot of information, so let me stop and see if you have any questions or if I can clear anything up for you."

The salesperson explains some additional details about how mutual funds work and how long it would take to set the account up.

Salesperson: "Sounds like you have made a great start into making sure your daughter can attend the right school. I think you've made a good decision and have picked out some great investments to get her on her way. Now that we've had a chance to discuss your daughter's account, tell me if you've been happy with the performance of your IRAs."

The customer discusses that he doesn't look at his IRAs much because he has never been serious saving for retirement up to this point. However, after starting a new, higher paying job, he is ready to start putting more away for the future. The salesperson and customer discuss the benefits of an NMF IRA account, including the simplicity of having everything on one, easy to read statement.

Customer: "I appreciate the information, but I think I'll just keep my IRAs where they are. I don't like the idea of having all my eggs in one basket."

Salesperson: "I don't blame you a bit. In fact, I hear that from a lot of customers. Just for my information, what exactly about having all your investments in one place don't you like?"

Customer: "Well, if NMF goes under, I don't want to lose everything. In fact, my accountant told me that I should never keep everything in one place."

Salesperson: "Good point. However, did you know that the strength of NMF has nothing to do with whether your money is safe? Your assets are required to be kept in a separate trust under the name of the fund. In fact, the government even insures your accounts up to $500,000, and we even have separate insurance bonds on our mutual funds that protect them. Of course, this doesn't guarantee against the performance of the funds, just the safety of your shares."

Customer: "So, you're telling me that I can't lose money with NMF?"

Salesperson: "Well, that would be great, but you could call any investment company and none of them would be able to guarantee that. You can lose value in addition to gain value, depending on the performance of the particular fund you chose. However, you are protected against fraudulent activity."

Customer: "I guess I didn't know that, but I would like something in writing. Can I also get that off your Web site?"

Salesperson: "Sure—in fact, you'll find it in the same place as the 529 application for your daughter. I know that we've gone over a lot of information today. Let me just confirm our plan so far: You're downloading the application for your daughter's 529 plan and your own IRA to transfer in. You'll also find information on the protection of your account in the same kit. After you fill it out, you'll attach your check and mail it to us at the address shown on the application. I'll also check in with you in a day or two to see if you have any problems filling out the paperwork. Does that sound OK?"

Customer: "Sounds OK to me. I appreciate your taking the time to talk to me."

Salesperson: "No problem, Mr. Cross; we're here to help. Just call us back if you have any problems downloading the applications. Thanks for calling and have a great day."

APPENDIX B TRADER-CUSTOMER CONVERSATION

Trader: "Thank you for calling NMF. This is Chris, how can I help you today?

Customer: "Hi—can you tell me what the market is at right now?"

Trader: "No problem. The Dow is currently down 56 for the day so far."

Customer: "Hmmmm—not really headed in the right direction, is it?"

Trader: "Well, I guess that depends on how you look at it. Are you interested in moving some of your investments around today?"

Customer: "Well, I was thinking about getting out of my XYZ stock. I bought it a few years ago and it just hasn't done much for me. But I don't want to sell it for a loss when the market's down."

Trader: "I can understand that. Let's take a look at what your stock is doing today. Do you have your account number handy?"

Customer: "Yes—it's 123-456-789."

Trader: "Great. And if I can just get another piece of information from you—can you confirm your mailing address for me?"

Customer: "Sure—it's 123 Main Street, Pittsburg, PA."

Trader: "Great—and who am I speaking with?"

Customer: "This is Robert Montgomery."

Trader: "Thanks, Mr. Montgomery. Looks like XYZ is currently at $25.06 per share, down right at $.24 from yesterday's close."

Customer: "That's what I was afraid of. Can you tell me what I paid for that originally?"

Trader: "Sure—looks like you only made one purchase of XYZ and you paid $23.96 for 25 shares, so you've actually made a little money on it. Tell me—were you planning on using this for anything?"

Customer: "Not really—I just play around a little with this and may use it to help with another down payment on our next house in about five years."

Trader: "I see. Well, if you want, you can place a limit order where you specify a price that you want to sell XYZ for, if you want to wait and not sell it until you've locked in a good enough profit. The only problem is, if the market and possibly your stock continue to go down, you may want to think about locking in the small profit you made on it already. Do you feel like XYZ may go lower than what you paid for it?"

Customer: "I wish I knew. I've just heard so many reports that we may not have hit the worst part yet. I guess I should go ahead and sell it today and worry about what to do with the money later."

Trader: "No problem. I can put in a market order for you, which basically means you'll get the next available price today. It's no guarantee that you'll get the $25.06 I quoted you, but it should be close. In fact, just looking at it again, looks like XYZ is down to $25.03 per share right now."

Customer: "Well, why don't you go ahead and sell it with a market order. I guess I should be happy that I made any money off of it."

Trader: "No problem. Let me just confirm this for you. I'm going to sell all shares, or 25 total, of your XYZ stock at the market today. The total commission on this will be $27.50, and will be deducted from the proceeds. Is this correct?"

Customer: "Yes—let's go ahead and process it."

Trader: "OK—I went ahead and put that in. You should be receiving a confirmation within four to six days, which will have all the details, or you can call back after market close to get the details. In fact, if you want, you can also look it up yourself on our Web site."

Customer: "Yeah—I've done that before. I'll just take a look at my account on the Web later on tonight."

Trader: "Sounds good, Mr. Montgomery. By the way, did you know that you can make stock trades over the Web as well?"

Customer: "Yeah—I know that it's pretty easy and the commissions are even a little lower, I just prefer talking to someone when I trade."

Trader: "I understand. While I have you, are there any other transactions I can handle for you today?"

Customer: "No, just give me one more quote. What's ABC company at right now?"

Trader: "Looks like ABC is currently at $56.36, down $1.29 from yesterday's close."

Customer: "Great. I think that covers everything for me today."

Trader: "Well, thanks for calling in, and we appreciate your business, Mr. Montgomery. Have a nice day."

POWER AND MOTION INDUSTRIAL SUPPLY

It was 7:00 on Sunday evening when Hal Maybee returned to his office. He had spent the afternoon golfing with one of his customers, and he now had to decide what he was going to tell the head office on Monday morning with regard to new salaries for the sales staff at his branch.

Hal had just been appointed Atlantic Region District Manager for one of Canada's largest industrial distributors. His appointment was made only two weeks before, following the sudden death of Fergie McDonald, who, at 48 years old, had been in charge of the company's most profitable branch. About 70 percent of the sales in Atlantic Canada, including the four most profitable product lines, were for manufacturers that the company did not represent on a national basis. There were many manufacturers in Ontario and Quebec that served central Canada with their own sales forces and used distributors for the east and west coasts due to the distances from their head offices and the geographical dispersion of customers in those regions. Although Power and Motion had sales agreements with over 400 North American manufacturers, only about 100 manufacturers were involved in 80 percent of the sales.

It was a complete surprise to Hal when he was promoted, and he knew there were people at the branch who thought they deserved it more. Exhibit 1 shows the performance evaluations that Fergie had completed on the six salespeople just before he died. Head office had intended to send only five forms to Hal, but one of the

This case was prepared by H. F. MacKenzie of Memorial University of Newfoundland, Canada. The case was prepared as a basis for class discussion and is not intended to illustrate effective or ineffective handling of a management situation. All names in the case have been disguised.

EXHIBIT 1 Evaluation of Salespeople

		Rating						
Salesperson	*Evaluation Criteria*	*Far Worse Than Average*			*About Average*			*Far Better Than Average*
Dave Edison	Attitude	1	2	3	4	⑤	6	7
	Appearance and manner	1	2	3	4	5	⑥	7
	Selling skills	1	2	3	4	5	⑥	7
	Product knowledge	1	2	3	④	5	6	7
	Time management	1	2	3	④	5	6	7
	Customer goodwill	1	2	3	④	5	6	7
	Expense/budget	1	2	3	④	5	6	7
	New accounts opened	1	2	3	④	5	6	7
	Sales calls/quota	1	2	3	④	5	6	7
	Sales/quota	1	2	3	4	⑤	6	7
	Sales volume	1	2	3	④	5	6	7
	Sales growth	1	2	3	4	⑤	6	7
	Contribution margin	1	2	3	4	5	⑥	7
	Total score: 61							
Comments: Current salary $52,000. Territory is Cape Breton Island and the city of Moncton, N.B. Needs more product knowledge but has learned a lot since hired. A bit aggressive, but he has developed some excellent new accounts through attention to detail and follow-up support.								
Arne Olsen	Attitude	1	2	③	4	5	6	7
	Appearance and manner	1	2	③	4	5	6	7
	Selling skills	1	2	③	4	5	6	7
	Product knowledge	1	2	3	④	5	6	7
	Time management	1	2	③	4	5	6	7
	Customer goodwill	1	2	③	4	5	6	7
	Expense/budget	1	2	3	4	⑤	6	7
	New accounts opened	1	2	③	4	5	6	7
	Sales calls/quota	1	2	3	4	5	⑥	7
	Sales/quota	1	2	③	4	5	6	7
	Sales volume	1	2	3	④	5	6	7
	Sales growth	1	2	③	4	5	6	7
	Contribution margin	1	2	③	4	5	6	7
	Total score: 46							
Comments: Current salary $44,500. Has been calling regularly on his existing accounts in southern New Brunswick (except Moncton). Although he has increased the number of sales calls, as agreed at our last review, sales have not gone up accordingly. Some concern with product knowledge. Arne knows all of our major product lines very well, but has not shown much effort to learn about many of the new lines we have added that may become our best product lines in the future. Further concern with his contribution margin. This is the fourth year in a row that it has dropped, although it is almost the same as last year.								
Hal Maybee	Attitude	1	2	3	4	⑤	6	7
	Appearance and manner	1	2	3	④	5	6	7
	Selling skills	1	2	3	④	5	6	7
	Product knowledge	1	2	3	4	⑤	6	7
	Time management	1	2	3	4	5	⑥	7
	Customer goodwill	1	2	3	4	5	⑥	7
	Expense/budget	1	2	3	④	5	6	7
	New accounts opened	1	②	3	4	5	6	7
	Sales calls/quota	1	2	3	④	5	6	7
	Sales/quota	1	2	3	4	⑤	6	7
	Sales volume	1	②	3	4	5	6	7
	Sales growth	1	2	③	4	5	6	7
	Contribution margin	1	②	3	4	5	6	7
	Total score: 52							

EXHIBIT 1 (continued)

Salesperson	*Evaluation Criteria*	*Rating*						
		Far Worse Than Average			*About Average*			*Far Better Than Average*

Comments: Current salary $38,500. Although still the Office Manager, Hal has taken over Newfoundland as a territory and travels there four times a year. Hal also travels to northern New Brunswick with me occasionally due to his expert product knowledge on electric and pneumatic products, which we sell to the mines and pulp mills in the two areas. Hal is very focused and successful with the big sales but needs to develop knowledge of and interest in some of the lower sales volume, less technical products, as they are generally higher-margin items. Hal has a lot of respect in the office and our efficiency has improved greatly, as has the general work atmosphere within the office.

Salesperson	Evaluation Criteria							
Tanya Burt	Attitude	1	2	3	④	5	6	7
	Appearance and manner	1	2	3	④	5	6	7
	Selling skills	1	2	3	4	⑤	6	7
	Product knowledge	1	2	③	4	5	6	7
	Time management	1	2	3	4	⑤	6	7
	Customer goodwill	1	2	3	4	⑤	6	7
	Expense/budget	1	2	3	④	5	6	7
	New accounts opened	1	2	3	4	⑤	6	7
	Sales calls/quota	1	2	3	4	⑤	6	7
	Sales/quota	1	2	3	4	⑤	6	7
	Sales volume	1	2	3	④	5	6	7
	Sales growth	1	2	3	4	⑤	6	7
	Contribution margin	1	2	3	4	⑤	6	7
	Total score: 59							

Comments: Current salary $36,000. Very impressed with her performance. Has good knowledge of product pricing and sourcing but needs to learn more about product applications. Tanya sells mainly maintenance and operating supplies, but she has a number of accounts that buy large annual volumes, as her territory is the Halifax-Dartmouth area surrounding our warehouse. Tanya is dedicated and dependable. She has opened many new accounts for us, and I predict good success for her as she continues to develop her knowledge and selling skills.

Salesperson	Evaluation Criteria							
Jim Stanley	Attitude	1	2	③	4	5	6	7
	Appearance and manner	1	2	③	4	5	6	7
	Selling skills	1	2	③	4	5	6	7
	Product knowledge	1	2	3	④	5	6	7
	Time management	1	②	3	4	5	6	7
	Customer goodwill	1	2	③	4	5	6	7
	Expense/budget	1	2	③	4	5	6	7
	New accounts opened	1	②	3	4	5	6	7
	Sales calls/quota	1	2	3	④	5	6	7
	Sales/quota	1	2	3	4	⑤	6	7
	Sales volume	1	2	3	④	5	6	7
	Sales growth	1	2	3	4	⑤	6	7
	Contribution margin	1	2	3	4	⑤	6	7
	Total score: 46							

Comments: Current salary $42,000. Jim seems to be performing quite well, but there is concern with his behavior. I hope that a salary increase and some direction from me will improve his performance next year. He has been making some suggestions that he might like to move back to office management because everyone thinks I will be promoting Hal to full-time sales and letting him take over my territory as well as Newfoundland. I really do not want Jim back in the office, and I think he should be a good salesperson. His sales and contribution margin are good, but part of his sales increase this year came from a new customer that has a manufacturing plant in his region but actually buys from an office located in Tanya's territory. Tanya and Jim have agreed to split the credit for the sales, as Tanya must do the selling but Jim has to service the account.

Salesperson	Evaluation Criteria							
Buck Thompson	Attitude	1	2	3	④	5	6	7
	Appearance and manner	1	2	3	④	5	6	7
	Selling skills	1	2	3	4	⑤	6	7
	Product knowledge	1	2	3	4	5	⑥	7
	Time management	1	2	3	④	5	6	7
	Customer goodwill	1	2	3	④	5	6	7

EXHIBIT 1 (Continued)

Salesperson	Evaluation Criteria	Rating						
		Far Worse Than Average			About Average		Far Better Than Average	
	Expense/budget	1	2	③	4	5	6	7
	New accounts opened	1	②	3	4	5	6	7
	Sales calls/quota	1	2	③	4	5	6	7
	Sales/quota	1	2	3	④	5	6	7
	Sales volume	1	2	3	④	5	6	7
	Sales growth	1	2	3	④	5	6	7
	Contribution margin	1	2	3	④	5	6	7
	Total score: 51							

Comments: Current salary $49,000. Sells in Pictou Country, N.S., where we have a very established customer base and a variety of industries. Buck knows all of his customers very well, as he has lived in the area all of his life. He has very good selling skills and product knowledge and has been the main reason we have done so well in his territory.

secretaries mistakenly included Fergie's evaluation of Hal as well.

Nearly three weeks previously, Fergie and Hal were making some joint calls on some pump mills in northern New Brunswick, the territory that Fergie kept for himself, even though head office wanted him to stop selling and spend more time on sales administration. During the trip, Fergie told Hal that he was given 6 percent of the total sales staff salary to be divided among them for the coming year. This was the customary way of giving salary increases at the branches, as it gave the head office the discretion to decide the total increase in the salary expense, but it gave the district managers responsibility for allocating salary increases. Fergie was told that nationally, sales increases would average about 3 percent, but his branch was among the lowest paid in the company and had been the best performing branch for several years.

Hal did not want to express his opinions, as he knew he and Fergie would disagree. However, he did allow Fergie to express his own thoughts on the staff. There were two salespeople that Fergie had a real problem with. He viewed Jim Stanley as his biggest problem. Jim actually had seniority at the branch. He had been hired, as shipper, order desk salesperson, and secretary when the branch was only large enough to support one person other than Bob Laird, the first salesperson the company had in Atlantic Canada. Bob and Jim operated the branch for almost two years when Bob decided to hire Fergie as a salesperson to help develop the territory. When Bob retired, Jim thought he would get the position as District Manager, as he had seniority, and he had experience with all aspects of the business including managing the office and warehouse, which had grown to include seven people. He was very disappointed when the head office gave the position to Fergie, as he had no experience other than sales.

Within a year, Jim decided he wanted to get into sales. He was finally resigned to the fact that office management was a dead-end job, and the only possibility for advancement was through sales. Now, after five years, Jim was not performing as well as he should. In fact, he hated selling and spent an increasing amount of time drinking while away from home. He hinted that he wanted to get back into the office. However, when these rumors started to spread, the staff let it be known that they did not want to work under Jim again if there were any alternatives.

Fergie was thinking about giving Jim a good salary increase. First, it might make him appreciate his job more, and may be he would put more effort into selling. Second, it would make the position more attractive than a possible return to the office, as he would not want to take a tremendous salary cut.

The other problem was Arne Olsen, the other senior salesperson. As the territory developed quickly, the branch hired a secretary just after Fergie was hired. A month later, a warehouseman was hired and Jim was promoted to office manager. Jim immediately hired Hal Maybee as an order desk salesperson. Within a year, another salesperson, Arne, was hired, along with a second secretary. The branch growth slowed but was steady from that point on. Arne was always an average salesperson. He never really had much motivation to perform, but he always did whatever he had to do, so that he was never in any serious trouble as far as his job was concerned. Lately, he was starting to slip a bit, and rumor had it that he was having at least one affair.

He also recently bought a Mazda Miata that he drove on weekends, as he was not allowed to drive anything but the company car through the work week.

Dave Edison was with the company for just under one year. If he had had a few more years with the company, Hal knew he would have probably been the new District Manager. He came to the company from the life insurance industry, and rumor had it that he was slated for a national sales manager position within the next year, as the company was rumored to be taking on a new line of capital equipment from Europe that would be sold nationally, but would have one person at head office responsible for national sales.

Tanya Burt was also in sales for only a year. She had been hired as a secretary, but it soon became apparent that she had exceptional telephone skills. She was promoted to order desk salesperson within a year, and three years later, she requested and was given an outside sales territory. There was some concern with her product knowledge but no concern with her attitude or sales ability. Tanya was the first and only woman to be promoted to one of the company's eighty outside sales positions.

Buck Thompson had a very solid, established territory. He needed little direction, as he was doing most things very well. Fergie was a bit concerned that he was not making enough sales calls, but he certainly was performing well.

As Hal reviewed the performance evaluations, he agreed that Fergie had been very thorough and accurate in his assessment of each of the individuals. Hal wondered about the amount of salary increase he should give to each person. While he had to make this decision immediately, Hal realized there were other important decisions he would have to make soon. He recognized some of the problems Fergie had trying to decide salary increases, and these were more important for Hal, as he had to get the support of the sales staff before he could hope to overcome some of these problems. He also had to start thinking about hiring another salesperson to cover Newfoundland and northern New Brunswick, as the head office was determined that he give up responsibility for all accounts in the region. He would, however, be allowed and encouraged to call on customers with the sales staff.

QUADO SYSTEMS GROUP

In August of 2000, Andrew Thorby, president of Quado Systems Group, was considering a sales opportunity at Taylor Corporation, a retail chain in North America and Canada. A meeting was scheduled with Taylor's chief financial officer in one week to present Quado's proposal for the project. In two weeks, Quado would make a presentation to Taylor's entire project team outlining Quado's approach to the project and to address any concerns the project team might have. The problem is that Thorby had not yet made up his mind whether this was the right opportunity for Quado at this time. Quado had grown to $20 million in sales last year and had set an objective of $25 million in revenues for 2000. Synectics, a competitor of Quado, had already estimated the project at $9 million. Thorby was very concerned whether Quado could successfully deliver on a project of this size without straining the organization and taking away potential revenue from other accounts. On the other hand, the project was in an area, the Internet, that Quado had targeted for future growth and in which they needed to build a reputation.

The Taylor opportunity had come to the attention of Mike Chaffin, one of Quado's sales representatives, several months after Synectics, a large information systems consulting firm with over $1 billion in revenue, had already established its presence at Taylor. Taylor wanted to design and build an Internet infrastructure to connect all of its remote stores and prospective customers in order to provide online access to catalogs, inventory, and employee certifications. The objective of this project was to allow Taylor to meet some of its

This case was prepared by Michael Chaffin of Quado Systems Group, James Boles of the Georgia State University, William L. Cron of Texas Christian University.

strategic repositioning objectives, along with reducing costs and improving customer service.

Despite the attractive size of the project and its fit with several of Quado's strengths, Thorby kept coming back to the comment made by Alan Boyer, a project manager with Quado.

> With our existing customers' demands for more from our people, we need to focus on supporting their needs. Furthermore, the retail environment has not been the most pleasant working environment for our consultants.

INDUSTRY OVERVIEW

The term *systems integrator* is a broad characterization for companies that provide information technology related and consulting services. A systems integrator could be industry-focused such as with information technologies used in the oil and gas exploration industry; information technology-focused such as with Internet application development, data warehouse, and so on; or, a mix of both.

Competitors in the systems integration business are divided into two groups of firms depending on their size. On the one hand, there are a limited number of very large systems integration firms consisting of companies such as IBM, Accenture, Deloitte & Touche, and Synectics. Each firm has a worldwide presence with several thousand consultants.

There are also a large number of smaller systems integration firms. The Houston, Texas, market alone is home to over 2,200 technology consulting firms. There are at least two reasons for the large number of small systems integration firms. First, there is very little barrier to entry into this business, as the initial capital requirements are minimal. Second, most large systems integration organizations will not look at projects that are less than $7 to $8 million in size. These smaller firms fill the void created by large firms not taking on the smaller projects.

The large and small systems integration firms also differ in their operating models. The large firms follow a leveraged model where they provide one senior consultant and several junior consultants. This process helps to ensure high quality and consistency, while achieving scale economies. This approach is also attractive to people early in their careers or those who just received their MBAs; they are usually more risk adverse and still learning the ropes. Despite its advantages, customers' experiences with this approach are somewhat mixed.

> A number of our customers have told us that they have to provide parking for the school bus when the large systems integration firms show up. Even though this frustrated many of our customers, they had several projects that required an enormous amount of people. The large systems integration firms could provide these resources on a moment's notice, whereas the small boutique systems integrators could not—Chaffin

The smaller firms, on the other hand, tend to attract top-level, experienced talent because these individuals are confident in their ability due to their experience. They also have the opportunity to make a big return should the company successfully go public. This may make smaller firms more attractive to customers because of the quality of the human resources put on each project.

The average number of consultants who are not assigned to projects for the large systems integration firms is typically around 15 to 25 percent of their workforce, whereas the unassigned in the smaller firm is usually around 5 percent or less. The large systems integration firms are the more expensive alternative, but from the customer's perspective are potentially the least risky in regard to their own job security. Management rarely gets fired should a project fail when they utilize a large systems integration firm.

> It seems that our customers have a much more pleasurable experience working with us. They have a lot of involvement with our projects and they get to work with senior people. The large systems integration firms can be frustrating to their clients at times when they send 20 people to do a project and don't involve the customer.—Boyer

Small systems integration firms have to be more creative with their approach to marketing. Small firms might utilize independent contractors or engage in joint ventures in order to gain client referrals and muster the resources necessary to compete with the larger firms.

Like most consulting and service industries, the key resource in this industry is the expertise and experience of the firm's human capital. Salary requirements for individuals with similar experience, for instance, vary widely. The large demand for consultants has increased their demands for pay, benefits, and stock.

> In 1990, compensation for a technical consultant ranged from $35,000 to $50,000. By 2000, the range grew from $60,000 to over $100,000 depending on their area of expertise. One of our customers has an information systems staff of over 700 people. Three hundred of those people are consultants on assignments from numerous systems integration firms.—Chaffin

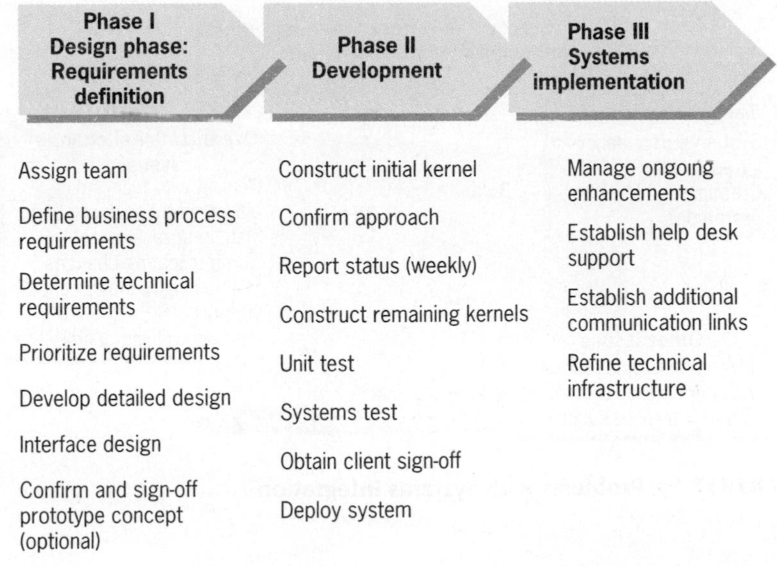

Phase I
Design phase:
Requirements
definition
Phase II
Development
Phase III
Systems
implementation
Assign team
Define business process requirements
Determine technical requirements
Prioritize requirements
Develop detailed design
Interface design
Confirm and sign-off prototype concept (optional)
Construct initial kernel
Confirm approach
Report status (weekly)
Construct remaining kernels
Unit test
Systems test
Obtain client sign-off
Deploy system
Manage ongoing enhancements
Establish help desk support
Establish additional communication links
Refine technical infrastructure

EXHIBIT 1 Project Phases

A TYPICAL PROJECT

A typical project in the systems integration industry has three distinct phases (see Exhibit 1). The first phase is to define the technical and organizational change requirements of the project. The first phase, often referred to as the design phase of each project, requires generalists in five categories: business analysis, technical architecture, application architecture, data architecture, and change management (Exhibit 2). At the end of phase 1, there would be a minimal switching cost to change systems integrators should there not be a fit between the organizations. Phase 1 averaged about 10 percent of each project's total effort.

The second and third phases are systems development and implementation (Exhibit 1). Typically, the bulk of the consultants during these phases are specialists in each of the previously mentioned categories. While the first phase utilized a smaller number of resources (three to five people on average), the latter phases for large projects may require in excess of twenty consultants.

Prior to receiving approval for the project, a systems design firm would usually spend some time with the potential client to develop accurate numbers to present to the client's management team so that they could determine a project's return on investment (ROI). Systems integrators would usually spend a week or more, depending on the size of the project, performing a high-level analysis (usually at no cost) to determine the overall size of the project (all three phases). In addition to giving the client an understanding of the general size of the project, it would also give the systems integrator a chance to sell itself and give the prospective clients a comfort level with the systems integrator before moving ahead with the project.

EXHIBIT 2 Design Phase Team

Business Analysis—determines the business requirements for the project

Technical Architect—determines the computer hardware platform to support the business requirements. This position is a generalist who understands a wide range of computer hardware platforms.

Application Architect—determines the development architecture and toolsets. This position is also a generalist who understands a wide range of development toolsets (i.e., PowerBuilder, Visual Basic, etc.).

Data Architect—models the data requirements for the project and makes recommendations on the type of database required for the project (i.e., Oracle, DB2, etc.).

Change Management—determines the people factors that might impede the success of the project and how to correct them.

THE INTERNET

The Internet has had an important impact on the systems integration industry. Historically, information

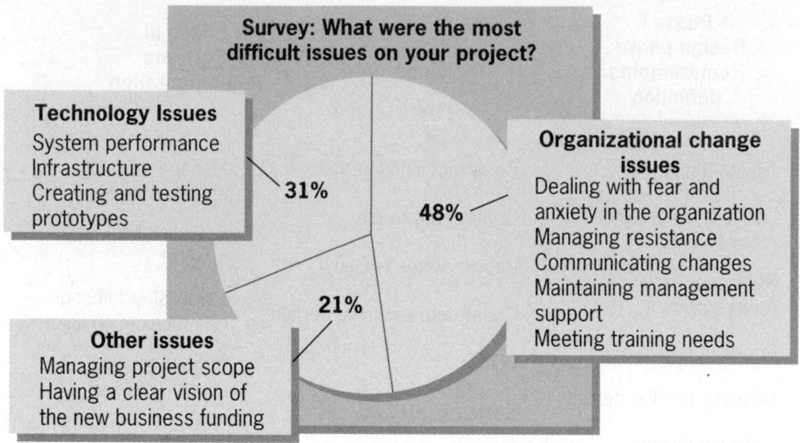

EXHIBIT 3 Problems with Systems Integration

systems departments had developed applications such as order entry and accounts payable that their business units had to use. The end-users of the application were well defined and their needs fairly easy to see. The Internet, on the other hand, did not have well-defined users, nor were the users required to use the system. This created much more pressure for organizations to focus on the user side of the process. Who would be using the system? What would they need from the system? What are their personal preferences? Exhibit 3 shows the human factors and how they connect the Internet to an organization's existing infrastructure

> The Internet spawned the introduction of many new small Internet development companies that are very good at the technical requirements needed to develop an Internet site. Most of these firms had the creative talent and developers, but lacked the experience to connect the Internet with their customers' existing systems, or to understand the human factor needs for projects of this nature. As the Internet moves from more of a passive medium to an interactive one, the smaller firms will need to partner with firms like ours to compete.—Boyer

THE QUADO SYSTEMS GROUP

In late November 1992, Kaushik Shah and Andrew Thorby, two independent consultants, sat around the dinner table discussing the current systems integration industry's business model.

> Our customers always complained about the way the large systems integration firms worked. They felt that they were paying a lot of money for inexperienced people to build their large scale mission critical systems. We saw an opportunity to build an organization with seasoned consultants. Unfortunately we did not recognize that, as much as our customers despised the large systems integration firms, they viewed them as job security.—Thorby

With this in mind, Quado was born. Quado built its practice rapidly; by 2000 it had grown to approximately $20 million in sales with over 125 employees. With more and more organizations looking for industry-specific expertise, Quado had narrowed its focus to three: energy, telecommunications, and financial services. Quado also narrowed its product offerings to management consulting and custom application development. Within management consulting, Quado focused on business process reengineering and change management. Within the custom application development, Quado wanted to shift its focus toward the Internet due to strong growth potential.

> The Internet is the fastest growing segment in the market. Quado as a company has limited experience in this area. We need to get some experience quickly in order to stay even with or slightly ahead of our competition.
>
> Our management consulting practice is extremely competitive with the large systems integration firms. The projects we typically go for are considered small in the eyes of the larger systems integrators. When we compete against them, they often send in the "B Team" while we send in our "A Team." They frequently use a direct strategy to sell against us, by showing the customer how many references they have. For the first phase of any project, however, we can compete against anyone.—Boyer

Quado's objective was to do an initial public offering (IPO) within the next eighteen months. It was critical for Quado to maintain revenue growth and high profitability in order to have a successful IPO. However, well-publicized project failures could have an adverse effect. Since everyone at Quado had stock options, opportunities were scrutinized to avoid any high-risk projects. A large part of Quado's past success derived from its ability to attract and retain experienced consultants. Offering the opportunity to work on interesting and leading edge projects is considered important to future recruiting.

THE TAYLOR CORPORATION

The Taylor Corporation traced its history back to 1919 as a wholesaler of woolen products. The company survived the Great Depression and following World War II opened its first two retail stores specializing in wool products. This was the beginning of a successful retail and mail order chain store business that eventually grew to $6 million in sales. In 1963, Taylor acquired a small, virtually bankrupt company that was an electronics retailer. The company had nine retail stores and a mail order business that sold primarily to ham operators and electronic buffs. Since 1963, Taylor has grown to more than 7,000 locations throughout the U.S. and over $5.6 billion in annual sales.

Taylor Corporation has undergone a lot of changes in the past five years, spinning off several unsuccessful business ventures and consolidating and refurbishing its retail outlets. They also experienced a large information systems project failure in the previous year, causing the business units to be less than confident in the ability of their internal information systems department.

> Our organization was not prepared to take on a project of that nature. People were comfortable supporting our older systems. They were not ready for change. Unfortunately, management did not recognize this soon enough. The project was 100% over time and budget before anyone even thought to look at the problem. The technology was ultimately blamed for what I think was clearly a people issue.—Former information systems employee

Senior management had brought in a whole new team to revamp the information systems department. The new chief information officer (CIO), Teri Sullivan, was determined to tear down any walls that had been built between her new department and the business units. The proposed project had to be successful in order to regain the confidence of the business units.

> Being a retail organization, the company is fairly price-sensitive and willing to accept a bit more risk in order to save a dime. This is why we had a high failure rate.—Former information systems employee

This was Taylor's first attempt at building an interactive Internet site, so the technology portion of the project was viewed as very complex. Taylor felt that it was important that the systems integration firm involved in this project should have experience with large-scale Intranet projects. Taylor's current company-information only Intranet site was relatively inexpensive to create and could only be accessed within Taylor by certain employees. This experience established expectations with Taylor's senior management that the costs for this Internet project would be relatively low.

> Taylor's senior management expected hardware costs to be the most expensive item on this project. Early estimates from our hardware vendor were approximately $750,000 for the necessary hardware.—Boyer

> Teri was previously the vice president of human resources so she had an appreciation for the human factors involved in the project. The project team for Taylor was made up of information system technical and project management resources. Teri gave the project team significant input into the decision process. The project team's decision criteria were the following: Can the vendor deliver? And can we team with them to enhance our skills? While the project team wanted to insure a successful implementation, they appeared concerned that by bringing in Synectics, their roles in the project would be substantially reduced, therefore limiting their professional growth with the Internet.—Chaffin

A project of this nature is a significant undertaking for Taylor. The technologies are new, and this is the first time its information systems department would be building a system for customer use. While technical issues associated with developing the screens that the individuals saw will present some challenges, Thorby felt that this was not the main challenge of the project. Understanding how end users (customers and employees) would want to interact with the system and organizational issues associated with building and supporting the new systems he considered to be most critical to the success of the project. This played into several of Quado's strengths, particularly its experience in change management.

THE TAYLOR OPPORTUNITY

After spending a week interviewing all the senior management at Taylor, Synectics, one of the large integration firms, had put together some rough estimates for the entire project. The estimate was $9 million for full implementation of the project. Taylor was certainly shocked by Synectics' initial cost estimate. Taylor's management was considering this proposal when Quado was introduced to the CIO through a current customer of Quado.

While Quado did not have experience with large-scale Internet projects, this could be a great opportunity for Quado to gain the references it needed in the Internet practice. This may also be an opportunity for Taylor to reduce its cost. Quado had a much lower overhead than the larger systems integration firms and a low price offer might be considered the cost of entry for Quado into this growing business.

The Quado team had spent some time reviewing notes from the original interviews but did not have enough information to propose costs for the entire project. There were also concerns as to whether Synectics had captured all of the requirements or estimated the project cost at a realistic number. Two meetings had been scheduled for Quado to walk through its approach with Taylor. The first meeting, scheduled for next week, will be a 30-minute session with Taylor's CIO. In this meeting Quado would be expected to present its overall approach to the project and its cost estimates. The CIO's confidence in Quado's ability to deliver and the recommendation of Taylor's project team will be critical for Quado's to have an opportunity to win. The second meeting, two hours with the entire project team (12) from Taylor, was to discuss Quado's approach and allay any concerns the project team might have with Quado. This meeting is scheduled for two weeks from today.

This is a very tight schedule for Quado and not at all typical of how the selling cycle of most projects develops. Commenting on this opportunity. Mike Chaffin explained:

> When we first entered the sales process, it appeared that we had such a remote chance of winning that we didn't pay much attention to what happens should we win. Because of the size and strategic nature of this project, most people at Quado thought we were wasting our time because we had no Internet client references. My company felt that we were being used by Taylor to get a better price from Synectics. I think Quado is now beginning to worry that we might actually win this project. We're still the underdog, and we have to develop a "win theme" to present to the executive sponsor and project team.

It was also clear that Quado's sales approach would have to be well thought out to have any chance of succeeding. This would not be a straightforward features-benefits comparison type of presentation. Neither Mike nor his boss Rudy George, sales director at Quado, felt that they could slug it out with Synectics standing toe-to-toe and win the sale. In summarizing the situation, Mr. George commented:

> Synectics has positioned itself with Taylor as an Internet specialist. They have been in the account longer than we have, they have a lot more experience as a company with the Internet than we have, and they have the resources on board now to do the entire project. Synectics will attack us directly on our lack of Internet technology experience and our size. Based on our competition successfully positioning this project as strictly Internet-only with Taylor, the customer has to view Synectics as the least risky alternative because of its number of Internet references compared to Quado. We need to find a way to position this opportunity to allow us to compete.

Not only did Mike and Rudy need to develop a sales strategy for Taylor, but also they realized that they would need to sell the merits of the project internally to Quado.

> This is considered a large project for Quado and a mid-to-small size project for Synectics. Unfortunately, we have one large and several medium- to small-size projects that we are currently working on. All of our consultants are currently involved in these projects. The latter phases of the project for Taylor would eventually require a bunch of people over the next two years. Staffing it with all new people would raise our risk of delivery. But they pay me based on a percentage of revenue from new customers, not to be risk-averse. A project of this size would take care of my quota for next year.—Mike Chaffin

WHAT SHOULD QUADO DO?

Thorby realized that he had to make a decision with respect to Taylor before things developed too far and events made the decision for him. Due to the size of the project and its Internet focus, Thorby recognized that this sale had to be considered strategic in nature:

> We will be only a $20 million company this year and could be putting $9 million of next year's projected revenue of $25 million on one customer. Can we deliver a project of this size successfully without straining the organization or taking away potential revenue from a strategic account? This opportunity is not in an industry that we typically pursue. Although this service offering is an area that we want to get into, we currently don't have the experience Taylor desires. They have clearly stated that relevant Internet experience is required. Should we expend the resources chasing something that we are not well positioned to

> win or successfully take on? We would have to substantially increase the size of our company to take on the latter phases of this project not counting the growth that will be required to service our existing customers.

It is clear that Quado is coming into the game late, and Thorby was wondering if it was too late. It was even questionable whether Quado had enough information to accurately estimate the price for the entire project. Thorby's concern was that any numbers given to Taylor could be invalid and could potentially set their expectations too high.

When talking to sales, Thorby got the impression that it was very important to win this opportunity. This is a multiyear project involving a service offering in which Quado had no current experience. On the other hand, Quado has several people who have the requisite experience from previous jobs. Should Quado win this project, the customer has a recognizable name, which can be used as leverage with other prospective clients.

But Thorby also recognized that he had to consider the big picture. Was this opportunity right for Quado, and how could they minimize their risks? "We have revenue goals for sales," he thought, "low turnover goals for human resources, and delivery goals for our consultants. Is this business aligned with those goals?"

CASE 19 ROMANO PITESTI

Events had come to a head in Tickton-Jones Ltd. and the Marketing Director, Jack Simpson, had called in his Consumer Products Sales Manager, David Courtney, to sort out the problem.

> "To come straight to the point, David," said Jack, "I'm about up to here with this sales rep of yours. Romano Pitesti. . . . Am I sick of hearing the guy's name! Everywhere I go, someone bends my ear about him. Last week it was the receptionist complaining about his making personal telephone calls during company time. Yesterday it was the security people about his untidy parking habits. And this morning, the accounts department is abuzz with outrage over his expense returns. Quite frankly, David, these are not isolated instances—he's out of control and I want to know what you intend to do about him, before the whole company is in uproar."

BACKGROUND

Tickton-Jones Ltd. was formed two years previously, when Tickton Flexible Products Ltd. acquired Samuel Jones Ltd., a local family-owned company. At the time, Tickton's annual sales were approaching $12 million and they employed 230 people, compared with Jones' $4.5 million and 110 people, respectively. Tickton was well established as a compounder of polyurethane and rubber materials and had its own molding facility for a wide range of industrial components. Jones, after years of steady business as a manufacturer of shoes, ladies' handbags, and travel goods, had recently moved successfully into sports shoes and for the first time had made an impact in the export field.

Ben Jones was the chairman and majority owner of Samuel Jones Ltd. He was the grandson of the founder and the last of the Jones family line with an active participation in the business. At age 63, he wanted to sell out and retire to the Channel Islands with his wife, who had a health problem. The remaining two senior directors were willing to accept early retirement on generous terms.

Ben Jones had been very happy to accept Tickton's offer and was satisfied that the new company would not involve too much upheaval for his employees. He was a paternal chairman with a strong Protestant work ethic but in recent years this had softened, and the organization had become somewhat looser in all aspects of its operations.

Not everyone on the Tickton Board had been in favor of the acquisition, largely because it represented a major diversification into consumer products. But the Managing Director had swayed the decision on grounds of too much current dependence on declining customer industries (e.g., motor vehicles, railways, general mechanical engineering). Jones was considered

This case was prepared by A. F. Millman of the Conventry Polytechnic, England.

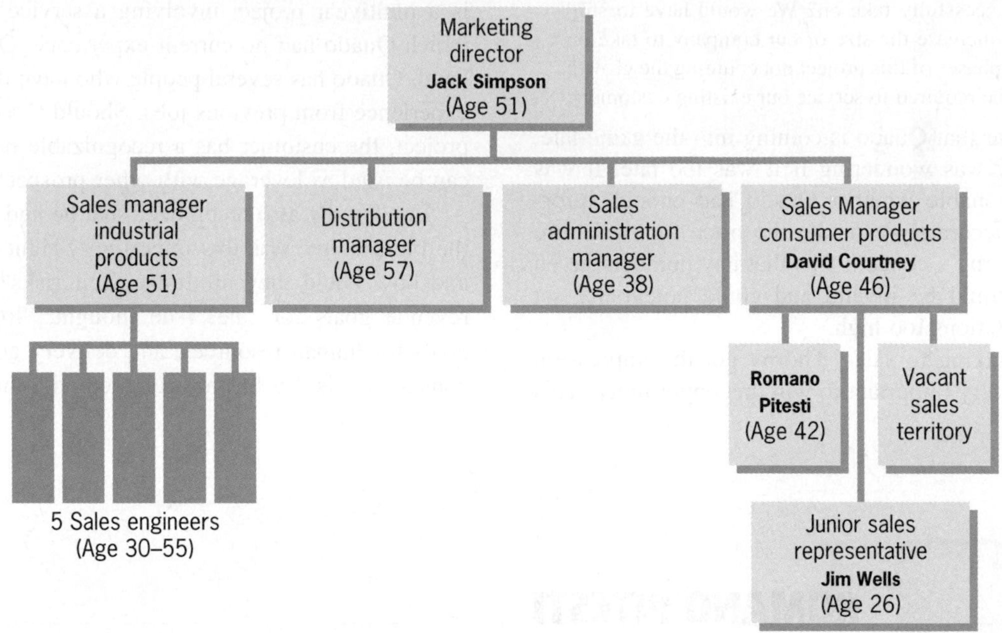

EXHIBIT 1 Organization of the Tickton-Jones Marketing Department

to have good products in growth markets. In the words of Tickton's Managing Director: "An opportunity like this might never pass our way again. Ben Jones assures me that he has a sound labor force and, like our own, they're not strongly unionized. The sports and leisure shoe business looks particularly attractive. Put our expertise in molding technology alongside their distribution network, and it could be one of our main product lines in five years. It's now or never—it would be virtually impossible to find equivalent facilities within a 5-mile radius." Within four weeks, the acquisition was agreed upon.

Due to the departure of Jones's senior directors, integration of managerial staff provided few problems. Jones's production manager, Bill Thompson, was retained and placed in charge of the Jones site, which was effectively reduced to a manufacturing operation. All nonproduction staff, including the sales manager, David Courtney, were moved to the Tickton site.

However, the absorption of middle/lower-level administrative staff had not been easy, and there were still cliques of former Jones employees who felt aggrieved. For example, certain secretaries had found themselves reporting to managers of lower status; friction in the sales administration office and accounts office caused internal divisions; and there was growing rivalry among the industrial sales engineers and the consumer sales representatives.

The organization of Tickton-Jones' marketing department is shown in Exhibit 1. From the marketing point of view, Jack Simpson had merely added another arm to his departmental organization—the Consumer Products Group under David Courtney.

Prior to the acquisition, David Courtney had been very much a field sales manager. He was responsible for the usual sales management tasks of forecasting and budgeting, and spent most of his time dealing with major existing accounts or on the road developing new accounts. David Courtney, Romano Pitesti, and Jim Wells were all paid a salary plus commission. The commission element accounted for 20 to 25 percent of their annual pay. On joining Tickton-Jones' salary structure they received salary only, though in money terms this did not constitute a loss of total pay.

On the question of company car policy and day-to-day business expenses, there were major differences. Indeed, since at Samuel Jones Ltd. they applied to so few people, there were no formal procedures and Ben Jones signed off on everything, almost without question. In contrast, Tickton had a written document clearly setting out the type of car applicable to particular grades; spending limits for travel and entertainment, and so on. There was also a handbook covering Tickton's general conditions of service, which automatically became the Tickton-Jones handbook.

ROMANO PITESTI

To say that Romano Cesare Pitesti was different from the industrial sales engineers would be an understatement. While they "toed the line" and had quite similar training and attitudes, Romano "sailed close to the wind."

Romano liked to feel that he was an individualist and repeatedly proved disruptive in formal group situations. Though basically conscientious and hardworking, he operated in bursts of enthusiasm that usually came to nothing but sometimes, through sheer tenacity on his part, brought the company an important order.

He was the master of the instant opinion and often entered into conversation on a range of issues of which he had only cursory knowledge and experience. This led him into a number of embarrassing situations, reflecting his gullibility and boyish naiveté.

There were occasions when he could be charming, understanding, and a good listener, especially in female company. And even more so in the presence of Sheila Jones, his previous chairman's wife! It was well known that she had a soft spot for Romano and had once saved him from serious trouble following an incident involving a secretary after the office Christmas party.

Romano was flamboyant in all things, yet beneath this facade lay a caring and deeply sensitive person. His colleague, Jim Wells, summed him up as "part hero, part villain, and part clown."

From the day he transferred to Tickton-Jones, Romano was regarded as a curiosity and a "figure of fun." The reasons were not hard to find. He dressed impeccably and in the height of fashion. Some would say that he overdid it for a 42-year-old, and he was soon dubbed "The Great Gatsby," "Peter Pan," and "The Aging Lothario."

In his first year with Tickton-Jones, Romano married Wendy Churchill, a 28-year-old set designer with a regional television company. This brought him in contact with numerous television personalities and turned him into a prolific name dropper. The stories he told provided unlimited ammunition for the industrial sales engineers, who cruelly taunted him at every opportunity. But Romano, unperturbed, shrugged off their remarks, usually with some witty return.

Despite all these oddities and eccentricities, Romano's sales performance was exemplary.

THE MEETING WITH DAVID COURTNEY

With Jack Simpson's words ringing in his ears, David Courtney summoned Romano to a meeting. Romano insisted that it would upset his call schedule, but after some cajoling agreed to attend the following morning.

David opened the meeting with firm words: "Romano, something has to be done about the way you operate in this company. It has been put to me that you are out of control. I'm taking the kicks at the moment and I don't like it! I've got a list of incidents to review with you—and you had better have good answers."

1. **David:** Your time-keeping leaves a lot to be desired, and you've been accused of wasting your own time and other people's. The normal starting time is 8:30 A.M. and not some time after 9:00 A.M. when you can make it!

   Romano: That's all very well, but I'm entitled to a little freedom on time. Only yesterday I left home at 6:00 A.M. to visit a customer and didn't return home until late in the evening. How many of those complaining about my time-keeping would be prepared to join me at such times of the day and night without overtime payments?

   David: And what about time wasting? You seem to spend a fair amount of time with secretaries and typists.

   Romano: No more than anyone else. It's just that other people spread their time over the week and mine's more concentrated. You know how much importance you attach to letter and report writing. Well, they all have to be typed.

2. **David:** That brings me to the time you claim to spend report writing. Taking Fridays off is a favorite for sniping by the industrial sales engineers.

   Romano: If you want me to write reports, you have got to allow me time to write them—it's as simple as that.

   David: The industrial sales engineers write their reports over their lunch break or between sales calls. Why can't you? There's a rumor circulating the company that you played golf last Friday.

   Romano: Yes, that's right. I played golf with Arthur Dixon—you know, Singleton's Purchasing Manager. I'm pretty close to a regular order from them. I'm playing with Arthur again on the 29th—should I cancel it?

   David: No, no—I only wish you to make yourself a little more visible on Fridays. Not every Friday, just now and then.

3. **David:** Are you aware that you have higher claims for replacement of damaged clothing than anyone in the company? Why?

   Romano: I can't help it if I wear trendy Italian suits and shoes. That damaged briefcase I claimed last month really was two-tone crocodile skin and cost me $180. I can't visit my customers dressed like those scruffy Herberts in the Industrial Group. They wouldn't let me on the premises.

David: OK, OK, just try to moderate your claims in future. I'm the poor guy who has to sign them off.

4. **David:** The biggest problem, as always, surrounds your company car. It's like a big orange blotch on the company landscape!

Romano: I can't see what you have against my car, David. It's only a Ford Escort 1.3 and bought within the company rules. We have very little flexibility on choice of model. After all, it's my mobile office—I live in it for 15 hours per week.

David: Yes, but do you have to choose bright orange and add all those accessories? The industrial sales engineers all have more sober colors such as bottle green and navy blue. Do you really need two large spot lamps with checkered covers, a rear spoiler, and whiplash radio aerial?

Romano: I paid for the accessories myself. You could do the same if you wish. Incidentally, there's a nice vivid green in the Ford Sierra right now!

David: I can almost bear the color with my sunglasses on—but not when you park your car on the double yellow lines near the reception area.

Romano: I knew it! That receptionist has got it in for me. It would be her who complained and not the security people. I only popped in to the switchboard to collect my telephone messages from the overnight answering machine.

David: I can accept that as an isolated incident. But your car is so obvious—everywhere you go, it's instantly recognizable. Which leads me to a very serious issue—did you or did you not use your company car to ferry voters to the local council elections?

Romano: Yes, I did. I had my doubts about it and was on the verge of opting out. Then I realized Bill Thompson, the production manager, was using his company car for the Labor party, so I thought, what's good enough for Labor is good enough for the Liberals.

David: Perhaps I had better have a word with Bill about the matter. We'll pick this one up later.

5. **Romano:** You've mentioned all these minor irritations, David. Have you ever had cause to question my sales performance? I'm the best salesperson in this company, and you know it! When did I last fail to meet my targets? And have you received any complaints from customers? I was the same at Samuel Jones. Don't forget, we're a rep short at the moment. A few more salespeople like me and we would be a market leader in no time. Who was it who secured the Milan export order?

But at that particular moment there was an interruption. Romano's telephone paging beeper was signaling an incoming call, and he picked up David's telephone. It was Joe Pinkerton. Romano's number-two customer, with an urgent query.

Romano sat back in his chair, put his feet on David's wastepaper basket, and entered into a drawn-out conversation. Twenty minutes later he was still engrossed in conversation. David shook his head and decided to abandon the meeting. Romano gave him a wry grin as he left the office.

SKATA, INC.

One snowy Saturday in January 2004, Mary Reid was reviewing the performance of her field sales force. Mary was the national sales manager for Skata Inc. Skata produced vinyl siding and plastic plumbing supplies for the construction industry. Their products were sold to 120 distributors in the United States, who made them available to lumberyards, hardware stores, and contractors. The company employed fifty-six salespeople who worked with the distributors and made calls on contractors, retailers, and architects. Skata had organized its sales force into five geographic districts headed by sales managers. The

This case was prepared by Douglas J. Dalrymple of Indiana University.

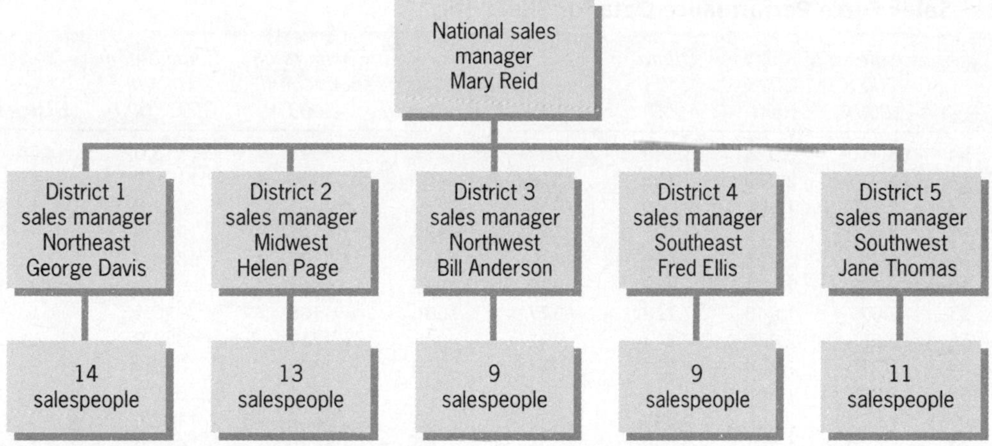

EXHIBIT 1 Skata Sales Organization

five sales managers reported directly to Mary Reid (Exhibit 1). Siding and plumbing fixtures were shipped by truck from company warehouses to distributors and directly to large buyers.

Salespeople were assigned fixed territories and were responsible for increasing sales in their areas. They were given quotas based on potential and past company sales in their areas. Territory performance was also measured by the penetration ratio. This ratio compared company sales with published industry data showing the volume of building contracts awarded in each territory. Salespeople who exceeded their quotas were eligible for recognition awards, larger territories, and promotions.

Field reps were paid a straight commission that ranged from 1 to 3 percent of sales. The size of the commission varied according to the experience of the salesperson. In addition, salespeople received an expense allowance that averaged $8,500 per year. The five district sales managers were paid a salary and a bonus based on the volume produced in their districts.

Consolidated sales of Skata, including the overseas division, totaled $355,670,000 in 2003. Although sales were up in 2003, net profits had declined. These results were partially due to increased competition and price cutting. Reid wanted to learn more about her sales force because she was under considerable pressure to improve profits in the new year.

Reid decided to start her analysis by calling up some basic sales force performance data on her desktop computer. These figures are shown in Exhibit 2. The territory sales quota, penetration, and contribution margin are given for twelve months, even though a few salespeople worked for less than a year. As a result, Reid adjusted calls and commissions to make it easier to compare salespeople with one another.

Next, Reid transferred her data files to the new spreadsheet analysis program that she had acquired. This program allowed her to create new variables and perform a variety of evaluations on her field salespeople. Reid decided to calculate some simple correlation coefficients among her control variables (Exhibit 3). Age appeared to be related to sales, and there were some interesting correlations with other variables. Reid decided to focus on the most significant associations to see what effects they might have on sales force supervision. Based on a review of the numbers in Exhibit 3, she decided to plot some of the variables to give a performance matrix for evaluation.

Skata's marketing manager had been asking for some recommendations on sales managers and salespeople who could be honored at the national sales meeting scheduled for February. Although it would be very easy to rank them on sales achievements, Reid wondered if she should prepare some sort of composite index that would evaluate the sales force on a variety of factors.

Reid had recently come across an article in a marketing journal suggesting that salespeople follow a career path that resembles the product life cycle. According to the article, salespeople start off exploring the sales field, go into a development phase, mature, and then experience declining performance measures as they approach retirement. The suggested relationship is shown in Exhibit 4. Note that sales are lowest in the exploration phase, grow rapidly in the development

EXHIBIT 2 Sales Force Performance Data for Skata, Inc.

Name	*Age*	*Sales 2003 (000)*	*Sales 2003 (000)*	*Quota 2003 (000)*	*Penetration 2003*	*Calls 2003*	*Commission per Month 2003*	*Contribution Margin 2003 (000)*	*Sales District*	*Months of Work 2003*
Field	54	$3.710	$2.943	$3.548	702	917	$6928	$1318.0	1	12
White	29	2.971	2.070	2.300	419	467	4990	1149.7	2	8
Evans	35	2.927	2.364	2.749	1948	1219	4075	1041.8	1	12
Long	37	2.428	1.773	2.107	315	880	4125	903.8	2	12
Hunt	30	2.298	1.753	1.899	710	1213	4905	854.9	3	12
Reed	32	2.741	2.421	2.879	2820	935	4967	977.0	1	12
Knight	33	2.577	1.948	2.228	527	1096	4198	920.4	5	12
Quinn	36	2.565	2.432	2.847	297	807	4752	961.9	2	12
Reilly	34	2.278	1.684	1.899	957	939	4305	833.8	3	12
Adams	33	1.872	1.308	3.016	338	889	3851	699.4	2	12
Zimmer	37	2.982	2.399	2.649	644	1165	5618	1105.4	3	12
Smith	27	1.669	1.751	2.098	225	780	3250	635.9	4	12
Miller	37	3.589	3.272	3.698	368	1091	6030	1329.2	2	12
Hall	51	3.755	3.322	3.739	306	1181	7107	1366.6	4	12
Vance	29	1.928	2.054	2.391	580	866	3684	698.3	3	12
Martin	27	1.292	.914	1.777	343	1178	3659	465.1	5	10
Sharp	48	3.884	3.301	3.798	1490	1354	6726	1375.9	1	12
Jones	43	3.500	2.836	3.150	1960	1180	6565	1219.1	3	12
Baker	26	2.944	2.256	2.738	571	402	4251	1120.9	2	12
Queen	37	1.945	1.886	2.248	506	492	3402	704.6	2	8
Kelly	35	2.068	1.932	2.141	342	825	4883	759.0	2	12
Lewis	60	1.501	1.295	1.339	448	1199	4466	535.1	5	12
Young	57	2.693	2.067	2.421	1123	806	6070	979.0	1	12
Isom	27	1.551	1.612	1.878	246	832	3137	584.7	2	12
Urban	38	1.099	.716	.962	231	353	3706	387.4	2	12
Green	40	1.262	1.071	1.309	453	1313	3876	468.4	5	12
Scott	67	2.243	2.042	2.767	550	968	5535	793.6	2	12
Norris	33	2.448	2.225	2.558	453	1060	4129	905.5	4	12
Ward	34	2.713	1.567	1.998	267	958	4960	996.7	4	12
Wood	45	2.541	2.670	2.811	873	1260	4918	899.3	1	12
Upchurch	49	2.759	2.583	3.086	365	969	6056	1008.8	4	12
York	65	2.606	2.400	2.697	497	1147	5352	986.7	4	12
Grant	33	2.786	2.400	2.197	441	1461	4279	1009.6	5	4
Taylor	38	2.965	2.174	2.448	1151	1373	5473	1075.8	5	12
Carter	63	3.716	2.704	3.128	1332	1047	6920	1347.0	1	12
Wolf	64	2.384	1.990	2.281	3000	614	6202	835.8	1	12
Olsen	43	2.126	2.050	2.200	455	1173	4240	785.2	5	12
Edwards	47	2.203	1.930	2.600	141	882	5870	818.8	5	8
Summers	32	4.078	2.762	3.183	602	767	6725	1472.1	1	12
Black	53	2.742	2.434	2.682	931	945	5976	998.6	3	12
Allen	38	2.617	2.475	2.898	300	938	3353	968.1	4	8
Owens	32	3.595	3.323	3.848	1861	1135	5339	1346.2	1	12
Day	63	3.358	2.801	3.282	1133	1604	8265	1205.7	1	12
Parsons	38	1.790	1.842	2.105	203	941	4029	655.9	4	12
Dunn	49	2.596	2.372	2.796	310	1162	5089	927.9	5	12
Thomas	39	1.678	1.571	1.812	907	1281	3136	608.5	3	12
Voss	30	2.192	1.875	2.469	166	673	5824	829.3	4	7
Stone	48	1.879	1.711	2.032	990	1182	5124	679.4	5	12
Zorn	30	2.011	1.739	2.281	243	568	3657	742.2	2	11
Jackson	33	1.903	1.894	2.161	450	840	3790	701.3	3	4
Nichols	36	1.609	1.690	1.898	381	1307	2527	583.3	5	12
Irwin	30	2.631	2.170	2.560	199	697	3803	987.9	2	10
Page	47	3.047	2.939	3.298	806	1200	5846	1099.6	1	12
Cook	37	2.328	2.054	2.398	664	933	4665	859.6	1	12
Walker	39	2.055	2.043	2.399	519	1099	3594	735.9	3	12
Fox	28	3.411	2.689	3.248	3322	706	5335	1187.5	1	12

EXHIBIT 3 Correlations Among Sales Force Performance Factors, 2003

	Age	*Sales*	*Sales Growth 2003/2002*	*Sales to Quota*	*Penetration*	*Calls*	*Commission per Month*	*Contribution Margin Percent*	*Sales per Call*	*Contribution per Call*
Age	1.00	.21	−.09	.04	.16	.30	.59	−.39	−.15	−.17
Sales	.21	1.00	.22	.45	.39	.17	.76	−.15	.52	.51
Sales growth	−.09	.22	1.00	.64	.08	−.19	.22	−.05	.35	.35
Sales quota	.04	.45	.64	1.00	.19	.03	.34	−.09	.36	.35
Penetration	.16	.39	.08	.19	1.00	.08	.34	−.53	.19	.17
Calls	.30	.17	−.19	.03	.08	1.00	.22	−.28	−.68	−.67
Commission/month	.59	.76	.22	.34	.34	.22	1.00	−.27	.29	.25
Contribution percent	−.39	−.15	−.05	−.09	−.53	−.28	−.27	1.00	.18	.23
Sales/call	−.15	.52	.35	.36	.19	−.68	.29	.18	1.00	.99
Contribution/call	−.17	.51	.35	.35	.17	−.67	.23	.23	.99	1.00

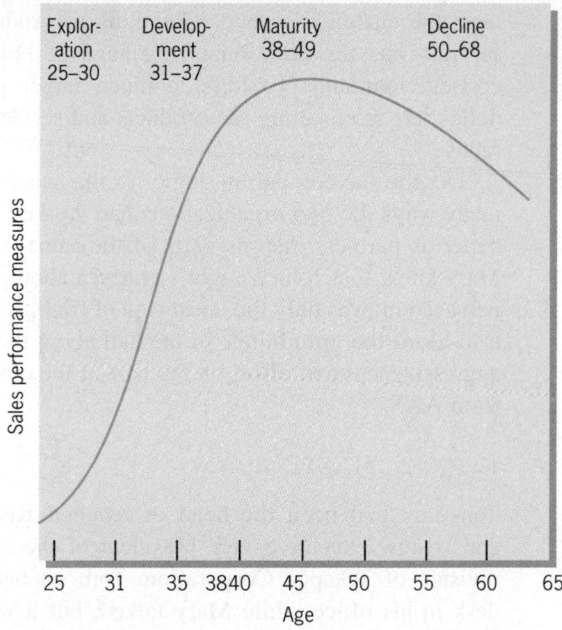

EXHIBIT 4 Sales Force Career Path Life Cycle

stage, level off in the mature phase, and drop off in the decline stage. Mary wondered whether the career life cycle concept described in Exhibit 4 applied to Skata salespeople. Skata employed a variety of sales reps ranging in age from 26 to 67; the median age was 37. Reid thought it would be useful to calculate an age distribution of the sales force to see if there was anything meaningful to be learned.

To help find out whether the career life cycle applied to Skata, Mary decided it might be instructive to calculate the means of various performance factors for groups of salespeople divided according to the career categories described in Exhibit 4. Mary was sure that there was something to be learned about the sales force from the performance data if she just kept her computer humming. The data in Exhibit 2 also gave an indication of the turnover rate in the sales force in 2003, and Reid wondered if some adjustments were needed in the compensation program. Reid was concerned that the results of her performance matrix and career life cycle analyses would require some changes in terms of hiring, firing, training, and motivation.

TEKSPAN CORPORATION

Mary Stramm sunk back into her first-class seat. The perks of flying with the CEO weren't bad, but she knew that there was no such thing as a free lunch. She would soon be on another "special assignment." Mary was officially the vice president of human resources at Tekspan Systems, a developer of software for middle-market companies, but unofficially was CEO's John Vaught's troubleshooter. He called her in on all sensitive customer issues, and this one definitely fit the bill. They were flying home after a tense meeting with Dave Cowley, CIO of Barnett Engineering, an important account. Dave was entertaining a competitor's offer.

After a few minutes in the air, John started to recap the meeting, "Dave has a legitimate gripe. Our people seem to be driving him nuts trying to sell additional projects left and right. We're disrupting things too much by trying to stimulate demand for changes that his company doesn't want and can't handle. We're taking up too much of Barnett's management's time. I need you to look into this.

"No problem," Mary responded.

"I called Tom Lay before this trip and he gave me an earful. Start by calling Tom and get your impression of the situation. Frankly, I wonder if our sales compensation program isn't part of the problem."

"That could be," Mary offered cautiously.

"With sales of product slowing, we need to sell more services. That's where the growth is, but we don't want to abuse our customers in the process."

Mary looked out the window thinking about the next step.

BACKGROUND

Ten months earlier, Tekspan had acquired the systems-integration and consulting firm Applied Knowledge Systems (AKS), which had been one of Tekspan's alliance partners. The acquisition seemed to offer great opportunities for synergy. Tekspan hoped to sell more software, which is a natural by-product of an AKS consulting engagement. AKS, on the other hand, would benefit from the wider range of companies with which Tekspan has relationships and the aggressive new customer acquisition competencies of the Tekspan sales force.

After the acquisition, the organization had spent a lot of time developing "solutions," which consisted of standard bundles of products and services for the market. It has been Tekspan's experience that neither products nor services alone fully solved a customer's problems, but that it took the application of the right mix of products and services bundled together to meet the customer's needs. Bundling of products and services has the additional advantage of being both cost-efficient and providing a much larger potential dollar sale than selling the products and services separately.

Despite the compelling logic for the acquisition, in many ways the two organizations had worked together better as partners than as parts of the same company. Mary knew that John Vaught's concern about the Barnett account was only the latest sign of friction. She had also heard the grumblings in the hall about the lack of aggressiveness and effort on the part of the consultants from AKS.

THE CONSULTANTS' VIEW

Tom Lay had been the head of Applied Knowledge and is now executive vice president of the Solutions division of Tekspan Corporation. Tom sat behind the desk in his office while Mary talked, but it was clear that he had been stung by John's concern about the Barnett account. "Look, this really isn't about all those sales calls on his people," he said defensively. "Dave Cowley is upset because his boss has been taking my suggestions to improve his operations. He is just jealous because I have better access to his boss than he does because I run with him on the weekends. CIOs don't like it when consultants have better access than they do." Mary couldn't help glancing at the number of marathon medals displayed in Tom's office. "John should recognize that it's because of this special access that Barnett purchased the HR package they signed up for last month. The account manager had nothing to do with the sale—his commission is a gift."

This case was prepared by William L. Cron of Texas Christian University and Thomas E. DeCarlo of Iowa State University.

"Oh, I see, we don't need account executives anymore, do we?" Mary asked, knowing Tom could take the gentle jab.

"I'll admit, the account execs are great at getting us in the door," Tom continued, "especially when we have had no prior relationship with the contact. They also are good at selling an initial financial software package, which is usually what prospects purchase first. But the account execs don't help much in growing the account because they lack the technical knowledge needed to sell the add-on business.

"Take Barnett, for instance, if it weren't for the extra effort of Dick Carlson during the final month of the rollout for the basic finance package, we may have lost the sale," Tom said, referring to the principal consultant on the engagement. "I was there a lot myself. That's how you get to really know the people and to understand a client's business. Between you and I, the account managers only know how to push product. Selling a solution designed to meet a client's needs takes a consultant's perspective."

"All right," Mary said, sighing, "but this gets us nowhere. What was the point of our combining these two companies if the customer contact philosophies are incompatible?" After taking a breath, she added, "Tom, you just made a remark about the commissions. Do you think there is something wrong with our incentive program?"

"Well, think about it," Tom said with an admonishing tone. "The current compensation plan rewards the sales force for all the work sold into an account—forever! It doesn't matter if they contributed to the sale or not. On the other hand, our people—the consultants in Solutions—have to sell to keep billable, but the salesperson who won the account gets the commission, even if it was years ago that they won the account and had nothing to do with the current sale at all. Does this make sense to you?"

"But the salespeople's contributions are important to our success, aren't they?" asked Mary.

"Of course they are. At least sometimes. But there are big holes in the plan." Tom glanced up and saw Lola Krammer passing his door and called for her to come in his office. Lola was in charge of the consulting group that implemented the facilities portion of the solutions package that Barnett purchased. Facilities management software and services accounted for only a small fraction of the company's revenue, and in the current economic climate few customers signed up for it. Mary knew Lola, and considered her to be very professional and levelheaded. She was someone that could be counted on to be objective.

After Lola walked in the office, Tom asked, "Lola, Dave Cowley at Barnett has complained that they are seeing too many of our people. What would happen if we waited for the account reps to sell work for us?"

"If I waited for that, I might as well start looking for another job," responded Lola. "The price of a facilities implementation is about a quarter of the price of any other package. Our projects are tiny, especially in today's economy. Understand, it is going to take the account rep just as much time to sell for us as it would take to sell any other package. Besides, he would have to build relationships with people in the client's facilities department—people he has no other reason to get to know otherwise. He'd much rather be selling a high priced financial, HR, or sales package instead due to the commissions."

"So you have to sell it?"

"Right. But, I don't blame the account execs for being uninterested, I just can't wait around. I won't be able to hang onto the team I've built up over the past years if I can't keep them busy. So I sell."

"I sense that you would rather not," responded Mary.

"I don't really mind," Lola shrugged. "Besides, I have a natural advantage on the account execs. I know the facilities people and belong to their associations. The account reps don't really understand what we do. We are not alone in this. There are several small units in AKS—excuse me, I mean in Tekspan—that suffer from this problem. I've asked if the company is really interested in our practice areas and I'm told it is and that we are needed so that the firm can offer a complete array of products and services—one stop shopping."

"What do you think of the compensation plan?" chimed in Tom.

After a long pause, Lola said, "I don't really understand it. But I figure that the higher-ups have their reasons."

'Thanks for stopping in, Lola," Tom said. "And keep up the great work."

Just as she was about to leave, Lola turned and added, "The funny thing is that before the acquisition, I was always considered a hero at AKS for going out and selling my own work. Now it upsets people. Good luck with your investigation, Mary."

After Lola had left the office, Tom added, "In this market, facilities software isn't all that popular with clients. But when the economy turns again and companies are expanding, there's a lot of interest. Lola has to keep things going until then. When the turn comes, I'll bet the account execs will take notice of us."

THE ACCOUNT EXECUTIVES' VIEW

Knowing that she needed to hear the sales organization's point of view, Mary set up a meeting with Shannon Moncrief, vice president of sales and marketing at Tekspan. When she showed up for the meeting she was stunned to see the cast on his leg.

"You would think I'd know better by now," he said with a laugh. "I was at one or our customer's company picnics and they invited me to join in the 'big' softball game. Now why would anyone slide into home during another company's softball game? I don't even know the final score." He laughed again and asked, "So what is this changing the compensation plan for my account execs about?"

Mary knew not to take Shannon's easy manner at face value. Tekspan owed a lot of its success to his relentless drive and ability to manage and lead people. She proceeded to describe what she had heard from Tom Lay and the consultants.

"I've known Tom for over ten years, and I'm a big supporter of his," Shannon said. "He is one of the brightest guys I know. As you know, I pushed hard for the acquisition of his firm. But he doesn't understand sales."

"Boy, I have to say that Tom is a pretty good salesman, based on his record," Mary responded.

"Sure. Sure. Of course he is. One of the best. It's because of Tom and one or two others that we bought AKS. I mean he doesn't understand what it takes to manage a sales force. For all of Tom's posturing, Solutions sales are only 22 percent of the business. We are hard-charging salespeople who are well rewarded for our efforts to make the numbers. The reality is that the Solutions camp can't deliver the goods. Aside from Tom and a few others, most of them feel selling is unprofessional. They don't want to dirty their hands.

"The Barnett account you mentioned is a good case in point. Philip Davies worked for two years to get us into Barnett. Sure, the basic financial package they purchased was a little disappointing in terms of the size of the sale, and he wouldn't have had much to show for his efforts. But now, Barnett is generating all kinds of revenue and profits for Tekspan. Those consultants would not even have known who Barnett was if it weren't for Philip and the work he put in on the front end. I don't question the job that Tom Lay and Dick Carlson did there, but you can't screw Philip out of his commission on last month's HR implementation. We would lose him if all he got was commission on the initial package."

Mary recalled at least two other occasions when she had been threatened with the loss of "Prince Philip." "Yes," she said, "but if he didn't really contribute to the HR sale. . ."

"Mary, you have to understand how sales really works. Sometimes you work your butt off, do everything right, cross every 't' and dot every 'i', and you still don't win. Sometimes it comes too easy. It all nets out. Philip knows how to maximize his time and talents. He knew things were going well at Barnett and he felt he could spend his time more productively elsewhere. And you know what, he uncovered Westenhover Electric, which, by the way, is about to sign up for an HR and a planning implementation program this week. Do you really want to penalize him for doing the right thing? Oh, by the way, Dick Carlson is the project principal on that account too. You think he worked hard on it? No! He was too busy at Barnett to be bothered with Westenhover. Philip knows you have to stay in front of your customers to move them through the pipeline."

"Tom said Dick practically lived at Barnett for a month to help with that rollout."

"I know. But look, the consultants get compensated, and well compensated, on utilization. The more the customer uses the system the more they get paid. They have an ongoing stream of income. They didn't do much to sell the extension work at Westenhover, but they'll still get paid for the work they do there. They want it both ways."

"How much of the first sales to Barnett was product and how much was services?" Mary asked.

"You've been talking with Tom, I can tell. He's always accusing my people of 'pushing product' rather than 'crafting solutions'—nothing pejorative about that language, is there? He may have a point, though. Maybe the account execs do need more training in selling solutions, but while you are at it, train Tom's consultants to sell anything at all. At least my guys can sell product. Most of the consultants couldn't sell sunscreen at a nudist colony."

Mary had to laugh, in spite of herself. The idea of some of the more introverted techie consultants in that type of situation was amusing, she had to admit.

ON THE BRIGHT SIDE

That night, bits and pieces of the conversations Mary had that day kept coming to mind. She found herself wondering just how big a problem she was addressing. Was the merger just not working? She quickly dismissed this thought, however, because she knew that some of the account exec and project consultant teams were working well. She decided it was time to look into these to determine why some teams were working when others were not.

On Friday afternoon, she met with Vickie Morgan, a project consultant from Solutions, and Dirk Tyson, the account executive assigned to the Weatherford National Bank (WNB) account. Mary explained her purpose for meeting with Vickie and Dirk and asked, "You two have succeeded wildly at WNB. Has the compensation system helped or hurt?"

"I try not to think about it," joked Vickie. "If I did, it might just break up our team."

Laughing, Mary asked, "Do you agree with that, Dirk?"

"I've never seen a sales compensation plan that worked perfectly. This one's OK, I guess."

"So how do we create more successes like WNB?"

"Hire more account execs like Dirk," said Vickie.

"Could you elaborate on that a little?"

"Yeah, I'd like to hear more about that, too," Dirk said.

"I can trust him," Vickie said. "I can't say that for everyone I've worked with. I remember, just after the acquisition, I took an account executive, who will remain nameless, to meet with the president of one of my old accounts. We were there to explain why the two firms had come together and to ensure him that it would enhance the relationship we had with his company. The client was very gracious and the meeting was going along nicely, until the president mentioned a need he had. The account exec pounced on it and went into full sales mode. My client gave me a look as if to say, 'What's going on here?' He hadn't agreed to a sales pitch, and we were out of there in about 2 minutes. I called him up and apologized.

"Dirk would never make such a mistake. He knows how to listen, when to come to me and my consultants, and how to ask us to support him. Meanwhile, he's out there pounding the paving, which I don't have time to do. We've have sold more product at WNB than at any other account of its size as a result. I'll bet we can do the same for other companies we've targeted."

"Dirk, is this how you see it?"

"Actually, I could say similar things about Vickie. If I spend six months getting a customer to the point where he wants a meeting, I can trust her not to cancel on short notice because a current customer has asked for the same time slot. And when I introduce her to the client, she knows how to present herself and the technology. She doesn't go on about the latest technical fix till their eyes glaze over. She listens to their problems. She doesn't drop the ball."

Impressive, thought Mary when she left them, but how do we replicate that?

WHAT TO DO?

"Well," asked John, "what have you found out?"

"John, this may go deeper than compensation. The account execs provide broad market coverage, while our project consultants provide excellent content knowledge and deep working relationships. We need both. We just don't seem to have developed a way to sort out the two of them.

"Compensation can really clarify different people's priorities," John observed.

"Yes, but I think that the people with Tekspan and AKS prior to the merger were better suited to their old organizations than to the new solutions selling program. We are going to need to start recruiting to some new job profiles.

"I understand Mary, but we can't turn over a majority of the workforce in the next year without causing more problems than we solve. I need results before then."

THE SULLIVAN GROUP (A)

Bob Mitchell, Director of Risk Management for Madison Energy, a publicly traded firm that focuses on the servicing of producing oil and gas wells, picked up his phone and heard his secretary say, "A Mr. Matthew Kincaid of the Sullivan Group is here to see you."

"Send him in," Mitchell replied.

BACKGROUND INFORMATION

Madison Energy is a rapidly growing company, and the complexity of its risk management needs is increasing accordingly. The major assets Madison Energy needs to protect are its oil and gas wells, workers in the field, and the heavy equipment used on the wellsites. In fact, the company has now reached a level financially where it requires an array of insurance products and services, including some more exotic services such as those related to kidnapping, to adequately handle its growing exposure to loss. Given this exposure to risk, the company had hired in the past year Bob Mitchell as Director of Risk Management.

The usual first step of the selling process for insurance products and services is for a brokerage company to call on Madison Energy directly to try and setup a meeting with Bob Mitchell, Director of Risk Management. If Bob Mitchell felt that the situation warranted further investigation, he would set up a meeting between the broker and someone in Accounting Operations to gather information. A tour of the facilities would also take place to ensure familiarity with Madison's needs. Following information gathering, the broker would develop a proposal that would be presented to Mitchell. If he felt it was a viable and attractive proposal, he would pass it along to the Chief Financial Officer (CFO). If approved at this point, the CFO would present an overview of the proposal to the Audit Committee of the Board of Directors for final approval.

Matthew Kincaid, an Account Executive of the Sullivan Group, is about to discuss his company's insurance services and its specific experience with oil and gas clients. The only previous meeting between Bob Mitchell and Matthew Kincaid came two weeks ago at a local charity event. Mitchell invited Kincaid to come by the office to discuss what the Sullivan Group might be able to do for Madison Energy.

THE INTERVIEW

Mathew Kincaid enters Bob Mitchell's office and hands him a business card.

KINCAID: Good to see you again, Bob. Thanks for giving me some time to tell you about the Sullivan Group. We are a leader in risk management and insurance solutions, and we have developed the most effective program specifically for oil and gas companies like yours. Our program, based on exceptional client service, will improve your claims handling and save your company time. I think you will see that through this solution we can make you more efficient in your operations.

MITCHELL: Good. And please have a seat.

KINCAID: Thanks. At the Sullivan Group we work hard to truly understand the business of our clients. You see ...

Kincaid spends several minutes elaborating on the Sullivan Group's ability to get competitive quotes for energy companies, focus on client service and claims handling process..

KINCAID: As I was saying, what sets our firm apart is our total commitment to client service. We have our own 24/7 claims service. This is unique in the industry.

MITCHELL: Well, Matt, that all sounds great; however, we have been approached by a number of other firms touting the same services the Sullivan Group provides.

KINCAID: Well, the difference is really in our firm's expertise with oil and gas companies. Our brokers have written articles and presented on various topics of insurance relating to the energy industry. In fact (rummages in his briefcase), here are some brochures that talk about our services and experience in more detail.

Kincaid places two brochures on Mitchell's desk. Kincaid continues ...

KINCAID: These brochures explain our firm's philosophy, our experience in the energy business, and some of our latest rankings and awards.

MITCHELL: Ok, so what are we looking at cost-wise for all these services and for the insurance plan as a whole?

KINCAID: Well, here is a table that breaks down the insurance companies we represent (Kincaid has risen and places a paper on Mitchell's desk. He continues:

KINCAID: We can get quotes from each of these companies for you in just a matter of weeks.

At this point, a 15-minute discussion ensues between the two men on the information the Sullivan Group will need to get quotes for Madison Energy. After the conversation draws to a close, Mitchell rises and shakes hands with Kincaid.

KINCAID: Bob thanks again for your time. I'll give you a call in a couple of days. If you want any more information, you can reach me on my e-mail or direct number, and I encourage you to explore more about our firm on our Web site.

DISCUSSION QUESTIONS

Assume that the decision to use the Sullivan Group as your company's insurance brokerage firm would involve a minimum bottom line expense of $250,000.

1. You must now decide whether to send Mr. Kincaid of the Sullivan Group to see the Accounting Operations people. Would you send him?
Yes _______ No _______
2. How confident are you about your answer to Question 1?
Very _______ Fairly _______ Not so _______
3. Given the service (the design of risk management and insurance plans) and its expected use by Madison Energy, how would you evaluate the Mr. Kincaid's presentation?
Good _______ Average _______ Poor _______
4. How would you evaluate Mr. Kincaid in terms of his knowledge of Madison Energy's problems and operations?
Good _______ Average _______ Poor _______
5. Suppose instead of sending Mr. Kincaid on to the CFO, you personally had full responsibility for deciding whether your company would use the Sullivan Group as the company's insurance broker. Would you use the firm?
Yes _______ No _______
6. How confident are you about your answer to Question 5?
Very _______ Fairly _______ Not so _______
7. How would you evaluate Mr. Kincaid in terms of his likability?
Very likable _______ Fairly likable _______ Not so likable _______
8. How would you evaluate Mr. Kincaid in terms of his knowledge of the service he is selling?
Very knowledgeable _______ Fairly knowledgeable _______ Not so knowledgeable _______
9. How would you rate Mr. Kincaid in terms of his overall competence?
Very competent _______ Fairly competent _______
Not so competent _______
10. How would you rate Mr. Kincaid in terms of his trustworthiness?
Very trustworthy _______ Fairly trustworthy _______
Not so trustworthy _______

THE SULLIVAN GROUP (B)

Bob Mitchell, Director of Risk Management of Madison Energy, a publicly traded firm that focuses on the servicing of producing oil and gas wells, picked up his phone and heard his secretary say, "A Mr. Matthew Kincaid of the Sullivan Group is here to see you."

"Send him in," Mitchell replied.

BACKGROUND INFORMATION

Madison Energy is a rapidly growing company and the complexity of their risk management needs is increasing accordingly. The major assets Madison Energy needs to protect are its oil and gas wells, workers in the field, and the heavy equipment used on the well-sites. In fact, the company has now reached a level financially where it requires an array of insurance products and services to adequately handle its growing exposure to loss.

The usual first step of the selling process for insurance products and services is for a brokerage company to call on Madison Energy directly to try and setup a meeting with Bob Mitchell, Director of Risk Management. If Mitchell felt that the situation warranted further investigation, he would set up a meeting between the broker and someone in Accounting Operations to meet to gather information. A tour of facilities would also take place to ensure familiarity with Madison's needs. Following information gathering, the broker would develop a proposal that would be presented to Mitchell. If he felt it was a viable and attractive proposal, he would pass it along to the Chief Financial Officer (CFO). If approved at this point, the CFO would present an overview of the proposal to the Audit Committee of the Board of Directors for final approval.

Matthew Kincaid, an Account Executive of the Sullivan Group, is about to discuss his company's insurance services and its specific experience with oil and gas clients. The only previous meeting between Bob Mitchell and Matthew Kincaid came two weeks ago at a local charity event. Mitchell invited Kincaid to come by the office to discuss what the Sullivan Group might be able to do for Madison Energy.

THE INTERVIEW

KINCAID: Good to see you again, Bob. How are things?

MITCHELL: Great, Matt. Please, have a seat.

KINCAID: Thank you.... Bob, we work with executives of oil and gas companies like yourself who from time to time find themselves frustrated with the effectiveness of the insurance programs in terms of cost and time it takes to accurately resolve claims issues. But before we go any further I wanted to ask you some questions to get to know Madison Energy a bit better. Is that okay with you?

MITCHELL: Sounds great.

KINCAID: Good. First off, Bob, I know Madison has experienced a lot of growth over the last few quarters, so how does this new business vision relate to your needs from an insurance and risk management standpoint?

MITCHELL: Put simply, Matt, our business is just a lot more complex—not just because we are three times as large as we were this time last year, but also because we have some very significant assets now that require solid protection; perhaps the biggest being our people in the field. You know how dangerous this business can be, and you also know how expensive coverage like workers compensation can be. We need the peace of mind knowing that we have a great risk management program that still enables us to remain financially competitive to our competitors.

KINCAID: Absolutely. Now, let's talk a bit more about some of these new complexities Madison is facing. I did a little research before our meeting today and talked to a few members of your safety and environmental departments to determine if they were seeing an increase in the number of complex insurance claims. They mentioned that because Madison recently launched an extensive five-year growth plan, both the number and complexity of claims has indeed increased significantly—which is perfectly ordinary for a firm of your size. We talked a bit further and they estimated that it works out to about 70 hours per week of their collective time devoted to handling these claims with the insurance company. So Bob, what I'm wondering is, relative to all other issues Madison's safety and environmental group is already dealing with, is the potential offload of 70 hours per week worth looking into any further?

BOB: Well, those guys are right; they have had to spend way too much time on the phone with insurance companies and adjusters to properly close claims. We really need them in the field. So, yes, I think it is definitely worth exploring.

KINCAID: Bob, what I would suggest is that you recommend a few of your top people to me—what I like to call your brain trust. These people represent the functions that are impacted by this situation. Usually, I speak to a key person in safety, finance, and operations. I have conversations with these individuals, get into more detail with them, and figure out what this situation is costing you and how realistic it would be for your organization to create a partnership that could offload that work—saving you both time and money. Then, I'll come back to you with an analysis of those costs. Would that be helpful?

MITCHELL: Yes. That sounds like a good idea to me.

KINCAID: Great. If I may, I would also like to ask you just a couple more questions before I get started with your core team members.

MITCHELL: Sure.

KINCAID: Bob, as you look at the entire process of creating a new partnership with an insurance brokerage firm—starting with the installation of a new risk management program—which part of this process concerns you the most?

MITCHELL: As you are aware, the growth plan for our company calls for rapid expansion. So, my concern: Are we going to be able to properly address all areas of Madison's exposure to loss quickly enough and be able to mitigate any claim issues that do arise?

KINCAID: Can you help me understand what "quickly enough" would be in your situation?

MITCHELL: Well, Matt, ideally, we would like to have a new insurance broker implementing a competitively priced plan that protects our company's major assets by the start of next quarter—which is next month. Also, it sure would be nice to get our safety guys back to doing safety work instead of calling insurance companies as soon as possible.

KINCAID: What seems to be the key contributing factors to making that transition a smooth one and a quick one?

MITCHELL: I would say it is effective communication with each department of Madison Energy that is involved with the insurance and risk management program. Getting our broker on the same page with each division is very important. If we can make a smooth transition, especially with the time pressures we are dealing with, it will be a big help in the kickoff of our growth plan.

At this point, Mr. Kincaid asks Mr. Mitchell a few more questions about Madison's new growth plan. Finally, Mr. Kincaid rises and shakes hands with Mr. Mitchell.

KINCAID: Bob, thanks again for your time. Knowing that time is of the essence, I will report back in ten days, if that is okay with you. Meanwhile (Kincaid hands Mitchell his business card), please don't hesitate to call me if you have any other questions or information you would like me to obtain for you.

DISCUSSION QUESTIONS

Assume that the decision to use the Sullivan Group as your company's insurance brokerage firm would involve a minimum bottom line expense of $250,000.

1. You must now decide whether to send Mr. Kincaid of the Sullivan Group to see the operations people. Would you send him?
   Yes _______ No _______
2. How confident are you about your answer to Question 1?
   Very _______ Fairly _______ Not so _______
3. Given the service (the design of risk management and insurance plans) and its expected use by Madison Energy, how would you evaluate the Mr. Kincaid's presentation?
   Good _______ Average _______ Poor _______
4. How would you evaluate Mr. Kincaid in terms of his knowledge of Madison Energy's problems and operations?
   Good _______ Average _______ Poor _______
5. Suppose instead of sending Mr. Kincaid on to the Board, you personally had full responsibility for deciding whether your company would use the Sullivan Group as the company's insurance broker. Would you use the firm?
   Yes _______ No _______
6. How confident are you about your answer to Question 5?
   Very _______ Fairly _______ Not so _______
7. How would you evaluate Mr. Kincaid in terms of his likability?
   Very likable _______ Fairly likable_______ Not so likable _______
8. How would you evaluate Mr. Kincaid in terms of his knowledge of the service he is selling?
   Very knowledgeable _______ Fairly knowledgeable _______ Not so knowledgeable _______
9. How would you rate Mr. Kincaid in terms of his overall competence?
   Very competent _______ Fairly competent _______ Not so competent _______
10. How would you rate Mr. Kincaid in terms of his trustworthiness?
    Very trustworthy _______ Fairly trustworthy _______ Not so trustworthy _______

VENTURE INSURANCE CORPORATION

Johnny Ramone groaned to himself as he reread the letter from Murry Fine, the attorney for Andrew Farriss. The letter threatened both a lawsuit for wrongful termination and a complaint to the Equal Opportunity Employment Commission. Andrew Farriss had been fired by Joni Mitchell, the sales manager of the Texas sales district, at the end of 2004.

A call to the head of the Venture Insurance legal staff provided a recommendation that Johnny gather information on Andrew Farriss, Joni Mitchell's record as a sales manager, and information on the performance of other salespeople in the eighteenth district. The attorney also recommended that all of the information be gathered within two weeks. This would allow Johnny to review the information and see if there actually was a problem. After Johnny reviewed the information, he would have a meeting with the legal staff to decide what to do.

VENTURE INSURANCE CORPORATION

Venture Insurance was established in Columbus, Ohio, in 1946 after the end of the Second World War II. Venture sells health, fire, theft, personal injury, and other types of business insurance to business owners and corporations. It also sold insurance policies to businesses to cover the disruption in operations from the death of key managers. Until 1976, Venture issued policies only in Ohio, Illinois, Michigan, and Indiana.

In 1976 Venture started expanding geographically in the United States and Canada. In late 2000, Venture completed this expansion when it received permission to issue policies in Texas. In 2001 the eighteenth sales district covering Texas was opened in Dallas with Joni Mitchell as sales manager.

Venture's sales operations are divided into eighteen sales districts. There are between eight to fifteen salespeople per district. A sales manager supervises each district. Johnny is one of two regional managers and he oversees 9 sales districts. He reports to the national sales and marketing manager.

Venture's target market are the owners of small and medium size businesses. A typical policy will cover a company of $35 million in sales and 30 employees. Currently, Venture does not have any policies with Fortune 1000 companies.

Originally, the entire sales staff was white males. In the 1940s and 1950s most business owners were males, and Venture thought having a sales staff who related well to customers would be most effective in the field. The first female sales representative was hired in 1958. Venture also had a strong company ethic of promoting from within. The most outstanding employees in the company were groomed for advancement. Only when special circumstances arose did the company hire outside management talent.

Changes in federal law in the 1960s and 1970s, along with increasing numbers of businesses owned by women and minorities, resulted in a radical shift in Venture's recruiting policies. Venture's market share declined from 1975 to 1985. Part of this market decline was attributed to outdated recruiting policies. Although an increasing number of small businesses were owned by women or minorities, Venture's sales staff was 90 percent male in 1985. Venture's top management decided to aggressively diversify its sales staff. For the next ten years 80 percent of all new hires were females or minorities. By 2000, the sales staff was 60 percent male, and eight of the eighteen sales managers were female. These personnel changes, combined with several other strategy changes, caused Venture's market share and sales to increase. Venture's revenue growth averaged 9 percent higher than the average growth in the industry from 1986 to 2003.

These personnel policy changes did not occur without problems. Until 1985, Venture had always promoted the most successful field sales representatives to sales manager. However, due to Venture's outdated hiring policies, this meant that only one of the sixteen sales managers in 1985 was female. In order to diversify its management team, Venture hired several female sales managers from outside of the company. Venture also promoted to sales management positions several females whose performance was somewhat weaker than the best male salespeople. However, all of the female managers were qualified sales management candidates. Due to these changes in promotion policies, Venture lost about 10 percent of its top-performing male salespeople to competitors or other business opportunities between 1985 to 2004.

Exit interviews with these departing male salespeople sometimes uncovered considerable hostility toward Venture. One salesperson who departed after being in the top 5 percent of sales for seven years in a row commented, "I got three offers of management positions within a month of looking for another job. I was turned down for promotion at Venture three times in the last three years for people outside of the company or for women with weaker sales performance. The names of the Top 15% Club and the Top 5% Club are published in the company newsletter, so I know that my performance was better than ***** and *****. I was never going to get ahead at Venture regardless of my performance. You're lucky you have not been sued yet for reverse discrimination. I was stupid for staying at Venture for as long as I did."

Venture's mission statement has an emphasis on profitability, customer service, and diversity. Diversity is an important goal because it helps Venture better relate to customers from different backgrounds. Diversity provides Venture with a better understanding of customers, which in turn allows Venture to better serve the needs of it customers.

GENERAL SALES TRAINING AND SELLING POLICIES

Venture salespeople are paid a base salary plus a 7 percent commission on the premiums of policies sold. Each salesperson has a responsibility to cover a specific geographic territory. Salespeople are responsible for selling new policies, maintaining current policies, handling customer problems, and doing the initial investigation of payment claims.

Each salesperson goes through an intensive two-month training program in Columbus. After successfully completing the training program, each salesperson is assigned a sales territory. Existing salespeople are also given training on new insurance policies, changes in insurance coverage and policies, and selling techniques during district sales meetings for one or two days every month.

Because the sales job requires considerable maintenance and support for existing policies, there is a substantial salary component of total pay. To encourage salespeople to generate new business as well as maintain current policies, they receive a 7 percent commission on the premiums paid by customers within their territory. Unlike many other insurance companies, Venture does not pay a bonus when new policies are issued. Venture tries to maintain a balance of providing excellent service to existing customers while also aggressively seeking out new business. Venture's management team believes that providing bonuses for new policies could decrease the emphasis on providing excellent service to existing customers.

Salespeople are formally evaluated by their sales manager three times a year. These reviews have several objectives. First, they provide the opportunity for one-on-one sales coaching and sales training. Second, they are used to provide warnings to poorly performing salespeople. Third, they are used to gather suggestions for improving Venture's information about customers, competitors, and marketing strategy. Salespeople are provided a brief written evaluation (usually one page or less) and more extensive verbal feedback during these review meetings.

SALES MANAGER POLICIES AT VENTURE INSURANCE

All people selected for sales management at Venture come from a background of insurance sales. New sales managers undergo a variety of training. First, if they are not experienced Venture salespeople, they undergo the same classroom training given to new recruits. They then spend two weeks studying Venture's policy and procedure manual. This is followed by an intensive three-day seminar by Venture's legal staff covering fine points of internal policy and procedures. Next, the new sales managers spend a week with the Head Claims and Adjustment Officer to learn the more difficult parts of filing, reviewing, and investigating insurance claims from policyholders. They then spend two weeks shadowing an experienced sales manager. During this shadowing process, the new sales manager conducts a monthly training session and also sits in on triannual reviews. The experienced sales manager also acts as an official mentor for the new sales manager for the next eighteen months. After shadowing the experienced sales manager, the management recruit spends a week with his or her regional sales manager learning the allocation of sales territories, evaluation of employee performance, motivational techniques for the sales force, and other topics.

The training process for new sales managers lasts six weeks for experienced Venture sales reps to fourteen weeks for recruits lacking sales experience with Venture. Venture's sales manager training program was honored as exhibiting Best Practices in the Industry at the 2003 meeting of the Business Insurance Trade Association.

Sales managers are responsible for training existing sales reps, handling customer problems, doing initial investigation of insurance claims within their district, conducting triannual reviews of salespeople, designing and assigning sales territories, allocating salary increases, and setting sales quotas. Sales managers recruit new salespeople. Sales managers are also responsible for ensuring salespeople follow Venture policy. Most important, sales managers are responsible for meeting Venture's financial performance standards. If a district consistently underperforms financial goals, the sales manager is replaced with someone else. Sales managers are paid a salary plus a bonus based on overall district performance.

Because retaining current clients is important and also because a significant portion of salesperson compensation is salary, sales mangers at Venture Insurance are required to conduct performance reviews three times a year with each salesperson. These performance reviews contain a brief written evaluation (usually one page or less). This written evaluation is signed by the sales manager and the salesperson. A copy of the evaluation is retained by the company and a copy is also given to the salesperson. A more extensive verbal review is also given during the face-to-face meeting with each employee. The average meeting will last somewhere between 15 minutes and two hours.

Although preparing the evaluations and conducting the triannual review sessions is time consuming, Venture thinks they are important to ensure that the sales managers keep up with the activities of the salesforce. These meetings also provide salespeople an opportunity to provide information about clients, competitors, and selling strategies that could help Venture improve its marketing efforts. Every effort is made by the sales managers to have these review sessions three times a year with each employee. But illness, client needs, and scheduling difficulties will sometimes interfere with the ability to schedule and hold these review sessions.

Venture believes in the Three Rights in maintaining a highly effective sales staff. These are Recruiting the Right People, Giving the Right Training, and Supplying the Right Feedback. The sales manager plays a vital role in recruitment and in supplying feedback. Sales managers are also vital to ongoing training of existing staff. Right recruiting, training and feedback helped make Venture profitable and also keep salesperson turnover to 5 percent annually.

Venture feels that it is essential that sales managers follow the letter and spirit of company policies. Sales managers who fail to do so are either provided written reprimands or terminated.

Employee Satisfaction Survey

Venture conducts brief, periodic anonymous employee satisfaction surveys. These surveys are used to monitor employee satisfaction and also uncover potential problem areas within the company. Although the surveys contain only seven questions, the information from the surveys has been helpful in the past in identifying areas where managers are best motivating their subordinates. The last two surveys for the company were conducted in 2005 and 2002. Overall results, as well as results within each specific manager's domain that contained at least six employees, are given to the core management team as well as each individual manager.

Salesperson Rewards

Sales managers have several tools to reward outstanding salespeople. First, the highest performing salesperson within a district is usually given the opportunity to take over a better sales territory when one opens up due to someone leaving or being terminated. An informal policy at Venture is that the top-performing rep within a district gets the right of first refusal when a new district opens up. Doing this allows the best salespeople to gradually move into the territories with the highest sales levels. This both increases the commissions going to the best salespeople and also provides the best service level to the most important territories.

Second, the sales manager has total control over the allocation of salary increases. It is Venture's policy that salary increases are given for merit only. Venture believes in pay for performance, not cost of living pay increases. Better performing salespeople will gradually see their salary increase over time.

The third possible reward for outstanding salespeople is promotion to sales manager. Although it is the stated company policy that sales managers be drawn from the ranks of the best company salespeople, Venture also desires a diverse management team. These two goals will sometimes come into conflict. Since there are relatively few sales manager positions, not all outstanding sales reps can be promoted.

Venture has a salesperson recognition program. Salespeople who perform in the top 5 percent of company sales are inducted into the Top 5% Club for the year. Salespeople who perform in the top 15 percent of sales are inducted into the Top 15% Club. Salespeople gaining this recognition receive a plaque, have their names and photos in the e-mailed newsletter sent to all Venture employees, and also are honored at the national sales meeting. In addition to all of the honors given to members of the Top 15% Club, members of the Top 5% Club have their photo taken with the Vice President of Marketing, the CEO, and the Chairman of the Board. They also are given luxury accommodations at the annual sales meeting.

SALESPERSON CONTROLS

There are three primary control procedures used by sales managers. First, the sales manager sets sales quotas. At Venture, it is expected that all salespeople will make their sales quota. Failing to make sales quotas is a serious shortcoming. However, it is also Venture policy to set the sales quotas to both motivate the sales staff to high levels of performance, but also not to set the sales quotas so high that they are not possible to obtain by experienced salespeople with good work habits. New recruits are usually given to the end of their second year to make their sales quotas, but failure to make significant progress is grounds for termination. In sum, Venture expects the sales managers to carefully set quotas so they motivate outstanding performance, are achievable by experienced reps with good work habits, and also weed out reps who significantly underperform.

The second control procedure is Venture policies and procedures. Business insurance is a complicated product. Venture expects the salespeople to be highly knowledgeable about Venture insurance policies. Venture expects the sales representatives to follow all local and state laws and to operate in a highly ethical manner. Intentionally misrepresenting the content or coverage of Venture insurance policies to current or potential clients in order to get a quick sale is a firing offense. Venture also expects sales reps to follow all company policies in all areas. This includes filing accurate and timely reports, following all expense account procedures, and operating their company car in a safe fashion. Salespeople with outstanding sales performance who also intentionally violate important company polices can be immediately terminated by their sales manager.

The third control procedure is the triannual reviews. Sales managers are expected to identify any serious weakness of individual salespeople on the written review. This is especially important if the sales rep is performing so poorly that he or she could be terminated. Sales managers are also expected to praise good performance and also to provide coaching suggestions for improvement. Much of the coaching and suggestions for improvement are handled verbally during the individual meeting with the sales rep.

SALESPERSON SANCTIONS

Sales managers have a variety of sanctions they can impose on poorly performing salespeople. They can provide negative verbal feedback during performance appraisals. They can give negative written performance appraisals. Sales managers can withhold salary increase from poorly performing reps. The sales manager can also fire sales reps who perform poorly or violate the law or company policy.

ANDREW FARRISS

Andrew Farriss was hired in late 2000 and was one of the initial salespeople in the Texas sales district when it was formed in January 2001. Andrew held the San Antonio territory during his entire employment with Venture. Andrew was named to the Top 15% Club for his performance in 2001, 2002, and 2003.

Andrew was terminated by Joni Mitchell for failure to make his sales quota at the end of 2004 and replaced by Michael Anthony.

The letter from attorney Murry Fine charged that Joni Mitchell had wrongfully terminated Andrew in violation of Venture's own internal policies. Andrew claimed that Joni had: (a) failed to provide notice of poor performance that could result in termination in triannual reviews; (b) failed to conduct Andrew's triannual reviews; (c) given Andrew a poor territory and withheld the opportunity to have high commission income; (d) imposed much higher sales quotas on Andrew than those given to other salespeople in the district, and (e) denied Andrew promotion to sales manager.

The letter further claimed that Joni had systematically provided poor territories and thus low commission income to male employees. Joni was also charged with creating a hostile work environment for men by failing to hold required performance evaluations and by making disparaging comments toward male salespeople. The letter also claimed that Venture had systematically denied opportunities for promotion and advancement in sales management to male employees and instead had promoted more poorly performing women.

The letter also contained the last four performance evaluations given to Andrew Farriss. The written evaluations were very, very brief. A quick check of the records confirmed that these were the performance evaluations given to Farriss and that no evaluations were omitted.

> December 31, 2002 Andrew, I am delighted with your continued outstanding sales record. You beat your quota by 9%. I'm pretty sure that in January you will be named to the Top 15% Club for the second year in a row. You are also getting a $3,000 merit salary raise that will raise your total salary to $26,000 effective January 31, 2003. Keep up the good work!

> April 28, 2003 Andrew, your overall first quarter sales results are excellent. You do need to push a little harder in order to pick up a few more quality new customers. You have plenty of money in your expense account for prospecting, and I have confidence that you can achieve this goal.

> April 30, 2004 Sorry we were unable to coordinate schedules last quarter. I'm sure that you noticed the extra $4,000 in merit salary raise that kicked in at the end of January. You beat quota again in 2003.
>
> You need to spend more time traveling outside of San Antonio in order to pick up some new clients. You have plenty of money for a few more road trips.
>
> Congratulations for making the top 15% club for the third year in a row.

> January 2, 2005 Mr. Farriss, you are being terminated from the Venture Company for failing to make your sales quota. I have warned you repeatedly about the importance of hitting the company's financial targets. Your termination is immediate, and you will be granted the standard one month severance pay.

Phone Interview by Johnny Ramone with Joni Mitchell, January 22, 2006

JOHNNY: Tell me about Andrew Farriss.

JONI: Andrew initially did well. Unfortunately, his performance continued to slip after a great start.

JOHNNY: What did Andrew do well?

JONI: His initial sales levels were tops in the district. Unfortunately, he continued to slide after the first year. He beat quota by 20 percent in 2001, 9 percent in 2002 and only 2 percent in 2003. He also made the Top 15% club a couple of times, but was never good enough to hit the Top 5% club. Andrew just would not follow my recommendations.

JOHNNY: What do you mean?

JONI: Just like company policy states, I reminded him every evaluation that hitting his sales quotas was critical. But he expected to become a manager after only one year—and that year was not that

EXHIBIT 1 Sales and Sales Quotas 2001–2005

	2001 Sales	*Sales to Quota*	*2002 Sales*	*Sales to Quota*	*2003 Sales*	*Sales to Quota*	*2004 Sales*	*Sales to Quota*	*2005 Sales*	*Sales to Quota*
Andrew Farriss	420000	1.2	435000	1.0875	450000	1.022727	465000	0.978947	T	
Garry Gary	275000	0.785714	T							
Donita Sparks	320000	0.914286	370000	1.013699	400000	1	430000	1.02381	460000	1.045455
Michael Hutchence	370000	1.057143	380000	1.013333	398000	0.995	419000	0.997619	450000	1.022727
Jesse Valenzuela	280000	0.8	350000	0.921053	T					
Suzi Gardner	360000	1.028571	385000	1.026667	415000	1.0375	440000	1.047619	475000	1.055556
Phillip Rhodes	390000	1.114286	430000	1.075	490000	1.139535	T			
Bill Leen	377000	1.077143	390000	1.026316	420000	1.02439	430000	1.02381	460000	1.045455
Doug Hopkins	410000	1.171429	420000	1.05	440000	1.047619	460000	1.045455	485000	1.021053
Robert Becker	400000	1.142857	425000	1.089744	460000	1.069767	490000	1.042553	540000	1.058824
Jennifer Finch			340000	0.918919	385000	0.9625	T			
Gail Greenwood					392000	1.005128	425000	1.011905	440000	1
Janis Tanaka							390000	0.975	410000	0.931818
Dee Palakis							440000	1.1	490000	1.088889
Michael Anthony									440000	1.1

T = Terminated or Left the Company

great. He never got into the 5% club, but expected to be promoted after only one year.

JOHNNY: What recommendations did you give him?

JONI: He needed to make quota every year. He did not pick up enough accounts. He also did not spend his expense budget. I kept telling him that if he could travel more outside of San Antonio, he could pick up more business. He had the money to do it, and his district was compact, but he just would not travel much. His performance kept slipping until he failed to make quota.

JOHNNY: Seems like you missed a couple of evaluations with him.

JONI: You know how difficult it is sometimes to coordinate schedules. If you have an uncooperative employee, it is all the harder. I make 80 to 90 percent of my evaluations every year. My district has also always hit company financial targets! As you tell me in our meetings, my job is to follow policy and make lots of money for Venture. My district is in the top 30 percent in financial performance year in and year out.

JOHNNY: Andrew claims that he had a poor territory.

JONI: Bull!

JOHNNY: Bull?

JONI: Yeah, bull. He made more commission money than most people in the district.

JOHNNY: Andrew also claims that you did not treat men well.

JONI: Andrew is a crybaby. The men in my district make more than the women. Their commission income is higher. It is just like him to blame someone else for his failure to follow good advice.

JOHNNY: Thanks for the information. I will get back with you on this.

Phone Interview with Roy Moffitt: Venture Staff Attorney

JOHNNY: Hello, Roy. Did you get the fax with all of the information?

ROY: I have your interview with Joni Mitchell and the last four performance evaluations of Andrew Farriss. I also have the following information from the Texas district for 2001–2005: sales and sales quota information; the pattern of Joni's triannual performance evaluations; expense account spending by salesperson; total sales rep pay; and the results of the last two employee satisfaction surveys. (See Exhibits 1–5).

JOHNNY: What do you think?

ROY: I'm not sure what to think. Andrew missed quota and Joni fired him. Andrew's evaluations are pretty good up until the last one. The big question is do you think that Joni is following company policy? You have gotten a lot of good data together, but only you can determine if Joni's actions follow company sales policy.

JOHNNY: You're dumping this on me?

EXHIBIT 2 Triannual Performance Evaluations

		2001			2002			2003			2004			2005		
	Sex	*1st*	*2nd*	*3rd*	*1st*	*2nd*	*3rd*	*1st*	*2nd*	*3rd*	*1st*	*2nd*	*3rd*	*1st*	*2nd*	*3rd*
Andrew Farriss	M	C	C	M	C	C	C	C	M	M	C	M	T			
Garry Gary	M	C	C	T												
Donita Sparks	F	C	C	C	M	C	C	C	C	C	C	C	C	C	C	C
Michael Hutchence	M	C	M	C	C	M	C	C	M	C	C	C	M	C	M	C
Jesse Valenzuela	M	M	C	M	C	C	T									
Suzi Gardner	F	C	C	C	C	C	C	C	C	C	C	C	C	C	C	C
Phillip Rhodes	M	C	M	M	C	C	C	C	C	T						
Bill Leen	M	C	C	C	M	M	C	C	C	C	C	C	C	C	C	M
Doug Hopkins	M	C	C	C	C	C	M	M	C	M	C	C	C	M	C	C
Robert Becker	M	C	C	C	C	C	M	C	C	C	C	C	C	C	M	C
Jennifer Finch	F				C	C	C	C	C	T						
Gail Greenwood	F							C	C	C	C	C	C	M	C	C
Janis Tanaka	F										M	C	C	C	C	C
Dee Palakis	F										C	M	C	C	C	C
Michael Anthony	M													C	C	C

C = Completed Evaluation
M = No Evaluation Completed
T = Termination or Left Company

EXHIBIT 3 Expense Account Spending 2001–2005

	2001	*2002*	*2003*	*2004*	*2005*
Andrew Farriss	9800	9950	10500	10750	T
Garry Gary	11900	T			
Donita Sparks	10900	11000	11300	12700	13000
Michael Hutchence	12000	12500	13000	13400	14000
Jesse Valenzuela	12000	12500	T		
Suzi Gardner	11490	12100	12800	13100	13900
Phillip Rhodes	11700	12100	12600	T	
Bill Leen	11250	12200	12900	13400	13900
Doug Hopkins	11700	12100	13000	13100	13900
Robert Becker	11850	12500	12750	13490	14000
Jennifer Finch		9900	11100	T	
Gail Greenwood			13000	13100	13900
Janis Tanaka				13500	14000
Dee Palakis				13400	13900
Michael Anthony					13500
Spending Cap	12000	12500	13000	13500	14000

ROY: I have to. You are responsible for half of the company's sales managers. You handle day-to-day policy implementation. If Mr. Farriss sues, you will be interviewed and all of the information you sent me would have to be turned over to Andrew. I don't know if Joni's actions are out of line or not.

JOHNNY: Why don't you know if Joni's actions are right?

ROY: The critical issue is if Joni followed Venture's sales and management policies and treated everyone reasonably equally. If she did, then we don't have a problem. You can fire someone for not hitting quota, but if you single him out for bad treatment, he might win in court. Nobody expects a manager to be perfect, but if Joni singled out Andrew for bad treatment, and especially if she

EXHIBIT 4 Total Sales Representative Pay

	2001 Pay	*2002 Pay*	*2003 Pay*	*2004 Pay*	*2005 Pay*
Andrew Farriss	49400	53450	57500	62550	T
Garry Gary	39250	T			
Donita Sparks	42400	50900	57000	63100	70200
Michael Hutchence	45900	50100	54860	58330	63500
Jesse Valenzuela	39600	45500	T		
Suzi Gardner	45200	52950	59050	65800	73250
Phillip Rhodes	47300	55100	63300	T	
Bill Leen	46390	50300	55400	60100	66200
Doug Hopkins	48700	52900	56800	62200	68950
Robert Becker	48000	54750	61200	67300	75800
Jennifer Finch		48800	55950	T	
Gail Greenwood			55440	63750	68800
Janis Tanaka				59300	64700
Dee Palakis				62800	72300
Michael Anthony					64800

T = Terminated or left company

EXHIBIT 5 Employee Satisfaction Survey

	2002 Total Salesforce	*2002 Overall for District 18*	*2002 District 18 Males*	*2002 District 18 Females*
Overall Job Satisfaction	5.2	4.65	4.5	5
Satisfaction with Supervisor	4.5	4.6	4	6
Satisfaction with Training	6	5.7	6	5
Satisfaction with Pay	3.78	3.6	3	5
Satisfaction with Company Policies	4.4	5.3	5	6
Satisfaction with Co-Workers	5.9	6	6	6
Satisfaction with Customer Relations	3.9	4.15	4	4.5
	2005 Total Salesforce	*2005 Overall for District 18*	*2005 District 18 Males*	*2005 District 18 Females*
Overall Job Satisfaction	5.3	4.75	4	5.5
Satisfaction with Supervisor	4.4	4.75	3	6.5
Satisfaction with Training	6.1	5.25	5	5.5
Satisfaction with Pay	3.9	4	2.5	5.5
Satisfaction with Company Policies	4.2	4.75	4	5.5
Satisfaction with Co-Workers	5.9	6.25	6.5	6
Satisfaction with Customer Relations	3.85	4	4	4

Mean scores. 7 = totally satisfied; 1 = totally dissatisfied

systematically treated males badly, Venture could be in trouble.

You also have a responsibility to the company. If Joni is not following policy, you will either have to reprimand her or fire her and find a replacement. If Andrew was fired appropriately, then you should back up Joni.

I can't tell from looking at the data if Joni was out of line or not. You will have to decide this. You have to make a decision, we can't punt a complaint like this one.

JOHNNY: You can't imagine how happy I am to hear this.

ROY: Sorry. Just doing my job. I need a decision from you one way or another within the next two weeks. That will allow us to start putting together our case. Call me back if you have any other questions.

Johnny had a headache. He was going to have to review Joni's performance and decide whether to back her up, reprimand her, or fire her. Maybe Andrew was just a troublemaker? But according to the employee satisfaction survey Joni was much more popular with the female sales reps. Joni's district did hit all of the financial targets, though, and that was very important. It looked like he was not going to be able to pass the buck to the legal staff and he needed to make a decision.

CASE 25 WHITE ELECTRONICS

White is a medium-sized electronics company that specializes in the manufacture of circuit boards, customized computer chips, and test equipment. The electronic components are sold by company salespeople directly to original equipment manufacturers (OEMs), and test equipment is handled by a second group of independent reps. Bill Hicks was recently appointed national sales manager at White to supervise the company's salespeople and the independent reps.

Company sales for the Electronic and Test Equipment divisions amounted to $135 million in 2003. Test equipment sold for relatively high prices and made up the major portion of sales revenue. Independent reps were paid straight 6 percent commissions on all White equipment sales in their territories. The volume of test equipment shipments had increased 15 percent the previous year, and Bill was satisfied with the performance of the reps. Also, the reps' compensation plan made it difficult for White managers to direct their day-to-day activities. About all Bill could do with the independent reps was to replace them if they failed to push White's equipment. White's testing products were only one of several lines of equipment carried by these reps.

Bill Hicks was convinced, on the other hand, that a review of the Electronics Division's sales force would be quite useful. White currently covered the U.S. electronics market with eighteen company salespeople. The assignments of individuals and descriptions of their territories are given in Exhibit 1. Electronics salespeople acted as consultants to OEMs and helped them solve product design problems using White boards and customized chips. They were paid a base salary plus a commission and an annual discretionary bonus. Since electronics salespeople did a great deal of developmental work, their base wage amounted to about 60 percent of their total compensation. Commission rates varied from 0.3 to 1.0 percent of sales, depending on the products sold. The highest commissions were paid on items with the largest gross margins. In the past, bonuses had been based on sales increases, with some attention to profitability. Each salesperson was also given a company car and an expense account to cover travel and entertainment costs.

White's sales of electronic components increased in 2003, but profits were relatively flat. Price competition was intense, and Hicks had been brought in to improve sales force productivity and profits. Bill began his analysis by collecting some performance data on his electronics sales force (Exhibit 2). After reviewing these numbers, he thought it might be useful to calculate some additional control factors such as sales per call, expenses to sales, sales growth, dollars of gross margin, and sales to potential. White measured potential by the number of manufacturers who used electronic components in each sales territory and the value of their finished product shipments. These numbers were derived from U.S. Census of Business data using SIC codes and territory boundaries. Bill decided to calculate penetration by dividing territory sales by the total value of electronics shipments in each area.

To help with his analysis, Hicks called up the new spreadsheet software that he had recently installed on his computer. He then retrieved the White file. The next step in Hicks' sales force analysis was to calculate simple correlation coefficients among his

This case was prepared by Douglas J. Dalrymple of Indiana University.

EXHIBIT 1 Descriptions of Sales Territories

Territory Number	*Salesperson Assigned*	*Area Included*
1	Mary Holmes	Vermont, New Hampshire, Rhode Island, Massachusetts, Maine
2	James Potter	Connecticut, upstate New York (Rochester and east; includes Westchester County)
3	Harvey Stewart	Long Island (Nassau and Suffolk counties), western Pennsylvania (Altoona and west)
4	Jane Thomas	New York City (New York, Kings, Queens, Richmond, and Bronx counties), north Jersey, western New York from Buffalo to Rochester
5	Chad Hunter	Eastern Pennsylvania to Altoona, south Jersey, Maryland, Delaware
6	Harvey Phillips	Ohio, West Virginia, Kentucky
7	Greg Lewis	Indiana, Michigan
8	Anne Forbes	Missouri, Nebraska, Kansas, Iowa
9	Bill Fredericks	Illinois, Wisconsin, Minnesota, North and South Dakota
10	Sally Smith	California north of Santa Barbara, Oregon, Washington, Idaho
11	Fred Reilly	Los Angeles north to Santa Barbara (includes Santa Barbara, Ventura, and the western part of Los Angeles County)
12	Marilyn Reed	California south of Los Angeles (includes Orange, Riverside, San Diego, and Imperial counties)
13	George Pardo	Los Angeles (most of Los Angeles County and part of San Bernardino County)
14	Henry Dodds	Colorado, Arizona, New Mexico, Utah, Wyoming, Montana
15	Todd Young	Texas, Oklahoma, Arkansas, Louisiana
16	David Wood	Mississippi, Alabama, Tennessee
17	Tammy Cook	Virginia, North Carolina, South Carolina
18	Brad Wolf	Georgia, Florida

control factors. The correlations that came up on the screen varied from 0.0 to ±1.0, and they showed the direction and intensity of associations among the performance variables. For example, a strong positive correlation observed between sales and dollars of gross margin (+0.806) was expected because gross margin dollars is simply sales minus the cost of goods sold (Exhibit 3).

Once his sales analysis was complete, Hicks had a number of decisions to make. The annual sales meeting was scheduled in two weeks, and he needed to identify the best salespeople in each district and nationwide so that "Salesperson of the Year" awards could be made. He wondered whether these choices should be made on the basis of sales alone or whether he should use some combination of performance variables. He also had to identify salespeople for retraining and for possible termination. If the data showed evidence of plateauing among his middle-aged salespeople, then changes would be needed to correct this problem. Hicks would have to specify the topics needed to be covered for those picked for retraining. In addition, Bill had $55,000 in annual bonus money that he had to allocate among the electronics salespeople. He was also concerned about whether changes were needed in basic wage levels and commission rates. Another strategic question was whether White had enough electronics salespeople. If extra salespeople were hired, Bill had to decide how old they should be when hired and how much experience was necessary. In addition, he had to decide if the present sales territories needed to be redesigned. A reallocation of the territories would have to consider where to place any new salespeople. The more Bill thought about these problems, the more he was convinced that he needed one of those new computerized territory design programs he had seen advertised. Without a computer program, he would have to draw some maps to analyze the existing territories and plan for possible added salespeople.

Beyond these decisions, Hicks had to make decisions concerning the factors he wanted to emphasize to motivate his electronics salespeople to reach corporate objectives. Bill knew that his goals were unlikely to be reached if he asked his salespeople to improve on ten different control factors all at the same time. Besides, improving some of the factors conflicted with the achievement of others. What he needed was a short list of prioritized factors to highlight at the upcoming sales meeting.

EXHIBIT 2 Sales Force Performance Data[a]

							Potential						
Territory Number	Sales, 2002 (millions)	Sales, 2003 (millions)	Gross Margin (%)	Calls, 2003	Years of Service	Age	Territory Size in Miles^2 (000)	Total Number of Firms	Total Value of Shipments (millions)	Salary, 2003	Commissions, 2003	Expenses, 2003	District
1	$1.839	$2.214	40%	770	2	32	58.4	1965	$9959	$34,100	$16,500	$ 4269	1
2	2.398	2.411	38	660	6	40	44.2	1461	10190	40,150	17,710	7036	1
3	2.497	2.640	33	1250	25	50	16.7	1023	4719	35,860	21,450	9510	1
4	1.509	1.739	36	900	7	34	8.7	2601	10360	37,950	11,440	15628	1
5	2.167	2.686	31	678	20	49	46.7	2264	16287	33,330	22,330	13027	1
6	1.183	1.190	44	610	3	40	104.8	2286	21195	33,000	10,450	9785	2
7	2.232	2.431	37	870	12	38	92.9	2465	23010	33,000	16,610	11797	2
8	1.561	1.632	45	580	16	46	283.3	1601	14240	33,000	11,660	22425	2
9	2.147	2.032	42	630	14	48	334.9	3306	25600	31,900	18,370	12014	2
10	2.012	2.621	40	492	3	32	356.3	3329	17980	39,600	17,380	12523	3
11	.831	.885	52	600	2	26	4.6	136	540	27,500	8,470	4741	3
12	1.658	2.251	28	1030	6	39	16.4	994	4047	33,000	12,100	4938	3
13	1.377	1.146	39	540	5	38	4.0	2127	10590	46,200	6,600	3477	3
14	1.058	1.081	49	480	2	26	662.9	1407	6407	33,000	10,560	14165	3
15	1.898	3.083	37	460	2	29	427.3	3130	26280	33,000	12,100	19431	4
16	1.856	2.578	25	820	5	36	139.1	1603	12303	33,000	14,520	18747	4
17	2.090	2.317	23	820	20	50	118.7	2167	18840	38,500	16,280	9602	4
18	1.224	1.565	39	830	5	28	112.2	2479	13232	28,050	10,340	25394	4

[a]Data are in file yorkdat.sav.

EXHIBIT 3 Correlations among Sales Force Control Factors

	2002 Sales	*2003 Calls*	*Sales/ Calls*	*Expenses*	*Exp/ Sales*	*Exp/ Calls*	*Years Service*	*Age*	*GM (%)*	*GM ($)*	*Terr. Size*	*No. of Firms*	*Value Ship.*	*Penetration*	*Sales Growth*	*Commissions*
Sales	1.000	.285	.718	.140	−.435	.115	.346	.332	−.666	.806	.000	.353	.389	.279	.637	.738
Calls	.285[a]	1.000	−.430	−.112	−.221	−.492	.499	.371	−.562	−.047	−.583	−.318	−.343	.725	.071	.358
Sales/call	.718	−.430	1.000	.254	−.204	.517	−.079	−.035	−.174	.810	.447	.576	.587	−.203	.611	.355
Expenses	.140	−.112	.254	1.000	.807	.875	.061	−.124	−.021	.174	.428	.369	.359	−.337	.436	−.060
Exp/sales	−.435	−.221	−.204	.807	1.000	.714	−.121	−.302	.379	−.282	.445	.082	.048	−.386	.026	−.412
Exp/call	.115	−.492	.517	.875	.714	1.000	−.120	−.241	.207	.301	.718	.425	.450	−.452	.440	−.147
Years of service	.346	.499	−.079	.061	−.121	−.120	1.000	.874	−.429	.120	−.216	−.030	.117	.249	−.211	.640
Age	.332	.371	−.035	−.124	−.302	−.241	.874	1.000	−.478	.098	−.284	.057	.244	.180	−.297	.599
GM(%)	−.666	−.562	−.174	−.021	.379	.207	−.429	−.478	1.000	−.117	.356	−.111	−.125	−.354	−.420	−.430
GM ($)	.806	−.047	.810	.174	−.282	.301	.120	.098	−.117	1.000	.248	.486	.472	.064	.478	.631
Territory size	.000	−.583	.447	.428	.445	.718	−.216	−.284	.356	.248	1.000	.333	.331	−.326	.174	−.075
No. of mfg.	.353	−.318	.576	.369	.082	.425	−.030	.057	−.111	.486	.333	1.000	.846	−.570	.238	.192
Value ship.	.389	−.343	.587	.359	.048	.450	.117	.244	−.125	.472	.331	.846	1.000	−.630	.203	.236
Penetration	.279	.725	−.203	−.337	−.386	−.452	.249	.180	−.354	.064	−.326	−.570	−.630	1.000	.116	.271
Sales growth	.637	.071	.611	.436	.026	.440	−.211	−.297	−.420	.478	.174	.238	.230	.116	1.000	.131
Commissions	.738	.358	.355	−.060	−.412	−.147	.640	.599	−.430	.631	−.075	.192	.236	.271	.131	1.000

[a]Correlations of .320 and larger are significant, with a probability of error of <.10.

WINSTON LIU, BOOKMAN

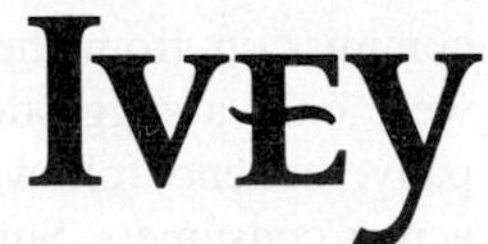

Every day, in every way, I get better and better. I feel happy, I feel healthy, I feel terrific!

Winston (Winnie) Liu repeated the mantra to himself, as a young woman wearing a salwar suit answered the door he had just knocked on. Almost three months after starting his own business selling children's books door-to-door, Winnie was working through a wealthy neighborhood in Edmonton, Alberta. Surrounded by enormous houses and manicured lawns, he reflected for a moment about the promising summer that now found him hungry, lonely, and desperate for a sale.

Anita Howard, a sales manager with the Southwestern Company, recruited Winnie during his first year at the University of Western Ontario (Western). He filled out a card he had received in a chemistry class indicating he was interested in running his own business during the summer. After meeting with Winnie, Anita believed his work ethic, persistence, and friendly personality combined with his passion for education would make him an excellent salesperson. She asked Winnie to consider starting his own business selling books, and Winnie agreed, excited about the possibility of being his own boss and making a lot of money. Between January and April, Winnie memorized the prepared sales talks and attended sales training meetings given by students who had sold books before. His enthusiasm for a rewarding summer grew.

THE SOUTHWESTERN COMPANY

The Southwestern Company, located in Nashville, Tennessee, was founded in 1855. The U.S. Civil War exhausted the fortunes of many Southwestern American families, and in 1868 the company began helping students finance their school expenses through selling books door to door. Over the years the company realized that educational materials were more profitable than Bibles and more consistent with the image of college students.

At present the educational books and software were sold to families in their homes by students during their summer breaks. Students were independent contractors and had the opportunity to run their own businesses by purchasing products from Southwestern at wholesale and selling them at retail. Students relocated away from home to a different part of the country for the summer, away from distractions that might drain attention and profits from their business.

In 1998, Southwestern recruited 3000 students from over 300 universities across Canada, the United States, and Europe. The average 1998 summer profits of Southwestern Student Dealers who sold for three months (US$) were:

First summer students: $6,994
Second summer students: $12,891
Third summer students: $17,189
Fourth summer students: $23,364

After the first summer, students could be selected for student management. Many students worked four, five, six or more summers, gaining invaluable experience by developing their own sales organizations throughout their university careers.

THE BOOKS

The two main products sold by the students were the Student Handbook (a fourbook set, USA) and the Volume Library (a three-book set, Canada). These books were study guides designed to complement, not replace, encyclopedias and CDROMs. The Student Handbook and the Volume Library contained practical "how to" information for subjects ranging from math and chemistry to grammar and geography, from the grade 1 to grade 12 level. Students in Canada sold the Volume Library set for $320 retail, taking a 40 percent

Sam Barnhart prepared this case under the supervision of Donald W. Barclay solely to provide material for class discussion. The authors do not intend to illustrate either effective or ineffective handling of a managerial situation. The authors may have disguised certain names and other identifying information to protect confidentiality.

commission from the sales price. Though the prices were only a suggestion from the Southwestern Company, students followed the guidelines for consistency across consumers. Since several students would be selling in every city, it was very likely that friends and relatives might buy the books from different students. Consistency also helped maintain the image of Southwestern, which was critical in this door-to-door sales context.

SUCCESS

The first of two keys to students' success in selling children's books was establishing themselves as legitimate education consultants in the community. Students sought to understand the strengths and weaknesses of the schools and teachers in the community, and the attitudes of parents toward the teachers, schools, and school board. This allowed them to better understand customer needs and to connect quickly during a sales call.

The second key to success was financial planning. Students submitted a high portion of their earnings to the Southwestern Company to secure delivery at the end of the summer (time and experience had demonstrated that students were not good credit risks), so planning was essential to ensure cash flow to cover expenses during the summer.

WINNIE'S SUMMER

After a week of sales training at company headquarters in Nashville, Winnie drove to Edmonton, Alberta, with seven students. He found a place to live with Holden McArthur, who had also just completed his first year at Western, and Seymour Burke, a student from British Columbia, who had sold books during the previous two summers. Winnie and Holden competed against each other daily, not just for sales, but for what they called "feel gooders." These included positive attitude, random acts of kindness, and the number of people they had cheered up during the day.

Winnie had been successful in all ways until the third week of June. He began working in a much wealthier area than he had been in before. His knowledge of local schools, teachers, and students was unusable because these schools and people were unfamiliar and unrecognized. The children in this neighborhood went to private schools. On Wednesday morning Winnie looked over his sales stats for the past two days: 94 calls, 41 demonstrations, and no sales. Every day without a sale meant stretching his meager food budget a little further. He had been eating peanut butter and jelly for a week straight. For the first time Winnie allowed himself to think about quitting and going home.

Now Winnie was sitting in the home of Ravish and Kavita Patel, successful stockbrokers and parents of three children. Halfway through the demonstration Ravish asked his wife to bring in the friends they were entertaining in the backyard. These four couples, all wealthy descendants of hardworking immigrants, lived in the immediate neighborhood, and all had children ranging in age from 7 to 13. All of their children attended Temple, the private school of choice for parents in this neighborhood.

Each of the parents liked the study guides. More importantly, their children were enthusiastic about the books too. Ravish moved to face Winnie and said, "Okay, you've sold us, so no fancy close, Winnie. How much for the set?" Prepared for the no-close close that a fellow salesperson usually called upon, Winnie replied confidently, "It's not the hundreds or even thousands that these study guides would cost if you bought them by subject individually. All three books for $320. With tax (7% GST) and shipping, the total is only $343. That's pretty good, isn't it?"

Ravish turned to the other four couples and spoke briefly in a language Winnie did not entirely understand but recognized as Hindi. After a brief exchange, Ravish turned to Winnie and said, "Here's the deal. Winnie, what do you make from these, 20 percent? That's about $65 per couple here, $325 for you. We'll pay you cash, up front, and cover shipping. Don't charge us tax, we'll pay $310 each. We want just a 10 percent discount. If you don't pay tax, you only give up $50 and you get five sales now. Boom."

Winnie did the math in his head. Ravish had underestimated his margin by one-half (Winnie normally received 40 percent of the retail price) and he would actually be giving up about $140 for the sale. But the potential profit was about $500, not the $325 Ravish had calculated.

Winnie responded, less confident now, but sure that Ravish was not objecting to the price. "Everyone pays the same price. There are other students in the city running their businesses and they charge the same price. I've charged the same price to everyone so far and I'm going to charge the same price for the rest of the summer. Besides, wouldn't you feel cheated if you found out your neighbor got 20 percent off? That's why I charge the same price to everybody."

Ravish spoke slower now, "No one has to know, Winnie. Think about $1,550 in your pocket right now. For overlooking a silly tax and giving us a small break. You can call it a 'Volume Discount for Volume Libraries.' " His guests chuckled at Ravish's pun. Ravish continued, "Come on, Winnie. We're salespeople too. This is no big deal." He sat back in his plush chair and sighed softly, "If you don't like the deal, you should leave now."

Winnie considered the offer. The names of these families and their children would open doors in this neighborhood. He desperately needed information about Temple, which these people could give him. Next summer, the Southwestern company would send students out to work in this area again, just as he was now working in a territory where someone had sold books in the previous summer. The information he collected would benefit them tremendously, as would the testimonials they would be able to obtain from five families of book owners.

Ravish was right, no one had to find out about this discount. It was only a small discount. Winnie also felt that the GST was a silly tax. And $500 would end his peanut butter and jelly marathon immediately. He could almost taste a steak dinner and chocolate milkshake. Winnie took a slow, deep breath, and spoke to Ravish.

CREDITS

Chapter 1

Figure 1-3: Adapted from *The Chally World Class Sales Excellence Research Report: The Route to the Summit*, (HR Chally Group, 2007), p. 3–4.

Figure 1-4: Ginger Canton, Lisa Napolitano, and Mike Pusateri, Unlocking Profits: The Strategic Advantage of Key Account Management (Chicago, IL: National Account Management Association, 1997), p. 44.

Figure 1-5: Thomas Muccio, "Procter & Gamble: Allocating Resources," in Unlocking Profits: The Strategic Advantage of Key Account Management, Ginger Canton, Lisa Napolitano, and Mike Pusateri (eds.), (Chicago, IL: National Account Management Association, 1997), p. 66.

Team Exercise "The Prima Donna" adapted from "Sales and Marketing Challenges," *Sales & Marketing Magazine* (May 2007), p. 48.

Figure 1-7: Adapted from "Sales Career Path Model" in recruiting material presented for Procter & Gamble, 2003.

Chapter 2

Figure 2-1: Adapted from Andris Zolgners, Prabhakant Sinha, and Greggor Zoltners, *The Complete Guide to Accelerating Sales Force Performance*, (New York: AMACOM, 2001), p. 67.

Figure 2-3: Adapted from William Cron and Michael Levy, "Sales Management Performance Evaluation: A Residual Income Perspective," Journal of Personal Selling & Sales Management (August 1987), p. 58.

Figure 2-4: Adapted from Stanley Slater and Eric Olson, "Strategy Type and Performance: The Influence of Sales Force Management," *Strategic Management Journal*, 21, 2000, p. 813–829.

Figure 2-5: Adapted from Zoltners et al., 2001, p. 8.

Figure 2-6: Adapted from Zoltners et al., 2001, p. 12.

Figure 2-7: Adapted from Zoltners et al., 2001, p. 18.

Figure 2-8: Adapted from Zoltners et al., 2001, p. 21.

Figure 2-9: Adapted from Rajendra Srivastava, Tasadduq Shervani, and Liam Fahey, "Marketing, Business Processes, and Shareholder Value: An Organizationally Embedded View of Marketing Activities and the Discipline of Marketing," *Journal of Marketing*, 63 (Special Issues 1999), p. 170.

Figure 2-10: Adapted from Srivastava et al., 1999, p. 170.

Figure 2-11: Adapted from Srivastava et al., 1999, p. 170.

Figure 2-15: Adapted from "Data Watch", Velocity (Spring 1999), p. 3.

Sales Management Resource: Estimating Potentials and Forecasting Sales

Table SMR2-1: "2004 Survey of Buying Power," Sales & Marketing Management (September 2004), pp. 12, 18, 21, 32.

The production employee data in Table SMR2-2 are from the 2002 Census of Manufacturers, Geographical Area Series, North Carolina, p. NC 1 and 2.

Management Resource: Sales Force Investment and Budgeting

Figure MR2-1: Adapted from Zoltners et al., 2001, pp. 70–71.

Figure MR2-2: Adapted from Zoltners et al., 2001, p. 74.

Figure MR2-3: Adapted from Zoltners et al., 2001, p. 75.

Figure MR2-4: Adapted from Zoltners et al., 2001, p104.

Table MR2-1: Adapted from *Sales Force Compensation Survey* (Chicago: Dartnell Corp., 1999), p. 9.

Figure MR2-6: Adapted from discussion with Mr. Robert Conti, Principal, The Alexander Group Inc., April 16, 2001.

Chapter 3

Table 3-2: Dartnell Corporation, *30th Survey of Sales Force Compensation*, Dartnell Corporation 1999, p. 117. Industry groups reflect categories selected and reported by Dartnell Corporation. The overall average has been calculated based on data from all industries studied.

Figure 3-1: Adapted from Raymond LaForge, David Cravens, and Clifford Young, "Improving Salesforce Productivity," Business Horizons (September–October 1985), p. 54.

Figure 3-3: Adapted from Robert Miller, Stephen Heiman with Tad Tuleja, *Strategic Selling,* New York: William Morrow and Company, Inc. (1985), p. 235.

Figure 3-4: Fenemore Group, as reported in *Sales & Marketing Magazine*, March 1998, p. 96.

Chapter 4

Figure 4-2: Adapted from Rackam and DeVincentis, 1999, p. 67.

Figure 4-3: Adapted from Atlee Pope and George Brown, "Growth is a Project," *Velocity*, (Q1 2003), pp. 22–25.

Figure 4-4: Adapted from Jeff Thull, *Exceptional Selling*, (Hoboken, NJ: John Wiley & Sons, Inc., 2006), p. 218.

Team Exercise "Different Strokes" based on Roger Kerin and Bob Peterson, *Strategic Marketing Problems*, 11th edition (NY: Prentice Hall, 2007), pp. 235–244.

Figure 4-4: Adapted from Robert Dwyer, Paul Schurrr, and Sejo OH, "Developing buyer-Seller Relationships," *Journal of Marketing*, 51 (April 1987), pp. 11–27.

Chapter 5

Figure 5-2: Adapted from Jeff Thull, *Exceptional Selling*, p. 29.

Figure 5-4: Adapted from material from the Wilson Learning Corporation, *The Counselor Salesperson* (2002).

Team Exercise "Why Beat a Dead Horse?" Adapted from Jeff Thull, *Exceptional Selling*, (Hoboken, NJ: John Wiley & Sons, Inc., 2006), pp. 194–195.

Team Exercise "What Does Ms. Williams Hear" was adapted from Thull, *Exceptional Selling*, p. 86.

Chapter 6

Figure 6-2: Source: Economist Intelligence Unit and Andersen Consulting: A survey of more than 200 leading executives in North America, Europe and Asia, as reported in Velocity (Summer 1999), p. 3.

Figure 6-9: Peggy Moretti, "Telemarketers Serve Clients," Business Marketing (April 1994), pp. 29, 31.

Figure 6-12: Adapted from Philip Kotler, Neil Rackham, and Suj Krishnaswamy, "Ending the War Between Sales and Marketing," *Harvard Business Review*, (July–August 2006), p. 77.

Management Resource: Territory Design

Figure T-1: Adapted from Zoltners et al., 2001, p. 136.

Chapter 7

Figure 7-1: Source: Used by permission of Federated Insurance.

Figure 7-3: Source: Used by permission of Federated Insurance.

Figure 7-4: Source: Used by permission of Federated Insurance.

Chapter 9

Table 9-2: Source: William Keenan, "The Nagging Problem of the Plateaued Salesperson," *Sales and Marketing Management* (March 1989), p. 38.

Table 9-3: *Sales Force Compensation Survey* (Chicago: Dartnell Corporation, 1999), p. 171.

Chapter 11

Table 11-2: *Sales and Marketing Management* (February 1990), p. 82.

Figure 11-3: "What Makes Great Sales People," *Sales and Marketing Management* (May 1994), pp. 82–92.

Figure 11-4: William L. Cron, "Industrial Salesperson Development: A Career Stages Perspective," *Journal of Marketing,* 48 (Fall 1984), pp. 41–52.

Figure 11-7: Developed by Thomas E. DeCarlo, Thomas Powers, and Gouri Gupte, "Sales Manager Training Practices: New Perspectives," *University of Alabama at Birmingham Paper 0-101* (March 2008).

Chapter 12

Table 12-1: *Sales Force Compensation Survey* (Chicago: Dartnell Corporation, 1999), p. 43.

Table 12-3: Joseph Kornik, Maggie Rauch, and Rebecca Arounauer, "What's It All Worth? 2007 Compensation Survey," *Sales and Marketing Management* (May 2007), pp. 27–39.

Table 12-1: *Sales Force Compensation Survey* (Chicago: Dartnell Corporation, 1999), p. 121.

Chapter 13

Table 13-6: Erin Anderson and Vincent Onyemah, "How Right Should the Customer Be?" *Harvard Business Review* (July-August), pp. 59–67.

Table 13-11: Douglas Dalrymple and William M. Strahle, "Career Path Charting: Frameworks for Sales Force Evaluation," *Journal of Personal Selling and Sales Management,* Vol. 10, No. 23 (Summer 1990), pp. 59–68.

Table 13-12: James S. Boles, Naveen Donthu, and Ritu Lohtia, "Salesperson Evaluation Using Relative Performance Efficiency: The Application of Data Envelopment Analysis," *Journal of Personal Selling and Sales Management,* Vol. 15, No. 3 (Summer 1995), p. 44.

KEY TERM AND SUBJECT INDEX

AUTHOR INDEX

COMPANY INDEX

CASE INDEX